# Corporate Encounters

Ethics, Law, and the Business Environment

⊥

Clarence C. Walton
*College of Commerce and Finance
Villanova University
and
The America College*

The Dryden Press
A Harcourt Brace Jovanovich College Publisher

Fort Worth   Philadelphia   San Diego   New York   Orlando   Austin   San Antonio
Toronto   Montreal   London   Sydney   Tokyo

## To Betty,
## who surrounds my life with enchantments.

Acquisitions Editor:  Robert Gemin
Project Editor:  Kelly Spiller
Production Manager:  Barb Bahnsen
Permissions Editor:  Doris Milligan
Director of Editing, Design, and Production:  Jane Perkins
Text and Cover Design:  Melissa Morgan
Indexer:  Leoni McVey
Compositor:  Impressions, Inc.
Text Type:  10/12 Times Roman

---

**Library of Congress Cataloging-in-Publication Data**

Walton, Clarence Cyril, 1915–
    Corporate encounters: ethics, law, and the business environment / Clarence C. Walton. — 1st ed.
      p. cm.
    Includes bibliographical references and index.
    ISBN 0-03-074822-4
    1. Social responsibility of business—United States.  2. Business ethics—United States.  3. Trade regulation—United States.  4. Industry and state—United States.  5. Corporation law—United States.  6. Commercial law—United States.  I. Title.
HD60.5.U5W35  1992
174′.4—dc20                                     91-33544

---

Printed in the United States of America
234-090-987654321
Copyright © 1992 by The Dryden Press

All rights reserved. No part of this publication may be reproduced or transmitted in any form or by any means, electronic or mechanical, including photocopy, recording, or any information storage and retrieval system, without permission in writing from the publisher.

Requests for permission to make copies of any part of the work should be mailed to: Permissions Department, Harcourt Brace Jovanovich, Publishers, 8th Floor, Orlando, FL 32887.

Address orders:
The Dryden Press
Orlando, FL 32887

Address editorial correspondence:
The Dryden Press
301 Commerce Street, Suite 3700
Fort Worth, TX 76102

The Dryden Press
Harcourt Brace Jovanovich

Cover Source: Scott Barrow/Superstock, Inc.

# The Dryden Press Series in Management

Bartlett
**Cases in Strategic Management for Business**

Bedeian
**Management**
*Second Edition*

Bedeian and Zammuto
**Organizations: Theory and Design**

Boone and Kurtz
**Contemporary Business**
*Sixth Edition*

Bowman and Branchaw
**Business Report Writing**
*Second Edition*

Bracker, Montanari, and Morgan
**Cases in Strategic Management**

Calvasina and Barton
**Chopstick Company: A Business Simulation**

Czinkota, Rivoli, and Ronkainen
**International Business**
*Second Edition*

Daft
**Management**
*Second Edition*

Donaldson
**Key Issues in Business Ethics**

Dyer, Daines, and Giauque
**The Challenge of Management**

Efendioglu and Montanari
**The Advantage Ski Company: A Strategic Simulation**

Foegen
**Business Plan Guidebook with Financial Spreadsheets**

Forgionne
**Quantitative Management**

Gaither
**Production and Operations Management**
*Fifth Edition*

Gatewood and Feild
**Human Resource Selection**
*Second Edition*

Gerhart
**Midwest Aeronautical Products, Inc.**

Gibson and Hodgetts
**Readings and Exercises in Organizational Behavior**

Greenhaus
**Career Management**

Higgins
**Strategy: Formulation, Implementation, and Control**

Higgins and Vincze
**Strategic Management: Text and Cases**
*Fourth Edition*

Hills
**Compensation Decision Making**

Hodgetts
**Management: Theory, Process, and Practice**

Hodgetts
**Modern Human Relations at Work**
*Fourth Edition*

Hodgetts and Kroeck
**Personnel and Human Resource Management**

Hodgetts and Kuratko
**Effective Small Business Management**
*Fourth Edition*

Hodgetts and Kuratko
**Management**
*Third Edition*

Holley and Jennings
**The Labor Relations Process**
*Fourth Edition*

Huseman, Lahiff, and Penrose
**Business Communication: Strategies and Skills**
*Fourth Edition*

Jauch, Coltrin, and Bedeian
**The Managerial Experience:
Cases, Exercises, and Readings**
*Fifth Edition*

Kemper
**Experiencing Strategic Management**

Kuehl and Lambing
**Small Business:
Planning and Management**
*Second Edition*

Kuratko and Hodgetts
**Entrepreneurship:
A Contemporary Approach**
*Second Edition*

Lee
**Introduction to Management Science**
*Second Edition*

Luthans and Hodgetts
**Business**
*Second Edition*

McMullen and Long
**Developing New Ventures:
The Entrepreneurial Option**

Matsuura
**International Business: A New Era**

Mauser
**American Business: An Introduction**
*Sixth Edition*

Montanari, Morgan, and Bracker
**Strategic Management:
A Choice Approach**

Northcraft and Neale
**Organizational Behavior:
A Management Challenge**

Penderghast
**Entrepreneurial Simulation Program**

Rudelius and Erickson
**An Introduction to Contemporary Business**
*Fourth Edition*

Ryan, Eckert, and Ray
**Small Business: An Entrepreneur's Plan**
*Second Edition*

Sawyer
**Business Policy and Strategic
Management:
Planning, Strategy, and Action**

Schoderbek
**Management**
*Second Edition*

Schwartz
**Introduction to Management:
Principles, Practices, and Processes**
*Second Edition*

Tombari
**Business and Society:
Strategies for the Environment
and Public Policy**

Varner
**Contemporary Business Report Writing**
*Second Edition*

Vecchio
**Organizational Behavior**
*Second Edition*

Walton
**Corporate Encounters: Ethics, Law,
and the Business Environment**

Wolford and Vanneman
**Business Communication**

Wolters and Holley
**Labor Relations:
An Experiential and Case Approach**

Zikmund
**Business Research Methods**
*Third Edition*

# Preface

All authors know—and few readers care—about the agony and ecstasy that go into writing. During periods of frustration brought on by poorly written or poorly organized materials, thunderclaps and clouds create the dreary atmosphere of dank pessimism. Then come the moments of sparkling sunlight when things fall in place and Tennyson's line sounds sweetly to the ear: "God's in his heaven, all's right with the world."

All will be right in the reader's world if this author's intention is always remembered—an intention explained by one word: *question*. On every possible occasion in this text, analysis is followed immediately by questions. What is insider trading? Is it ethical? What did the country's founding fathers think of human nature? Were they correct? If so, what are the implications for managers and organizations? Do we have a capitalistic economy? Do we really want one? Are labor unions passé? Does the Sherman Antitrust Act unfairly hobble American businesses in global competition? Is tort law a mess? Advertising deceitful? Manufacturers careless?

Only by struggling to find answers the magnitude of the manager's challenges is appreciated. And by such responses do we begin to identify in practical ways the values we ourselves espouse. Behind all questions and analyses is the belief that changing circumstances require constant attention to our laws and that statutory changes are best effectuated when laws march to an ethical beat.

Explicit mention must be made of two important items, namely, the author's intended audience and the book's overall organization.

## *Audience*

Readers for whom this book is intended include advanced undergraduates and graduate students in business who are at either the master's or doctoral levels; specialists in such functional areas as accounting, marketing, and engineering who, feeling that their educational background in the humanities has been inadequate, wish to expand their own intellectual horizons; and mid-managers on a career path toward more senior levels of responsibility who know from experience that a little knowledge is a dangerous thing. Finding this book useful will be university professors, personnel managers of in-house training programs, and directors of university-sponsored executive programs.

## *Organization*

The book is organized into four parts. The first part is designed to provide a common base on which the country's political and economic institutions have been built. Part One should be especially helpful, therefore, to those specialists in business who have majored in fields outside of the liberal arts. For this reason Part One deals not only with our basic institutions but with the institution-builders and the values they brought to their important projects.

Once the foundations have been described, Part Two moves into the way institutions have evolved—with particular attention given to the importance of market competition and how competition has been defaced by such practices as insider trading, bribery, industrial espionage, and by such structures as monopoly and, sometimes, oligopoly. Part Three then directs attention to those who are directly affected by the ways corporations operate, namely, the worker and the consumer. In this part, explanations are offered on the current state of unions, the concerns of employees, the instruments they employ to protect their interests, and managers' countermoves. While workers sometimes have different interests, consumers are always driven by a common desire to get good products and services at good prices. If consumers are harmed by certain advertising practices or manufacturers burdened by confusing and costly tort laws, the market system is again jolted.

Part Four is directed to two questions that arise when national boundaries no longer confine problems to one people in one nation. The two are environmental dangers and the role of multinational corporations. In light of these developments, the foundations described in Part One will have to be reexamined and, when necessary, restructured. In the formidable task of restructuring, business managers will obviously be involved. But in the reexamination, everyone has a stake which will be protected only by the knowledgeable and the involved.

To reaffirm this book's emphasis on questioning, the conclusion uses an Abelardian technique of confronting readers with specific problems to which a yes-or-no response is sought. And what is conclusion for the writer is commencement for the reader.

To further the writer's goal two other features of the book are worth noting: (1) the use of critical questions at the end of each chapter and (2) the use of ethical quandaries. The quandary is intended to relate and clarify a general theme developed in the chapter.

Short scenarios are also incorporated into the body of some chapters to encourage critical analysis. Discussion of the scenario can highlight a significant point in the analysis as well as clarify possible ambiguities. Every possible opportunity has been seized to illustrate a general proposition through the reader's response to a related and practical problem. Each scenario is related to a chapter's specific point.

There are, finally, some housekeeping chores relating to bibliography and to coverage, respectively. Bibliographical notes are an author's bane. However, ample citations provide useful starting points for professors who wish to strengthen their mastery of materials in certain areas, for students contemplating term papers or theses, and for anyone sufficiently intrigued by a topic to do further reading on it.

## *Acknowledgments*

It is now time to give thanks. Of the many who helped, special notes of gratitude go to Samuel Weese, president of The American College, Jane Dawson, the college's research librarian, as well as Patricia Perillo, Virginia Marzano, and Loretta Cipolla from the college's word processing center. Others who helped are Helen Schmidt, J. R. Walton, Brian Kennedy, Esq., and most particularly, Kathleen Walton of the Congressional Quarterly Library, and Anthony Amato, whose editing skills clarified certain inadequately written portions that first flowed from the author's pen. Gratitude is also due to members of the Villanova University School of College and Finance: Dean Alvin Clay, faculty colleagues, and the many able graduate students it was my pleasure to teach. I would also like to thank everyone at The Dryden Press for their help and encouragement, especially Kelly Spiller and Jean Berry, copyeditor extraordinaire.

Always helpful is my wife, Elizabeth. She makes no pretense to a special scholarship. She need make no pretense to a special wisdom because it is superabundantly hers. To live with her is to learn.

*Clarence C. Walton*
*Rosemont, PA*
*November 1991*

# About the Author

Experiences on corporate and university boards along with work as a university dean and president, teacher, and scholar uniquely equip Clarence Walton to speak authoritatively to questions of interorganizational ethics. Dr. Walton has held chairs in business at Columbia University and at The American College in Bryn Mawr. Currently he is serving on the faculty of Villanova University as professor of management.

Dr. Walton's contributions have brought him a wide variety of recognitions: 16 honorary doctorates, the Beta Gamma Sigma Award in 1976 for significant work in business scholarship, the Summer Marcus Award in 1988 from the Academy of Management for his contributions to management and ethical theory, and the Huebner Gold Medal from the life insurance industry in 1989 for advancing professionalism in that field. Dr. Walton has taught in executive development programs at Columbia, IBM, General Electric, Prudential, Alcoa, USX, and other major corporations. He also served as an elected school board director in Scranton, his native city, director of the Governor's commissions studying the housing needs of the poor in Pennsylvania, and as chair of President Nixon's Panel on Nonpublic Education.

Author and editor of 14 books and numerous scholarly articles, Dr. Walton has at times been called the "father of contemporary business ethics."

# Contents

**Introduction**    1
   Institutional Impact on Values    1
      *Distinctions and Caveats 1    Birth of Modern Morality 2*
   Catalog of Change    4
      *Demographic Changes 4    Cultural Changes 5
      Economic/Business Changes 6    Political Changes 8*
   Time for Whine or Roses?    8
      *The Pessimists' Assessment 8    The Optimists' Assessment 10
      Opportunity and Challenge 11*

## PART ONE
## Foundations

CHAPTER ONE
**The Political Foundation**    14
   The Constitution    16
      *The Intellectual Heritage 16    The Framers 18    The Testing Time 20    The Present 22*
   Elected Officials    22
      *Political Parties 23    Interest Groups 24    Money Interests 26*
   Appointed Officials    28
      *The Supreme Court 28    Federal Regulators 34*
   Summary    37

CHAPTER TWO
**The Business Foundation: Corporations, Unions, and the Commercial Professions**    44
   The Corporation and Capitalism    46
      *Early Corporate Forms 47    Managerial Capitalism 49
      Institutional Capitalism 49    Corporate Power over
      Employees 50    Corporate Power over Society: Federal
      Charters and CSR 53    Noncorporate Businesses 60*

## Workers and Labor Unions — 61

*The Nature of Unions 61   Characteristics of Unions 62
Evolution of Unions 63   Legitimacy Problems of Unions 65
The Murky Future 66*

## The Commercial Professions — 66

*The Emergence of Professions 66   Main Characteristics of Professions 70*

## Summary — 75

CHAPTER THREE
# The Moral Foundation — 82

## American Culture — 83

*Definition of Culture 83   The Infant Nation: Manifest Destiny 84   Adolescent America 86   The Civil Religion 90*

## Moral Responsibility in a Changing World — 91

*Cosmopolitanism 91   Economic Productivity 92   Family Structure 93   Social Fragmentation 94*

## America's Moral Future — 95

*Failures of the Prophets 95   A Cry for Values 96*

## Moral Philosophies — 97

*The Challenge for Philosophers 97   Self-Oriented Philosophies 99   Utilitarianism 100   Deontology 101   A Parting Word: Face 102*

## Summary — 103

PART TWO
# Intercorporate Relations

CHAPTER FOUR
# Competition: Ethical and Legal Rules — 110

## The Evolution of Economic Competition — 112

*Positive Aspects of Competition 112   Impediments to Competitive Capability 113   Negative Aspects of Competition 115*

## Ethical Criteria — 115

*Independent Initiative 116   Constructive Effort 116
Respect for the Rules 117   Level Playing Field 118
Respect for Referees 118*

## Legal Criteria — 120

*Antitrust Acts 120
The Two Critical Elements 122*

## Selected Problem Areas — 122

*Horizontal Price Fixing 122   Vertical Price Fixing 125
Throwing out the Bathtub 126   Exclusive Dealings 127
Tying Agreements 129   Restrictive Covenants and Predatory Pricing 130   Administered Pricing 131*

## Summary — 133

CONTENTS xi

**CHAPTER FIVE**
**Ethics of Size: Mergers and Takeovers** 138
   Merger Movements 139
      *The First Three Waves 139   The Fourth Wave 141*
   Hostile Takeovers 142
      *Bids and Greenmail 142   The Phillips Petroleum Story 143
      Leveraged Buyouts and Junk Bonds 145   The Drexel-Milken
      Saga 145   Negotiating Patterns 149   Defensive Tactics 152*
   Economic and Ethical Assessments 155
      *Economic Gains and Losses 155   The Ethical Ledger 159
      Newton's Law 160*
   Suggested Reforms 161
      *Internal Reform 161   Extenal Regulation 162*
   Summary 162

**CHAPTER SIX**
**Information Gathering: Clean or Dirty Tricks?** 168
   Capsule History of Snooping 169
   Sources and Kinds of Information 170
      *National Espionage 172   Political Intelligence 172
      Commercial Intelligence 173   Industrial Espionage 174*
   Special Problems in Information Gathering 175
      *Electronic Crooks 176   National Security 177   Globalization
      of Industrial Espionage 178   Business Costs of Security 180
      Intellectual Property Rights 183*
   Summary 185

**CHAPTER SEVEN**
**Insider Trading, Bribes, and Payoffs** 194
   Insider Trading 195
      *A Sense of the Problem 196   Dimensions of the Problem 200
      Definitional Examples 202   Ethical Assessment 205*
   Bribes and Payoffs 206
      *Definitional Examples 207   Making Distinctions 212
      Moral Assessments 217*
   Summary 220

**PART THREE**
# Workers and Consumers

**CHAPTER EIGHT**
**Union-Employer Encounters** 226
   Ethical Criteria 229
      *The Principle of Reasonable Disclosure 229   The Principle
      of Proportionality 230   The Principle of the Innocent
      Bystander 231   The Principle of Moral Suasion 231*

## CONTENTS

Collective Bargaining — 232
*Sham or Serious? 232   Bargaining Theory 233   Adversarialism 234*

The Big Guns: Strikes, Boycotts, and Lockouts — 236
*The Early Years 236   Definitions 237   Arbitration and Strikes 238   Positional Power 238   Recent Union Tactics 239   Recent Management Tactics 243*

Strikes by Professions and Government Employees — 244
*Doctors 244   Teachers 245   Traffic Controllers   247*

The Years Ahead — 250
Summary — 253

### CHAPTER NINE
## Advertising — 262

The Nature of the Industry — 264
*The Stakes 264   Definitions 265   Truth: Who Cares? 266*

Deceptive Advertising — 268
*FTC Rulings 268   Government and Industry Definitions 270   The Knowing-It-When-You-See-It Concept 271*

Special Forms of Advertising — 271
*Comparative Advertising 272   Puffery 273   Harmful-Product Advertising 274   Advertising to Children 278*

Institutional Controls — 279
*Intervention 279   Self-Policing 281   Two NAD Investigations 283*

Ethical Appraisals — 285
*Scrutiny of the Industry 285   Advertisers' Accountability 287   Specific Issues 288*

Summary — 289

### CHAPTER TEN
## Tort Law — 294

Evolution of the Law — 297
*Early Views 298   Critical Dates 299   The Current Scene 300*

Consumer Opposition to Protective Legislation: Three Examples — 302
*Motorcyclists 302   Saccharinites 303   AIDS Victims 303*

Judicial Trends and Ethics — 304
*Fault and Strict Liability 304   Admissible Evidence 307   The Law's Reach 310   Deep Pockets 312   Single and Collective Liability 317*

Guidelines — 322
*Fuller's Counsel 322   FDA Guidelines 323*

Summary — 324

CHAPTER ELEVEN
**Tort-Related Issues** 330

    Punitive Damages 332

        *Origin of the Doctrine 332   Problems in Application 333*
        *The Constitutional Question 335*

    Defense Tactics 336

        *Withdrawal from the Market 336   Bankruptcy 337   Shifting the Blame 343   Institutional Reform 347   Ethical Input 348*

    Life's Monetary Worth 349

        *Economic Theories 349   Legal Theory 352*
        *Moral Theory 352*

    Summary 355

PART FOUR
# The World Stage

CHAPTER TWELVE
**Multinational Corporations** 362

    Multinationals: What They Are 364

        *Multinationals Defined 364   Evolution of an MNC 366*

    Relations with Host Countries 367

        *The Scope of the Problem 367   Liberation Theology versus Liberating Theology 368   Ethical Considerations 370   Practical Steps for Improvement 373*

    Multinationals and Advanced Countries 374

        *The Rise and Fall of Nations 374   The MNC-versus-Government Struggle 376   Quasi Public vs Private Multinationals 377*

    American Multinationals and the European Community 381

        *Early Mistakes of American Multinationals 382   European Economic Interest Grouping 382*

    Strengths and Weaknesses of MNCs 383
    Summary 384

CHAPTER THIRTEEN
**The Environment** 390

    Threats to a Safe Environment 394

        *Domestic Dangers 394   Global Phenomena 396*
        *Technology's Side Effects 398*

    Key Questions Concerning the Common Good 401

        *How Safe Is Safe? 401   Do We Know What to Do? 402   Will Americans Pay for Their Own Safety? 405   Is Industry Doing Enough? 405   Will Americans Sacrifice for Others' Safety? 406*

### Contents

Toward a New Environmental Ethic ... 408
  *Two Ethics? 408   Rolston's Maxims 409   A Short Checklist 411   Short-Term Problems: Two Examples 413*
Summary ... 415
Appendix 13A. Protection of the Ozone Layer: Chronology of Key Events ... 419

**Conclusion: An Abelardian Valedictory** ... 421
  Why Abelard? ... 421
  Yes and/or No: Sic et Non? ... 422
  A Final Comment ... 432

**Index** ... 435

# 1. Introduction

## Institutional Impact on Values
### *Distinctions and Caveats*

Modest but important distinctions enable readers to sense the structure and goal of this book. The first distinction involves value analyses that might be called *interorganizational ethics* and *intraorganizational ethics*, respectively. An interorganizational analysis examines corporate encounters with other business organizations, with consumer and environmental groups, and with labor unions and government agencies. Intraorganizational ethics, on the other hand, deals with employee rights, performance appraisals, hiring and promotion policies, compensation packages, leadership styles, management-board relationships, and other practices and beliefs that define the organization's corporate culture.

A second distinction arises from the difference between *macroethics* and *microethics*. The latter draws attention to individuals—their rights and obligations, their needs and desires, their ambitions, and their frustrations. In contrast, macroethical analysis deals with the ways organizations interact with one another, the constraints that society puts on them to prevent such encounters from being dysfunctional, and the criteria used to justify such societal constraints—antitrust laws, environmental regulations, rules for disclosure, and the like.

This book is in the interorganizational and macroethical genre and therefore is concerned with the environment in which business operates. The novelty of the book is seen in the way the business environment is influenced by legal *and* ethical criteria.

Because of the range of topics covered in this text, specialists in any given area may take exception to certain interpretations and generalizations. To illustrate, some historians—Gary Wills is among them—have recently challenged the orthodox view that John Locke was the great teacher of the nation's constitutional fathers; some older economists—Kenneth Arrow among them—feel that the neoclassicists have ignored the importance of agency theory in constructing their theories of the firm; and some young economists—Paul Krugman is one—challenge the traditional wisdom that protectionism through high tariffs is a bad policy. Numerous other examples could be used, but the point is clear: specialists will find holes in a generalist's presentation. The author hopes that the holes discovered will be few and will be easily repaired.

A third distinction is related to a view well expressed by W. Michael Blumenthal, former Secretary of the Treasury and former CEO of Unisys. In a 1990 interview, the 65-year-old Blumenthal said of his rich and varied experiences, "My mistakes came when I put intelligence and energy ahead of morality."[1] The goal of this text is to encourage future corporate leaders to recognize the importance of all three—intelligence, energy, and morality. The instrument used to reach the goal is dialogue. Instead of conclusions, the author presents questions for analysis.

Morality is a composite of values. The question thus arises whether a science of values is possible. This query reflects in part the scramble of every scholarly discipline to earn or snatch the label scientific, which presumably gives to its postulates and principles the aura of infallibility.[2] As traditionally defined, science presupposes two things: (1) an objective causal order that is independent of human commitments, interests, and beliefs and (2) laws (also independent of the human observer) that explain the nature of the objective world.[3] Science aims, therefore, to propound theories that adequately represent the laws and to provide criteria for assessing the adequacy of various theories. The two presuppositions make up the so-called canonical definition of science.

If there is a science of values, are there then criteria for selecting what is good (or better or best) among objects, actions, ways of life, and social and political institutions and structures? Or do legal criteria alone provide the bases of judgments? Behind the questions are two other assumptions: (1) values affect individuals, institutions, and entire societies and (2) societies and the values on which they are built go through cycles of growth and decay, construction and destruction.

These assumptions flow from observations that show that every social organization, including corporations, stipulates roles to encourage behavior that reflect those values. Consequently, the individual's values are constrained by the character of the social institutions and the social order in which the individual lives. When the socioeconomic and political orders change in their fundamentals, we usually speak of a new epoch—the Greek word for a turning. The Renaissance and Reformation were epochs in Western civilization; so, too, were the Enlightenment and the Industrial Revolution. In each, society turned to embrace new values. A comparison of the feudal order of the Middle Ages and the technological order of today shows how this phenomenon reveals itself.[4]

## Birth of Modern Morality

During the Middle Ages, lords controlled the land and serfs worked on the lords' property, turning over a fixed proportion of the yield in exchange for protection. Serfs could not sell their services to potential bidders, and the lord could not sell his land to potential buyers. In this environment the nature of the dominant social values governed how serfs worked; and how they worked, in turn, governed their values. Work involved diversified activities and was integrated into the rest of their day. The rhythm was adjusted to the seasons. Serfs never left home for the factory, never worked on a 9-to-5 schedule, never did the same thing all day every day, and never followed detailed orders issued by superiors who disallowed flexibility and personal decision making. Sons knew what their fathers did. Daughters knew what their mothers esteemed. "Breaking away" was the last thing serfs thought of—or did. Customs counted!

The industrialization process, on the other hand, began to subordinate custom to innovation. Bureaucracy replaced personal spontaneity to become the major influence on worker behavior. Americans were programmed under the scientific management approach conceived by Frederick Winslow Taylor, who assumed that tradition impeded efficiency. Manufacturers adopted techniques to control worker behavior that they believed would be as effective as techniques used to operate machines. Soon people were treated like cogs in the machines they tended. Henceforth, the only influence on workers' willingness to produce was money owned by others.

Not surprisingly, bosses had enormous difficulty in motivating workers who, rebelling against stern discipline, malingered constantly, absented themselves often, and quit when they could. But the important point is this: slowly and steadily the problem of inducing workers to put up with the unpleasant factory conditions disappeared. What for one generation was the wrenching out of a complex network of customs and social relations was for their sons "only natural." The old system was destroyed by the new.

One result of scientific management was bureaucratic structures, and one result of capitalism was a get-what-you-can mentality. Society embraced, albeit unconsciously, new practices that defined the moral worth of a person. The virtuous person was not the altruist or the saint but the economic maximizer and, in time, virtuous people become indistinguishable from rational economic agents: children become commodities; home ownership is an investment; marriage is a risk in which partners hedge their bets. *By transforming the practices that make up social life, society created the conditions under which the person was formed and by which its conception of human nature became the true one.* One set of norms for judging morality was destroyed and another substituted.

Although cultural determinism does not alone define what is good and what is true, it invariably plays a significant part in the formation of values. In this process the power of governments and corporations cannot be ignored. Corporations, if not precisely moral persons or moral agents themselves, can "create" moral persons or agents whose values and goals are aligned with their values and goals.

The way in which organizations compete affects not only other organizations but individuals as well; the way unions define their goods and their values shapes the goods and values of workers; the way economic entities treat the environment influences the individual's attitudes toward nature; the way nation-states view other nation-states shapes the citizen's evaluation of the moral worth of "alien" people. Cataloging some of the changes even now evident provides a sense of the opportunities and the difficulties that will be encountered by the coming generation of businessmen and businesswomen. To understand how a value represented by our profligate consumption of energy will be altered, we need only to look at energy. Each American citizen uses two and a half times as much energy as his European or Japanese counterpart but is not two and a half times better off. Each American citizen generates two and half times as much pollution and had two and a half times as much to worry about when oil prices doubled in 1990. Attitudes (as much as shortages) are Americans' energy problem. The problem is not likely to be solved by science alone. More parsimony in consumption and more respect for the environment will become new values. Other changes may induce modifications in old—and introductions of new—values. Corporate leaders will increasingly watch the nation's heart as carefully as they take the market's pulse.

## Catalog of Change

Nineteen hundred and eighty was a momentous year: Japanese manufacturing productivity caught up to American productivity. The rest of the decade was spent in an American come-from-behind effort that was slowed by the continuing depressed investment levels of the 1970s. Henry Kissinger, secretary of state in the Nixon administration, said that if the United States did not improve its productivity, narrow its deficits, and retain its industrial competitiveness, it would be the weakest in the new economic triad made up of Europe, Japan, and the United States.[5] From being the strongest to being the weakest was not a happy prospect.

Although relative productivity declines have been attributed to an erosion of the American work ethic, the main problem lies in overemphasis on short-term returns, restrictive work practices, bonus and pay increments unrelated to productivity gains, the revolutionary changes in the work force from blue- to white-collar employees, the graying of America, et cetera. The "et cetera" will be cataloged briefly and incompletely. Even an incomplete list of the changes, however, represents a stunning array of challenges.

### *Demographic Changes*

- Demography, only recently directed primarily to the study of baby boomers and the elderly, now has turned to the middle-aging phenomenon of the world's population. Indeed, the changes are so momentous that the very definition of gerontology is being transformed from the study of the aged to a study of the aging process.[6]
- Overall U.S. population growth for the 1990s, projected to be only about 7 percent, is at a record low.

- A high proportion of children will finish high school as functional illiterates.
- Lessened job opportunities for unskilled or quasi-skilled workers will lead certain groups of workers to oppose other groups of workers more intensely than they oppose management.
- The outflow of people from the Northeast and Midwest to the South, Southwest, and West will continue.
- No-growth areas age more rapidly than others. Pennsylvania, for example, which will lose 100,000 residents in the coming decade, is already the second oldest state in the nation in terms of population: half of its people are over age 35 as compared with the national median of 33. Pennsylvania will be one of the first states to experience more deaths than births.
- By the year 2000 native-born white males will compose under 10 percent of the net addition to the labor force; 57 percent of the net work force growth will come from minority groups.
- Metropolitan areas are no longer big cities but metropolitan webs, choked by freeways on which motorists fume on the way to and from work.
- Possibly the most important element is the influx of immigrants, the biggest since the 1920s. But it is not size alone that makes this tide of new people so important; it is its composition, the nature of which is captured by Peggy Noonan, former speech writer for President Reagan:

  *In a single block in the East 60s in Manhattan, an area chosen not scientifically but because it's my neighborhood, the two brothers who own and run the stationery store are from India, the picture framer is from Afghanistan, the place where they do my nails is run by Koreans, the custom tailor shop is owned and run by a man from the Dominican Republic, the shoe repairman is from Russia and the cleaners is run by women from Hong Kong. They have, together, made New York that anomaly, a vibrant and successful Third World city.*[7]

  The United States may not become a Third World nation, but it surely will be different from the one that exists in the last decade of the 20th century.[8]

## Cultural Changes

- Developed societies have become so risk averse that technology is often seen as the Mephistopheles of the 21st century. Not long ago individuals were drawn toward technological benefits perceptions; today they are drawn more to risk perceptions.[9]
- Related to risk aversion is the idea of immediate gratification. Roger Smith, former chairman of General Motors, said that "in virtually every aspect of society—from three-minute fast-food restaurants to empty sav-

ings accounts, to slip-knot marriages—it is clear that we have become a society of short-term pleasure seekers with a very low tolerance for delayed gratification of any kind."[10]

- Seen as the tip of a moral-psychological iceberg are the growing activities of the proeuthanasia Hemlock Society, which has been particularly active on the west coast in trying to get a "death with dignity" amendment on the ballot.
- Ethical relativism may be seen as a very attractive option when citizens are bewildered by conflicting claims over euthanasia, abortion, and capital punishment. Relativism, however, can fracture the already fragile basket of beliefs carried by the "civil religion" to a point where moral chaos occurs.
- Children are increasingly viewed as commodities. Once the connection between sexual intercourse and procreation was broken, it became possible to choose when to have children. From that point on, it made sense to treat children in some ways as products, the purchase of which could be planned as one planned the purchase of other expensive items.[11]
- A continuous conflict is seen between the values of Western civilization (market exchange and economic rationality as the ultimate criteria) and the values of societies embracing a Confucian set of beliefs.

## *Economic/Business Changes*

- The European Community will give Americans sturdier competition than they ever faced when the countries of the continent were politically separated.
- Economic relations will be more between trading blocs than between countries. A North American trading bloc may emerge during the 1990s in order to compete more successfully with the East Asian bloc and the European Community.
- More joint ventures and alliances will come as one way to compete with the Japanese, whose capital costs are around 5 percent, whereas European and American companies are paying up to 20 percent for their money.
- A new class of executive, the global manager, will emerge. Already in the Pacific Rim a demand for international executives has spawned growing interest in American- and European-style managements. The Wharton School at the University of Pennsylvania, sensitive to this problem, established in 1988 the so-called SEI Center for Advanced Studies to research the international management skills needed for the next decade.
- Paralleling the need for the global manager will be the need for the global worker. As an example of things to come, AST Research Corporation, a computer maker in California, was looking for an advanced-computer engineer and found him in Taiwan.

- The Sherman Antitrust Act of 1890, which prohibited certain forms of cooperation and price fixing, will be modified in the face of global competition: other countries permit activities that disadvantage American businesses.

- Increased attention will be given to professional codes of ethics. Symptomatic of the trend is Emerson Pugh, who, upon taking office in 1989 as president of the Institute of Electrical and Electronic Engineers (IEEE), declared that the association's first priority was reform of its code of ethics.[12] Other professions (law, accounting) have already wrestled with the problem of reform.

- The "knowledge" worker will force a drastic restructuring of organizations so that fewer levels of bureaucratic controls will be necessary. Participatory management may grow initially but in a competitively driven world economy, the pendulum will swing back to more management control over fewer people.[13]

- Despite return of power to the center, more jockeying for advantage will take place as each special interest (marketing, finance, production) vies for power.

- More and more business will be done where people want to live rather than where corporations want to locate. The working spaces will not be restricted to American shores. (Even now Metropolitan Life Insurance Company sends claims to Ireland for processing via daily air shipments. Farming out by business will be as common as farming out is in baseball.)

- Extension of profit-sharing pension-fund programs will, by giving workers a stake in the corporation, change the nature of ownership. People are less inclined to destroy what they own.

- Large corporations are in a sense going more private in that they are putting themselves under the control of a small number of institutional investors.[14]

- Experiments with the free market system will continue in the Soviet Union, Eastern Europe, and China and, like all experiments, some will fail. Dealing with the failures will be just as important a challenge to business as dealing with the successes.

- With the fall of the Berlin Wall in 1990, Germany became *the* economic power in Europe and German banks the dominant financial institution. The deutsche mark may possibly replace the dollar as the world's reserve currency—a startling reversal to Brooks Adams' famous prophecy that the economic center of the world would rest within American shores.[15]

- The modern world has lived through three great technological revolutions: steam power in the 18th century, electricity in the 19th, and electronics in the 20th. The last is changing the concept of markets from places (Amsterdam for oil, New York for capital) to networks formed by computers, telexes, fax machines, and the like.

- To keep technologically ahead, corporations will be forced to ally themselves more completely with commercial banks, underwriters, and hardware manufacturers like IBM.

## *Political Changes*

- The economically integrated world and the fragmented political world will constitute one of the major disequilibria factors in the coming decades because the nation-state is "too small for the big problems of life and too big for the small problems of life."[16]
- The United States, ever more vulnerable because most of the earnings of its corporations depend on investments and sales abroad, will be forced into more international deals.
- Changes in tort law will come through legislative action after a bitter lobbying fight between tort attorneys and others, especially insurers.
- Narrowly focused interest groups will continue to upset political stability.
- Public Action Committees will be curtailed.
- A few venturesome U.S. states will enact legislation to prevent "life tenure," that is, assured reelections, for their congressmen and congresswomen. But reformers' zeal will decline if other states do not go along. The reason is that limitations on terms reduce chances for seniority for the reform state's representatives, and seniority is important to getting key chairmanships in the House and the Senate.
- Fear of ozone pollution and global warming will spur efforts to develop a new form of collective bargaining in which nations will—as unions and managements have done domestically—enter into time-specified contracts with predetermined expiration dates for renegotiations, as well as with provisions for grievance procedures and compulsory arbitration.
- The remarkable international traffic in legal ideas (American lawyers helping governments in Eastern Europe draft new constitutions) will change the international political climate, thus making the establishment of new international agencies more palatable to American leaders.[17]

## Time for Whine or Roses?

Given recent tumultuous changes, contrary assessments of America's performance and prospects, are understandable. Such assessments, in turn, influence career choices. Coleridge reminded us that vision is clouded by the "film of familiarity"; yet, the blur intensifies when the unfamiliar is encountered. It is salutary to review how the changes have been assessed.

### *The Pessimists' Assessment*

Scholars, and especially historians, are attracted as flies to honey to certain dates that they believe mark the beginning of a new epoch. Some, for example, have set the World War I of 1914 as the date when an old order vanished. The war ended one of history's greatest periods of a measured form of tranquility—a calm due to rationality, respect for the past, and a finite view of both man and the universe. The year "1914 may have changed all of that—changed it so devastatingly, so powerfully and so lastingly," wrote distinguished sociologist-historian Robert Nisbet, that he ended one of his essays with this somber confession:

> *I wish I could conclude ... with a ringing declaration of faith, with torpedoes of rah-rah-rahs for NO Decline, NO Decadence and for, at the same time, another miracle.... But, if I did this, it would be so patently insincere as to be recognized by the smallest child. What we know is that in diverse respects—philosophy, literature, education, property, family, language, art, etc.—the age that has followed the horrifying Great War has been one of visible decline of quality and of standards. Decline, too, I believe, of patriotism, of private citizenship, even, if not apparent, of strength as opposed to mere corpulence of government. What we do not know, cannot know, is when—or even whether—the approaching millennium, or anything else, will reverse the decline."*[18]

If Americans are basket cases, all that remains is for the battered body to be carried to either the emergency ward or the morgue. If dead, there are pallbearers aplenty to carry the caskets. The pessimists point to a nation with many ills: states that boast as their major industries mob-allied gambling enterprises, quickie-divorce mills, and even child prostitution rings; rich Texas with a prison system staffed by only one doctor for every 17,000 inmates; burgeoning cities of the South and West that blindly follow the dangerous practices of nonplanned Eastern cities. Examples are many: Houston, the only major city without zoning laws, is a town of 27 significant buildings surrounded by trivia. Atlanta is without any master plan. Denver has massive traffic problems and air pollution. Nevada has not only federally subsidized water supplies for Las Vegas and Reno, but government approved developers who ruin lakes and rivers in "the most appalling assault of God-given natural beauty on the American continent."[19]

Every example cited represents an ethical decision by someone. Editors of *Fortune* magazine, scarcely a bastion of left-wing radicalism, wrote: "With homelessness, poverty, violence, drug addictions, inadequate health care, and the well-known woes of its education system, America presents an ugly face to the world. Many Europeans and nations feel there is little they have to learn from the U.S.—and much that it could learn from them—about combining a more civil society with economic prosperity."[20]

The pessimists continue by noting the massive national debt, trade imbalances, the snapping up of American companies by foreigners (Firestone by Japan, Bloomingdale's by Canada, The Farmers Insurance Group by Britain) as examples of America's decline. Further, say the pessimists, foreigners are buying America at bargain basement prices—witness the Japanese purchase of Rockefeller Center in New York and Columbia Pictures in Hollywood. The mood of the 1980s seemed only to be a continuation of the mood of the 1960s, which the architect Edward Durrell Stone once defined as "an America of catch-penny materialists devoted to blatant insistence on materialism. If you look around and you give a damn, it makes you want to commit suicide."[21]

## *The Optimists' Assessment*

The optimists, on the other hand, place confidence in the imaginative and innovative genius of the American people. For example, Ralph Gomory, former head of research at IBM and currently president of the Alfred P. Sloan Foundation, predicted that "the computers would become one hundred times cheaper in the next two decades and that the riches of the information revolution have yet to be tasted."[22] Achievements in the field of biology during the coming 30 years will parallel the golden period of physics. Nor, say the optimists, is the economic picture nearly so bleak as the worrywarts have painted. In 1987 the stock of American foreign direct investments (in factories, offices, or brands as opposed to paper assets) was $309 billion compared with foreign investments in America, which were $262 billion. During 1987, both kinds of investments had grown, but American investments had grown faster. As a matter of fact, by the mid-1980s, America's foreign investments had risen faster than either Japan's or Britain's.[23]

Talk of an American economy endangered by foreign investments, therefore, is at best a half-truth. Pessimists, according to optimists, fail to acknowledge an important shift in power when the United States moved from its immediate postwar position as the world's *preeminent* nation to the world's *leading* power. This shift from preeminent to leading power should not be seen as evidence of decline but evidence of a healthy development for others. It means that more industrialized nations can carry a bigger share of world responsibilities, especially toward the developing world.[24]

Other facts are marshalled. By 1988 the rate of America's industrial production was 40 percent above the previous cyclical low and 24 percent over the previous cyclical high. Even the highly criticized manufacturing sector contributed about the same proportion of the total input to the American economy as it did three decades ago.[25] Expenditures for research and development in the United States have annually exceeded the combined totals of Japan, Germany, France, the United Kingdom, and Sweden.[26] Above all, the United States will continue to lead the world because of its political and economic flexibility. Unlike homogeneous Japan, a pluralistic society like the United States readily absorbs new ideas as fast as it absorbs new people. If power is considered in its broadest meaning, the United States has entered the 1990s as the world's greatest single player. In short, America is bound to lead.[27]

To optimists, no apocalypse is in the making—challenges, yes; decline, no. In current dollars, the GNP is $5.5 trillion, a substantial increase over the $1.6 trillion of 1950. It is two and a half times Japan's GNP and five times that of Germany. And yet when things are so good why do many Americans feel so bad?

## *Opportunity and Challenge*

Answers will come. The hope is that coming generations will give positive ones. To do so requires the skills of Janus (the Roman god who simultaneously looked backward and forward) and the wisdom of Minerva. Knowing what is coming is made easier by knowing what has happened—how the political, economic, and moral foundations of the nation were built; how they have been repaired by successive generations; and how they can be used to forge a more secure future. Crisis is not a new word to Americans. Neither is courage. One is surely coming. The other is certainly needed.

## *Notes*

1. Jerry Flint, "Master of the Game," *Forbes*, May 28, 1990, 200–207.
2. Jacques Barzun, *The Culture We Deserve* (Middletown, Conn.: Wesleyan University Press, 1989), 145.
3. The traditional distinctions are made between speculative and practical sciences, respectively. Both types seek knowledge through causes, but the former expresses its findings in universals—that is, laws that apply to all objects under its purview—while the latter seeks knowledge of what people can do or make. See Ernest Nagel, *The Structure of Science* (New York: Macmillan, 1961).
4. This analysis relies on the article by Barry Schwartz, "The Creation and Destruction of Value," *The American Psychologist* 45 (January 1990): 7–15. A fascinating variation on this theme is Michael Thompson's *Rubbish Theory: The Creation and Destruction of Values* (Oxford: Oxford University Press, 1979). Thompson shows how transient values can become enduring values—as values are sociologically defined.
5. Henry Kissinger, "The Impact on the United States of All the Changes Going On in the World Now." *Board Room Reports* 19, April 1, 1990, 1. This view was buttressed in a study by the MIT economist Paul Krugman, *The Age of Diminished Expectations* (Cambridge: MIT Press, 1990).
6. Davis W. Gregg and Neal E. Cutler, "Financial Gerontology and the Middle-Aging of People and Populations: Implications for Future Planning in Insurance Worldwide." Paper presented at the 26th International Insurance Seminar, July 10, 1990, Paris, France.
7. Peggy Noonan, "What New Americans Need to Know," *The Wall Street Journal*, November 21, 1990, A-14.
8. Julian L. Simon, *The Economic Consequences of Immigration* (London: Basil Blackwell, 1990).
9. Margaret Maxey, *Managing Environmental Risks: What Difference Does Ethics Make?* (St. Louis: Washington University/Center for the Study of American Business, 1990), 14.
10. Roger Smith, "Address at Wake Forest University," unpublished paper, 5. Presented at Winston-Salem, N.C., April 14, 1987.
11. Barbara Katz Rothman, "The Products of Conception: The Social Context of Reproductive Choices," *Journal of Medical Ethics* 11 (1985): 191.
12. Concern with ethics is spreading to others in the engineering community. See, for example, the essays by Cynthia Mascone, A. G. Santaquiliani and Charles Butcher, "Engineering Ethics: What Are the Right Choices?" *Chemical Engineering Progress* 87 (April 1991): 61–63 and by Fred Ordway, "Judging the Judges," *The Chemist* 68 (January 1991) 10.
13. Peter Drucker, *The New Realities* (New York: Harper and Row, 1989): 180–186. See also, John Naisbitt, *Megatrends: Ten New Directions Transforming Our Lives* (New York: Warner Books, 1983).

14. Michael C. Jensen, "Takeovers: Folklore and Science," *The Harvard Business Review* (November–December 1984): 109–112.
15. Brooks Adams, *America's Economic Supremacy* (New York: Macmillan, 1900), especially 217–222. Adams was wise enough to recognize that American hegemony would not last forever.
16. Daniel Bell, "The World and United States in 2013," *Daedalus* 116 (Summer 1987): 1–32.
17. Richard Thornburgh, "The Soviet Union and the Rule of Law," *Foreign Affairs* 69 (Spring 1990) 13–27. See also *The University of Chicago Law Review* 58 (Spring 1991) which was given entirely to this issue: "Approaching Democracy: A New Legal Order for Eastern Europe." Students interested in comparative legal systems will find great help in Don Alan Evans, The *Legal Environment of International Business: A Guide for United States Firms* (New York: McFarland & Company, Inc., 1990).
18. Robert Nisbet, "Reversing the Decline," *Crisis*, November 1988, 18.
19. Neal Peirce and Jerry Hagstrom, *The Book of America: Inside Fifty States Today* (New York: W. W. Norton, 1983).
20. Staff editors, "An American Vision for the 1990s," *Fortune*, (March 26, 1990), 16.
21. William Borders, "Edward Durrell Stone Deplores 'Mess' We've Made of Country." *The New York Times*, August 27, 1964, 35.
22. Staff editors, "An American Vision For the 1990s," *Fortune*, March 26, 1990, 14.
23. "America Still Buys the World," *The Economist*, September 17, 1988, 71–72.
24. An excellent study of the foreign direct investment issue and its relation to America's economic health is by Edward M. Graham and Paul R. Krugman, *Foreign Direct Investment in the United States* (Washington: Institute for International Economics, 1990).
25. Murray Weidenbaum, *The Myth of the Hollowed-Out Corporation* (St. Louis: Washington University/Center for the Study of American Business, 1989), 2–3.
26. Murray Weidenbaum, *Rendezvous with Reality: The American Economy after Reagan* (New York: Basic Books, 1988).
27. Joseph Nye, *Bound to Lead* (New York: Basic Books, 1990).

PART ONE

# Foundations

CHAPTER ONE
**The Political Foundation**

CHAPTER TWO
**The Business Foundation**

CHAPTER THREE
**The Moral Foundation**

CHAPTER 1

# The Political Foundation

### The Constitution
The Intellectual Heritage
The Framers
The Testing Time
The Present

### Elected Officials
Political Parties
Interest Groups
Money Interests

### Appointed Officials
The Supreme Court
*Judicial Review*
*Innovators and Originalists*
*The Power of the Court*
Federal Regulators
*Origins of the Administrative State*
*Hostility toward Regulators*
*Legitimizing the Administrative State*

### Summary
Questions for Discussion
Ethical Quandary

*W*hen, in the late 18th century, Americans created their own country, they joined a parade that had begun roughly three centuries earlier when the first nation-states began to appear. The nation-state was the result of the most massive merger in history. Its appearance meant the elimination of the petty baronies and fiefdoms that characterized feudalism during the Middle Ages. Burgundy and Normandy, for example, disappeared with other provinces into the superstate called France. Wales, Scotland, and England were combined to form the United Kingdom. In America the state-building process was almost the same: New York and Pennsylvania, along with the other 11 states, became one part of one nation.

While the emergence of the nation-state brought indubitable advantages—elimination of toll barriers at every stream and river, uniform currency, a common judicial system, greater security, and the like—it also brought with it a malignancy called nationalism. Nationalism was the expression of a tribal ethic that treated foreigners as inferiors, the home country as God's special creation, and the gentry as the moral elite. Since the end of the World War II, nationalism has intensified. Between 1945 and 1968 sixty-six new states came into being as Europe's colonial empires were interred. Each struggle for independence was marked by a rise in nationalism that gave power to the unifying effort. If unification was not achieved, then hatred of the outsider intensified. Aggrieved peoples—whether the two million Lithuanians, Latvians, and Estonians who joined hands across the Baltic to demand freedom; the Ukrainians calling for a "free Ukraine"; or the South African blacks who want, not an end to the nation-state, but an end to white dominance over it—spoke to and from a particular history, language, culture, and wounded sense of collective identity. The nation-state became the church and, too often, people's only God.

Yet dangerous as nationalism can be for world stability, it is also a virtue that provides a given people a sense of identity and mission. The story of the North American nation-state is the story of a people who successfully identified themselves and defined, with uneven success, their own mission. That identification was legally established by the Constitution. The national mission has been spelled out by the president and members of Congress, by Supreme Court justices and federal regulators, by political parties and pressure groups, by corporations and unions, and by other informed entities such as consumer groups, environmental elites, lawyers, and accountants. ■

*The purposes of this chapter are:*

1. To give a sense of the long intellectual heritage that the Founding Fathers exploited when they began work on Constitution building in 1787.
2. To note the urgent problems they confronted.
3. To identify the most salient features of the polity that the Constitution sought to protect.
4. To demonstrate the power (and abuses thereto) of elected officials.
5. To examine the power (and abuses thereto) of the nonelected officials like judges and regulators.

## The Constitution

### *The Intellectual Heritage*

One of the most extraordinary qualities of the nation's Founding Fathers was that they were politically multilingual: they knew something of Plato and Aristotle, and they could speak the language of conservatives and liberals—political philosophers like Bolingbroke, Montesquieu, Locke, Hume, and many others—"whichever seemed rhetorically appropriate to the particular argument at hand."[1] They understood that if the Constitutional Convention of 1787 was to succeed, a compromise had to be worked out or extraordinary means of persuasion had to be applied. They were, in short, an intellectual elite with political savvy.

Thus, to begin the political story of the United States is to throw an intellectual curve ball at American students if they are indeed as bereft of philosophical understanding as one distinguished political philosopher said they were.[2] It is, therefore, opportune to identify the cast of characters who, fleetingly but measurably, played key roles as mentors to the framers. Viscount Bolingbroke (1678–1751), England's notorious rake and political opportunist, nevertheless wrote one of the most astute essays on the weaknesses of political parties. Perhaps that is why the founders never mentioned them in their document. Montesquieu (1689–1755), an acquaintance of Bolingbroke and possibly an equally active sensualist, wrote the *Spirit of the Laws* to argue, among other things, that individual liberties were best preserved when political power was divided among three independent branches: legislative, executive, and judicial. The founders embraced Montesquieu's proposition with enthusiasm.

John Locke (1632–1704), so revered by the framers of the Constitution that they called him the "Great Mr. Locke," was possibly as much an intellectual father to them as he was to the Whigs who fought to diminish the power of the monarchy. From Locke's *Letter Concerning Toleration* (1689) the Americans learned the importance of religious tolerance and from his *Two Treatises on Government* (1690) they absorbed into their very marrow the conviction that political power depends on the people's confidence that governments would protect them and their property. Locke dominated American political thought as no other thinker anywhere dominated the political thought of a nation: he is, said one writer, "a massive cliché."[3] From David Hume (1711–1776), Adam Smith's friend, the framers learned (1) how a nation's prosperity depended on its ability to use *all* its raw materials to its best advantage (and the framers sought to assure this in Section 8 of the first article of the Constitution) and (2) how political and commercial transactions had important moral consequences. The organization of the economy was therefore not a morally neutral enterprise.

As much as by those 17th and 18th century men who lived through England's Glorious Revolution of 1689, the vocabulary of the founders was formed by both ancient and medieval philosophers. They had, for example, an easy familiarity with Plato's *Republic*, giving particular attention to the importance of joining political power and intellectual wisdom without which there could be "no rest from troubles for the cities."[4] When, therefore, a constitution is framed that protects liberty and justice it will be "for the people" a robe of many colors embroidered with all the flowers of the field."[5] Nor did they forget Aristotle's injunction in the *Politics* that a state's greatest need was not for generals or merchants but for civic virtue.

Plato's "flowers of the field" were also found in the West's religious traditions. The Old Testament spoke of the idea of covenant, as distinct from contract; St. Thomas Aquinas defended liberty against those who would confine the making of the conscience to churchmen; the practical advice he gave to the King of Cyprus in his *Governance of Princes* on the administration of justice through impartial investigations and procedures hinted at what was to become known as due process.

The idea of the state as a covenant received particular emphasis during the Protestant Reformation, when believers returned to careful rereading of Scripture. Of the many names associated with covenanting, two that merit special attention are Heinrich Bullinger (1504–1575) of Zurich and Johannes Althusius (1557–1638) of Westphalia. The influence of Bullinger was felt in the Dutch revolt against Spain and the formation of the United Provinces as a federal republic based on covenant. Althusius applied the idea of religious covenant more explicitly to the political language when he wrote:

> *Politics is the art of consociating men for the purpose of establishing, cultivating, and conserving social life among them. Whence it is called "symbiotics." The subject matter of politics is therefore consociation, in which the symbiotes pledge themselves—each to the other—by explicit or tacit covenant, to mutual communication of whatever is useful and necessary for the harmonious exercise of social life.*[6]

Althusius, had he been alive in 1787, might well have written the preamble to the Constitution. Certainly his thought has been kept alive by another distinguished theologian, H. Richard Niebuhr, who wrote:

> *One of the great common patterns that guided men in the period when American democracy was formed, that was present both in*

*their understanding and in their action ... was the pattern of the covenant or of federal society.... It is not meant that this was the exclusive pattern. None of our symbols, save in fanaticism, is likely to be exclusively employed and there are few periods, if any, in human history when a dominant pattern of interpretation does not have its rivals. What is suggested is that a fundamental pattern in American minds in the seventeenth, eighteenth, and early nineteenth centuries was the covenant idea ... [emphasis added].*[7]

Niebuhr's point is the position of those who believe that "two thousand years of political theorizing and practical experience crystallized in Philadelphia in the summer of 1787 in the most brilliantly sustained intellectual and oratorical achievement of history."[8] This is merited praise for meritorious men. The Constitution, in sum, was the work of philosophically multilingual men who were conservative in their commitments to a covenant based on respect for justice and liberty and radical in the instruments they innovated to make these ideals meaningful. In a real sense they were, so far as government mechanisms are concerned, heretics in the 18th century world because they believed in the following:

- Consent of the governed
- Control of the governed by making the amendment process very difficult
- An independent and tenured judiciary whose word was final on the Constitution's meaning
- Checks and balances to prevent abuses of power by president and legislators
- Political equality with the 13 original colonies when the territory became a state—something that even so experienced a colonial power as England did not accept until 1931 in the Statute of Westminster
- Promotion of interstate commerce, which Western European countries brought into existence in 1992
- A Bill of Rights to protect individual liberties

The Constitution, as a human artifact, was not, is not, and never will be a perfect document. African-Americans, Native Americans, and women were excluded from the original political covenant; it allowed states to deny the vote to many on the basis of property and religion; it made the governing processes ponderously slow—even suspect when it moved quickly. This said, the nation's founders were well read, well seasoned, and brilliantly inventive, and these characterizations provide an easy transit to the story of constitution making.

## The Framers

The preceding discussion gave some sense of the building materials available to the framers: a long moral tradition presupposing that the basic rules governing human conduct were discoverable by reason, that justice and liberty were the goals of government, that concentration of power threatened those goals, and that human nature could be trusted, up to a point. But they also shared a conviction, best expressed by James Madison, that although Americans had a decent regard for traditions and for other nations, they did not blindly venerate the past. Common sense told them that government under the Articles of Confederation was showing signs of wear and tear. Only two years after the Revolutionary War ended and only four years after the Articles had been approved, serious problems surfaced. Boundary disputes among the colonies, duties imposed by one state against its neighbor (New York taxed cabbages from New Jersey and firewood from Connecticut), and the issuance of useless "rag money" had brought painful aching to the body politic. Then, in 1786, the event most dreaded occurred: revolution. In Massachusetts, Captain Daniel Sharp led an armed force of angry farmers to stop foreclosures and tax hikes.

Affairs were not so desperate as the conservatives, anxious to protect their lands and their loans, claimed. They pounced on any weakness in the Confederation to support their desire for a strong central government. Victory seemed to be in their grasp when Virginia, the most populous state, called for a convention, which met at Annapolis, Maryland, in 1786. Only nine of the thirteen states appointed delegates and only five of the nine were actually represented. It was a fiasco, rescued from disaster by a young New Yorker named Alexander Hamilton. Hamilton persuaded the delegates to adopt a report he had written calling for a convention "for the sole and express purpose of revising the Articles of Confederation."

The Continental Congress, fearful of signing its own death warrant, reluctantly agreed to ask the various state legislators to send delegates to Philadelphia—a good choice. Philadelphia was home to the Continental Congress, unofficial capital of the Confederation, and North America's largest city. John Adams wrote to his wife, Abigail, that Philadelphia was "a happy, peaceful, elegant, hospitable and polite" metropolis. The adjectives were well merited. The city boasted well-appointed houses, the country's best tavern, charming and cultivated hostesses, a tradition of exciting dinner parties that were small replicas of Paris's salons, and a Quaker reputation for enlightened social policies.

In 1787 Philadelphia also had its most scorching heat wave; humidity drained energies; wagons bounced along unpaved streets; swarms of insects stung sweating pedestrians. Philadelphia was no paradise even if Abigail Adams was led to think so. The meeting place—the State House—had been constructed a half century earlier along graceful Federal architectural lines; a high seven-foot wall protected the secrecy that the 55 delegates had imposed upon themselves. It is impossible to imagine contemporaries letting the framers "get away" with things we now routinely accept: leaks to the inquisitive, press conferences, popular elections, no hidden agenda (a determination to scrap, not scrub, the Articles). Distinctly upper crust (lawyers were especially numerous), the assemblage was not likely to spark support among the disenfranchised small farmers and city workers.

Although silenced, the public was well served by the talented men who came to work in Philadelphia with job descriptions they were prepared to ignore. Every state, except Rhode Island, sent delegates. Pennsylvania's 81-year-old Ben Franklin lent wisdom and prestige to the gathering despite a physical condition that limited him to five minutes of talking. James Wilson, another Pennsylvanian and one of the foremost lawyers at the convention, compensated for Franklin's silence by talking more than any other delegate except James Madison and Gouverneur Morris. There were other "greats," of course—men like John Adams of Massachusetts; Roger Sherman, the wily politician from Connecticut; and Alexander Hamilton and John Jay of New York. But for numbers and brilliance Virginia took first rank: George Washington, a silent commanding force as the convention's president; James Madison, scrawny, pale, and brilliant, whose detailed notes of the proceedings published in 1840 helped earn him the title of "Father" of the Constitution; Edmund Randolph, scion of a celebrated Virginia family who refused to sign the document but later rallied to its defense when Patrick Henry (who refused to go to Philadelphia because he "smelled a rat") began to vent his wrath at the framers' work.

An intriguing exercise is guestimating the number of Patrick Henrys who might be found among contemporaries. One way is to imagine being polled by workers from the George Gallup or Louis Harris organizations on these questions:

1. Would you be willing to compromise the interests of your nation (and state) for the sake of a more stable and prosperous international community?
2. If you see the tide running toward such a compromise, what would you do to protect American interests?
3. Would you support an international congress whose members would be elected on the basis of one nation, one vote, and/or population?
4. Would you support that part of the United Nations' charter of human rights that stipulates that every able-bodied person has a right to a job, health care, and public education?
5. Would you support an international court of justice with power to override the acts of Congress?

Any comparison of 18th century life in the 13 colonies to 20th century life is a limping analogy. Americans spoke the same language, fought together in a war for independence, lived in a compact area along the Atlantic coast, knew the English common law, and were predominantly white Protestants. But to minimize the magnitude of the framers' challenge is to miss the high drama and the extraordinary political achievement of 1787.

## *The Testing Time*

On September 17, 1787, their work done, the 39 delegates who signed the Constitution bade farewell to one another, fully aware that the battle for ratification that they intended to wage would be a difficult one. Reasons for opposition were expressed by farmer Amos Singletary of the Massachusetts legislature: "These lawyers, and men of learning, and moneyed men, that talk so finely, and gloss over matters so smoothly, to make us poor illiterates swallow down the pill, expect to get into Congress themselves; they expect to be the managers of the Constitution, and get all the power and all the money into their own hands, and then they will swallow up all us little folks."[9]

Faced with such formidable threats to their handiwork, Alexander Hamilton, John Jay, and James Madison joined forces to write a masterly set of essays called *The Federalist*, wherein they sought to persuade their countrymen that the Constitution was good for them and for their children. As in many of the nation's historic debates, there was considerable public apathy. But among the interested, there was great passion. Riots broke out in New York and Pennsylvania. Rhode Island and North Carolina swore they would never approve—and did not do so until some months after the new government was in operation. New Yorkers gave a squeaky three-vote margin of approval. Virginia joined only after New Hampshire's ratification assured victory—and then only by a ten-vote margin out of a total 168 votes. Table 1.1 records the dramatic story.

**Table 1.1 Ratification of the Constitution**

| State | Date | Vote in Convention | Rank in Population | 1790 Population |
|---|---|---|---|---|
| 1. Delaware | December 7, 1787 | unanimous | 13 | 59,096 |
| 2. Pennsylvania | December 12, 1787 | 46 to 23 | 3 | 433,611 |
| 3. New Jersey | December 18, 1787 | unanimous | 9 | 184,139 |
| 4. Georgia | January 2, 1788 | unanimous | 11 | 82,548 |
| 5. Connecticut | January 9, 1788 | 128 to 40 | 8 | 237,655 |
| 6. Massachusetts (including Maine) | February 7, 1788 | 187 to 168 | 2 | 475,199 |
| 7. Maryland | April 28, 1788 | 63 to 11 | 6 | 319,728 |
| 8. South Carolina | May 23, 1788 | 149 to 73 | 7 | 249,073 |
| 9. New Hampshire | June 21, 1788 | 57 to 46 | 10 | 141,899 |
| 10. Virginia | June 26, 1788 | 89 to 79 | 1 | 747,610 |
| 11. New York | July 26, 1788 | 30 to 27 | 5 | 340,241 |
| 12. North Carolina | November 21, 1789 | 195 to 77 | 4 | 395,005 |
| 13. Rhode Island | May 29, 1790 | 34 to 32 | 12 | 69,112 |

When the votes were totaled, euphoria replaced exhaustion. An American orator proudly listed the lessons his country had taught the world:
1. A large country could be ruled by a republican form of government without monarchy or an aristocracy.
2. Religious worship needed no legal establishment: "To allow all to think freely for themselves in matters of religion, and to worship God according to the dictates of their own Consciences is the best policy."

3. Church and state could comfortably exist without formal alliance.
4. Mild punishment (especially for political crimes) tends to reduce criminality.
5. People are happier and more content under a mild and equitable government, which is far stronger than arbitrary governments and in less danger of being overturned.
6. Most Americans believed, as one contemporary observed, that to admit "the Jews to all the privileges of natural-born subjects is far from being the dangerous experiment that had been generally supposed."[10]

## *The Present*

The Constitution, like the Bible or Tolstoy's *War and Peace* or Margaret Mitchell's *Gone with the Wind*, was not meant to be read in one sitting. But it was meant to be read. The fact is that, except for possibly lawyers and scholars, relatively few Americans have ever read the Constitution in its entirety. National holidays celebrate major events and figures—Veterans Day, Presidents Day, Labor Day, Martin Luther King, Jr. Day, the Fourth of July—but there is no Constitution Day. Yet it is that great document that provides the groundrules according to which live 250 million people of different origins, races, and religions. It is inspiration to millions more throughout the world who seek the freedom and justice it assures.[11] It reveals many of the hopes of its framers for a stable order, hopes made explicit in *The Federalist Papers* by James Madison, who warned how instability

> *poisons the blessings of liberty itself. It will be of little avail to the people that the laws are made by men of their own choice if the laws be so voluminous that they cannot be read, or so incoherent that they cannot be understood; if they be repealed or revised before they are promulgated, or undergo such incessant changes that no man, who knows what the law is today, can guess what it will be tomorrow.... Another effect of public instability is the unreasonable advantage it gives to the sagacious, the enterprising, and the moneyed few over the industrious and uninformed mass of the people. Every new regulation concerning commerce or revenue, or in any manner affecting the value of the different species of property, presents a new harvest to those who watch the change, and can trace its consequences."*[12]

Stability comes through a system of checks and balances that inhibits precipitous action, through a Senate whose low turnover rate countered any surge of unwise public opinion, through an independently elected strong president with veto power and, finally, through a Supreme Court that could be employed against Congress itself.[13]

## Elected Officials

Weaknesses in implementing the Constitution were first systematically exposed by Alexis de Tocqueville, the insatiably inquisitive and enormously perceptive Frenchman who visited the United States during the 1830s, only one generation after the framers had completed their work. Despite the founders' intent to establish a powerful presidency, Tocqueville wrote that the "Americans have not been able to counteract the tendency which legislative assemblies have to get possession of the government"; as a result, the executive branch had become "an inferior and dependent power" and the process of electing and reelecting presidents "a national crisis"—"a sort of revolution," which slowed the wheels of government and turned the executive into "an easy tool in the hands of the majority."[14] Particularly dangerous was the middle class, whose quest for wealth threatened even their own freedoms.

Tocqueville's fears about structured weaknesses in the government have often been borne out. When a financial crisis engulfed the world in 1987, the response of the American government was not only indifferent, but incoherent. Other major issues, ranging from massive budget deficits to environmental and energy policies, extend the list. Dangerous stalemates occur when there is a Republican president and a Democratic Congress. Compounding the problem is the fact that, midway through the president's term, part of Congress may be replaced, and the replacements have their own agenda. Paralysis sets in much too easily—a lesson Tocqueville learned when the French could not make up their minds about reprisals against the English when they moved to claim Oregon, territory which, in the French view, was theirs.[15]

Frustration with the American system has influenced some people to look wistfully at England's parliamentary arrangement. Under it, politicians are tested over long years of public service; the climb to the prime minster's post is steep; decisive action can be taken in crisis because England's leader has a majority in Parliament; courts cannot frustrate the will of the MPs.[16] But paralysis in America is never complete. Only a short time after the Oval Office was deemed quasi-impotent, Richard Nixon was roundly denounced as the "imperial president." Long indeed is the list of powerful presidents—Jackson, Lincoln, and Teddy Roosevelt in the 19th century and Roosevelt, Truman, and Johnson (in his first term) during the 20th. Strength, of course, depends on effective political support.

## *Political Parties*

George Reedy, President Lyndon Johnson's press secretary, said it did not take long "to discover that politics is a form of warfare and that politicians have the psychology of warriors."[17] When the combatant's strength is divided, which is usually the case in American politics, compromise is inevitable and compromise means bargaining. One of the fundamental questions, therefore, is how gains from the bargain should be distributed to people who have different ideas about needs and priorities. Politics, in short, is largely a question of who gets what, when, how.[18] Although the Constitution did not mention political parties and although George Washington deplored them, the need for political parties became evident one year after the first national election in 1790, when Hamilton and Jefferson clashed over fiscal policy and foreign affairs. The Federalists supported Hamilton and the Democrat-Republicans were pro-Jefferson; the Federalists favored rule by a propertied elite whereas the Democrat-Republicans supported rule by the informed masses; the former advocated loose interpretation of the Constitution and the latter strict interpretation; the Federalists were pro-British and pro-protective tariffs while the Democrat-Republicans were pro-French and supporters of freer trade. From the nation's first days politicians knew the importance of organized groups. Soon party identification became important to voters and voter loyalty became important to candidates.[19]

If our first politicians were issue oriented—so much so that winning a vote that enhanced the country's interest was more important than personal ambitions—the same is not said of today's politicians. Issues, to be sure, remain important but personal ambition is even more so: "Careerism, rooted in an egoistic, utilitarian philosophy, is considered to be the primary motivation in almost all management theory" and politicians have embraced the new dogma wholeheartedly.[20] Party leadership was, in the past, respected because it could deliver votes when important issues faced Congress. But the "Class of '74" provided the *coup de grace* to the old autocrats of Congress and, in so doing, gained power for subcommittees and their increased professional staffs.

In the recent past, the bulk of important business in the Congress originated in the 15 standing committees of the Senate and the 20 committees of the House. Today, there are about 150 subcommittees in each, and they have become major forces. In fact, the House in 1973 passed a "Subcommittee Bill of Rights" that enhanced their influence. Membership on these subcommittees consists mainly of individuals who have a special interest in the topics to be considered. A former cabinet officer, Clifford Hardin, put it this way: "The zeal of members to develop their power base more quickly has led Congress to modify the rules and structure of the Congress to such an extent that it is becoming difficult for our national legislature to take actions that promote 'the general welfare.' Instead, promotion of special interests prevails on Capitol Hill."[21]

The new breed has shaped Congress in ways that encourage political entrepreneurship, shrewd use of media, and skills in fund raising. Whether it is coincidental or causal, the fact is that fragmentation of power in Congress has been followed by fragmentation in political parties. In what was then the most extensive survey of American voters ever conducted, the 1987 Gallup poll showed that the body politic had split into 11 diverse sectors ranging from feminists and environmentalists to religious and pro-business groups.[22]

## *Interest Groups*

Americans face a chicken-egg-first question: Is the multiplication of new interest groups the result of the successes by older and more entrenched interest groups? Or have special interest groups taken advantage of the political fragmentation in Congress? In his famous essay Number 10 in *The Federalist,* Madison wrote of factions:

> *By faction I understand a number of citizens, whether amounting to a majority or minority of the whole, who are united and actuated by some common impulse of passion, or of interest, adverse to the rights of other citizens, or to the permanent and aggregate interests of the community. . . . The latent causes of faction are sown in the nature of man; and we see them everywhere brought into different degrees of activity, according to the different circumstances of civil society. . . . So strong is this propensity of mankind to fall into mutual animosities that, where no substantial occasion presents itself, the most frivolous and fanciful distinctions have been sufficient to kindle their unfriendly passions, and excite their most violent conflicts.*
>
> *But the most common and durable source of factions has been the various and unequal distribution of property. Those who hold, and those who are without property, have ever formed distinct interests in society. Those who are creditors, and those who are debtors, fall under a like discrimination. A landed interest, a manufacturing interest, a mercantile interest, a monied interest, with many lesser interests, grow up of necessity in civilized nations, and divide them into different classes, actuated by different sentiments and views. The regulation of those various and interfering interests forms the principal task of modern legislation, and involves the spirit of party and faction in the necessary and ordinary operations of Government.*

In Madison's view, factions would be curbed because no single one of them could control either voters or Congress. Factions might kindle a flame within their particular states but would be unable to start a general conflagration. Madison's half-true prophecy may not be harshly criticized. He did not have television, national newspapers and magazines, and PACs that would make easy the creation of power bases. At first blush it would seem that legislators, drowning in a sea of bills, would be too confused to know "who was pushing what." In New York State alone, 23,000 bills are introduced in every legislative session. Only a few thousand are considered and only a thousand, if that many, ever become law. What is true of the Empire State is true of other states and of Congress. Lobbyists turn the situation to their own advantage by lobbying early in the legislative session when representatives have more time to see them.[23] Finally, there is general agreement among politicians that information provided by lobbyists on complex issues is necessary because they themselves lack sufficient expertise to make sound public policies.

As will be demonstrated in the chapters on competition and the environment, special interests do get results; if they did not, there would be no point in organizing and funding them. Thus there is the persistent question: Does congress represent more the collective or the special interest? Despite widespread belief that special interest groups prevail in most cases, evidence exists that legislators continue to vote according to their constituencies' respective preferences on issues related to public goods (that is, goods that are available for, and consumed by, all individuals in a manner that consumption by one person does not diminish its consumption by others). Of course, a single interest can unite the legislator's electorate—oil in Texas and Oklahoma, coal in West Virginia, environmental protection in Alaska, and so on. But this does not nullify the thesis that the complete constituency, more than a part thereof, influences the legislator.[24] Even the unorganized are represented by organized interest groups because the latter, wisely, work to influence a legislator only on issues toward which the voters have been—or are—indifferent. The thesis is this: those who say nothing say something.[25]

## *Money Interests*

As the late Jesse Unruh, the experienced Californian leader, once said, "money is the mother's milk of politics." The message was not lost on top corporate executives who increasingly travel to Washington ready to offer sweet talk and hard cash. Unions have also responded and have used "rebate dues" to amass money for use in election campaigns; it took 12 years for Harry Beck to win his case in 1988 against the Communication Workers of America to halt the practice. In the traditional view, political parties were seen as either (1) well organized enough to control the recruitment of candidates as well as the campaign's major issues or (2) having little relevance in an era of incumbency-dominated legislatures (once elected, rarely defeated).

Today political parties are seen as intermediaries in candidate recruitment, research/communication entities, and instruments for fund raising. In 1984 Republicans spent $10.5 million on House candidates and in 1986 they spent $6.7 million. Democrats spent over $13 million in 1984 and $2.8 million in 1986.[26] In the flow of green, Political Action Committees have played an increasingly important part. In 1976 PACs spent $5 million on Senate elections; in 1987 they spent $45 million on the Senate campaign alone. In 1989 PACs increased their contributions by 24 percent over the 1987 figure and most of the $68.7 million went to House Democrats because they controlled the chairs of the important committees and subcommittees. The importance of money in politics can be gleaned from the speech Dale Bumpers, the Arkansas Democrat, made in the Senate on February 19, 1988.

> Last year when I ran for reelection I spent about $1,500,000. I never dreamed in my wildest imagination that I would ever be able to raise $1.5 million.... That was the eighth election I have been in since I ran for governor the first time in 1970, and $1.5 million is precisely twice as much as I had spent in the other seven combined. Do you know something else? Our polls showed we were going to win and win rather handily, and I kept telling my staff and my financiers, "Let us save some of that money...." But we did not save it. Do you know why? You do not raise it to save it. You raise it to get reelected and you have this inordinate fear that if you do not spend every dime of it, and say you have $2,000 or $3,000 left in the bag, and you lose, you really look

*stupid. You say, "Well, if I had just spent that last money I could have won...."*

*When I ran for governor the first time and saw how much cash floats around in a campaign, I was absolutely traumatized. A lot of people who I had never seen before in my life came in and handed me ten $100 bills.... Most of those people [and corporations] would say, "All I want is good government." After I got elected, I found out some of those people wanted just a little bit more than good government.*[27]

The experience should not have traumatized the governor. In politics givers expect to be getters. The corporations, the professions, and the unions are givers, and sweet charity is not among their motives. While unsafe to make sweeping generalizations on the basis of one Senator's confession, the old story (August 1960) told in *Reader's Digest* still has a ring of truth. Writing on how payola works in politics, Assemblyman X (widely believed to be the same Jesse Unruh quoted earlier) told of his freshman year in the California legislature when the election of the Speaker promised to produce a sharp partisan fight. The Speaker had as much power as the governor. Lobbyists who initially ignored Mr. X now courted him to vote for their preferred candidate. Only after he had repeatedly received offers from donors to clean up his campaign debts did he realize that "I was being offered a bribe. Other legislators were approached in less subtle ways." Slowly, but steadily, X began to play the game because building a power base meant compromise and cash—hence the dilemma:

*If I had stayed away from the lobbyists I would have been ineffective. If I take their money and give them nothing for it, I am a cheat. If I do their bidding, I could be cheating the public. I find myself rationalizing what I have done. The tragedy is that I may wind up serving the very elements I set out to beat—yet not even know that I have changed.*[28]

Campaigns and cash have become so wedded that reformers fear the marriage will lead to maimed offspring because bought elections mean puppet legislators. One publicized effort on damage control came on April 28, 1988, when Archibald Cox, a former Solicitor General and the first Watergate special prosecutor, urged Senate subcommittees to strengthen congressional rules through five steps:

1. Ban honoraria for members of Congress. Using honoraria to supplement congressional pay is a way for special interest money to be funneled directly into the pockets of public officials. Like other special interest money (PAC campaign contributions), honoraria fees are destroying the institutional integrity of Congress.
2. Tighten the rules on travel and reimbursement by establishing clear restrictions against using reimbursed travel as paid vacations.
3. Tighten the restrictions on members' financial holdings through such mechanisms as divestiture of certain kinds of holdings tailored to committee assignments, and establishing blind trusts.

4. Remove the "grandfather clause" in current law that allows members of Congress in office on January 8, 1980, to keep their surplus campaign contributions for personal use after leaving Congress.
5. Tighten the rules regarding the use of campaign funds for noncampaign purposes.

Congress, to date, has not found the menu very palatable. And while the country hopes for reforms in Congress, others are worried about power and performance of nonelected officials.

## Appointed Officials

In Abraham Lincoln's memorable words, the United States is a nation "of the people, by the people, for the people." The phrase captured the attention of Americans because it buttressed their belief that they elected their president and their Congress and that, if affairs were poorly handled, they could throw the rascals out. Two powerful governing bodies, however, are beyond their reach—federal judges and federal regulators. The first can undo the work of Congress. The second can do things Congress may never have intended. Both deserve to be better known.

### *The Supreme Court*

Before 1801, the year John Marshall became Chief Justice, the Supreme Court was the puny dwarf of the three branches of government. Personality and politics were to shape Marshall's career as a judge as well as the character of the government itself in ways few imagined when the Constitution was ratified. During the Revolutionary War when he was among the shivering soldiers at Valley Forge, Marshall came to loathe the weaknesses of a decentralized government. It was, therefore, not surprising that Marshall viewed with deep concern the coming to the presidency of Thomas Jefferson whose preference for state power was well known. Their differing political philosophies turned into personal animosities when Marshall allowed Aaron Burr—whom Jefferson, with good reason, despised—to escape conviction as a traitor. In this atmosphere of conflicting ideologies and personalities the *Marbury v. Madison* case arose.[29]

In the final hours of his administration, John Adams had named a number of "midnight judges," one of whom was William Marbury; however, Marbury's formal commission was not delivered to him and he therefore asked Madison, now Secretary of State in Jefferson's administration, to deliver it. Madison refused. Marbury then appealed to the Supreme Court to issue a mandamus, a power the Court had under the Judiciary Act of 1789. Marshall refused, insisting that the act was unconstitutional. Outraged Democrat-Republicans denounced Marshall as incompetent (he had only six weeks of formal legal training), politically ambitious, crafty, and cunning. But John Marshall had something presidents and congressmen had not—tenure. And for another 30 years this "incompetent" and "crafty" judge made history in a series of decisions that assured respect for the seemingly novel doctrine of judicial review.[30]

**Judicial Review.** Judicial review existed in colonial times, when it was practiced by the Privy Councils. Eight state constitutions explicitly provided for judicial review and, by 1803, at least 18 decisions by state courts had declared state laws in conflict with state constitutions. The Judiciary Act of 1789 gave federal courts authority to review *state laws* and *state constitutional provisions* to determine whether they conflicted with the federal Constitution; however, in several cases prior to 1803, federal circuit courts had held state *and* federal statutes unconstitutional.[31] The Marbury decision unsettled many and vindicated Tocqueville, who had noted the trend.[32]

Since Marshall's time Americans have experienced bitter debate over the authentic meaning of judicial review. Despite his political motivations, Marshall stuck closely to the language of the Constitution in reaching his decision. The question today is whether Marshall's approach or a more commodious interpretation of judicial review is necessary in a society made complicated by technological and scientific advances. Should less attention be given to words and more to the document's "penumbras and emanation"? The Marshallites recall Justice Harlan's 1969 dissent in *Reynolds v. Sims* when he noted trenchantly that the Constitution is not a panacea for every blot on the public welfare; as a consequence the Court, ordained as a judicial body, should not be thought of as a general haven for reform movements.[33] This sense of judicial restraint has been reflected in the opinions of other renowned jurists like Learned Hand, Felix Frankfurter, and Hugo Black.

But the question has been put another way: How can we best achieve the ends of a modern representative democracy that includes both popular self-government and the protection of essential minority rights?[34] Judicial review's meaning became particularly urgent during the Warren Court years of the 1960s. Before Warren—and after Franklin Roosevelt's court-packing scheme had been earlier scuttled—the Court began to defend the spread of regulatory powers to the point that presidents and judges seemed to be working as one. The lesson for liberals was that the presidency and the courts could best live in peace when the judges accepted Harlan's dictum by limiting their sphere of jurisdiction. The White House was power; the Supreme Court was servant.

The Warren Court steadily and systematically breached these self-imposed constraints. The abstention doctrine (a federal court should decline to exercise jurisdiction when a constitutional issue rested on unsettled questions of state law) was consigned to the scrap heap. Rules governing determinations of mootness were relaxed to promote the court's view of the public interest. One example was the Supreme Court's intervention in the reapportionment policies of state legislatures. Reapportionment had been a cherished political power of jealous states that the Court itself had recognized in 1946.[35] This judicial acknowledgment of state power, however, did not disturb the Court when it later produced the "one-man one-vote" rule.[36] To the Court's great satisfaction, the ruling was embraced by the Kennedy administration, the AFL–CIO, the Americans for Democratic Action, and the NAACP. The political vision now was of an activist presidency and an activist Court. If frustrated by the president or Congress, forces dedicated to racial equality, environmental protection, abortion, and court reform could "go to court"; class action suits opened the gates even wider because claims that appeared minuscule when asserted by individuals became very substantial when aggregated against a common defendant.

The Warren Court made another seemingly technical change that had enormous practical consequences. Instead of defining injunction as an extraordinary writ, federal judges were allowed to issue injunctions on matters that formerly were handled in the political arena—jail overcrowding, teacher strikes, public toilets, social agencies, and union governance. The result was predictable: when a group could not secure legislative support, it sought judicial relief. Supporters of causes that did not evoke wide public support—prison reform is one example—now marshaled their strengths for appeals to the Supreme Court.[37]

One of the more controversial decisions came in April 1990 (*Missouri v. Jenkins*). By a 5 to 4 vote, the Supreme Court sustained the right of federal judges to order increased tax levies when affirmative action programs needed more money than voters were ready to provide. The decision related to federal judge Russell Clark's effort to provide the best public schools for all Kansas City youngsters. In the judge's opinion, between $500 and $700 million was needed to make the city's school system one of the best in the country. The Kansas City Missouri School Board (KCMSB) itself wanted the new revenues but Missouri's constitution mandated a two-thirds vote to raise property taxes. The school board was unable to get the necessary margin. The frustrated judge then ordered the tax increase. The minority opinion, delivered by Justice Anthony Kennedy, held the following:

> *The power of taxation is one that the federal judiciary does not possess. In our system "the legislative department alone has access to the pockets of the people" for it is the legislature that is accountable to them and represents their will. The [judicial] authority that would levy the tax at issue here shares none of these qualities. Our federal judiciary, by design, is not representative or responsible to the people in a political sense; it is independent. . . .*
>
> *Perhaps it is good educational policy to provide a school district with the items included in the KCMSB capital improvement plan, for example: high schools in which every classroom will have air conditioning, an alarm system, and fifteen microcomputers; a 2,000-square-foot planetarium; greenhouses and vivariums; a 25-acre farm with an air-conditioned meeting room for 104 people; a Model United Nations wired for language translation; broadcast-capable radio and television studios with an editing and animation lab; a temperature controlled art gallery; movie editing and screening rooms; a 3,500-square-foot dust-free diesel mechanics*

room; 1,875-square-foot elementary school animal rooms for use in a Zoo Project; swimming pools, and numerous other facilities.

But these items are a part of legitimate political debate over educational policy and spending priorities, not the constitution's command of racial equality. Indeed, it may be that a mere twelve-acre petting farm, or other corresponding reductions in court-ordered spending, might satisfy constitutional requirements, while preserving scarce public funds for legislative allocation to other public needs, such as paving streets, feeding the poor, building prisons, or housing the homeless. Perhaps the KCMSB's Classical Greek theme that schools emphasizing forensics and self-government will provide exemplary training in participatory democracy. But if today's dicta become law, such lessons will be of little use to students who grow up to become taxpayers.[38]

Decisions reached by the activist Court were, in the main, very laudable. Hitherto excluded groups could seek support that the majority was unprepared to give. But the gains also had a price: politicians could duck difficult issues; political ideology, possibly even above legal competence, often prevailed when nominations to the Court were made; and the nonelected could become the self-annointed.

The great debate over the relative weight of legal competence and ideological preferences occurred during the fall of 1987 when President Reagan nominated Robert Bork for a seat on the Supreme Court. Bork failed to secure Senate confirmation because the Senate majority saw in the president's action a deliberate attempt to reintroduce conservatism into the Court and downgrade the Court's image.[39] In the heat of the Bork battle, *The New York Times* editorialized that Americans had

created a Constitution, added a Bill of Rights, and amended the Constitution repeatedly to embrace persons previously excluded. By their very breadth, whole concepts like equal protection and due process of law guard against abuses by the majority and invite generosity to the underdog. That's the Constitution most Americans honor. Does Judge Bork? His earnest but inadequate answers say no. So should the Senate.[40]

Bork's supporters countered that the Bill of Rights, as well as amendments thereto, were to be resolved in the political, not judicial, arena. Court intrusions were seen by Bork's defenders as unacceptable because the Court had frequently ruled either contrary to, or without guidance from, constitutional meaning and purpose. It had become more the maker than the interpreter of the law.[41] But ideological differences had become so frozen by the time the Senators came to examine Bork's credentials that he was, according to columnist Edwin Yoder, Jr., "the victim of a slur campaign. . . . You would gather from this shameful barrage that the role of justices is to cast more or less predictable political votes on the bench, as senators and congressmen do in the halls of Congress."[42]

The intensity of the Bork debate and the line of judicial thinking initiated by the Warren Court have tended to obscure one important fact: the

Court had historically oscillated between restraint and activism. During the first quarter of the 20th century judges overturned statutes that they considered threats to economic freedom, including child labor laws, minimum wage and hour regulations, and the income tax. In the 1930s it rejected several pieces of New Deal legislation. Because the debate over the Court's philosophy has important implications for everyone, including business, unions, and professions, it is helpful to review the environment in which the present dialogue has taken place.

**Innovators and Originalists.** As earlier indicated, behind the Bork battle was the fundamental question: how *should* judges interpret the Constitution? Two common responses may be classified as either (a) innovative or (b) originalist. The innovative school argues that the Constitution is a living document that must be nourished by rulings that meet modern problems; without such innovation the Constitution would soon wither.[43] Guidance should be sought in the ambitions and goals of the framers and not solely their intent as expressed in a written product. Montesquieu's spirit of the law should be the spirit of the Court, a judicial spirit that has muted the differences between the "liberal" Warren Court and the somewhat "conservative" Burger Court. The 21st century citizen cannot be frozen in an 18th century ideological ice pond.

Advocates of the "original intent" thesis, on the other hand, note that what is at stake is nothing less than the question of how the country should be governed in regard to basic issues of social policy: should such issues be decided by elected representatives, largely on a state-by-state basis, or, as has been the case for the past three decades, primarily by a majority of the nine Justices of the United States Supreme Court?[44] The words of a noted scholar, the late Edwin S. Corwin, ring in the ears of the originalists: "What a judge cannot prove he can still decide."[45] And, say proponents of original intent, judges should decide according to rules explicitly stated or clearly implied by the document itself. This means several things, first of which is a return to the philosophy firmly stated by a Justice whom all view as decidedly liberal, Louis Brandeis. In a series of "will nots" Brandeis wrote:

> *The Court* will not *pass upon the constitutionality of legislation in a friendly, nonadversary, proceeding . . .* will not *anticipate a question of constitutional law in advance of the necessity of deciding it . . .* will not *formulate a rule of constitutional law broader than the precise facts to which it is to be applied . . .* will not *pass upon a constitutional question if there is also present some other ground upon which the case may be disposed of . . .* will not *pass upon the validity of a statute upon complaint of one who fails to show that he is injured by its operation . . .* will not *pass upon the constitutionality of a statute at the instance of one who has availed himself of its benefits. . . . When the constitutionality of an act is challenged, this Court will first ascertain whether a construction of the status is fairly possible by which the question may be avoided.*[46]

It follows, therefore, that in the resolution of cases (congressional redistricting; the meaning of a contract, will, or statute—and even the Constitution itself), the framers' words govern. Bork had defined "original intent" not as a rule applicable only to circumstances specifically contemplated by the framers but rather as accepted rules of legal construction that reflect what the text says. When further interpretation is needed, the most logical inferences from the most plausible meanings of the words should be used. Bork defended this concept of originalism by saying that there was "no principled way in legal reasoning to decide that one man's qualifications are more deserving of respect than another's or that one form of gratification is more worthy than another."[47] Such determinations belong to the elected branches of government.

**The Power of the Court.** When a political institution takes a major step to expand its powers it is unlikely to retreat. During Warren's tenure, for example, 19 federal statutes were held invalid, and under Chief Justice Burger even more were declared unconstitutional. The Court's power to limit Congress was demonstrated in 1983 when the justices not only declared a specific law unconstitutional, but invalidated all acts of Congress that included legislative vetoes of decisions by the executive branch related to the bill.[48] The effect was to nullify over 63 bills with legislative vetoes already passed.

Business now deals with a Court whose decisions influence its operations as much as—possibly more than—the laws passed by the country's elected officials. Cries for reform are heard: limit the judges' term in office, elect judges, give veto power to Congress. Such suggestions seem unlikely to be passed. For the present, at least, Supreme Court judges hold center stage. And all constituencies, including business, have a stake in knowing who the actors are and the lines they will, in all probability, speak. What the Supreme Court has explicitly given to some groups it takes implicitly from another. Since Justice Warren's time, the disadvantaged have gained slightly while the privileged have lost slightly. Yet the happy paradox is that both will gain in the long run. However, judicial review continues to stir passionate debate, especially in light of a 1958 case that placed everyone, whether or not party to the litigation, under the watchful eyes of the judicial ringmasters.[49] And the ringmasters, lamented federal judge Frank Easterbrook, have used a form of reasoning that "makes judicial reason and modern constitutional theory incompatible."[50]

It may be time to reconsider three criteria for judicial decision making that were advanced by law professor Herbert Wechsler, who felt that judges should (1) rely on *neutral* principles (by which is meant "reasoning with respect to all the issues in the case, reasons that in their generality and their neutrality transcend any immediate result that is involved");[51] (2) apply only the enduring principles stipulated by the Constitution and placed beyond the power of the majorities; and (3) avoid efforts to solve judicially the major social evils of society.

The norms are interconnected and this interrelatedness means that, while a neutral and durable principle may be "a thing of beauty and a joy forever, if it lacks connection with any value the Constitution marks as special, it is not a constitutional principle and the Court has no business imposing it."[52] The three norms are hard to apply because the phrasemakers in Philadelphia were smart enough to realize their need for selected delectable ambiguities. The framers had at least some prior experience with judicial review. They had little or no experience with the "administrative state."

## Federal Regulators

**Origins of the Administrative State.** The common belief is that the federal bureaucracy originated either during the New Deal days of Franklin Roosevelt or during the period immediately following World War II. In reality, bureaucracy came in 1887—exactly a century after the Constitution was completed—when Congress passed the Interstate Commerce Act. Unlike 1787, no cannons boomed, no flags waved, no toasts were drunk. But an acorn was sown and the mighty administrative oak grew rapidly. Another giant step was taken in 1890 when Congress passed the Sherman Antitrust Act. With time, squadrons of regulatory agencies have become ubiquitous. When, for example, the Consumer Product Safety Commission (PSC) ordered the recall of some children's toys, only a few theorists (and a very worried toy manufacturer) asked, "Why should some bureaucrat nobody ever voted for be able to do this?" Most people probably responded instead, "Those greedy toymakers will do anything for a buck." If government agencies are so intrusive, why were they established in the first place? Why have they been allowed to proliferate? The answer is the same today as it was in 1887: a problem or need arose that required the kind of constant attention that elected officials could not provide. In practice, however, the line between necessary oversight and unnecessary intrusion is often blurred.

**Hostility toward Regulators.** The popular view is easy to state: public administrators are second-rate people who, if more intelligent, would be "hacking it" in the business and professional world;[53] they are greedy for power they cannot earn in open elections; they identify too quickly with the special interest they are asked to control or, alternately, they get in the way of the legitimate work that the regulated must do; they sabotage the policies formed by the elected officials. Hostility to bureaucrats is bipartisan. Little differences can be discovered between the negative views toward regulators of Arthur Schlesinger, Jr., and Theodore Sorensen of the Kennedy administration and John Erlichman and H. W. Haldeman of the Nixon years.

Bureaucrats are butts for jokesters and targets for novelists. Illustrative is Anthony Burgess's short story about an 80-year-old man named Paxton who loved to travel but who hated customs and immigration officers. One day at an airport he engaged in conversation with a traveling businessman who was startled when Paxton threw his passport into a trash can. Surprise turned to consternation when the stranger discovered that Paxton's plastic folder was crammed with airline tickets to Rio, Sydney, Honolulu, Moscow, Tokyo, and New York. Asked how he could enter a country without a passport, Paxton cheerily informed his newfound friend that, on arrival at his destination, he always retreated to the travel lounge to freshen up before his next flight was called. "You'll be always traveling without arriving," said the acquaintance.[54] The Burgess story ends with Paxton being hauled away by men in white coats—with no passport needed and no bureaucrats to ensnare him.

The public often see bureaucrats as parts of a hostile elite who are not held accountable through the political process and can be restrained only by the federal courts which, in 1935, twice ruled regulatory bodies unconstitutional. The two cases (*Schechter Poultry Corporation v. United States* and *Panama Refining Company v. Ryan*) are often considered by contemporaries as ending of one of the darkest ages of constitutional history, the era in which the courts threw prudence and reason to the winds in their zeal to protect laissez-faire capitalism.[55] Two years later, however, the Court reversed itself when it agreed that Congress did indeed have power to establish agencies beyond the president's control.

Particularly irksome are the so-called *independent* agencies like the Federal Reserve Board, the National Labor Relations Board, the Securities and Exchange Commission, and, more recently, the Environmental Protection Agency (EPA) and the Office of Safety and Health Administration (OSHA). When regulators err, as they did during the savings and loan crisis of 1988–1990, the taxpayers pay a fearful price. Independent agencies especially have aroused the ire of presidents and their staffs.

**Legitimizing the Administrative State.** The real question is whether large-scale bureaucracy has become a power so inflexible, so untouchable, and so immovable that it is a menace to the constitutional order. The answer is no—for five reasons: efficiency, the "pluralized" presidency, the "sophisticated" Congress, "judicialization" for the agency, and the resurgence of the states. Illustrations suggest the story.

*Efficiency.* Government bureaucrats are not wolves in sheep's clothing; they are simply people who help the country run.[56] As such, they have the legitimacy Woodrow Wilson perceived they would have when the Interstate Commerce Commission came into being. In his celebrated book, *The Study of Administration,* Wilson did not hold that the bureaucracy would promote democratic values; rather, like Max Weber, he said that bureaucracy could become a tool for efficiency in government as it was a tool for efficiency in private corporations.[57] The bureaucrat was not "a murderous fellow sharpening a knife cleverly."[58] Although not needed when most Americans lived on farms, traveled by horse and buggy, and behaved according to the ethic of individualism, bureaucracy was absolutely essential when Americans lived in cities, traveled by trains and planes, and lived by the organizational ethic of the large corporation.

***Pluralized Presidency.*** Every president likes to be thought of as a leader. But the best of leaders cannot always be the best informed. If the expertise exists in some bureaucratic agency that is largely insulated from presidential control, the chief executive wants to have his own experts on the White House staff. These aides know what the president wants, what public opinion will support, what Congress will accept. Sometimes a staff member may challenge the president—as Donald Regan challenged Ronald Reagan—but when confrontations occur, the aide "retires." And when two sets of experts clash, dislike of one for the other increases exponentially. During the disastrous Bay of Pigs incident, for example, President Kennedy thought he could run the campaign solely with help from his own appointees; after all, he had brought the "best and the brightest" to his White House. But the best and brightest gave advice that some of the unconsulted bureaucrats knew was dead wrong. Presidents also make great use of task forces composed of knowledgeable outsiders to make important policy recommendations. Whether by appointed staff or by outsiders, the decision-making process now includes a large number of smart people, evidently in reliance on the old maxim that "two heads are better than one." It is realistic, therefore, to see presidential decision making as pluralized in nature.

***The Sophisticated Congress.*** Threatened by experts from the bureaucracies and from the White House, and overwhelmed by a deluge of complicated problems, Congress sought—and secured—its own core of experts. Individual members of Congress have expanded their own staffs, as have congressional committees and subcommittees. The value of these experts to Congress became evident when the reports of the Congressional Budget Office were given as much credence as those of the president's Office of Management and Budget. Their essentiality to Congress was even clearer in a phenomenon that has evoked both praise and criticism, namely, the incumbents' success in running for reelection. Such success is due in no small part to the ability of congressmen to resolve problems their constituents encounter with bureaucracies like Social Security and the Veterans Administration.[59] Staff members do the real work. Legislators get the credit. Finally, better staff enables congressmen to write better bills or, if not better, bills in technical areas where they previously had to remain silent. There is, however, a bleak side to the story. The fear now is that Congress has become a prisoner of its own hired hands—legislators who look and act more sophisticated than they really are.

***Judicialization.*** Judicialization is an awkwardly coined word that can be understood in two ways. It can mean a law that forces the agency to provide oral hearings on its recommendations and to make its decisions only on the basis of the written record. This was the case for the FTC when the Magnusson-Moss Act was approved in 1974 as a response to the FTC's assumption of rule-making powers in 1962.[60] Judicialization can also mean the increased jurisdiction of the courts, particularly in such areas as environment, fair employment, and civil rights. Agencies like the EPA, OSHA, and EEOC have issued rules that federal judges later struck down as inadequate. If a given agency appears to be either too somnolent or too "hyped," the courts often intervene. The whole point of judicialization is that bureaucrats do not wield, as a general rule, the awesome powers the electorates fear and the elected officials decry.

**The Role of the States.** The states present a less clear picture of what bureaucracy has meant to the federal order. In the constitution the police power of the state (jurisdiction over health, welfare, and education) was deemed sacrosanct. When these powers were threatened in the 19th century, the country went to Civil War. Since Roosevelt's New Deal, there has been a massive power shift from state capitals to Washington—so much so that states appeared to be neglected stepchildren of an autocratic father.[61] From the federal government, however, they learned important lessons. When states began to establish their own bureaucracies—often as mirrors of the federal prototypes—their citizens learned to seek relief for local ills from bureaucrats. A proposal to increase bus fares, enlarge taxi companies, or hike gas and electric costs brought hosts of citizens to state bureaucrats to approve (or protest) the proposed actions. In a sense, therefore, the administrative state increased rather than diminished citizen participation.

# Summary

What, then, is history's probable verdict on the bureaucratic state? The first answer is that it has become one of the major instruments for change. While focus has been on the courts, the bureaucracy has also transformed the face of government. One scholar encapsulates the exciting story in words worth quoting in detail:

> *There is perhaps nowhere in American political life where the rise of bureaucracy has been accompanied by more changes than in the operation of the federal system. Since the 1930s state, local, and national agencies have been laced together by intricate bureaucratic networks carrying on domestic programs that are federally financed and locally administered. Some observers see this development as centralizing in its effect—transferring power from state and local to national agencies. Others argue that it has opened up authentic opportunities for decentralization, as opposed to the illusory opportunities that had previously existed, by providing states and localities with the resources to undertake many activities they could not otherwise afford. But both sides would certainly agree that the bureaucratization of intergovernmental relationships within the political system represents a fundamental change in the character of American federalism.*[62]

Every branch of government has been changed and the changes, on balance, can benefit the public, especially when cost-benefit analyses and judicial processes are factored into the rule-making procedures of the agency.

As never before, the way agencies operate, how they are constituted, and how they are staffed are important to the business community. *The appointed have become as important as the elected.* That explains why confirmation hearings will become more partisan, more political, and more acrimonious.

## *Questions for Discussion*

1. Upon completion of your studies, you are offered two jobs: (1) staff director of your state's political party and (2) an employee of a major corporation at a comparable level of importance and income. Which would you take?
2. You are a 45-year-old corporate vice president earning good money. You are offered a job on a Washington-based regulatory commission that deals with issues on which you have expertise. Would you accept?
3. You are a successful executive who is offered a job as CEO of a reputable West European company. One of the conditions is that you must become a citizen of the host country. Would you accept?
4. A bitter senatorial contest involves one candidate who favors an "international court of commerce" with authority to decide all disputes involving international business and another candidate who insists that this amounts to "giving away the store to foreigners." All other things being equal, whom would you support?
5. In your judgment, which of the following is true? Why do you think so?
   a. PACs should be outlawed.
   b. Independent agencies like the Federal Reserve Board and the Federal Trade Commission should be held accountable to Congress or the president because it is the elected official who must respond to public criticism.
   c. Bork got a raw deal when his nomination for the Supreme Court was rejected by the Senate.

## Ethical Quandary

### *Executive and Politics*

You are a young executive with a Milwaukee-based corporation. Having been impressed by a report from the Business Roundtable on the substantial deficiencies of the public school system, you decide that it is your civic duty to try to improve the educational system of your own city. You run for school director and are elected.

Shortly after your election you are visited by Polly Williams, a state legislator, who advocates vouchers for the city's poor children. Under the plan a child could go either to a public or to a nonpublic school. Because Williams is African-American, her position is important. Just as you are making up your mind to support vouchers, you are visited by representatives of the local public-school teachers, who tell you that voucher systems (1) are unconstitutional, (2) drain scarce resources from already financially strapped public schools, (3) are divisive, and (4) "dump" problem children on the public schools. You ask the teacher representatives to explain why nonpublic school students outperform their cohorts in the public schools. Their answer is that parental involvement is high in the nonpublics and relatively low among the publics.

Reviewing the situation you conclude that competition among types of schools, even if limited, is a good thing. When you make your pro-voucher decision known, your CEO is inundated by phone calls and letters denouncing you for your positive position on vouchers. It becomes clear that your superior would be happy if you would simply resign from the board "for personal reasons."

## Question

- What would you do?

## Notes

1. Forrest McDonald, *Novus Ordo Saecolorum: The Intellectual Origins of the Constitution* (Lawrence, Kans.: University Press of Kansas, 1986), 235. See also Gary Wills, *Explaining America: The Federalist* (Garden City, N.Y.: Doubleday, 1981); and Gordon S. Wood, *The Creation of the American Republic* (Chapel Hill, N.C.: The University of North Carolina Press, 1969). These two books have the added virtue of putting into stark relief the founders' emphasis on community rights versus individual rights. Finally, a good article by William D. Liddle on Bolingbroke shows his great influence: "A Patriot King, or None: Lord Bolingbroke and the American Renunciation of George III," *Journal of American History* 65 (March 1979): 951–995.
2. Allan Bloom, *The Closing of the American Mind: How Higher Education Has Failed Democracy and Impoverished the Souls of Today's Students* (New York: Simon and Schuster, 1987).
3. Louis Hartz, *The Liberal Tradition in America: An Interpretation of American Political Thought Since the Revolution* (New York: Harcourt, Brace, and World, 1955), 140.
4. Eric Warrington and Philip Rouse, eds., *Great Dialogues of Plato* (New York: The Great American Library/Mentor Books, 1956), 273. Trans. W. H. P. Rouse.
5. Ibid., 356.
6. Quoted from Charles McCoy's fascinating unpublished essay, "Federal Theology and the Constitution: Religious Thought and the Idea of Covenant in the American Political System" (Berkeley Calif.: Pacific School of Religion/Graduate Theological Union, 1984), 10.
7. H. Richard Niebuhr, "The Idea of Covenant and American Democracy," *Church History* 23 (June 1954): 129 and 130.
8. Page Smith, *The Shaping of America* (New York: McGraw-Hill, 1980), vol. 3, xvi.
9. E. S. Morgan, *The Birth of the Republic* (Chicago: University of Chicago Press, 1956), 149.

40   PART ONE   Foundations

10. Quoted from Michael Kraus, *The United States to 1865* (Ann Arbor: University of Michigan Press, 1959), 255–265. The list is interesting to cultural historians interested in America's "antis": anti-semitism, anti-Catholicism, anti-minorities, and so on. It has been recently argued, for example, that Jews are still systematically excluded from top positions because of prejudice. Abraham Korman, *The Outsiders: Jews and Corporate America* (Lexington, Mass.: Lexington Press, 1983).

11. If reading the Constitution should inspire desires for deeper understanding of its evolving meanings, a step in that direction would be to consult Leonard Levy and Kenneth L. Karst, eds., *Encyclopedia of the American Constitution*, 4 vols. (New York: Macmillan, 1986).

12. James Madison, *The Federalist Papers* (New York: The New American Library, 1961), no. 62.

13. Alexander Hamilton, *The Federalist Papers* (New York: The New American Library, 1961), no. 73. See also John A. Rohr, "Public Administration, Executive Power, and Constitutional Confusion," *Public Administration Review* 49 (March–April 1989): 108–114; and Thomas H. Hammond and Gary T. Miller, "The Core of the Constitution," *American Political Science Review* 81 (December 1987): 1154–1174.

14. Alexis de Tocqueville, *Democracy in America* (New York: Vintage Press, 1945, 2 vols.), vol. 1, 126 and 142–43. Edited by Phillips Bradley. The first volume, which appeared in 1835 when he was only 30 years old, made Tocqueville famous.

15. Jean-Claude Lamberti, *Tocqueville and the Two Democracies* (Cambridge: Harvard University Press, 1988).

16. Peter Smithers, "Presidential Paralysis and the Constitution," *The Wall Street Journal*, December 24, 1987, A6.

17. George Reedy, "A Matter of Perspective: Politicians Versus the Press," *Ethics: Easier Said than Done*, 1 (Spring–Summer, 1988), 21.

18. Harold Lasswell, *Politics: Who Gets What, When, How?* (New York: Meridian, 1958).

19. Robert S. Erikson and James A. Stimson, "Macropartisanship," *American Political Science Review* 83 (December 1989): 1125.

20. H. George Frederickson and David K. Hart, "The Public Service and the Patriotism of Benevolence," *Public Administration Review* 45 (September–October 1985): 547.

21. Clifford Hardin, "Congress Is the Problem," *Choices* (Spring 1986), 6. For a detailed treatment, see Burdett Loomis, *The New American Politician: Elected Entrepreneurs and the Changing Style of Political Life* (New York: Basic Books, 1988).

22. Norman Ornstein, "How to Win in '88," *U.S. News and World Report*, October 12, 1987, 31–33. See also Dee Allsop and Herbert Weisberg, "Measuring Change in Party Identification in an Election Campaign," *American Journal of Political Science* 32 (1988): 996–1017.

23. Marcia Calicchia and Ellen Sadowski, *The Lobbying Handbook: A Guide to Effective Lobbying in New York State* (Ithaca, N.Y.: Cornell University/New York State School of Industrial and Labor Relations, 1989). For the national scene, see A. Lee Fritschler and Bernard Ross, *How Washington Works: The Executive's Guide to Government* (Cambridge, Mass.: Ballinger/Harper, 1987).

24. John E. Jackson and David C. King, "Public Goods, Private Interests and Representation," *American Political Science Review* 83 (December 1989): 1143–1164.

25. Arthur T. Denzau and Michael C. Munger, "Legislators and Interest Groups: How Unorganized Interests Get Represented," *American Political Science Review* 80 (March 1986): 89–106.

26. Paul S. Herrnson, *Party Campaigning in the 1980s* (Cambridge: Harvard University Press, 1988), especially chs. 3 and 4.

27. *Congressional Record* (February 19, 1988), 985.

28. Assemblyman X, "As Told to Lester Velie," *Ethics: Easier Said than Done* (Spring–Summer 1988): 57–58.

29. Marbury v. Madison, 1 Cranch 137 (1803).

30. The major cases strengthening the Court's power were McCullouch v. Maryland (1819), where the concept of implied powers was used to justify the right of the federal government

to establish national banks that could not be taxed by the states; Cohens v. Virginia (1821), reaffirming the court's appellate jurisdiction; and Gibbons v. Ogden (1824), placing the power over interstate commerce in the federal government.

31. See Vincent Blase, *The Burger Court: The Counter Revolution That Wasn't* (New Haven, Conn.: Yale University Press, 1983).
32. Tocqueville, *Democracy in America*, 100.
33. Reynolds v. Sims (1969).
34. Christopher Wolfe, *The Rise of Modern Judicial Review from Constitutional Interpretation to Judge Made Law* (New York: Basic Books, 1986), 11.
35. Colegrove v. Green (1946).
36. The impact of the revised judicial thinking on state elections is told in Malcolm E. Jewell and David Olson, *Political Parties and Elections in American States* (Chicago: Dorsey Press, 1988), ch. 5.
37. Donald Horowitz, *The Courts and Social Policy* (Washington, D.C.: The Brookings Institution, 1977) provides a good survey of the events. See also, Marc Silverstein and Benjamin Ginsberg, "The Supreme Court and the New Politics of Judicial Power, *Political Science Quarterly* 102 (Fall 1987): 371–388.
38. Missouri et al. v. Jenkins et al., 110 S.Ct. 1667 (1990).
39. Henry Abraham, *Justices and Presidents* (New York: Oxford University Press, 1983).
40. "Against Robert Bork," The *New York Times*, October 5, 1987, Sec A, 22.
41. Bernard H. Siegan, *The Supreme Court's Constitution* (New Brunswick, N.J.: Rutgers University/Transaction Publishers, 1987).
42. Edwin M. Yoder, Jr., "The Public Mugging of Bork," *The Philadelphia Inquirer,* September 18, 1987, 23A.
43. Stephen Halpern and Charles Lamb, *Supreme Court Activism and Restraint* (Lexington, Mass.: Lexington Books, 1984).
44. Lino Graglia, "How the Constitution Disappeared," *Commentary* 81 (1986): 19.
45. Edwin S. Corwin, *The President's Removal Power under the Constitution* (Ithaca, N.Y.: Cornell University Press, 1981), 339.
46. Ashwander v. TVA (1946).
47. Robert H. Bork, "Neutral Principles and Some First Amendment Problems," *Indiana Law Journal* 47 (1971): 10. One should note that original intent has been defined in various ways. Professor Leonard W. Levy, for example, has suggested that original intent would have the framers speaking from "the grave to run our lives." *Original Intent and the Framers of the Constitution* (New York: Macmillan, 1988). This writer thinks that Professor Levy, a distinguished scholar and Pulitzer Prize winner, is wrong in this view.
48. Immigration and Naturalization Service v. Chadha (1983).
49. Cooper v. Aaron (1958).
50. Frank H. Easterbrook, "The Influence of Judicial Review in Constitutional Theory" in *A Workable Government? The Constitution after 200 Years,* ed. Burke Marshall (New York: W. W. Norton, 1987), 175.
51. Herbert Wechsler, *Principles, Politics and Fundamental Law* (Cambridge: Harvard University Press, 1961), 688.
52. John Ely, "The Wages of Crying Wolf," *Yale Law Journal* 82 (Winter 1975): 949.
53. "Popular opinion has it that bureaucrats are great time-serving nonentities who care more for rules and job security than they do for their citizen clients." David K. Hart, "Public Administration, the Thoughtless Functioning and Feelinglessness," in *The Revitalization of the Public Service,* eds. Robert B. Denhardt and Edward T. Jennings (Columbia, Mo.: The University of Missouri Press, 1987), 77–97.
54. Anthony Burgess, *The Devil's Mode* (New York: Random House, 1989), 142.
55. Stephen L. Carter, "The Beast That Might Not Exist: Some Speculations on the Constitution and the Independent Regulating Bodies," in *A Workable Government? The Constitution after 200 Years,* ed. Burke Marshall (N.Y.: W. W. Norton, 1987).

56. Barry Karl, "The American Bureaucrat: A Sheep in Wolves' Clothing," *The Public Administration Review* 47 (January–February 1987): 26–34.
57. Woodrow Wilson, *The Study of Administration* (New York: Academy of Political Science, 1887).
58. J.W. Doig, "If I See a Murderous Fellow Sharpening a Knife Cleverly . . . the Wilsonian Dichotomy and the Public Authority Tradition," *Public Administration Review* 43 (March–April 1983): 292–304.
59. Morris P. Fiorina, *Congress: Keystone of the Washington Establishment* (New Haven, Conn.: Yale University Press, 1977).
60. William F. West, "Judicial Rule Making Procedures in the FTC," *Public Policy* 29 (January 1981): 196–217.
61. Malcomb E. Jewell, "The Neglected World of State Politics," *Journal of Politics* 46 (1982), 638–657.
62. Francis E. Rourke, "Bureaucracy in the American Constitutional Order," *American Political Science Review* 102 (Summer 1987): 228.

CHAPTER 2

# The Business Foundation: Corporations, Unions, and the Commercial Professions

## The Corporation and Capitalism
Early Corporate Forms
Managerial Capitalism
Institutional Capitalism
Corporate Power over Employees
Corporate Power over Society: Federal Charters and CSR
*CSR*
*Evolution of CSR*
*The Case for CSR*
*Future Stages in CSR*
Noncorporate Businesses

## Workers and Labor Unions
The Nature of Unions
Characteristics of Unions
Evolution of Unions
Legitimacy Problems of Unions
The Murky Future

## The Commercial Professions
The Emergence of Professions
*The Legal Profession*
*Professions Defined*
Accounting: The Watchdog Profession
Main Characteristics of Professions
*The Criteria*
*The Dark Side*

## Summary
Questions for Discussion
Ethical Quandaries

*O*ne of the most important decisions a society can make is its choice of the economic system through which it seeks to assure its survival. The choices are limited. Whether in Babylonia under Hammurabi or in Greece under Pericles, whether in medieval Italy or in modern America, only three possibilities exist: traditional, command, or market economy.[1] The traditional economy, usually self-sufficient, existed when producer and consumer were one and the same. Jobs held by the father were assigned to the son; sharp distinctions existed between a man's work and a woman's work; stability meant more than economic growth; the elders were esteemed for their wisdom and adolescents for their muscle.

The second of the three economic systems is the planned economy—found among the Egyptian pharaohs of old and among communists today. A centralized agency (the politburo in Russia) determines what will be produced and who will do the producing; wages are set and not negotiated; cooperation is honored and competition is condemned. For nearly a half century after World War II, the Russians lived under this system. Then, with a suddenness that caught even the experts unprepared, Michail Gorbachev (who became the Soviet leader in 1985) publicly acknowledged the failure of communism as an economic system and his country's need for some form of capitalism.

The chief features of capitalism, which is the third way of organizing an economy, are the following:

1. Individuals are primarily motivated by self-interest.
2. Individuals themselves perceive and achieve their goals more rationally than others can do this for them.
3. Rational decision making requires "breathing space" for all individuals and must be respected unless the users interfere with the breathing space of others.
4. Long-term investment in making products is better than immediate consumption.
5. Production and distribution are organized rationally.
6. An established enterprise is a better way to get things done than ad hoc ventures.
7. The market, indifferent to religion, race, and color, relies on a stable network of laws.
8. Capitalism and urbanism go "hand in hand."[2]

*One important thing about capitalism is that its working is rarely geared in any consistent fashion to the theoretical postulates attributed to it, providing ambiguities that make it less and less useful "for honest intellectual currency. It is liable to become a mere word, lacking any coherent meaning, and with which one can perform the most astonishing conjuring tricks."*[3] *How capitalism has worked in theory has been the interest of economists; how it has worked in practice has been the focus of historians, philosophers, and other social scientists. In pre-business capitalism—the longest period of economic history—most people made things for themselves; when they learned to make more things than they needed for their own use, they began to sell and buy. Exchange and specialization came to characterize this elementary form of capitalism. As exchange became a regular feature of life, markets were established and market pricing practices followed. "Petty capitalists" came to be the term used to describe a small businessman who usually had complete control over his own operations, owned the capital, and did most of the work himself.*[4]

*The contours of capitalism were changed by two great revolutions—the commercial revolution and the industrial revolution, respectively. The roots of the commercial revolution are found in the 13th century but it was not until the 15th century that its most dramatic manifestations were clearly visible: villages were transformed into new towns and old towns into bustling cities; local markets were complemented by international markets; banking became more sophisticated and bankers more powerful.*[5] *In this exciting world the business corporation was born; during the industrial revolution the corporation matured.* ■

## *The purposes of this chapter are:*

1. To compare early corporations and their 20th century successors.
2. To consider early unions and their successors.
3. To look at the origins and nature of the primary commercial professions: law and accounting.

## The Corporation and Capitalism

The words corporation and capitalism have become so identified in the public mind that corporation's more commodious meaning has been lost. The corporate form was known in Rome, but not until Norman England was the idea of a corporate personality first developed. The variety of corporate personalities is impressive. Charitable organizations like UNICEF, nonprofit corporations like Harvard, municipal corporations like New York, and religious corporations like the Chicago Archdiocese are some examples. As the form of capitalism evolved over the years so, too, did the form of business organization. The corporate form took on a new importance with the creation of the Muscovy Company in 1555 and the Dutch East India Company in 1602. Seeing new markets for new products, restless entrepreneurs went out to capture them while the established capitalists grew fat and contented in the security of the home city. The key element of commercial capitalism was the restorative power brought to it by market-oriented men ready to take great risks for great rewards.[6]

## Early Corporate Forms

America was born when the commercial revolution was in full flower. Not surprisingly, the city merchants—the bourgeoisie—became more influential than the farmers who constituted the overwhelming majority of workers. American entrepreneurs took to commerce as ducks would to water. Making their splash easy were the excellent harbors that dotted the Atlantic coast, the navigable rivers in the interior, an abundance of natural resources, and awareness that fortunes could be made by the risk takers. As commerce increased, competition intensified and individual entrepreneurs found themselves unable to raise funds necessary to build shops and warehouses and to buy equipment and stock. The consequence was the formation of corporations in the banking and turnpike-construction industries.

The need for a rather precise legal definition of the corporation was becoming more important, and John Marshall provided the answer in his famous Dartmouth College decision: "A corporation is an artificial being, invisible, intangible, and existing only in contemplation of law. Being a mere creature of law, it possesses only those properties which the charter of its creation confers upon it, either expressly, or as incidental to its very existence . . . among the most important (of which) are immortality and, if the expression may be allowed, individuality; properties by which a perpetual succession of many persons are considered the same, and act as a single individual."[7] A contemporary wrote that a "corporation had no anatomical parts to be kicked or consigned to a calaboose; no conscience to keep it awake all night; no soul for whose salvation the parson may struggle; no body to be roasted in hell or purged from celestial enjoyment."[8]

But corporations did have two qualities that worried legislators: immortality and limited liability. As a result, states were somewhat hesitant to grant corporate charters—and then only on quite restrictive terms. New York, for example, required a separate legislative act for each corporation, and not until 1811 was the secretary of the state empowered to grant charters without legislative debates. The predictable thing happened: corporations favored those states where the process was fast, the supervision moderate, and the demands minimal. New Jersey, the first favorite, was dislodged from its leadership as a chartering state in 1913 when Delaware (and to a lesser extent Maryland and Maine) became the favorites.

More important than the commercial revolution in its impact on the corporate form was the industrial revolution, which grew rather unspectacularly in England between 1770 and 1840 and jumped astronomically after that date. One easy way to appreciate the meaning of industrialism is to focus on the year 1869. Two events—the opening of the Suez Canal and the completion of the first transcontinental railroad in the United States—signaled the significance of steam-powered locomotives and ships. Thomas Newcomen set the pattern when he invented the first successful steam engine in 1712 but it was James Watts who made the engine practicable in 1769.

Yet if the industrial revolution's beginnings can be located in one industry, it was in textiles, not transportation or mining. Richard Arkwright's roller spinning process, patented in England in 1769, provided a new manufacturing system for cotton. This combination of mechanization in the textile industries and steam engines in transportation constituted the greatest achievements in technology following the invention of the weight-driven clocks in the Middle Ages. Unlike the early Chinese, who used their great technological skills largely for entertainment—the production of kites, puzzles, and fireworks—Westerners used their skills primarily for the production of practical things.

Coal and iron had many auxilaries: copper and tin, aluminum and concrete. If these materials formed the body of industrialism, electricity was its soul. That soul seemed noble when expressed in electric lights, telephones, high-speed turbines, and sewing machines. It appeared perverse when electric chairs became approved as the instrument for state-ordered death sentences. As machines multiplied, factories expanded. Those who knew how to use the new instruments and those who provided necessary capital made fabulous fortunes. And it was not long until these captains of industry were seen as the chieftains of society. If their profits begat envy, their power spawned fear. The post-Civil War period was consequently characterized by a struggle between Wall Street, on one side, and factory workers and farmers, on the other.

The new industrial capitalism required a larger view of the corporation.[9] To early observers, the key figure of the industrial age was the engineer, a title used initially to describe someone who built military fortifications and weapons. Later it came to mean those who built the railroads and turnpikes, bridges and canals, and invented such useful things as the Bessemer converter in steel manufacturing. But it was the investor who lubricated the machines the engineers made. To them flowed massive profits that were now measured in gold. Until 1870 only Great Britain had used this precious metal as the exclusive currency. France, on the other hand, and many other European countries used gold and silver. Shortly after 1870, others followed the British pattern: Germany (1871), Scandinavia (1872), the Netherlands and the United States (1873), and France, Spain, and Italy (1878). Only so-called backward countries like Mexico, China, and Ethiopia maintained silver as their currency. One unhappy by-product of the gold standard was that, as the precious metal became more scarce, money became extraordinarily expensive. Creditors and traders prospered; debtors and farmers suffered.

In sum, capitalism developed in uneven stages from individual ownership to partnerships, from partnerships to joint stock companies, from joint stock companies to corporations. Unlike their predecessors the new capitalists had little or no personal relationship with the workers who produced their profits. Rockefeller, Ford, and Carnegie were great. J. P. Morgan was legendary. The bricks were being laid systematically for a highway leading to two new kinds of capitalism: managerial and institutional. Each had enormous strengths and substantial weaknesses.

## *Managerial Capitalism*

When the Great Depression hit America with devastating effect in 1929, observers began to note a singularly important development in corporate structure. Designed originally as wealth-getting instruments for the people who formed them, the corporations had come under the control of highly trained professionals. The new breed was university trained, had relatively little stock in the companies they managed, controlled the selection of directors, set the agenda for board meetings, and was psychologically prepared to move to new jobs when the inducements were right. These corporate managers constituted a new class and their coming was itself a revolution.

This was the exciting theme propounded in 1932 by Adolf Berle and Gardiner Means.[10] Without ever using the now popular term agency theory, they noted how management interests often collided with stockholder interests. The thesis (separation of ownership from management) was often challenged, but it did call attention to the key quality of corporate capitalism—a managerial revolution had taken place.[11] The results have been well documented: tensions between manager and investor became more acute; bureaucracy grew; midmanagers routinely emasculated the power of top executives; responsibility became fragmented and diffuse; executive mobility became more pronounced; and notions of entitlements, job security, and assured salary increases became part of the club mentality. For the rest of the century CEOs acted as the corporation's field generals, stockholders were the supply corps, and workers were the foot soldiers.

## *Institutional Capitalism*

Recently a new form of capitalism has arisen that is inadequately termed institutionalism. This brand differs from managerial capitalism in the sense that those who control enormous pension funds, both public and private, are taking increasing control of the corporation. Peter Drucker called the phenomenon "pension fund socialism."[12] Managers of institutional pension plans tell workers how much of their income will be saved, invested for the future, and where their earnings will be put. Institutional investors now own over half the shares listed on the New York Stock Exchange and account for three-quarters of the trading. The annual turnover rate of the listed shares on the exchange has jumped from 14 to 95 percent. These institutional investors trade intensively in index baskets of stock and no particular company matters very much for very long. The transactional costs of all this trading are very high, amounting to approximately 16 percent of the after-tax profits of corporate America. One consequence is that the largest corporations now faced a new environment of guerrilla warfare in which "the behemoths were in danger of being nibbled to death."[13] The short-term mentality that replaced the long-term corporate outlook of former years is a danger to the business system.[14]

How to reinvigorate corporate capitalism is today's major challenge. And who or what will be the "invigorators" if managements become complacent? Will it be the hostile raider? leveraged buyouts by outsiders or by managements? reorganization of corporate boards? changes in corporate policy that require pension funds to be managed for the long-term interest of investors and employees? Clearly the frenzied dance of the contemporary corporate world needs to be moderated and modulated. The reason is not simply in the interest of investors or the economy. An additional concern is that, regardless of whether the economy is in the stage of managerial or institutional capitalism, corporations may have powers over their employees that even exceed those exercised by the state over its citizens. In addition, corporate power influences society as a whole. Concern about the internal power of corporations has led to a call for corporate constitutionalism. Concern about their external powers has brought demands for corporate social responsibility. Each theory has its passionate supporters and equally fervid criteria.

## *Corporate Power over Employees*

The current debate over the organization's power over its employees is between those who say that the modern corporation must be "constitutionalized" and those who insist that doing so is both unnecessary in voluntary organizations and a threat to economic efficiency. For brevity's sake the two camps will be referred to as the *constitutionalists* and the *economizers*, respectively. The first expression of constitutionalism was found in colonial corporations that exercised large political powers. The first charter of the Virginia Company in 1606, for example, vested in "certain loving and well-disposed subjects, Knights, and Gentlemen not only the right to take up part of the royal domain in America for a colony, but to exercise in it some of the powers of the Crown, including the creation and management of military forces and the coinage of money." Three years later a second charter gave the company "full and absolute Power and Authority to correct, punish, pardon, govern, and rule such Subjects of Us as might journey to Virginia and come under the jurisdiction of the local company." In much the same way the first charter of Massachusetts in 1628 created "one body, corporate and politique, in fact and name" and gave to the "Governor and Company of the Massachusetts Bay in Newe England" the right to exercise the powers of the public authority. Today, the corporation's political legitimacy is not derived from the State's benediction. The legitimizing source is private property.

Property, being essential to freedom, was sacrosanct in the gospel of John Locke and few indeed were the corporate leaders who left Locke's classroom. Ford owned his company, Rockefeller his, and Carnegie his. Each could use his property for his own self-interest so long as other property owners were not harmed. It mattered little then that workers were exploited, legislators bought, and judges seduced. Symptoms of public unease—intensified during the Great Depression of the 1930s—were muted during the World War II and the postwar boom, but never left permanently. Even when Carter entered the White House in January of 1977—and despite a booming economy—a feeling existed that the economy was out of control and that those who managed large corporations were also out of control. The public began again to issue its own writs, asking by what warrant do corporations wield their powers. The answers seem to have been unsatisfactory if measured by opinion polls, which repeatedly recorded declining confidence in business and other basic institutions.[15]

Critics asserted that the root cause of such loss of confidence is corporations' use and abuse of power. Corporations are the enforcers of rules for an industry; they administer justice for millions of workers; they disenfranchise the stockholders. Corporations have even been said to have secured a constituent power that they have preempted from the state in ways that violate the prevailing values of the American democracy: "Corporation charters permit the disenfranchisement of the qualified through manipulation of the voting rights of owners of various classes of stock; they institutionalize minority rule through the diffusion of stock ownership and the separation of ownership and control; and they deny the principles of due process in the adjudication, within the corporation, of relative rights, such, for example, as those of dealers, minority stockholders, workers, and consumers."[16]

Even before political scientists became interested in problems of power and its use in private systems of governance, sociologists like Max Weber and Emile Durkheim described the operation of large organizations and the problems their managers faced, particularly in the area of value conflicts. Four premises were laid down by the sociologists:

1. Because modern societies are pluralistic and functionally differentiated, authorities must mediate employees' competing beliefs and competing goods to maintain order. To mediate is necessary. To mandate is wrong.
2. Beliefs and interests once shared in common by managers have become more differentiated so that the exercise of authority has become more difficult.
3. Since there is no overarching common value system within the elites, the employee's core beliefs and economic interests are always potentially divisive.
4. Conflict is endemic to modern societies.[17]

Managing conflict among subordinates when the values of managers themselves clash is a major challenge. There are, it seems, only three ways to structure organizations: collegial, bureaucratic, and constitutional. Examples of the first are universities and professions; examples of the bureaucratic form are modern corporations; examples of the constitutional form are democratic states. Managers themselves now ask whether corporations should move toward the third form of organization, possibly along lines similar to—but not identical with—the codetermination patterns of Germany.[18]

Proponents of constitutionalism argue that good reasons exist in both organizational theory and in history for managers to take the big step toward constitutionalism and that the nation's first moral mentor, John Locke, shows them the way. In his famous *Second Treatise on Government* Locke described two paths that people followed in establishing a state. The first was the social contract theory and the second, less appreciated, was an evolutionary process that came about through "insensible changes." Corporations fit both patterns: they result from social contracts and they are passing through a series of insensible changes.[19] Insensible changes occur when capitalism, evolving through the successive stages of managerial and investment capitalism, respectively, embraces constitutionalism. Reaching it is not through explicit codes of conduct but through propositions that establish the general framework for operations. Such a framework avoids the authoritarianism implicit in bureaucratic structures when it meets these tests:

1. General statements, not ad hoc dicta
2. Available to all affected
3. Prospective rather than retroactive
4. Clear and understandable, at least to those trained in rule making
5. Free from contradiction
6. Infrequently changed
7. Congruent with the actual administration of the rules as presently or prospectively developed[20]

The distinctive attributes of organizational constitutionalism are so similar to societal constitutionalism that they may be treated by nonexperts as one. This form of constitutionalism specifies a threshold of procedural institutionalization that is *voluntaristic, irreducible,* and *grounded.*[21] It is voluntaristic because the very notion of constitutionalism exists to restrain the arbitrary exercise of power; it is irreducible because if procedural integrity is not preserved integration is impossible, regardless of the organization's ideology or society's beliefs and rituals; finally, constitutionalism is grounded because, rather than downplaying the material bases of conflict, it accepts them and assumes that, if basic issues are not mediated, the only other recourse is manipulation or coercion. But manipulation and coercion are counterproductive because employees will eventually rebel.

Important in this evolution is management's recognition that, in every organization, collegial bodies must exist in some of its sectors. The trick is to recognize them, use them, and gradually transform other parts of the organization into collegial bodies.[22] A first step in the direction of collegiality could be the appointment of an ombudsman, defined as a "senior official who would receive all complaints—which could be made on a confidential basis—of allegedly improper or illegal corporate conduct whether from the public, employees, whistle-blowers, anonymous letter writers, or others. The ombudsman would be appointed by the Board of Directors, but to insure that she or he would have support at the top, the CEO should have the power of veto over any proposed nominee."[23] A legitimate worry is whether veto power by the CEO means subservience by the ombudsman, a question best answered by experiment and experience.

To some economists, however, the very thought of politicizing the corporation is subversive.[24] To them arguments from the "politicalizers" and the "socializers" are palaver lacking proof. The corporation was, is, and should be an economic instrument best conceived to meet society's material needs. Its strength is its record—one of the highest living standards in the world. It has enabled the United States to post an outstanding record of generosity toward Western Europe when England and France, Germany and Italy were on their knees; it offers an unprecedented degree of personal freedom because workers are not vassalized; it exploits the country's natural abundance to create even more abundance; it joins the state in having annual R&D investments that, as noted, exceed the combined totals of Japan, Germany, France, Sweden, and the United Kingdom.[25] Finally, in the titanic battle between the superpowers, the United States has outlasted the Soviet Union because the market economy has allowed corporate bodies to perform miracles that consumers now believe are routine.[26] The message from corporate apologists is simple: let the corporation alone to continue its great work!

## *Corporate Power over Society: Federal Charters and CSR*

If some Federal Charters concentrate on the organization's power over its employees, others worry about the corporation's power over society. To restrict such influences, proposals have been made to introduce federal chartering in the United States. In this line of reasoning, by placing corporations under the direct control of the Congress or one of its agencies, uniform rules would apply to large, federally chartered organizations. States like Delaware, which has a reputation for generosity toward corporations, would be held in check. The presumption is that federal chartering would lead to more consistent interpretations and application of such issues as the business judgement principle, disclosure rules, corporate structures, and board interlocks.

Reasons for introducing federal chartering, according to Ralph Nader and his associates, are "because (a) our largest corporations have such harmful market and nonmarket impacts; (b) state chartering laws, downgraded by the Delaware syndrome, have failed to restrain corporate abuses; (c) the governing ethos of our giant firms more resembles an autocracy than a democracy; (d) the officers of these corporations lack individual accountability for their actions; (e) corporate secrecy has overwhelmed the need for corporate disclosure; (f) these firms routinely violate the rights of their employees; (g) widespread market concentration insulates most of our largest companies from the rigors of competition; (h) there is occurring an outbreak of corporate payoffs and other crimes; and (i) our chronic economic conditions amply demonstrate that these corporations are not performing well even by their own standards—there is an obvious need to fundamentally reform the giant corporation in America. Federal chartering is an effective means to that goal."[27]

The precise content of a Federal Chartering Act, then, is crucial. The act would require a full-time outside board of directors, with a full-time staff available to it, to monitor executive performance. It should provide for the following:

1. More detailed disclosure of toxic substances in the workplace, minority employment by job and income categories, and ultimately multinational firm job exportation
2. Protection of the civil liberties and civil rights of both union and non-union workers by adopting an Employee Bill of Rights
3. Substantiation of major advertisements by federally chartered firms, expanded class action rights for consumers, and general reduction of prices through deconcentration of primary industries
4. Corporate disclosure of congressional and executive lobbying contacts and federal tax returns and contracts
5. Reports of polluting plant discharges
6. Compliance schedules and the issuance of a "community impact statement" when a plant is relocated

The Supreme Court has been rather consistent in preventing the individual states from interfering with the internal affairs of a corporation so long as it has been organized under, and is governed by, the laws of a single state. But what are internal affairs? Answering the question was a "hazardous venture," Justice Cardozo said in a 1915 case.[28] Harold Williams, when he was director of the SEC, told an audience at Carnegie Mellon University on October 27, 1979, that it was indeed a hazardous venture.[29] There is, however, another school of thought that insists that more restrictive measures over the corporation overlook the real issues, namely, the corporation's power to block society from—or to nudge society toward—higher forms of achievement. To act as a positive force, corporations should voluntarily accept greater social responsibilities.

**CSR.** The corporate social responsibility doctrine (CSR) has led to both definitional and ideological problems.[30] So far as definitions are concerned, CSR has appeared in five guises.

***The Austere Mode.*** Working from the premise that every firm consists only of two elements (the ownership group and the resources group), advocates of the austere mode insist that the owners are entitled to the profits—all of them. Channeling money away from owners, even for laudable purposes, is both illegal and immoral.

***The Household Mode.*** The key word is *oeconomia*, the Greek word for household management. All who live and work for the household are in the *charondas* (companions of the cupboard) and consequently have claims on the larder. In contemporary terms, this means that managers and workers share just as completely in the profit sharing as do stockholders.[31]

***The Vendor Mode.*** If the household mode of CSR accords priority to industrial policy (employment opportunities, incomes, and rights) over financial policy (profit maximization), the vendor mode thrusts the consumer into the picture as the forgotten man of modern economics—forgotten because big business and big unions have produced a species of accommodations in which the rewards of increased productivity are shared with these groups rather than with the consumer. Financial and industrial policies look inward to the stockholder and to the worker, respectively. Market policy looks outward to the rights, interests, and tastes of the consumer. Some of these rights are protected by laws enforced by agencies such as the Federal Trade Commission or through the policing of private agencies such as the Better Business Bureaus. But some things, like planned obsolescence or substitutability of inferior materials, can still go undetected. A responsible enterprise eschews such practices.

***The Artistic Mode.*** Creative business managers should not restrict their abilities and their organization's capabilities solely to corporate interests. Neil Chamberlain of Columbia's School of Business caught the spirit of the artistic mode when he wrote that the real fun in managing a business lies in projecting one's own creative imagination into realms that none of the participating parties dream of.[32] Although relating the creative concept mainly to the household mode, Chamberlain's insights can be extended to include a helping hand to the institutions and to the people who spend their whole lives in artistic endeavors. Richard Eells, formerly with General Electric, phrased the issue this way:

> *I do not think it is a passing phase, a transient interest of some business leaders in cultural programs that have caught the nation's imagination. . . . It is, rather, an indication of some deeper current in the development of the modern corporation as a major social institution involved in America's expanding cultural aspirations, now in the ascendancy. Witness the growing number of orchestras, dance companies, opera and ballet companies, choral groups, recordings, museums, books, libraries, drama groups, and the increasing amount of people in all walks of life who are now attending concerts, listening to good music, viewing ballet and dance, participating in the arts of one kind or another. A more responsible and humane society is in the making, and the business executive is quick to sense the interdependence of all facets of that responsible and responsive community.*[33]

***The Civic Mode.*** The content of the civic mode was captured in Adolf Berle's talk to a group of senior executives in New York City: "You make money, yes. But you don't know what your efforts cost the community around you. If those costs were added to your costs, businesses very much in the black now would find themselves in the red, and vice-versa. This means, in substance, that we are all cogs in a vast machine. Sometimes the cogs are very big—but big or little, there is no escape from your being in the machine."[34] Being in the machine means being in a larger society—and that fact requires economists and managers to understand the causes and consequences of things people do that transcend the scope of free exchange: "In a broad sense the great task of the theorist (and managers) of our tremendously dynamic age is to substitute an economics of responsibility for the economics of irresponsible conflict."[35] Like individual citizens, corporate citizens cannot be content simply to vote or obey the law. They must actively engage in activities that promote a better society—and assume those initiatives voluntarily, not through government coercion.[36]

The austere, household, and vendor models involve obligation. Stockholders can press their legal rights in courts of law and can withdraw their investments in particular firms if dissatisfied. Unions protect workers under the household mode. Regulatory agencies, plus consumer preferences in market decisions, make corporations aware of their duties under the vendor rules. But the last two modes—creative and civic—allow for infinitely more discretion. Whether a company supports education and whether it behaves like a good citizen toward communities that have supported it are largely matters for management's judgement. How the civic mode came to the fore illustrates how managerial values change.

**Evolution of CSR.** Roughly a half century ago, two events occurred that, though given relatively little public attention at the time, may well have been the harbingers of major ideological changes in the world of corporate America. The first was a 1950 act by the New Jersey legislature that declared it public policy that "corporations organized under the laws of this State should be specifically empowered to contribute such monies as, in a judgment of the governing boards, will conduce to the betterment of social and economic conditions, thereby permitting such corporations, as creations of this State, to discharge their obligations to society while, at the same time, reaping the benefits which essentially accrue to them through public recognition of their existence within the economic, social, as well as within the legal, structure of society."[37]

In the same year, New York University celebrated the golden anniversary of its business school. The theme selected for its commemorative Bernays Lecture Series was devoted to the social responsibilities of management. The topic in itself appeared to have no particular significance until it is realized that the university's business school had begun—as had most early schools of business—as an institution established to prepare students for careers in commerce, accounting, and finance. Management as a particular area for study was ignored. The new theme revealed a faculty moving beyond its original functional areas of instruction and toward the managerial aspects of business, including the then somewhat novel doctrine of social responsibility.

With the legislative framework having been established in New Jersey, and with the issue's importance having been stated by New York academics, the rest of the scenario was predictable. Three years after both events, a case came before the New Jersey Supreme Court that was to challenge legal precedent in a very significant way. At that time, corporate executives behaved circumspectly within a legal fence built by the courts in the famous *Dodge Brothers v. Ford Motor* case.[38] The case was precipitated by Henry Ford's decision to cut dividends to a "paltry" 200 percent of invested equity per year in order to raise wages and reduce prices—and by so doing, to behave responsibly by sharing profits with employees through better wages (the household mode) and with customers through reduced prices (the vendor mode).

The Michigan Supreme Court told Ford that his motives were simply wrong because a corporation existed to maximize returns to the shareholders. The reasoning of the Dodge case continued to prevail in executive suites until midcentury so that managers simply did not think of such adventurous possibilities as company donations to private institutions. But this was precisely the issue raised in the Smith Manufacturing case. And the operating premise—or, at least, the hope—was that New Jersey would prove more amenable to corporate philanthropy than the old Michigan law had allowed. It is appropriate to capture here the flavor of that important decision by quoting Judge J. C. Stein:

> *I cannot conceive of any greater benefit to corporations in this country than to build, and continue to build, respect for, and adherence to, a system of free enterprise and democratic government, the serious impairment of either of which may well spell the destruction of all corporate enterprises. Nothing that aids or promotes the growth and service of the American university or college in respect to matters herein discussed can possibly be anything short of direct benefit to every corporation in the land. The college-trained men and women are a ready reservoir from which industry may draw to satisfy its need for scientific or executive talent. It is no answer to say that a company is not so benefitted unless such need is immediate. A long-range view must be taken of the matter.*
>
> *A small company today might be under no imperative requirement to engage the services of a research chemist or other scientist, but its growth in a few years may be such that it might have available an ample pool from which it may obtain the needed service. It must also be remembered that industry cannot function efficiently or enjoy development and expansion unless it has at all times the advantage of enlightened leadership and direction. The value of that kind of service depends in great measure upon the training, ideologies, and character of the personnel available.... What promotes the general good inescapably advances the cor-*

*porate weal. I hold the corporate contributions to Princeton and institutions rendering a like public service are, if held within reasonable limitations, a matter of direct benefit to the giving corporations, and this without regard to the extent or sweep of the donor's business. The benefits derived from such contributions are nation-wide and promote the welfare of everyone anywhere in the land.*

*Here then, are supportive actions in behalf of a cause that is intimately tied to the American way of life. Such giving may be called incidental power, but when it is considered in its essential character, may well be regarded as a major, though unwritten, corporate power. It is even more than that. In the court's view of the case, it amounts to solemn duty.*[39]

What happened was that the old Puritan tradition of *personal* responsibility of the rich toward the needy was being extended into an *organizational* responsibility to others who had no legal claims on it. The question was, of course, different: could boards of directors take earnings that properly belonged to stockholders and, in the board's discretion, use a portion of those funds for causes they deemed essential to the public good and to the organization's welfare? The Smith case gave a resoundingly affirmative answer.

In view of the assault on a long philosophical tradition and on legal precedent, it is not surprising that counterattacks would be mounted. Given Henry Ford's prominence in the early days of the century, it was somewhat ironic that Thomas Reid, a Ford executive, should later express skepticism toward the corporate social responsibility movement when he declared that the job of an executive was to respond swiftly and efficiently to consumer wants as expressed in the marketplace. Managers are well advised to stick to their knitting, mind the store, and guard their interests.

Substantial representations from the academic community also voiced opposition to the new concept. Theodore Levitt of Harvard, Milton Friedman and Frederick Hayek of Chicago, Ludwig von Misis of New York University, and Ben Lewis of Oberlin were among those who spoke out against management's use of corporate income for purposes other than stockholder benefit. Three threads (not necessarily reinforcing) were entwined in their critiques: (1) corporate oligarchs already had too much power and were using corporate responsibility as a way to soothe troubled consciences; (2) corporations were extending their "tyranny" over other sectors of society; and (3) corporate executives had little expertise in questions of public policy, of education, or of art.

**The Case for CSR.** Disturbed by the ambiguities that surrounded the initial articulations of the idea of corporate responsibilities, scholars like William Frederick urged abandonment of the term responsibility and substitution of the word response. The new coinage had certain advantages. A reactive posture relieved the corporation of any charge that it intended to manipulate the form and shape of contemporary society. Since manipulation was the "ugliest face of power," corporate executives simply could not afford to present such a face to the public. The response method was also less threatening to other organizations because it also allowed them to become the initiators of change. Finally, the response method provided rich opportunities for social audit trails.

Perhaps the most singular advantage of the response mechanism—and its supporting arguments—was its flexibility. Managers respond to threats as well as to opportunities. Perceived threats are everywhere—abroad and at home. Such agencies as the United Nations Conference on Trade and Development, the Food and Agriculture Organization, the United National Industrial Development Organization, the Economic Commission for Asia and the Far East, and similar commissions for other areas of the world had transmitted vast literature hostile to market capitalism. Preservation of the system itself had become a social responsibility of business leaders in all countries. And because America was the most powerful capitalist nation in the world, the heaviest obligation fell on it.

Yet there are conceptual weaknesses in the "response" rationale. A response is nothing more than an answer to questions raised by others, framed by others, and judged for adequacy by others. In a subtle but real sense, business is locked in. Efforts to move the debate from any kind of CSR-1 (defined as responsibility) to CSR-2 (defined as response) have not been overwhelmingly successful. This does not suggest that the response mechanism is unusually defective; insofar as it goes, it is quite helpful. But it does suggest that responsibility, which is a moral quality, is needed to round out the picture. The difference between seeing corporate responsibility as response and viewing it as the product of virtuous leaders is easy to suggest. Whereas response is more passive, virtue is more active; response urges us to stop, look, and listen before moving. Virtue pushes individuals toward risk; response enjoins people to do no harm; virtue impels individuals to do some good.

The ill-defined outside world is the heart of the problem. What responsibilities have business organizations for the health of public ones? Should higher education have high priority? If so, is the relatively niggardly support (the 5 percent deductible allowed under tax laws) a reflection of caution or confusion? Should the bulk of support go to public tax-supported institutions? To the private voluntary sector? To both evenhandedly? One conclusion is inescapable: defining, prioritizing, and publicizing the corporation's sense of its own missions is probably as hard as the actual fulfillment of that mission. But CSR is fairly well entrenched today as part of the corporate mission.[40]

**Future Stages in CSR.** If you want to know what is new in the modern world, said James Coleman, "it is the modern corporation."[41] But is the new known? As noted in the introduction and worth repetition here, philosophers, who once saw the corporation as a simple monolith when compared to the complex motivations and sensibilities of the average person, are now suggesting that "the moral nature of the corporation is moving toward a level more nearly commensurate to those of responsible individuals.[42] Does the forward movement, however, warrant calling the corporation a moral person? Some philosophers have no hesitancy in answering affirmatively.[43] Others insist that the corporation is not an organism but a machine designed by humans, modified by humans, operated by humans, and like anything controlled by the few, works for the prime benefit of the few. Only on humans do major moral responsibilities rest. Only people are moral persons.[44] Nevertheless, corporations do create distinctive types of culture. And because all cultures are value laden, all who work within them are influenced. Managers may be interested in the philosophers' debates, but they continue to focus on the legal attributes that John Marshall posited for them in 1819—immortality and limited liability. The managers also focus on productivity and innovation, as well as on personnel and morale.

Corporations will be around a long time and durable organizations exist by doing things right—right in the fullest sense of word. Limited liability will be turned more toward moral accountability. Critical examinations of the capitalist system in which the corporation is nested will continue—and this despite capitalism's apparent victory over socialist economies in Europe and despite new incarnations in East Asia. Capitalists are essentially disturbers of the economic peace and capitalism is the ideology that justifies their disturbances. Creative destruction, as economist Joseph Schumpeter once used the term, is endemic to capitalist societies. With characteristic optimism Americans expect more creation than destruction from their economic system. The hope will be measured within the perspective of the nation's industrial success between 1880 and 1949 when the most distinctive feature of America's manufacturing exports was intensity in nonreproducible natural resources.[45] Preserving nonreproducible natural resources is a major part of the coming challenge, a relatively new stage in the unfolding drama of CSR.

## *Noncorporate Businesses*

The billion-dollar sales figures of the nation's top ten corporations blind observers to the importance of other forms of business organization—sole proprietorships, partnerships, and cooperatives. Of the three, cooperatives tend to be most ignored even though they represent a substantial percentage of American sales. Unlike the Fords and the General Motors of the world, cooperatives are nonprofit associations organized to promote the interests of their members. Although outwardly similar to business corporations in structure, they differ from them in their articles of incorporation and in their bylaws, especially in rules pertaining to the admission of new members, the way earnings are distributed and, above all, in their belief that social progress comes best through mutual efforts.

The cooperative movement originated in England during the industrial revolution and was the product of urban workers who had been expelled from their small landholdings during the enclosure movement. The cooperative took hold after 1820 when Dr. William King (known as the poor man's physician) and social reformer Robert Owen pushed the cooperative as the best way for laborers to accumulate enough capital to establish a fair measure of economic independence. But King and Owen asked too much sacrifice from the membership and their efforts failed. In 1844, however, in Rochdale, England, the cooperative movement received its distinctive (and successful) format.[46]

Because the Rochdale principles became the operative philosophy of the international cooperative movement, they are worth noting: (1) membership open to everyone without regard to sex, race, or creed; (2) democratic control (one vote for each member); (3) selling at market prices; (4) profits distributed in proportion to a member's purchases; (5) limited low interest on capital; (6) religious and political neutrality; (7) nothing sold on credit; and (8) strong support for education.[47]

With time, the cooperatives began to add production to consumption. In this respect American farmers played a leading role, seeing in cooperative production a means to improve efficiency and reduce purchasing costs for tractors and other heavy equipment. By 1869 more than 400 cooperatives were involved in processing dairy products, building grain elevators, marketing hogs, and buying supplies. The National Grange, founded as a fraternal organization to promote farm interests, took the lead in establishing cooperatives in the Midwest. And when the Grange faltered because of mismanagement, the Farmers Union (1902) and the American Farm Bureau Association (1919) resurrected and reinvigorated the movement.

Large-scale associations were also established to foster the processing and sale of such items as citrus, fruit, and walnuts; soon American consumers took for granted brand names like Sunkist, Sunmaid, and Eatmor. Today there are 15,000 credit unions, 668 electric power cooperatives, 250 rural electric co-ops, and about 4,000 consumer cooperatives representing such widely disparate fields as housing, manufacturing, food processing, metallurgy, and chemicals.[48] In a real sense this small business segment is Big Business. The cooperatives' economic strength is considerable. Their political clout is potent. Their philosophy is appealing.

## Workers and Labor Unions

Since nine of every ten Americans works for somebody else, a brief note on why some workers unionized early while others did not is relevant to the history of business. American unions are interesting because of their nature, unique characteristics, their evolution, and liabilities.

### *The Nature of Unions*

Some observers wonder whether labor unions exist primarily (a) to meet the workers' sociopsychological needs, (b) to serve as instruments for acquiring political power, or (c) to provide the worker with sufficient income to live decently. In the first view, trade unions are essential to workers in the Aristotelian sense that a person's fulfillment comes through community living.[49] The Athenian would challenge Americans like Emerson and Thoreau who praised rugged individualism even before Carnegie and Rockefeller saw its values in the business setting. A second interpretation sees unions as necessarily concerned with politics: who gets what, when, and how. Premised in the unions' political outlook is the notion of an adversary society in which groups fight other groups for a share of the economy's spoils. Unions battle employers, other unions, nonunion workers, and even minority groups who threaten them. They are also political in the sense of seeking to influence public policy. Unions care who is elected, what laws are written, and who is appointed to regulatory agencies and nominated for judgeships. Further, they are political in the crude Machiavellian sense of trying to manipulate other groups and other people: power and status count. No union leader could succeed—although he or she may survive—unless that person was a skillful politician. Quite obviously, there are different styles of leadership. John Lewis, Walter Reuther, and Jimmy Hoffa had their own particular behavior patterns, but all were political. A criticism of Lane Kirkland, head of the AFL-CIO, is that he is not political enough.

In the third view, labor unions are depicted as being overwhelmingly economic in nature because their goals are bread-and-butter ones: better wages, better working conditions, better health and pension benefits, and better job security.[50] Actually, unions combine sociopsychological elements (togetherness), political elements (power), and economic elements (earnings). Overarching the composite is a distinctive quality that has set American unions apart from their European counterparts.

## Characteristics of Unions

A distinctive feature of the American labor movement is the absence of the ideological uniformity found in European unions. During the 1950s, union leaders themselves recognized their differences. The arch-conservative Bill Hutcheson of the carpenters' union had no sympathy for the socialism of Dave Dubinsky of the garment workers' union, yet they worked closely together as vice presidents of the American Federation of Labor (AFL). Even when the younger leaders of the CIO came to power, the differences between Emil Rieve of the Textile Workers and Walter Reuther of the UAW likely would have disrupted European trade-union organizations; but they did not do so in the United States.

Nor is American unionism a proletarian movement committed to class warfare. This does not mean that American unions are not militant. Their militancy, however, has been used to achieve status, security, and full citizenship in a capitalist society, not to achieve a socialist state. The worker is a middle-class member of a middle-class society—in the plant, in the local community, and in the economy. At the same time, unions have shown great hostility to management. And even with shrinking membership, workers in the United States are still among the most militant in the world.[51]

## *Evolution of Unions*

Throughout the colonial period, wage-earning workers were the least numerous and least important segment of the American work force. Three out of every four workers were—or had been—indentured; one out of every six was a slave.[52] As more and more slaves were brought from Africa, conditions in the South quickly began to change. Slavery quickly displaced the indenture system. A free laboring class was born in seaport towns and in cities because traveling artisans wanted roots for themselves and for their families. By 1715, colonial newspapers were carrying want ads for scores of different types of free workers, ranging from watchmakers to furriers.

Furthermore, after returning home from Revolutionary War battlefields, America's ex-soldiers found themselves in a disturbing predicament: if they fought for political freedom during war, should they not fight in peace for economic freedom? In their political campaigns, however, the working class was handicapped because the right to vote was usually restricted to property owners. Only when workers began to think in terms of independent political action was the idea of a labor union born. This *idea* of collective action was probably the workers' major accomplishment in the 18th century.

In the early 1830s, workingmen's parties held the balance of power in New York and Philadelphia. After a time of slumber, unionism spread and resulted in 1867 in the National Labor Union; five years later, this union collapsed. Its successor was the Knights of Labor founded by Uriah Stevens but led by Terence Powderly. This union began a spectacular growth after 1879, and by 1886 over 700,000 Knights seemed to think that their organization was impregnable. Yet its demise came as fast as its growth and by 1896 membership had fallen to 75,000.

The primary reason for the Knights' decline was the founding of the American Federation of Labor (AFL), which came into being largely through the joint actions of such national organizations as the Molders Union, the International Typographical Union, and other independent locals who saw the need for a coordinated labor organization. The question facing AFL leaders was whether to organize the skilled *and* unskilled into one association or to select *only* the craftsmen because they, being most essential to employers, could cripple a firm through a strike. The question was answered: the AFL was to be only for the skilled. It was a historic decision.[53] While organizations of only skilled workers gave union leaders a stiletto to pierce the corporation's heart by denying it the kind of worker most needed, the strategy led to isolation from the more numerous less skilled and unskilled workers who lacked the bargaining power and job control that craftsmen were able to wield.[54] History was to show that numbers would count as much as skill in the growth of labor organizations.

The name of Samuel Gompers is practically synonymous with the AFL. From the 1880s to his death in 1924, Gompers towered over the labor scene. His answer to the question—what do workers want?—has become legendary: More! If the "more" maxim dominated his thinking, two questions arose: (1) more for whom and (2) more gotten how? The first he answered easily:

more for the minority of skilled workers. The "how" question vexed him, but the depressions of the 1870s and the 1890s convinced Gompers that the rigid ideological views prevailing in most European labor organizations were not appropriate for the United States. Staying out of politics meant staying in power.

Both answers led to problems. For four decades the skilled workers prospered under Gompers' leadership, but by 1920 the AFL was largely an organization without clout because it excluded millions of workers in the new steel, automobile, and rubber industries. His answer to the second question (should unions be involved in politics?) was to ignore it—another mistake when political power was flowing to Washington. Gompers kept the AFL on the sidelines while the real power game was being played by others in the national and state capitals.[55]

Gompers' answers—exclusiveness in membership and isolationist in politics—vexed other craft unions whose leaders were forced to adapt to the demands of semiskilled and unskilled workers. Adaptation was necessary because technology affected different sectors of the economy at different times and in different ways. As a consequence craft unions were forced to adopt widely differing structures to include unskilled workers, who were now often as much needed as were the craftsmen. To illustrate, the carpenters' union was originally composed only of construction workers, but by 1902 it had begun to admit others because of problems imposed by technological changes in the woodworking industry. To achieve its goal, the union expanded its jurisdiction to cover "all that's made of wood" and, by 1914, anything "that ever was made of wood." The first expansion took the union into the woodworking industry; the second led the union to organize workers in metal-fitting manufacturing firms, where it clashed repeatedly with the unions affiliated with the AFL's Metal Trades Department. Another step the carpenters took was to enter the lumber industry in order to gain control over the basic raw material of many of the industries in which the union was active. This resulted in their organizing woodworkers in railroad repair and maintenance shops. Each adaptation of jurisdictional policy meant alterations in the union's structure. While successfully widening its control, the United Brotherhood of Carpenters and Joiners (UBCJ) continued to organize only those less-skilled workers who could add to its own power base.

Responses by its affiliates put great pressure on the AFL, but Gompers continued to favor national unions of the pure craft type, and between 1886 and the early 1900s he had encouraged the formation of as many autonomous craft unions as possible. The jurisdictional boundaries between these small groups of skilled workers were frequently rather narrow. Side by side, for example, were the Pocket Knife Grinders and the Table Knife Grinders, the Watchcase Makers and the Watchcase Engravers, each with its own charter as a national union. The result was constant squabbling.

The International Association of Machinists (IAM) and the UBCJ, fearing splinter groups, pressured AFL leadership to stop chartering small units.

They proposed, instead, that different groups of skilled workers be placed under the jurisdiction of the major craft in an industry or trade. Acceding to these demands, the AFL approved in 1911 the chartering of one organization for one trade. From this date forward the AFL favored rather than pure craft unionism, single organizations containing *all* the strategic workers of a particular trade or industry. AFL's chance of becoming the dominant labor force disappeared when it gave autonomy to its own constituencies. The whole became less than the sum of its parts.[56]

The story of the AFL was, in a nutshell, rigidity at the top and adaptability at the bottom. Even then, affiliates did not deal with overall needs of workers in industries in which the labor force was predominantly semi-skilled or unskilled—as it was throughout most of mass production. These industries remained unorganized until the unions that were to found the CIO grew tired of the vacillation of other AFL affiliates. The United Mine Workers (UMW), determined to preserve its monopoly over coal mining, extended its control over steel, the major industry using coal, and launched the Steel Workers' Organizing Committee in 1936; it also supported organizations of workers in the automobile industry.[57] Because the CIO's achievements were in sharp contrast to the AFL unions in the major manufacturing industries, many observers concluded that the AFL was living in stunned inactivity. However, numbers tell a different story. In labor's great forward leap in 1936 (when 1,673,000 new workers were unionized) the CIO registered 53 percent of the total membership gains (886,000), while the AFL unions enrolled 46 percent (768,000).[58] Stunned inactivity could not explain such stunning results. Nevertheless, the unions as organizations always had the problem of public suspicion.

## *Legitimacy Problems of Unions*

Arguably outsiders (government, business, and the general public) caused the problems of union legitimacy before 1930 but workers themselves have created most of their own headaches after that date. In the 19th and early 20th centuries, the public read newspaper stories and saw pictures that depicted unionized labor as organized groups of thugs. Beginning with the New Deal, however, workers gained government support, and with passage of the Wagner Act of 1933 a new era began. The Great Depression shifted public opinion from an antilabor to a prolabor stance. The 1930s were good years for unions. Nevertheless, other things plagued the movement—charges of violence and racketeering along with claims that many among the teamsters were, if not Stalinists, at least "leftists"; that communists were active, especially at Westinghouse and General Electric; and that "bossism" was simply the expression of organizational totalitarianism. Fortunately, labor (with nudges from the government) has begun to clean up its act and prospects for an authentic form of union democracy seem brighter than ever before.

## The Murky Future

Today union membership is down and continues to fall. In 1956, roughly 40 percent of the work force in the private sector was unionized; 30 years later, the figure was under 14 percent. A perceived union weakness has encouraged some managements to wage such a virulent antiunion campaign that the number of unfair labor practices has increased nearly fourfold since 1960—the year when the talk was of big government, big business, and big labor. In view of certain union excesses, it is easy to become antiunion. However, if unions continue their steady decline, the free world may be less free. The public-at-large has a stake in the outcome.[59] As the Catholic bishops declared in their 1987 Labor Day statement: "through unions, workers cannot only have more—they can be more."[60]

## The Commercial Professions

To think of the foundations of business is to think of powerful boards, well-known executives, and large bureaucracies. Doing so, however, overlooks the vast powers over company policies that professions exercise. Few executives would ignore the lawyer's "no-no" advice on a proposed course of action; most worry about a CPA audit, particularly if there is any possibility of a qualified report. Less powerful, but still significant, are advertisers whose comparative advertising strategies start the gastric juices flowing in executives of the targeted company; public relations firms can help or hurt the corporate image; insurers can appraise property values or raise premium costs in ways that create cash flow problems.

The main commercial professions are still law and accounting, even though emergent professions (stockbrokers, insurance agents, investment bankers, advertisers, public relations experts, and others) clamor for entry into the golden circle—a circle made possible by the power they exert over business, the revenues they generate for themselves, and the state-protected monopolies they have created. A truncated history of the development of law and accounting provides opportunity to understand their roles in American business—as well as a chance to contrast professional ideals with current performances.

### The Emergence of Professions

A first step in understanding the nature of a profession is to acknowledge that professionals do not a profession make. Babe Ruth and Joe Namath, lionized by New York fans and paid well by their employers, made neither baseball nor football a profession. Money is part—but only a part—of a profession's meaning. And meaning evolved slowly as distinctions were made between the *learned men* in teaching and preaching and the *learned professions* like law and medicine.

In the early life of this country the clergy constituted the dominant profession. Ministers were most admired and most sought after; they taught the young, sometimes served as physicians and legal advisers, wrote treatises, and served as molders of public opinion. During the colonial period the notion of a profession was one of a "calling": the Lord summoned the minister to perform pastoral duties in a single congregation for the rest of his life. It was one life in one place. Harvard and Yale were founded to educate ministers for the Congregationalists, Princeton served the Presbyterians, Rutgers educated the Dutch Reformed, and Columbia tutored the Anglicans. Even at the end of the colonial period, when secular interests were stronger than they were at its beginning, most American college students were planning a career in the ministry. The country honored its learned men.

**The Legal Profession.** By the time Andrew Jackson was elected to the presidency, the ministry had been nudged to the sidelines by lawyers and by doctors. The here-and-now seemed more important than the hereafter. Learning and character continued to be important but other characteristics were coming to the fore: work for pay, expertise, state licensure, and peer control. The "power hitters" were the lawyers. Although there were no lords or barons and no Oxfords or Cambridges in the United States, it looked for a while as if American lawyers would become elitists like their British counterparts—if not in titles and schools at least in status and income.

When the Revolutionary War ended, many Americans, because of their strong hostility toward the British, urged the adoption of Continental legal codes rather than the English Common Law. When it became clear that the latter would indeed become the American pattern, fear was widespread that the law would be used in this country as it had been used so often in England—as an instrument for preserving and defending the property rights of the upper classes. The fear was deepened by the emergence of closed guilds that, by controlling admissions to the bar, prevented outsiders from gaining entry—unless such outsiders shared common friendships, marriage connections, economic means, or a "respected" paternal occupation. As late as 1830, the lawyer class in a state like Massachusetts and in a city like Philadelphia operated within guild systems. The message to those who had little money and few social connections was clear: stay out!

For over a half century lawyers disdained to serve the masses. At the outbreak of the Civil War, however, numerous lawyers knew that their old tactics of crying wolf before barbarian invaders were not going to work. Rather suddenly—in law magazines, in public speeches, and in general notices—lawyers began to emphasize their lowly origins, their industriousness, and their role as public servants. In 1849 the American Legal Association was founded with the avowed purpose of furnishing the names of at least one trustworthy lawyer to businessmen and businesswomen of every township in the country.

This new sense of professionalism by lawyers occurred at a time when the country's industrialization processes were under way. Rather than argue for the corporation or for capitalism, the legal fraternity's rhetoric emphasized equal opportunity for all Americans, protection of everyone's private property, individual freedom, and support of the citizen against public or private monopoly. After the Civil War period it was clear that lawyers were indispensable to businesses that wanted to incorporate, to form a partnership, to buy or sell property, to file for injunctions against striking workers, and the like. If one lesson emerged from the tangled story of the legal profession it is the importance of public opinion and public respect. Without these, all claims by any profession for a special status were seen as self-serving. So professions sought public approval by proclaiming their expertise, their noble aspirations, and their commitment to the common good.

**Professions Defined.** Developments in medicine produced the most famous definition of a profession. In 1782 Harvard put its prestige and power into medicine by establishing a medical school. Yet 50 years later a contemporary concluded that medicine's ranks were filled by doctors deficient either in abilities or requirements—too stupid for the Bar and too immoral for the pulpit. Even when doctors greeted the 20th century, criticism remained intense. Finally the profession acted. Between 1900 and 1917 the American Medical Association (AMA) worked to organize itself more effectively. Its leader was the extraordinary Joseph McCormick, who traveled throughout the country urging physicians to improve their skills, end their squabblings, and unite. He persuaded the AMA to expose the highly variable standards employed for admission to medical schools and he lobbied successfully for the creation of state licensing boards composed exclusively of allopathic physicians. Eventually medicine developed a state-sanctioned monopoly over the provision of a defined set of health services. To the first three characteristics of a profession (expertise, moral probity, and a client-first philosophy) was now added a fourth—monopoly over a particular activity.

But McCormick and his associates, still needing help in their unfinished crusade, turned to the Carnegie Foundation for further support. The decision was understandable: the organization was highly respected, possessed substantial resources, and had no vested interest to protect. To study the field and prepare a report, the foundation hired Abraham Flexner, a German-trained psychologist. His "Bulletin Number 4," published as a paperback in June 1910 by the Carnegie Foundation, was to become one of the most famous education reform documents in the history of the United States. The hard-hitting Flexner Report was accorded something like a Talmudic status. What had become obvious to Flexner was that, in the evolution of a profession, education needed to be formalized within a university setting. Training in the necessary technical areas to assure expertise, credentialing, the transmission of knowledge, the extension of knowledge frontiers, and the inculcation of an understanding of the professional culture—all attested to the need for formal educational institutions.

As universities accepted the challenge, the distinction mentioned earlier between *learned men* and *learned professions* was indelibly established. The learned men were the theologians, historians, and philosophers whose purpose was to advance general understanding. The learned professions, on the other hand, were law and medicine, whose primary purpose was to meet specific social needs. Because of the differing emphasis, it was not uncommon to find tension on American campuses between liberal arts faculties (the learned men) and professional schools (the learned professions). The former often resented the intrusion of pre-professional training into the curriculum and sought to resist it. If the resistance was strong enough, or if the need for the professional service was mounting, it was not uncommon for professors in a new profession to break entirely from the liberal arts faculty. The Wharton School at the University of Pennsylvania is one example of this process. When it sought to provide professional education for business students, the learned men resisted, yet the need was so apparent that the Wharton faculty eventually won the support of the university's trustees.

**Accounting: The Watchdog Profession.** This capsule history cannot, of course, ignore the accountants. Having the benefit of history, accountants often sought to encourage universities to establish separate schools of accounting—and, by and large, they were rebuffed. They did, however, succeed in having separate departments established in universities; they encouraged the formation of state licensing boards; they established a quasi-monopoly in accounting for CPAs and created a code of ethics. The latter is especially interesting because it came early in the profession's development, not rather late as in law and medicine. In 1906 the American Association of Public Accountants (AAPA) formally established a committee on ethics to develop standards. That it took a decade for this committee to receive power to consider violations of the code is an index of the resistance that has always characterized reform in a profession.

The stock market crash of 1929 caught many professions—lawyers, investment bankers, accountants—in a web of professional carelessness, even chicanery, that led to a high level of public disdain. To recapture public trust for accountancy the leaders announced (after approval by the membership) that even the possibility of a violation of an ethical rule by an accountant would henceforth be investigated.[61] The restatement of the Code of Professional Ethics in 1973 was still another example of the accountant's determination to make of theirs a fully defined profession. The effort reflected awareness that theirs was, indeed, a special profession so far as the public interest was concerned. The former Chief Justice of the Supreme Court, Warren Burger, emphasized this point in a sharp distinction he made between lawyers and accountants:

> *The private attorney's role is as the client's confidential adviser and advocate, a loyal representative whose duty it is to present the client's case in the most favorable possible light. An independent certified public accountant performs a different role. By certifying the public reports that collectively depict a corporation's financial status, the independent auditor assumes a* **public responsibility transcending any employment relationship with the client.** *The independent public accountant performing this special*

*function owes ultimate allegiance to the corporation's creditors and stockholders, as well as to the investing public. This public watchdog function demands that the accountant maintain total independence from the client at all times and requires complete fidelity to the public's trust.*[62]

What all of this means to business is clear: monitoring of the firm's financial condition by outsiders; publication of its performance to investors whose capital may be sorely needed; internal restructuring to give the comptroller some voice in decision making; representing the enterprise before the IRS or tax courts; and other related activities. The point at issue here is that one profession introduced for itself a role as a moral watchdog. That the accountants have, by and large, met the challenge is revealed in the way corporations behave as compared to their behavior in some other countries. The overall result of the public accountant's oversight has not transformed corporate executives from sinners to saints; it has simply meant that the sinners sin less.

## *Main Characteristics of Professions*

The best way to understand what theorists say about professions is to take Flexner's basic catalog and add to it certain characteristics that have evolved as professions sought to respond to changing social needs.

**The Criteria.** The full set of criteria developed to define a profession include the following:

1. Because a profession uses a body of knowledge that is more than ordinarily complex, those who work with routine or simple skills (or those whose competencies are accessible to any person of reasonable wit) are not members of a profession.

2. Since a profession is necessarily an intellectual enterprise that trains practitioners to avoid hit-or-miss solutions (the hunch, the lucky guess, and the like), there has to be a secure theoretical grasp of the phenomena with which it deals. Surgeons, for example, once deemed unworthy to join the medical profession, achieved admission only after they wedded their manual dexterity to a knowledge of biological sciences.

3. The theoretical and complex knowledge is used to provide practical solutions to social and human problems; knowledge does not simply remain at a theoretical level—it has to be pragmatic and worldly. Those who pursue pure research or pure science do not qualify for membership, however rigorous their academic preparation and however brilliant their minds.

4. No profession is worthy of the name unless it increases the stock of knowledge in its field.

5. To be a profession, members must pass on what they know to coming generations in a deliberate and formal fashion. The chief means of transmission is the university or some other institution of higher learning.

6. Anyone entering a profession has to be credentialed by a qualified educational institution that provides the long and rigorous preparation necessary. The institution attests to the intellectual integrity of the credential itself.
7. Professions require associations to promote the health and stability of the profession. Since other organizations—such as trade or lobbying groups—also form associations, it is important to distinguish between a professional association and others. Business and trade organizations are lobbies organized for corporate self-advancement whereas professional associations exist to promote self-improvement by their members.
8. Every profession exercises large measures of self-regulation through its code of ethics. It defines legitimate professional conduct, which is used as a negotiating base with other professions and with the general public.
9. The profession provides its members with a means to earn a living—the art is practiced for pay.
10. To qualify as a profession, members are to be imbued with an altruistic spirit, defined as a client-first ideology; therefore, a profession is an antonym to words like commerce or business.
11. Because their ideology is one of service, and not profit, the professions must establish a special relationship of trust and confidence with users of their services.
12. Beneficiaries are rarely described as a customer, even when they purchase the services indirectly: they are patients or clients, important words that emphasize the dependence of the user on the knowledge of the expert. Benefits conferred, rather than quid-pro-quo, are the keys. The attitude of business is that the customer is always right; the attitude fostered by the professions is almost the opposite.
13. No matter where or how they provide their services, members of a profession retain their professional identity. Doctors see themselves as doctors whether engaged in fee-for-service activities or working for a health maintenance organization; lawyers identify themselves as lawyers whether they have their own practice, work for a large firm, or are salaried employees of a corporation; CPAs may work for a business firm but they continue to distinguish themselves from other accountants.
14. While the purpose of professional practice is to serve particular clients, such service is generally subordinated to larger social ends. Doctors treat individual patients but are expected to contribute to the preservation of public health; lawyers help clients but work to foster the "social health" by peacefully resolving disputes and conflicts; accountants are responsible to the investing public even more than to their clients.
15. Every profession has a monopolistic character. Society strikes a bargain with a specific group by saying that, if the profession performs a func-

tion society deems essential, it will grant a monopoly so that very few others may practice. Doctors and lawyers enjoy a clear monopoly; CPAs exercise a quasi-monopoly.

Problems, however, remain. Is money making (item 9) superior to, equal to, or subordinate to altruism (item 10)? Is criterion 14 internally consistent? If criterion 13 is true, why do practicing attorneys take a smug attitude toward in-house corporate lawyers? The questions suggest that, despite tremendous advances made by Flexner and his successors, inconsistencies or ambiguities exist that subject the professions to heavy strain when change is underway. The term profession, therefore, is not fixed in concrete.

Congress sought through the Taft-Hartley Act (1947) to remove some of the ambiguities by giving its understanding of a profession. The term "professional employee" meant one engaged in work described as follows:

1. Predominantly intellectual and varied in character as opposed to routine mental, manual, mechanical, or physical work
2. Involving the consistent exercise of discretion and judgment
3. Of such a character that the output cannot be standardized in relation to a given period of time
4. Requiring knowledge of an advanced type in a field of science or learning customarily acquired by a prolonged course of specialized intellectual instruction and study in an institution of higher learning—as distinguished from a general academic education, apprenticeships, or from training in the performance of routine mental, manual, or physical processes

**The Dark Side.** Codes of ethics, advanced university education, state licensure, publicly accepted monopoly, continuing education—are all important to a profession's standing. Clouds continue to hang over the profession's performance, however. Several examples tell the story:

- Doctors have been accused of playing the unbundling and exploding games that annually cost patients, employers, and insurance companies hundreds of millions of dollars. Unbundling occurs when a doctor codes a hysterectomy as a number of separate procedures—exploratory operation of the abdomen, removal of ovaries and tubes, removal of scar tissues, and the like. Exploding occurs when the doctor itemizes a series of tests that are all done on a single sample of blood—thereby turning a $25 analysis into a $150 fee.[63]
- Lawyers are close to the bottom of the barrel in public esteem according to attorney Peter Megargee Brown because unrestrained greed is their bottom line. Today's law firms, according to Brown, are "run by professional manager-accountants—the new barbarians—who, with some exceptions, have no real knowledge of the profession.[64]
- Lawyers lose further public confidence when they wail over—and rail against—government efforts to secure the names of clients who make

large cash payments, the usual practice for money launderers and tax evaders.[65]
- Stockbrokers have been sneaking their way into the National Association of Securities Dealers' list of registered brokers by hiring surrogates to take the entrance test—the so-called "Series Seven" examination.[66]
- Prestigious accounting firms have not escaped suspicion. To cite one example: Arthur Young, for nearly a century, had an enviable reputation for prudence and care, so much so that it could boast the smallest out-of-court legal settlements of any big accounting firm during the 1980s—less than $4 million. But during the spring of 1990 regulators and congressmen asked why this firm gave unqualified opinions in 1986 and 1987 to Lincoln Savings and Loan shortly before its collapse.
- Five of the Big Six accounting firms in the United States (with Price Waterhouse the exception) have been banned from participating in the thrift industry's reorganization work by the Resolution Trust Corporation created to clean up the mess because federal policy prohibits hiring accounting firms being sued by the government for allegedly shoddy audit work with the thrifts and with the banks.[67] These firms face a loss of business estimated to be $100,000,000. Coming at a time when competition is intense, the potential loss is staggering.
- Thrown in doubt is accountants' capacity to regulate themselves because names of the miscreants are kept secret from the public. John Burton, who had worked as chief accountant for the SEC and who had served as dean of Columbia University Graduate School of Business, expressed the public's view when he said that "self-regulation of accountants cannot work without scalps of offenders who fail to adhere to professional standards hanging on the belts of the regulators."[68] Incidentally, the profession's practice differs sharply from the self-regulatory program of the New York Stock Exchange, which since the early 1970s has published the names of expelled members. The defense by Robert Mautz, a member of the Public Oversight Board, of secretive disciplinary procedures (on grounds that publication of the malefactors' names would feed ammunition to overly zealous lawyers) is not persuasive. If, as Chairman Peter Scanlon of Coopers & Lybrand insisted, the purpose of self-regulation is preventative and not punitive, recent revelations raise doubts about the effectiveness of prevention processes.

Savvy business executives have learned that foot-dragging by organizations in need of reform leads to foot-stamping by the government. Professions need to master the same lessons. While not an endangered species in any Darwinian sense, professions are endangered in terms of public respect. And on such respect rests the legitimacy of every profession in a free society. Lack of responsiveness to the need for internal reform prompted sociology professor Eliot Friedson of New York University to define the major professions as a delinquent community.[69] To him the only kind of reform that will effectively raise the moral as well as the technical quality of professional service lies in the development of norms appropriate to a community dedicated to serve the public—norms that the professional community must in some way be taught or be persuaded to develop. Instead, professions tend to be communities bound together by the norms of mutually protective professional etiquette. Only when the norms of etiquette and their associated conceptions of propriety have been changed, only when all agree that it is appropriate to judge what a colleague does and to discuss differences of opinion with the aim of resolving them—only then will the problem of the social control of the professional community be adequately addressed.[70]

While Friedson's depiction of the professions as delinquent communities may be too harsh, publishing the names of culprits may be necessary. Revised codes of ethics are necessary. These are only part of the answer, however, because codes never reconcile standards with the individual's needs; they lag behind change and they are ambiguous. Nevertheless, codes are a profession's heroic effort to remind its members that principles do transcend self-interest. And this transcendent quality is related to the client's rights and needs.[71]

In the 15 years that have elapsed since Friedson called for reform, some professions have heard and heeded.[72] The law profession established the Kutak Committee, and the accountants created the Treadway Commission. Further steps, however, appear necessary if the public good is to be served more effectively. The 1979 discussion draft of the code for lawyers, for example, required disclosure of plaintiff's intentions to commit acts that could result in death or serious physical harm to others; it also permitted disclosure to prevent or rectify the consequences of other wrongful acts. However, in the face of strong protest, the final version had not reversed but actually strengthened the confidentiality requirement of the older code. Lawyers are permitted, but not required, to reveal information necessary to prevent imminent death or substantial bodily harm; moreover, they are now even forbidden to reveal information necessary to prevent substantial financial loss to innocent third parties from a client's wrongful conduct. Nor can they reveal past crimes, except where their services were involved. In the words of the Commission Chairman Robert Kutak, "by narrowing the exceptions for disclosure, the principle of confidentiality has been strengthened not only in the adversary system, but in the general practice of law."[73]

Two questions arise: (1) Is the public sufficiently protected by the lawyers' rule or is it a denial of the rights of others? (2) Should any profession have absolute right to establish its own rules of the game? A similar question about confidentiality exists in the accounting profession, which refuses to release a culprit's name to the public. To a distrustful public, this appears to be "stonewalling" or cover-up. The work of reform might come more quickly if nonprofessionals were involved in such reform efforts. The lay person's role is to protect the public's right from infringement by zealous professionals who also write their own job descriptions and enforce their own prescriptions. This "separatist thesis" will be challenged.[74]

CHAPTER TWO   The Business Foundation   75

## Summary

Insofar as the primary commercial professions are concerned, both law and accounting exercise a powerful influence over the way business is conducted in the United States. The ethical balance sheet suggests that their influence has been beneficial. But warning flags fly. If the monitors are careless in monitoring themselves, can they be trusted to monitor others? If their accrediting agencies disrupt—as they sometimes do—the normal operations of a university that educates their future members, have their powers gone too far? If a profession takes stands on public issues unrelated to its field, is the public well served? If the American Bar Association approves or disapproves nominees to judgeships on ideological grounds, is its action reprehensible? If lawyers serve on boards of corporations that are their clients, do they create conflict-of-interest problems? Do professions really care about the moral character of their entrants? Or is class standing in a prestigious university more important? Do some lawyers serve or exploit clients? Do some doctors exploit patients? One inescapable conclusion is that when, as noted, Professor Friedson called the professions the delinquent community, observant scholars and worried citizens are trying to tell the professions that all is not well. In such a time of unwellness, professions can more easily catch and transmit other moral viruses.

## *Questions For Discussion*

1. Do you favor the introduction into the corporate world of such government practices as due process, trial by peers, and free speech?
2. Should the same procedures be introduced into labor unions?
3. Can you think of businesses that could be better run on a cooperative rather than a competitive basis?
4. Are labor unions essential to an effective capitalist society?
5. Should professions be required to conduct their disciplinary investigations in public?

## Ethical Quandaries

### *The Baffled Builder*

As a management consultant specializing in the field of business ethics, you received a letter from a client that includes these salient paragraphs:

> We are building a high-rise condominium project that, of necessity, is an "all union" job. Nearing completion of the project,

certain units were about to be sold to individual owners who felt that they had a right to decide whether their "customizing" should be done by union or nonunion workers. The cost of union labor is substantially higher. These buyers threaten to back out of the sales if they cannot have the work done nonunion.

When union members found out about nonunion labor working in individual units, they sabotaged the elevators, threatened subcontractors, refused to let them unload supplies at the loading dock, etc. After personally being stuck in a sabotaged elevator for over an hour, I met with the union stewards. We negotiated an agreement whereby we could have a certain number of units customized by nonunion workers without harassment. Once this number was met, all additional units would be customized by union contractors. If I failed to comply, the union would shut down the building. If I see that the agreed-upon limit is about to be exceeded (even though the amount of customized work by the owners is small), should I notify the union stewards? Or simply let the work go on?

## Question

- What advice would you give?

## The Generous Town

You are the CEO of a firm that has benefited enormously by relocating in Shallow Brook ten years ago. The town, hard-pressed economically, gave land and tax breaks to attract the company. In the decade since, no strikes, no work stoppages, and no slowdowns have occurred to hurt the company. Profits have been respectable.

Now, however, figures from a study authorized by the company's vice presidents for finance and production, and which you approved, clearly show that profit margins can be improved by moving out of state to Jillsville, another financially hard-pressed community. Thus far, there have been no complaints from stockholders, no lowering of credit ratings, and no dissatisfaction among workers. You know, however, that savvy investors will pull out if they ever discover that the company is not doing its very best to increase dividends, even if it means leaving generous Shallow Brook.

## Question

- What would you do?

## *Notes*

1. Robert Heilbroner, *The Worldly Philosophers* (New York: Simon & Schuster, 1953), ch. 1.
2. It has been argued that Protestantism, more than urbanism, goes hand in hand with capitalism. Max Weber, *The Protestant Ethic and the Spirit of Capitalism* (New York: Charles Scribners, 1958). Trans. Talcott Parsons.
3. Wilhelm Röpke, *Civitas Humana: A Humane Order of Society* (London: William Hodge, 1943), 1. Trans. Cyril Spencer Fox, from the German.
4. N. S. B. Gras, "Capitalism: Concepts in History," *Bulletin of the Business Historical Society*, 16 (April 1942): 21–34.
5. N. S. B. Gras, *Business and Capitalism: An Introduction to Business History* (New York: Crofts, 1947).
6. Henri Pirenne, *Stages in the Social History of Capitalism* (Stanford, Calif.: Academic Reprints, 1953).
7. Trustees of Dartmouth College v. Woodward, Henry Wheaton, *Report of Cases in the U.S. Supreme Court, Feb. Term 1811,* (NY: Banks & Bros., 1887), 634.
8. Walton Hamilton, *On the Composition of the Corporate Veil* (Philadelphia: Brandeis Lawyers Society, 1946), 4.
9. Thomas C. Cochran, *Basic History of American Business* (Princeton, N.J.: Van Nostrand, 1959). For a delightful exploration of business history, with special emphasis on the movers and shakers in the capitalist economy, see Peter Baida, *Poor Richard's Legacy* (New York: William Morrow, 1990). Not to be overlooked is the superb study by Alfred D. Chandler, *Strategy and Structure: Chapters in the History of Industrial Enterprise* (Cambridge: Harvard University Press, 1955).
10. Adolf Berle, Jr., and Gardiner Means, *The Modern Corporation and Private Property* (New York: Macmillan, 1932).
11. Ibid., 21–28.
12. Peter Drucker, "Pension Fund Socialism," *The Public Interest*, Winter 1976, 3–46.
13. Louis Kraar, "Your Rivals Can Be Your Allies," *Fortune Magazine*, March 27, 1989, 66–78.
14. Elmer W. Johnson, "Ethics in Corporate Governments in the Age of Pension-Fund Capitalism", unpublished paper, 11. Presented at Columbia University School of Business Seminar, New York, October 25, 1989.
15. Clarence C. Walton, *Management Rights and Prerogative: Quo Warranto?* (State College, Pa: Penn State University School of Business, 1986). The classic work on the question is Jurgen Habermas, *The Legitimacy Crisis* (Boston: Beacon Press, 1973).
16. Earl Latham, "The Body Politic of the Corporation," in *The Corporation in Modern Society*, ed. Edward S. Mason (Cambridge: Harvard University Press: 1960), 221.
17. David Sciulli, "Voluntaristic Action as a Distinct Concept: Theoretical Foundations of Societal Constitutionalism," *American Sociological Review* 51 (December 1986): 752. See also, Robert A. Dahl, *Dilemmas of a Pluralist Democracy: Autonomy vs. Control* (New Haven: Yale University Press, 1982).
18. Bob Barber and Rachelle Tower, "Worker Participation in the United States," in *The State Trade Unions and Worker Participation in the United States* eds. Gyorgy Szell, Paul Blyton, and Chris Cornfort (New York: Walter de Gruyter, 1989), ch. 2.
19. Jeremy Waldron, "John Locke's Social Contract versus Political Anthropology," *The Review of Politics* 52 (Winter 1989): 3–51.
20. Lon L. Fuller, *The Morality of Law* (New Haven: Yale University Press, 1969), 46–84. While teaching at Harvard, Fuller began to exercise great influence in the 1950s and 1960s through his discussions with H. L. A. Hart, the British legal theorist, on this question: On what is legality ultimately based?
21. Sciulli, "Voluntaristic Action," 755–760.
22. On this point, see the classic article by Robert K. Merton, "Social Structures and Anomie," *American Sociological Review* 3 (1938): 672–682.

23. Victor Futter, "An Answer to the Public's Negative Perception of Corporations: A Corporate Ombudsman," *The Business Lawyer* 46 (November 1990): 35.
24. Milton Friedman, *Capitalism and Freedom* (Chicago: University of Chicago Press, 1982).
25. Murray Wiedenbaum, *The Myth of the Hollowed-Out Corporation* (St. Louis, Mo: Washington University's Center for the Study of American Business, 1990), 3.
26. Joseph Nye, *Bound to Lead* (New York: Basic Books, 1990). Expanding (and challenging) Nye's thesis are many of the essays edited by Stephen A. Marglin and Juliet B. Schor, *The Golden Age of Capitalism: Reinterpreting the Postwar Experience* (New York: Oxford University Press, 1990).
27. Ralph Nader, Mark Green, and Joel Seligman, *Taming the Giant Corporation* (New York: W. W. Norton, 1976), 252–254. Three articles that balance out the story are by Gary M. Anderson and R. D. Tollison, "Myth of the Corporation as a Creature of the State," *International Review of Law and Economics* 3 (Spring 1983): 107–120; Norwood P. Beveridge, "The Internal Affairs Doctrine: The Proper Law of a Corporation," *The Business Lawyer* 44 (May 1989): 693–719; and Herman Kripke, "The SEC, Corporate Governance, and the Real Issue," *The Business Lawyer* 36 (June 1981): 173–206.
28. Travis v. Knox (1915).
29. Commissioner Williams's main theme was to invite analysts to consider ways to match the corporation's great power with equally great responsibility.
30. Used with the permission of PWS-Kent Publishing Co., Boston, Mass. Clarence C. Walton, *Corporate Social Responsibility* (Wadsworth Publishing Co., 1967), ch. 5.
31. "Aristotle's Politics," in Leonard Dalton, *Masterworks and Government* (Garden City, N.Y.: Doubleday, 1947), 83.
32. Neil Chamberlain, "The Public Side of Private Business," *Challenge* 14 (June–February 1966): 4–6.
33. Richard Eells, "The Impact of Corporate Giving on the Corporation, the Arts, and the Community," in *The Business of America*, ed. Ivar Berg (New York: Harcourt Brace World, 1966).
34. Adolf Berle, "Corporate Social Responsibility—Too Much or Not Enough?" *The National Industrial Conference Board Record*, April 1964, 10.
35. John Maurice Clark, "The Changing Bases of Business Responsibility," *The Journal of Political Economy* 24 (March 1916): 220. For a detailed exposition of Clark's views, see *Alternates to Serfdom* (New York: Knopf, 1948).
36. Christopher Stone, *The Culture of the Corporation: Where the Law Ends* (New York: Harper Row, 1983).
37. Quoted from the *A.P. Smith Manufacturing Company v. Barlow et al.* (May 19, 1953). New Jersey Sp. Ct. Chancery Division, *Atlantic Reporter*, 197.
38. How the changing ideology affected business since Dodge has been traced by George Cabot Lodge, "Managerial Implications of Ideological Change," *The Ethics of Corporate Conduct* (Englewood Cliffs, N.J.: Prentice-Hall, 1977). Ed. Clarence C. Walton.
39. Smith Manufacturing Company v. Barlow et al., 199.
40. E. B. Dunkel et al., *Special Report to General Electric Management* (New York: McGraw-Hill, 1970), 116.
41. James Coleman, *Power and the Structure of Society* (New York: W. W. Norton, 1974), 14.
42. James B. Wilbur, "The Foundations of Corporate Responsibility" in *Proceedings of the Second National Conference and Business Ethics*, ed. Michael Hoffman (Waltham, Mass.: Bentley College, 1984), 235–250.
43. Kenneth E. Goodpaster and John B. Matthews, Jr., "Can a Corporation Have a Conscience?" *Harvard Business Review* (January–February 1982), 132–141. See also Peter French, "Morally Blaming Whole Populations," in *Philosophy, Morality, and International Affairs*, eds. Virginia Held et al. (New York: Oxford University Press, 1974), 266–285. Useful, too, is the short article by Raymond J. Pfeffer, "A Central Distinction in the Theory of Corporate Moral Personhood," *Journal of Business Ethics* 9 (June 1990): 473–480.
44. Manuel V. Velasquez, "Why Corporations Are Not Moral Persons," *Business and Professional Ethics Journal* 2 (Spring 1983): 1–16. Because firms represent different things to

different observers, continued efforts are being made to develop new theories that have the virtues of accuracy and political neutrality. For an exposition of one such effort, see William W. Bratton, Jr., "The Modern Business Corporation: A Critical Appraisal," *Cornell Law Review* 74 (1987): 407–465.

45. Gavin Wright, "The Origins of American Industrial Success 1879–1940," *American Economic Review* 80 (September 1990): 651–668.

46. One of the classics on British cooperatives is F. T. Hall and W. P. Watkins, *A Survey of the History, Principles, and Organization of the Cooperative Movement in Great Britain and Ireland* (Manchester, England: Holyoake Books, 1937).

47. W. P. Watkins, *Cooperative Principles: Today and Tomorrow* (Manchester, England: Holyoake Books, 1986), 6.

48. U.S. Department of Commerce, *Statistical Abstract of the United States, 1990* (Washington: Government Printing Office, 1991), 530.

49. Frank Tannenbaum, *A Philosophy of Labor* (New York: Alfred Knopf, 1951).

50. Selig Perlman, *A Theory of the Labor Movement* (New York: Macmillan, 1928).

51. "The U.S. Labor Movement," *Fortune Magazine*, February 1951, 37.

52. Philip Foner, *History of the Labor Movement* (New York: International Publishers, 1962), 19. See also, Richard B. Morris, ed., *A History of the American Worker* (Princeton: Princeton University Press, 1983). The fact that some of the essayists in the Morris book have had both academic and shopfloor experience makes this collection very valuable.

53. David J. Saposs and Sol Davison, "Employee Organizations and Elections: The Structure of AFL Unions," *Labor Relations Reference Manual* (Washington, D.C.: Government Printing Office, 1940), vol. 4, 1044 and 1047.

54. Lloyd Ullman, *The Rise of the National Trade Union: The Development and Significance of Its Structure, Governing Institutions, and Economic Policies* (Cambridge: Harvard University Press, 1955).

55. Stuart Kaufman and Harold C. Livesay, *Samuel Gompers and Organized Labor in America* (Boston: Little Brown, 1978).

56. Michael T. Hannan and John Freeman, "The Ecology of Organizational Mortality: American Labor Unions 1836–1935," *The American Journal of Sociology* 94 (July 1988): 25–52.

57. The unions that left the AFL in 1936 to form an independent CIO (United Mine Workers; United Mine Workers, District 50; United Textile Workers; Amalgamated Clothing Workers; International Ladies' Garment Workers; Mine, Mill and Smelter Workers; Iron, Steel and Tin Workers; Oil, Gas and Refinery Workers; United Automobile Workers; Fur Workers; Flat Glass Workers; Rubber Workers; Newspaper Guild) had a total membership of 1,104,900.

58. Christopher L. Tomlin, "AFL Unions in the 1930s: Their Performance in Historical Perspective," *The American Historical Review* 65 (March 1979): 1035. See also, Walter Galenson, *The CIO Challenge to the AFL: A History of the American Labor Movement, 1935–1941* (Cambridge: Harvard University Press, 1960).

59. Richard Freeman, "Can American Unions Rebound?" *The Wall Street Journal*, December 8, 1987, 36.

60. *Freedom, Future and the Role of Unions* (Washington, D.C.: U.S. Catholic Conference, 1989).

61. For an excellent summary of the profession's history, see Herman J. Lowe, "Our 100-Year History," *Journal of Accountancy* (May 1987): 79–87.

62. *U.S. v. Arthur Young et al.*, Supreme Court Reports, April 26, 1984.

63. Rhonda L. Rundle, "How Doctors Boost Bills by Misrepresenting the Work They Do," *The Wall Street Journal*, December 6, 1989, A–1.

64. Peter Megargee Brown, "Professional Responsibility," *The ABA Journal* (December 1989): 38. For details, see his book *Rascals* (New York: Benchmark Press, 1989). See also Norman Bowie, "The Law: From a Profession to a Business," *Vanderbilt Law Review* 41 (May 1988): 741–758.

65. P. Cohen and Martha Brannigan, "Law Firms Must Disclose Sources of Big Cash Payments," *The Wall Street Journal*, March 14, 1990, B5. The usual cry of criminal defense

attorneys is that the ruling invades attorney/client relationships, according to Neal Sonnett, president of the National Association of Criminal Defense Lawyers. Lawyers are now hiring public relations experts, whom they once scorned.

66. Ann Hagedorn, "U.S. Probes Alleged Scam in Brokers Test," *The Wall Street Journal*, March 15, 1990, Cl.

67. The objects of government suits included Ernst & Young, Deloitte & Touche, Coopers & Lybrand, Peat Marwick, Arthur Andersen, and Grant Thornton.

68. John Burton, "CPA Self-Regulation: Contradiction in Terms?" *The Wall Street Journal*, August 19, 1986, A12. Very helpful overviews are Michael Bayles, "Professional Power and Self Regulation," *Business and Professional Ethics Journal* 5 (November 1987): 26–46; and Louis Lombarde, "Self Regulation: Business and the Profession," *Business and Professional Ethics Journal* 5 (November 1987): 68–86.

69. Eliot Friedson, "The Social Control of Professions" (New York: Columbia University, Seminar Report, 1975), 121–127. For his detailed analysis, see Eliot Friedson, *Professional Powers* (Chicago: University of Chicago Press, 1986). For a Marxist critique, see Magali Sarfatti Larson, *The Rise of Professionalism: A Sociological Analysis* (Berkeley: University of California Press, 1977).

70. Friedson, *Professional Powers*, 127.

71. Alan H. Gothman, *The Moral Foundations of Professional Ethics* (Totowa, N.J.: Rowman and Littlefield, 1980).

72. Paul Camenisch, *Grounding Professional Ethics in a Pluralistic Society* (New York: Haven Publishers, 1983).

73. Robert Kutak, "The Adversary System and the Practice of Law," in *The Good Lawyer*, ed. David Luhan (Totowa, N.J.: Rowman and Allenheld, 1983), 185.

74. Alan Gewirth, "Professional Ethics: The Separatist Thesis," *Ethics* 96 (Summer 1986): 282–350.

CHAPTER 3

# The Moral Foundation

### American Culture
Definition of Culture
The Infant Nation: Manifest Destiny
Adolescent America
*Individualism*
*Social Darwinism*
*The Role of Education*
The Civil Religion

### Moral Responsibility in a Changing World
Cosmopolitanism
Economic Productivity
Family Structure
Social Fragmentation

### America's Moral Future
Failures of the Prophets
A Cry for Values

### Moral Philosophies
The Challenge for Philosophers
Self-Oriented Philosophies
*Survival Ethics*
*Expediency Ethic*
*Ego Ethic*
Utilitarianism
Deontology
A Parting Word: Face

### Summary
Questions for Discussion
Ethical Quandaries

*In 1986 the editors of the* Harvard Business Review *gave to Sir Adrian Cadbury, head of the English candy manufacturing concern, its Ethics in Business prize for his article "Ethical Managers Make Their Own Rules."*[1] *The title was somewhat misleading for Cadbury was really saying that since "there is no single, universal formula for solving ethical problems, we have to choose from our own codes of conduct whatever rules are appropriate to the case at hand...." Making rules and choosing rules are not identical. The former suggests the moral autocrat who forges rules for himself and forces them on others. Choosing, on the other hand, results in following one course of action among other options that have already been established, promulgated, and accepted. The rules may be found in the Bible, in church dogmas, in philosophical treatises, and in political constitutions. The manager's task is not to* make *the rules but—as Cadbury wrote—to choose the appropriate guide. Having the ethical choice become operational is the manager's moral assignment.* ▮

*The purposes of this chapter are:*

1. To define in broad terms the meaning of culture.
2. To describe the American culture.
3. To emphasize the special role that "civil religion" plays in the United States.
4. To note fissures in the culture occasioned by such things as global economic competition and the fragmentation of family life.
5. To illustrate the difficulties inherent in trying to anticipate the future.
6. To define the various moral philosophies individuals may select to confront change in the culture.

## American Culture

### Definition of Culture

Over 30 years ago a highly respected historian, Michael Kraus, began his book with a dedication to "my immigrant parents who taught me the meaning of America before I ever learned it from books."[2] The dedicatory note is an important reminder of how values are learned. Experience may or may not be the best teacher but it certainly is the first. These first experiences, shaped as they are by parents, teachers, and friends, form the lived ethics or culture that itself is the result of a learning process about things people like and dislike, find good or bad.[3] Cultures are, therefore, "ways of life that are normative, that is, constructs that enable people to ask such basic questions as, For what and to whom am I responsible? How do I hold others accountable? Choices among ways of life—the institutionalized embodiment of rules specifying how individuals ought to live with each other—are moral choices. Thus, moral rules do not exist only on pages—they are part and parcel of institutions that grade and constrain behavior."[4]

Over time, these experiences "form the shared values that legitimize social practices."[5] Because the sharing of these basic values may be very shallow or very deep among different groups, the idea that culture means a constellation composed of firm, consistent, and authoritative values has been challenged; they should be seen, rather, as important signals of general directions.[6] It is nevertheless clear that without shared core values (respect for individual rights, some agreement on what is appropriate and good, procedures for arriving at just decisions, and so forth), no society can long hold fast. Indeed one of the nation's most profound challenges is to shore up the values necessary to sustain a communal life before further erosions transform community into chaos.

Various kinds of culture coexist: the high culture of opera and art and the low one of football and baseball; regional cultures represented by the North and the South;[7] national cultures that, in the minds of their devotees, are vastly superior to others (DeGaulle provided a good example of this); tribal cultures like the one that led Apache Indians to believe that raiding was better than working; city cultures and farm cultures. The list is almost inexhaustible. For present purposes, however, *culture is best understood as that collection of basic and shared values that make a country or community what it is.*

## *The Infant Nation: Manifest Destiny*

America's moral story began with a man who never saw these shores but in whose footprints the first Americans trod. The man was the 16th century religious reformer John Calvin, who taught that some individuals were predestined by God for heaven and others for damnation. As a frustrated rhymester of those times put it:

> *You can and you can't*
> *You will and you won't*
> *You'll be damned if you do*
> *You'll be damned if you don't*

Despite frustrations among those who were unsure what spiritual basket they themselves were placed by the Almighty, the Puritans believed that they alone were selected for special missions on earth. Puritans who thought that the Church of England was being corrupted became known as the

CHAPTER THREE  The Moral Foundation

Separatists—a sturdy, fearless, God-fearing people, some of whom crowded aboard the Mayflower and landed on a rocky New England coast—far from their destination in Virginia, where they had hoped to link forces with the first settlers in Jamestown. The Puritans, now strictly on their own and totally isolated, had to be self-dependent. In their rugged independence they took four steps toward a distinctive culture.

One of the necessary first steps was to write rules of the game, and this they did in the Mayflower Compact which provided for majority rule—step one in forging a distinctive political culture. Within a few years the hard-pressed Puritans decided to complete a friendly merger with the better-financed Massachusetts Bay Colony of Boston—step two; frustrated there by the oligarchic rule of Governor John Winthrop, the Pilgrims curtailed the governor's power through annual elections—step three; driven by the necessity of survival in a harsh wilderness and by their fierce commitment to do God's will in their everyday labors, they established the famous Puritan work ethic—step four. By opting for majority rule, regular elections, limited government, and a philosophy of hard work, these Americans were becoming a different people, a fact they themselves recognized well before the 18th century dawned.

The Americans' unanalyzed assumption of distinctiveness was validated by two French visitors: shrewd Hector de Crevecouer and the brilliant Alexis de Tocqueville. The former answered his own question, "what, then, is an American?," by pointing out that "unlike Europe where the poor did not live, but only vegetated, individuals feel themselves members of a special community." Unlike the English, for example, where upper-class males wore bowlers and dined in their exclusive clubs while the workers wore caps and ate in the local pubs, Americans felt free to wear what they liked and eat where they chose. There were, of course, class distinctions in America but the distinctions were less marked—and always removable with money.

Although creating their own brand of community, the colonists had learned from Mother England that the nation-state was here to stay. While these political communities could owe their existence to friendly mergers (the Hanseatic League in Germany was an example) or to hostile takeovers (Cromwell in Ireland), there was general agreement that the nation-state was the political organization best suited for modern times. Neither fiefdoms nor city-states counted for much in the New World order. Building a nation-state led Americans to see the values of a common frontier, a common language, a common memory (especially of wars), and a common religion. They saw, too, how nation-states in Western Europe had become the "churches" where the faithful participated in a secular liturgy, sipping wine from grapes fermented in their own vineyards. The wine was often intoxicating, even dangerous, when people of one land, drunk with success, came to believe they were innately superior to all others. The disease was called nationalism.

With the nation-state came the Enlightenment, which changed the focus of philosophy from what was good to what was useful, from the transcendent to the existent, from primacy of faith to primacy of reason. Virtue and vice as causes of happiness and unhappiness were replaced by Enlightenment thinkers, like Rousseau, with pairings like integrity/alienation, authentic/spurious, sincerity/insincerity. Because the pairings were psychologically and not theologically rooted, it meant that Americans would henceforth live in tension between their biblical and secular legacies.[8]

The tension explains in part why Americans rejected a state church, an aristocracy of blood, and a landed gentry. They had their own special mission and the slogan "Manifest Destiny" was no accident. By the end of the 17th century the colonists thought of themselves as Americans, not Europeans; by the time the Revolutionary War began, the thought had become a conviction. Even their language became different as Americans borrowed from the Indians (skunk, terrapin, hickory), from the French (bureau, prairie, portage), and from the Dutch (stoop, cruller, scow).[9]

The import of certain words had its counterpart in other imports—the delicate wrought-iron fences from French craftsmen, songs and poems from England, sturdy furniture and good beer from the Germans. As with words, however, these imports either took on a distinctive American quality or failed to survive. Many did not. New France produced no Moliere, New England no Milton, New Spain no Cervantes. Nevertheless, at the same time, Boston had become second only to London in book publishing in the English-speaking world; stagecoaches ran between Philadelphia and Boston; New York's Fraunces' Tavern and Williamsburg's Raleigh Tavern provided quality accommodations for weary travelers and ambitious politicians. Newspapers, found first in Boston in 1704, appeared in local communities and were of sufficiently high quality to make Americans "newspaper nuts"; doctors practiced medicine and politics; lawyers, initially disliked, gained status when able young men who ordinarily would have entered the church joined the bar.

Americans were on the move. Change was their daily experience as forests were turned into farms, farms into villages, and villages into towns. By 1776, they found familiar what elites in the Old World found strange, namely, the idea that all men were created equal and endowed by their Creator with certain inalienable rights to life, liberty, and the pursuit of happiness. Because of their early experiences, Americans were psychologically ready for a written constitution—they had written them before; ready for a union of states—they had merged before; ready for regular elections—they had used them before; ready for other political innovations (checks and balances, judicial review) because change had become second nature to them.

## *Adolescent America*

What Crevecouer had said about the distinctiveness of the American people in the 18th century was confirmed with greater precision by Tocqueville in the 19th. In the fourth chapter of *Democracy in America,* Tocqueville wrote:

> *The inhabitant of the United States learns from birth that he must rely on himself to combat the ills and trials of life; he is restless*

> *and defiant in his outlook toward the authority of society and appeals to its power only when he cannot do without it. The beginnings of this attitude first appear at school, where the children, even in their games, submit to rules settled by themselves and punish offenses which they have defined themselves. The same attitude turns up again in all the affairs of social life. If some obstacle blocks the public road, halting the circulation of traffic, the neighbors at once form a deliberative body; this improvised assembly produces an executive authority which remedies the trouble before anyone has thought of the possibility of some previously constituted authority beyond that of those concerned. Where enjoyment is concerned, people associate to make festivities grander and more orderly. Finally, associations are formed to combat exclusively moral troubles: intemperance is fought in common. Public security, trade and industry, and morals and religion all provide the aims for associations in the United States. There is no end which the human will despairs of attaining by the free action of the collective power of individuals.*[10]

This perception of the tension between individualism and collective action requires further comment.

**Individualism.** Individualism, a key concept in the American culture, was used by Tocqueville to describe a new social philosophy concerning the relationship of the individual to society.[11] *Individu* in French had a negative, antisocial connotation and Tocqueville, like most European elitists of his time, could envision no outcome other than chaos when social relationships and social obligations were ruptured. Individualism not only made every "man forget his ancestors, but hid his descendants and separated his contemporaries from him; it threw him back forever upon himself alone and threatened in the end to confine him entirely within the solitude of his own heart." However, what Europeans despised, Americans exalted. Emerson expressed the national feeling when he wrote: "The antidote to the State is the influence of private character, the growth of the individual."[12]

What was celebrated, however, at the start of the 19th century was quite different from what Americans celebrated at the 20th century's beginning.[13] It was not the self-made man of farm and frontier—rivermen and cowboys—but the Vanderbilts, Carnegies, and Rockefellers who counted.[14] Individualism meant even J. P. Morgan, who, born with a silver spoon in his mouth, was nevertheless celebrated by *The New York Tribune* as the embodiment of the successful self-made man. A development so devoid of logic in Morgan's case and so compelling in Carnegie's meant one thing—the new brand of individualism needed a new definition and a new justification.

The first came more easily than the second. Individualism now meant that personal fulfillment was to be found in cooperating with other employees (echoes of Tocqueville's idea of association) in large firms. People who wanted more of everything had to pay a price for something—and the price was acceptance of managerial authority and its expression through large bureaucracies.[15] Frederick Winslow Taylor's successful experiments at the Bethlehem Steel Company in the 1890s—which increased productivity enormously—required meticulous planning, including planning for the planners themselves. The first result was bureaucracy; the second was a new definition of individualism: obey directions that benefited the firm and the worker.[16]

Justification for this new brand of individualism came from the one man who best exemplified it: Andrew Carnegie. This shrewd little Scotsman, who began work in a cotton mill for $1.20 a week, saw the advantages of bringing Minnesota iron ore to Pittsburgh, where Pennsylvania's coal and limestone could be used with it to make iron by the Bessemer process. Carnegie outlined his philosophy in a talk to a group of young men: "Aim for the highest; never enter a barroom; do not touch liquor, or if at all, only at meals; never speculate; never indulge beyond your surplus cash funds; *make the firm's interest yours* [emphasis added]; break orders always to serve owners; concentrate; put all your eggs in one basket."[17]

In 1889, near the pinnacle of success, Carnegie published his gospel of wealth in *The North American Review*. At the time when farmers were in revolt against eastern financiers, and when workers remembered the brutal way strikers were crushed during the Haymarket riots in Chicago, it might have appeared to most corporate leaders an inopportune time to praise themselves. Carnegie had no such apprehension. His message was blunt: Some people will make it big and some people will not! The real question is what the shakers and movers should do with the shaken and stuck. Carnegie answered that the successful should behave as agents for their poor sisters and brothers by bringing to them the wisdom of their superiors; by so doing "the laws of accumulation will be left free; the laws of distribution free. Individualism will continue, but the millionaire will be a trustee of the poor."[18] Bishop Lawrence of Massachusetts gave theological support to the gospel of wealth when, in his Sunday sermons, he told his rapt congregation that only to the man of morality did wealth come. Godliness is in league with riches.[19]

**Social Darwinism.** One problem with the secular gospel of service was that others in business—the Jay Goulds and the Jim Fisks—found an alternative in the gospel of greed. If Carnegie's version could be defended on the trusteeship principle, what could rationalize the Gould–Fisk gospel? The answer was social Darwinism, a prepackaged import "manufactured" by Herbert Spencer, the English sociologist, on the scientific conclusions he found in Charles Darwin's *On the Origin of Species*. Social Darwinism meant a ruthless struggle between business competitors, between labor and management, and even among nations. Only the fittest survive.[20] Social Darwinism fired the American nationalism that eventually expressed itself in Manifest Destiny; it permeated the reasoning of the Supreme Court as it turned back worker attempts to organize themselves; it slowed the Populist drive to control big business; it justified government callousness toward the poor at a time when 10 percent of the populations in big cities lived in dirty tenements owned by slum landlords.[21]

Despite its crudities, the doctrine found favor with segments of the intellectual elite. Yale Professor Charles Sumner, for example, preached the doctrine most vigorously: governments are meddlesome; bureaucrats are bunglers; public assistance to the poor encourages indolence; tariff protection is a disguised handout to inefficient businesses.[22] Nevertheless, two contrary doctrines gnawed at the American psyche: (1) the difference between Calvin's and Carnegie's ideas of trusteeship and (2) the two versions of the gospel of wealth—the "give" of Carnegie and the "get" of Gould. By the end of World War II the purer version seemed to be taking hold but the Dennis Levines and Ivan Boeskys of the 1980s showed that Gould's gospel of greed was far from dead.[23] Twentieth century Americans were thus left with several ambiguous, possibly contradictory, messages:

1. Individualism meant fulfillment in large organizations *or* individualism meant fulfillment through one's own entrepreneurial skills.
2. Financial success required a sense of obligation to the less fortunate *or* financial success was reward for the self.
3. Economic growth required business concentration (a law of nature) *or* economic growth depended on small independent merchants.
4. Nationalism rested on Enlightenment principles *or* on biblical values.
5. Labor unions were anathema because they hampered both the employer's and worker's freedom *or* labor unions reflected the worker's natural instinct for associations that Tocqueville had earlier identified.

By the 20th century the old moral tradition was beginning to crease, if not crack.

**The Role of Education.** If there were debates over what young Americans should learn, there were no doubts about the need for learning itself. Even self-made men were not produced by half-made boys. Girls were ignored. Interest in education was instinctive in a people who sought to follow God's will. And reading the Bible required a reasonable amount of literacy. That the Puritans had distributed over a million copies of the *New England Primer* is evidence of widespread literacy in the infant nation. Private schools existed for the elite and tax-supported schools for the commoner. Higher education was pushed vigorously. The Congregationalists established Harvard in 1636 and Yale in 1701; the Anglicans founded William and Mary in 1693; the Presbyterians made Princeton their educational cornerstone in 1746. The momentum never ceased.

At the lower level—even before the Civil War—the ideal of tax-supported elementary schools had begun to take hold, despite opposition from the "privates." Horace Mann (1796–1859) pushed his successes with tax-supported schools in Massachusetts to other states so effectively that he was able to persuade legislatures to invest in teacher training (normal) schools. A generation after his death in 1900 the literacy rate had jumped from 10 to 20 percent; little red schoolhouses resounded to the voices of youngsters reading *McGuffey Readers*; selections from English poets and novelists were used to inculcate patriotism and temperance, obedience and industry. Every tale had a moral lesson. Few questioned the value of public schools, except the Catholics who, perceiving public schools as enclaves of Protestantism, established their own network of parochial schools. Only the African-Americans and Native Americans were lost in the shuffle—a loss painful to them and disastrous for all.

## The Civil Religion

In the midst of construction and conflict came a hunger for a statement of certain basic values that embodied what most Americans accepted. It was found in the civil religion.[24] The concept was first explored by Jean Jacques Rousseau, the previously mentioned French writer, whose ideas have been most closely associated with progressive education. In Rousseau's formulation, the civil religion consisted of four essentials: (1) acceptance of God's existence, (2) belief in a life hereafter; (3) reward for virtue and punishment for evil and, finally, (4) religious toleration. All other religious opinions were beyond government interests. People could believe in a unitary or triune God, think the Messiah had come or was coming, feel that miracles were possible or not. But the four essentials must be present if the civil religion was to play a vital role in the culture. That it has played such a role may be seen in the similarities between constitutional interpretations and theological doctrines—even though the constitution provided no moral code.[25]

Given the perceived relationship of the Constitution to the civil religion, it is not surprising to find political leaders in the camp of those who profess the civil religion. A starting point is Ben Franklin's *Autobiography*, where this observation was made:

> *I never was without some religious principles. I never doubted, for instance, the existence of the Deity; that he made the world and governed it by his Providence; that the most acceptable service to God was the doing of good to men; that our souls are immortal; and that all crime will be punished, and virtue rewarded either here or hereafter. These I esteemed the essentials of every religion; and, being to be found in all the religions we had in our country, I respected them all, tho' with different degrees of respect, as I found them more or less mix'd with other articles which, without any tendency to inspire, promote or confirm morality, serv'd principally to divide us, and make us unfriendly to one another.*

The same message appeared in John F. Kennedy's 1961 inaugural address:

> *We observe today not a victory of party but a celebration of freedom—symbolizing an end as well as a beginning—signifying renewal as well as change. For I have sworn before you and Almighty God the same solemn oath our forebears prescribed nearly a century and three quarters ago.*

> *The world is very different now. For man holds in his mortal hands the power to abolish all forms of human poverty and to abolish all forms of human life. And yet the same revolutionary beliefs for which our forebears fought are still at issue around the globe—the belief that the rights of man come not from the generosity of the state but from the hand of God. . . . Finally, whether you are citizens of America or of the world, ask of us the same high standards of strength and sacrifice that we shall ask of you. With a good conscience our only sure reward, with history the final judge of our deeds, let us go forth to lead the land we love, asking His blessing and His help, but knowing that here on earth God's work must truly be our own.*

From Washington's inaugural address in 1789 to Bush's inaugural address in 1989 the same themes have been sounded—belief in God and an afterlife, a final judgment, and religious toleration.

## Moral Responsibility in a Changing World

Three major periods of testing the vitality of the civil religion occurred in the United States: (1) the Constitutional Convention in 1787, when the issue was a people's capacity for self-government; (2) the Civil War, when the primary issue was political unity and racial equality; and (3) the present domestic revolution for social justice, accelerated by global economic competition and by the developing countries' cry for the material and spiritual things Americans have already attained.[26] But what is moral responsibility in a revolutionary world? And what "attainments" are involved? Is cosmopolitanism one answer?

### *Cosmopolitanism*

Does the nation's changing culture mean Americans must become, in Nietzsche's lyrical words, the

> *cosmic dancers who do not rest heavily in a single spot but lightly turn and leap from one position to another. . . . The cosmic dancer, the world citizen, will be an authentic child of his parent culture but related closely to all. He will not identify his whole being with any one land however dear. Where he prides himself on his culture or nationality, as he well may, his will be an affirming pride born of gratitude for the values he has gained, not a defensive pride whose only device for achieving the sense of superiority it pathetically needs is by grinding down others through invidious comparison. His roots in his family, his community, his civilization will be deep, but in that very depth he will strike the water table of man's common humanity and, thus nourished, will reach out in more active curiosity, more open vision, to discover and understand what others have seen. For is he not also man? If only*

*he might see what has interested others, might it not interest him as well? It is an exciting prospect. The classic ruts between native and foreign, barbarian and Greek, East and West, will be softened if not effaced. Instead of crude and boastful contrasts there will be borrowings and exchange, mutual help, cross-fertilization that leads sometimes to good strong hybrids but for the most part simply enriches the species in question and continues its vigor.*[27]

If indeed Americans are to become cosmic dancers on the world stage, it is necessary to know the rhythms of the dance. From what is already evident, dancers may sway to the stately waltz and shake to the pulsating rock.[28] The analogy is possibly too awkward a way of saying that Americans are going to dance to new and strange songs, the lyrics for which are written in words related to productivity and family life, respectively.

## *Economic Productivity*

The Harvard Business School *Study on Productivity* used a simple example to pinpoint what its investigators thought was this nation's most serious economic problem: sloppiness. "The failure rate of air conditioners made by the worst producers were 500 to 1,000 times greater than those made by the best producers. The worst producers were American and the best producers were Japanese. The Japanese with the best quality records also had the highest productivity per worker. The extra cost of making higher quality Japanese goods was about half of what American manufacturers spent on fixing defective products."[29] Also singing the blues was the report from distinguished participants who met under the auspices of the American Assembly of Columbia University in 1987:

*America's economy is growing more slowly than it used to, more slowly than we need it to, and more slowly than our competitors' economies. We are consuming far more than we produce and earn—and we are having growing difficulty paying the bills. Our prosperity is threatened, as is our capacity to provide world leadership and to achieve a more just and competitive society. The evidence is unmistakable. We have the largest budget deficit, trade deficit, and foreign debt in our history. Individual debt, corporate debt, and government debt are all perilously high, while our savings rate is among the lowest in the industrial world. We cannot long continue on this path without profound consequences.*[30]

As has already been made clear, the dismal assessments are not shared by all. But they do come at a time when Americans face greater challenges from Western Europe and from the Pacific Basin countries. So far as the continent is concerned, a 1987 Bank of England report said that the "sheer size of the European Community makes it impossible for any international business to ignore [it] when formulating its strategic plan.[31] France and Italy were the top investment targets because of their size and wealth; Spain is another hot favorite but West Germany is seen as a prickly pear—difficult to get into but juicy once in. Among the concerns cited in the report were corporate shareholding structures, long-established banking relationships, and local market practices. Claude Bebéar, chairman of Axa Midi Assurance Company, one of Europe's largest, wrote that the global dance floor now has "room only for the big companies or niche players. Size is extremely important."[32]

Meaningful new economic dancers are joining—or have joined—the global party. The initial configuration of expansion was the Mediterranean Basin, then the Atlantic Rim, and now the Pacific Basin. Japan has few resources but Australia has large deposits of coal and uranium, and China has more of everything. With a population of over a billion people, China may become the 21st century's strongest and largest country in the world. While all of this is going on, America is losing one of its chief levers of power as capital is internationalized.[33]

## Family Structure

Moving from international economics to domestic demographics may seem like too wild a leap for even the most talented cosmic dancer to make. But the reality is that the nation's material prosperity is directly related to the strength of its family structure. And on this, too, comes stark news. Dr. Armand Nichol, Jr., of the Massachusetts General Hospital and the Harvard Medical School, conducted extensive research that led him to conclude that the breakdown of the family is contributing significantly to America's other major problems. Research data make unmistakably clear the strong relationships between broken families and (1) the drug epidemic, (2) the increase of out-of-wedlock pregnancies, (3) the rise in violent crime, and (4) the unprecedented epidemic of suicide among children and adolescents. The trend toward quick and easy divorce has a strong bearing on family life in this country (13 million American children have one or both parents missing from the home), and this ever-increasing divorce rate subjects an ever-increasing number of children to physically and emotionally absent parents. Among Nichol's other findings—and substantially in his own words—are these:

- The increasing number of married women who have joined the labor force and work outside of the home has a profound negative effect on young children. Two-career families compound the problem of emotional inaccessibility. Single-parent families, in which the mother is burdened with providing the children both emotional and economic support, are an overwhelming problem.

- A tendency exists in many colleges and universities to convey the notion that the role of parent is passé, and to settle for such a role is to settle for second-class citizenship. Many young women no longer feel free to stay home with young children. Unless they can pursue a career while raising the family, they consider their lives a failure. Said Nichol: "My clinical experience indicates clearly that no woman with young children can do both *at the same time* without sacrificing one or the other—the quality of work or the quality of child care. Many professionals know this—but few have the courage to say it."

- The tendency to move frequently also imposes great stress on families. Our society has become extremely mobile. Parents often travel long distances to their work. Because of such travel, a father may be absent from home for many days or for weeks at a time. The job also frequently causes the whole family to move. We have only begun to understand the enormous psychological uprooting that a move can have on a family.

- The intrusion of the television set into the American home has had an effect on the family that we have not yet even begun to fathom. Television acts as a two-edged sword: it both results from and causes parental inaccessibility. When parents are home physically, television often interferes with the meaningful interaction between members of the family even in our most affluent homes. *Cross-culture studies show that U. S. parents spend considerably less time with their children than parents in almost any other country in the world.*

Dr. Nichol said that his interest in the impact of parental absence began while he was conducting research on college students. "At that time I noticed a cluster of psychiatric symptoms that occurred among a rather significant number of undergraduate men." The syndrome included the following:

- Unusual preoccupation with motor vehicles, especially the motorcycle
- A history of accident proneness that extended to early childhood
- Persistent fear of bodily injury
- Extreme passivity and inability to compete academically, athletically, or in any other area of life
- A defective self-image
- Poor impulse control and a propensity for heavy use of drugs and alcohol
- Impotence and intense homosexual concerns
- A distant, conflict-ridden relationship with the father[34]

If Nichol's analysis is correct, many successful executives will live with seriously disadvantaged offspring; corporate recruiters will snare many losers into their nets; firms will pay high prices in turnover ratios and sick benefits; lawsuits will increase when discharged employees claim that the cause of their unsatisfactory performance is the employer, not themselves or their parents. Broken humans lead to fractured corporations.

## *Social Fragmentation*

Fragmentation of family life is paralleled by fragmentation of social life. Two distinguished sociologists, Talcott Parsons and Gerard Platt, wrote that "for a modern society there is no possibility of uniformity in roles, personalities, and styles of life; tolerance of diversity must exist in a pluralized environment."[35] The traditional two-parent nuclear family is less than one-third of all households; increased politicalization of universities and public schools is symptomatic of deeper divisions over values; the populations of most modern societies have become more multiethnic due to decolonization and labor immigration, and this contrasts sharply with the once relatively homogenous countries like France and Germany.

Today it does not seem possible to specify substantive qualities of French, British, German, or American cultures that are clear and not ambiguous or controversial. Moreover, it seems unlikely that there are substantive qualities of life which allow people to specify when a social order is based upon latent coercion or manipulation (which may be legitimated electorally) or when it is based upon nonauthoritarian social integration. This being the case, modern societies—to hold together—have accepted increasing coercion by the state.

The gravity of the fissures in the culture has become apparent in the number of cases over basic values that have reached the Supreme Court in the past two decades: questions of privacy, libel, pornography, and free speech. Probably the most divisive issue is over abortion as both supporters and foes have mounted massive campaigns to have their respective views accepted by the justices.[36] Also demanding attention are minorities, some of whose voices (women and African-Americans) have already been heard and others, like the Hispanics, which will be heard. The Native American continues to be the forgotten minority. Unanswered is the most important question in public and private policy: Which is coming—integration by government coercion? Disintegration through group autonomy? Or a satisfactory amalgam of old and new values?

## America's Moral Future

### Failures of the Prophets

Prophecy, say the wags, is best applied to the past. They have a point. Confident predictions had been made about things that turned out far different from the futurist's script. To illustrate, the famous Club of Rome (composed of prominent academics and business leaders) said in its report, *Limits to Growth,* that the world would run out of mercury by 1985, tin by 1987, zinc by 1990, gold by 1991, petroleum by 1992, and copper, lead, and natural gas by 1993. All have been wrong. Another prophecy, in a throwback to Malthus, said population growth was so out of hand that only famine or pollution could stop it; yet even at the time the prophecy was made population growth had peaked and was gradually slowing down. The consensus among demographers today is that a century hence the world's population will be around 10 to 12 billion, a manageable level for the industrialized countries but a potential nightmare for the developing nations.

More arresting is the development of modern science. Few of the world's greatest scientists foresaw how one simple equation ($E=MC^2$) would change the face of warfare and contribute to an ominous cold war, how understanding radio waves would alter communications networks, or how the ability to control bacterial growth would lead to a population explosion in underdeveloped countries. The rapidity of scientific advances alone spurs wild speculation. As such seemingly small things as the pill and the automobile have upset the traditional mores of sex, so, too, will science affect longevity, health, and diet. And these, in turn, will influence government and business policies toward child-care centers, retirement patterns, and so on. The discoveries have unhinged the culture in its ideological configurations and public patterns—and more is yet to come.

Indeed, the coming changes may make excusable the failure of the prophets to foresee the collapse of the old colonial systems (British, French, and Dutch), the rupturing of Soviet power in Russia and Europe, the rise of Third World countries, the transformation of Mideast politics by Khomeni, the changing balance of power signalled by Iraq's invasion of Kuwait, or the use of terrorism as an instrument of national policy. Yet despite errors, policymakers need the prophets and the citizenry relies on them.

Every American carries a bag of questions. What is the meaning of the generally peaceful disintegration of the Soviet mid-European empire and democratization of Eastern Europe? What will happen in the drug war? in public education? in America's infrastructure? in South Africa? in the European Community? Educated people, and most particularly their leaders, know that disciplined efforts are needed to identify structural changes—even in the face of the overwhelming weight of political and cultural imponderables and the irrational tides of hatred and anger. Prophesy is much like "holding a small candle in a hurricane to see if there are any paths ahead and how to go forth. But if one cannot light and hold even a small candle, then there is only darkness before us."[37]

## *A Cry for Values*

Impressive in the above assessments on productivity, product quality, and family structure is a common emphasis on values. The same American Assembly that dealt with productivity ended its report with a reminder that *"values of integrity, social justice and moral leadership are not only necessary in themselves but lead directly to competitive advantage* [emphasis added]."[38] The Harvard Study on Productivity concluded that one of the nation's major problems is management's misguided view that business realities dictate that "standards of integrity and ethics are properly left in textbooks and classrooms."[39] Dr. Nichol finished his report on family life by urging contemporaries to read the Bible "objectively, free from the aura of religiosity... so repugnant to most of us [and] find there wisdom about how to lead our lives with meaning and fulfillment."[40]

Is there a clue to Americans' moral future in the *Good Housekeeping Magazine* editors' prediction that the 1990s will be known as the "decency decade"—a decade marked by what the editors trumpeted as the *Journal*'s leading role in the New Traditionalism: "better day care, better health care, better education, maternity leave, flextime, and advancement opportunities for working women." Or, as one columnist remarked, is much of the New Tradition opposed to the Old Tradition?[41] The question is one no American

can avoid. How it is answered depends heavily, though not completely, on the philosophical premises that each person takes to the analysis. Since what each takes is what has been learned (or will be learned), it is useful to peer into the philosopher's corner.

## Moral Philosophies

Everyone philosophizes—and the questions raised in normal conversation reveal the extent to which each one of us does so. Why am I here? Where am I going? What do I need to be happy? How do I get what I need? Sometimes overwhelmed by change, the individual—to reverse Reisman's famous thesis—is the "crowded lonely." Help is needed from professionals who extend Everyman's questions and provide greater systematicity in arriving at the answers. A common criticism of philosophers, however, is that they are too diffident when questions are asked about specifics and too bold when questions are asked about universals. Often the truth falls between the two.

### *The Challenge for Philosophers*

Ethicists are wisely diffident on specifics because they know that problems in particular areas are generally best understood by those in that field; they recognize that sound moral theory needs postulates from social scientists, especially from psychologists who track the child's socialization process from infancy to adulthood. Few moralists, for example, ignore the work of the famous Swiss psychologist Jean Piaget[42] or of the American Lawrence Kohlberg.[43] The latter claimed that everyone can pass—albeit may not pass—through three irreversible levels of moral growth: the obey-or-pay level, the give-and-get level, and the reflect-before-react level.[44] Possibly more influential than either Piaget or Kohlberg is B. F. Skinner's carrot-without-stick hypothesis: good results come more from rewarding good acts than by punishing bad acts.[45]

There remains, nonetheless, an important corner in the world of theory for moral philosophers because, whereas psychologists *describe* behavioral patterns, moral philosophers *prescribe* for them. Driven to the defensive by criticism by managers and economists because of their reluctance to quantify, they counterattack by pointing to the imprecision of their critics. Consider, for example, the differences on projected deficits between the administration's Office of Manpower Budget (OMB) and the Congressional Budget Office (CBO), as shown in Table 3.1. Both are staffed by large numbers of economists and statisticians—and remember that these experts are talking about differences in the *billions*. Imprecision is not the philosopher's monopoly.

Not surprisingly, moral philosophers feel more confident in their judgments about how individuals ought to behave then economists feel in their predictions about how the economy will behave. So philosophers examine

**Table 3.1  Deficits Projected by the Office of Manpower Budget (OMB) and the Congressional Budget Office (CBO)**

| Year | OMB | CBO |
|------|-----|-----|
| 1990 | $123.8 billion deficit | $138 billion deficit |
| 1991 | $63.1 billion deficit | $138 billion deficit |
| 1992 | $25.1 billion deficit | $135 billion deficit |
| 1993 | $5.7 billion surplus | $141 billion deficit |
| 1994 | $10.7 billion surplus | $130 billion deficit |
| 1995 | $9.4 billion surplus | $118 billion deficit |

the findings of sociologists, anthropologists, and other social scientists on the meaning of a specific culture to discover how—or whether—individuals should mold their private lives according to society's dominant values. To do this philosophers ask key questions:

- What should I believe?
- What life and career goals should I set?
- What is life's purpose?
- What am I really worth?
- Is the market system ethical?
- How should conflicts between personal and role values be reconciled?
- How do I know if I am right on moral questions?
- Is obedience to the law the best ethic?[46]

If legal rules come from legislatures and judges, where do moral rules come from? Nearly a quarter century ago, when Raymond Baumhart made the first systematic effort to find how managers answered the question, he discovered that most of them felt that ethics came from intuitions—"what my feeling tells me is right."[47] Nearly a quarter of the respondents said their intuitions flowed from their religious convictions.[48] While acknowledging the importance of intuition, philosophers deem it inadequate. Hitler intuited a moral code for Germany; Khomeni forged his own version of Islamism for Iran; de Sade intuited a sexual "code" for males. Intuition must therefore be reinforced by reason, which, in our friend Tocqueville's view, "reckons with a standard above the will of the majority—and even above the usually morally binding constitutions."[49]

The message is clear: everyone needs "moral space," that is, moral rights of the kind the Founding Fathers recognized but did not create in Philadelphia.[50] Foremost among rights are equality, liberty, and the justice that results from their proper exercise.[51] If laws do not define the amplitude of moral space, neither does ethics. Ethics does, however, require *systematic reflection about what is right and wrong, good or bad, benign or baleful.* As a subfield of moral philosophy, *business ethics concentrates on the nature and operation of the market system, the corporation as a moral agent,*[52] *the behavior of those who work within it, the meaning of fiduciary responsibility, conflicts between role values and personal values, and the cluster of issues related to them.*

The question of integrity is of particular interest to business ethicians.[53] Integrity includes such moral virtues as "industry, reliability, justice, a sense of social responsibility, empathy and courage, the possession of which leads to a clear sense of identity, principled consistency and self-control."[54] These qualities lead managers to act in such a manner that one person's "expression of integrity must increase, not decrease, the likelihood that other individuals will be able and willing to express [their] integrity."[55] This modest excursion into the meaning of integrity is enough to show that rights and wrongs do not come in bunches like grapes; they do, nevertheless, come with sufficient frequency that people, especially those in leadership positions, continually ask whether their moral decisions are logically defensible. Trouble immediately begins with the word logical.

- Is it logical to accept the anthropologists' argument that moral values are culturally relative?
- Is it logical to accept the conscience-is-king argument when two different consciences whisper two different moral messages?
- Is it logical to believe that this country's ethical pluralism means that the individual's only secure refuge is in society's civil religion?
- Is it logical to agree with those moral absolutists who believe that all moral principles (basic and derivative) are the same for all people at all times?
- Is it logical to think that morality is simply an attempt by human beings to adopt principles to govern human society in ways that help them to live together and abide by the rules that all of them, in their reasonable and objective moments, would accept?[56]

## *Self-Oriented Philosophies*

Summarizing possible answers to each of the foregoing questions exposes the contradictions inherent in both cultural morality and ethical relativism. What remains to be considered are the values reached by individuals in their reasonable and objective moments that hold a community together (social integrity) and themselves together (personal integrity). Among the candidates are (1) the survival ethic, (2) the expediency ethic, (3) the egoist ethic, (4) the utilitarian ethic, and (5) the deontological or duty ethic.[57] Only the last two are given serious attention here, but it is necessary to tell what the others are and why they are found wanting.

**Survival Ethics.** A variation of previously discussed Social Darwinism, survival ethics needs only minimal comment. Propounded by Herbert Spencer (1820–1903), who applied Darwin's theory of survival of the fittest in the animal kingdom to humans,[58] the survival ethic justified a dog-eat-dog behavior. John D. Rockefeller, one of the great survivors and a shrewd practitioner of the jungle ethic in his business affairs, said that the "growth of big business is merely the working out of a law of nature and a law of God."[59] But the evils justified by Darwinian ethics have been documented by so many historians that it is not generally defended as adequate for today's business world.

**Expediency Ethic.** The expediency ethic has been attributed, some say unfairly, to Niccolo Machiavelli (1469–1527), who learned how to cope in the mad Florentine world of his times.[60] Seeing so many good men destroyed by bad men, he urged princes to learn how to be cunning, even cruel, when the occasion required it. Parallels between the Machiavellian state and the modern corporation have been made by management theorists;[61] if climbing the corporate ladder requires stepping on a rival's face, let it be done.[62] What is required for success, not merely survival, is the ethical guide.

**Ego Ethic.** The ego ethic has been identified with many economists and philosophers. Not surprisingly, one who was both economist and philosopher was most generally, and wrongly, associated with it. The man is Adam Smith and his book, *The Wealth of Nations*. Largely ignored by economists and philosophers is Smith's *Theory of Moral Sentiments*, which accords high priority to benevolence. This temerarious infatuation with self-interest has been forcefully expressed by Ayn Rand.[63] To her, business is the primal expression of human nature—people love themselves so much that conventional moralities of religion and societies are irrelevant to the objective realities of life. Forget Jefferson's talk about pursuing happiness unless the pursuit is for the acquisition of wealth. The ethical *ought* comes from the *is*, not the other way around. Lucid writing and lucid argument enhance Rand's appeal. The implications, however, are disturbing: virtue resides in the rich and vice in the poor; benevolence is unnecessary; society is an aggregation of self-serving individuals and fear of atomization and anomie is unjustified. Rand's is a harsh philosophy but, to millions, a true one. Lincoln's ethic of charity toward all is overwhelmed by Rand's ethic of charity toward none.[64]

The cursory survey of the foregoing philosophies shows that each contains a kernel of truth—and the kernel grows bigger and tougher with the progression from the survival to the egoist ethic. Yet each shares in common an addiction for a moral philosophy that begins with the self and ends with the self—and always on the assumed premise that "what is good for me" is good for others. The two philosophies that most directly attack this view—and emphasize the needs and rights of others—are utilitarianism and deontology.

## *Utilitarianism*

Utilitarianism has several intellectual fathers, chief of whom are David Hume (1711–1776), Jeremy Bentham (1749–1832), and John Stuart Mill (1748–1832). Hume never suggested the kind of moral philosophy found, for example, in Ayn Rand. To him, what was moral was that which, after careful reflection, was approved by the self and by others. In his *Enquiry Concerning the Principles of Morals* (which Hume said was "incomparably my best"), he argued that it was human nature to laugh with the laughing and to grieve with the grieving; therefore, concern for others was innate. Hume's morality took others into account. But how many "others"? Bentham tried to answer the question by saying it was the greatest good for the greatest number. Because human nature is driven to seek pleasure and to avoid pain—the meaning of utility—the object of any act, individual and institutional, is to add to the pleasure of as many people as possible.

Distinctions have been made between *act* utilitarianism and *rule* utilitarianism. The first required the actor to go through several complicated steps: fact gathering, identifying people who would be affected, gauging long- and short-term consequences, and so forth. Rule utilitarianism, on the other hand, simplified the decision-making process by holding the analytical process to an evaluation of the correctness of an ethical principle by judging the results that would occur by following it. Always present in both forms of utilitarianism was concern for the greatest good of the greatest number.[65]

Utilitarianism gained great support from American judges, politicians, and business managers, all of whom are results oriented. It also had a strong hold on economists because of its insistence on measuring utilities; it was attractive to many philosophers because it motivated people to seek consequences that are good for others.[66] But it has some problem in determining what consequences will flow from a given course of action, as the dramatic story of the *Komsolets* demonstrates. On April 7, 1989, this Soviet submarine, while spying on the U.S. submarine fleet in the Norwegian Sea, caught fire. When the flames spread, Captain Yevgeniv Vanin had to decide whether to turn a form of freon gas on the flames in compartment seven, where the explosion had occurred. Captain Vanin knew that at least one sailor (possibly more) was trapped inside the compartment. Turning on the freon meant certain death for some of his crew. Two thoughts entered his mind: (1) those endangered crew members might be already dead and (2) the *Komsolets* might be already doomed. On the other hand, to do nothing meant certain destruction of the ship with a consequent loss of more lives.[67] The captain turned on the freon. The ship sank. Was Vanin's utilitarian ethic wrong? The answer necessarily involves distinctions between what may be logically correct under some circumstances and what is ethically wrong in all circumstances.

## *Deontology*

Results interest the utilitarians. But, ask others, suppose the results bring pleasure to many and unnecessary pain to few. Suppose the minority's rights are trampled. Suppose duties to others become lost in the shuffle. The overriding concern with obligations led Immanuel Kant (1724–1804) to propose deontology (*deon*–duty, and *ology*–study). Starting with two premises—(1) everyone is morally equal to everyone else and (2) everyone can figure out moral obligations—Kant offered his famous *categorical imperative: what individuals believe is right for themselves they should believe is right for all others.* By so thinking, ethical principles are universalized. Motives take precedence over consequences.[68]

Individuals may therefore never be treated as means but rather as ends having full access to such fundamental rights as freedom and justice, equality and truth. From these basics all other rights (to property, privacy, contract, freedom of speech) are derived.[69] Individuals are not free when they are coerced by others, especially by the leviathan state.[70] What favorably impressed Harvard law professor Charles Fried about deontology was that it was "solicitous of the individual's. . . claim to preserve his *moral integrity*," which goes back to the word previously emphasized.[71]

In the practical order, contrasts exist between the utilitarians and the deontologists. When utilitarians would bend the moral rules to get positive results for the community, deontologists would answer that every bent rule bends someone's back or breaks someone's heart; consequently the individual's rights take priority. Utilitarians prioritize the community's wellbeing whereas deontologists stress the autonomy of each person; utilitarians emphasize the necessity of testing the moral maxims by results; deontologists point out that during the testing period people's lives and property may be jeopardized. However, differences between the two do not obliterate their similarities. They agree that (1) good principles usually bring good results, (2) specific situations require determination of the preferred moral principle to be applied, and (3) principles and consequences are inextricably connected.[72] Decision makers are more comfortable when these three elements are united than when each is treated separately.

Managers, by virtue of their roles, must consider consequences because administrative decision making (unlike judicial decision making which looks backward in a who-done-it mode) looks forward. Why else have managers? Managers are more than prophets because they are in the business of both seeing *and* manufacturing the future. As they go about their high-risk business the successful among them learn what economic competition is and how to turn it to their advantage; they learn when to have their enterprises grow and, most difficult of all, when to have them shrink; they know the direction that tort law is taking; they confront the environmentalists, who have learned a few tricks of their own; they bargain with workers in ways that seek to protect short-term gains from baneful long-term consequences; they deal with elected representatives and with nonelected judges and regulators. Managers, the cosmic dancers of this story, perform in two big ballrooms: domestic and global.

## *A Parting Word: Face*

Present in our everyday vocabulary is an interesting word: face. Face the facts, face the competition, face the music, face the future. Perhaps managers' first priority is to face themselves. But what is the face? It is unique, for no two faces are identical; it is in the face that we recognize each other, and identify ourselves; it is the face that is shown on passports and identification papers. The face is physical and therefore personal and intimate. Yet the face is also "made up," "put on," and subject to fashion. It is public, but also intensely private. With its 80 mimetic muscles, the face is capable of over 7,000 expressions. The face reveals the age, gender, and race of the self with reasonable accuracy; it often shows the person's health and socioeconomic status; it conveys moods and emotions, even perhaps one's character and personality. The face is also the site of our five senses and the source of verbal and nonverbal communication. The face indeed symbolizes the self, more than any other part of the body.[73] The face can be mask or mirror. The first conceals, the second reveals. It is time to see what the symbolic face of American business reveals about those who run it, participate in it, profit from it, depend upon it.

## Summary

Accustomed to seeing Roman bridges or roads that were built before the world was introduced to Christianity and to worshipping in cathedrals erected in the Middle Ages, Europeans are inclined to smile, sometimes smirk, at Americans' sense of history—five centuries since Columbus, three centuries since the first permanent settlement at Jamestown, two centuries since the historic events at Philadelphia. Yet the United States has compressed in its relatively short life what Europe has experienced in its long life: revolutions for political independence, business revolutions (commercial, industrial, and electronic), and cultural revolutions (individualism, social Darwinism, and organizationalism). In dealing with these upheavals, some business sophisticates like James Patterson and Peter Kim, managers at the J. Walter Thompson advertising agency, surveyed 2,000 Americans, asking them to answer 1,800 questions about ethics and morality. They found that

> *nine out of ten people lie on a regular basis. Twenty percent of the nation's children lose their virginity by the age of 13. There is little faith in the institution of marriage, with one-third of the respondents saying they are not sure they love their spouse, and one-third admitting to having an affair. And, religion plays a minor role in shaping our lives, with only 13 percent of the respondents believing in all ten of the biblical commandments. Overall the authors see that 'there is absolutely no moral consensus at all in the 1990s.'*[74]

The disquieting results are open to question. But there is no question that the United States is at a crossroads in its value systems, where choosing the right route to its future is difficult, where staying on course is an ordeal, and where business cannot escape playing a role. For those already in business as well as those preparing for a career in business, the journey promises to be exciting, even tumultuous.

## Questions for Discussion

1. Individualism has always been a buzzword in the American ideology. How would you define it today? Is there a good fit between individualism as you define it and your career preferences?
2. As a general rule, do you believe that firms engaged in necessarily dangerous work—for example, heavy construction or steel processing—should avoid hiring accident-prone workers?
3. Does the expanded jurisdiction of the Supreme Court over what were once viewed as private matters (abortion, privacy, women's rights in the workplace, and so forth) mean that the American value system is in danger of collapse?
4. Would the Puritans be comfortable with the work ethic of contemporary Americans?
5. Does a globalized economy mean the end of Americans' perception of themselves as a unique people?
6. Would you welcome the secularization of church-related universities?
7. Should corporations place private universities before state universities in their financial-support programs?

## Ethical Quandaries

### Wooden's Loyalty

Jim Wooden, a highly respected executive in his company and your good friend, sought your advice on how to deal with a situation involving Barry Selden, from whom his company had been buying executive insurance for more than a decade. When Selden developed cancer, the illness was thought to be so serious that his days were numbered.

Wooden decided to restructure the insurance package through another agency. Its CEO, Ted Axel, is on the board of Wooden's company. Negotiations were almost complete when Selden suddenly appeared in Wooden's office, asking to keep the business on his books. Selden looked ghastly, walked haltingly, and spoke slowly. But he made business sense. Furthermore, he appealed to Wooden's emotions by saying that his personal financial picture had been darkened by expenses occasioned by his illness.

Wooden knew that Axel's agency had expended considerable time and energy on restructuring the package. When Wooden told Axel that Selden was back at work and wanted the business to be continued with him, Axel protested. His agency had done all the work; further, Selden perhaps knew the costs of the new package and would underbid on it.

Wooden responded: "My ethic is the golden rule. Do unto others as you would have them do unto you."

## Question

- Should Selden get the contract?

## The Jays' Lifestyle

Jim and Anne Jay, both MBAs from State University, had successful careers in a manufacturing firm and in an advertising agency, respectively, when they reached their 30s. Jim was earning $65,000 a year and Anne $72,500. They decided it was time to have children. They planned to take nonpaid parental leaves sequenced so that one parent would be always at home for three months after the baby was born. Then they would place the baby in a nursery.

Shortly before the baby was due, Anne's parents visited. They asked how Anne would care for the child and were told of the plan. Both of Anne's parents began by saying, "I know it is none of my business." They nevertheless protested that children should come before cash and that Jim's salary was enough for the family to live on until the baby was at least three years old. As the argument intensified, Anne was reminded that sacrifices had been made for her; her mother recounted how she retired from a teaching position she loved and returned to the profession only after Anne left for college. When asked if Jim was forcing her to continue work, Anne exploded, telling her parents she wanted to work because it fulfilled her.

The parents' acid comments were: "Fulfill yourself and deprive the child. Young people today want everything and will sacrifice nothing."

## Question

- With whom do you agree?

## Notes

1. Sir Adrian Cadbury, "Ethical Managers Make Their Own Ethical Rules," *Harvard Business Review* (September–October 1987): 64–73.
2. Michael Kraus, *The United States to 1865* (Ann Arbor, Mich.: The University of Michigan Press, 1959).
3. Robert Axelrod, "An Evolutionary Approach to Norms," *The American Political Science Review* 80 (December 1986): 1095–1112. See also Axelrod's book, *The Evolution of Cooperation* (New York: Basic Books, 1984).
4. Aaron Wildavsky, "If Institutions Have Consequences, Why Don't We Hear about Them from Moral Philosophers?" *American Political Science Review* 83 (December 1989): 1343.
5. Aaron Wildavsky, "Choosing Preferences by Constructing Institutions: A Cultural Theory of Preference Formation," *American Political Science Review* 81 (March 1987): 3–32.
6. David Laitin, "Political Culture and Political Preference," *American Political Science Review* 82 (June 1988): 589–597.
7. Samuel Hill, Jr., has noted how "nearness" and "farness" of value preferences have influenced the relationships between the North and the South. *The South and the North in America* (Athens, Ga.: University of Georgia Press, 1980).

106    PART ONE    Foundations

8. The new nationalism was not found in religiously oriented societies: patriotism may have flourished in the old, but not nationalism. Gerald Newman, *The Rise of Nationalism: A Cultural History, 1740–1830* (New York: St. Martins Press, 1987), 87.

9. Americans never went as far as, say, the French who, to a degree unmatched by other countries of Western Europe, used language and literature most fully to identify their culture. Visitors to France are often surprised how names of leading writers appear on French banknotes and on city streets and boulevards. Priscilla Parkhurst, *Literary France: The Making of a Culture* (Berkeley: The University of California Press, 1987).

10. The author believes that no American's education is complete without reading Tocqueville's magnificent *Democracy in America* (New York: Alfred A. Knopf, 1945). Trans. George Lawrence, ed. J. P. Mayer.

11. The word "individual" was in use some 15 years before Tocqueville made it popular.

12. Stephen E. Whicher, ed., *Selections from Ralph Waldo Emerson* (Boston: Houghton Mifflin, 1957), 139.

13. John William Ward, "The Ideal of Individualism and the Reality of the Organization," in *The Business Establishment*, ed. Earl Cheit (New York: John Wiley, 1964), 45. The author's treatment relies heavily on Ward's careful analysis.

14. Ibid., 51–52.

15. Relevant are William E. Nelson, *The Roots of American Bureaucracy, 1830–1900* (Cambridge, Mass.: Harvard University Press, 1982); and Kenneth Boulding, *The Organizational Revolution* (New York: Harper, 1953).

16. Taylor ran tests to decide the optimum shovel load for a first-class worker. The results were fascinating: (1) a variety of kinds of shovels had to be designed to handle the different kinds of materials; (2) to eliminate the wasted motion of wandering about so large a yard meant organizing and planning work at least a day in advance, so that when men checked in they would be at that day's work; (3) this meant building a labor office for a planning staff—a bureaucracy. The results were startling. After three years under scientific management the work force dropped from roughly 500 to 140 men; savings amounted to $78,000 a year, and wages increased 60 percent. Frederick Winslow Taylor, *The Principles of Scientific Management* (New York: Harpers, 1911), 133.

17. Quoted from Foster Rhea Dulles, *The United States Since 1865* (Ann Arbor: University of Michigan Press, 1959), 61.

18. Andrew Carnegie, *The Gospel of Wealth and Other Timely Essays* (New York: The Century Co., 1900).

19. In this message the Massachusetts clergyman found rapport with Pennsylvania clergyman Russel Conwell, *Acres of Diamonds* (New York: Harpers, 1915).

20. Richard Hofstadter, *Social Darwinism in American Thought* (Boston: Beacon Press, 1955).

21. A firsthand account of life in a New York tenement was given by immigrant Jacob Riis, *How the Other Half Lives: Studies of Tenements in New York* (Boston: Hill and Wang, 1957).

22. William Graham Sumner, *Folkways* (Boston: Ginn, 1906).

23. Clarence C. Walton, *Corporate Social Responsibility* (Belmont, Calif.: Wadsworth, 1967). Reflections on this book led the author to seek refinements. See my *Reality's New Face and the Corporation's Future* (Minneapolis: University of Minnesota School of Business, Kappel Lecture, 1955) and "Corporate Social Responsibility: The Debate Revisited," *Journal of Economics and Business* 34 (1982): 173–187.

24. Usually credited with popularizing the term is Robert N. Bellah, "Civil Religion in America," *Daedalus* 117 (Summer 1988): 97–118. It is interesting to contrast Bellah's account with the way other sociologists have analyzed the topic. See Peter H. Rossi and Richard A. Berk, "Varieties of Normative Consensus," *The American Sociological Review* 50 (1985): 333–346.

25. Sanford Levinson, *Constitutional Faith* (Princeton: Princeton University Press, 1988), 90.

26. Bellah, "Civil Religion in America," 113.

27. Huston Smith, *The Religions of Man* (New York: Harper & Row, 1958), 6.

28. Perhaps bebop is, as one music critic said, "the music of the future," to which people dance in increasing isolation and bounce vertically because crowding prevents horizontal

movement. It may have been youth's way of expressing its own form of individualism. Despite the same music and the same partner, each dancer "did his or her thing." Richard B. Woodward, "Can Lesser Mortals Play the Jazz Masters' Works?" *The Christian Science World Monitor*, February 1990, 72.

29. David Garvin, ed., *Study on Productivity* (Cambridge: Harvard Business School, 1986).

30. *Running Out of Time*, Preliminary Report, 5. Presented at the Seventy-fourth American Assembly of Columbia University, New York, N.Y., November 19–22, 1987.

31. *The Single European Market—A Survey of the UK Financial Services Industry* (London: Bank of England, 1989).

32. *International Insurance News Letter* (New York: Price Waterhouse, 1990), no. 1, 3.

33. Daniel Bell, "The World and the United States in 2013," *Daedalus* 116 (Summer 1987): 1–32.

34. Armand Nichol, Jr., *The Family in America* (Boston: Harvard University Medical School, 1989).

35. Talcott Parsons and Gerard Platt, *The American University* (Cambridge: Harvard University Press, 1973), 199.

36. For an example of how the pro-choice people coordinated their legal campaign, see Attorney Kathryn Kolbert of the ACLU, "The *Webster Amicus Curiae* Briefs: Perspectives on the Abortion Controversy and the Role of the Supreme Court," *American Journal of Law and Medicine* 15 (1989), 153–168. In early 1990 the Supreme Court grappled with another sensitive issue, namely, affirmative action. The most recent cases involved the actions of the Federal Communications Commission, which awarded a license to the 90-percent Hispanic-owned Rainbow Broadcasting Company and denied a license to the black-dominated Astrolene Corporation in Hartford.

37. Daniel Bell, "The World and the United States in 2013," 31.

38. *Running Out of Time*, 11.

39. This view that ethics is unnecessary because business has its own autonomous rules was first popularized by Albert Z. Carr, "Is Business Bluffing Ethical?" *Harvard Business Review* (January–February 1968): 143–152.

40. Nichol, *The Family in America*, 35.

41. Cal Thomas (Los Angeles syndicated writer), "Unfinished Agenda on the Home Front," *Arizona Republic*, January 16, 1990, A11.

42. Jean Piaget, *The Moral Judgment of the Child* (New York: The Free Press, 1965).

43. Lawrence Kohlberg, *Collected Papers on Moral Development and Moral Education* (Cambridge: Harvard University, Center for Moral Education, 1973).

44. Lawrence Kohlberg, "Moral Development" in *The International Dictionary of Social Sciences* (New York: Crowell, Collier and Macmillan, 1968).

45. B. F. Skinner, *Beyond Freedom and Dignity* (New York: Knopf, 1972).

46. On the last question, Oliver Wendell Holmes wrote something that provides a contrast between legal and theological ethics: "When men live in a society a certain average of conduct, a sacrifice of individual peculiarities going beyond a certain point, is necessary to the general welfare. If, for instance, a man is born hasty and awkward, is always having accidents and hurting himself or his neighbors, no doubt his congenital defects will be allowed for in the courts of heaven, but his slips are no less troublesome to his neighbors than if they sprang from guilty neglect. His neighbors accordingly require him, at his proper peril, to come up to their standard, and the courts which they establish decline to take this personal equation into account." Oliver Wendell Holmes, Jr., *The Common Law* (Boston: Little Brown, 1881), 108. To theologians, motive and willing are always relevant.

47. Raymond Baumhart, S.J., *An Honest Profit: What Businessmen Say about Ethics* (New York: Holt, Rinehart and Winston, 1968), 11–12. A later survey showed relatively little variation in the pattern of responses. Steven N. Brenner and Earl A. Mollander, "Is the Ethics of Business Changing?" *Harvard Business Review* 43 (January–February 1977): 57–71.

48. J. Irwin Miller, "How Religious Commitments Shape Corporate Decisions," *Harvard Divinity School Bulletin* (February–March 1984): 4–7.

108    PART ONE    Foundations

49. Robert P. Kraynak, "Tocqueville's Institutionalism," *American Political Science Review* 81 (December 1987): 1194. See also Sanford Kessler, "Tocqueville on Civil Religion and Democracy," *Journal of Politics* 39 (1977): 119–146.
50. Lorene Lomasky, *Persons, Rights and the Moral Community* (New York: Oxford University Press, 1987), chs. 2 and 3; and Hadley Arkes, *First Things: An Inquiry into the First Principles of Morals and Justice* (Princeton: Princeton University Press, 1986).
51. Burton Zwieback, *The Common Life: Ambiguities, Agreement and the Structure of Morals* (Philadelphia: Temple University Press, 1988). To this writer equality is the prerequisite, not a consequence, of the common good (p. 63). His view of equality moves from its conceptual to its economic meaning: decent housing, adequate education, health care, etc. (pp. 159–160).
52. The broad outline of the debate has been noted in the Introduction.
53. Suresh Srivasta and Associates, *Executive Integrity: The Search for High Human Values in Organizational Life* (San Francisco: Jossey-Bass, 1988).
54. Nancy J. Adler and Frederick B. Bird, "International Dimensions of Executive Integrity: Who Is Responsible for the World?" in Srivasta, *Executive Integrity*, 247–248.
55. Chris Argyris and Donald A. Schoen, "Creating Conditions That Encourage Personal and Organizational Integrity," in Srivasta, *Executive Integrity*, 307ff.
56. Richard De George, *Business Ethics,* 2d ed. (New York: Macmillan, 1986), 39.
57. For nonphilosophers, one of the most concise accounts of the different philosophies was given by Edward Stevens, *Business Ethics* (New York: Paulist Press, 1979). This writer is indebted to Stevens.
58. Herbert Spencer, *Social Statics* (New York: Augustus Kelley, 1851).
59. Quoted by W. J. Ghent, *Our Benevolent Feudalism* (New York: Macmillan, 1902), 29.
60. Niccolo Machiavelli, *The Prince* (New York: Mentor Classics, 1952).
61. Anthony Jay, *Management and Machiavelli: An Inquiry into the Politics of Corporate Life* (New York: Bantam Books, 1967).
62. Michael Korda, *Power! How to Get It and How to Use It* (New York: Ballantine, 1975).
63. Ayn Rand, *The Virtue of Selfishness* (New York: The New American Library, 1965). Of her influential writings, her novel *Atlas Shrugged* (New York: Random House, 1957) is the best known.
64. William O'Neill, *With Charity toward None: An Analysis of Ayn Rand's Philosophy* (New York: Philosophical Library, 1971).
65. Very helpful in understanding in detail the nature of act and rule utilitarianism is the work of Richard Brandt, *A Theory of the Good and the Right* (New York: Oxford University Press, 1979).
66. Russell Hardin, *Morality within the Limits of Reason* (Chicago: University of Chicago Press, 1988).
67. William M. Carley, "How Secret Soviet Sub and Its Nuclear Arms Sank North of Norway," *The Wall Street Journal*, March 14, 1990, A-1 and A-8.
68. Immanuel Kant, *Groundwork of the Metaphysics of Morals* (New York: Harper & Row, 1964), 70–105. Trans. H. J. Paton.
69. Alan Gewirth, *Reason and Morality* (Chicago: University of Chicago Press, 1976), 255 ff. Relevant is the essay by Harry Frankfurt, "Equality as a Moral Ideal," *Ethics* 98 (October 1987): 21–43.
70. Robert Nozick, *Anarchy, State and Utopia* (New York: Basic Books, 1974). Nozick's introduction outlines his theme clearly.
71. Charles Fried, *Right and Wrong* (Cambridge: Harvard University Press, 1978), 2. See also, Bernard Mays, *The Philosophy of Right and Wrong* (New York: Routledge, Kegan Paul, 1986).
72. Clarence C. Walton, *The Moral Manager* (Cambridge, Mass.: Ballinger-Harpers, 1988), 110–112.
73. Anthony Synott, "Truth and Goodness, Mirrors and Masks," *The British Journal of Sociology* 40 (December 1989): 607.
74. James Patterson and Peter Kim, *The Day America Told the Truth* (Englewood Cliffs, N.J.: Prentice-Hall, 1991).

PART TWO

# Intercorporate Relations

CHAPTER FOUR
**Competition: Ethical and Legal Rules**

CHAPTER FIVE
**Ethics of Size: Mergers and Takeovers**

CHAPTER SIX
**Information Gathering: Clean or Dirty Tricks?**

CHAPTER SEVEN
**Insider Trading, Bribes, and Payoffs**

CHAPTER 4

# Competition: Ethical and Legal Rules

### The Evolution of Economic Competition
Positive Aspects of Competition
Impediments to Competitive Capability
*Litigiousness*
*Health Care*
*The Tax System*
*Education*
Negative Aspects of Competition

### Ethical Criteria
Independent Initiative
Constructive Effort
Respect for the Rules
Level Playing Field
Respect for Officiating Parties

### Legal Criteria
Antitrust Acts
The Two Critical Elements

### Selected Problem Areas
Horizontal Price Fixing
*Analytical Tools*
*Ambiguities*
*Indirect Price Discrimination*
Vertical Price Fixing
Throwing Out the Bathtub
Exclusive Dealings
Tying Agreements
*How Tie-Ins Work*
*When Tie-Ins Exist*
Restrictive Covenants and Predatory Pricing
Administered Pricing

### Summary
Questions for Discussion
Ethical Quandaries

*If* ever a web of interconnected strands between law and ethics existed, it is surely in the area of market competition. The degree to which statutory law and ethical norms overlap is a source of disagreement between those who argue that identifying one with the other is a serious mistake and those who insist that, at least in business, the law **is** the ethic. Typical of the first view is Christopher Stone, who has stipulated not only the limited reach of the law but also that immoral actions not deemed wrong under prevailing legal standards cannot be punished once the law is brought into conformity with ethical prescriptions.[1] To illustrate: after the Civil War no southern farmer was ever jailed for once having owned slaves and no northern industrialist was brought to book for having exploited child labor before the practice was outlawed in 1938. Focusing explicitly on the market, philosopher Norman Bowie said that anything that was blatantly coercive (such as monopoly and price fixing) is unethical.

> A business transaction is unfair if it is coercive or if one of the parties to the transaction lacks essential knowledge in protecting his or her interests in the transaction. . . . Economists are fond of pointing out that the benefits of exchange require that exchanges be noncoercive and that parties to the exchange have perfect knowledge.[2]

In this sense arguments are on solid moral ground. However, there are modifications. Taking a firm stand in favor of the obey-the-law ethic is Nobel Laureate Milton Friedman, who chides philosophers for their ambiguities. What is coercion? What is perfect knowledge—and who is primarily responsible for getting it? Are all exclusive dealings immoral? Only when the people speak through their elected representatives or through acceptance of court rulings are the rules for fair competition established. Asking people to go beyond the law is dangerous nonsense to the Friedmanites in a pluralistic and morally relativistic society because each participant may march to the moral beat of a different drummer.[3] The law may be incomplete in its coverage, inadequate in its definition, and uneven in its sanctions. The remedy, however, is not to encourage corporate managers to "impose" their moral views on others. When the community's moral sense is offended, old laws will be modified or new ones introduced. Business is a game played for high stakes. Law provides the necessary and sufficient rules. Reliance on the golden rule is counterproductive. One businessman put it this way:

*So long as a businessman complies with the laws of the land and avoids telling malicious lies, he is ethical. If the law as written gives a man a wide-open chance of making a killing, he would be a fool not to take advantage of it. If he does not, somebody else will. There is no obligation on him to stop and consider who is going to get hurt. If the law says he can do it, that is all the justification he needs. There is nothing unethical about that. It is just plain business sense.*[4]

*The foregoing observation raises the stark question: Do "plain business sense" and plain moral sense remain in different spheres until the law speaks? What follows is an attempt to demonstrate that the two spheres interact of necessity, not from the choice of business do-gooders.* ■

## The purposes of this chapter are:

1. To provide the specific ethical criteria that apply to economic competition.
2. To review the technicalities of the major laws and court decisions that define business competition.
3. To invite comparisons between ethical and legal criteria as they pertain to the market.

## The Evolution of Economic Competition

To begin thinking about competition is to realize how much the so-called miracle of capitalism is related to the miracle of Greece. When Adam Smith institutionalized competition in the marketplace he did for economic activity what the Greeks, alone of all ancient people, had done in all activities: potters vied with potters, craftsmen with craftsmen, beggars with other beggars, and minstrels with other minstrels. The tradition of the great athletic games at Olympia, Delphi, and elsewhere have become our tradition. Competition produced innovation and Athens honored her innovators.

### Positive Aspects of Competition

Smith's genius consisted in transferring social, artistic, and athletic competition to the English economic scene, demonstrating how countries that embraced it moved ahead of their rivals—even as Athens had moved ahead of Sparta in its world. When John Bodin (1530–1576) outlined his notion of the nation-state, he placed absolute power in the hands of the monarch, who made all key appointments, assigned markets, and often set prices. England, on the other hand, took a different direction by putting power in people and giving markets to merchants. The results astonished the Western

CHAPTER FOUR   Competition: Ethical and Legal Rules   113

world. Despite advantages in certain natural resources, France steadily fell behind England in economic progress and thoughtful men began to ponder the reasons for the disparity. A contemporary named Dean Tucker sought to provide an answer in a 1750 pamphlet in which he wrote that France's first disadvantage was its arbitrary and despotic government; merchants would not choose to live under it if they knew the sweet smell of liberty in England, where subjects could go to court against the Crown as easily as they could against private subjects.

After the death of Louis XIV in 1750, the French began to ask more insistently why England's prosperity was greater than their own—especially when England was failing to compete successfully in nearly all other endeavors. No English monarch compared to the brilliant Louis XIV; English art and English music were generally deemed inferior to French art and music; the vast continental market was more accessible to French than to British merchants. Why, then, was one country distinctly pulling ahead of the other in material prosperity? Adam Smith answered: free governments and free markets.

Competition has many assets: it spurs efficiency; it is vastly superior to conflict and aggression, which seek to destroy rivals; it is done without violence or bloodshed; its ideology is the belief that competition forces all to do their very best; it disciplines the inefficient and thereby contributes to the optimum allocation of resources; and, above all, it helps customers, who get what they want at prices they are prepared to pay. Competition can sometimes work in strange ways. Coca-Cola was anything but efficient in running Columbia Pictures but sold it in 1984 at a windfall profit for $1.2 billion.[5] Of course, the parent company was immensely effective in selling its beverages so that, on balance, the efficient competitor was still the victor. The first question for every firm and every nation, therefore, is the effectiveness of its competitive efforts.

## *Impediments to Competitive Capability*

Much has been said and written about America's alleged decline in competitiveness. Among various reasons given are the erosion of the work ethic coupled to rampant hedonism, mismanagement of organizations, a short-term investment mentality, the takeover and walkaway philosophy of corporate raiders, and antitrust legislation that is obsolete in a global economy. There are, in addition to these variables, certain other factors that adversely affect the nation's competitive capability. The former Colorado governor, Richard Lamm, specifically noted some of these "overhead features" when he addressed an American Assembly session in the fall of 1987. Four merit repetition.

**Litigiousness.**   Japan trains 1,000 engineers for every 100 lawyers; the United States trains 1,000 lawyers for every 100 engineers. With a population half that of the United States, Japan produces about 50 percent more engineers each year than does the United States. Of the 700,000 lawyers in the United States, 100,000 graduated between 1981 and 1986. Each year American institutions graduate as many lawyers as exist in all of Japan. Two-thirds of all the lawyers in the world practice in the United States. Our rate of litigation far exceeds that of any other industrial society. In 1966, cases filed in the federal courts numbered 70,906, but by 1986 the number of cases had exploded to 254,828. Lloyds of London estimated that, while only 12 percent of its business was in the United States, 90 percent of its insurance claims were there. This litigiousness adds to the cost of American goods as assuredly as does any inefficient management and inefficient labor.

**Health care.** The cost of health care is as much a component of American productivity as are raw materials. The United States spends eight times more than many of its international competitors on health care. In 1950 the United States was spending approximately $1 billion a month for health care; in 1987 it spent well over $1 billion a day. Health care costs are growing at a rate over twice the rate of inflation, putting American goods at a competitive disadvantage. In 1987, for example, Chrysler spent $317 per automobile on health care, which meant that the corporation had to produce 82,000 automobiles a year just to pay for its health-care compensation package.

**The tax system.** The complexity of our tax system is also a factor in the decline of American competitiveness. The jury is still out on whether the 1987 tax simplification effort made the tax system any better. Simplification may well have made it more complex. Senator Bill Bradley of New Jersey noted the number of tax shelters had risen from 11,000 in 1975 to 263,000 in 1985. Approximately 300,000 of the nation's best and brightest young men and women are employed to advise Americans about tax shelters. U.S. taxpayers spent more than 541 million hours in 1987 filling out forms, and more than 45 percent of the 95 million taxpayers sought help from the nation's 80,000 tax lawyers and accountants. Those who did their own taxes spent an average of 8.12 hours each on preparing their returns. Tax shelters became a $20 billion a year industry, and there is no reason to believe this figure is diminishing under the new legislation. Tax avoidance and evasion have become a part of American mores. The system breeds contempt.

**Education.** An average eighth grader in Japan knows more mathematics than an MBA in the United States. An average 17-year-old American knows half as much math as an average Swedish 17-year-old. Homework in Japan is about two hours a day, compared to approximately half an hour in the United States. Japanese students go to school 240 days a year while U.S. students go 180 days a year. By the time a Japanese student graduates from high school, he or she has experienced as much classroom time as an American college graduate. The net effect is that average students graduating from Japanese high schools score significantly more IQ points than average American students and the percentage of their graduates is around 95 percent while in this country the number is 75 percent, many of whom are functionally illiterate.

## *Negative Aspects of Competition*

To think of competition as being influenced solely by markets risks misreading reality. In the world of theory, perfect competition exists when no single firm can significantly influence prices other firms charge; when many buyers and sellers trade; and when there are free exits and entrances to the markets. In theory, buyers do not care from whom they buy because at equal prices the commodities of each seller are similar. And, in theory, the cost of production, having been paid by the seller, is offset by the rise and fall of prices without government interference.

The realities, however, not having the lovely symmetry that theorists so much admire, pose ethical problems. In theory, competitors see their rivals as participants in a game played under rules prescribed by law and defined by tradition. Competition may not involve fraud, violence, or force. Unlimited competition is a contradiction in terms. Often, however, the killer instinct surfaces. Ruthlessly practiced, competition becomes exploitive of others. Furthermore, the quest for maximum profits encourages extravagant consumption of scarce resources. There is always a price to pay because humans deplete the ecosystem faster than the economic systems replenish them. This is an important point. Because capitalism is committed to change, and because change comes faster than society's capacity to adjust, competition itself can become dysfunctional; it is then that factories are closed, people are idled, and psychological disturbances arise as incomes fall.

Contrary to a common belief, competition promotes a basic kind of cooperation because it requires that competitors agree in advance to rather explicit legal rules for playing the game: free elections in politics and free markets in business. Behind the legalities, however, are ethical concepts that businesses encounter when dealing with issues for which no clear precedents have been established. In such instances judges are frequently inclined to look at history *and* philosophy.[6]

## Ethical Criteria

The litigious society that is America is inclined to believe that courts are its best friends even though, as in the competitive world of business, somebody wins and somebody loses in the adversarial world of law. All in all, the belief is not misplaced. Without courts the country's momentous upheavals in race relations might have become very bloody; without courts, intricate changes in labor law might not have come about; without courts the business world could well drift toward the jungle ethic of social Darwinism. But a neglected and intriguing question could also be asked: if Americans lean on the judges, whom do the judges lean on? A good case can be made that moral philosophers provide much of their support.

The Western legal tradition, based heavily on old canon law and medieval philosophy of the Catholic church, was never entirely jettisoned in the British common law, in the European continental law, or in American statutory law. To illustrate, in the *Henningsen v. Bloomfield Motors* case the plaintiff suffered injuries when the car she was driving ran off the road. When Mrs. Henningsen sued Chrysler and Bloomfield Motors on grounds that the car was defective, the defendants argued that there was no legal contract and therefore no moral responsibility. But the New Jersey Supreme Court, appealing to the general principles of justice more than to a specific statute, ruled in the plaintiff's favor on the grounds that the dispute that pitted a corporate giant against a purchasing pygmy was inherently unfair when harm was done to an innocent buyer.[7]

If the relationship between man-made law and moral philosophy is close, what general guidelines emerge from ethics? With considerable skill and insight, Lynn Sharpe Paine, who is both a philosopher and a lawyer, answered that fairness in a competitive environment requires respect for five principles that she called (1) independent initiative, (2) constructive effort, (3) deference to the rules, (4) the level playing field, and (5) respect for referees.[8] With such respect, competition's tendency toward destructive conflict is restrained. Instead of speaking of competition only in economic terms, it is more realistic to include a moral category that can be defined as encapsulated competition.[9] A brief review of the five ethical principles gives a sense of their relevance.

## *Independent Initiative*

The principle of independent initiative *means that competing units should work individually to produce the artifacts or services upon which they are judged.* All competitors are free to exploit society's common knowledge and property within the limits laid down by the rules, but they are not free to take from one another certain types of internally generated knowledge and information. This principle puts a premium on qualities such as originality, self-reliance, and effort, as well as on respect for the independence and privacy of competitors; and it is closely related to the idea of integrity in the sense that a competitor's endeavors are linked at the core by a unity of purpose. Independent initiative is more likely to promote an economy based on innovation than one based on a copycat mentality. Economic theory itself recognizes the importance of innovation to growth.[10] A central problem with the principle of independent initiative is allocating legal rights to protect and exploit innovations in ways that promote the greatest social good while simultaneously protecting the innovator.

## *Constructive Effort*

The principle of constructive effort *holds that the best businesses are those that succeed by their own positive efforts rather than by undermining and downplaying the competition.* This principle requires that competitors focus on their own strengths rather than on their opponents' weaknesses; it prohibits sabotaging a rival's operations, reputation, or relationships in order to create a competitive advantage.

A sad example of a company's violation of the principle came to light in a long exposé carried in *The Wall Street Journal* in September 1990.[11] It involved the American Express Company's effort to ruin the reputation of banker Edmond Safra, founder of the Geneva-domiciled Trade Development Bank and the Republic National Bank of New York. James D. Robinson III, chairman of American Express, saw Safra's organization as an archrival that had to be brought down. The actual operation was carried out by Robinson's top aide, Harry Freeman, who hired a private detective and a public relations practitioner to spread rumors that Safra was involved in drug trafficking, money laundering, and murder; with criminals heading Columbia's Medelín drug cartel–and with the Mafia. The story rivals the most sophisticated spy thrillers: secret meetings in plush European restaurants; tailing suspects; trashing garbage cans of suspected informants; and using a former associate producer for ABC news, Susan Santor. Despite repeated denials and threats of libel suits against the *Journal*, American Express, a company with an unrivaled reputation for integrity, finally admitted that it had engaged in a protracted two-year campaign to smear Mr. Safra. With the admission came the announcement that American Express would agree to pay $8 million to Mr. Safra and to the charities he selected.

Because the principle of constructive effort concerns appropriate attitudes and motivation, it is difficult to enforce through law. Nevertheless, the purely motivational aspect of the principle is seen in the body of law governing the improper use of business tactics that are normally quite legitimate. The test of improper use lies in the purpose for which the tactics are employed, a classic illustration of which is seen in an old Minnesota incident, in which a banker was held liable for setting up a rival barbershop with the sole motive of driving a personal enemy out of business.[12] Normally, of course, setting up a competitive business is not legally actionable but, in this case, the competitor's purpose was judged to be legally improper because it was ethically suspect. Other conventional business tactics whose misuse has been the basis of liability include selling below cost and refusals to deal.

Although such cases are rare, courts have looked at the relative strength of the improper motivation, the degree of the rival's injury, and the extent to which there is public harm. The principle of constructive effort is also recognized in the doctrine against commercial disparagement—the making of false statements about the quality of a business's products or services with intent to cause financial harm to the business. In summary, the principle of constructive effort calls for competition directed toward self-improvement and conducted in a spirit of respect for one's rivals.

## Respect for the Rules

Respect for the rules is *so important to fair competition that businesses should see it as self-evident.* Unfortunately, some firms deliberately play as close as possible to the legal edges, especially when intense competition threatens profitability. Two centuries ago Montesquieu wrote of the "spirit of the law," by which he meant a profound respect for a statute's fundamental purpose even when its details allow loopholes for unethical acts. The spirit of competition means such respect for others that all are taken seriously. What creates moral problems is not competition itself but the temptation to use "dirty tricks" to achieve superiority. Boxing is a case in point. As originally conceived, boxing was a match between two men who sought to outpoint the other through superior skills. Professional boxing today emphasizes gouging, the knockout, and the concentration of blows to an opponent's bleeding eye. A sport has become a sickness. The spirit of competition, therefore, includes fiduciary honesty, honoring contracts, respecting the property of others, and, indeed, respect for all relationships.

## *Level Playing Field*

The level playing field principle *seeks to prevent certain inequities by preventing competitors from using advantages like size, or practices like "buying in,"* which involves bidding below cost in competitive bidding contests—such as occurred in the defense industry. Although strict equality among competitors is rarely required, adjustments are frequently made to ensure that disparities in abilities and resources are not too great. The principle has its roots in the ethical notion of formal equality, which requires that the rules of the activity be applied to all competitors alike. In competitive bidding, for instance, the principle finds expression in the requirement that all bidders receive the same information at the same time and that all be held to the same deadlines.

The principle received endorsement from the Supreme Court in May 1988 when it ruled that manufacturers' decisions to stop supplying a price-cutting dealer do not necessarily violate the Sherman Antitrust Act. Price-cutting practices could easily degenerate into cut-throat practices, the effects of which are to destabilize the competitive playing field. The court case involved Sharp Inc., a manufacturing concern, which decided to terminate its business with a discount firm named Business Electronics because BE was undercutting the prices of Gilbert Hartwell, Sharp's only other dealer in the Houston area. The decision could make it more difficult for discount retailers to obtain products they want if they undercut the prices of larger authorized dealers in the same products. In delivering the 6-2 opinion Justice Scalia referred to the "free rider" argument that discount firms should not benefit from lower costs because they have not had the same promotional expenses as do the authorized retailers. The main goal of public policy is to encourage competition between dealers in different brands of products—different makes of electronic calculators, for example—and not competition between different dealers in the same brand.[13]

## *Respect for Referees*

The principle of respect for officiating parties *relates to relationships between competitors, on one hand, and the referees (regulators and judges) on the other. Efforts to influence or mislead government officials and the officials of self-regulatory agencies are prohibited.* Firms may neither mislead customers nor coerce them into buying; attempts to bribe or in other ways exert excessive influence over legislators, judges, and other government officials who have power to affect competitive relations also violate this principle.

An intriguing question deals, therefore, with the likely culprit: Who in the organization—engineers, controllers, counsel, senior management—are most vulnerable to temptations to breach them? Over a quarter century ago, the American Marketing Association wrestled with the problem because of the early findings of Raymond Baumhart that five of the top eight problems that most worried business itself were related to marketing.[14] Twenty-five years after the Baumhart study, a survey of 462 marketing managers produced the result shown in Table 4.1.[15]

**Table 4.1 Market Managers' Ranking of Issues Related to Competition**

| Rank | Issue | Frequency | Percent |
|---|---|---|---|
| 1 | Bribery | 41 | 15 |
| 2 | Fairness | 40 | 14 |
| 3 (tie) | Honesty | 33 | 12 |
| 3 (tie) | Price | 33 | 12 |
| 5 | Product | 32 | 11 |
| 6 | Personnel | 29 | 10 |
| 7 | Confidentiality | 13 | 5 |
| 8 (tie) | Advertising | 12 | 4 |
| 8 (tie) | Manipulation of Data | 12 | 4 |
| 10 | Purchasing | 8 | 3 |
|  | Other | 28 | 10 |
|  |  | 281 | 100 |

Source: L. B. Chonko and S. D. Hunt, "Ethics and Marketing Management," *Journal of Business Research*, 13 (August 1985), 344.

Although bribery was the single issue that received the highest percentage of negative comments, aggregating the next four (fairness, honesty, price, and product) is probably more useful for prioritizing issues related to competition because they are so interrelated. These four issues attracted nearly 50 percent of marketing managers' attention. Initially, however, it was not the tampering with prices or products that aroused public indignation. It was the problem of size, with the "big boys" seen as the bully boys, grinding down people and driving out rivals.

Throughout the 1920s and 1930s, for example, DuPont fought competition by acquiring firms making cellophane, rayon, pigments, titanium dioxide, insecticides, plastics, heavy chemicals, paints, and rubber-coated fabrics. DuPont's appetite was curbed only when the company aroused the wrath of Congress. Because today's problems with size (related as they are to mergers, hostile takeovers, and leveraged buyouts) are so important, they will receive special treatment in the following chapter. Suffice it to say for the moment that fears of gargantuan size have been voiced by economists, legislators, and social philosophers, the last of whom advanced the so-called principle of subsidiarity—the small-is-good paradigm promulgated among contemporary economists by B. F. Schumacher.[16]

## Legal Criteria

Americans have found that when ethical criteria stand alone and naked in the public square, they are not effective. The competitive edifice requires support from two other pillars, namely, self-discipline and government regulation. By showing callous disregard for the first, 19th century corporate executives literally wrote the regulatory script for themselves. And the law, albeit slowly and clumsily, revealed the search for practical ways to incorporate the five ethical principles moralists found relevant. In examining the laws governing competition, therefore, it is prudent to maintain awareness of the ethical principles on which they were built.

### *Antitrust Acts*

In 1890 Congress passed the Sherman Antitrust Act, a statute so delectably ambiguous that lawyers have feasted on the fat crumbs falling from that legislative table ever since. The law declared that anyone (a) who contracted or conspired to restrain trade or (b) who monopolized (or conspired to monopolize) trade or commerce among the several states or with other countries was guilty of a felony. Except for Pennsylvania and Vermont, which relied on the English common law to outlaw such practices, every other state subsequently passed legislation patterned after the Sherman Act.[17]

Sherman has had a twisted history. Under Theodore Roosevelt, the acclaimed trustbuster, the antitrust division of the Justice Department monitored corporations with a staff of five lawyers and four stenographers. It was a David-Goliath story whose outcome was substantially different from the biblical tale—the Goliaths invariably won. Despite cutbacks during the Reagan years in the White House, the antitrust division today is itself big business, employing thousands of lawyers and economists and having jurisdiction over hundreds of cases annually. Observers have correctly said that "once the United States had an antitrust movement without antitrust prosecutors; in our time there are antitrust prosecutors without an antitrust movement."[18] Obviously the very existence of so many government monitors led to busy courts, and busy courts have ground out increasingly complicated decisions.

During the first 30 years of antitrust activity, ingenuity in evading the law was such that Adam Smith could have been seen as a shrewd prophet when he wrote that "the interest of dealers in any particular branch of trade or manufacture is always in some respects different from, and even opposite to, that of the public. To widen the market and to narrow the competition is always the interest of the dealers."[19] When Adam Smith spoke of the trader's instinct to play fast and loose with the moral rules, he was echoing something voiced by Aristotle in ancient times, picked up and promulgated by the church fathers in the early Christian era, and articulated by Aquinas for medieval merchants.

When the Sherman Act, however, became shrill in its articulation and still in its implementation, and when the traders' wit outmatched the lawmakers' wisdom, Congress found it necessary to strengthen the controls. In 1914 it passed the Clayton Act, which established the Federal Trade Commission (FTC) to enforce prohibitions against (a) stock acquisition by a corporation where its effect may lessen competition, (b) certain interlocking directorates, (c) price discrimination, and (d) sales based on the condition that the buyer cease dealing with the seller's competitors. The Clayton Act was the first federal statute to make certain forms of price discrimination unlawful.

When inadequacies again developed, new remedies were sought through the more comprehensive Robinson-Patman Act of 1936. Congress now declared it unlawful for sellers in certain circumstances to discriminate in prices between two buyers and (very important to the judicial process) that the burden of proof was on the defendant once a *prima facie* case of price discrimination had been shown. The seller could not provide products, handling, promotion, or advertising unless the same or equivalent benefits were afforded to all buyers.[20]

History has treated Robinson-Patman peculiarly. It became a stepchild because, for 30 years, the Justice Department failed to institute a single Robinson-Patman suit; the last FTC action involving the law was filed against Boise-Cascade in 1984. Despite its relative nonuse, the law is still a powerful weapon in the government's antitrust arsenal, especially for private parties seeking treble damages and injunctions. Nevertheless, the wording of Clayton still permitted suppliers to provide favorable treatment for one—or for a limited number of customers—without violating the statute if commerce is within the state where the selling occurs.[21]

Intrastate commerce remained unaffected until the federal courts ingeniously produced a stream-of-commerce theory, placing under federal control the state-based enterprises that manufactured goods obtained from or returned to other states. Furthermore, although price discrimination is outlawed, suppliers who make clear to all customers that concessions depend on the purchase of a specific minimum quantity of goods will probably go unchallenged so long as the minimum is within the economic reach of most customers.

Even what seems like a straightforward requirement (merchandise sold contemporaneously by the same seller to different purchasers must be at the same price) can be circumvented. The one-price-for-all still permits what is called functional discounts—that is, one price if customers intend to resell the commodity and a different price if the customers themselves intend to use the commodity. It is important only that all competing customers be treated the same way for functional pricing to apply. Exceptions to what was viewed as a tightly constructed statute again demonstrated how the best of regulatory models dropped quickly to the lowest common ethical denominator when respect for the spirit of the law was absent.

## The Two Critical Elements

Over time the courts established two principles for determining violations of antitrust provisions: (1) the rule-of-reason principle, which required the government to demonstrate that motive, methods, or market impact of alleged violators were suspect, and (2) the per se rule, which meant that certain actions automatically violated the law. The two rules apply to the following areas:

- Price fixing, horizontal and vertical
- Exclusive dealings
- Tying agreements
- Restrictive covenants and predatory pricing
- Monopolistic prices

Managers constantly scanned the horizons to see if others were using one or more of these techniques against them, and their organizational codes of ethics were designed largely to make sure their own personnel were not playing with illegally loaded dice. Although the law has spoken voluminously on each of the foregoing, it is sufficient for present purposes to concentrate only on selected areas in which law and ethics have clearly interacted.

## Selected Problem Areas

### Horizontal Price Fixing

**Analytical Tools.** Price fixing, having few if any redeeming features, comes *under the per se rule*. Horizontal price fixing flows from restraints imposed on actual and potential competitors at the same level of distribution.[22] A classic example of horizontal price fixing occurred in Pennsylvania two decades before the Sherman Act was passed when five coal companies agreed to divide their markets, sell at prices previously agreed upon, and share the excess profits with those who received less. Although the agreement had been made in New York State, the Pennsylvania Supreme Court took an unusual step in 1871 by voiding the arrangement under a common law doctrine, even though there was a specific New York statute prohibiting just such a practice.[23] The Pennsylvania jurists noted that the agreement enabled the conspirators to fix coal prices in markets stretching from the Hudson to the Mississippi River and from Pennsylvania to the Great Lakes. As a result, it brought economic power no single corporation could achieve under fair competition and, therefore, was injurious to competitors and to the buying public. Legally indefensible and morally inexcusable, it was a per se violation of hallowed common law principles and, specifically, of the level playing field concept of ethics.

The per se rule was also applied under the Sherman Act of 1927 case involving the *United States v. Trenton Potteries*. The Sanitary Products Association, headquartered in New Jersey, was a trade group of manufacturers of vitreous pottery for bathrooms and lavatories. By 1922 the 22 member firms had come to represent 80 percent of the market and the association was determined to protect that share. Its vigilance included insistence that members forward information to the Trenton headquarters regarding the number, type, and price of their orders as well as the geographic location of the customers. Each firm, having received the information, would then distribute bulletins describing discounts and surcharges and, on the basis of surcharges, prices were raised or lowered. The defendants contended that their prices were reasonable and therefore not harmful to the public.

Speaking for the court, Justice Stone wrote that agreements to fix prices are not justified simply because the prices themselves are reasonable: "Whether this type of restraint is reasonable or not must be judged, in part at least, in the light of its effect on competition; whatever difference of opinion there may be among economists of the social and economic desirability of an unrestrained competitive system, it cannot be doubted that the Sherman Law—and the judicial decisions interpreting it—are based on the assumption that the public interest is best protected from the evils of monopoly and price control by the workings of competition."[24] The association's policy was conspiracy and whether or not it protected its members or whether it helped or hurt consumers was irrelevant. In its decision the jurists followed a deontological approach by reasoning that price fixing was intrinsically evil. Fidelity to the Sherman Act's intent required condemnation of the practice and the condemnation mirrored the intent of the *constructive effort* principle of ethics.

**Ambiguities.** Despite these two analytical tools, enough ambiguities remained that some business executives gambled that exploiting loopholes would bring substantial payoffs. As noted, under the Robinson-Patman Act sellers could not charge different prices for goods of like grade and quality; however, physically identical goods that often carried brand names raised the question whether brands might be priced higher than nonbrands. In its response, the courts eschewed deontology in favor of a utilitarian approach by looking at the customer's willingness to pay higher prices for brand names. The justices concluded that, since such willingness existed, the price differentiation between brand and nonbrand was justifiable—even when the goods were of similar grade and quality.[25] The reasoning made eminent sense from the lawyer's and economist's viewpoint, but a different conclusion could be reached by the moralist, who would argue that consumer

sion could be reached by the moralist, who would argue that consumer ignorance could easily be removed by truthful advertising and by accurate packaging information.

Again, the ingenuity of sellers was not exhausted by judges. If conspiracy was the danger, why not invent schemes in which there was no need to conspire? Seeking to answer the question, a man named Makin moved in 1947 to acquire control of several Yellow Cab companies as well as the Checker Cab Manufacturing Corporation. He then ran both as a single business, with the cab companies purchasing all their vehicles from Checker. When the Justice Department took action against Makin, the Supreme Court endorsed the government's position on grounds that Makin's behavior constituted conspiracy to restrain trade. To justify its position, the court invented what became known as the bathtub theory, the idea of supplier and user being in one tub that others could not use.[26] Reason and imagination had been used by the courts to support the previously discussed ethical principle: respect for the spirit of competition.

**Indirect Price Discrimination.** Price discrimination occurs indirectly when sellers provide better services to some buyers than to others. These services relate to credit terms, return privileges, and delivery services. Courts and commissions have struggled with these issues, but rather than detail the many cases bearing on definitions of price discrimination or conspiracy, it is, from moral perspectives, more fruitful to focus on certain bare-bone issues that can be developed in the brief examples that follow.

1. A manufacturer whose product was used daily by millions sold it only to wholesalers, who then sold either to small retailers or to five large chain stores. Because selling by the carload was cheaper than selling by the case, wholesalers gave a discount to purchasers of very large quantities. Any buyer could qualify by buying enough at one time, but only wholesalers who dealt with the five large chains were able to meet the quantity standard and hence obtain the best price. The chains were able, in turn, to sell at retail cheaper than the independents that competed against them. Small retailers cried "foul."

## Ethical Question

- Was the manufacturer's pricing practice ethical?

2. A major oil company sold supplies at the same price to its many franchises throughout the country. When one encountered stiff competition from a private dealer, the parent lowered the price for the beleaguered outlet—but not for its other dealers.

## Ethical Question

- Was the oil company's action ethical?

3. Five national brewing companies (including the AB Brewery) were locked in bitter competition. The industry practice was for each large brewer

to sell its beer across the country at a price slightly higher than the one asked from regional or local buyers. When unions made heavy wage demands on all five, four felt that added labor costs would hurt them so grievously they must accept a strike. AB, however, made wage concessions and, with competitors' plants shut down, began to dominate the national market. When the strike ended, the four nationals broke industry practice by increasing prices except in the region where AB had its brewery. To meet that threat, AB lowered prices in its own home region below those of its four national competitors; however, AB increased prices elsewhere to get the additional revenue needed to offset wage increases given to its unionized workers. While the price increase resulted in a decline in national sales, AB continued to prosper in its home region.[27]

## Ethical Questions

- Were the four nationals unethical?
- Was the AB Brewery guilty of unfair pricing in its home territory?

## Vertical Price Fixing

Vertical price fixing *occurs when the making and the selling of a product are under one control*, a practice that led to some curious results. To illustrate: Congress, spurred by concern for small businesses, passed legislation in 1931 to allow states to approve resale price maintenance (RPM) provisions through so-called fair-trade laws. Between 1931 and 1941, 45 states passed fair-trade laws that permitted manufacturers to link their wholesale prices to dealers to the retail price charged by such dealers to their customers. Retailers were compelled to charge the price set by manufacturers for their products. The alleged justification was the fear that, without RPMs, cutthroat competition would bring monopoly.

In time, Congress became convinced that fair-trade laws were actually unfair-trade laws because they (1) did not encourage retailers to pass along the savings to customers, (2) prevented more efficient allocation of resources, (3) blocked innovations in retailing, and (4) implied that although price competition was acceptable between manufacturers of similar products, it should not exist between different sellers of the same products. When Congress voted in 1975 to outlaw fair-trade laws, outraged manufacturers argued that RPMs actually encouraged competition because (1) consumer pressure was directly on them and (2) RPMs enhanced customer education and service for the reason that only retailers who guaranteed the higher prices would be able to provide such benefits.[28]

Throughout the debate, little was said of the moral issues that touched significantly on the fact that RPMs were unilaterally fixed and gave consumers no choice to shop around to determine the reasonableness of the established prices. It might be added, too, that these laws had come about through extraordinary lobbying efforts by manufacturers. Beginning in 1982, the courts began to back away from applying the per se rule to RPM practices, especially when wholesalers reduced their price to enable their dealers, in turn, to reduce their retail prices to meet competition. Tradition here is that the dealer must pass along the price breaks to the purchaser.

Another practice was to set the wholesale price at a percentage of the suggested retail price and then to vary the wholesale price if the dealer charged a price other than the one suggested by the wholesaler. An example was the *Lewis Service Centers v. Mack Trucks* case, in which the court sustained the trucking company's sales assistance program under which dealers could apply for wholesale price reductions when they believed it necessary to reduce their retail prices in order to meet competition. In pure logic it seems difficult to distinguish between the old and new interpretations of the law—whether the manufacturer set the arrangement or whether the retailer requested the arrangement. However, resale price maintenance does not now automatically warrant application of the per se rule.[29]

The issue arose again in 1984 when the Spray Rite Service Corporation sued Monsanto on grounds that Monsanto had refused to continue supplying herbicides because Spray Rite was a price-cutter. The Justice Department and the FTC both wanted to use the rule-of-reason principle on grounds that its flexibility could be applied selectively as the facts warranted it. The National Mass Retailing Institute and the Association of General Merchandise Chains countered that suppliers who cut off a discounter in response to complaints from the discounter's competition automatically violated the Sherman Act. Dissenting from the official government position was FTC Commissioner Michael Pertschuck, who argued that the professed benefits of resale price maintenance could be achieved in ways less anticompetitive than vertical pricing. In the commissioner's view, if the manufacturer wanted his dealer to have a showroom or provide warranty service, he could require it as a condition of supplying the retailer. If, further, the manufacturer wanted his retailer to promote the product, he could always provide promotional allowances.[30]

## *Ethical Question*

- Are RPMs ethical?

## *Throwing Out the Bathtub*

Noted earlier was the Supreme Court's ingenious introduction of the so-called bathtub theory, which outlawed any intraenterprise activity deemed to have deleterious effects on competition. For example, if Company A owned Company B, A could not force B to buy exclusively from it because the policy would create an intraenterprise conspiracy. From ethical perspectives the complicated story of the Copperweld Corporation is intriguing. Copperweld had purchased in 1975 the Regal Tube Corporation, a totally owned subsidiary of Lear Siegler. Under the purchase agreement, Lear Siegler was precluded for five years from competing in the manufacture of steel tubes.

Shortly after the acquisition, a former Lear Siegler executive formed an entirely new corporation called Independence Tube to compete in the steel

CHAPTER FOUR  Competition: Ethical and Legal Rules    127

tubing business. When he contracted with Yoder Corporation to construct a plant for his new firm, Copperweld worried over possible competition because Independence, nonexistent when the contract was signed, was not necessarily precluded by the noncompetitive provisions of the acquisition agreement. When Copperweld (and Regal) threatened Yoder with legal action to protect trade secrets acquired from Lear Siegler, Yoder voided its construction agreement with Independence, an action that caused a nine-month delay for Independence in opening its plant. When Copperweld also used that interval to discourage banks and real estate firms from doing business with Independence, Independence went to court.

To establish its legal position, Independence had to prove that Regal and Copperweld were distinct economic units who conspired to pressure firms not to deal with Independence. Regal had exploited its relationship with certain steel suppliers and mill manufacturers to block construction of Independence's mill. Copperweld had used its banking and realty contacts to harass Independence. In Independence's view, Copperweld and Regal were guilty of conspiracy.

Copperweld countered the charge by holding that, since distinctions between a parent company and its wholly owned subsidiary were artificial, the old intraenterprise conspiracy doctrine was illogical. If maintained, said Copperweld, the law would deter efficiencies that flow from separate incorporation that benefit the firm, its employees, and the consuming public. Consistent with the bathtub theory, however, the federal district court ruled that Copperweld and Regal were guilty. Both companies then appealed to the Supreme Court, which in June 1984 did something it had done rarely in antitrust cases: it broke precedent. By a 5-to-3 margin the court ruled that intraenterprise conspiracy was nonsense because a single corporate body could not conspire against itself.[31]

Thirty states joined forces to say the majority's ruling seriously jeopardized their ability to protect consumers, taking their cue from Justice John Paul Stevens' dissent, which held that the decision would haunt Americans because two "predatory" corporations had been allowed to escape liability simply by "working for the same godfather." Words like predatory and godfather seem pejorative; but Copperweld's motive in buying Regal was suspect and its tactics rather ruthless. And the founder of Independence was also less than angelic because he knew of the restrictive covenant in the sales agreement between Copperweld and Regal before deciding to establish his own company.

## Ethical Question

- From ethical perspectives, should one party—or both—be censured?

## Exclusive Dealings

Exclusive dealings *are agreements wherein a buyer consents to purchase from only one seller.* In defense of this practice, it is said that such arrangements result in the following:

- More stable market arrangements
- Reduced selling costs because sellers have less need for large sales forces
- Discounts for buyers, which mean lower prices for consumers
- Dealer loyalty
- The right of manufacturers to protect investments made in dealers' training and counseling

The classic case arose in 1949 with Standard Oil of California. Standard (the largest refiner and oil supplier for Arizona, California, Idaho, Nevada, Oregon, Utah, and Washington) had exclusive dealing contracts with approximately 6,000 independent filling stations. The contract provided that the stations buy from Standard alone one or more petrol-related products, a common practice among suppliers. Despite evidence that the rule of reason might be applicable, the Supreme Court (in a 5-4 decision) used the per se rule to find Standard guilty. The court embraced what was later labeled the *quantitative substantiality* test, that is, the percentage of the market hindered by the exclusive dealing agreement. In this case, the court decided that foreclosure of nearly 7 percent of the market was substantial.[32]

In 1977 a somewhat different issue arose in a case involving Sylvania's policy of selective distribution for its television sets. All franchise agreements had a clause requiring retailers to stay in their own locations unless granted specific permission to move out. When a dealer claimed violation of the Sherman Act, the Supreme Court ruled that, even though Sylvania's franchise terms reduced the amount of intrabrand competition for Sylvania color television sets, the practice increased Sylvania's capacity to engage in vigorous competition with other companies. The net result, reasoned the court, was a generally more competitive marketplace that was good for consumers.

From moral perspectives, one could speculate that both utilitarians and deontologists would support the decision—the former because the consequences seem so clearly in favor of the greatest good for the greatest number, and the latter because the dealers had freely entered the Sylvania contract because of perceived benefits to themselves. Contractual obligations, plus the argument that going beyond one's own territory could harm another Sylvania franchise (the do-no-harm principle), provide ammunition for a deontological logic.

Related to rules on exclusive arrangements for territorial distributions are *exclusive dealerships*, which occur when a buyer agrees not to use—or deal in—goods handled by competitors of his or her own suppliers. An early example involved a Pennsylvania mining company that obligated a shipper to keep half its coal-carrying capacity for the exclusive use of the coal company. In return, the coal company pledged to the shipper an assured level of toll revenues that would be calculated on the basis of the prevailing market price for coal. Finding no injury to the public, the court allowed the contract to stand.[33] In this instance the jurists relied on a utilitarian interpretation of exchange justice by presuming that no injury would come to other producers or to consumers. Deontologists would, in all likelihood, challenge such reasoning on grounds that benefits to a few suppliers should not come at the expense of other suppliers whose handicaps had been created by other producers in the same field. Furthermore, whether the public was unharmed by a contract that assured shipping facilities to the coal company, and barge business to the canal company and not to others, is problematic.

## *Tying agreements*

Tying agreements *are arrangements whereby a manufacturer sells one product to a customer (tying) on the condition that the buyer also purchase a different (tied) product or agrees not to purchase that product from any other supplier.*[34] To get one product, the customer must buy two.

**How Tie-Ins Work.** Manufacturers like tying arrangements for many reasons. They promise greater profits by setting a relatively low price on the first item but a higher-than-competitive price for the tied item; they provide cost savings because products are sold in packages rather than separately; and they enable the manufacturer to disguise the price because two products are sold as a package. Finally, tying agreements allow manufacturers to stipulate that their repair service must be used by the buyer to ensure the product's proper functioning.

Clearly the buyer is being coerced, and moralists put this matter bluntly: Tie-ins represent a form of theft against customers because they take money for a product that customers may not at the time of purchase want or need or, indeed, may never use. Related to tying contracts is *full-line forcing,* which requires a dealer to purchase an entire product line when only part of the line is really desired. Again, this practice is ethically suspect because it usually works after the manufacturer has already gained considerable power over the buyer.

This element of tie-in power has also been used in the field of financial services, an area rarely mentioned when tying arrangements are discussed. A senior executive of the National Association of Life Underwriters, Jack Bobo, told the story of seeking from a Phoenix bank a $10,000 loan. To give Bobo the loan the bank insisted he open a checking account and, because he obviously needed the loan, Bobo did not object. About a week after completing the loan, he received a two-year decreasing term life certificate covering the loan and a statement indicating that the premium for this coverage was $232, which had been added to the interest. No discussion of such coverage had taken place and, because he had an adequate personal insurance program, he called the loan officer for an explanation. Bobo was told that the application had been among the forms he had signed. When Bobo indicated that, based on current rates, the coverage the bank provided was worth about $45, the bank official seemed unmoved. However, after a call to the bank's president, Bobo successfully obtained a refund. His comment is relevant: "An isolated incident? Not by a long shot! Parallel examples occur on a daily basis. No banker that I know would regard the requirement of a checking account as a condition for a commercial loan as a tie-in sale, and yet that is precisely what it is."[35]

**When Tie-Ins Exist.** Determining when tying agreements actually exist presents a thorny legal and moral problem. Two examples (the second of which was suggested by the Atlantic Refining Company's case against the FTC) underscore the difficulties.[36]

1. A company sells products that represent 80 percent of the market in one area. The CEO knows, therefore, that he is vulnerable to antitrust charges if he attempts to tie a related and newly introduced product to the old item. The R&D team, however, insists that the new line, which is more expensive to make, be tied to the older product line. If it is not tied, profits may be adversely affected.

## *Ethical Question*

- Does the CEO face a strictly marketing decision? Or are ethical problems involved?

2. Company A manufactures several products that complement its chief product, which is sold, solely and directly, by its own retail outlets. Company A asks Company B to help its marketing effort by having B's outlets promote the sale of A's other products. Company B agrees. Knowing that Company A's products are of the highest quality, B asks A to package two other unrelated products in one unit and provide B with commissions on the sales. A agrees to B's request.

## *Ethical Question*

- Did Company A act ethically?

## *Restrictive Covenants and Predatory Pricing*

Restrictive covenants *are agreements not to compete and typically supplement employment or sales contracts for a business.* Sellers see them as protecting their business and its goodwill,[37] employers like to use them for workers in positions to know trade secrets or having valuable personal contacts with the company's competitors. Covenants are deemed reasonable if they are no broader than necessary in their restrictions on time, territory, and product lines; but they may not be used to punish workers or stifle competition. Court decisions have tended to favor such agreements but, as usual, there are either exceptions or ambiguities to contend with.

A case in point is *Ingredient Technology v. Nay*.[38] In 1979 Nay sold his firm, Seasoning Mills, to Ingredient Technology (IT) with an agreement not to compete with IT in the spice-selling business for a five-year period. Within a year, Nay reentered the business in direct competition with IT and regained the customers he had cultivated during his 40 years at Seasoning Mills. The court granted IT's request for an injunction. Despite IT's failure to show irreparable harm, the court held that what the purchaser lost when

CHAPTER FOUR  Competition: Ethical and Legal Rules    131

the seller solicited former customers was the opportunity to cement the loyalties of the new customers to itself. Customer preferences are part of an organization's goodwill, an asset so fragile that potential harm to the new proprietor's business must be considered irreparable.

In addition to restrictive covenants, there is predatory pricing, which comes in two varieties. *One occurs when a company cuts prices below costs in order to drive out competitors*—after which price levels generally rise to a point at which previous losses on sales are more than recouped.[39] It was believed, for example, that the old A&P grocery chain sometimes engaged in such practices. A utilitarian argument might be invoked to defend the practice on grounds that customers garner short-term gains whereas sellers take substantial risks that the strategy will backfire. And even if it did not, when prices were eventually raised, customers would only be "paying back what was due" the seller in the first place. The strained argument collapses when tested by moral criteria: the price-cutter's intent was evil; the result ultimately hurts customers and competitors; the practice, if unchecked, could lead to oligarchy or monopoly.

Predatory pricing *also occurs when a seller charges competing reselling buyers different prices for the same merchandise.* Prohibited by the Robinson-Patman Act of 1936, suppliers who attempted to gain unfair advantage over competitors by discriminating among buyers were put on notice. While this instance provides a good example of law and morality working together, it has already been noted that some ambiguities in the law allowed businesses to play the competitive game close to the ethical edge.

## *Administered Pricing*

No analysis of pricing problems is complete without mention of administrative pricing policies developed in 1924 by Donaldson Brown, then with DuPont and later with General Motors. An administered price *occurs when a company—seeking returns that will (1) support production and marketing costs, (2) provide funds for research and development as well as for capital expansion, (3) satisfy stockholders and workers, and (4) stay within the requirements of the Sherman and Robinson-Patman Acts—sets the price long before demand makes its force felt in the market.* The administrator assumes responsibility for weighing and establishing priorities among the various claimants: stockholders, workers, customers, and the managers themselves. The administered price may turn out to be above, below, or equal to the price that would have been established by the free market. At the time it is fixed, however, administered pricing seems to represent sound industrial policy.[40]

Problems arise, however, when a declining market generates conflict between sound industrial policy (full use of all resources) and sound business policy (maximized profits). Administered prices are established on an estimate that so many units can be sold at the predetermined figure. If the calculation proves defective, the executive has to determine whether to cut prices or to cut production. Whereas a viable industrial and moral policy seeks optimum use of all resources, business policy aims to provide satisfactory profits. In the face of falling demand, the tendency has been not to lower prices (when gains from additional sales are marginal), but to cut both costs and production in order to reach the targeted profit level. But "good" business policy can result in idle people and idle plants. This clash however, between industrial and business policy has had some unusual terms.

For example, Esso's administered price for oil in 1946, was below what the normal market would have afforded and consequently yielded a profit less than what would have been realized by adhering to normal market operations. The country was then fighting a serious postwar inflationary threat and Esso felt that higher prices would not bring out a greater supply of oil because transportation facilities were unable to meet the demand. Esso decided to hold the price line. President Truman's assistant, John Steelman, hailed the company's action as a patriotic service; other oil firms and independent jobbers, forced to buy in markets with higher prices, called "foul" and appealed to Congress to protect small business. Debate still erupts when the question is asked whether Esso did the "right thing."

A more dramatic case was the famous confrontation between President John Kennedy and Roger Blough of U.S. Steel in April 1962. The facts were clear: the steel giant was operating below full capacity, meaning that the sound industrial policy of full resource utilization had not been achieved. Production had fallen from 117 million tons of ingots in 1955 to 98 million tons in 1962. On April 10, 1962, the executive committee of U.S. Steel decided to raise the prices by about $6 a ton—despite the government's argument that such action would set off a new wage–price spiral, aggravate unemployment, cut into export sales, weaken the dollar, and possibly intensify the outflow of gold. On the other hand, the company said that it had not had any overall price adjustments since 1958, that it was forced to spend over a billion dollars for modernization during the 1958–1962 period, that the dividend rate had not been increased in five years, and that costs had risen perceptibly. In order to meet competition, both at home and abroad, the company declared that it must raise prices.

The fact that the price hikes were eventually revoked precluded testing Steel's judgment of the market. Although the company's arguments were fairly persuasive, the case illustrates the dangers to which administered pricing policies are exposed: (1) likely subordination of industrial to business policy, (2) an unsophisticated perception of the public's pulse, (3) a neglect of possible consequences for future wage negotiations, and (4) an "ostrich" view of the nation's stake in foreign trade.

Perhaps no area of managerial entrepreneurship is more difficult to depict accurately, assess fairly, and prescribe for realistically in terms of morality than the domain of administered pricing. Responsibility often seems to fall as much on the administrator as on the market. Yet the market system cannot be expected to operate promptly as a countervailing force against overpricing. If an administered price can be maintained below what the market would reasonably allocate, as it was by Esso in 1947, it can also be maintained above what the market would allocate. The interesting question is whether administrative pricing is intrinsically unethical. Used to promote the firm's and the economy's health, administered pricing may actually foster social justice. On the other hand, such pricing practices are like the previously discussed RPMs, unilaterally established to assure profits that might not come through fair competition.

## Summary

The recurring theme of this chapter on competition is that human law and moral law are locked indissolubly together. The idea that differing interests of individuals and/or companies automatically mesh into one organic network is rejected. Also rejected is the belief that obedience to law is business's only ethical obligation.

A look at the evolving law on competition suggests that lawyers and courts have struggled to reconcile law and ethics into a meaningful relationship. The principle of constructive effort was evident in the Supreme Court's decision in *Tuttle v. Buck*; the level playing field concept was clearly one inspiration for the Sherman Antitrust Act and the subsequent congressional efforts to improve it. Ambiguities remain in such areas as administered pricing and fair trade law. Possibly of greater relevance than specifics is the constant interplay between deontological and utilitarian reasoning—the kind that goes on when corporate managers, sales personnel, and advertisers seek to balance positive consequences for their firms and for their society.

## *Questions for Discussion*

1. Is the Supreme Court's second view of the bathtub theory more defensible on ethical grounds than its first interpretation?
2. If you were asked to devise ethical rules to govern regulators of business like those in the Federal Trade Commission, what would you suggest as the best way to promote the principle of respect for the officiating parties?
3. If a specific company in a specific industry follows administrative pricing policies that consistently result in below-market prices for consumers, are the policies ethical?
4. Are manufacturers acting ethically when they insist that maintenance services be provided only by their technicians when others with comparable training are available?
5. Do you think antitrust laws should be applied to American corporations doing business abroad when the host countries have no statutes similar to ours?

## Ethical Quandary

*PowerMaster*

G. Heilleman Brewing Company of Chicago in 1991 announced plans to market PowerMaster, a malt beer containing 5.9 percent alcohol—31 percent more alcohol than the company's top-selling Colt 45 malt beer. Regular beer contains about 3.5 percent alcohol. Malt drinks are especially popular with male teenagers who like their macho effect and, with the poor who cannot afford hard drinks. According to Hugh Nelson, Heilleman's marketing director, PowerMaster was the company's response when research convinced him that drinkers wanted even more bang for the buck. For decades, malt advertising has held out the promise of manhood in a bottle. Coming to mind are the Schlitz malt–liquor bull crashing through a wall and Billy Dee Williams' pitching Colt 45 among snarling pit bulls, white stallions, and hip-grinding go-go dancers. Malt makers are commonly believed to aim their products at the most vulnerable populations: low-income, inner-city African-Americans who suffer disproportionately from alcohol-related diseases.

Hearing the news about PowerMaster, the Reverend Calvin Butts of the Abyssinian Baptist Church in New York said he was "outraged and frightened" over the prospect of new and more powerful malt and that he planned to launch another campaign to whitewash liquor and tobacco billboards promoting such products. The previous year Reverend Butts' grass-roots whitewashing attracted considerable press coverage, turning him into something of a folk hero. George Hacker, director of the National Coalition to Prevent Impaired Driving, echoed the theme: "Basically, PowerMaster is substituting destructive power for social justice."

You, a New Yorker, are on Heilleman's board. You are also on the board of the Harlem Youth Club, an organization formed to help African-American youngsters avoid drugs and get jobs. At the Heilleman board meeting you ask pressing questions: Is PowerMaster aimed particularly at the poor? Will it not increase drunkenness? Should the macho image be played up in a violence-prone society? May not Heilleman itself lose out when it becomes known that the company's Colt 45 is already a financial success and that the new beverage is designed to solidify Heilleman's hold over the malt industry?

The answers you are given are these: The higher alcohol segment of the malt beer industry had been growing annually at the astronomical rate of 25 to 30 percent and Heilleman will either tap this market or be outstripped by others. Furthermore, consumers are still the best judges of their own wants and needs. Michael Rodriguez, a Colt 45 drinker, was reported to have said that he felt pleasantly mellow after 12 cans a day, but he could still do his building superintendent's job. The intended message of the Rodriguez story is clear to you: Not everyone will like a stronger malt but, for those who do, PowerMaster would be ready to serve. You are also told that

PowerMaster is aimed not only at the poor. In affluent suburbs, college crowds show evidence of preferring strong malts over weaker ones.

You leave the board meeting convinced that PowerMaster is coming to the market no matter what stand you take.

## Question

- What should you do next?

## Notes

1. Christopher Stone, *Where the Law Ends* (New York: Harper & Row, 1975).
2. Norman E. Bowie, "Fair Markets," *Journal of Business and Professional Ethics* 7 (1988): 80–98.
3. Milton Friedman, *Capitalism and Freedom* (Chicago: University of Chicago Press, 1982).
4. Albert Z. Carr, "Is Business Bluffing Ethical?" *Harvard Business Review* (January–February (1968): 130.
5. Betsy Morris, "Coke's Windfall...," *The Wall Street Journal*, September 26, 1989, 1A and 18A.
6. See Ronald Dworkin, *Taking Rights Seriously* (Cambridge, Mass.: Harvard University Press, 1977).
7. Claus Henningsen v. Bloomfield Motors, 161 S. Ct. N.J. A.2d 69 (1960).
8. Lynn Sharpe Paine, "Ideals of Competition and the Gathering of Commercial Intelligence," in *Enriching Business Ethics*, ed. Clarence C. Walton (New York: Plenum Press, 1990), ch. 4.
9. Amitai Etzioni, *The Moral Dimension: Toward a New Economics* (New York: The Free Press/Macmillan, 1988), ch. 12.
10. Joseph Schumpeter expressed the innovation-productivity link in the idea of "creative destruction" in *Capitalism, Socialism and Democracy* (New York: Harper & Row, 1942). For a more sophisticated treatment of the concept, see Schumpeter's *Theory of Economic Development* (Cambridge: Harvard University Press, 1934). Trans. Redvers Opie.
11. Daniel Bourrough, "How American Express Orchestrated Smear of Rival Edmond Safra," *The Wall Street Journal*, September 24, 1990.
12. Tuttle v. Buck, Minn. Sp. Ct. (1909).
13. *The New York Times*, May 31, 1988, 1a and 18. In his dissent, Justice Stevens said the majority's decision is a restraint of trade whose only purpose is to stifle competition.
14. R. C. Baumhart, "How Ethical Are Businessmen?" *Harvard Business Review* 36 (1961): 6–9, 156–157. See also Wroe Alderson, "Ethics, Ideologies, and Sanctions," *Report of the Committee on Ethical Standards and Professional Practices* (Chicago: American Marketing Association, 1964), and Steven N. Brenner and Earl A. Molander, "Is the Ethics of Business Changing?" *Harvard Business Review* 55 (January–February 1977): 55–71.
15. Relevant are the articles by Lawrence B. Chonko and S. D. Hunt, "Ethics and Marketing Management: An Empirical Examination," and James H. Leigh and Charles M. Futrell, "From the Trenches to the Command Post: Perceptual and Attitudinal Differences among Levels in the Marketing Management Hierarchy." Both articles appeared in the *Journal of Business Research* 13 (1985), 511–536 and 339–360 respectively.
16. B. F. Schumacher, *Small Is Beautiful: Economics As If People Mattered* (New York: Harper & Row, 1975).
17. One of the classics is James Atwood and Kingman Brewster, *Antitrusts and American Business Abroad* (New York: Shepard/McGraw Hill, 1981), 2 vols. Helpful are Ernest Gellhorn, *Antitrust Law and Economics in a Nutshell* (Minneapolis: West, 1981); and Edwin M. Epstein, "Regulation, Self-Regulation and Corporate Ethics—Mutually Rein-

forcing Conditions for Achieving Social Responsibility and Publicly Accountable Business Behavior," presented at the symposium on business ethics, Woodstock Theological Center, Georgetown University, February 28, 1986.

18. Richard Hofstadter, "What Happened to the Antitrust Movement?" in *The Business Establishment*, ed. Earl Cheit (New York: Wiley, 1964), 114. For superb insights into the history of U.S. regulation, see Thomas K. McCraw, *Prophets of Regulation* (Cambridge: Harvard University Press, 1984). The prophets were Louis Brandeis, James Landis, Charles Francis Adams, and Alfred Kahn. A detailed legal analysis is found in Robert G. Harris and Thomas M. Jorde, "Antitrust Market Definition: An Integrated Approach," *California Law Review* 72 (January 1984): 1–67.

19. Adam Smith, *The Wealth of Nations* (New York: The Modern Library, 1973), 250. Quoted so frequently as to be instantaneously recognized is Smith's comment that "people of the same trade seldom eat together even for merriment and discussion" without the conversation ending in "a conspiracy against the public (p. 128)."

20. A rather elementary treatment was provided by Earl Kitner, *A Robinson-Patman Primer* (New York: Collier-Macmillan, 1970).

21. Irving Scher, "How Sellers Can Live with the Robinson-Patman Act," *The Business Lawyer* 41 (February 1986): 553–554.

22. Charles Price, "Vertical v. Horizontal Restraints," *National Law Journal*, August 12, 1985, 15–17, 19.

23. Morris Run Coal Company v. Barclay Coal Company, 68 Pa. Sp. Ct. 173 (1871), 187.

24. A. D. Neale, *The Antitrust Laws of the United States* (New York: Cambridge University Press, 1974), 21.

25. For a delightful story of one consumer's confusion in dealing with brand and nonbrand purchasing, see John Philip Jones, "Competition and the Emergence of Brands," *Syracuse Scholar* (1984): 37–41. See also the old study by Almarin Phillips, *Market Structure, Organization and Performance* (Cambridge: Harvard University Press, 1962). Above all, one should include the two studies by Oliver E. Williamson, *Markets and Hierarchies* (New York: The Free Press, 1975), and *The Economic Institutions of Capitalism* (New York: The Free Press, 1984).

26. Janet L. McDavid, "The Courts Welcome Demise of the Bathtub Conspiracy Doctrine," *The National Law Journal*, July 23, 1984, 22–24. See also Kenneth P. Quinn, "Intra-Enterprise Conspiracy Doctrine: Toward an Equitable Approach," *DePaul Law Review* 33 (Spring 1983): 113–131. Students interested in this area might find it helpful to review the court's thinking as it evolved in Kieffner-Stewart v. Joseph Seagram (1951); and Perma Life Mufflers v. International Parts Corporation (1968).

27. The first example approximates FTC v. Morton Salt Company (1943). In this case, the corporation was found guilty of promoting anticompetitive practices by favoring the "big boys." The second parallels a 1963 Sun Oil Company case in which the Supreme Court sustained an FTC contention that local competition meant the seller's not the customer's, need. The last reflects Pearl Brewery v. Anheuser-Busch (1980). In this case the court rejected the FTC accusation and said there was no proof the brewer used its size to engage in predatory pricing in the St. Louis area. Prior to 1980, it was generally held that using the wholesale price to affect the resale price was a violation of the law.

28. Richard Posner, "Market Power in Antitrust Cases," *Harvard Law Review* 94 (March 1981): 937–996; and "Next Step in the Anti-Trust Treatment of Restricted Distribution Per Se Legality," *University of Chicago Law Review* 48 (1981): 871–994.

29. Jay Greenfield and James Rubinger, "Is Basing Wholesale Prices on Resale Prices Legal?" *The National Law Journal* (June 17, 1985), 22–25.

30. The court again applied the quantitative substantiality rule in Tampa Electric Company v. Nashville Coal Company (1961). When Tampa Electric decided to expand its facilities, it contracted with the Nashville Coal Company to provide the expected coal requirements for a period of 20 years. Nashville agreed but later reneged, whereupon Tampa sued for performance of the contract. The court decided that the impact on Tampa's maximum anticipated requirements would be insubstantial.

31. Copperweld v. Independence Tube Corporation 496 U.S. 927, 83 L. Ed. 2d 257 (Oct. 29, 1984).

CHAPTER FOUR  Competition: Ethical and Legal Rules   137

32. Standard Oil of California v. FTC 71 S. Ct. Reporter 240–259 (Jan. 8, 1951).
33. Stephanie G. Spauling, Pennsylvania's Antitrust Law: What is the Commonwealth's Policy on Competition? *Duquesne University Law Review* 19 (1980–81), 731–760.
34. Richard Craswell, "Tying Requirements in Competitive Markets: The Consumer Protection Issues," *Boston University Law Review* 62 (May 1982): 661–700. Although the leverage theory of tied good sale has been sharply criticized, a recent analysis suggests that tying can indeed serve as a mechanism for leveraging market power. Michael D. Whinston, "Tying, Foreclosure, and Exclusion," *American Economic Review* 80 (September 1990); 837–895.
35. Jack Bobo, "Costly Insight," *The American Council of Life Insurance Review* 9 (January–February 1984): 5.
36. The commission had condemned an agreement between Atlantic and Goodyear under which Atlantic promoted sales of Goodyear batteries and accessories to its wholesale and retail service stations in return for a commission on such sales. The Supreme Court upheld the FTC ruling, saying that, while the arrangement was not technically a tying agreement, it had the characteristics of one.
37. William F. Gray and Jeffrey L. Liddle, "Proof of Damages for Breach of a Restrictive Covenant or Noncompetitive Agreement," *Antitrust Law Journal* 52 (1983): 455–460.
38. Ingredient Technology Corporation v. Florence Nay, Daniel Nay, and Food Processing Ingredients, Inc., 532 F. Supp. 627–634 (Feb. 8, 1982).
39. Joseph C. Bradley and George A. Hay, "Predatory Pricing: Competing Economic Theories and the Evolution of Legal Standards," *Cornell University Law Review* 66 (April 1981): 740–803.
40. Clarence C. Walton, *Ethos and the Executive* (Englewood Cliffs, N.J.: Prentice-Hall, 1969), 207–210.

CHAPTER 5

# Ethics of Size: Mergers and Takeovers

**Merger Movements**
The First Three Waves
The Fourth Wave

**Hostile Takeover Techniques**
Bids and Greenmail
An Example: The Phillips Petroleum Story
Leveraged Buyouts and Junk Bonds
An Example: The Drexel-Milken Saga
Negotiating Patterns
Defensive Tactics
*Pensions*
*Poison Pills*
*Pac-men*

**Economic and Ethical Assessments**
Economic Gains and Losses
The Ethical Ledger
Newton's Law

**Suggested Reforms**
Internal Reform
External Regulation

**Summary**
Questions for Discussion
Ethical Quandary

*T*he number and scale of corporate acquisitions during the 1980s surprised even the experts. From a 1980 total of 1,165 deals the number jumped to 3,165 in 1985. In 1981 nine of them were valued at a billion or more dollars; in 1985 twenty-six reached that figure. Corporate giants like Gulf Oil, once thought impregnable, have fallen. Small companies have swallowed others three times their size. Arbitrageurs and lawyers have made decisions that have more affected the outcome than those made by managers themselves. The climax of the story is hard to determine, but clearly the levels of approval and disapproval of the merger-acquisition-takeover movement indicate that important economic and ethical qualities are involved.

The temptation to make sweeping definitive judgments is strong, but the facts are simply too convoluted for simplistic assessment. Companies can become big by being good. Companies can become big by being greedy. Drawing the line between the two is what ethical reasoning about corporate size is all about. It is appropriate, therefore, to look at arguments, both pro and con, on the merger-takeover movement from both economic and moral perspectives.[1] When corporate size is achieved more through financial wizardry than through technological or marketing skill, the public becomes rightly suspicious—and this despite the fact that small firms are doing very well under corporate capitalism. ■■

## *The purposes of this chapter are:*

1. To trace the history of the four most recent waves in the merger movement.
2. To examine the nature of hostile takeovers and the game plans followed by the chief players.
3. To offer both economic and moral assessments of the merger-takeover phenomenon.

## Merger Movements

### *The First Three Waves*

The United States has gone through four waves of intense merger activity. The first occurred during the last quarter of the 19th century and was characterized by companies merging to reduce competition and create monopoly. The growth of the railroads following the Civil War (by 1914 the U.S. boasted more railroad mileage than all of Europe), and a concurrent revolution in production techniques had opened a previously closed national market. Large local and regional producers with large production capacities suddenly found themselves in direct competition with similar firms from other regions in the country. These firms began to merge to reduce competition and, once merged, adopted decentralized organizational structures to operate with improved efficiency. The American Tobacco Company and Standard Oil were products of this era. By the end of the 19th century, huge merged firms dominated such industries as oil, tobacco, steel, whisky, and sugar. These monopolies inspired fear of unrestrained corporate power and prompted Congress to pass the Sherman Antitrust Act in 1890.

The second swell hit America between 1925 and 1930, when moderately sized firms doing business in the same industry were combined; these mergers produced no monopolies but rather large companies that competed successfully against monopolies. Bethlehem Steel, for example, challenged U.S. Steel. A similar pattern developed in transportation when Cornelius Vanderbilt, looking at the railroad industry, saw how the Harlem Railroad thrust into the heart of New York City, how the Hudson Line stretched from the city to Albany, and how the New York Central linked Albany to Buffalo, gateway to the developing Midwest. By combining the three into the New York Central, Vanderbilt created a sturdy rival to the hitherto unchallenged Pennsylvania Railroad.

During this period the public began to accept big business as a fact of life; however, worry over corporate power reappeared after World War II and, in response to public fears, in 1950 Congress passed the Cellar-Kefauver Act, which voided the Clayton Act's asset loophole and practically eliminated large mergers between competitors and between related businesses. Although the Cellar-Kefauver Act greatly reduced merger activity at the time, it placed no restrictions on large mergers between unrelated companies.

The third wave rolled over the business coast in the 1960s. In contrast to the monopolistic mergers of the late 19th century and the vertical mergers of the late 1920s, many acquiring firms used price-earnings (PE) ratios to exploit tax laws and accounting conventions in order to realize instant profits. Financial wizards used PE magic to add a company worth two to a company worth two and a half to form a conglomerate worth five. Between 1960 and 1968, five obscure companies (Gulf-Western, LTV, International Telephone and Telegraph, Tenneco, and Teledyne) acquired over $1 billion in assets through the PE approach. To illustrate, 70 percent of the 500 largest American industrial companies earned most of their income from one business in 1949; by 1969, little more than 30 percent of the top 500 companies did so. The stock market's fall put an end to the epidemic of PE magic transactions in 1964, when investors learned that conglomerates often realized profits by manipulating financial reports, not by producing something of real economic value.

## The Fourth Wave

The fourth wave engulfed the business world during the 1980s. As was noted, the merger movement slowed around 1968 because of changes in tax laws, stricter antitrust enforcement, fear that organizations were becoming so large as to be unmanageable and, finally, evidence that mergers did not always result in happy marriages. By the mid-1980s the situation had reversed itself and the new wave, lashed by hurricane forces of investor and management daring, imagination, and often greed, left relatively few big companies untouched. By and large, reasons for combining companies relied on a similar logic—economies of scale. Sometimes the purpose was to acquire new technologies or product lines by buying small and successful firms.[2] At other times, the reasons dealt with bankruptcy avoidance, "evening out" business cyclical patterns, managerial fears or ambitions, or acquirers' greed and, of course, tax breaks.

The fourth wave soon reached such proportions that the 1968 high clearly would be surpassed.[3] In 1981 Wall Street itself experienced a tumultuous year when the prestigious investment house of Dillon Read, unable to compete against such heavily capitalized firms as Solomon Brothers and Merrill Lynch, was acquired by the Bechtel Group, a construction and engineering firm based in San Francisco. Dean Witter was taken over by Sears, Salomon Brothers by Phibro, Bache Halsey Stuart by Prudential and, most dramatic of all, Shearson by American Express.[4]

The pace quickened and by 1985 companies were being acquired, in whole or in part, at the frantic rate of 11 per day, well ahead of the 1968 record. The dollar value paid in 1983 for completed transactions surged to over $73 billion, up nearly $54 billion from the 1982 mark. A look at 1984's postings gives a sense of what was going on. For traditional and solid reasons (investment opportunities, diversification) General Motors bought Hughes Aircraft for $5.2 billion; General Electric purchased RCA for more than $6 billion; and Phillip Morris took over General Foods for $5.7 billion. For more speculative reasons, GAF, a midsized maker of chemicals and building materials, went after Union Carbide for $4 billion; Pantry Pride Supermarkets swallowed a reluctant (and three times larger) Revlon for $2.7 billion; and Ted Turner ensnared MGM for $2.5 billion.

The high numbers of mergers (2,800 in 1985 and 2,300 in 1986) were unique to the 1980s in terms of money. Between 1969 and 1980, only 12 transactions were valued at more than a billion dollars each; by 1985, over 30 such deals were consummated, leading the public to wonder what was actually going on. Dozens of the country's biggest businesses wooed, wrangled, and battled for one another in the strongest outbreak of the urge-to-merge fever in U.S. history. As the 1980s drew to a close, questions multiplied: Was the rash of mergers good for American business? for stockholders? for the country? And just how far could it go before it went too far?[5] Responses will come later in Part Four.

The Reagan administration, confident that the movement was good for the United States, had taken a relaxed position toward the antitrust issue, and the guidelines announced in 1982 by Assistant Attorney General for Antitrust William Baxter emphasized only one theory of economic harm: monopoly price–fixing between direct competitors. Mergers were allowed between large companies in unrelated industries and between direct competitors; Chevron, for example, was able to absorb Gulf Oil for a record $13 billion when it agreed to sell some holdings that violated antitrust laws. This relaxation had essentially returned antitrust policy to that prior to the Cellar-Kefauver Act. Government tranquility is best illustrated by the fact that the Justice Department and the Federal Trade Commission initiated only three cases between 1980 and 1988 to enforce the Sherman Act's ban on monopoly, the lowest in any eight-year period since 1900. However, the merger binge raised both economic and ethical questions.[6]

## Hostile Takeover Techniques

Owners and potential purchasers financially joust with one another in multiple ways, especially when owners do not want to sell and buyers are determined to acquire. Techniques include (1) greenmail and two-tiered bids, (2) leveraged buyouts and junk bonds, and (3) "shark repellents."[7] A comment on each exposes its essential components.

### *Bids and Greenmail*

Two-tiered bids and greenmail have been especially identified with Ivan Boesky, Carl Ichan, and T. Boone Pickens, the feared raiders who always worked under a cloak of secrecy in approaching their unsuspecting targets. Because the words "secrecy" and "unsuspecting" are pejorative, objectivity requires us to look at the practices before jumping to conclusions. The raider secretly buys up a sizable portion of the targeted company's stock through either brokers or through private investors. To maintain secrecy, the raider pays top dollar to sellers within the first tier in order to amass shares as expeditiously as possible. Obviously, astute stockholders reap handsome benefits when bidders have paid, as they sometimes have, almost 13 times earnings for target companies. When the acquired amount of the target company's stock requires that the Securities and Exchange Commission be notified, the raider moves to the second tier by announcing his intention to make tender offers for the remaining stock at a price lower than that offered in the first-tier stage.

The obvious problem with front-end, two-tier offers is that even if investors feel that the offer is inadequate they cannot afford to refrain from tendering because they must protect themselves against receiving the lower back-end price for their shares if the bid succeeds. The technique substitutes coercive market pressures for objective judgment; the short time that an offer is required to remain outstanding denies shareholders the benefit of an informed public discussion of such important issues as values, alternatives, reputation of the bidder, and reliability of finance capabilities, especially when junk-bond financing is involved.

Accompanying second-tier offers is greenmail—often called legalized blackmail—which occurs when the purchaser exhibits an ill-concealed zeal to sell back stock he has already bought at a handsome profit. Ivan Boesky, for example, garnered an 8.7 percent stake in CBS at an average price of $95.50 a share, but a week before the public announcement he had offered privately to sell back his holdings to CBS at a market price of $105 a share.[8] Carl Ichan is another who has employed the buy-me-out or face-a-takeover ploy. In May 1985 he launched an attack on Uniroyal by offering $18 a share for stock that had not moved appreciably from the $10 per share of the previous year. The company arranged a leveraged buyout that would bring the holders $22 a share, an offer that Ichan promptly accepted at the same time that he promised to be a nice boy by calling off his raid. His greenmail amounted to $6 million from Uniroyal to compensate for "expenses." Uniroyal management was happy; Uniroyal stockholders were happy; Ichan was happy.

The only flies in the euphoric ointment went to owners of Uniroyal's preferred stock, who were not bought out under the program. Immediately after the news became public, the price of preferred dropped from $68 to $50 a share. At least one set of Uniroyal owners saw the company's managers and board as Benedict Arnolds.[9] The box score on Ichan's other maneuvers is interesting: nearly a $7 million profit when Chesebrough-Ponds bought back its shares, $8 million when Dan River did the same thing, $11 million on a Marshall Field's bid, and $31 million on Hammermill Paper. Injured parties asked what Ichan had contributed to increasing the nation's productivity or to long-term stockholder equity for his own $57 million gain.[10]

One of the notables in the takeover drama is T. Boone Pickens of Mesa Petroleum in Texas. Pickens had perfected the heads-I-win-tails-you-lose technique in applying the two-tiered bid system. In June 1981 Pickens moved against Cities Service, which eventually bought back his holdings at a $40 million gain for Mesa. Then, in March 1983, Pickens pocketed nearly a $32 million profit with his two-tiered bid for Superior Oil Company; in October 1983 he made his famous move on Gulf Oil and, despite protracted and unsuccessful maneuvering by both sides, Pickens walked off with a $590 million gain. In all, Pickens' "defeats" netted $762 million profit on three of the five deals.

## *An Example: The Phillips Petroleum Story*

The best way to understand how takeover specialists operate is to follow the Phillips Petroleum story, which provides ingredients out of which large legends and big profits are made. The story began on December 4, 1984, when T. Boone Pickens attempted a takeover of Phillips Petroleum, a company roughly 37 times larger that Mesa, Pickens' own company. The ant wanted to swallow the elephant. Phillips' CEO, William Douce, sought the aid of attorney Michael Lipton, a seasoned veteran of takeover fights. Lipton told Douce to fight, shrewdly estimating that Pickens, despite pledges not to accept greenmail, would prefer cash to combat. While Lipton was right,

Pickens was able to walk off with a bundle ($53 for each share which he purchased at around $40), plus $25 million in expenses. Investment bankers at Morgan Stanley and First Boston took another $45 million for their brief but pivotal role.

But the story had not ended. Carl Ichan, whom friend and foe described as one of the greediest men on earth, smelled opportunities when the Phillips group showed signs of fatigue. Ichan once spelled his business philosophy out in these words:

*It is our opinion that the elements in today's economic environment have combined in a unique way to create large profit-making opportunities with relatively little risk . . . It is our contention that sizable profits can be earned by taking large positions in "undervalued" stocks and then attempting to control the destinies of the companies in question by:*

    *a) trying to convince management to liquidate or sell the company to a "white knight";*
    *b) waging a proxy contest, or;*
    *c) making a tender offer and/or;*
    *d) selling back our position to the company.*[11]

Having secured financial backing from Drexel Burnham Lambert of junk bond fame, Ichan intensified his efforts to complete the takeover by offering Phillips' shareholders a rather handsome price. When Douce and the Phillips' band fought back, Ichan sought the assistance of attorneys from Paul, Weiss, Rifkind and Garrison who, three years earlier—when representing Dan River—had called Ichan a racketeer and market manipulator. Politics is not the only place for strange bedfellows!

At this point Lipton introduced a poison pill strategy to prevent partial two-tier takeover bids. Because Lipton's pill allowed shareholders to redeem their shares for substantial gains the moment anyone bought more than 30 percent of the company, it would mean rich rewards for Phillips even if Ichan bought the company. Lipton's ploy enabled Phillips to fight off the man whose ethic was articulated in his famous "I'm not a Robin Hood . . . interested in the welfare of widows and orphans."[12] It may have been a Pyrrhic victory because Phillips became burdened with a huge debt. After the event Lipton warned Senator Proxmire, who was investigating the takeover entrepreneurs, that the institutional investors and takeover artists were interested only in the short-term and therefore posed an immediate threat to "every large company that sells in the stock market for less than its liquidation breakup value. . . ."[13] Attorney Lipton's bitter blast against Drexel (one of the most powerful financial institutions in the world) proved poor prophecy—so poor, in fact, that Drexel and its star performer, Michael Milken, will be given extended treatment after leveraged buyouts and junk bonds are discussed.

## Ethical Questions:

- Was Lipton's poison pill strategy not only financially defective but morally defective as well?
- Is greenmail blackmail? If so, should the practice be outlawed?
- Is Ichan's greed unethical? Or immoral?

## Leveraged Buyouts and Junk Bonds

When the early takeover laws were enacted in the 1920s, leverage and high-risk debt were the wonder of the day. In those years leverage (huge debt controlled by minuscule stock holdings) allowed Samuel Insull to build a vast Midwestern utilities empire of such complexity that he could not possibly have understood it himself. And it allowed Ivar Kreuger to build an industrial domain in Europe through the creation of an enormous amount of debt, some of it in bonds that he had forged and issued against the assets of unwitting creditors. Also in those years, exploiting the miracle of leverage, Goldman Sachs created the Goldman Sachs Trading Corporation, which then established the Shenandoah Corporation, which next created the Blue Ridge Corporation, at each step selling bonds to buy stock for the next step. When the day of reckoning came, Samuel Insull went into exile in Greece, Kreuger to Paris where he shot himself, and Goldman Sachs—its breathtaking innovations all but worthless—retreated to a greatly chastened conservatism.[14]

*An LBO occurs when borrowed funds are secured on the basis of the targeted company's assets, which then can be used to magnify a gain (or minimize a loss) on the amount of money invested.* A rule of thumb in leveraged buyouts is that the would-be purchasers can borrow nine dollars for every dollar of their own. By projecting sharply higher returns, the device popularized by the New York investment banking firm of Drexel Burnham Lambert, purchasers could borrow 100 percent of the necessary money even before beginning a takeover drive through the use of securities especially issued for that purchase. Such securities come from junk bonds, normally offered by a shell company formed, with no assets, by the raider; the shell uses large amounts of debt securities to raise funds for the takeover, securing the debt with the stock it intends to acquire. Pickens had used, as noted, a shell company in Mesa's bid for Unocal. By having the total purchase amount, the raider can ignore the banks if a bidding war erupts and also can make unexpected strikes. Although the practice of engraving securities to swamp the market for the purpose of destroying or undermining another organization is morally reprehensible, court decisions and generous forms of financing give special advantages to unwelcome suitors. How the game is played is best understood through example.

## An Example: The Drexel-Milken Saga

Capitalism's strength lies in its capacity for what one great economist, Joseph Schumpeter, called creative destruction, that is, the emergence of new firms—as well as better ways of production and distribution—to replace old firms and traditional modes of operations. Drexel's financial wizard, Michael Milken, played the key role in this process during the 1980s by bringing to the financial market $200 billion for companies that showed promise for growth. Because the computer industry held such promise, Drexel looked upon it with great favor. Other industries—such as telecommunications and entertainment—soon followed in Drexel's favor. This switchover of media, with video going increasingly over wires and voice going increasingly over the air, promised a vast increase in the power of information and telecommunications technology throughout the world. Whole new industries in manufacturing, entertainment, education, telecomputing, and defense appeared. And although all were hungry for capital, not one was able to offer the collateral demanded by traditional lenders.

Drexel and Milken accepted the challenge to provide needed venture capital. The company's big opportunity came when William McGowan, leader of MCI's phone fiber network, needed $3 billion. When he turned to traditional lenders they blanched. But he found the answer in high-yield, high-risk junk bonds pioneered by Drexel, to whom he paid tribute: Drexel "is a big reason why America has produced so many new business pioneers in the last decade and why America has produced so many new industries—cellular phones, cable television, the personal computer and our own field of phone service.... It could not have happened without the opening of the nation's capital markets to emerging companies."[15] Drexel made the difference.

Toward the end of the 1980s the firm's stunning successes came to a grinding halt. Drexel and a group of its officers and employees failed to report as much as $850 million of taxable income in 1987. The tax burden arose because of the way Drexel and some of its insiders structured a 22.5 percent stake in the leveraged buyout of Beatrice Company. Drexel's problem originated with Kohlberg Kravis Roberts' April 1986 leveraged buyout of Beatrice. At the time, the $8.2 billion LBO—with Drexel serving as key underwriter for most of the relevant financing—was the biggest and potentially most lucrative LBO ever. KKR staffers had boasted during the summer of 1987 that breaking up Beatrice and selling off its assets would produce a stupendous $3.8 billion in profits, roughly nine times the $417 million in equity that KKR and its associates had invested in BCI Holdings, the company that took Beatrice private.

Drexel's significant ownership stake in BCI Holdings, however, was kept secret for more than a year. An elaborate prospectus was filed in April 1986 for the public offering of 99,000 limited partnership interests in BCI Equity Associates, which had been established to acquire the warrants. Although that document stated that Drexel Burnham proposed to offer the limited partnership interests directly to the public, subsequent filings made it clear that these limited partnership interests were not really offered to the public. However, the IRS had earlier established its Gregory doctrine, which held that when the form of a transaction was intended to camouflage its true substance, the IRS would proceed on the basis of the substance. In upholding the Gregory doctrine, the Supreme Court had said that to rule otherwise would exalt artifice above reality. Drexel's troubles had multiplied so rapidly that Standard & Poor downgraded Drexel's commercial paper to a speculative grade. The Big Daddy of junk bonds suddenly looked like a weeping adolescent. When cries for help to big commercial banks and to the SEC elicited no response, Drexel, on February 14, 1990, declared itself bankrupt. The inevitable result was fear among the 12 to 15 companies that had committed to issue $4 billion in junk bonds and now had no investment banker to sell them.

The early verdict on Drexel was a concatenation of contradictions. "Drexel got what it deserved for its greed and for its mismanagement," opined *Fortune* magazine on March 12, 1990.[16] On the other hand, *The Wall Street Journal* blamed the firm's collapse chiefly on government errancies (S&Ls were abruptly forbidden to buy junk bonds even though those that did so had better results than those investing in real estate), and on the Justice Department's "extortion" under RICO of a half billion dollars in an out-of-court settlement.[17] The respective positions of both the castigators and the defenders have an element of truth.

To the critics, Drexel's behavior at the end of the story was symbolic of its erratic behavior. Frederick Joseph, Drexel's head, was so unprepared for the firm's demise that he hired bankruptcy lawyers only three days before the news became official. Joseph's eyes had been glued on the raucous conflict among his senior aides over who would get the biggest bonus. Peace was bought by Joseph's giving $15 million to his merger chief and $11 million to his new junk-bond chieftain—even though the firm had lost money for over a year. Bonuses totalling $260 million were offered the other top officials, despite the fact that other Drexel employees thought the bonuses were unwarranted. Money lust had induced management lunacy.[18]

For its part, the *Journal* editors stuck to their position that Drexel and other junk bond issuers had assisted many budding companies, had created jobs four times faster than the economy as a whole, and by so doing helped fuel economic prosperity. Moreover, no one ever claimed that no defaults would ever occur or ever denied that junk bonds were riskier than investment-grade bonds. However, it is pure myth that there is no risk in bonds approved by the sages of the rating agencies. An investment-grade rating, for example, did not stop the spectacular $2.25 billion default by "Whoops," the Washington Public Power Supply System.[19] Risk always exists; the bottom line is whether it is correctly priced.

Before Drexel's collapse, the firm's own archangel, Michael Milken, had already been ensnared in a web of conspiracy. Milken had originated and orchestrated the company's high-yield junk department in ways that drove the country's largest arbitrageurs to take illegal stock positions, to hide from the investing public the plans and activities of corporate raiders, to help his Drexel colleague David Solomon to evade income taxes by creating losses for him, to conspire with Ivan Boesky to hide the identities of the real owners of securities held in Boesky's name, and to cheat Drexel clients by reporting lower prices at which their securities had been sold. Milken's department pocketed the difference. In one year alone he pocketed $550 million.

Faced with allegations of 98 crimes and with mounting evidence that many of the government charges would hold up in court, Milken agreed on April 24, 1990, to pay the government $200 million in fines for its investigative costs and to repay $400 million to his cheated clients. In his statement to the court, Milken said: "I transgressed certain of the laws and regulations that govern our industry. I was wrong in doing so and knew that at the time, and I am pleading guilty to these offenses."[20] But the government was not satisfied with Milken's confession and persuaded the sentencing judge to impose a ten-year prison sentence. The sentence still provokes debate. Dean Henry Manne of the George Mason University Law School held that the government's use of RICO (under which Milken's assets could be put in escrow even before guilt was established) was a legal travesty about which the vocal guardians of civil liberties had been surprisingly silent.

*The advance leaks to the press about the new complaint against Mr. Milken were only the latest in a long and dishonorable series of deplorable government tactics. The SEC and the Justice Department have long known the source of these leaks and have condoned or even authorized many of them. The government's questionable behavior has even included advance disclosure of the SEC's "Wells request," a procedure expressly designed to let defendants rebut charges before they become public.*[21]

Manne said that the government's purpose was to persuade the public of the defendant's guilt before one iota of evidence had been presented in a court of law; defendants faced with such coercive tactics often find it prudent to agree to a settlement or guilty plea they would not otherwise make. Manne concluded: "This may seem to be just a legal cat-and-mouse game to cynics, but it is really a totalitarian tactic that should not be tolerated in a society dedicated to the rule of law." Implicit in Manne's views was the warning voiced in 1940 by Robert Jackson when he was attorney general of the United States:

*Prosecutors have more control over life, liberty and reputation than any other person in America. . . . If the prosecutor is obliged to choose his case, it follows that he can choose his defendants. Therein is the most dangerous power of the prosecutor: that he will pick people that he thinks he should get, rather than cases that need to be prosecuted. With the law books filled with a great assortment of crimes, a prosecutor stands a fair chance of finding at least a technical violation of some act on the part of almost anyone. In such a case, it is not a question of discovering the commission of a crime and then looking for the man who has committed it, it is a question of picking the man and then searching the law books, or putting investigators to work, to pin some offense on him. It is in this realm that the greatest danger of abuse prosecuting power lies. . . .*[22]

If the government hurt Milken even as Milken hurt himself, the question of his contributions to the country's welfare remain. Palomba Weingarten, the head of the Pilgrim Group of Mutual Funds, whose parent company was a client of Drexel, wrote in *The Wall Street Journal* on May 2, 1990: "Mr. Milken will be remembered as a man who created a revolution that allowed small and medium-sized companies to finance their growth. He was forced to plea bargain because otherwise he would have been blamed for things that had nothing to do with him, including Drexel's going out of business and people losing their jobs."[23]

For every voice of support, there was a counter voice. In the same *Journal* issue,[24] Rabbi Arnold Jacob Wolf of Chicago said Milken "should be hung by his thumbs for years and years and years," a view expanded by a fellow Chicagoan, novelist Studs Terkel, who used the case to indict American society as a whole: "Milken is reflective of our society at this time. But he probably won't be criticized in the history books [because] people have lost their sense of outrage." A people not outraged by egregious behavior is a people who have lost their moral moorings. This pair's assessment puts into stark relief two questions.

## Ethical Questions

- Do Milken's contributions to this country's economic growth outweigh his moral lapses so that no prison sentence (or at most a very minor one) should have been imposed?
- Did the federal prosecutors behave ethically?

## Negotiating Patterns

Another development worth noting was the chicken-or-egg quality of questions about the dealing-wheeling techniques of the 1980s. Had the number and size of mergers changed the way negotiations were handled—or did changed bargaining styles escalate the number and size of mergers? One way to appreciate the shifts between 1975 and 1985 is to follow a story told by a prominent New York lawyer named James C. Freund. In Freund's account, negotiations a decade ago were handled in lengthy discussions carried out in a gentlemanly way.

> There was a one-step merger transaction that, after approval by the seller's board and a majority of its stockholders, bound all stockholders. There were, of course, hostile takeovers in which the raider made a tender offer that, if successful, resulted in the purchaser's obtaining enough shares to gain control of the board and eventually to merge the target into the raider's subsidiary. But that world of friendly mergers and hostile takeovers was far removed from the 1980s phenomena. What was once considered crude and vulgar had become so respectable by 1985 that techniques perfected for corporate warfare were now applied to peaceful encounters and the gentility that formerly characterized much of the American business community is in relative tatters today.[25]

Even in all-cash arrangements (which are far simpler than stock and hybrid deals) six steps are regularly followed—and in each lurks potential for an ethical misstep as different ground rules are applied. The new rough-and-tumble rules are these:

1. Accept nothing but a binding agreement before any public announcement is made.
2. Put teeth in the agreement through a no-shopping clause that requires the seller not to solicit, cooperate with, or print confidential information to a competing bidder—plus substantial "bust-up" fees should the deal be topped or otherwise sidetracked. This differs from pre-1975 practices when a public announcement went out immediately after a meeting of the minds.
3. Insist on a lock-up deal, in which the purchaser seeks immediate control over large amounts of the seller's stock by offering a price well above the stock's prevailing market price—and at the same level as the total merger price will be. In return, the seller agrees to vote in favor of the one merger and no other. A prime example occurred in 1985 when a New York corporation named SCM was under siege by Hanson, a British company, which opened its negotiations with a $60-per-share cash tender offer in August. SCM's directors then solicited white-knight support from Merrill Lynch, which demanded a lock-up right to purchase two of SCM's most profitable business lines if another bidder blocked the merger. In short, SCM would be stripped of its most valuable assets.[26] A decade ago, dealing with stock on such a piecemeal basis was as rare as were pledges not to take other steps on behalf of the stockholders' interest. Comparative shopping has diminished in the current culture.
4. Demand a "crown jewel," which guarantees to the buyer the right to acquire a particularly successful part of the seller's business if some outside party successfully outbids the first negotiator. The crown-jewel technique has, of course, a chilling effect on other interested buyers because it means that the seller has already given away one of his diamonds.
5. Make an immediate cash tender offer for some or all of the shares of the seller at the merger price level. This action saves paperwork and avoids the seller's calling special meetings to secure stockholder approval. Purchasers making tender offers on one day can begin actually purchasing shares ten business days later, and in 20 business days will probably own a majority of the seller's stock, either obviating the owners' vote on the final deal or making it a mere formality. The effect is to muffle the stockholder voice.
6. Pay attention to the need for speed, which puts enormous pressure on all of the negotiators, with certain residual side effects. The due diligence of yore is attenuated, and understanding the target's financial health comes more from possibly suspect public filings than through investigation.

CHAPTER FIVE   Ethics of Size: Mergers and Takeovers   151

Congress tried to protect stockholders in 1985 through the Hart-Scott-Rodino law, which requires that big deals cannot be closed before the Justice Department and Federal Trade Commission have had opportunities to investigate their antitrust implications. In addition, the SEC moved in the summer of 1985 to force more disclosure about merger talks—a decision, incidentally, criticized by some corporate lawyers and investment bankers because of its potentially chilling effect on merger discussions and praised by others for the protection it gives to the average stockholder.[27] Disclosure raises one of the more important ethical questions, namely, the obligation of the negotiating parties toward others of the investment community.

When news of merger or takeover strategies become public, the market volatility of stock prices usually intensifies. And in the volatile stages millions can be made by those who know something others do not. The truth issue erupted in 1978 when irate stockholders of Basic, Inc., a specialized chemical company, accused management of claiming that it was not holding merger negotiations with Gebas, a subsidiary of Combustion Engineering. The plaintiffs asked damages on grounds that they sold their shares for less than the true value because they relied on Basic's statements that it was having no talks. In times past, such denials did not violate the law.

Attempting to rectify the situation the court applied a major principle for fair competition (the ethic of the level playing field) to a terrain of hills and valleys. In *Basic Inc. v. Levinson* (1988) the Supreme Court ruled that misleading statements or veils of secrecy were not acceptable.[28] Of the two, the second was more unpalatable to the business taste because it was so often difficult in secret negotiations for the negotiators to know when prospects for the merger were bright enough to warrant disclosure.

Executives themselves have turned more and more to the leveraged buyout techniques of raiders with their own management buyouts (MBO). One example was the Fred Myers Company, a respected Oregon food retailer and general merchandiser whose annual sales were close to $1 billion in fiscal 1982. Shares were trading around $28.81, a little over eight times actual earnings, and when an MBO was completed shareholders received $55 per share, or two times book value. But the process was interesting in its total results. Senior executives who had been with Myers since 1976, and the top two who had been with the company since 1947, did not invest any meaningful amount in the purchase but they received over $5 million in cash or stock options. Moreover, Myers also agreed to provide senior management with another $2.5 million ten-year, interest-free loan to help meet the group's additional tax liabilities, plus a supplemental cash payment plan that added another $3.5 million over the ten-year payout period.

Obviously, the managers had reason to smile. But the buyout did not bring the expected efficiencies. Instead, profit margins remained about constant; worker morale was shaken; interest expense grew from $1 million in 1981 to $29 million in 1983; during the new Myers' first full year operating expenses rose 155 percent. By the end of 1983 the company had accumulated $13 million of net operating losses and its $2 million of unused investment tax credits would keep it in a net loss position for tax purposes for an indeterminate period of time. The long and short of it was that Myers was no more successful before the buyout than after it. What really happened was that managers had taken very good care of their own interests.

## Ethical Question

- Were the managers' actions immoral in a business system predicated on self-interest?

## Defensive Tactics

**Pensions.** The staid old Wall Street investment firms have been changed by the rules introduced by Drexel and its *Wunderkind* Michael Milken. The old order called for careful judicial monitoring to make sure no laws were being breached. To thwart aggressors today, increasing numbers of companies seek to use their pension funds. Between 1980 and 1985, over 400 firms actually terminated their pension plans, recapturing almost $5 billion. Taking pension-fund surpluses and using them for other purposes often makes the company less attractive to a potential raider because the existence of large amounts of excess pension cash can alone be a reason to buy.

## Ethical Question

- Is this strategy morally neutral, morally permissible, or morally objectionable?

The U.S. Chamber of Commerce argued that such strategies as using pension fund surpluses are completely moral because (a) the excess is company property and (b) companies taking the risks are entitled to reap investment benefits. Bad investments do not excuse companies from obligations to pay specific retirement benefits. Labor, of course, does not share the Chamber's view. Burke Seidman of the AFL/CIO strongly criticized the strategy, arguing that workers generally lose pension benefits when terminations occur. Senator Howard Metzenbaum called the United Airlines termination of its pension program an "outrageous rip-off."[29] From a moral perspective it initially appears that the Chamber of Commerce argument possessed the greater logic: Companies own the excess, do take the investment risks, and when investments go sour, still must meet their fiduciary obligations. However, the argument is based exclusively on the idea of commutative (exchange) justice; missing from it is the idea of distributive justice, which rests on a concept of sharing.

**Poison pills.** Poison pills, which come in a wide variety, have also stimulated court action. As noted, *the basic strategy of poison pills involves a company's giving its stockholders the right to buy shares at a special price or get other benefits when a hostile bidder tries to take over the company.*

This makes takeover prohibitively expensive for the would-be acquirer. Poison pills raise the cost of acquisition of the company, increase the directors' bargaining power against the raider, create uncertainties, raise the cost of negotiations, and deter partial bids and market accumulations by providing benefits to stockholders other than the aggressors. The ultimate goal is to transfer bargaining power from the aggressor to the target company. In late 1985, for example, Cluett Peabody (CP), known for its Arrow shirts and Gold Toe socks, sought to ward off separate bids by Californian Paul Bilzerian and by Texan Craig Hall. The former, after acquiring control of 26.4 percent of CP's 8.4 million shares, offered $40 for each of the remaining shares. When Cluett Peabody responded with an offer of $45 a share, observers shivered over what the offer would do to the company's debt burden.[30]

A second example is Household International, an Illinois conglomerate incorporated in Delaware, which developed a plan whereby a poison pill would automatically activate during any hostile takeover. Because the pill would cost nearly $6 billion, Joseph Moran, a former Household director, went to court to protest the action of his former colleagues in what was considered the most important corporate law case of 1984. It involved the business judgment rule: how far could a board go with defense measures that might adversely affect stockholder rights?

When the Delaware Supreme Court ruled that the business judgment rule protected the directors in such cases, former DuPont chairman Irving Shapiro, who represented Moran, said that the decision was "incomprehensible." It was in reality an invitation to other companies to rush toward so many poison-pill techniques that corporate lawyers would have their greatest bonanza in history.[31] Shapiro's dismay was short-lived because, little more than a month later, the second U.S. Court of Appeals held in January 1986 that a bargain sale of assets approved by the directors of the SCM Corporation to fight a hostile takeover in 1985 was *not* a reasonable exercise of the business judgment rule. Because of the enormous implications for corporate governance, for the business judgment rule, and even for the corporate social responsibility doctrine, it is important to trace the main outlines of recent judicial reasoning on the hallowed meaning of the business judgment principle.

The key players were Hanson Trust and SCM Acquisition in the first case and Revlon pitted against MacAndres & Forbes Holdings Company in the second. The second U.S. Circuit Court of Appeals (applying New York law) and the Delaware Supreme Court invalidated the use of asset "lock up" options by target companies fighting hostile takeover bids. Both courts seemed to say that the business judgment rule does not apply when defensive tactics usurp the right of stockholders to determine the corporation's ultimate destiny. Directors bear the burden of proving the reasonableness of the defensive measure and the fairness of the result to the stockholders.

The Hanson case grew out of a battle for control of SCM Corporation waged between Hanson Trust and SCM Acquisition Inc., the acquisition vehicle formed by members of SCM's management and Merrill Lynch.[32] Hanson started the bidding for SCM with an all-cash tender offer for all shares at $60 per share. Then there ensued a series of moves and countermoves until the SCM board finally approved a deal. But did company directors act prudently? The court summarized the critical board meeting as follows:

> *The SCM directors, in a three-hour late-night meeting, apparently contented themselves with their financial advisor's conclusory opinion that the option prices were within the range of fair value although had the directors inquired, they would have learned that Goldman Sachs had not calculated a range of fairness.*
>
> *There was not even a written opinion from Goldman Sachs as to the value of the two optioned businesses.... Moreover, the Board never asked what the top value was or why two businesses that generated most of SCM's income were being sold for one-third of the total purchase price of the company under the second LBO merger agreement, or what the company would look like if the options were exercised.... There was little or no discussion of how likely it was that the option "trigger" would be pulled, or who would make that decision—Merrill, the board, or management.*[33]

The court, in rejecting the directors' argument that they had properly relied on legal and investment banking advice, stated that directors had some oversight obligations to become reasonably familiar with an opinion, report, or other source of advice before they were entitled to rely on it. The court was particularly critical of the board's reliance on the oral opinion of Goldman Sachs as to the purported fairness of the option price.

If the court had ended its discussion of the duty of care at this point, the Hanson case would represent simply the New York analog of Delaware's *Smith v. Van Gorkom*. The greater significance of the Hanson decision lies in the court's two additional thoughts—management's self-interest in the proposed LBO and the board's usurpation of shareholder rights—that were not traditionally included in the "duty of care." The concurring opinion by Judge James L. Oakes highlighted the point:

> *The directors' duty of care is, if anything, heightened when the favored buyer obtaining the lock-up is a consortium including within it the management who will have a substantial participation in the future equity of the potential buyer and whose interests, by virtue of that participation, at that stage, are to favor the buyout at the lowest price. Management interests are then in direct conflict with those of the shareholders of the target corporation.*[34]

Facts in *Revlon Inc. v. MacAndres & Forbes Holdings Inc.* closely parallel those in the Hanson case. Here the Delaware court reemphasized the concern it expressed in the 1985 *Unical Corporation v. Mesa Petroleum Company* that, when the board adopts antitakeover tactics, there is the omnipresent specter that a board may be acting primarily in its own interests, rather than those of the corporation and its shareholders. After approving the board's initial defenses (the issuance of the poison pill, thereafter redeemed, and the exchange offer), the court turned to the lock-up option. It concluded that, upon Revlon board's authorization of merger negotiations, the board's duty changed from the preservation of Revlon as a corporate entity to the maximization of the company's value at a sale for the stockholders' benefit. In other words, the directors had changed from defenders to auctioneers whose duty it was to get the best price for stockholders. They should not, therefore, act in ways to block out other bidders.[35] For directors and for executives, clear inferences flow from the decision: lock-up options are limited, total reliance on financial and legal advisers is dangerous, and the anything-goes ethic is unacceptable.

**Pac-men.** An especially intriguing problem arises when an adage (minnows can swallow whales) is involved. To prevent such outcomes larger firms are using a Double Pac-man defense when pursued by smaller firms. In the Double Pac-man the pursued firms turn on the pursuing firm, putting it on the defensive. This strategy was used in the Bendix and Marietta case, as well as the Cities Services and Mesa Petroleum affair. In these two instances the concerned parties attempted to acquire 51 percent of each others' stock. Often the Double Pac-man defense leaves both firms vulnerable to white or grey knights. This defense, available to the giant Gulf Oil Corporation in its fight with the much smaller Mesa Corporation, was not used. There is, finally, the scorched-earth policy as another form of counterattack. Under the scorched-earth policy the defending firm retaliates by making itself a lesser prize by selling off its most valuable possessions: asset stripping becomes the torch.

## Economic and Ethical Assessments
### *Economic Gains and Losses*

Friendly mergers and hostile takeovers are cousins that must be judged on their separate merits. Because each is part of the general family of consolidations, however, initial comments address both equally. From economic perspectives, merger activities fall into three broad categories: (1) those that are justified because the whole, measured in value, is larger than the sum of the parts; (2) those of neutral value; and (3) those that are purely speculative in that the aggregate has actually diminished in true value.

Falling somewhere within the first two are a company's use of profits. Six ways are open to each firm: reinvest in its own business, distribute the profit to shareholders in the form of higher dividends, start new enterprises, invest the money in securities, share the profits with the employees, or acquire new firms. The first five options are sometimes incapable of consuming profits when firms find themselves in the position that reinvesting in their own businesses will not promote growth. Consider Coca-Cola's position in the saturated cola market. When Coke waged war on Pepsi with a large advertising budget, Pepsi matched Coke's promotional campaigns. The results were negative because both companies spent more money to keep their respective market share of an already saturated market. Eventually, Coca-Cola changed its strategy and decided to use its excess profits to buy Minute Maid, wine companies, and Columbia Pictures. But there are times when increased market shares can come more quickly through acquisitions than through investing internally—as when Procter & Gamble purchased Richardson-Vicks for $1.2 billion to get Nyquil and Oil of Olay.

Contrasting the gains and losses recorded in the economic story often leads to inconclusive results. For affirmative positions toward takeovers, five claims are made: (1) mergers can work, (2) the federal government approves, (3) global competition requires efficiencies of scale, (4) stockholders gain, and (5) management is made more accountable. Instead of overheated critical rhetoric, Americans should remember how good mergers and takeovers have been for the United States. For one thing, they force managers to slash bloated bureaucracies and thus improve efficiency. Economist Michael Jensen made this point when he wrote that takeovers "provide unique, powerful, and impersonal mechanisms to accomplish the major restructuring and the redeployment of assets continually required by changes in technology and consumer preferences."[36] In addition, takeovers force managements to do the following:

1. Cut employee overloads.
2. Open the investment market to small investors through so-called junk bonds.
3. Provide tax savings. (Interest payments are tax deductible and dividends are not.)
4. Use debt to increase wealth. (U.S. corporations are still only half as leveraged as their major foreign competitors.)
5. Put surplus capital to immediate use.[37]

Critics are not mollified by the foregoing arguments and find holes in every strand of the pro-merger/takeover thesis. Rejecting the "mergers work" hypothesis, they point out that conglomerates of the 1970s (like Gulf-Western and International Telephone & Telegraph) divested themselves in the mid-1980s simply because they found gargantuan size and the "mix" unmanageable.[38] There are other disadvantages. When it is alleged that stockholders usually profit, two points must be noted. First, it is necessary to know which class of stockholder walks off with the juiciest plums. Most large corporations have three different sets of shareholders: (1) the arbitrageurs, whose full attention is given to short-term gains through exploitation of slight changes in a stock's value; (2) institutional holders interested in immediate profits, who collectively own 50 percent of American industry and whose proportion of activity on the New York Stock Exchange represents 65 percent of the public share volume value; and (3) long-term stockholders, often many past and present employees, who are less sophisticated

CHAPTER FIVE  Ethics of Size: Mergers and Takeovers    157

than the other two sets of owners. These nonsophisticates are constantly bombarded by complicated notices loaded with complex legal jargon that is absolute gobbledygook. Meanwhile, sophisticated institutional investors can have a field day.[39]

The basic question then is how directors and mangers can act in the best interests of all investors when the classes of stockholders may have different interests.[40] Conveniently omitted by defenders of the merger and takeover movement is that, in noting stockholder gains, they concentrate only on the acquired firm and ignore growing evidence that shareholders of the aggressor are no better off than before the union took place.

The bondholders' position during mergers and takeovers can be clarified by a few simple but not widely discussed facts. In the traditional view, bondholders are creditors and stockholders are owners. Contract law is for the bondholder and corporate law is for stockholders. Indenture protects the bondholder and directors protect the stockholder. But these tidy and traditional concepts no longer apply. When major industrial corporations need money, few seek private loans from banks or insurance companies; rather, they depend on the public capital markets—commercial paper for short-term and bonds for long-term needs.

Relying on large amounts of debts, especially junk bonds, to secure cash for takeover battles meant that the targeted company, to ward off the threat, also began to substitute debt for equity—and with little attention to its impact on existing bondholders. The consequences, however, are significant: old bondholders are forced to provide a partial subsidy for the handsome premiums paid to new stockholders. In all cases bondholders are big losers.[41] Recent studies have found losses ranging from 3 to 5 percent in market values one year after the acquisition, and as much as 28 percent within five years, relative to comparable companies on the New York Stock Exchange. Bondholder losses are stockholder gains. Economists call it the bondholder rip-off. Compounding the problem is the fact that in leveraged buyouts, company obligations can instantly turn from gems to junk. In 1985 Standard & Poor lowered a record 272 corporate ratings, topping the previous peak of 246 downgrades set in the recession year of 1982, and the number of 1990 downgrades was higher than the 1985 figure.

In a basic sense, the issue is one of justice: Should stockholders be allowed to transfer wealth from bondholders to themselves, especially when stockholders show little inclination to stay with the corporation in which they have fractional ownership? Because stockholders move in and out of the corporation without any feeling of loyalty, what is the rationale for blurring differences between investors? Those why buy stock and those who lend money have the same motivation, namely, to make money on a capital investment.[42] If contract law is failing to protect bondholders, the likely next step is to include bondholders among the fiduciary obligations of directors and managers. The courts are moving in this direction. In the largest corporate reorganization in American history—the breakup of American Telephone & Telegraph—the courts held that management had a fiduciary duty to protect all those with interests in these companies, including creditors.

Emerging is a duty of loyalty, possibly even more than the duty of care, which says that an agent who acts in a transaction involving two principals must be fair to each. Therefore, if managers take actions that inevitably cause stock prices to rise and bond prices to fall, they have violated their duty of loyalty. This new bondholder-protection principle replaces the old caveat emptor ethic of the common law. The courts, invoking at least four legal theories to protect the bondholders, were seeking to raise the moral standards of executives and directors: breach of fiduciary duty (corporate law), breach of an implied covenant of good faith and fair dealing (contract law), fraud (tort law), and unjust enrichment (equity).

Examples of the trend include decisions on the Rockwell Corporation, which failed to give adequate notice to bondholders of a redemption call and, as a result, many bondholders failed to convert into stocks, which had a market value greater than the redemption price of the bonds. The corporation was held liable.[43] In a 1983 case involving the Baltimore & Ohio Railroad the Third Circuit Court held the corporation liable because it failed to give notices of a spin-off of shares of a subsidiary.[44]

Quite obviously, greater responsibilities fall on directors when their fiduciary duties are spread to cover bondholders: if stockholders are not usually expected to protect themselves, neither should bondholders be required to erect their own defenses. The working premise is easy to state: "The exclusive focus of corporate law and stockholders is too narrow for modern corporate finance. Bondholders and stockholders are all security holders in the enterprise and equally deserving of board protection."[45] At this point, law and ethics join forces. In the future, directors and managers have three choices: maximize stockholders wealth, maximize bondholder wealth, or maximize combined stockholder-bondholder wealth; however, only the third is a legitimate choice because the manager's duty is to make the firm richer, not to take one investor's property and hand it over to another.

To summarize, critics claim that hostile takeovers do the following:

1. Divert management from its primary goal, which is to increase the long-term profitability of the company.
2. Provide short-term benefits to stockholders of the acquired firm and little benefit to owners of the acquiring firm.
3. Saddle the merged companies with enormous debt.
4. Drive corporate America to a mind-boggling debt of approximately $50 billion. (Before the 1980 decade ended, nonfinancial companies had debts of $1.8 billion.)
5. Raise the specter of increased bankruptcies.

Finally, there is the untold drama of suffering by workers and their hometowns.[46] Although blue-collar workers (as in the steel industry) consistently lost ground over a decade, there was, at least, some time for adjustments. The results of mergers and takeovers, on the other hand, are swift and brutal. In a classic case, Pittsburgh suddenly lost the purchasing and taxing power of an estimated $75 million as 1,400 Gulf employees in Pittsburgh were dismissed or transferred to Chevron's San Francisco headquarters within weeks, and Gulf's art-deco landmark in downtown Pittsburgh was sold to a New York real estate firm. A second example is the takeover of Gardner-Denver Company by Cooper Industries. The local headquarters was shut down unceremoniously, benefits shrank, and the work force was reduced. One executive observed that, when told his job was terminated, he went through mental and physical torment, trauma, ulcerous symptoms, and total loss of a grasp of reality. For those who had devoted their whole lives to a beneficent company that had suddenly become a monster was too much to bear.

## *The Ethical Ledger*

Before making moral judgments, we must understand the economic and financial climate of the 1980s, which defied the prayerful admonition "lead us not into temptation." The 1980s were times of temptation. When long postwar economic expansion had lulled many companies into a why-take-a-risk slumber, a few investors realized that an expanding economy made the debt-carrying capacities of companies relatively easy. Takeover specialists also realized earlier than most others that parts of many companies were so undervalued by the market that chunks often equaled the value of the whole. So they borrowed to buy, confident that the sale of parts of the acquired company meant quick reduction of the debt and retention of the financially "juiciest" sector of the acquired company. Helped by a weakened dollar, the big gamblers became the big buyers. Once having convinced bankers that they were right, the takeover cliques had easy sailing. Riding the new wave was glorious fun.

However, what was economic fun to some could be moral pain to many. Philosophers asked whether two basic assumptions of the takeover specialists were true: is the decision-making process adequate and rational? does the corporation act as a single person moving to promote its own self-interest? They also inquired whether key actors in takeovers wanted to promote stockholders' or managers' self-interest (ethical egoism), whether they weighed the impact of their decisions on workers and communities (utilitarian ethics), and, finally, whether corporations reflect contractual or covenantal relationships (deontological ethics).

Taking the last question as a point of departure, it should be recalled that contract obligations require directors to distinguish among different classes of stockholders—individual, institutional, and arbitrageur. People who move in and out without any concept of duty of care and loyalty to others are often at moral risk without even being aware of it. Contract law also requires management attention to labor relations in mergers, an issue given relatively little public attention. If, for instance, an aggressor acquires a unionized business, it incurs labor-related cost because change in ownership does not usually relieve the new owner of obligations under previous labor contracts.[47] From a moral standpoint the law's silence on the acquirer's duty to seek to preserve or find jobs for its predecessor's work force is disturbing—even though refusal to hire as a device to avoid a bargaining obligation violates the Wagner Act. Employees of the acquired company, of course, may complicate moral judgments by refusing to work for the new owner because they do not like the acquirer's terms of work or its reputation. Without endorsing situationalist ethics, the point is that ethical judgments must be informed by the full facts. The general rule takes on special meaning in complicated takeover cases.

The most critical factor in moral assessments of the fevered world of mergers and takeovers is the way that such judgments insinuate themselves into (1) the realm of justice, (2) the inner logic of the economic system, and (3) the national culture. So far as justice is concerned, all that needs to be noted is a market's dependence on trust. But today's mergers and takeover negotiations rely on relationships between minimally trusting people, leading one philosopher to ask: "What is a trust-tied community without justice but a group of mutual blackmailers and exploiters?"[48] The old robber barons were greedy, selfish, ruthless, but they built their fortunes by building things useful to the community—railroads, banks, and oil refineries. Some even had a social conscience. Marked differences are seen in today's crop of wheeler-dealers. Perhaps Robert Jacoby, former chairman of Sunrise Savings and Loan enterprise (which was declared insolvent on July 18, 1985), put it aptly: "I have a pretty wife, a Jaguar, a Mercedes, a beautiful home, a yacht. I want a Ferrari, a bigger house, and a bigger boat."[49] This code relies on two simple rules: (1) more is moral and (2) greed is good.

## *Newton's Law*

One of the most ingeniously argued defenses for hostile takeovers came from an individual who fundamentally had scant sympathy with them, Lisa Newton.[50] Her argument proceeds mainly along the propositions related to greed, fiduciary responsibility and need for investments.

- *Greed* (Proposition G): The maximizing principle of business rewards the greedy.
- *Fiduciary obligation* (Proposition F): A person hired by others to manage their assets has an obligation to do everything to ensure that the client becomes as rich as possible.
- *Investment pressure* (Proposition P): An enterprise expected to maximize wealth, at least over the long run, requires the investment of resources at the outset of the enterprise for the tools, buildings, lands, livestock, or other durable assets that will be employed to produce that profit.

In Newton's argument nothing can slow the hostile takeover machine because the raiders are simply responding to the G factor. In this respect they are like managers who think they own the company. The lethargic, but money-driven, stockholders play into the hands of management because they, too, are motivated by the G principle. Accountability, therefore, has to be brought back to corporate America. If defenders of the corporate status quo cannot do it, and the raiders will not do it, how will reform be achieved?[51] The answer is that if motivations cannot be changed, they must be controlled. As the nation's Founding Fathers recognized in 1787, human nature is fairly constant; the job is to create institutional mechanisms that keep certain human instincts from becoming dominant. Steps in this direction are reflected in recommendations that follow.

## Suggested Reforms

### *Internal Reform*

Suggestions for internal reform include an overhaul of corporate boards as well as the following specifics.

1. Encourage directors to become significant shareholders. One way to reach the objective is to pay directors in common stock and require such shares to be retained during the individuals' tenure on the board.
2. Limit the number of inside directors and make the chairman of the board a nonexecutive director.
3. Require potential directors to state publicly their views of what a trustee should do, so that stockholders could judge the director's qualifications and perspectives on corporate policy.
4. Create two classes of stock—one freely traded and carrying a dividend equal to the current dividend rate, and the other, registered directly in the name of the actual owners, paying dividends that increase over time at a rate higher than those of the first class. Shares of the second class could not be sold or transferred but could be converted fully into the regularly traded type of shares, with the proviso that dividend premiums would not carry over to the new owner.
5. Establish an ESOP plan that places approximately 20 percent of the firm's ownership in the hands of management and employees.[52]
6. Change the corporate charter to guarantee that:
    a. No one be permitted to vote more than 5 percent of the outstanding shares unless such concentration had been approved by a majority of the stockholders. Shares owned by the purchaser would obviously not be allowed to vote on this particular issue.
    b. Require companies to call a stockholder meeting promptly when merger talks reached a serious point to determine whether stockholders actually approve the merger.
    c. If the merger is approved, set controls over voting concentration.
    d. Voting concentration restrictions would also apply to third-party purchases of existing shares and to shares newly issued by the company.

e. The repurchase of voting securities by the company in excess of 5 percent of the outstanding voting power (greenmail) would be subject to stockholder approval.

## External Regulation

Changes in the law should be made to correct the imbalances that favor takeovers.[53] These changes might include the following:

1. Outlaw or limit front-end-loaded, two-tier offers.
2. Adopt the British practice of allowing active and informed debate about the merits of the proposal. The principle itself might require a precise timetable that included these checkpoints:
   a. A three-month merger review period begins after the formal announcement by the aggressive firm.
   b. Within 40 days, the acquiring firm must advance an economic and social justification for the proposed merger.
   c. Forty days later (80 into the merger review period) the target firm's management must submit a response to the acquiring firm's proposal.
   d. Also at 80 days opinions obtained from the SEC and the Justice Department on the antitrust and social implications of the proposed merger must be considered.
   e. One hundred days into the review period, the acquiring firm's management must submit responses to the target firm's responses and to the government's opinions.
   f. The merger review period ends with stockholders of both the acquiring and the target firms having the right to approve or disapprove.

## Summary

Although mergers are not a new phenomenon in American business history, the merger movement of the 1980s was marked by strategies so widely followed and by tactics so innovatively and energetically pushed that it deserves to be seen for what it was—a watershed in the nation's business drama. Greenmail, poison pills, and Pac-man became part of the business vocabulary. People like Levine, Boesky, and Milken became the topic of popular talk shows on television.

Debate still rages over the impact of the merger movement on the investing public. Equally spirited debate rages over the question of whether corporate raiders like Ichan and Pickens and investment bankers like Boesky and Milken were good for the business community. Suspended judgments on these questions tend to blur sound ethical judgments. Despite the fad, it seems clear that many were unnecessarily harmed by a few, that corporate

CHAPTER FIVE  Ethics of Size: Mergers and Takeovers   163

boards will be held to higher fiduciary standards (Hanson case), that stockholders will gain a larger share of decision making on merger questions, and that bondholders need—and will get—greater protection from corporate directors. In sum, the ill winds that blew with gale force during the 1980s are bringing some good to American business life.

## *Questions for Discussion*

1. Nobel Laureate economist Harry Markowitz, of Baruch College said that "the blanket condemnation of the 'greedies' of the 1980s is not just silly, but destructive," as reported in *The Wall Street Journal* (May 11, 1991).
Would blanket praise be equally silly and destructive?
2. Markowitz also said, "Crimes were committed during the 1980s. But I know of no study that shows that, per person with comparable opportunity, the financial industries of the 1980s had more lawbreakers than other industries or other times."
In your judgment is this a good ethical defense?
3. Is a takeover attempt ethical when the primary motive of the intruder is greenmail?
4. Would you be willing to work for men like Ivan Boesky and Michael Milken?
5. Do you agree that selling junk bonds is a respectable activity because the junk bond market provides a major source of capital for American businesses?

## Ethical Quandary

### *Secret Negotiations*

Company Able approaches Company Baker to suggest a merger. The CEO of Baker is very interested and says that, in his judgment, Baker's board would probably approve if the price is right. Baker's board is scheduled to meet a month later and, to avoid the confusion that calling a special meeting might cause, the CEO tells Able that the normal schedule will be observed but that he will call the board's executive committee to meet once a deal seemed likely. The first two weeks were devoted to intensive management discussions regarding a variety of technical matters. During the negotiating period the head of a local investment house called Baker to inquire if "anything special" was going on that could explain the convening of the executive committee. The CEO gulped. Did the inquirer know of a pending deal? Should he give an honest answer on the basis of strict confidentiality? Had

Able leaked the news? If so, for what reason? So the CEO put off the inquirer by saying he was meeting at that moment with his top people to deal with a variety of pressing matters.

After the phone call, the executive immediately contacted the company's lawyers to narrate the story and seek advice. One supported the CEO's delaying tactics by saying that premature disclosure could scuttle a deal that Baker wanted badly. The second lawyer did not disagree with his colleague but pointed out that a prominent New York acquisitions lawyer from the prestigious law firm of Sullivan and Cromwell, George C. Kern Jr., (who had represented Allied Stores during its unsuccessful effort to fight off a hostile takeover by Campeau Corporation) was in trouble with the SEC for not disclosing "material information" under the agency's tender-offer rules.[54]

## Question

- How should the CEO handle future inquiries regarding a potential merger?

## Notes

1. Mark Lange, "Artful Acquisitions: Who Profits?" *Wharton Alumni Magazine*, Spring 1986, 29–34.
2. Good background materials may be found in Michael Keenan and Lawrence J. White, eds., *Mergers and Acquisitions* (Lexington, Mass.: Lexington, 1982); and J. Fred Weston and Eugene F. Brigham, *Managerial Finance*, 7th ed. (Hinsdale, Ill.: Dryden Press, 1981).
3. Walter S. Morris, "Corporate Takeovers and Professional Investors," *Financial Analyst Journal* 39 (January–February 1983): 75–80.
4. Tim Carrington, *The Year They Sold Wall Street* (New York: Houghton Mifflin, 1986).
5. John Greenwald, "Let's Make a Deal." *Time*, December 23, 1985, 42–47.
6. The Bendix-Martin Marietta struggle was a classic example of confused and conflicting economic and ethical issues.
7. James C. Freund, *Anatomy of a Merger: Strategies and Techniques for Corporate Negotiations* (New York: Law School Press, 1975), 22–26.
8. Before being jailed Ivan Boesky had created tremors on Wall Street in the spring of 1986 when it was learned that this feared arbitrageur was expected to close deals that would provide him with a billion dollars in subordinated debt and equity to finance new forays in the takeover field. *The New York Times*, March 13, 1986, D-1.
9. Floyd Norris, "Not the Preferred Treatment," *Barron's*, June 17, 1985, 45.
10. Norman S. Poser, "The Law and Ichan's Tactics," *Investment Dealers Digest*, March 1, 1985, 14.
11. Quoted from Steven Brill, "The Roaring Eighties," *The American Lawyer*, May 1985, 11.
12. Ibid., 12.
13. Ibid., 18.
14. John Brooks, *The Takeover Game* (New York: E. P. Dutton, 1987). See also Connie Bruck, *The Predator's Ball: The Junk-Bond Raiders and the Man Who Staked Them* (New York: Simon Schuster, 1989).
15. Quoted by George Gilder, "The Drexel Era," *The Wall Street Journal*, February 16, 1990, A12. Economist Glenn Yago also made a spirited defense of Milken and the junk bond industry in his book, *Junk Bonds* (New York: Oxford University Press, 1991). A totally different view is given by James B. Stewart, *Den of Thieves* (New York: Simon and Schuster, 1991).

16. Brett Duval Fromson, "Did Drexel Get What It Deserved?" *Fortune*, March 12, 1990, 81–88.
17. Editorial, "Fall of the House of Drexel," *The Wall Street Journal*, March 19, 1990, A-18..
18. *The New York Times* deplored the bonus binge on its editorial page on Feb. 22, 1990, A-22.
19. Credit-rating agencies cracked down hard on over-leveraged companies holding WHOOP bonds. *The Wall Street Journal*, May 30, 1990, C-1.
20. Laurie P. Cohen, "Public Confession" *The Wall Street Journal*, April 25, 1990, A-1-6.
21. Henry Manne, "Due Process?" *The Wall Street Journal*, Feb. 13, 1990, A–20.
22. Excerpted from *The Wall Street Journal*, May 2, 1990, A–17.
23. L. Gordon Crovitz, "Milken's Tragedy: Oh How the Mighty Fall Before RICO," *The Wall Street Journal*, May 2, 1990, A–17.
24. Ibid.
25. James C. Freund, "Mergers and Acquisitions," *The National Law Journal*, November 11, 1985, 12–26.
26. The results of asset stripping can be devastating on stockholders. For a good overview, see Victor Brudrey, "Equal Treatment of Stockbrokers in Corporate Distributions and Reorganizations," *California Law Review* 71 (July 1983): 1072–1134.
27. Floyd Norris, "A Basic Truth: Supreme Court Rules Firms Shouldn't Lie," *The Wall Street Journal*, March 8, 1988, 1 and 50.
28. Basics v. Levinson, 56 U.S.L.W. 4232, 4341 (March 7, 1988).
29. *U.S. News and World Report*, July 29, 1985, 65.
30. "Cluett Rejects Offer," *Washington Post*, October 22, 1985, 1–B.
31. Martha Middleton, "Court Supports Poison Pill," *The National Law Journal*, December 2, 1985, 24.
32. Hanson Trust, P.L.C. v. SCM Acquisition Inc. 781 F.2d.264 2d Cir (1986).
33. Ibid. 276.
34. Ibid. 279. See the analysis by S. P. Lamb and A. J. Turezyn, "Revlon and Hanson Trust," *The Delaware Journal of Corporate Law* 12 (No 2, 1987): 497–525.
35. Based on the analysis by Dennis L. Block and Nancy E. Barton, "Board's Role in Hanson and Revlon," *The National Law Journal*, April 21, 1986, 19–23. See also Mark A. Stegemoeller, "Misapplication of the Business Judgment Rule in Contests for Corporate Control," *Northwestern University Law Review* (February 1982): 983–1004.
36. Michael Jensen, "Takeovers: Folklore and Science," *Harvard Business Review* (November–December 1984), 109–120. Supporting Jensen's view is the analysis by Kenneth Lehn, *The Economics of Leveraged Buyouts* (St. Louis: Washington University Center for the Study of American Business, 1987). See also the two articles in the *Journal of Management* 16 (1990): Virginia Blackburn, James Lang, and Keith Johnson, "Mergers and Shareholder Returns: The Roles of the Acquiring Firm's Ownership and Diversification Strategy," 769–782; and William B. Carper, "Corporate Acquisitions and Shareholder Wealth: A Review and Explanatory Analysis," 807–823. Louis Lowenstein combined his experiences as CEO, practicing attorney, and law professor to the analysis and contended that the merger movement, especially through MBOs, was not good for the country. "Lessons from Main Street to Wall Street," *Columbia Magazine*, October 1989, 27–30.
37. Murray Wiedenbaum and Stephen Vogt, *Takeovers and Stockholders: Winners and Losers* (St. Louis: Washington University Center for the Study of American Business, 1987). To round out the optimistic story, readers will find helpful the largely nontechnical essays by the following: Robert H. Hayes and David A. Garvin, "Managing As If Tomorrow Mattered," *Harvard Business Review* (May–June 1982): 70–79; Dennis E. Logue, "Counter Evidence on Management's Investment Myopia," *California Management Review* 28 (Fall 1985): 175–176; and Stephen A. Hochman, "Takeovers: Boon to the Economy," *The National Law Journal*, August 19, 1985, 15–26.
38. P. Dodd, "Merger Proposals, Management Discretion, and Stockholder Wealth," *Journal of Financial Economics* 8 (June 1980): 105–138.

39. *Fact Book* (New York: New York Stock Exchange, 1983), 54. Indeed, the portfolio turnover rate reached such a point that observers were disturbed by the stock market itself. For example, the *Forbes* 1984 honor roll showed that from 1974 to 1983 turnover rates were so high that no one could deny that institutional stockholders, motivated by short-term strategies, were doing well at the public's expense.
40. Warren A. Law, "Letter to the Editor," *Harvard Business Review* (January–February 1985): 172.
41. Stephen Prokesch, "Merger Waves: How Stocks and Bonds Fare," *The New York Times*, January 7, 1986, 1 and D4. For a good in-depth analysis, see Michael Bradley, "Interfirm Tender Offers and the Market for Corporate Control," *Journal of Business* 53 (October 1980): 345–376.
42. Here the decision is Pareto superior if it makes someone better off without making anyone worse off; it is Pareto optional if no one can be made better off without making someone worse off. When managers act to maximize the value of the firm, they are likely to achieve Pareto efficiency between bondholders and stockholders and to serve the interests of both groups better than if managers pursue any other objective.
43. Broad v. Rockwell International Corp. (1981).
44. Baltimore & Ohio Railroad v. Pittsburgh Terminal Corporation, 509 F. Supp. 1002 (1981).
45. Morey W. McDaniel, "Bondholders and Corporate Governance," *The Business Lawyer* 41 (February 1986): 456.
46. Roy Serpa, "The Often Overlooked Aspects of Mergers," *Journal of Business Ethics*, 7 (1988): 359–362.
47. Lee E. Miller and Ronald A. Lindsay, "Mergers and Acquisitions: Labor Relations and Employee Relations," *Employee Relations Law Journal* 9 (1983–84): 427–443.
48. Annette Baier, "Trust and Antitrust," *Ethics* 96 (January 1986): 253.
49. *The New York Times*, April 26, 1985, B2.
50. Lisa Newton, "Charting Shark Infested Waters," *Journal of Business Ethics* 7 (1988): 81–87. *The New York Times* showed remarkable objectivity (?) by noting that "*even* Republican leaders are disturbed by debt financed takeovers." *The New York Times,* November 1, 1988, sec. 3, 1.
51. James D. Richman, "Merger Decision Making: An Ethical Analysis and Recommendation," *California Management Review* 27 (Fall 1984): 177–184. In this brilliant essay, Richman could be faulted only for ignoring the deontological argument. Compare Richman's approach to the legal analysis provided by F. H. Easterbrook and D. R. Fischel, "The Proper Role of a Target's Management in Responding to a Tender Offer," *Harvard Law Review* 94 (April 1981): 1161–1204.
52. Joseph Fogg, "From the Boardroom," *Harvard Business Review* (November–December 1985): 30–40.
53. "Guidelines for Directors," *The Business Lawyer* 41 (November 1985): 208–221. For a brief overview, see Ira K. Millstein, "Takeover Reform Commission: Common Sense from the Common Law," *Harvard Business Review* (1986): 16–21.
54. *The Wall Street Journal*, June 7, 1988, 3.

CHAPTER 6

# Information Gathering: Clean or Dirty Tricks?

**Capsule History of Snooping**

**Sources and Kinds of Information**
National Espionage
Political Intelligence
Commercial Intelligence
Industrial Espionage

**Special Problems in Information Gathering**
Electronic Crooks
National Security
Globalization of Industrial Espionage
Business Costs of Security
*Export Controls*
*Security Consultants and Equipment*
*Freedom of Information*
Intellectual Property Rights

**Summary**
Questions for Discussion
Ethical Quandaries

*B*y their very interdependence, corporations need to know the capabilities of other business organizations. When the interdependence is characterized more by competition than by cooperation, the need-to-know intensifies. Finally, when innovation characterizes the competitive world, disaster is inevitable for anyone who falters. The net result of these factors is to put the "snooping machines" in high gear.

Nothing is intrinsically wrong with gathering information, but it becomes morally unacceptable when the procedures involve espionage directed toward acquiring trade secrets and technological breakthroughs, recruiting highly knowledgeable employees from a rival for the sole purpose of acquiring data not yet in the public domain, tapping of private phone conversations, and the like. In contemporary times, knowledge is a company's prime asset. Stealing this asset is simply wrong.

But is acquiring information always stealing? Are its methods always stealth? What are the responsibilities of the organization to protect its own secrets? When may employees who are privy to company secrets leave the organization with clear consciences? ■

*The purposes of this chapter are:*

1. To describe what information gathering is and the various ways used to carry it out.
2. To distinguish between information gathering by nations and information gathering by corporations.
3. To note the more vigorous prosecution of snoopers, including company sanctions.

## Capsule History of Snooping

Gathering information about people and things is part of human nature. When scientists seek to extract the secrets of nature and when historians seek to extract the secrets of diplomacy, the intelligence gathering instinct is at work. Operating at lower levels are the rumormongers who, in a somewhat paradoxical way, are criticized and cultivated. Leaking information in

Washington has become a high art and a low ethic. When big stakes are involved—a nation's security or a company's prosperity—the instinct to protect information from foes and garner it from competitors becomes irresistible.

The Chinese were so eager to preserve the secret of silk making that they prescribed death by torture for revealing it to outsiders. The Vatican Library's vast collection was open to only a few trusted investigators until Pope Leo XIII broke the tradition in 1895. What some zealously protected, others zealously pursued. Fire was stolen from one primitive tribe by another; silk and porcelain making were stolen from the Chinese by the French; the English in turn stole the secret from the French; and the English got their comeuppance when Germans stole the British secret for steel production.[1]

The military has always been acutely aware of the importance of intelligence. An illiterate genius named Genghis Khan led the Mongols to victory over armies three and four times their size because he managed to secure "foreknowledge."[2] Not until the late Renaissance did Europe match the Eastern world's sophisticated practice of intelligence gathering. Sir Francis Walsingham, who served as Queen Elizabeth's secretary of state, is generally credited with being the initiator of the most extensive and most successful political intelligence system in the European world. Later, Cardinal Richelieu in France and John Thurber, secretary of state for Cromwell, developed elaborate networks of secret agents to gather information.

In the commercial world, the German House of Fuggers amassed large fortunes in textile manufacturing (and later in silver, copper, and iron mining in central Europe), which it then used to develop its vast banking system. The Fuggers developed the first "manuscript newsletters," detailed reports of political and commercial information, which they used to disseminate private commercial information and on which they made their most important decisions. In a similar fashion, the Rothschild family used institutions in five major parts of Europe to gather information and to coordinate policy.

In the United States the first cotton yarn factory was built in the 18th century when Samuel Slater memorized the layout of an English factory in order to evade the British trade laws.[3] Francis Cabot Lowell, described as a shining light in early 19th century New England, a "visionary entrepreneur, and an adventurous risk taker, was a master of industrial intelligence."[4] And what Lowell copied, Lowell built. Two things are certain in today's world: (1) as the numbers of people involved in manufacturing or in transactions increase so, too, do the holes in the information sieve; and (2) intense new competitive pressures from all over the world are driving executives to exploit information to gain a competitive advantage.[5]

## Sources and Kinds of Information

Wide differences exist between legal and illegal forms of information gathering and between information and intelligence. Legal sources and ways to accumulate a fact book are varied. A salesperson can enter a competitor's

## CHAPTER SIX  Information Gathering: Clean or Dirty Tricks?    171

store to check prices and brands; promotional literature that comes unsolicited to company mailboxes can be studied; manufacturers can purchase a rival's product; important government reports are available (many of them free) to all and sundry; seminars and business conferences provide rich sources of material; full reports from company sales personnel are routinely requested; consultants and research firms can be hired; technical journals can be scoured. The list goes on.

So seemingly small a thing as counting the corrugated boxes purchased by a shipper or the number of trucks leaving a plant can give an observer a good idea of the volume of plant shipments. The people who do the firm's day-to-day work can often give information on how to find what the investigator is seeking. To illustrate, a bank teller could help a spy to determine the types of services the bank offers and the level of transactions it is completing. The teller may also have received information from customers who have shopped around or have been dissatisfied with competing services. A financial statement can be built by taking available public data and interpolating the rest of the figures through use of financial ratios, credit reports, and interviews. Even when the credit reports are incomplete, a combination of techniques can provide a reasonably accurate financial picture. An expert can use financial ratios to project an income statement by applying industry ratios from a matching company to a few specific figures on the known company. The figures can then be verified and modified through informational interviews.

Telephone directories and Yellow Pages can be used to number and identify competitors in regions where the firm operates. Data can also be derived on product line and market size, as well as on suppliers and distributors. Although the white pages are usually not as up-to-date as the Yellow Pages, they sometimes contain more geographic data on the company's location relative to competitors and suppliers. People working nearby in nonrelated businesses are often sources for valuable information. For instance, employees of a restaurant near the targeted company may be able to give a good estimate of its hiring or firing status because the restaurant employees have almost daily contact with the employees of the firm under surveillance.

Visual sightings (as mentioned in the corrugated-box example) can reveal estimates on production costs, shipment volume, and plant capacity. Aerial photographs of companies can show expansion or a shutdown. This type of information can then be used by the marketing department or senior management of the inquiring firm to predict industry trends or to prepare a promotional campaign. Other creative sources include snooping around at trade shows, scrutinizing buyers' guides, tracking want ads, analyzing environmental impact statements, and many others. One popular technique is to buy a few shares in a company in order to attend stockholder meetings and raise probing questions.

The information seeker, then, is like the detective or investigative reporter who seeks facts from as many sources as possible. The intelligence gatherer must often have something to offer, such as other information or money, for the information he or she is seeking. A trade-off, therefore, exists between information gained and time and money spent. Decisions on what information to seek—and how to use it—are part of the intelligence operation. For example, during World War II, before certain Japanese codes were broken, American counterintelligence would watch for any unusual change in radio communication patterns. If a sudden flurry of messages from Tokyo to some island outpost occurred, American intelligence would alert all regional commands to possible danger.

*Intelligence gathering is, therefore, an analytical process that transforms raw data into relevant, accurate, and usable strategic knowledge.* The information is about (1) a company's position, performance, capabilities, and intentions; (2) the driving forces within the market; (3) specific products and technology; and, finally, (4) economic, regulatory, political, and demographic influences.[6] What happens at the organizational stage is the transformation of disaggregate data into a composite picture that shows, quite accurately, the competitor's capabilities, goods, and performance. Respectable and moral ways therefore exist to gather information about rivals, but the line between the acceptable and the unacceptable is often blurred.

## *National Espionage*

National espionage and its subspecies, military espionage, have been particularly active ever since the 16th century, when the nation-state was coming into prominence. In the 20th century a fascinating exercise is to read government documents published after the outbreak of World War I. Lord Haldane, the British foreign minister, and Kiderlen von Waechter, his German counterpart, used their respective ambassadors as legitimate sources of information. Ambassadors were spies in high hats who, as intelligence gatherers, were greatly respected by their home governments. During the second World War Japanese codes were consistently broken by American counterintelligence and some code breakers received medals for their work. On the other hand, the victimized country experiences righteous anger when its vital information is revealed or stolen. Philby in England and Wolk in the United States are high on the lists of English and American traitors.

## *Political Intelligence*

Political intelligence is essential to a candidate's success in an electoral campaign. When a person announces intention to run for public office, the rival party launches a systematic effort to find out as much as possible about that individual's sexual preferences, drinking habits, credit rating, circle of friends, health records. The search is never undertaken for benign purposes. Occasionally party operatives, carried away by excessive zeal, go overboard; Watergate is a classic example. Sometimes government investigators use sting operations to entrap unsuspecting officials in ways that have legal and political implications. In 1990 Washington Mayor Marion Barry's drug experiences were exposed in an FBI sting.

## Commercial Intelligence

Commercial intelligence and its subspecies of technological, marketing, and financial intelligence gathering have increased dramatically during the past two decades as more companies have learned how cheap and effective they are. U.S. corporations known to collect intelligence on competitors include Ford Motor, Westinghouse Electric, General Electric, Emerson Electric, Pfizer, Motorola, Eastman Kodak, Rockwell International, Celanese, Union Carbide, and Gillette. Both Digital Equipment Corporation and Wang Laboratories have batteries of information analysts. Nor is snooping limited to companies that make highly sophisticated engineering hardware. Enterprises such as Chemical Bank, the Revlon Research Center, the specialty grocery products group of Del Monte, General Foods, Kraft, and J.C. Penney are all busy monitoring what competitors are doing.[7]

The legitimate sources of information are public government documents and reports, as well as information that can be found under the investigatory rights established by the Freedom of Information Act (85 percent of inquiries to the Food and Drug Administration come from other businesses), along with competitor's annual reports, consultants, the company's own sales personnel, private research organizations that sell data for profit, patent applications, employees who have left other companies, and the like. A good example of what now routinely occurs in commercial intelligence gathering is provided by the Washington Researchers firm founded by Stuart Feldstein, a former business journalist, and Mark Kamm, an erstwhile private investigator. The company tracks and digs information for business clients who are willing to pay as much as $60,000 for checks on a competitor. Some of Feldstein's clients included Citicorp, Bank of America, Prudential, and G.E. Credit. One client of SMR Research, the New Jersey-based concern of Feldstein and Kamm, wondered why Citicorp's Person-to-Person consumer loan operation was pricing its loans so low. Was it because the unit was trying to build market share or because its cost of funds was low? "That kind of information is imperative in order to compete with Citicorp subsidiaries, whose results are seldom discussed by Citicorp itself," Feldstein said.[8]

In addition, electronic data bases that store information to be retrievable by computer are proliferating. One, called Economic Information Systems and published by a subsidiary of Control Data Corporation, lists the names and locations of industrial facilities as well as calculations of each plant's dollar volume of output, work force, and the share of market that its production represents. Another data base, called Investext—published by Business Research Corporation of Brighton, Massachusetts—gives subscribers the full text of research reports on companies by security analysts and investment bankers. Some services even now monitor such data bases for specific clients. Selective dissemination of information, offered by data base distributors such as Dialog Information Services, provides subscribers with surveillance and periodic reports on competitors' performances.

## Industrial Espionage

Unlike legitimate information-accumulating processes, industrial espionage is the stealing of a competitor's secret, with secrets broadly defined as proprietary information or trade secrets. Proprietary information includes patents and copyrights, which are protected as property rights for a specific number of years. Trade secrets may be formulas, patterns, devices, or compilations of information used in a business that give owners an advantage over competitors who do not know of them. Because this description is necessarily vague, companies must define their own trade secrets rather specifically. If not so defined, the courts will not recognize trade-secret claims.[9]

The Restatement of Torts, which incorporated principles from the English common law on property, said that a trade secret simply cannot be comprehensively defined. For nonlawyers the question is this: does the company have something not generally known in the industry that gives it a competitive advantage? One distinction between a trade secret and a patent is disclosure. With the latter, disclosure is "safe" to the company because it has the right to exclude others from making, using, or selling the invention. Trade secrets, on the other hand, have no such protections and getting them invariably includes forms of industrial espionage.

Espionage is thievery. According to Jerry Woll, a reserve officer in military intelligence and a member of the American Society for Industrial Security, it is on the rise.[10] Executives from industrial security firms like Pinkerton, Burns and Wackenhut say that unwillingness to wash a company's dirty linen in public often causes unsuspecting managers to underestimate the extent of the industrial espionage threat. Herchell Britton, an executive vice president at Burns, stated that not only is industrial espionage a thriving, booming business, but it is also a highly organized one. It is itself "big business."[11] Costs for protection were estimated to rise from $5.7 billion in 1980 to $23.5 billion by 1995. Such expenses, compounded by the value of business and product losses attributed to trade-secret theft, raise the cost of industrial espionage in this country to billions of dollars a year—a cost that is ultimately passed on to consumers. It may be much larger because the generally accepted standards for accounting do not allow the balance sheet to employ a heading called "espionage expenses."

Industrial espionage can be accomplished through bribery, bugging, blackmail, and planting moles. The tactics are limited only by the operative's imagination. Sensitive information can leak from any part of a company—mailroom and boardroom. Common sources are sales personnel because of their many contacts with customers doing business with their competitors. In the high-tech fields especially, salespeople often pay customers to inquire about a competitor's latest design. This, of course, is a two-way street, because the salesperson is as often used as not. Salespeople are not the only ones caught with their guards down. One vice president who played tennis after work and later showered in the clubhouse had his conversations taped by a janitor who sold them to the vice president's competitors. Listings of "soiled sources" usually highlight the following practices.

CHAPTER SIX  Information Gathering: Clean or Dirty Tricks?   175

- Employment interviews with individuals who worked for a competitor during which the discussion touches on the competitor's know-how, manufacturing costs, and other proprietary information
- Camouflaged questioning and "drawing out" of competitors' employees at technical meetings
- Direct observation of a device or equipment (usually involving surreptitious photography)
- False job interviews with a competitor's employee when there is no intention to hire
- Breach of confidentiality in negotiations for a licensing agreement in which access to a trade secret is acquired
- Hiring a professional investigator to obtain a trade secret or using prostitutes to get information
- Hiring an employee away from a competitor to obtain specific know-how or other secret information
- Trespassing on a competitor's property in the course of a clandestine espionage operation
- Bribing a competitor's supplier or employee to obtain trade secrets
- Planting an agent on a competitor's payroll for the purpose of securing trade secrets
- Eavesdropping on competitors by wiretapping or bugging
- Theft of drawings, samples, documents, and similar confidential property
- Blackmail of key employees who have been deliberately compromised through sexual indiscretions
- Penetrating a competitor's computer system to scrutinize, manipulate, or extract secret, proprietary information
- Inducing customers to put out phoney bid requests

One of the preferred ways is to encourage key customers of a competitor to talk. In every industry companies show new products to certain important customers, who, "loyal" to a competitor, phone it as soon as the salesperson has left the office. For example, Gillette told a large Canadian customer the date on which it planned to begin selling its Good News disposable razor in the United States. The date was six months before Bic Corporation was scheduled to introduce its own disposable razor in America. When the Canadian distributor promptly called Bic and told it about the impending product launch, Bic mounted a crash program and was able to start selling its razor shortly after Gillette did.[12]

## Special Problems in Information Gathering

Compared to the late 20th century, the late 19th was a time of limited access to information sources and, in some respects, to limited numbers of people interested in the other person's business. The world is different today. A number of examples could be used to establish the point but the following are sufficient.

## *Electronic Crooks*[13]

Wiretapping has become an art. The three commonly used methods for tapping a telephone are inductive pickup devices, direct wire taps, and wireless radio taps. The most common is a wireless radio tap called a drop-in tap that can be purchased all over the world at relatively low prices. Although there are legitimate uses for these taps, retailers have no control over their final use. One interesting instrument is an infinity transmitter, which spies install on their telephones to hear conversations in other homes. After dialing a direct number, the transmitter deactivates the ringer and opens the microphone on the phone to which the snooper has dialed. Any conversation in the same room as the telephone can be heard through the telephone's microphone. The eavesdropper would not even be charged for the call because it bypasses the switchboard. Other people have used this device to reduce their long-distance phone bills. Former Federal Research Bank board employee Theodore Langevin, who took a job with E. F. Hutton in New York, illegally tapped into the Fed computer to obtain secret information in 1980 about the nation's money supply. He was caught, pleaded guilty to wire fraud, and was sentenced to one year's probation. This time the tap was on the wrist.

A leading source of information in the intelligence gathering drama is *Washington Post* writer Mary Thornton, who told two stories as illustrations of the problems introduced by electronics.[14] The first occurred on January 18, 1980, when a New York air traffic controller, angered by the Soviet invasion of Afghanistan a month earlier, momentarily took over an incoming Aeroflot jet carrying Soviet Ambassador Anatoliy F. Dobrynin. He transferred control to his computer, deleted a signal identifying the aircraft as a large jet, then returned control to the main console. Without the signal, the jet looked like a small private aircraft on other controllers' monitors. It landed safely, but only after flying through heavily traveled airspace without proper controls for 20 perilous minutes. The controller was fired but not prosecuted. In the summer of 1983 a second drama began when a group of young Milwaukee computer enthusiasts (nicknamed "the 414s" after their telephone area code) was raided by FBI agents after 414s had gained access to more than 60 computer data banks, including those at New York's Memorial Sloan-Kettering Cancer Center, the Los Alamos laboratory in New Mexico, and a California bank.

These incidents, one potentially deadly and the other apparently playful, are examples of a phenomenon that has triggered growing concern among law enforcement officials and corporate managers: computer crime and abuse. Computers and advanced copiers have made easy the forging of documents such as banknotes, passports, stock certificates, and savings bonds. Wire tapping was facilitated by computers and new levels of sophistication have been reached by their users. Specialists can now alter tapes either to convey messages different from those intended or use old recordings to construct new tapes with new meanings. Such "doctoring" is detected only by highly skilled and experienced sound engineers; without detection the public believes the tape to be genuine.

Other tape crimes occur when thieves copy artists' music and package it differently for sale in other countries, profiting from songs they never helped to produce and thus unencumbered by the expense incurred by the artist and the recording studio. Tapes were also used for dictating important letters and for storing confidential information. Careless companies that left office doors open—or did not remove tapes from machines sent for repair—were easy prey. One example occurred in 1980 when San Francisco's Wells Fargo Bank discovered that it had lost $21 million in a year, allegedly to two boxing promoters who, with a bank employee's help, used a computer for illegal transfers.

Richard P. Kusserow, inspector general for the Department of Health and Human Services, finished the first survey of crimes involving the federal government's 650,000 microcomputers and 16,000 large mainframe computers in 1982. He concluded that there is in business and government an extraordinary vulnerability to crime: "The government has become the biggest user of computers in this country," he said, and "an information explosion is going on that has come so quickly the bureaucracy hasn't had time to respond."[15] The study found 172 cases of fraud and abuse in 12 government agencies during a four-year period. One employee diverted $24,000 in unauthorized benefits checks to himself and erased the evidence; in another case, three clerks stole $150,000 worth of food stamps because their supervisor left a key in the computer terminal. These instances, however, are relatively insignificant when compared to the country's position in the international field.

## *National Security*

The United States is faced with two main outflows of technology, one to Russia and the other to Japan. Until recently—and even this is uncertain—Russian efforts were thought to more directly threaten national security. Their success at obtaining technology saved them billions of rubles and forced the United States to increase its spending. The Soviets were particularly adept at purchasing what they could not get in the United States through Japan and neutral countries. Soviet assurances that a dual-use item would not be used for military purposes have been worthless in the past; and whether the thaw in Eastern Europe will change the picture is purely conjectural. Japan and Sweden, for example, sold the Soviets two floating dry docks on written assurances that they would be used only for their merchant fleet. Instead, the dry docks were used to service the aircraft carrier *Kiev* and other Russian warships. The Russians have even turned neutrality into a weapon. An Austrian company named C.F.M. is the world's leading manufacturer of continuous forge casting for tubing, axles, and cannon barrels. The Russians argued that it was impossible for a neutral nation to export these items to the United States and not to Russia. This machinery is currently producing cannon barrels for Soviet T-72 tanks.

What the Soviets could not purchase legally they bribed to acquire. The concentration of electronic firms in the Silicon Valley has brought spies like bees to honey. The Soviet consulate in San Francisco, headed by Alexksandr Chivaidze, a trained engineer and chairman of the Soviet Union's Committee on Science and Technology, directed as many as 60 KGB agents in the valley. The Central Intelligence Agency has placed agents in the Silicon Valley to keep tabs on foreign agents and prevent theft of secrets by Soviet and Eastern bloc agents. But the 1983 Hitachi scandal reinforced what many San Francisco Bay area executives believed: the Japanese are certainly as big a threat—perhaps bigger—than the Russians.

## *Globalization of Industrial Espionage*

The vast increase in foreign trade has heightened the need by foreigners and Americans for intelligence. Here in the United States there are many sources of information on foreign companies and, conversely, many sources of information for foreigners on Americans. Such domestic sources include foreign banks with U.S. offices, branch offices of foreign companies, trade shows, foreign financial texts, and magazines. Additional sources include *The Wall Street Journal*, business school cases, regional magazines, and packaged management programs. Unfortunately, industrial espionage also plays a role.

One of the most exciting episodes involved Assistant U.S. Attorney Gregory Ward, who had his hands more than full running the San Jose office of the Justice Department.[16] Crimes in Silicon Valley were not the routine sort, yet there were only three lawyers to handle the heavy caseload of erupting white-collar crime. Before 1982 both the FBI and the Justice Department had failed to gather enough information to secure indictments but at long last, Ward found his opportunity: the leaking of IBM confidential information by individuals who had access to the company's top-secret documents—documents that described in detail the design of an about-to-be-marketed IBM mainframe computer. It was first thought that the information had been stolen for the Soviet Union and the investigators were surprised to learn that they were dealing with IBM's top competitor—the Japanese conglomerate called Hitachi.

The first hint that IBM had a serious security problem came in an August 12, 1982, phone call to the company from Martin Alpert, president of Tecmar, a Cleveland electronics firm. Alpert said that his company had been approached by IBM's William Erdman, a systems design expert, with an offer to provide what appeared to be confidential information. IBM officials persuaded Alpert to play along with Erdman and covertly tape their negotiations. Erdman discussed the deal several times by phone and once met in the IBM manager's Stamford, Connecticut, home. As Erdman talked, Alpert taped. The negotiations climaxed in a September 4 meeting at Tecmar's Cleveland office when Erdman left a draft contract for Alpert to sign.

CHAPTER SIX  Information Gathering: Clean or Dirty Tricks?   179

Working with another consulting firm called Paylon Associates, Ward learned that Kenji Hayashi and Isao Ohnishi, two Hitachi executives, had approached Paylon seeking additional Adrondaik workbooks, the top-secret program for IBM's 3081 mainframe. It had been rumored that Paylon was actually an undercover operation for IBM itself although this was not certain at the time. Richard Callahan, an IBM employee and former FBI agent, was called to assist in this case. Because Hitachi was a major competitor to IBM, Callahan had good reason to focus on that company.

The case, however, had complications. Because Japan outlawed undercover operations (except in drug cases), any arrest in the covert operation would not be considered legitimate by the Japanese. This, coupled with the embarrassment of the arrest for the Japanese government, made the likelihood of extradition remote. Ward knew, therefore, that those who were to be apprehended must be in the United States at the time of the arrest (although Hitachi's top executives had avoided visibility in all transactions) and that the conviction of Hitachi's highest executives would provide greater deterrent to white-collar crime than the arrest of lower level employees.[17] The question was how to convince the top executives to visit this country.

After unsuccessful efforts to entice the targeted men to visit America, government officials conceded defeat and reluctantly focused their attentions on Hayashi and Ohnishi. The sting operation progressed as planned and the arrests were made in June of 1983. The news hit Tokyo like a thunderclap. For the first time the Japanese cabinet debated a scandal that had rocked computer-technology circles throughout the world and aggravated trade tensions between the United States and Japan. How Japanese and American managers handled the problems revealed important differences between Japanese and American cultures. At the annual shareholders meeting of Mitsubishi, part of the Hitachi conglomerate, president Nihachiro Katayama asked stockholders to treat the espionage case with "understanding." While apologizing for concerns raised by the case, Katayama assured his stockholders of his confidence that Mitsubishi employees were not criminals.[18] The company also canceled its advertising campaigns in Japan and the United States, a move that, from American perspectives, might be seen as retaliation. Actually, the company was following the Japanese tradition of showing public restraint after a scandal or accident. For example, Japan Air Lines had halted all advertising after one of its planes crashed into Tokyo Bay, killing 24 people. It resumed advertising only after four months had passed.

Hitachi had acknowledged paying $546,000 and Mitsubishi about $20,000 for computer technology secrets. However, both denied wrongdoing, saying they believed they were purchasing information through a legitimate company that turned out to be an FBI front. The attorney for the defense made an interesting observation toward the close of the hearing when he said that the American "government had basically rented out the investigation process to IBM. This violated all Justice guidelines. I'm also convinced that the [U.S.] antitrust case against IBM and the Hitachi matter were linked."[19] The defense went on to claim that the government settled quickly in order that the relationship with IBM not be disclosed. The prosecution disputed this claim.

IBM's management, in contrast to the Japanese, behaved so firmly and aggressively that the signal from corporate America was clear: no more avoiding the espionage issue to save face. In September 1982, three months after joining the FBI's sting operation, company officials confronted three high-ranking employees at their desks, charging them with trying to sell secrets about IBM's new personal computer. They fired them on the spot. Later the same day the firm sued the three employees in a New York State court in an effort to block them from using confidential IBM information for personal profit.[20]

The case also provides a glimpse of IBM's elaborate security apparatus. The company spends more than $50 million annually to guard its internal secrets. Hundreds of in-house detectives monitor employees suspected of being security risks, keep confidential information out of the hands of those who do not need it, and even enter offices at night to make sure that desks are locked. Although such measures sometimes thwart the outright theft of classified documents, they are less effective in preventing employees with trade secrets stored in their heads from either jumping to competitors or starting their own firms. Since 1970, ex-IBMers have launched several highly successful computer companies, including Amdahl Corporation, which makes equipment that plugs into IBM systems.

In the past, IBM and other computer companies had tended to accept this practice as part of the competitive game, but now they take ex-employees to court more often. For example, Microcomputer Systems Corporation of Sunnyvale, California, won a preliminary $2 million judgment against two former employees who had started a rival firm. In the multibillion-dollar computer business, trade secrets have become too valuable to be given up without a fight.

## *Ethical Questions*

- If American authorities pressed for extradition of involved Hitachi and Mitsubishi officials, would this be unethical in view of the fact that the Japanese had no treaty with the United States governing such matters?
- Though legal, are entrapments unethical?
- If corporations (like IBM, for example, which knew that employee thievery was extensive) took no legal action in order to "save face," were they "sinning by omission"?

## *Business Costs of Security*

Faced by staggering costs occasioned by the loss of critical information, each country and each company has taken—or is taking—steps to protect itself. Because the United States and its corporations are in positions of industrial, technological, and financial preeminence, they are in the vanguard for security about vital information. Examples make the point.

**Export Controls.** Government leaders find themselves in a paradox. Cutting the flow of critical technology to unfriendly nations makes the business community unhappy. Loss of market share and sales abroad reduces the profits needed to remain competitive. But the transfer of technology is also saving other countries, including the Russians, billions of dollars in research and development because they can reap the benefits without any of the work. The Export Administration Act of 1979 reflected the confusion between increased trade with the Russians and concern about their growing power. From the Commodity Control list was compiled over 100,000 items not considered exportable. Even if the item was not on the list the Commerce and State Departments—as well as the CIA and NASA—may disapprove an export of a specific product. The length of time involved in getting clearance can cause American companies to lose sales to foreign competitors; on the other hand, sales to Iraq later led to the bitter U.S. involvement of 1991.

J. Fred Bucy, president of Texas Instruments, would change the focus of government attention by having federal agencies concentrate on keeping out of unfriendly foreign hands not products but processes of design, joint ventures, technical exchange agreements—what Bucy terms the active transfer mechanisms that most help this country's rivals. What foreigners are often barred from getting directly from the United States can be picked up in the equivalents of a Radio Shack in Hong Kong, Singapore, and Venice. It is almost impossible to stop the smuggle of microchips when thousands can be placed in a shoebox or the suit lining of a foreign agent. Bucy alluded to a perennial sore point when he said: "Few American allies are willing to make sacrifices as large as we are; U.S. trade with the USSR and with the Eastern bloc countries is marginal, but for Western Europe it's big time."[21]

The Western allies have cooperated in export control through the Coordinated Committee for Multilateral Export Controls (Cocom), whose members are NATO allies and Japan. Cocom has its own secret export control list but it is shorter than the U.S. list of prohibited exports; as a consequence America is constantly trying to push its larger list on Cocom members, a highly unwelcome effort. Possibly the United States could get support from Cocom and neutral nations if it used Bucy's suggestions and clamped controls only on technologies with probable military application. These technologies are ones in which the United States has a distinctive lead and are important to national security, such as submarine sound detection devices and very high speed integrated circuitry. These restrictions, generally favored by most NATO countries, are easier to enforce.

One important action undertaken to prevent internal abuses was Operation Exodus, an interagency working group consisting of the FBI, CIA, and several cabinet departments. Early efforts included the launching of more than 50 technology theft investigations; intercepting illegally exported electronic devices; and sabotaging equipment—forcing the recipients to take months to figure out and make necessary corrections. However, one restriction government agents want changed is the current statutes that prohibit customs officials from searching suspected violators until they actually export the item. For example, custom officials in New York believed that a certain Austrian businessman was carrying around the gun sight used on F-4 fighter planes. But they could do nothing until after the Austrian went through the exit-processing procedures at Kennedy Airport. Had he chosen to stay in New York for some time, customs might have waited months to act. The elapsed time would have provided opportunities for the culprit's associates to tip him off.

**Security Consultants and Equipment.** Corporations have instituted programs undreamed of 15 years ago. They have elaborate security devices that are as sophisticated as the products that they make. Much of the precautions are taken against bugging. No one knows with certainty how much industrial bugging really goes on but, judging from sales of eavesdropping devices manufactured in foreign countries, as many as 50 to 100,000 bugs may have been planted in the United States in one five-year span, 1975–1980.[22] As a result, the fear of being bugged has soared. The view of the security officer of one multinational corporation is typical: "We never found a bug, but we are sure they're there."

The fear of being bugged has been cornucopia for security consultants. Companies have been willing to spend between $800 to $20,000 a sweep to find bugs and for $300,000 to $400,000 companies could build electronically shielded walls around conference rooms or offices. Also available are machines that blur conversations with background noises imitative of falling rain. Problems remain. Even good equipment may not provide the security firms need. Electronically shielded walls can be circumvented by drilling holes through the wall or simply by opening a window. The most thorough antibug sweep is nullified if someone plants another bug five minutes later. One reasonably successful security firm, seeking to halt an attempt to plant moles, provided detailed background checks on all job applicants to make sure the applicant's answers corresponded to the facts. Although polygraph tests are legally restricted, courts will allow the asking of certain questions whose aggregated answers provide important clues to the investigator.

**Freedom of Information.** One especially vexatious problem for business is the Freedom of Information Act (FOIA) which too often had become a vehicle for surveillance by competitors, at public expense, of the private affairs of commercial enterprises.[23] The National Association of Manufacturers, a leader in efforts to amend the act, argued that the requests under the law have been aimed to get private data rather than information on government activities. More than three of every five requests for information are made by companies and the result of such openness has led corporations to become very reluctant in giving information to the government. The quality of that information has been thereby diminished.

Numerous attempts to modify the act have been made. Senator Robert Dole has sought to amend the FOIA by safeguarding proprietary information and by requiring the federal agency holding such information to notify the targeted company of impending disclosure. Dole's purpose is to give the target an opportunity to show why the information should not be released. Opponents of change argue that actual damages caused by the act are grossly overstated and that the real reason why businesses are balking is because they are not used to working in the open.

## *Ethical Question*

- In the "no holds barred" world of industrial espionage, should corporations be allowed to determine what technical information will be provided to the government, the only exception being technical data developed with the help of public funding?

## *Intellectual Property Rights*

How the question of intellectual property is phrased largely shapes the answer to the issue of release of information by former employees of one company to present employers of a company in competition with the worker's old firm.[24] If it is asked, "Who owns what is in an individual's head?", a rather straightforward answer is to say that it is the individual. If, on the other hand, this question is asked, "Who owns information the individual has acquired when paid to work on a secret project with other equally competent employees?", the answer is less clear. Senior managers and research scientists are usually involved in this second group but market specialists, salesmen, lawyers, advertisers, and public relations personnel are also often privy to guarded company material.

There is a third way of phrasing the question: "Who owns confidential information when an employee joins a firm for the sole purpose of acquiring restricted data to improve changes for getting a high-level job with a competing firm?" An example is the job applicant who said, "I wasn't eager about going to IBM or TI because of all the bureaucracy that went with it, but I knew it would be a good ticket to my future because when I left I could bring along valuable information to my new employer."

In times past, companies may not have been pleased when key employees jumped ship to join a competitor, but they learned to grin and bear it. Now they are going after employees suspected of stealing the family jewels. Evidence of this pursuit is seen in the way large law firms are forming departments to deal exclusively with illegal acquisitions of computer trade secrets. During the Hitachi sting, IBM sued a group of former employees who started the Cybernex Corporation, which set up a production plant in less than eight months to make thin film read-and-write recording heads. A year later Cybernex started to market the product. IBM argued that it was inconceivable that an organization could have developed such technically complex recording heads in so short a period when it took IBM four years of trial and error to perfect the process.

In a parallel case Guardian Industries, by hiring three former employees from the Manville Corporation, was in the fiberglass insulation business in 18 months, using the same technology that Manville had spent $9 million in R&D over a seven-year period to develop. Manville prosecuted the trio. The actions of both IBM and Manville were meant to signal to all employees and would-be spies that swift retaliatory action would be taken.[25]

Long before get-tough policies existed, the Goodrich Tire Company of Akron had taken a protective step that anticipated future toughened policies by other companies. The incident involved one Donald W. Wohlgemuth, a manager of the company's space-suit department, who resigned to take a better paying job in the space-suit department of the competing International Latex Corporation of Dover, Delaware.[26] Goodrich sought to obtain an injunction against Wohlgemuth to prohibit his going to work in the space-suit department of International Latex on the grounds that a competitor would benefit from trade secrets known to Wohlgemuth and paid for by Goodrich stockholders. The Court of Common Pleas of Summit County, where Goodrich was situated, refused to enjoin Wohlgemuth on the grounds (1) that, since no disclosure of trade secrets had yet occurred, an injunction was premature, and (2) that Wohlgemuth's new employment was in a geographical area outside the jurisdiction of that court. Goodrich then took the case to the District Court of Appeals, which did restrain Wohlgemuth from divulging any trade secrets to his new employer, but leaving him free to remain in the new job. Wohlgemuth was thus left in the awkward position of being subject to legal penalties for any slip of the tongue, even though nobody had ever been able to establish what constituted a trade secret. The dilemma here was over whose property was being pirated—the individual's or the company's.

## *Ethical Questions*

- Given the great value of research in contemporary society, were any of the Goodrich-Wohlgemuth court decisions ethical ones?
- Did Latex behave unethically?
- Do individuals have an absolute right to move to a new job at any time of their choosing?
- If knowledge—once held to be exclusively and uniquely the person's own—is no longer susceptible to such an interpretation, does this represent an improvement in business ethical practices?

That companies have continued to behave aggressively to protect their confidential data was shown in the sequence of articles that appeared in *The Wall Street Journal* over a period of one year:

- Ashton-Tate took action against its former chief scientist, Wayne Ratelief, who had pilfered the firm's popular data base product.[27]
- Pratt & Whitney accused a former employee of stealing secret pricing information and selling it to Electromethods for $220,000.[28]
- Service Corporation International sued Hillenbrand Industries for more than $100 million, claiming that Hillenbrand was behind a plot to steal

CHAPTER SIX   Information Gathering: Clean or Dirty Tricks?   185

Service's trade secrets. In this case, a former Hillenbrand employee (who was previously with the FBI) was accused of searching Service Corporation's trash for copies of cost and pricing information, as well as merger plans.[29]
- Boeing was awarded $3.2 million by the Washington State Supreme Court from Sierralin Corporation for misappropriation of trade secrets.[30]
- Lotus Development Corporation secured a court order to prevent its advertising agency from telling its secrets to competitors.[31]
- Microsoft Corporation cried "dirty tricks" when Borland International hired a former Microsoft executive, Rob Dickerson. The settlement limited Dickerson's work to certain projects as Borland's vice president of product management.[32]
- Apple Computer sued its former president, Steve Jobs, for using company secrets in computers intended for the education market.

To protect themselves companies have required employees to sign nondisclosure agreements; however, companies may not need such arrangements because nondisclosure is always enforceable under the "fiduciary duty of loyalty" concept. Employees who possess sensitive information can still enter the job market but the legal principal does provide former employers with judicial recourse against workers who join a competitor and "spill the beans." But problems remain, as the Auerbach example illustrates.

Harvard professor Joseph Auerbach used the hypothetical case of a physicist doing paid research for a firm on nuclear power plants, who signed a standard agreement that all inventions he produced belonged to the firm and that his notebooks were to be left behind should he quit. The notebooks included all his experiments—successes and failures. By keeping their notebooks, the company thought it could prevent former employees from duplicating successful experiments. When the physicist accepted an offer from a rival firm, he took his notebooks with him. The company sued.

## *Ethical Question*

- Even supposing that the court ruled in favor of the physicist, is the physicist's act ethical?

## Summary

To cynics, the talk among executives that people are the organization's most valuable asset is little more than pious cant. But senior managements are to be believed when they speak in a similar vein about their knowledge workers—the folks in research and development, the lawyers who file for patents, the production heads who know the manufacturing priorities, and the sales force who are taught the product's special capabilities. In a high-tech world, knowledge is a company's most important asset: knowledge of the enterprise's technological needs and capabilities as well as knowledge of the competitor's needs and capabilities. In a technologically driven society, therefore, managers want to know as much as they can as fast as they can. The temptation to engage in unethical forms of industrial espionage is often irresistible.

Also in such societies, individual employees are often as much involved in espionage as are companies. Selling their firm's trade secrets to a competitor is clearly unethical; but carrying trade secrets to a new employer for the purpose of advancing their own careers is more problematic, involving as it does the conflict between communal and personal property. Overprotection of the organization's property rights can violate the individual's property rights, and vice versa. In such cases, the facts influence the judgment. Here, if anywhere, the tenets of situationalist ethics may be applicable.

## Questions for Discussion

1. Your company is facing severe competition from companies widely suspected of engaging in industrial espionage. If you engage in counter industrial espionage, is your reaction ethical?
2. Does the magnitude of problems related to industrial espionage tell important things about the values of business? Of society?
3. Should companies about whom competitors seek information (under the Freedom of Information Act) be notified before the information is released?
4. If a company is careless in handling its trade secrets, may its competitors take advantage of such carelessness by making it the special target of industrial espionage?
5. If countries are justified in spying on other countries, are companies justified in spying on other corporations?

## Ethical Quandaries

### An Espionage Offer

1. An employee of a competing firm calls to inquire if you would be interested in earning some extra money simply by telling him how your company's high-performing product works. The money would be paid by him only if you brought along a copy of the plans. He mentioned a sum that was enough to make you financially secure for life. Would you cooperate?

2. Another competitor calls around the same time and makes the same request. Instead of asking for money, however, he threatens to tell the wife you love the fact you are in the midst of—as he says—a "torrid affair." What would you do?

CHAPTER SIX  Information Gathering: Clean or Dirty Tricks?   187

3. Assume that, in both situations, you know that whatever you tell the "other guys," they will believe. Would you deliberately give false information to the cash-hungry individual in order to collect the money yourself? Would you deliver false data to crush the threat of the gossip monger?

## Question

- Would your answer differ if management disapproved your plan to deceive the two spies?

4. An employee for the leading competitor telephones to say he would like to meet at some isolated location to talk about something that would help your company and probably advance your career? Would you go?

5. Assume that you go and find that he has some key plans of his company's new product that he is willing to sell for a price, payable in cash. Would you buy them?

## Questions

- What if he said, "If you don't accept, I'll shop around to find a competing firm that will buy them"? What would you do?
- Is it ethically consistent to condone military espionage and condemn industrial espionage?

## The Candid Camera[33]

A client who wished to remain anonymous hired photographers Rolfe and Gary Christopher of Beaumont, Texas, to take aerial photographs of new construction at the Beaumont plant of E.I. DuPont de Nemours & Company Inc. Sixteen photographs of the DuPont facility were taken from the air on March 19, 1969, and were later developed and delivered to the client. DuPont employees noticed the airplane and immediately began an investigation to determine why the craft was repeatedly circling over the plant. By late afternoon they knew that the craft was being used on a photographic expedition and that the Christophers were the photographers. DuPont contacted the suspected spies that same afternoon, asking them to reveal their employer's name. The Christophers refused, giving as their reason the client's desire to remain anonymous.

Having reached a dead end in the investigation, DuPont filed suit against the Christophers, alleging that they had wrongfully obtained photographs about DuPont's trade secrets which they then sold to an undisclosed third party. DuPont contended that it had developed a highly secret but unpatented process for producing methanol that gave DuPont a competitive advantage over other producers. This process, DuPont alleged, was a trade secret developed after expensive and time-consuming research—and a secret that the company had taken special precautions to safeguard.

The area photographed by the Christophers was the plant designed to produce methanol by this secret process. Because the plant was under construction, parts of the process were exposed to view from directly above the building site. Photographs would enable a skilled person to deduce the secret process for making methanol. DuPont thus contended that the Christophers had wrongfully appropriated DuPont's trade secret. In its suit, DuPont asked for damages to cover the loss it had already sustained and sought temporary and permanent injunctions prohibiting any further circulation of the photographs and prohibiting any additional photographing of the methanol plant.

The Christophers insisted that they had committed no legally "actionable wrong" in photographing the DuPont facility and passing these photographs on to their client because they conducted all of their activities in public airspace, violated no government aviation standard, did not breach any confidential relation, and did not engage in any fraudulent or illegal conduct. In short, the Christophers argued that for an appropriation of trade secrets to be wrong there must be a trespass, other illegal conduct, or breach of a confidential relationship.

## Question

- Did the Christophers behave ethically?

## *The Harvard B-School Caper*[34]

Like all of the 800 cases that form the core of the Harvard Business School curriculum, the case of Corporation Two is based on something that actually happened—not in the business world, as with most cases, but at the B-school itself. How the case was resolved (?) ignited an emotional debate over the emphasis that business professors should place on ethics—and where ethical considerations fit in the fast-track real world that B-students intend to enter.

The story revolves around first-year students taking part in Harvard's "business game." A clever computer simulation of a competitive marketplace, the game is designed to pull together all the elements of the first-year curriculum. Offered during the spring vacation, the game is an intensive and totally demanding experience concentrated in one week of 15-hour days. The first year at the B-school is often likened to boot camp and the business game to the first full-scale maneuvers. The class of 750 students is divided into nine sections of 80 to 85 students; each section takes the same four-hour courses together in the same room throughout the entire year. Because the school grades on the curve, the bottom 20 percent is constantly in danger of failing and the pressures are enormous. The trial by ordeal, however, fosters a tightly knit, if overwrought, *esprit de corps* within each section.

The game, scheduled just before second-term grades are released, gives students a chance to test what they have learned and what they can use

CHAPTER SIX   Information Gathering: Clean or Dirty Tricks?   189

against their peers, all the while having an exciting time in the process. Each section plays a separate game. The students divide into six teams of about 12 members each to run six corporations with different histories, characteristics, and starting market positions. Each team appoints a president and other executives. The amount of material to be mastered is formidable, and split-second decisions have to be made; there are two to three deadlines each day for entering new decisions into the computer in reaction to changes in the marketplace.

About midway through the week, Team Two, whose president was Dan Friedman, a Stanford graduate, got hold of Team Six's computer code, thus providing access to Six's private records. Later, some Team Six members speculated that Team Two had stolen the number by looking over someone's shoulder as the code was tapped into the computer. But Friedman said that a member of his team found the number on a computer printout sheet that Team Six had carelessly discarded on a table in the central computer room.

At first, only a handful of students on Friedman's team was privy to the discovery of Team Six's code, and they said they did not think much about the ethics of the situation. They simply used the computer password in every advantageous way they could. They obtained simultaneous printouts as Team Six typed its decisions into the computer; they passed on information to other teams that could use it better than they against Team Six; and they charged snoop reports—even some they did not need—to Team Six's account.

"We could not believe we had the other company's password, it was such a joke," said one member. "We never had a meeting over whether it was right or wrong to use the password. In the context of the game, once you have access to information, it would not make sense not to use it. It was a gift, like finding a notebook left on your doorstep."

The students on Team Two made one mistake—they were caught. Team Six had become suspicious that something was amiss when the team's early successes were suddenly jeopardized by seemingly inexplicable market reactions to its moves. Then a competing student tipped off Team Six that his group was receiving advance information—how and from whom was not clear. Team Six tightened security. On Friday morning each team entered its final decisions into the computer while champagne was chilling for the traditional postgame party. Champagne is for the winners—losers drink beer. With five minutes to go, Jonathan Nelson, a member of Team Six, thought some members of Team Two were acting oddly. Wandering over to their terminal, he saw his team's user-information number being printed out. He ripped off the sheet and raced back to his teammates. The game was up.

To some extent, the students on Team Two figured they had legitimately outsmarted their colleagues. If not an intended component of the game, industrial espionage was commonly practiced in the business world. As a matter of fact, an article in the B-school's student newspaper that appeared just before the game played up espionage as one of the more "exhilarating" aspects of the game. The article's author was a second-year student who claimed that in 1981 his team had captured the computer password of a competitor and had found it useful in diverting its costs for snoop reports to the other team.

Prior to the game—suggesting premeditation in the eyes of some students—Friedman discussed with Marie-Therese Flaherty, a young assistant professor who was to monitor his section, whether such espionage tactics were part of the game. According to Friedman, Flaherty said espionage happened in the real world and could happen in the game. (Flaherty later declined to be interviewed on the subject.) Friedman felt the implication of Flaherty's remarks was that such tactics were part of the game. As a joke, Friedman said his team put someone in charge of espionage. "It wasn't as though we were cheating," he said. "I thought part of the fun was doing things like espionage or collusion."

It may have been just a game to Friedman and his teammates, but the students on Team Six were irate. In their opinion Team Two's acquisition of the code was not like finding another company's confidential file on a doorstep and reading it; rather, it was like finding the key to another company's vault. The questionable behavior came with the decision to use that key to unlock the vault, tamper with accounts, and steal company secrets. What particularly upset Team Six was that the competitive atmosphere of the Harvard Business School seemed to suspend ethical considerations in the game, a particularly reprehensible attitude to show to people who routinely reached top management positions in Fortune 500 companies.

Some members of Team Six were also angry because the faculty stayed neutral, maintaining that the issue was one for the students themselves to resolve. James L. Heskett, the dean for educational programs, commented that the incident showed how well the case method worked, particularly with regard to ethics: an ethical question arose in a dynamic situation and the instructor tossed it back to the students to resolve. Heskett said that in not voting for Team Two, a leading contender at the end of the game, the students showed their disapproval of the team's behavior. "That's a cop-out," retorted members of Team Six. "The incident doesn't prove how the case method works, but where it goes wrong. If Team Two had not been caught, what would have been learned last year in terms of ethics?" The real problem, the students contended, was that ethical considerations involved in cases studied at the business school had not often been raised by the professors—a situation that changed markedly at Harvard around 1980. But the incident, not likely repeatable without sanction at Harvard, raised important questions.

The controversy over the game revived a touchy subject. Before the incident, critiquing the school in his annual report to the board of overseers, Harvard President Derek C. Bok questioned whether ethics received enough attention at the business school.[35] Bok disapprovingly quoted an official of an unidentified business school: "As far as ethics are concerned, we figure that our students either have them or they don't." After Bok issued that report, a business school advisory board released its own report, which concluded that the school's goals ought to be broadened to require an understanding of ethics and corporate responsibility.

CHAPTER SIX  Information Gathering: Clean or Dirty Tricks?  191

## Questions

- Did Team Two's members act unethically?
- If you found yourself in the same situation as Dan Friedman, would you have behaved differently?
- Do you think some on the Harvard business faculty behaved unethically?

## Notes

1. Richard Eells and Peter Nehemkis, *Corporate Intelligence and Espionage: A Blueprint for Executive Decision Making* (New York: Macmillan, 1984), 109. See also John Fuld, *Competitor Intelligence: How to Get It, How to Use It* (New York: John Wiley, 1985). Another excellent source is *Harvard Business Review* issues of November–December 1959 and November–December 1974.
2. Harry Howe Ransom, "Intelligence: Political and Military," *International Encyclopedia of the Social Sciences, vol. 7* (New York: Macmillan, 1964), 415–421.
3. Skip Derra and Ted Agres, "Competition Drives Market for Industrial Espionage," *Research and Development* 29 (June 1987): 63.
4. William K. Salmon, Mark A. Kurland, and Robert Spitalnic, *Business Competition Intelligence: Methods Used for Collecting, Organizing and Using Information* (New York: John Wiley, 1984), 55.
5. Michael E. Porter and Victor E. Millar, "How Information Gives You a Competitive Advantage," *Harvard Business Review* (July–August 1985): 149–161. Professor Porter's views have been detailed in two books, *Competitive Strategy* (New York: Free Press, 1980) and *Competitive Advantage* (New York: Free Press, 1985).
6. Kirk W. M. Tyson, *Business Intelligence: Putting It All Together* (Lombard, Ill.: Leading Edge Publications, 1986), 9.
7. Steven Flax, "How to Snoop on Your Competitors," *Fortune*, May 14, 1984, 29–34. See also William Cohen and Helena Czepiec, "The Role of Ethics in Gathering Corporate Intelligence," *Journal of Business Ethics* 7 (March 1988): 199–204.
8. Quoted by Steven E. Prokesch, "Keeping Tabs on Competitors," *The New York Times*, October 28, 1985, B1.
9. James Pooley, *Trade Secrets: How to Protect Your Ideas and Assets* (Berkeley: Osborne/McGraw-Hill, 1982), 12–16.
10. Salmon, *Business Competition Intelligence*, 31.
11. Robert W. Stewart and Michael A. Hiltzik, "Industrial Espionage Is Big Business," *Best of Business* 4 (Fall 1982): 91–101.
12. Lynn Sharpe Paine, "Indices of Competition and the Gathering of Commercial Intelligence," in *Enriching Business Ethics*, ed. Clarence C. Walton (New York: Plenum, 1990), ch. 4.
13. Robert Farr, *The Electronic Criminals* (New York: McGraw Hill, 1975). See also Gregory Parsons, "Information Technology: A New Competitive Weapon," *Sloan Management Review* 25 (Fall 1983): 3–14.
14. Mary Thornton, "Do You Know Where Your Computer Code Is?" *Washington Post National Weekly Edition*, June 4, 1984, 7.
15. Department of Justice, *Computer Crimes* (Washington, D.C.: Government Printing Office, 1982).
16. The Hitachi–IBM conflict was told in a lively fashion by James A. Stewart, *The Prosecutors* (New York: Simon and Schuster, 1987).
17. Ibid., 93. Ward worried over the prospect of the court dismissing evidence gathered from a sting operator.
18. The *Philadelphia Inquirer*, June 30, 1982, 15D.

19. Stewart, *The Prosecutors*, 122.
20. Charles Alexander, "Sting II: IBM Strikes Again," *Time*, September 27, 1982, 48.
21. Walter Guzzardi, Jr., "Cutting Russia Harvest of U.S. Technology," *Fortune*, May 30, 1983, 104. See also Robert Kuttner, "How 'National Security' Haunts National Competitiveness," *Harvard Business Review* (January–February 1991): 140–149.
22. *Data Communications*, August 1982, 49.
23. See the articles by Charles Marson, "On Obtaining Access to Government Files," and Morton Halperin, "Freedom of Information Act: How to Find Out More and Pay Less," *The Business Lawyer* 34 (March 1979) 887–914, and 1041–1048 respectively.
24. Kevin McManus, "Who Owns Your Brains?" *Forbes*, June 6, 1983, 168–179.
25. See Stanley Lieberstein, *Who Owns What's in Your Head?* (New York: Hawthorn Books, 1979).
26. Clarence C. Walton, *Ethos and the Executive* (Englewood Heights, N.J.: Prentice-Hall, 1969), 87.
27. "Ashton-Tate Sues Ex-Chief Scientist, Five Others over Gain," *The Wall Street Journal*, January 5, 1987, 32.
28. Staff reporter, "A Former Employee of Pratt & Whitney Is Charged with Fraud," *The Wall Street Journal*, February 27, 1987, 32.
29. News Roundup, "Service Corp. Is Suing Hillenbrand, Alleges Theft of Trade Secrets," *The Wall Street Journal*, March 4, 1987, 7.
30. Staff reporter, "Sierralin, Boeing Settle Litigation on Charge of Using Trade Secrets," *The Wall Street Journal*, June 5, 1987, 19.
31. "Lotus Gets Order Barring Ad Agency from Telling Secrets," *The Wall Street Journal*, December 14, 1987, 13A.
32. "Microsoft, Borland Settle Dispute over Trade Secrets," *The Wall Street Journal*, December 18, 1987, 14.
33. E. I. DuPont De Nemours & Co., Inc. v. Christopher, 431 f.2d 1012, U.S. Court of Appeals, 5th Cir. (August 25, 1970).
34. Thomas Moore, "Industrial Espionage at the Harvard Business School," *Fortune*, September 6, 1982, 72–82. Permission granted for text only. ©Time Inc. all rights reserved.
35. Walter Kiechel III, "Harvard Business School Restudies Itself," *Fortune*, June 18, 1979, 48–58.

CHAPTER 7

# Insider Trading, Bribes, and Payoffs

## Insider Trading
A Sense of the Problem
Dimensions of the Problem
Definitional Examples
*Winans*
*Chiarella*
*Dirks*
Ethical Assessment

## Bribes and Payoffs
Definitional Examples
*The Haitian Dealmakers*
*The Big Tipper*
*Operations Rescue*
*Embargo Aftermath*
*Miles Makers*
Making Distinctions
*Bribes and Gifts*
*Extortion and Payoffs*
Government Reactions
*The Foreign Corrupt Practices Act*
Moral Assessments
*American Justice and Fairness to Others*
*FCPA and Ethics*

## Summary
Questions for Discussion
Ethical Quandary

*The theme has been reiterated constantly that healthy economic competition depends on consistent observance of such basic ethical norms as respect for the umpire, constructive effort, independent initiative, and the level playing field principle. When any one of the norms is violated, people cry foul. The outburst has been particularly vocal in regard to insider trading at home and bribery abroad. What follows is an attempt to show the moral hazards each creates and the moral hazards of jumping too quickly to definitions that, on some occasions, are poor descriptions of reality. A sense of direction comes by (1) reviewing the unholy works of Dennis Levine, Ivan Boesky, and others; (2) analyzing the ethical implications provided through a few domestic scenarios; and (3) looking abroad to explore a few of the more interesting bribery cases.* ∎

*The purposes of this chapter are:*
1. To profile some of the more unsavory aspects of insider trading.
2. To illustrate the difficulty in defining it, using examples, congressional definitions, and court decisions when appropriate.
3. To distinguish between bribes and grease money.
4. To offer ethical perspectives within which other definitions may be weighed.

## Insider Trading

The flood of money available for lending caused many financial tributaries (banks, brokerage houses, pension funds, other institutional investors, and foreign bargain hunters) to overflow their banks. In the eddying flood waters, takeover activity and insider trading have become almost synonymous in the public's mind. That information is hot property on Wall Street is clear but the law relating to it has not been clear.[1]

## A Sense of the Problem

The following seven situations give a sense of the problem. Answering the questions on the basis of one's own values—and then comparing the responses later to those made by the public authorities—is a sensible way to view the floodwaters.

YES   NO

___   ___   Your best friend lives with the vice president of a large company. She wants to take you out to celebrate. Although she is not supposed to tell anyone, she lets you know that her company just landed a big government contract. Can you call your broker before the deal is announced?

___   ___   In a theater lobby at intermission you overhear a conversation between two men you know to be top executives in a big company. "Our stock should really jump when we announce those earnings tomorrow," said one. Can you buy call options now?

___   ___   A small textile company calls you in as a marketing consultant. Its president shows you samples of a new fabric that sheds dirt and almost never wears out. You are bowled over—but too busy to take on the account. Can you buy stock in the company?

___   ___   As the human resources manager of Mammoth Oil, you learn from the CEO that the company has just hit a gusher. Can you buy before the news becomes public?

___   ___   Your broker has an uncanny knack for picking takeover targets whose stocks always rise just before the public announcement is made. Either he is very smart or he is getting inside information. When he called to recommend Maximove, an obscure over-the-counter company, should you ask questions before your buy?

___   ___   You own stock in the company you work for, and you have been selling 45 shares each month to make payments on your new car. You learn that the next quarterly report will show a huge and unexpected loss. Can you sell before the bad news hits?

# CHAPTER SEVEN  Insider Trading, Bribes, and Payoffs  197

___  ___  As scientist at a research institute, you are going on television tomorrow to release a study showing that a major fast-food chain's hamburgers contribute to obesity, and a negative reaction on Wall Street is likely. Can you now sell the chain's stock short?

If the foregoing disclosures do not spark ethical fires the story of Metromedia should. Holding center stage was the German-born John Kluge who came with his family to the United States when he was only eight years old. Settling in Detroit young Kluge went to the public schools and upon graduation got a job on the assembly line at the Ford Motor Company. His academic accomplishments brought him a scholarship to Columbia University where he graduated in 1933 with a major in economics.[2] Kluge's competence in theory was subsequently complemented by a wizardry in financial practice.

Kluge's personal life was marked by a longing for comfort and privacy, both of which he found in his Waldorf Towers apartment in New York City. In his business life power and plaudits were his ambitions and both came in his career at Metromedia. For over a quarter century Kluge worked to develop and expand Metromedia and he did both so well that eventually he became the company's chairman and CEO. Metromedia's stockholders had reason to rejoice. The company's share price had jumped from $4.50 in 1974 to over $50.00 in 1984, making the firm a darling on Wall Street.

He was nearing 70 when he plunged into a series of activities that brought him big headlines and bigger bucks. How he accomplished both led one observer to dub him the magician who "pulled rabbits out of the hat. Using the hocus-pocus of leveraged buyouts, Kluge, right before your eyes, trebled his stakes (in Metromedia) while pocketing some $1.5 billion in cash and securities."[3] A clue to his tactics came earlier when he purchased the depreciation rights to $100 million of New York City's bus and subway system which, when complete, made the corporation's financial statements almost impenetrable—even to the experts. Impenetrabilities mounted when Kluge decided to mount a management leveraged-buyout program. Exactly how the plan was hatched and when the saga began is hard to determine but certain developments are clear in Kluge's strategy:

- In early 1984 Metromedia reported an 83 percent drop in fourth quarter earnings and a fall in net income from $221.5 million to $37.2 million. Stockholders were jolted.
- The numbers were later challenged by a prominent New York University accounting professor as being the result of a rather creative measurement technique.[4]
- The worried stockholders were offered by management what seemed to be a very good deal—$38 per share which was well above the then prevailing price. The prospectos failed to mention the true market value of Metromedia's seven television affiliates.

- The price was declared to be fair by the company's two major investment bankers, Lehmann Brothers and Bear Stearns, both of whom acknowledged that they had relied exclusively on information provided by Metromedia management itself. For its work Lehmann Brothers received $750,000 for a two-page opinion, with another $2 million to be paid if the deal went through. Bear Stearns received $500,000 for its opinion with another $2 million if the buyout went forward successfully.
- The company's law firm (Skaddin, Arps, Slate, Meagher & Sloane) found nothing wrong with the deal, and the accounting firm of Peat, Marwick and Mitchell saw nothing wrong with the company's books.
- On June 20, 1984 the stockholders bought the deal. A month earlier management members of the board had unanimously approved the MBO. A special meeting for outside directors met later and they, too, unanimously approved.
- Government regulators approved the leveraged buyout in late 1984.

Kluge was now king of the hill. Stockholders had received roughly $724 million in May of 1984 for a company estimated to be worth six times that amount just two years later. The estimate seems to be completely correct in light of Metromedia's subsequent sales. In late spring and early summer of 1985 Metromedia signaled its motives, motives clearly designed to enrich Kluge and his three associates (Robert Bennett, George Duncan and Stuart Subotmic). It sold its Boston television affiliate to Hearst Corporation and then quickly arranged another deal with Rupert Murdoch, the Australian newspaper king, and Denver oilman Marvin Davis for the sale of the remaining six stations. For the seven stations Kluge and friends received over $2 billion. The deal was overshadowed only by American Broadcasting System's sale of its affiliates to Capital Cities Corporation for $3.5 billion.

What is interesting about Metromedia's disposition of its big-city television stations was that a shrewd Rupert Murdoch was very willing to make the acquisition despite the fact that his ownership of the *New York Post* and the *Chicago Sun Times* was placed in jeopardy. This was because federal regulations prohibited one company from owning more than five percent of a broadcast station in the same city where it already owned a newspaper. It was also interesting that, as publicity increased over the transaction, Marvin Davis quietly pulled out of the arrangement on May 21, 1984. But Murdoch continued full steam ahead in pursuit of what he obviously thought was a good buy. It certainly was a good sale for Kluge and his friends.

Next on the chopping block was Metromedia's outdoor advertising business which it sold for $710 million in June 1986 to Patrick Joyce, founder and president of the Patrick Media Corporation. Around the same time Metromedia sold its paging and mobile phone business to Southwestern Bell for $1.65 billion. The fat cat had swallowed another elephant. Kluge's next move was to sell the Globetrotters and the Ice Capades for $30 million. The long and the short of it was that Kluge and friends netted about $3 billion in investments where Kluge had personally put nothing in. One of the country's wealthiest men seemed to be insatiable and for a man in his seventies, the quest for such vast wealth seemed inexplicable. Meanwhile, if the financial community showed any signs of restiveness, the Securities & Exchange Commission did not.

## *Questions:*

- Kluge is a modern Midas. Is he also a John Silver?
- Should society frown on billion-dollar fortunes for one person?
- What do you think of the behavior of the two investment firms, Lehmann Brothers and Bear Stearns?
- Was the prospectus issued by the sellers truthful?
- Where were the auditors when the evaluations of assets were made? If they were fooled by Kluge were they unethical?
- Did Metromedia's law firm represent management? Or stockholders? Whom should they have represented?
- If a law firm acts only on behalf of corporate management should it be punished severely?
- If you knew all details of Kluge's game plan and had a chance to be in his inner circle of friends would you join it?

Kluge's behavior contrasts sharply with past practices. During the 1930s, when most transactions in securities were effected by private investors, they were carried out mainly by professionals who, by and large, were associated with institutional investors. By contrast, as has already been noted, individual investors today account for only 10 percent of NYSE volume while institutions account for over 50 percent. And brokerage firms' own accounts may represent an additional 30 percent. In the 1930s there was virtually no cadre of professional investment analysts; today there are thousands, all sifting through mountains of data to discover clues to a company's future.[5] Where vast amounts of information are quickly available about corporate issuers, some scholars have argued that (1) the markets themselves, by promptly reporting what trading occurs, provide adequate counterchecks against early information advantages and (2) economic incentives allowing traders to use nonpublic information encourage and reward research initiative.

Others, however, see insider information as an unfair advantage even in today's impersonal, high-speed securities markets. Prior information about dividends, mergers, acquisitions, or products enables groups and individuals to turn hundreds of dollars into millions. With the flurry of merger-takeover activity, this temptation has been irresistible to many. Between 1983 and 1985, for example, 229 companies were involved in takeovers, mergers, and leveraged buyouts and of these 229, 72 percent had risen in price between the month before public announcement of the transaction and the day prior to the transaction. Is this accident or coincidence? If the stocks had followed the market, 52 percent would have risen. The odds that this occurred by chance are 1 in 50.[6]

Perhaps the temptations to wheel and deal are stronger for brokers. Although brokers and investment bankers have long lived on the same side of Wall Street, propinquity never led to marriage. Typically products of non-Ivy League schools like City College of New York and Fordham, brokers knew from experience that access to the inner sanctums of investment banking were closed to them. They were seen as freewheeling, aggressive types who hustled for business. On the other hand, long-established investment bankers like Salomon Brothers and Dillon Read, although they bought and sold stock, perceived their mission as raising venture capital to help industries to grow and prosper. They employed graduates of Yale, Columbia, and Princeton and gave them offices with paneled walls, mahogany desks, and lush carpeting, whereas brokers shared cubbyholes with Quotran machines. Neither group has been inclined to trade spaces.

## *Dimensions of the Problem*

The story might begin with a young man named Reich, a partner in the respected law firm of Wachtell, Lipton, Rosen and Katz. While Reich was described by his associates as hardworking and brilliant, the terms straight-shooting and ethical were never mentioned. Less than a year into his career, Reich met Dennis Levine, another brilliant performer not in law but in investment banking. Reich agreed to pass along tips of merger-takeover work being handled by the Wachtell firm. Less than five years later, Reich, now a 31-year-old whiz kid earning $500,000 a year as a Wachtell partner, felt the law's noose close around his neck. Called by his superiors to explain why the SEC was investigating him, Reich repeatedly denied each of the government's allegations. Told that his own law firm would not defend him, he broke down and cried. On October 9, 1986, Reich, pleading guilty to two counts of fraud, was ordered to jail and to pay nearly $500,000 in cash and property. One of the ironies of the story was that Reich took no money for his tips and seemed never to know the uses that Levine made of the leaked information. How a young man like Reich could reveal all and receive nothing gave a new twist to the word brilliant.

Levine, who took everything from Reich and gave nothing in return, was born in 1952 and grew up in the Bayside section of Queens. In 1972 he enrolled at Bernard Baruch College, a branch of the City University of New York, the first member of his family to attend college. At Baruch, Levine met a man who fueled his zeal for making money. The man was Jack Francis, a professor of economics and finance, who showed a great liking for Levine. During one of their talks the professor allegedly said, "Greed is a nice religion." The secular commandment paid off handsomely for Levine, who, between 1980 and the end of 1986, earned over $12 million in profits and interest through insider trading. The numbers became, in the words of one writer, "the stark epitaph of Dennis Levine's greed and compulsion, his imperious manipulation of friends and contemptuous betrayal of colleagues. But the numbers are only the cold facts of a story about how the optimism and desperation of one man's thirst for glory destroyed the course of some of Wall Street's brightest young stars, triggered the greatest scandal since the Great Crash of 1929, and proved that corruption in the stock market can have global repercussions."[7]

In a drama of squealing on friends that would have outraged the Mafia, Levine implicated Ivan Boesky, to whom he had funneled much of his own insider information, and Boesky betrayed Michael Milken. Ivan the Terrible was in a class of his own until November 14, 1986, when the SEC, on the basis of Levine-provided information, announced that the 49-year-old Boesky was also in the dragnet. With an estimated $1.25 billion in assets, Boesky headed the largest arbitrage firm in America. He had enrolled in three colleges before receiving his law degree but the law's appeal paled before the excitement of the investment world. This reward was a $200 million nest egg, a sum obviously inadequate to one of enormously high personal expectations. A member of university boards, generous benefactor of institutions of higher learning, and author of a well-received book, Boesky seemed to have it all.[8]

After government charges were made against Boesky, he played the same stonewalling game as Reich, agreeing to cooperate only after the SEC had confronted him with massive evidence of legal wrongdoing. Now the insider who exploited his friends on the financial front began to exploit them on the legal front. He secretly taped conversations with professional associates; he talked freely to government agents; he actually seemed grateful to pay $100 million in penalties and to return ill-gotten profits; he accepted banishment from the Street that was paved in gold for him. He did anything and everything to cut the penalty. Boesky epitomized the sighs-and-grunts theory of ethics.[9]

The Milken tale, reported in an earlier chapter, was simply the climax in a triple play that moved the ball from Levine to Boesky to Magnificent Mike. Milken made junk bonds popular, his employers at Drexel famous, and his earnings ($700 million in one year) unbelievable. But to seasoned observers it seemed that nowhere had ethical standards dropped more precipitously than in investment banking. A *Fortune* writer commented that "while other areas of business are in most respects no more unethical than ever, wrongdoing in this central arena makes a crisis of business ethics seem in full swing. And with investment banking now largely manned by the young, is the erosion of ethics here an early warning of imminent trouble elsewhere in business as this generation rises to power?" He amplified his views by stating that

> *insider trading is investment banking's most widely publicized sin, and since extra-sensory perception alone does not explain why the*

*stock price of takeover targets regularly rises in advance of official announcement, doubtless plenty of insider traders besides Boesky's confederate Levine remain uncaught. But much more pervasive, if less heralded, is the unscrupulousness that now infects relations with clients. Says Herbert A. Allen, Jr., president of the Allen & Co. Inc. investment banking firm: "A major disquieting factor is the loss of confidentiality, well short of illegality. Important clients can find out anything about other important clients."*[10]

Confidential information flowed freely from one investment house to others; the walls of constraint tumbled; fiduciary fidelity was mocked; cases appeared where one investment banker gave its client's plans to another of its clients. The financial skies poured acid rain on the unwary.

## Definitional Examples

Just what constitutes illegal insider trading remains confused. Congress has been cautious in defining it and courts have been inconsistent in explaining it. Some sense of the definitional problem can be better obtained from examples and court decisions than from reading the law. Twenty-five years ago the SEC amended its definition of insider trading from face-to-face dealings between buyer and seller to situations involving open-market transactions when there was no communication between buyer and seller.[11] The prevailing rule rests on the disclose-or-abstain principle, which means that someone having inside information has a duty to disclose the information or abstain from trading on the basis of it. But the problem becomes compounded when the question is asked, how did the individual secure inside information in the first place?[12] Three examples illustrate the problems that cloud the answers.

**Winans.** R. Foster Winans was hired in 1981 as a reporter for *The Wall Street Journal*, where he became one of the writers of the influential "Heard on the Street" column. Winans and David Carpenter were homosexuals who had been involved in a "spousal relationship" for over ten years. Carpenter also worked at the *Journal*, but for a briefer period than Winans. Referred by Winans, Carpenter was hired as a news clerk in December 1981. The practice of the *Journal* was to distribute to all new employees instructions on what amounted to the paper's code of ethics.[13] Winans was sent these instructions but later denied having ever received them.

In early January 1983, Winans started looking into the American Surgery Company as a possible topic for a future article. To improve his sources and increase his wealth, Winans purchased 100 shares of American Surgery stock for a brokerage account held in Carpenter's name at a cost of $1,814.17. After two favorable columns about the company were published in January and March 1983,[14] Winans sold the shares on May 17, 1983, for $4,673.64.

He also bought 1,000 shares of Institutional Investors stock in Carpenter's account on April 28, 1983, and after a favorable article appeared on June 1, 1983, the stock was sold five days later at a profit.

American Surgery remained a significant part of the story in that it indirectly led Winans to Peter Brant when Mark Delotte, a public relations consultant for American Surgery, put the two in touch. Delotte suggested Brant as a possible focus of an article about superbrokers. Brant was the number-one broker at Kidder Peabody, with a commission income of $1.8 million for the fiscal year December 1982 through November 1983. Brant and Winans met for the first time in mid-May of 1983; they met again on June 1, 1983, to tour the Racquet Club and have dinner at the restaurant 21. A third meeting on June 14 was intended to be an opportunity for Winans to observe Brant's meeting with a new client. When the potential client cancelled, the meeting turned into another general chat about Brant's phenomenal market success, his personal wealth, and his flamboyant lifestyle.

From June 1983 on, Brant became Winans' informant, confidant, and broker. Whenever Winans called his new friend, he used a pay phone outside *The Wall Street Journal* building in New York, identifying himself as Howard Cahn. Before Winans' article was scheduled to appear, Brant bought or sold stocks (depending on whether the story was positive or negative) prior to the article's appearance. After each transaction, Brant paid Winans a certain amount of money. This activity went on until mid-February 1984, when Winans told Brant he wanted no more meetings at the Racquet Club lest other *Journal* reporters see them together.

When the SEC began its investigation, Winans was called into the office of the managing director of Dow Jones & Company, which owns the *Journal*. Also present was corporate counsel. Both warned Winans not to give any false information to government investigators—a warning he did not heed. Winans denied having an interest in a brokerage account in someone else's name and further denied ever having received money from Brant, who also lied in subsequent statements to the SEC. Winans argued that what he did to his employer may have been unethical but that no law was violated—even though misappropriation of information was illegal.

## *Ethical Questions*

- Was *The Wall Street Journal* lacking in its monitoring and training programs, especially for new employees?
- Because Winans was not a fiduciary of a brokerage house or company, might his behavior be condoned?[15]

**Chiarella.** Vincent Chiarella was an employee of a printing company that handled confidential information for many firms, including forthcoming announcements of takeover bids. Chiarella used this information to purchase stock before the takeover announcements were made public. Over the course of 14 months, Chiarella realized a gain of more than $30,000 from 17 transactions based on inside information. When the facts became known, he was fired. Chiarella did not induce others to trade and made neither positive nor negative statements to others, but he was convicted by a district court for violating SEC regulations. On appeal, the Supreme Court overturned the decision, ruling that Chiarella had not violated section 10b–5 of the act. Even though Chiarella had possession of nonpublic market information, he had no legal duty to disclose his sources to the public; furthermore, no relationship of trust and confidence existed between each trading party. The justices also said that the lower court had failed to prove there was a fiduciary relationship between Chiarella and the sellers.[16]

## Ethical Question

- Does the Supreme Court's reasoning represent sound ethical reasoning?

**Dirks.** Raymond Dirks, a registered broker-dealer, had learned from a former employee of Equity Funding Corporation of America that Equity's funding successes were due in part to fraud. Although able to corroborate these allegations, Dirks was unable to convince the SEC to investigate or *The Wall Street Journal* to publish his story on Equity Funding's fraud. Dirks then informed his clients, who sold their holdings, causing the price of Equity stock to fall before the SEC finally began to investigate. The SEC then claimed that Dirks improperly disclosed material nonpublic information to his clients, who traded on the information. But, obviously confused by its application of a utilitarian ethic, the SEC limited its penalty to censure because Dirks had brought Equity Funding's massive fraud to light in the first place.[17] Dirks, a determined soul, went to the Supreme Court, which rewarded his persistence by reversing the SEC's sanction and vindicating Dirks' action. The court reached its decision on grounds that the purchasers of Equity Funding stock relied on neither Dirks nor his clients and that Dirks (and those who traded on the basis of his information) were outsiders. In vindicating Dirks, the Court offered three criteria for judging whether prohibited insider information existed:

1. *Derivative liability.* The "tippee" who receives material nonpublic information from the insider can, on the basis of this information, trade if the insider commits no breach of the fiduciary relationship between the insider and corporate stockholders. In other words, the outsider's duty to disclose or refrain is based upon—or derived from—the insider's duty to disclose or refrain. In addition, the insider does not breach any fiduciary duty to corporate stockholders if the disclosed information is meant to be used for corporate purposes, not personal gain.
2. *Misappropriation.* To reduce the risks of abuse, some lower courts have introduced the misappropriation theory, which extends liability to all who violate the duty owed to their own employers or to clients of their employers—even though such persons have no formal duty to the stockholders of a target corporation. But the Court added that, if the tipper

breached an obligation and the tipped knew that fact, liability would be incurred. The law's garment, however, has a wrinkle. If the misappropriator's employer is not itself a purchaser or seller of securities, the employer may not be able to bring action under the securities law. Under the moralist's microscope, however, the misappropriator, as well as the insider, is guilty of an unethical act.

3. *Constructive insider.* Under certain circumstances outsiders enter into a special confidential relationship with the issuer and become a fiduciary of its shareholders and subject to the duty to disclose or refrain from taking actions to benefit from the information.[18] This special confidential relationship occurs when a corporation has a right to expect outsiders to keep nonpublic information confidential. If they do not they are just as guilty as insiders who misappropriate confidential information. The key word in determining the illegality and impropriety of insider trading is Access.[19]

## Ethical Question

- Do these three legal criteria add to the ethical norms you have used in your previous analyses?

The Chiarella and Dirks decisions provide vivid contrasts between economic reasoning, which holds that the availability of information improves the efficiency of the market, and the SEC, which is concerned with fairness to investors—possible only when all information is available to all at roughly the same time. In current legal thought, outsiders like lawyers, accountants, and bankers could become insiders burdened by fiduciary responsibilities if they have access to information intended exclusively for corporate purposes. But the field is far from clear from both legal and ethical perspectives. To illustrate, if a corporate executive finds nonpublic market material information about another company, does he or she have any obligation to that corporation? Does a bank that learns, during an arm's-length negotiating session, about a proposed takeover have a duty to the targeted company's stockholders? Court decisions suggest that they do not.

## Ethical Assessment

Recognizing that it is not always easy to identify the actors (tipper and tipped) that are involved, what each knows about the other's intentions, or the effects that the exchange of information will have on other parties, Congress and the courts have been reluctant to make broad generalizations about insider-trading practices. The restraint is both understandable and laudable. Recognizing the restrictions, ethicists would nevertheless be prepared to say that there is a *prima facie* case for believing insider trading is wrong, independent of consequences, if any of the following occurs:

1. The tipper is careless in handling confidential information with anyone.

2. The tipper seeks personal gain even if the gain is not a pecuniary one.
3. The tipper knows that the informant is a responsible officer of one of the involved companies.
4. The tipper deliberately refrains from finding out the facts on grounds that "ignorance is bliss."

To these should be appended another fact, namely, the professional ethic that falls on individuals whose expertise and probity bring to their roles special privileges and special duties. If any act of a professional (1) infringes the moral rights of others, (2) erodes public confidence in the investment community and the profession, or (3) invites government discipline (when enforced voluntary codes of conduct could achieve the same result), the total result is baneful. To argue that economies are produced by inside trading is not enough. They well may be. But the means become, in ethical terms, the more critical criteria for judgment.

## Bribes and Payoffs

When governments grant subsidies to certain groups, the activity is legitimized on grounds that it has been approved by elected representatives who speak for all the people. The explanation often masks a quite different reality. Lobbyists for special-interest groups often draft the proposal that a willing congressional sponsor puts before the House or Senate. As we have seen earlier, each special favor is then defended on grounds that the favored group deserves to be shielded from the ill effects of market competition. In the private sector itself, efforts to modify or suspend the rules of competition take a variety of forms, one of which is in the form of payments. By and large, such payments are deemed illicit if they are bribes and are less clear in ethical terms if they are responses to extortion. A bribe is usually defined as a voluntary, self-initiated act taken to influence the decision of a person of trust in government.

By extension, bribery also covers gifts or payments made to influence the decisions of persons of trust in private organizations. However, when Congress passed the Foreign Corrupt Practices Act, it refused to extend the meaning of bribery to include efforts to influence managers of private organizations. Possibly the legislators took the restricted meaning of the word because they knew that in certain other countries bribery was a way of life. That way was noted by John McCloy, the man who looked into allegations of bribery by executives of Gulf Oil. Testifying before a Senate committee on April 5, 1976, McCloy quoted an SEC study that failed to identify a single country in the Mideast and the Pacific Rim that made bribery an illegal act. Moreover, previous American efforts to define bribery in legal terms were spasmodic and ineffective. Nevertheless, most Americans felt intuitively that the game of competition was being played unfairly by those who took the bribery route even though arguments have been made that bribes sometimes advance legitimate interests.[20] So indifferent were philosophers toward the question of bribery that, as late as 1984, not a single

CHAPTER SEVEN  Insider Trading, Bribes, and Payoffs    207

reference to the topic appeared in the *Philosopher's Index*. Yet long before the philosophers formally acknowledged their importance the giving of bribes to legislators and judges, to athletes and referees, to labor-union officials and corporate executives was widespread. How difficult it is to distinguish bribery from other forms of payment is best illustrated by examples.

## *Definitional Examples*

**The Haitian Dealmakers.**[21]   Imagine yourself a senior vice president of a company that has signed an agreement with Haiti for a 99-year lease to build a complex of hotels and entertainment facilities. You had headed the negotiating team and got along so well with Haitian government officials that you have been offered, without solicitation, a five-year, tax-free status for your company. It is clear that Haiti desperately needs an assured source of jobs and revenue. Everything proceeds swiftly: licenses and building permits are issued promptly; labor leaders cooperate fully; and local public opinion is favorable.

Thus encouraged, your company signs final papers and construction begins. Suddenly you are told by local officials that they want a $500,000 cash payment, implying that without the money, so much red tape would be placed in the company's way that construction would never be completed. When the company refuses to pay, it is told bluntly to leave Haiti. The estimated loss from such abrupt a departure is about $3 million. The company has never before made payoffs and you know your CEO and the board of directors enjoy good reputations for integrity. The company will not go broke if it forfeits the $3 million. But neither will it keep its enviable record of paying annual dividends to stockholders. A decision must be made promptly.

## *Ethical Question*

- What would you recommend to senior management? Why?

**The Big Tipper.**   Before ending a vacation in Halifax, Harry Smith contacted a Canadian friend to arrange a business dinner meeting in Saint John's, located on the western side of the Bay of Fundy. Arriving at the Nova Scotia debarkation point for the ferry only 15 minutes before departure, Smith was dismayed to discover a long line at the ticket counter. Minutes passed and the line barely moved. Smith realized that he had to act quickly or the boat would leave without him.

Canceling his scheduled business meeting in Saint John's was out of the question; it would embarrass him and, more important, would cost him a big deal. So he sauntered to the front of the line and politely said to the passenger who was about to buy a ticket, "It will only take a moment to pick up the reserved ticket being held for me." Winking at the clerk, he said loudly: "I'm here to pick up Smith's ticket," while pushing $50 toward the agent. Smith received the ticket and arrived in Saint John's at the appointed time. However, he had made no reservation at the restaurant and no table was available. He slipped $50 to the maitre d', and he and his guest were promptly seated in a prime location.

## Ethical Question

- Were Smith's actions ethical?

**Operations Rescue.** When famine struck a developing nation in the Third World, a number of leaders from various churches and synagogues gathered in New York to devise a strategy to raise $10 million. The money would come from modest contributions from individuals, who would be solicited from the pulpit. Collection envelopes were printed with the heading, Help the Hungry, and attractive brochures were distributed to encourage potential donors to be as generous as possible. Because the need was great and the time short, a crash program was planned. The effort was so well orchestrated that, before Thanksgiving, the $10-million goal was reached. Elated by its success the group determined to embark on a second multi-million-dollar drive.

In late November, a small staff was hired and headquartered in Chicago. This group, called Operations Rescue, dispatched a small professional team (along with a few volunteers) to the area targeted for aid. The team's job was to assure that food and medical supplies were actually delivered to the needy as promptly as possible. Heading this overseas unit was Matt Thornton, a man with long experience in social work. By January the team had begun preliminary operations in the host country. Contacts were made with government, business, and labor leaders in order to have everything in readiness for deliveries to the hungry when the shipments arrived. Though due in March, the first relief ship arrived in early February. Thornton and his colleagues were overjoyed because they knew that prompt distribution of food would save many more lives.

When Thornton's people arrived at the dock to supervise unloading from the arriving vessel, they were told that the harbor master wanted to see Thornton immediately in his office. There Thornton was told that official approval for the ship's unloading, and permits for the truck convoys to move, required "a modest gift of $250,000 in American dollars." In total shock and anger, Thornton declared he would never pay such blackmail. "It is," he said, "extortion from the dying and I shall never be part of such a scheme."

The harbor master, unruffled, went on to explain quietly that because his government was almost bankrupt, his duty was to take care of "my own people." When asked who his people were, the harbor master refused to specify, saying that to do so would jeopardize their position within the country. He added that, if the American made any effort to publicize the conversation, he would simply deny it—and his word would carry more weight than an alien's. He concluded the conversation by saying, "You either pay—or the food rots." Taken aback, Thornton decided to divulge the conversation to no one in his group, telling them only that there was confusion over needed government permits that he hoped to clear up within a day or so. Already accustomed to the circuitous modes of operation in the host country, the group took Thornton's explanation at face value. That night, Thornton cabled Chicago headquarters to outline the situation and to seek advice.

## Ethical Question

- If you were chief of the Chicago rescue operation staff, what would you tell Thornton to do?

**Embargo Aftermath.** Orin Akins, who had been head of Ashland Oil for 17 years, was forced out of office in September 1981.[22] His resignation came after a six-month private investigation commissioned by Ashland's directors to discover whether Akins had made unauthorized payoffs to get crude oil from Oman in 1980. The investigators concluded that neither Akins nor Ashland had violated any U.S. laws, but it criticized questionable payments Ashland had made to wealthy Libyans with ties to the Sultan of Oman, as well as other dealings with a Canadian adventurer who helped the sultan seize power in 1970.

The incident that triggered board action came after President Carter's embargo on Iranian imports, a move that cost Ashland a quarter of its total oil supply. Desperate to replace the loss, Akins paid a mystery man named Yehir Omar for help in securing crude oil from Oman. But Omar had one condition: Ashland must buy some of its oil from him and his associates at marked-up prices. In September 1980, Ashland entered into a contract with the Omani government to buy up to 20,000 barrels of crude oil a day. Ashland's internal investigators found no evidence that Omar helped to get the contract; he nevertheless demanded his share of the money connected to the Omani purchase. On Akins' direct order, the company wired $1,350,000 to an Omar-related concern called Mont d'Or. When an Ashland official named Bill McKay reported the payment to an outside director, who agreed that the payment was improper, Mont d'Or was pressured to return the money—which it did.

Akins argued that, because Omar was not an official of Oman, bribery could not have occurred under the Federal Corrupt Practices Act and that he sought only to serve Ashland loyally and well. He cooperated fully with the company's investigating committee, which concluded that Akins had not violated American law because Omar was, as Akins alleged, not an Omani official when he was paid off. Nevertheless, the board kept pressure on Akins until he resigned.

## Ethical Questions

- Was Akins treated fairly?
- If you think he was treated unfairly and you later learned he was fined for making illegal payments in the 1972 presidential campaign to both parties, would you change your mind?

- As you will read subsequently, when Akins was U.S. Ambassador to Saudi Arabia, he refused Henry Kissinger's order to facilitate bribery and paid the price by being fired. Does this influence your final judgment of the man?

**Miles Makers.** Following his discharge from the army after World War II, Jason Miles, a high school graduate, began working doggedly to build his own manufacturing company, Miles Makers. After a rocky start, the company turned the corner in 1953 and posted increased sales and earnings every year thereafter. As a result, Miles expanded operations from his first small plant in Pennsylvania to locations in Georgia and Alabama. He always followed a quadrilateral management philosophy: (1) build all plants according to the same design in order to cut building and maintenance costs; (2) run production along identical processes; (3) if change is needed, make it in all plants closely on the heels of the pacesetter; and (4) keep the size of every work force the same (about 300 employees) because this allows plant managers to know their people on a first-name basis.

In 1984 Jason Miles began to talk retirement to his son, Marty, a bright 42-year-old whose MBA was to him a signal of competence and to his father a badge of honor. In 1985 Marty suggested that starting one or two operations in a Third World country might be useful, not so much as a hedge against potential loss in domestic markets, but as a way to expand markets and increase profits. If successful, the project would provide jobs for needy people and add luster to the Miles' name as a socially responsible corporation. The father approved and, after considerable negotiation, plants were established in Nigeria and in Botswana—again along the precise module patterns of the domestic plants.

Within two years it was clear the plants were not going to meet expectations. Investigations showed that their American managers, strangers in a strange land, were naive about the local rules. The CEO of their major competitor, a subsidiary of a Paris-based corporation, made no effort to conceal the fact that his people regularly paid money to local officials, employed strategically placed government agents as retainers, and paid for memberships of local officials in the most select private clubs in the area.

Marty was persuaded that if Miles Makers played according to the same rules, it could outdistance its competitors by a substantial margin. However, when Marty urged Jason to take this approach, the father reacted angrily by saying that such practices violated not only the law but his conscience as well. Marty argued in vain that even the Federal Corrupt Practices Act made distinctions between grease money and bribery and that he simply needed grease to lubricate the machinery essential to the firm's success. When the father adamantly refused, the son backed off.

In late summer of 1991, Jason announced his retirement. Although the news came as no surprise, it caused a certain amount of dismay among workers who had deep respect for "the old man." Son Marty promptly arranged for a public dinner to honor his father, at which the mayor would give the principal address, and invited senior managers from the Alabama

CHAPTER SEVEN   Insider Trading, Bribes, and Payoffs   211

and Georgia plants to fly in for the occasion. The dinner was scheduled for December 17. Invitations had been accepted by the dignitaries, a large turnout was expected from local merchants, and nearly all workers in the original Pennsylvania facility planned to attend. The dinner promised to be the town's event of the year.

On the morning of December 15 Jason went to his son's office to check on a problem related to the Georgia plant. On the desk were notes on a phone conversation Marty had had several weeks before with the manager of the Nigerian plant. Even though it was in his son's handwriting and marked "strictly confidential," Jason felt comfortable about checking memoranda concerning the company's operations. He read:

*Phoned J.L. this morning and made explicit the following points:*
*1. In view of the deteriorating performance of our Nigerian operation, it is imperative to take aggressive steps to restore our competitive position. We need an imaginative use of tying arrangements with our French friends who are worried about competition from us. I want you to approach them with a deal whereby our retailers will be forced to buy one of their products and their retailers will, in turn, be forced to buy a product from us.*

*2. For products not covered by them, seek to establish exclusive trading areas. We will respect their turf if they respect ours. This will be tricky, I know, because both of us will want the best marketing area, but I think it can be worked out through some hard bargaining and realistic compromises.*

*3. Contact government people on a very quiet basis. Take the customs director out for lunch on occasion and, when the time is right, let him know that you have a "special fund" that can profit him for his assistance. Also follow our competitor's practice of hiring retainers who have influence in government. God knows we do not need them but these influence peddlers are in a position to hurt us if they slow down export licenses, interfere with franchise agreements, or recall shipping permits.*

*4. Let me know realistically how much cash you need so that on my planned year-end visit to you I can provide sufficient wherewithal for you to carry out the aforementioned projects.*

*5. One thing must be stressed: In no way can this information be shared with my father. In foreign operations he is simply out of his depth. But we must be realists and realism demands recognizing that laws passed for Americans working in America are not laws passed by Nigerians for Nigerians working in Nigeria. We must play according to their rules if we want to be in their ballparks.*

With trembling hand Jason put down the memorandum and slumped into a chair to await his son's return. Each minute he took a firm position, which he just as quickly abandoned. What would he say to his son? More important, what *should* he say? Questions swirled through his mind: Was he out of his depth? Were Americans imposing their moral rules on the Nigerians? If he acted precipitously to rescind his son's directive, would he cost the Nigerians their jobs? Might he even jeopardize the jobs of his own people—the solid kind who raised good families, paid taxes, went to church, and were the real pillars of the community? Finally, he muttered softly, "When it gets right down to it, should my moral code prevail when my son will soon be the new captain of the ship?"

## *Ethical Question*

- If Jason sought your counsel, what would you tell him?

## *Making Distinctions*

**Bribes and Gifts.** Some who analyze the foregoing examples may come to quick conclusions that to them are logically consistent and morally defensible. Inconsistencies in viewpoints are also possible. Considering bribes from historical perspectives may clarify matters, and traditional meanings of words provide clues to present problems. In early France, for example, to bribe was to beg. In England, to bribe was to steal, the degree of evil being determined by such factors as the thief's age, the intensity of his need, local mores, and the victim's wealth. But the presumption in England was always there: to bribe was to steal and to steal was evil. Although we can make the same presumption about bribery, factors such as time, intention, and local customs cannot be automatically dismissed.

Time and intention, for instance, are sometimes used to draw the line between gift and bribe. A gift is given to express gratitude for a legitimate service *previously* rendered even though the giver may hope that the same favoritism will be provided in the future. Bribery, on the other hand, is designed to influence a decision related to a *future* service contract, sale, or loan that the bribe giver would not get under fair and open competition. Gratitude for past favors is, of course, legitimate. But is gratitude that is used to shape future decisions legitimate? Often donors have mixed motives: to thank and to influence.[23] Although the ethical shadings in such cases are blurred, the ethical difference between gift and bribe is clear: the bribe is tied to a favorable future decision and neither donor nor recipient is in doubt about its purpose. Gift givers, on the other hand, have the benefit of the doubt; bribe givers and bribe takers do not. But is bribery an intrinsic evil? Consider the following incidents.

The eminent and respected German philosopher, Ludwig Wittgenstein, showed no hesitation in bribing certain Nazi officials to protect a sister living in Vienna under German occupation. The Rollins Corporation of Atlanta voluntarily disclosed to the SEC that it had passed $127,000 between 1971 and 1976 to municipal government officials in Mexico in connection with the company's outdoor advertising business. Rollins expressed its philosophy forthrightly: "In the company's judgment the discontinuation of such payments would adversely affect the operations of the company's subsidiary in the locations where such payments were made. Accordingly, the company will authorize such payments in the future where no reasonable alternative is available."[24] More interesting than the company's position was the response from Richard Rowe, director of SEC's Office of Corporation Finance, who said that Rollins would be required to make no further disclosures about its Mexican payments and, more important, that he would not object if the company continued to make similar grants in the future. With the admission came a typical regulatory warning not to take the Rollins situation as a precedent.

Clearly, bribery has been widely practiced, widely tolerated, and even vigorously defended in many parts of the world as a necessary way to obtain favorable treatment. In global markets, payments to local agents, consultants, middlemen, or foreign officials are often a prerequisite to business success. That bribes could properly enter the facilitative flow was openly acknowledged; a scratch-my-back-and-I'll-scratch-yours principle was the pure and simple logic of a possibly less pure and less simple ethic.[25]

**Extortion and Payoffs.** Extortion and payoffs are not like bribes. The motive of bribers is to bring beneficial results to which the briber is not entitled. The extortionist threatens evil to others, who have a rightful claim to press, unless payment is received. Among American longshoremen extortions are a way of life. Payoffs are a form of grease money to have done what should be performed but, absent the grease, is not likely to be done. Payoffs have been called transactional bribes, but the motives for giving—and the results sought—are so different from the briber's motive that subsuming them under the heading of bribery leads to mistaken ethical assessment.[26] The Gulf Oil incident is relevant.

Gulf Oil's chairman, Robert Dorsey, was told by the ruling powers in South Korea in 1970 that Gulf's continued prosperity depended on coming up with a $10 million contribution to their party. Payments were made and the story became front-page news. Dorsey came under heavy fire. A special investigating committee concluded, however, that the "donations" were not bribes: not initiated by Gulf, they were treated by the corporation as distasteful efforts by Korean officials to obtain contributions that Gulf had no desire to make. No one disputed the fact that money changed hands. The moral question was whether the payoffs represented grease money intended to lubricate the hands of officials to do their duty or were bribes designed to get concessions to which company was not entitled.

At the time of Gulf's first contribution, the Korean government was being encouraged, if not pressured, by American officials to move toward open and free elections. The Koreans who approached Gulf believed that responding to this "encouragement" would involve heavy campaign expenses that they could not meet. To them, therefore, it was natural that foreign investors, especially Americans, should help. The Gulf representative in Korea viewed the contribution as support for the development of democratic processes and communicated this attitude to the Pittsburgh headquarters.

Dorsey said that Korea's pressure left little to the imagination. In light of his company's huge investment there, Dorsey made the decision to contribute $1 million for what he "sincerely considered to be in the best interests of the company and its shareholders."[27] Eventually, Dorsey's mistakes (illicit political contributions and the like) caught up with him and he was summarily fired by Gulf's directors in January 1976.[28] The dismissal came after a top Korean official named S. K. Kim demanded a $10 million "gift" to help in the 1970 election—a demand Dorsey initially refused but later met with a compromise donation of $3 million.

Dorsey could appeal to history as well as to ethics to justify his actions. A century ago, responding to accusations of bribing public officials to expedite completion of his Southern Pacific Railroad, C. P. Huntington said: "If you have to pay money to have the right thing done, it is only just and fair to do it. . . . If a man has the power to do great evil and won't do right unless he is bribed to do it, I think the time will be well spent . . . to go up and bribe the judge."[29] And when Joseph Wharton (the Philadelphia nickel monopolist who established America's first business school at the University of Pennsylvania) was criticized for seeking special tariff favors from government officials, he responded tartly: "I am one of the men who create and maintain the prosperity of the nation and who enable it to survive even the affliction of wrong-headed and cranky legislators."[30]

Few corporate or political figures would today make similar statements. But the reality is that illicit payments tend to be ignored when nations experience bad years. During the Gulf episode, the United States deficits in international trade were costing American workers about three million jobs annually and American corporations billions of sales dollars—losses aggravated by the estimated $10 billion in exports lost annually because of government regulations alone. In such circumstances the government itself wanted American business to succeed.

For years, as Washington "solved" the problem of bribes and payoffs by ignoring them, the number of payoffs and bribes grew quietly under a lid of official discretion. The State Department had received cables over the years from American embassies describing bribery as a way of life in countries to which they were attached; indeed, in 1973 Ambassador James Akins was fired two weeks after being named ambassador to Saudi Arabia for refusing to abide by a cable signed by Secretary of State Henry Kissinger asking Akins to seek Saudi approval of a multimillion dollar payment by Northrop Corporation to facilitate a military arms sale. The *Chicago Tribune* had run a lead story on April 11, 1976, reporting that a high-ranking CIA official admitted that many of his operators daily reported tales of bribery to Washington—evidently with little effect.[31]

When, however, a Senate investigating committee discovered in 1975 that Lockheed Aircraft's overseas payments had reached into the Dutch royal family and into the highest level of the Japanese government, the lid of congressional indifference came off. Discretion became dismay and dismay turned to disgust. Suddenly payoffs and bribes threatened to unseat a queen, topple a government, and incriminate officials of at least a dozen friendly countries. Lockheed was only one of more than three dozen multinationals (ranging from munitions makers and oil producers to drug manufacturers and bank companies) that were eventually caught in the Senate's investigatory nets.

Lockheed was made the example because, as the largest defense contractor in the world, its reach was well-nigh universal, its war chest was substantial, and its vulnerability to pressures was known abroad because of its need for profits in the jungle warfare of defense contractors. Shortly after the end of World War II, Lockheed had learned from painful experiences in Indonesia that nonpayment to a demanding official meant loss of business; in this instance it was Indonesia's decision to buy French Caravelles instead of Lockheed Jetstars. At that time, Gordon Meyers, the company's marketing vice president, said the demand was discussed and rejected because "it just wasn't right." In the summer of 1970, Lockheed had received another jolt when it sought to sell two aircraft to the Philippines and the Pentagon thwarted the effort by offering 12 old C-119 models free. Lockheed officials decided that in the world of international business, payments to the powerful were simply dues for club membership.[32]

**Government Reactions.** The Lockheed decision was one of many by corporate executives that led Senator Frank Church (Democrat, Idaho) to launch a series of investigations. The first probe began on May 16, 1975, against the oil giants — Gulf, Exxon, and Mobil. Lockheed soon found itself in the public glare when Senator William Proxmire (Democrat, Wisconsin) said his Senate Banking Committee would hold public hearings on that company's overseas payments. The announcement sent shivers down the spines of Lockheed officers, who remembered the Senator's vigorous opposition to a federal loan needed to save the company from bankruptcy in 1971. Unhappily for the companies, the exposures coincided with the post-Watergate moral fervor.

President Gerald Ford reflected American public opinion when he said that the United States bore a clear responsibility to the international community to stop questionable payments. In Ford's opinion, "corrupt business practices struck at the very heart" of America's moral code and its faith in free enterprise. To protect both, the president appointed a cabinet-level task force, chaired by Commerce Secretary Elliot Richardson, to address the payoff issues effectively. The usual politicking occurred as the administration and Congress jockeyed for the central role in providing remedies. Even the Internal Revenue Service caught the fever. On March 7, 1976—despite the fact that American law did not require disclosure of books and records of their foreign subsidiaries—corporate executives found themselves subjected to long interrogations by revenue agents. Affidavits detailing management's knowledge of corporate slush funds, bribery schemes, and other financial information were demanded. Some executives called the IRS intervention a witch hunt, while others questioned the ethics of the agency's methods. Most, however, went along if the IRS hinted that approval of corporate tax returns would be delayed.[33]

Basing its policies on recommendations made by Richardson's commission, the Ford administration advocated full disclosure of questionable payments—but without criminal penalties. It was feared, however, that (1) disclosure's paperwork costs would mount astronomically, (2) noncriminal penal activities seemingly condoned bribery, and (3) the vital interests of foreign governments would be devastatingly affected. Many foreigners insisted that the United States should recognize that its moral responsibility must take into account the interest of its allies, who were long accustomed to the payoff game: American "puritanism" should not be foisted on others.

Despite the fears of Western European leaders, Senator Proxmire introduced a bill in July 1976 that closely paralleled an earlier and tougher SEC recommendation. It placed tight controls over accounting, required (for the first time) subject companies to keep books and records of its payments abroad, prohibited falsification of company records, made it a crime to deceive an auditor in connection with the financial review of a publicly held corporation, and provided penalties of up to $10,000 fines or two-year imprisonments upon the executive's conviction of bribery charges. The legislation was designed to tell the world that bribery by American companies was total unacceptable.

**The Foreign Corrupt Practices Act.** In December 1977 President Carter signed the Foreign Corrupt Practices Act into law.[34] The law made it a crime for the first time in history for corporations to bribe an official of a foreign government or of a political party to obtain or retain business in another country. Although similar to the 1976 proposals of Senators Proxmire and Church, the fines were stiffer—up to $1 million for corporate violations and up to $10,000 and five years in jail for individual violations. The bill was approved in the Senate by acclamation and in the House by a 349 to 0 vote.

Notwithstanding the scope of its potential impact, no significant business group opposed the bill because, in the post-Watergate moral climate, opposition would be interpreted as support for evil practices. The Corporate Law Section of the Criminal Bar Association and the American Institute of Certified Public Accountants did interpose objections but these were made largely on technical, not moral, grounds. A few critics noted with alarm that the precedent-making requirement for data keeping, the "books and records" stipulation, could be used subsequently by the SEC as a hook to justify the commission's intervention into corporate governance and other internal corporate affairs.[35]

Legitimate suspicions always surface when wide-sweeping legislation proceeds through Congress too smoothly: either the cause is so noble that no one can vote against it or the bill is so ambiguous that no one can understand it. There was something of both in the FCPA. Nevertheless, what had been denounced by critics as "a curious distinction" (bribes are forbidden and grease payments are tolerated) seemed to make sense. Although payments to reluctant customs officials to approve shipments, secure required permits, or obtain police protection are not permitted in the United States, they are commonplace elsewhere. In such cases American businesses may then play according to local rules. Corporate executives, however, were understandably concerned that such nice distinctions might not be understood by government field agents. In view of the law's ambiguity, Hewlitt-Packard's corporate counsel, D. Craig Norlund, expressed the rather common corporate opinion when he said that it was better to "put everything off limits rather than run the risk of somebody not understanding the distinctions of the law."[36]

## Moral Assessments

The high moral excitement that attended passage of the FCPA has subsided and will remain dormant until another major scandal comes to public attention. Beneath the calm, however, is a fair amount of continuing interest by the relatively few who desire a better moral climate for business but who differ over the means to achieve it. Not unexpectedly, the American penchant for legal "fixes" has motivated some people to suggest more institutional reforms. *The Wall Street Journal*, for example, used its editorial page on February 27, 1976, to urge the government to work with the Organization for Economic Cooperation and Development (OECD) to produce an international code of business behavior. The late Theodore Purcell had urged American firms to experiment with a board ethics committee whose director-secretary would ideally be a corporate officer—perhaps general counsel—as suggested by William Gossett, former president of the American Bar Association and former vice president of Ford Motor Company.[37]

Such proposals have the merit of forcing people to think about the moral rules that should go into an international code, or that should be enforced by a firm's director of corporate conduct. Concern for the appropriate moral rules will, in the light of the publicity the FCPA has drawn, begin with the bribery issue, but it cannot stop there. Other questions arise: Is the American legal system fair to non-Americans? Does the FCPA represent moral imperialism by Americans? If bribery is wrong, what other obligations fall on the corporation? The questions merit attention.

**American Justice and Fairness to Others.** In the past, trouble arose primarily over application of American antitrust laws to American firms doing business in other countries. Although U.S. courts and administrators had attempted to be very sensitive to the interest of other nations, Congress had been less so. Complicating the matter is the fact that antitrust legislation in the United States differs in many ways from its counterparts elsewhere: suits are time-consuming and very complex; the United States permits treble damages for successful private plaintiffs, a practice particularly offensive to foreign nations; extremely large sums are at stake; parties bringing the case often do so because of commercial interest not directly related to the lawsuit itself; and discovery and enforcement procedures used here differ in some respects from practices elsewhere.[38] Each difference is touched by ethics.

Consider, for example, the Westinghouse Electric Corporation. During the late 1960s and early 1970s, when the company signed contracts to construct nuclear facilities, it pledged to supply those facilities with uranium fuel for a fixed term at a fixed price, subject to an escalator clause pegged to the general rate of inflation. However, Westinghouse itself was not a significant producer of uranium and did not cover itself under future contracts to guarantee delivery. At the time of the contracts, the going price for uranium was between $6 and $8 per pound; by 1975 the price had reached $26 a pound, and by 1978 had jumped to $44 a pound. Facing multibillion-dollar losses, Westinghouse refused to honor its contracts and the utilities brought suit.

If the courts sustained the contract provisions, Westinghouse would be bankrupted; if excused from performance, the utilities themselves would suffer unexpected and significant cost increases. Westinghouse argued that its inability to meet the contract was caused by the operation of a foreign cartel formed by major uranium producers. To prove its case, it demanded documents from the accused parties in Australia, South Africa, England, and Canada. England's House of Lords flatly refused to honor the American petition, and the other three countries adopted specific measures to prohibit compliance with the discovery request.

The case was ultimately settled by the parties themselves, but the litigation had lasting repercussions. For one thing, there is a changed attitude on the part of the United States government. In the past, the State and Justice Departments accepted protests from foreign countries and then interceded, when appropriate, on behalf of the protesting nation. More recently, the foreign nations have been told that where private litigation is concerned they should appear in the courts as *amici*—a procedure that effectively puts the private parties of a foreign nation on the periphery. The FCPA exacerbated the problem and, by so doing, intensified the moral debate.[39]

**FCPA and Ethics.** At this point, the Foreign Corrupt Practices Act provides opportunities to suggest how the reasoning of different ethical schools of thought (utilitarians, situationalists, and deontologists) might be put to work. A strong case can be made that utilitarians would disapprove FCPA because of its possible harmful consequences to American society—jobs lost, trade deficits raised, antagonisms heightened. What is fair competition when non-Americans play under different rules? Hobbled by their inability to behave according to an ethically low common denominator, situational ethicists, on the other hand, could see the issue in the same terms but from different perspectives: FCPA is simply another example of America's indifference to particular situations. At issue was the old maxim, "When in Rome, do as the Romans do." However, because the ancient Romans were capable of all sorts of debaucheries, it may be asked—as Congress did indeed ask—whether the maxim made ethical sense. But situationalists would answer that "no matter how much we beat our breasts about honesty and integrity and ethical standards of business conduct, if American firms wish to do business in foreign lands, they must play by the foreigner's rules, not ours. Otherwise, they'll do no business at all."[40] Furthermore, if all the trips, promotions, and vacation incentives used by Americans to influence their own countrymen's businesses are incorporated into a situationalist ethic judgment, the percent of the sales dollar spent to influence domestic business is greater than the proportion used to influence business overseas.

Differing from both utilitarians and situationalists are the deontologists, who applaud congressional condemnation of bribery because bribes are given to get what, under ordinary rules of competition and fair play, would not otherwise be secured. A second deontological reason for supporting FCPA is that it discourages company efforts to conceal managerial incompetencies. The evil is further intensified when the bribe is given with full knowledge that the payment will end in private pockets, with the added costs passed on to unwitting consumers through higher prices.

To deontologists, the initiative is taken by the briber; the motive is circumvention of the rules; the method is perversion of public officials; and the result is exploitation of customers. Deontologists would also stress the fact that bribery of a public official is always unacceptable because it violates legal justice (respect for the law), frustrates exchange or commutative justice by subverting the explicit contract officials have with their governments, as well as the implicit contract governments have with merchants to treat them on equal terms.

Even if it is not always a *prima facie* wrong to offer and to accept bribes in all contexts, it is an intrinsic wrong to do so in morally "clean" societies. Accordingly, a bribe-offerer or a bribe-taker must defend the morality of the act either by showing that there are countervailing moral considerations in its favor or, alternatively, by showing that the moral context is so corrupt that the factors that generate *prima facie* duties do not apply here. This strategy of moral justification, of course, is not unique to bribery. It may hold in relation to a wide range of what are ordinarily taken to be *prima facie* duties.[41] On the issue of bribery, courts have been deontologically oriented. In two 1989 cases, for example, the judges held that the essential element was *intent* to influence.[42] Before 1977 Congress, sensing the difficulty in establishing intent, had been deliberately ambiguous, but with passage of the FCPA the legislators embraced the judicial interpretation of bribery.

In assessing the FCPA an interesting difference developed between philosophers and theologians. The former often condemned the statute because (1) it criminalized the act of trying to influence a public official and thereby assumed that foreign nations had the same assumptions about morality and free enterprise as Americans and (2) it neglected to examine the specific duties connected to special roles. Bribery is intrinsically wrong only if it attempts to have officials go contrary to their duties. Acting "contrary to their duties" cannot be determined on the basis of written regulations; indeed in some countries, when custom officials underestimate the value of imports after their palms are greased, the practice is widely known and ignored by other government officials. Here again the critical element is not intent but the *role* of the recipient of payments as defined by that culture.[43]

The view from the religious bridge, especially from the Jewish tradition, is somewhat different. More supportive of Congress, Rabbi Gordon Tucker argued that while inconsistencies between market theory and market practice exist, there is no legitimate reason to compound the problem by condoning a form of cheating that further undermines fair competition, itself a good thing.[44] One has only to look at reality to recognize that countries that ignore bribery are cursed with other forms of corruption. Commitment to a system of fair competition does not make Americans cultural imperialists when they insist that what is done to respect morality at home should be done to respect morality abroad. The lowest common denominator is not the way to go and resorting to means extraneous to fair competition is simply wrong.

Of the two positions reached through philosophical and religious reasoning, respectively, the second is better for corporations, which seek to base their legitimacy on economic and ethical criteria. And from a long-term perspective, the FCPA may be seen ultimately as an attempt to intensify board and management responsibility in the use of corporate assets by requiring tightened internal accounting mechanisms—even though it has been seen by managements as an unwarranted government intrusion.[45] FCPA can also be seen as an expansion of management's stewardship role, which, when met, contributes to the restoration of public confidence in business.

Good intentions need to be supported by good institutions. In addition to compliance with the law's requirement that payoffs must be reported to the IRS, there is need for some sort of international watchdog—a court of international commerce—to exercise jurisdiction over transactions among nations and to enforce provisions outlawing payoffs that violate the laws of the host countries. In a global economy, companies will themselves clean up their act—or governments will do it for them.

## Summary

At first blush it seems easy to distinguish between a bribe and a gift and between extortion and a payoff. However, the analysis and examples in the text show that the assumption does not hold up. Making distinctions difficult are motive and act. A bearer of gifts, for example, may have ulterior motives, reminding contemporaries that the Trojan horse story is still relevant to the world of international business.

Worth noting is the fact that Congress, for a long time, was reluctant to make important distinctions. And when it did so in the Foreign Corrupt Practices Act, many large firms thought it wiser to pay nothing to get business abroad than risk being caught up by regulators or judges over technicalities. Complicating the problem even further is the fact that applying the moral standards of Americans to foreign lands has led to outraged protests against this country's "ethical imperialism."

At the moment matters are quiet and voices still. While waiting for the next explosion to come, corporate executives and corporate lawyers are trying to figure out which form of ethical reasoning—situationalist, utilitarian, or deontological—makes the most sense.

## Questions for Discussion

1. In your judgment, does the Foreign Corrupt Practices Act unfairly interfere with a corporation's internal governance?
2. Should sensitivity toward foreign officials who are caught in a bribery deter the United States from blowing the whistle?
3. Is the United States too much of a puritan in controlling American corporations doing business abroad?
4. Do you think a better ethical climate would come to domestic business if insider trading was defined as including any person who gets confidential information about a company and uses such knowledge for his or her friend's purposes?
5. Would you continue to use a broker who has handled your investments brilliantly if you had good reason to believe he was getting inside information illegally?

## Ethical Quandary

### Politics in Canada

You have just been sent from your parent company in the United States to head one of its largest subsidiaries in Canada, where both major political parties expect corporate contributions to help finance their respective campaigns. Your company's policy prohibits political contributions. When approached for a company donation, you cite company policy, but are summarily told that such contributions are legal and expected. No threat is made but you feel a chill in the air—especially because your subsidiary is competing directly with an American-owned, Canadian-based company that makes political contributions.

To remain competitive you phone the home office to ask permission to make an exception to the company rule. "Policy is policy," you are told. Yet part of that policy is also market share and profit volumes. The targets, difficult enough without internal corporate obstacles, look even bleaker. Desperate, you decide to use part of the advertising and public relations budget for political contributions. You defend your decision by telling yourself that the budget had been approved by the home office to get business and that this is one way to get it.

### Question

- Are you acting ethically?

## Notes

1. "Who Engages in Insider Trading?" *University of Baltimore Law Review* (Spring 1984): 631–638. The legal underbrush was somewhat cleared away for nonexperts by Dennis W. Carlton and Daniel R. Fischel, "The Regulation of Insider Trading," *Stanford Law Review* 35 (May 1983): 857–895. See also, "Report of the Task Force Regulation of Insider Trading: Regulation under the Antifraud Provisions of the Securities and Exchange Act of 1935," *The Business Lawyer* 41 (1985): 223–272.
2. Donald E. Cuff, "Kluge: He Built Metromedia," *The New York Times,* May 7, 1985, 10D.
3. Allan Sloan, "The Magician," *Forbes,* 133 (April 23, 1984) 32–33.
4. Abraham Briloff, "Move on Metromedia: Abe Briloff Still Doesn't Like Its Accounting" *Barrons,* August, 1983, 32.
5. The deluge of data from large institutional investors overwhelms individuals. Michael Blumstein, "How the Institutions Rule the Market," *The New York Times*, November 11, 1984. Sec. 3.1.
6. Jeffery M. Laderman, et al., "The Epidemic of Insider Trading," *Business Week*, April 29, 1985, 72–78.
7. Willis W. Hagen III, "Insider Trading Rule 10b–5: The Theoretical Basis for Liability," *The Business Lawyer* 44 (August 1989): 13–42. The author gives nonlawyers a good understanding of two divergent legal views: (1) that liability occurs when any insider misappropriates information for personal gain and (2) that liability occurs only if insiders themselves break a fiduciary duty. See also, Douglas Frantz, *Levine and Company: Wall Street Insider Scandals* (New York: Henry Holt, 1987), 11.
8. Ivan Boesky, *The Merger Mania: Arbitrage—Wall Street's Best Kept Secret* (New York: Holt, Rinehart & Winston, 1985).
9. See *The New York Times* issues of November 11, 1986, D1, D20; and November 19, 1986, D1 and D8.
10. Myron Magnet, "The Decline and Fall of Business Ethics," *Fortune*, December 8, 1986, 63. When names like Oliver North, Robert McFarlane, Michael Deaver, Gary Hart, and Jim Bakker joined the gallery, *Time* magazine editorialized that, "taken collectively, the needless lack of restraint in their behavior reveals something disturbing about the national character. America, which took such back-thumping pride in its spiritual renewal, finds itself wallowing in a moral morass. Ethics, often dismissed as a prissy Sunday School word, is now at the center of a new national debate. Put bluntly, has the mindless materialism of the 80s left in its wake a values vacuum?" *Time*, May 25, 1987, 14.
11. In re Cady, Roberts & Company 40 SEC 907, 912 (1961).
12. The experience of Barry Switzer, the former head football coach at the University of Oklahoma, is apposite. While attending a track meet, Switzer overheard his friend and a Phoenix Resources Company director, George Platt, tell his wife of plans to visit New York for a meeting with Morgan Stanley to discuss liquidation of Phoenix. Switzer told a friend of the overheard conversation and the friend later informed other parties, some of whom purchased Phoenix stock. Did Switzer violate the law? The Western Federal District Court of Oklahoma held (SEC v. Switzer, 1984) that since Platt did not benefit from his inadvertent disclosure, he had not breached any duty owed to the shareholders of Phoenix and that Switzer could not be held liable for what he had overheard because he—and the others with whom he talked—had no way to know that the information was confidential.
13. U.S. v. Winans, et al., 612 F. Supp. 827 Southern District Court of New York (June 24, 1985).
14. "Heard on the Street," *The Wall Street Journal*, January 13, 1983, 55 and March 23, 1983, 57.
15. The court found Winans guilty of misappropriating his employer's property.
16. Chiarella v. U.S. 445 US 222 100 S. Ct. 1108, 1116. See also Karen Johnson, "A Corporate Outsider's Duty to Disclose under Rule 10b–5," *Texas Tech Law Review* 12 (1981): 542. See also, Harry Heller, "Chiarella, SEC Rule 14e–3 and Dirks: Fairness versus Economic Theory," *The Business Lawyer* 37 (January 1982): 517–558.

17. Dirks v. SEC 103, S. Ct. 3255, 3262 (1983).
18. Jennifer Moore, "What Is Really Unethical about Insider Trading," *Journal of Business Ethics* 9 (March 1990): 177–182, argues that ethical consideration of insider trading on grounds of misappropriation or harm to the uninformed are off base. The real reason why insider trading is unethical is because it undermines the fiduciary relationship that is at the heart of American business.
19. Steven R. Saliby, "A Legal and Economic Analysis of Insider Trading" *Business and Professional Ethics Journal* 8 (Summer 1989): 3–22.
20. Colin Lays, "What is the Problem about Political Corruption?" in *Political Corruption: Readings*, ed. Arnold J. Heidenheimer (New York: Holt, Rinehart, & Winston, 1970).
21. This narrative was prompted by the 1972 experiences of the Travelwear Company of Texas.
22. Paul Ingrassia and Richard Hudson, "Ashland's Oil Chief's Sudden Departure," *The Wall Street Journal*, May 16, 1983, 4.
23. Michael S. Sinkeldam, "Payments to Foreign Officials by Multinational Corporations: Bribery or Business Expense and the Effects of United States Policy," *California Western International Law Journal* 6 (1976), 360–381.
24. Jerry Landauer and Carol Falk, "Rollins Inc. Says It Will Continue Payoffs Abroad," *The Wall Street Journal*, March 3, 1976, 3.
25. The most comprehensive treatment of bribery is John Noonan, Jr., *Bribes* (New York: Macmillan, 1985). See also, W. Michael Reisman, *Folded Lies: Bribery, Crusades, and Reform* (New York: The Free Press, 1979).
26. Michael Philips, "Bribery," *Ethics* 94 (July 1984): 621–635; and John Danley, "Toward a Theory of Bribery," *Business and Professional Ethics Journal* 2 (Spring 1983): 19–39.
27. "Report of the Special Review Committee of the Board of Directors of the McCloy Commission," (Pittsburgh, Pa.: The Gulf Oil Corporation, 1975), 99.
28. Byron E. Calame, "Gulf Officers' Ouster was Boldly Engineered by Mellon Interests," *The Wall Street Journal*, January 15, 1976, A1.
29. Richard Hofstadter, *The American Political Tradition and the Men Who Made It* (New York: Alfred Knopf, 1948), 163.
30. Ibid., 165.
31. Bill Niekirk and John Maclean, "When Does one Man's Fee Become Another's Bribe?", *Chicago Tribune*, April 11, 1976, 2.
32. David Boulton, *The Grease Machine* (New York: Harper & Row, 1978), 261 ff.
33. Timothy Shellhardt, "Jittery U.S. Firms Face Scrutiny by IRS on Foreign Kickbacks," *The Wall Street Journal*, March 26, 1976, 1.
34. "Foreign Corrupt Practices Act of 1977 and the Regulation of Questionable Payments," *The Business Lawyer* 34 (January 1979): 672–684.
35. William L. Larson, "Effective Enforcement of the Foreign Corrupt Practices Act," *Stanford Law Review* 32 (February 1980): 561–579.
36. John Greenwald, "Let's Make a Deal," *Business Week*, September 3, 1979, 150.
37. *Chicago Tribune*, March 31, 1976, Sec. 3, 2.
38. Shelly O'Neill, "The FCPA: Problems of Extraterritorial Jurisdiction," *Vanderbilt Law Review* 12 (1970): especially 703–710.
39. Thomas W. Dunfee and Aryeh S. Friedman, "The Extra-Territorial Application of United States Anti-Trust Laws: A Proposal for an Interim Solution," *Ohio State Law Journal* 45 (1984): 883–932. See also, Douglas S. Sherwin, "The Ethical Roots of the Business System," *Harvard Business Review* 60 (November–December 1983): 183–192.
40. Bob Wiedrich, "Applying Our Ethics Abroad Won't Work," *Chicago Tribune* January 20, 1976, 4. See also, the *Chicago Tribune*, March 29, 1976, 8.
41. Philips, "Bribery," 631.
42. Minneapolis based Napco International was found guilty of intent to bribe Nigerian officials. *Washington Post*, May 5, 1989, B3. Good Year International was fined $250,000 for similar efforts in Iraq. *Washington Post*, May 12, 1989, F3.
43. Philips, "Bribery," 631.

44. Gordon Tucker, "Business from Jewish Theological Perspectives," in *Enriching Business Ethics*, ed. Clarence C. Walton (New York: Plenum, 1990). See also, Charles Chazen, "An Accountant Looks at the FCPA," *CPA Journal* 50 (May 1980): 7–38.
45. Joseph Conan, *The Foreign Corrupt Practices Act: Implications for Directors* (New York: Price Waterhouse, 1979), 5.

PART THREE

# Workers and Consumers

CHAPTER EIGHT
**Union-Employer Encounters**

CHAPTER NINE
**Advertising**

CHAPTER TEN
**Tort Law**

CHAPTER ELEVEN
**Tort-Related Fallouts**

CHAPTER 8

# Union-Employer Encounters

## Ethical Criteria
The Principle of Reasonable Disclosure
The Principle of Proportionality
The Principle of the Innocent Bystander
The Principle of Moral Suasion

## Collective Bargaining
Sham or Serious?
Bargaining Theory
Adversarialism

## The Big Guns: Strikes, Boycotts, and Lockouts
The Early Years
Definitions
Arbitration and Strikes
Positional Power
Recent Union Tactics
Recent Management Tactics

## Strikes by Professions and Government Employees
Doctors
Teachers
Traffic Controllers

## The Years Ahead
## Summary
Questions for Discussion
Ethical Quandaries

*D*eclining *membership, weakened political clout, and global economic competition have forced unions to make painful readjustments in their relationships with business and government. Not so very long ago, the odds for union success in a strike were high. The percentages have changed, leading some managers and labor experts to believe that unions are no longer a significant force in American society. Such beliefs are badly mistaken. Workers still take to heart the idea expressed by the former editor of the* Harvard Business Review, *David Ewing, who wrote that when a U.S. citizen steps through the plant or office door in the morning, he or she is essentially rightless until the end of the workday.*

*The arresting statement tells why unions exist, namely, to reduce the powerlessness of workers. Between management and labor, the major question is over decisions on wages and conditions of work, job safety and job security, management prerogatives and employee rights, and unemployment and retirement benefits. Other concerns include seniority, the nature of grievance procedures, worker participation, types of union, and modes of arbitration and mediation. Conflict is assumed to be part of organizational life and the modes and consequences of its resolution are critical to the success of all organizations.*

*The story of government and public opinion of unionism in the United States, as told in Chapter 2, went something like this: Unions are a conspiracy against the public. Unions are refugees for thugs. Unions are socialistic. Unions are corrupt. Unions want too much. Unions are violence prone—and so on. Surely American history shows a persistent and long-standing resistance to organizing efforts by workers. Threatened by a strike, managements (successfully in most cases) sought injunctions on the basis of breach of contract or on the basis of conspiracy. Contract law was interpreted to mean a voluntarily entered arrangement with managers to work at a certain wage for a fixed hourly rate. Ceasing to work at that wage breached the contract. The theory of conspiracy went even further by outlawing altogether attempts of workers to join forces. Its meaning was clearly expressed in the Philadelphia Cordwainers' case of 1806 when the Philadelphia Mayor's Court declared that "a combination of workmen to raise their wages may be considered in a two-fold point of view: one is to benefit themselves, and the other is to injure those who do not join their society. The rule of law condemns both."*[1]

*The first sign of modest relief from this harsh doctrine came in 1842 when Chief Justice Shaw of the Massachusetts Supreme Court declared that* the mere fact that workers agreed to act together was not a criminal conspiracy unless the unions' objective—or the means they employed—was unlawful.[2] A dramatic example of 19th century judicial activism happened during the Pullman strike of 1894 when employees, outraged by the company's wage-cutting policy, walked off the job. And members of the American Railroad Union (ARU), heeding the call of their socialist leader, Eugene Debs, refused to service passenger trains. Federal troops were called and blanket injunctions followed, leading Debs to complain bitterly that it it was not the army, or any other power, but simply the courts which broke the strike and the workers' backs. Debs said: "I have no hesitancy in declaring that money . . . has invaded the Supreme Court and left that august tribunal reeking with more stench than Coleridge discovered in Cologne . . ."[3]

Despite legal and judicial interventions, the common interpretation of the laborers' indifference to the broad social and political reforms that Debs advocated was that blue-collar workers freely accepted—and perhaps even supported—capitalism because it meant that labor could work out its own arrangements with management without fear of government oppression.[4] It was therefore incorrect to think that legal skirmishes diverted American workers from broad reform efforts. Laborers really never entertained such ideas. Union strategy was therefore directed at equalizing the power between unions and corporations.

Not until the early 20th century was the workers' right to organize recognized by what has been called labor's Magna Carta, the Wagner Act (officially the National Labor Relations Act). Three provisions of the Wagner Act were especially important to workers: (1) the right to organize without interference by management, (2) the establishment and definition of unfair labor practices and, (3) the creation of the National Labor Relations Board (NLRB) to police violations of the law. Congress had finally permitted what courts had consistently declared impermissible.

But workers' jubilation was dampened by the public antagonism when, immediately after World War II, strikes resulted in the loss of 113 million workdays. When the coal industry and the public utilities were paralyzed during 1946, the public's mood turned sour and, in 1947, Congress passed the Taft-Hartley bill over President Harry Truman's veto. Management hailed it as a freedom act. Labor denounced it as a slave act. The statute allowed the government to impose an 80-day cooling off period before a strike call went into effect; outlawed the closed shop and secondary boycotts, sympathy strikes, and jurisdictional strikes; forbade featherbedding; curbed excessive initiation fees or dues; prohibited labor to bargain in bad faith; and permitted states to outlaw union-shop contracts, thus permitting states to enact right-to-work laws.

When charges of union corruption were widely made, Congress in 1959 passed the Landrum-Griffin Act, which required unions to submit detailed reports to the Department of Labor regarding financial and nonfinancial matters and to conduct elections of officers by secret ballot. Other provisions forbade payments to union officials other than their salaries, and their use of union funds for personal interests. The pendulum effect—from warm public support to cool public condemnation—was obvious. Labor unions' coming of age was followed by new interpretations of the workers' beliefs. It is now agreed that workers were not, as previously thought, procapitalist and antireform but reform had to be scuttled before the need to survive judicial assaults.[5]

Assessments differ but the facts are that, over the years, the NLRB expanded its rules governing labor by requiring that managements *(1) make available to unions the names and addresses of employees eligible to participate in representation elections and (2) not threaten to fire workers or use epithets like "commies" or "subverters."* Managers were not completely crippled. *They could still tell workers that, if unionization comes, overtime might be reduced; that union dues represent a waste of employee money; and that other companies had relocated to avoid being unionized.* ∎

## *The purposes of this chapter are:*

1. To provide a few ethical principles that apply to bargaining relationships.
2. To describe the bargaining process.
3. To define the nature and meaning of strikes, boycotts, and lockouts.
4. To explore the nature of strikes by professionals like doctors and teachers.
5. To peer into labor's future.

## Ethical Criteria

As was useful in Chapter 4 which provided ethical background against which business competition and the laws governing it might be made, so, too, is it helpful to posit four principles against which labor-management conflicts might be judged.

### *The Principle of Reasonable Disclosure*

Bargaining, by definition, deals with differences over issues, strategies, and tactics. It also involves clashes of personalities. Because of this elementary fact, parties in the bargaining process cannot be held to courtroom standards for testimony where witnesses are sworn "to tell the truth, the whole truth, and nothing but the truth." Perjurers can be severely punished. Bargaining, on the other hand, imposes no such stringencies or sanctions. Negotiators may differ over facts, haggle over their meaning, prioritize one issue over another, and even withhold facts damaging to their respective causes. What is unethical is the presentation of materials known to be untrue. Withholding data essential to an honest resolution of differences skirts the ethical edges. Negotiators may bluster for effect, threaten to call off negotiations, detail the dire consequences that would flow from a strike or lockout—but blatant lying is off limits.

Years ago the General Electric Company outlined its position in these words: "There is a natural tendency for an employer to hold back something he might otherwise offer, and for a union official to press for a demand he might otherwise withdraw, in the expectation that the Federal intervener will seek concessions from both. Any such action on the part of General Electric as an employer would be, of course, completely contrary to our truth-in-bargaining approach where, after appropriate negotiations, we try to make available in our initial bargaining proposals everything that seems to be warranted at the time. Still, we are sometimes asked if the record of intervention over the last two years suggests the prudence of saving something from our offers to the unions for later bargaining with the interveners—something we could yield up later as a final concession to the unions in order to get a settlement. The answer to this must be a resounding, 'NO.' "[6]

The policy was known as Boulwarism after its architect, General Electric vice president Lemuel Boulware. Dismayed by the posturing that went on between management and labor, Boulware said that employers should put all of their cards on the table—and make the cards known to workers, because company negotiators were playing with a marked deck when union representatives were the only ones to communicate with employees. Although General Electric accepted Boulwarism as both an ethical and a practical bargaining policy, it died after a very short existence because (1) workers did not trust the company and (2) union leaders saw in it a weakening of their own status as fierce protagonists of workers' rights.

## *The Principle of Proportionality*

Demands cannot be made that, if secured, grievously damage either employer or employee. Wage demands far in excess of productivity increases are one example. Wage concessions unnecessary for reasonable profit margins are another. A striking example of a violation of this principle of proportionality occurred in October 1986 when 30,000 members of the International Longshoremen's Association walked off their jobs in northeastern ports. Management accused Thomas Gleason, president of the ILA, of breaking his promise to give a 60-day prestrike notice. As a result, retailers failed to stockpile certain kinds of goods that, if not replenished, could have disastrous effects on Thanksgiving sales. It was also feared that there would be heavy damage to the regional economy. What made the union's position difficult for employers to accept was that shipowners, battered by rate wars and overcapacity for years, were already reporting large losses—a fact the strikers knew. The result of the strike was an intensification of the drift from northeastern to southern and West Coast ports.

The steel industry provided another example of workers getting too much too fast and managers doing too little too late. The 1950s were marked by strident union demands and by management timidity, a timidity aggravated by the industry's unwillingness to embark on necessary modernization programs. On the other hand, textile owners provided examples of employers' unwillingness to listen to the largely reasonable demands of their workers.

## *The Principle of the Innocent Bystander*

This principle is particularly relevant when strikes or lockouts are used by teachers (students are hurt), by doctors or nurses (patients are jeopardized), or by police or firefighters (public security is endangered). Some would apply this principle to railroaders, airline pilots and mechanics, and public utility workers. However, a fine line exists between harm and inconvenience. The first is evil; in the second case (when an airline cancels flights without warning or railway workers strike), the moral judgment is more difficult to make.

Workers can also hurt other workers. As an example, in the late 1950s Pan American pilots threatened to strike. Their objective was not higher wages, not shorter hours, and not different working conditions, but rather the goal was to deny jobs and benefits to other pilots. Pan Am had just acquired American Overseas Airlines (AOA), but the parent company's pilots refused to allow AOA pilots to join the union except at the very bottom of the wage scale. Union leaders and government agencies both urged full acceptance of the seniority gained by the AOA employees during their years of service—but in vain. The Pan Am pilots asserted property rights to their job. Another example was the typographical union, which set up a priority system to protect preferred jobs for linotype operators—even if they were forced by illness to miss work for years or, as in World War II, left the industry for better paying jobs in the defense industry. Other individuals were denied work opportunities. In considering the innocent bystander rule it would be a mistake to conclude that all strikes, say, by teachers or nurses, are per se unethical. The principle only seeks to establish the gravity of certain kinds of behavior in certain kinds of essential services—a gravity that places a much heavier burden of justification on the shoulders of unions and managements.

## *The Principle of Moral Suasion*

A person's autonomy is violated by any form of coercion, the most blatant of which is, of course, physical violence. In the 19th century management used Pinkerton operatives to beat workers into submission; and in the 20th century unions like the teamsters regularly violated the principle of moral suasion. When, for example, Ronald Carey ran for union office in November 1990, he was threatened by lies about his behavior (such as claiming he was an adulterer) and by broad hints that his life was endangered. Even more illustrative violations of the principle of moral suasion involved the behavior of unions in Philadelphia and in New York.

The sobriquet of Philadelphia as the City of Brotherly Love was meaningless to the Philadelphia Roofers Union Local, which had a long history of sporadic violence and corruption. In the late 1980s, the local's boss, John

McCullough, was murdered in a Mafia hit and in the ensuing power struggle, the city's Mafia chief, Nicodemo Scarfo, put his muscle behind a McCullough lieutenant, Stephen Traitz, Jr. Traitz, easily elected, immediately began to repay his powerful benefactor: he collected Scarfo's debts, gave jobs to Scarfo's bodyguards, and allowed some contractors to pay below-scale wages if Scarfo favored them. Roofing contractors bought labor peace with "initiation fees" and other questionable payments to the union; if they did not, they risked property destruction or assaults by union goons.

Money embezzled by union officials was used for payoffs to nearly 50 Philadelphia-area public officials: judges, policemen, prison officials, and even employees of the Philadelphia district attorney's office and the Pennsylvania Department of Labor. When a contractor named Thomas Zimmerman tangled with the local, his veteran roofing employees were ousted by the union and replaced with union-designated workers. William Hargrove, another contractor, was beaten, his trucks torched, and his repair shop vandalized because he refused to dismiss his nonunion roofers. Today, the unholy alliance is dead: Scarfo is serving a life term for murder; 13 union officials and employees have been convicted under RICO of extortion, racketeering, and other crimes; Traitz is also in prison and his local was branded a criminal enterprise by federal Judge John Bechtle. Moral suasion meant nothing to these morally malformed musclemen.

New York City had its sorry episode when building contractors had to pay kickbacks to Ralph Scopo, who was president of the New York District Council of Cement and Concrete Workers Union and a member of the Columbo crime family. Scopo and the Columbo family extorted one percent of all concrete-pouring contracts up to $2 million; contracts exceeding $2 million were allocated among roughly six Mafia-designated contractors known as "the Club" who, in turn, paid two percent of their contracts in kickbacks to a fund that was split among four New York crime families. Contracts above $15 million were reserved for a company called S&A Concrete, in which Genovese crime-family boss Anthony Salerno held a secret interest. The FBI estimated that during the period of Mafia control, New York concrete companies overcharged builders by more than $40 million a year to offset their illegal payoffs. When the ring was smashed, Scopo and his Mafia bosses were sentenced in 1987 to 100-year prison terms for extortion and other crimes, and the District Council and Local Six of the Cement and Concrete Workers were placed under a court-appointed trustee. Moral suasion was again a casualty.

## Collective Bargaining

### Sham or Serious?

Is collective bargaining charade or reality? Columbia University professor Neil Chamberlain thought that the "contest had become largely a sporting one, for prizes which are as symbolic as the kewpie doll at a carnival sideshow, and that the reminder provided by the parties and the textbooks that management and the unions are engaged in deep conflict has the same uninteresting truth and half-truth as the equally frequent reminder that they have interests in common."[7] What occurs is a minuet danced to the music of the status quo. Neither unions nor managements take any real initiatives. Union leaders are particularly unimaginative, having never doffed the beggar's cap in petitioning for a fair share of the corporation's financial pie. In Chamberlain's view, therefore, American unionism can hardly be regarded as a movement because it has no sense of direction and is content to ride with the tide. Because unions are neither politically nor socially innovative, individuals who rise to the top look more like their staid management counterparts than like authentic workers' representatives. Preservation of their own power is what counts most.

Others, however, insist that the management-labor encounters are real and sometimes even vicious because the stakes are high for both parties. How, they ask, can labor representatives be indifferent to the results of bargaining when their success in the union elections depends on "bringing home the bacon" to their followers? Similarly, how can management be indifferent when labor costs are such a substantial part of operating expenses. The price for charade is simply too great and those who read labor-management bargaining in the context of posturing are badly deceived. Both sides insist that the contract is seriously negotiated because it affects job security (which, in turn, affects management's control over human resources), hours of work, holidays, overtime pay, absenteeism, vacations, incentive wages, layoffs, and a host of other items. Flowing from this interpretation of bargaining is the assumption that, because one party's gain is the other's loss, the tactics must not exclude deception. Herein lies the danger to the principle of reasonable disclosure.[8]

## *Bargaining Theory*

Because of the pervasiveness of conflict in human affairs, the disputants can either bargain or batter for a solution. Long before management was forced to the bargaining table by the Wagner Act, premiers and princesses of nation-states were forced to negotiate in order to avoid war, devastation, or dismemberment. Diplomacy, cynically called the "high art of lying," was practiced by only the most seasoned and educated politicians, on whose skill and cunning often rested the success and survival of their respective countries. Practiced by the many and studied by the few, diplomatic bargaining was a process often misunderstood and mistrusted. A breakthrough in theory came a quarter century ago when Thomas C. Shelling described bargaining as something like a game of chess:[9] players must make explicit their objectives, announce their values, and state forthrightly the power and resources they command.[10] Like the diplomats of old, who plied their trade without benefit of theory, management and labor continue to do much the same thing today.

Nevertheless, despite wide variations in the way bargaining is carried out, certain basics in the process are clear. There are (1) the prenegotiation stage, (2) the choice of negotiators, (3) the development of strategy and tactics, and (4) the fixing of boundaries for acceptable results. During the prenegotiating stage both management and unions probe into such things as corporate profitability, wage levels in similar organizations and industries, implications for the bargaining process when leadership in either the corporation or the union is in the process of changing, and the personalities of the chief negotiators. A team approach is used. For both sides lawyers are always present and CEOs always absent. Speaking for the unions are business agents, shop stewards, presidents of the locals, and spokespersons from the international union. Speaking for management are vice presidents, labor lawyers, and knowledgeable staff personnel.

One of the most critical decisions bargainers make is choosing appropriate strategies and tactics. For both management and unions the first step is to determine the maximum concessions that can be made by the other side. One part of the union's tactics is to so bargain that the leaders can announce victory. Running for reelection on their record requires victory flags. But it also means that demands on management cannot be too excessive—long strikes hurt workers as well as employers. From their side managers often stalled recognition of the union by challenging the fairness of an election, that is, until the courts restricted such practices;[11] they imply that plants may have to be closed; and they go public by buying newspaper space to air their views. When the parties finally get to the bargaining table, however, the assumption is that good-faith negotiations will begin. However, if the past is prologue, unions and employers still have reasons to question the good faith of the other.

## *Adversarialism*

A past marked by oppression and a present characterized by dissimulation seem surefire guarantees that when management and labor get together their mood will reflect profound distrust. A typical management view of the last century was expressed in 1851 by the editor of the *New York Journal of Commerce* who wrote: "Who but a miserable, craven-hearted man, would permit himself to be subjected to such union rules, extending even to the number of apprentices he may employ and the manner in which they shall be bound to him."[12] The adversarial ideology has not died. Workers note such recent things as the National Association of Manufacturers' effort (in which 450 member companies joined) to create a union-free environment; nor do they forget that over 400 consulting firms had been hired by companies to conduct antiunion programs in the early 1980s; and they vividly remember the long and costly J. P. Stevens strike of the early 1980s, the Pittston Coal Strike of the late 1980s, and the Greyhound strike of 1990. Finally, unions note the recent number of plant closings and employee layoffs that have often resulted from hostile takeovers because the major players in that game cared little for anyone except themselves.

Management, for its part, had reasons to complain about labor: featherbedding among railway workers, wildcat strikes, muscle men at corporate gates during organizing periods, decreased per-capita productivity, slowdowns, especially at critical points in the production process, and paddings of payrolls. One example of padding occurred in late 1983 when officials of Local 29 of the Blasters, Drillers and Miners' Union were accused of lying to a grand jury over the issue of no-show schemes and other-show jobs. In a no-show scheme, the unions put on the payroll the names of people who never appeared for work; in the other-show scheme, labor officials had work performed by persons who, for a variety of reasons (possible loss of welfare benefits, people who were down and out, relatives) did not work under their own names.[13]

No matter what the cause, labor and management found in both past and current practices reasons to fear and dislike the other. The bitterness with which each side frequently approached the other in bargaining seemed to contradict the basic notion that the production of goods and services is, by definition, a cooperative enterprise. Chrysler may compete with General Motors but the production of Chrysler cars results from a long series of interconnected and interdependent operations, none of which can long be sustained if parts of the team deliberately set out to subvert the process.

Therefore, a question arises: *Why should not the collective bargaining process use cooperative rather than competitive techniques?*[14] The man who asked the question, philosopher Norman Bowie, answered it by suggesting that collective bargaining should be seen as a form of family decision making between wife and husband in which each is treated as an equal. In the prenegotiation stage there should, therefore, be a consensus on the basic corporate goals (R&D, retirement benefits, capital investments) and, once a consensus is reached, both parties should behave like the heads of the family working to achieve a common goal. Because cooperation is based on trust there can be no lies, no deceits, and no bluffs. Bowie's analogy primarily reflects the principles of reasonable disclosure and of moral suasion. One of the other important aspects of this familial model of bargaining is its concern for third parties—the principle of the innocent bystander. Just as the family is constrained by a wider community (obey the law, harm no others, respect others' rights) so, too, are the corporation and the union constrained by the rights and needs of the public.

In light of multiple examples of bitter animosity between labor and management, there is a utopian strain in Bowie's prescription. Moving toward the same conclusion but working from different premises, industrial-relations experts argue that in an atmosphere of global competitiveness neither management nor labor can afford the luxury of continuing their intermural adversarialism. Their enemy is big government at home and big competition from abroad. They have, therefore, a profound and mutual need for cooperation. Nevertheless, despite occasional cooperative experiments in economically distressed industries, prospects for change are not bright.[15]

Taking a cooperative posture is especially difficult when workers fear unemployment. General Motors is determined to build and operate people-free plants; nevertheless high unemployment rates in the local labor market seem not to have elicited greater productivity. One study of a major U.S. automobile company with plants in Canada and the United States—all of which were covered by collective bargaining agreements and all of which had wide variations in labor-relations procedures and in productivity—raised this question: Why did not the company select only the best practices and apply them to all plants?[16] The answer seemed to be its past experience, which had frozen management and union positions into the adversarial molds.[17] The question of adversarialism is of such importance to the public that its continued presence creates constant concern. Experts differ over such issues as the relationship of strikes to future productivity, management competence, currency-exchange differences, and the like. But the relevance of labor-management cooperation to America's prosperity now gets serious attention in executive suites and in union halls.

## The Big Guns: Strikes, Boycotts, and Lockouts

### The Early Years

Strikes probably began with the Israelites' insurrection against the Egyptians. In modern times the English, being the first to industrialize, were the first to experience the strike. In 1810, thirty thousand Lancashire workers walked off the job and, in 1837, eighty thousand spinners and miners went on strike. However, not until 1871 in England, and not until 1884 in France, were worker associations given civil recognition. In the United States, even though striking was not considered illegal per se, conspiracy laws largely prevented their occurrence. It was only during the railroad industry's "great upheaval" of 1877 that the first large-scale strike occurred in the United States.

Railroading had become the nation's most critical industry. On July 16, 1877, when the Baltimore & Ohio Railroad cut employees' wages 10 percent (the second cut in eight months), disgusted crewmen abandoned their train in Martinsburg, West Virginia, and other workers refused to replace them. The strikers moved the locomotives into the roundhouse and then announced to railroad officials that no more trains would leave the Martinsburg yard until their former wages were reinstated. As news of Martinsburg spread, the strike came to encompass all divisions of the B&O Railroad and eventually gained the support of laborers everywhere. Only after federal troops were called were the strikes suppressed, but by then, a signal had been clearly sent to all managements—the individual worker was no longer helpless and no longer alone.

Surprisingly, even workers themselves did not initially condone striking, preferring instead arbitration to settle disputes. However, when a 5 percent pay cut was announced in the fall of 1878 for shopmen of Missouri Pacific Railroad (part of the larger Southwest System), the workers spontaneously struck. Like the strike of 1877, this one soon spread to all parts of the system. Unlike the previous year, this strike was well organized, due largely to support from the Knights of Labor. For the first time in American history, organized labor successfully dealt with owners on an "equal" basis. Another historic event happened in 1902 when the United Mine Workers (UMW) demanded a nine-hour day, a 20 percent wage increase, and recognition of their right to bargain as a union. When the mine owners urged Teddy Roosevelt to use federal troops to break the strike, the president refused, instead naming a commission to resolve the dispute. The overall result was a significant worker victory because this was the first time the federal government had ever intervened to protect the interests of *everyone*—strikers, employers, and the public. The courts, on the other hand, remained sturdily antiunion until the NLRB was established.

## *Definitions*

An old and basically unchanged definition is that a strike is an organized cessation of work on the part of a number of workmen in a firm or industry for the purpose of enforcing certain demands on the employer.[18] By refusing to work the strikers hope to disadvantage their employer to the point that his surrendering is wiser than continuing to struggle. Once seen as criminal acts (strike statistics started out as a branch of crime statistics), they are now seen as the workers' last and legitimate resort. But when is a strike a strike? The quick answer is: when the union leaders declare it and when the workers walk out. But the quick reply needs amplification. A Delaware court ruled in 1974 that "where acceptance of overtime assignments was an established past practice, the fact that overtime duties were voluntary did not preclude mass refusal to work overtime from constituting a strike."[19] Furthermore, a work stoppage that lasted only an hour was a strike if union workers refused to cross picket lines formed by their wives and their friends.

A *sympathy strike* occurs when a number of employees, having no grievance of their own, take action on the belief that another body of workers is not being fairly treated.[20] The American Railroad Union strike against Pullman provides a good example. Concern for others gives a high moral tone to the sympathy strike. Appearing less lofty are *wildcat strikes*, which occur when members of a union local walk out without authorization from the international or national union; such strikes invariably happen when members of the local feel that their interests are not being protected by absentee union chieftains.

Why wildcat strikes were so common—especially when both labor leaders and corporate executives decried them—is partially explained by laws that protect both union agents in the local and the wildcatters themselves from financial liability. Liability was placed on the union.[21] In addition to its financial liability union leadership had been told in 1976 by a lower federal court that it must take all reasonable steps to halt wildcat strikes.[22] When the ruling was modified by the Supreme Court in 1979, the wildcatters became more vulnerable—a vulnerability that became painfully clear when, in 1978, a federal court in Ohio ruled that individual employees might be held personally liable for damages suffered as a result of a wildcat strike.[23] In this case, the judge reasoned that the evidence left no doubt whatsoever that the defendants went on strike as individuals—and none took the stand to deny the fact. The court also noted that the plaintiff's plant was open and that employees had been notified to come to work. In addition, the two defendant unions had also notified the striking individuals, both in person and in writing, to go back to work. Despite both warnings, workers had placed signs saying that a strike was on. The judge reasoned that, because no worker was responsible for what others were doing, each wildcatter had to take the consequences: pay for breach of contract.[24]

## *Arbitration and Strikes*

The Supreme Court took a more active role in fashioning national labor policy in a case dealing with Local 174 of the Teamsters.[25] In this case, an employer discharged a union employee because of unsatisfactory work. To force rehiring of the worker, the union went on strike for eight days, even though the labor contract required that any difference arising between the employer and the employee be resolved through binding arbitration. The contract did not contain an explicit no-strike promise on the part of the union. After the dispute was resolved by an arbitrator in favor of the workers, the employer sued for relief on grounds that the union breached an implied no-strike promise.

The Supreme Court ruled in favor of the employer, holding that even in the absence of an express no-strike promise a union violates its collective bargaining contract when it strikes over a dispute that, under the provisions of the contract, should be settled through binding arbitration. The implication of a promise not to strike over arbitrable disputes, said the Court, was fully consistent with the principles of traditional contract law. Moreover, the Court stated that a contrary view would be completely at odds with the basic policy of national labor legislation, which was to promote the arbitral process as a substitute for economic warfare.

Union leadership has never been happy with the Court's ruling. The UMW, for example, has repeatedly tried to establish its right to strike over issues it had specifically agreed to arbitrate. Ironically enough, the UMW position had been taken because of headquarters' inability to control wildcat strikes. The union's position has been consistently rejected by the Supreme Court which, in fact, widened the range of impermissible strike activities by holding that, despite the Norris-LaGuardia prohibition against labor injunctions, they cold be employed in disputes in which the parties had agreed to arbitration. The combined results of court decisions, shifting circumstances, and public attitudes mean that labor leaders now give great attention to selecting the strategies that offer the most likely prospects for union success.

## *Positional Power*

The success or failure of a strike depends on the workers' positional power, that is, the ability of workers in a given industry to (1) disrupt production of other industries (up or downstream), (2) cause great public inconvenience

(Mike Quill's regular Christmas season threats to shut down New York City's subway system), or (3) pose direct threats to public health (doctors' and nurses' strikes) and public safety (police and firefighter strikes). Before a strike is called labor and management negotiators also take careful stock of their respective positional powers. Strategy is hobbled, however, when divisions exist ether in the union's ranks (locals dissatisfied) or in employer ranks (CEO under board fire). For unions this positional power may also be reduced by union-wide differences over the two-tier wage system—a development that merits rather specific comment.

In the more than 650 labor contracts negotiated between 1984 and 1989 new workers were placed on lower pay scales than prevailed for their senior coworkers in industries like airlines, metal fabrication, lumber, and retail food chains. The two-tier system has had, in some cases, dramatically negative effects for workers. For example, under the two-tier system accepted by the unions in 1983 with American Airlines, some new hires received 50 percent less pay than employees already on the payroll doing the same job. Union leaders find the constant complaints of the second-tier employees a klaxon to the ear and a burden to the conscience. What looked so promising during the 1980s may well be a casualty during the 1990s. In 1989, for example, only 6 percent of some 962 nonconstruction contracts contained two-tier plans, down from a peak of 11 percent in 1985. More disturbing about the two tiers is the fact that new hires get less insurance coverage, less vacation time, and less pension benefits. The long and the short of it is that positional power is effective in strategizing only when there is unity in the ranks.

Positional power is also influenced by the type of ownership. Absentee owners are quicker to shut down plants than the more risk-averse local firms; are more willing to take a strike because they do not live in the struck community; and are less financially overextended than the smaller local enterprises. However this represents a major change of heart. Union leaders, once highly critical of absentee owners, began to ask whether jobs preserved at some cost were not better than the jobs lost at higher costs when plants are closed. Absentee owners seemed to be more in tune with the market and more willing to restructure.[26]

## *Recent Union Tactics*

Some unions—like those for the miners, automakers, and teamsters—used muscle and threats of violence to get results. Others—like those for airline pilots, teachers, and nurses—used peaceful picketing and newspaper advertisements to advance their respective causes. One of the most interesting developments in the rough-and-tumble unions is their more sophisticated approaches to corporate boards, and management's counter tactics of using what labor calls whipsawing. A signal of the union's innovativeness came in 1987 when the autoworkers and the miners introduced the *selective strike* to close a particular facility, not the whole company. The UAW used it against 17 General Motors plants to put pressure on the company and relieve pressure within the union without the high cost, risk, and political backlash that a total walkout might have incurred. The miners found another use for the selective strike. After signing a tentative new contract with an association of major coal operators, the union immediately began walkouts against certain of the independents to persuade the holdouts to accept the master agreement. It was an important step in the mine union's drive to reestablish its grip on all the coal-mine work force.

At the same time that selective strikes were introduced, unions began to use the *boycott* more effectively. The word came from the name of a ruthless English land agent working in Ireland, Captain Charles Boycott. Two types of boycotts—primary and secondary—are available to workers. The first occurs when union leaders urge their members and their supporters not to buy goods produced by a company against which it is striking; a secondary boycott is directed against a noninvolved third party who uses products made by the striking company. Chavez had used this tactic against the United States supermarket industry. Boycotts seemed to be an effective technique and soon environmentalists, churches, and consumer groups followed the labor union practice. The number of boycotts rose from 39 in 1984 to 300 in 1990.

The public-interest boycotters knew that, although the likelihood of closing company operations was slim, even a small dent in company sales (a 5 percent decline) could have sufficient impact to force changes in corporate policy. These boycotters are interesting from a demographic standpoint. A 1989 Roper survey showed that they often came from two-income families, had college degrees, and were big spenders. This kind of boycotter knew that companies prized their image above all else—a fact that became clear when the H. J. Heinz Company was accused of trapping and killing dolphins in the netting of tuna. Although sales of the company's Star-Kist tuna brand were not hurt, Heinz changed its fishing techniques and began a public relations campaign to inform protesters of its new practice.

Not all corporations succumb to boycott pressures. For example, when Procter & Gamble was accused of indirectly supporting right-wing parties in El Salvador because it bought coffee beans used in Folger's coffee from that country, the company canceled its advertising at WAPH, a CBS affiliate in Boston, which carried advertisements of the boycotters. P&G's decision cost the station a million dollars in lost revenue. And the company did not stop in Boston; it said it would do the same thing to any other station that aired the boycotters' advertisement. Procter & Gamble's reverse boycott worked: no other station ran the boycotters' ads.

Another technique was perfected by the Clothing and Textile Workers to win their 17-year-old strike against J. P. Stevens. The union hired Ray Rogers, a former VISTA volunteer, to lead union members to bombard the company's outside directors with public criticism, always implying that a boycott could be mounted against their company. Rogers began by attacking corporate executives who sat on Stevens' board and those corporations having Stevens' managers on their board (Manufacturers Hanover Bank,

Sperry, Avon Products, the New York Life Insurance Company, and Metropolitan Life).

Particularly visible and vulnerable was Metropolitan Life, because it held 43 percent of Stevens' long-term debt. When the union threatened to place two names on the ballot for the Met's board of directors, Richard Shinn, the company's CEO, pointed out that a contested election might cost between $5 and $7 million. In October 1980 Shinn met with Whitney Stevens, the new chairman of the company, who had just replaced the feisty James D. Finley, the vociferous opponent of unionism. Although Shinn claimed to have exerted no pressure, Stevens' managers "realized that if, in the course of good business dealings, they could settle with the union, it would minimize the Met's election problem." Shinn added: "We were dragged into this (Stevens') thing in a roundabout way, and in that situation you feel pretty helpless.... I suppose the union would have contended that our lending money to Stevens wasn't in the public interest because Stevens had been anti-union.... But do we lend money to a company like Stevens that's a good credit risk, that's investing the money to modernize their plants and create jobs? Or do we also go behind them and raise judgmental questions about how they handle labor issues?"[27] Shinn may have been effective because Stevens finally signed an agreement that gave the union a two-to-three year contract for about 3,200 (10 percent) of Stevens' workers in plants where it had already won NLRB elections. If the other 73 plants were eventually unionized their workers would also have the same benefits as the 10 percent wage increase, retroactive pay, provisions for arbitration, and for the dues checkoff. The union, in turn, promised to halt its boycott.

More dramatic is the miners' strike of 1988–1989 against the Pittston Coal Company, a story rich in both irony and in sorrow. Before Pittston bought Clinchfield Coal Company, things were peaceful in the quiet Appalachian hills of West Virginia. A social contract of sorts existed between the miners (who lived in Dante) and officials of Clinchfield. Workers felt, however, the contract started to be breached the minute Pittston entered the picture. In 1972, waste dumped by Pittston at the head of West Virginia's Buffalo Creek led to the bursting of a dam that killed 125 and left thousands homeless. Prior to the incident, residents had repeatedly complained to the company about the unsafe situation, but no action was ever taken. When the dam broke, a company spokesman described it as an "act of God." The courts did not agree and ordered the company to pay $26 million in damages to survivors of the flood.[28]

Problems with Pittston worsened when Paul W. Douglas became the company's chairman in 1984. Douglas, a Princeton graduate and son of the famed liberal Democratic senator from Illinois, was an unlikely leader of a coal-mining company. When he arrived at Pittston, regaining control over the mines became his top priority. In the five years that followed, Pittston transferred a significant portion of its operations to nonunion subsidiaries and laid off 4,000 of its 6,000 miners. Prior to 1986, Pittston had been a member of the Bituminous Coal Operators' Association (BCOA), a multiemployer bargaining group that negotiated labor contracts with the

UMWA. In 1987, Pittston withdrew—a decision that seemed to make sense because, unlike most other coal companies, Pittston was a heavy exporter of metallurgical coal, a product whose prices had fallen by 50 percent between 1982 and 1989. Other BCOA members, on the other hand, were primarily producers of steam coal, which is sold domestically to utilities under the price protection of long-term contracts.

Pittston began bargaining for a new contract directly with the UMWA. On January 31, 1988, in a highly uncharacteristic move, the union declared that its employees would work without a contract to show its good faith. Shortly thereafter, Pittston decided to terminate medical-coverage benefits for 1,500 retirees, widows, and disabled miners. Pittston said that the company would have continued benefits if the UMWA had waived its right to strike. For 14 months negotiations dragged on while the miners worked without a contract. Pittston made its final offer—a dollar-an-hour raise in exchange for reduced pensions and reduced health benefits, a flexible work schedule that included mandatory overtime and working on Sundays. On April 5, 1989, the miners walked out. Union official Joseph Corcoran said: "You can talk about this as a labor-management issue, or as an issue of changing markets, as Pittston does. But what really is at risk is the viability of the union and a way of life in Appalachia. It is a moral and spiritual issue. And a nonviolent (striking) strategy is a moral and spiritual strategy."[29]

UMWA's "nonviolent" strategy included training in civil disobedience and a massive publicity campaign. Strikers wore camouflaged outfits as symbols of solidarity and hung signs proclaiming, "This is Southwest Virginia—not South Africa"; wives and daughters of the miners, calling themselves the Daughters of Mother Jones, gathered daily at the picket site and blockaded entrances to the mines; school children staged sit-ins at the courthouse; high-school pupils left classes to join the strikers; and Jesse Jackson urged the miners to buy Pittston from the "incompetent" executives who were ruining the company. One group of miners traveled to Pittston's corporate headquarters in Greenwich, Connecticut, to support the union lawyers, who were then engaged in what turned out to be a fruitless proxy fight.

Although federal mediators were summoned, the strike escalated. By the end of June 1989, 42,000 miners were off their jobs at dozens of mines in support of the 2,000 Pittston miners. At the end of July, a car bomb exploded at a Virginia coal company; in Kentucky, sympathetic strikers hurled rocks at coal-carrying trucks near the entrance to the Sydney Coal mine; and in Virginia, 300 wildcatters were arrested for blocking the entrance to a nonunion mine. The standoff continued. Coal production at Pittston dropped 35 percent. On July 11, 1989, the NLRB found Pittston guilty of unfair labor practices.

The UMWA had its own problems. Its leaders faced possible jail terms as well as multimillion-dollar fines for inciting acts of disobedience, among which were mile-long "rolling roadblocks" that prevented coal trucks from making deliveries. Thirty other companies in West Virginia sued the union for damages suffered because of wildcat strikes, even though the UMWA had not sanctioned such walkouts. The union resorted, therefore, to a different tactic: picketing banks that lent money to the company; questioning whether Pittston was returning enough equity to shareholders; and reminding companies on whose board Pittston Chairman Paul Douglas sat that they had a union buster in their midst. "The companies have changed so we've had to change," said UMW President Richard Trumka, whose flair for innovation had made the young lawyer one of the most influential leaders in the labor movement.[30]

Outside experts felt Trumka's move was foolhardy because the depression-ridden area of West Virginia had hundreds of workers ready to take the strikers' place. But the union's success changed the experts' assessments from foolhardy to brilliant. Until Trumka took over the UMW leadership in 1982, mine workers were seen as nothing more than barroom brawlers. During the Pittston campaign, however, the union was represented by white-collar, numbers-crunching experts, more at home in their tailored suits than in overalls and miners' hats. For example, David Blitzstein, who had helped coordinate the drive against Pittston, was then a 34-year-old, Ivy League-educated labor economist. For the miners, Blitzstein's briefings on the meaning of Pittston's balance sheet opened a new world. Miners' wives and UMW retirees, many of whom had never been out of the South, packed into buses headed for Connecticut, where the annual meeting was to be held in Greenwich. "These aren't pick-and-shovel days anymore," said Nina Mullins, whose husband worked at Pittston for 32 years. "That's why we're coming to Wall Street."[31] And come they did. And come they will.

## *Recent Management Tactics*

Pittston's management had not closed its eyes to the changed labor maneuvers. Its first move was to hire the Vance Security Asset Protection Company, a firm noted for its skill in provoking violence, which then became the excuse for counter violence; and Pittston terminated the workers' health benefits, hired replacements, and initiated a publicity campaign. The strategy of other employers was far more imaginative. In 1983 the owners opened a nonunionized mine in Illinois, once a union stronghold. They knew that the sons did not share the prounion sympathies of their fathers and grandfathers. At the Turris Coal Company, efforts to keep out the UMW began even before the mine was opened. Turris studied everything—from people's religious practices to their union sentiments—before concluding that a mine could remain nonunion despite UMW pressures. Turris also provided a pay package that not only competed with the UMW national contract but was better in its total wage and benefits.[32]

Another management tactic was to encourage intraorganizational competition. General Motors, for example, threatened to close two of its six Fisher body divisions, which made small parts like seat belts and car-door hinges, if productivity did not improve. To get GM to reverse the planned closing, the UAW agreed to boost hourly worker output by 20 percent; soon thereafter GM demanded matching gains at the four other plants, threatening to close at least one of them if workers did not go along. Worried about big job losses, local union officials acceded, even though some workers pleaded that they would not be able to keep up with the faster production lines. The result was that Fisher Body cut costs significantly without actually shutting any plants. "Whipsawing," howled the workers.[33] "Survival," answered the company. Union smashing and worker bashing may have diminished, but inexorable pressures from global competition is forcing managements to upset work patterns with their own cost-saving schemes. The net result is that bargaining will become harder than ever, especially in cases in which the rank and file reject cooperation with management.

Finally there are management's take-it-to-the-public tactic and renewed use of the *lockout*. For example, when Greyhound drivers first struck the company in 1983, management ran full-page ads in all major newspapers urging passengers and customers of the "14,000 communities we serve" to remember that its labor costs were between 30 and 50 percent higher than other major bus companies in America.[34] In the 1988–1989 strike Greyhound brought suit against the unions under RICO, the stiff law that imposes harsh conditions (putting funds in escrow even before the trial begins) on the defendant. There are also signs that management may revive its use of lockouts. Whereas a strike is started by employees, a lockout is initiated by employers who have grievances against their employees. The Pennsylvania Superior Court defined a "lockout as an employer's withholding of work from his employees in order to gain a concession from them and may be imposed by employer without physically closing his plant or forbidding access to it by his employees."[35] The most publicized lockout occurred in the spring of 1990 when baseball owners refused to open their training facilities unless the players made certain concessions—which they successfully refused to do.

## Strikes by Professions and Government Employees

By definition, a profession enjoys some form of monopoly because its members are expected to put the needs of others ahead of their own legitimate wants. Patients come before doctors; clients come before lawyers; and students come before teachers. That, at least, is the theory. The historic change in the work force from a blue- to a white-collar majority, coupled with the dramatic decline in union membership, meant that generally better-educated workers, who were strongly attracted to the professions, had to be recognized. With recognition often came unionization, and with unionization came strikes. Selective examples record the general trend.

### *Doctors*

The Ontario physicians' strike is a prime example of a strike by a venerable profession. The American health-care system is funded through various sources, such as government programs (Medicare and Medicaid), private health insurance companies, and prepaid health plans (HMO). In Canada, the federal and provincial governments finance the entire system through health insurance plans in which every resident can participate. Physicians are paid on a set fee-for-service basis and reimbursed directly from the plan. These fees are established through negotiations between the provincial government and the provincial medical association. Until 1984, every province permitted qualified physicians to extra-bill and these came usually from specialists in surgery, ophthalmology, and gynecology. In 1984, Prime Minister Trudeau succeeded in having the legislature pass the Canada Health Act designed to eliminate extra-billing. Provinces that allowed extra-billing would lose one dollar in federal support for every dollar a physician extra-billed. Unless the practice ended before April 1987, Ontario would have lost $100 million in federal payments.

The Ontario Medical Association (OMA) argued that as long as patients were told up front about the extra-billing and were willing to pay, no one was hurt. They also argued that extra-billing was often the only way to finance new treatments not covered under the government's list of insured services. When protests failed, over half of Ontario's physicians closed their offices, withdrew hospital services, canceled elective and nonemergency service, and shut down several emergency departments across the province. While only 12 percent of Ontario physicians overbilled, the OMA's major concern was that billing prohibition would represent the first step toward total government control of medicine.

## Ethical Question

- Did the strike violate the innocent bystander principle?

## Teachers

A teacher strike affects almost everyone, every government level, and, above all, the parents and students themselves. There have been over 3,500 public-school teacher strikes since 1971; in Pennsylvania alone (which had 23 percent of total strikes), 3.6 million students have been affected by teacher work stoppages; 250,000 Pennsylvania teachers have participated in strikes, causing 3.5 million idle work days.[36] Lead players are administrators, district board members (usually elected by the public), and union representatives. The public, parents, and students are not included in the negotiating process.

Before collective bargaining became popular in the 1960s, school boards determined teachers' wages and working conditions and dealt with teachers on an individual basis, not collectively. The right-to-strike feature of private-sector collective bargaining had not been widely accepted in public education.[37] Only nine states have given teachers the right to strike, and then only on the conditions that (1) serious negotiations have failed and (2) the strike does not create a clear and present danger to the health, safety, or welfare of the public. Twenty-three states have statutes prohibiting teacher strikes, while the remainder are without legislation.

Teacher strikes have some very unusual features. To begin with, only teachers are able to have their salaries made "whole" for time spent on strike. And because they work a shortened year (usually 185 days), the strikes merely delay the term to a later point. Moreover, makeup days permit most of the employee's strike days to be recaptured so that any financial loss is kept to a minimum. By contrast, in other industries a striking employee always faces possible loss both of job and of income. Because most teachers have virtually assured job security under the law, the balance of power has been crippled. Teachers have nothing to lose and everything to gain.

And so far as the school district itself is affected, it loses neither customers nor, over the long haul, revenues. Because the board enjoys a monopoly on providing education, it can sit tight until the strike is broken. This monopoly does not, however, immunize board members from significant negative impacts. If the board accepts the strikers' demands too quickly, it loses community respect because of the higher taxes its decisions bring. Moreover, because school boards possess limited financial resources, demands for improved salaries constitute one more pressure on communities already strapped by rising expenditures for supplies, textbooks, capital equipment, maintenance, and energy costs. As a consequence, the board and administration will lose something; the teachers, nothing. The effects on others can be devastating. One observer put the matter in these words:

> *Were there readily available educational alternatives and were those alternatives comparable in quality, cost, and ease of access to the public schools, the ethical balance of teacher strikes might be quite different. Thus, the most grave injustice accrues to those least able to influence the negotiating process: the children, their parents and the community. This feature, which provides the broadest perspective for making ethical judgments, is the qualitative and quantitative impact of decisions on the individuals and groups who themselves are not a part of the bargaining process. This ethical component is most readily identifiable with society's interest at large.*[38]

Studies show that students in strike districts score lower in achievement tests than students in nonstrike districts. But the more immediate concerns are high-school seniors seeking job opportunities or entrance to advanced education programs and, to a lesser extent, juniors waiting to take their college aptitude (SAT) tests. But not to be minimized is the psychological impact of teacher strikes on children. Many times students witness hostile picket lines, name calling, deceit, and even violence by striking teachers, administrators, and board members. Asking students to learn the importance of honesty, decency, cooperation, and respect for others from individuals who students feel have betrayed their sense of values is asking a great deal.

Teachers, however, are not without counterarguments. First is an indifferent, or even hostile, public who perceive public education as a mess; next is the low prestige attached to elementary and high-school teaching; and, of course, there are low salary scales and classroom violence to contend with. Teachers feel that parents have abdicated their duties by dumping on schools responsibilities for drug and sex education, driving courses, and other things not related to the school's mission or the teacher's job.

These factors go a long way toward explaining why the National Education Association (NEA) has become as militant as the American Federation of Teachers (AFT). The militants are generally career oriented, older, more experienced, and teach in a bureaucratic system. An interesting research finding is that AFT teachers most active in strikes have had the least effective communication with their students, principals, peers, and communities.[39] Although the NEA has always defined itself as a professional organization, its strikes have rarely been related to educational-outcome issues. The independence that striking teachers are generally able to maintain allows them to neutralize and, then, to enlist students and parents on behalf of their own interests. When criticized, teachers answer that their interests are legitimate, their demands just, and their services essential. Their positional power is strong.

The first case to involve higher education came in the late 1980s when faculty of Yeshiva University in New York decided to unionize and to demand collective bargaining. The university's administration, arguing that universities are not bureaucratic but collegial (meaning that professors have a large role in decision making), resisted the teachers. The case reached the Supreme Court, which ruled, in a 5 to 4 decision, that because faculties at the university perform managerial duties, they were outside of the protection of the NLRB.[40] However, the strike door has not been completely slammed in the face of teachers. If it can be shown that faculty do not participate meaningfully in decision making, and that a bureaucracy does in fact exist, the door may be reopened—as it has been at many institutions. This explained why the NLRB reopened the Washington University case regarding the managerial status of professors on grounds that the president had established too firm a hand over all decisions.[41] There is, in the case of teacher strikes, an important ethical conclusion, namely, that *effective participation by parents and teachers in decisions directly affecting them is itself of such value that to strike without their participation creates a presumption against the morality of teacher strikes.* If the negotiating process is changed to include all the key players, a different judgment could be made.

## *Traffic Controllers*

Presenting a difficult ethical problem are strikes by government employees engaged in essential services. That is why the traffic controllers' strike in 1981 is so important to the ethical content in public-policy debates. A key actor in the 1981 drama was the Federal Aviation Agency (FAA), established by Congress as an independent body in 1958.[42] Nine years later the FAA was placed under the Department of Transportation. The FAA's task, to ensure safety in all sectors of civilian aviation, required the agency to examine such diverse things as aircraft manufacturing, flight operations, airport management, pilot training, maintenance work, controllers' education, and other airline-related operations. Also within the agency's purview were matters like aircraft engine-noise abatement, communications with airplanes, certification of airplanes and pilots, determination of which hazardous materials may be carried on aircraft, and prevention of hijackings. In 1970, passage of the Airport and Airway Development Acts provided the agency with funds to foster development of newer technologies and to encourage further expansion of the industry.[43]

In the late 1960s, the aviation industry began to grow enormously and the number of airlines, passengers, routes, and airports increased almost exponentially. The FAA was slow to respond to this growth, especially in hiring and training new controllers and in acquiring the latest technology to assist them. The workload on controllers expanded significantly, with deleterious effects on morale. Whereas a close bond had traditionally existed between controllers and their managers, a more resentful and distrustful atmosphere developed. Controllers who considered themselves highly trained professionals and took great pride in their work were distressed as working conditions steadily deteriorated. Controllers were expected to work daily from eight to ten hours for six days per week, with compulsory overtime, and under the intense emotional pressure of knowing that a mistake could cost hundreds of people their lives.

In 1968, the Secretary of Transportation appointed a task force, known as the Corson Committee, to examine the controllers' complaints. The committee released its findings in 1970 and urged the FAA to reduce work hours, eliminate required overtime, revise pay criteria, and upgrade facilities and equipment. Concurrent with the commissioning of the task force, the controllers formed their own professional society, which they called PATCO. Within six months, membership in PATCO swelled to over 5,000 controllers, eventually topping out at over 18,000 members. In July 1968, PATCO announced the start of a campaign to work strictly by the book, causing a backlog of some 1,927 aircraft around New York City alone on July 19.

In early 1979, the disputes between PATCO and the FAA became more frequent and more contentious. The FAA contended that PATCO's strike fund of $600,000 violated an executive order prohibiting federal employees from striking or condoning such activity, and the agency unsuccessfully sought to have the fund declared illegal. In June, PATCO officials, testifying before the House Appropriations Committee on Transportation, claimed that continued shortage of controllers was endangering air safety. Nor did the FAA escape criticism for its role in equipment problems. Trying to bring newer technology into the control centers, the FAA encountered hardware and software difficulties. Media sympathetic to PATCO were quick to pounce on control-center computer outages as hazards to the traveling public's safety.

Congress also took the FAA to task over its equipment failures and frequent reports on the breakdowns. Congressman Robert Whittaker accused FAA Administrator Langhorne Bond of deliberately misleading the Congress on the number of computer outages and their duration. The FAA responded by accusing PATCO of attempting a publicity stunt. Sensing the probability of a strike, management had developed contingency plans to keep at least one-third of all scheduled flights operational. Among others, these plans included accommodations for altering peak travel times, providing a set daily schedule to each airline, and protecting control centers and nonstriking controllers.

In April 1980, PATCO distributed a strike plan to its membership, and on June 17, 1981, rejected a proposed contract from the Reagan administration. Although formal talks with the FAA were broken off, informal talks continued. Arguing that a controllers' strike was a first threat to public safety, the government secured a permanent injunction, which the courts refused to lift. Facing a threatened nationwide strike on June 22, the FAA and PATCO agreed to a tentative contract that had four key elements: (1) controllers would be paid for 42 hours work for each 40 actually worked; (2) night shift differential would rise from 10 to 15 percent of base pay; (3) pay-cap limitations for premium pay would be removed; and (4) a retraining allowance of 14 weeks pay for medically disqualified controllers ineligible for retirement would be made available. First-year cost of the government's new package was approximately $38 million, far less than the $700 million package under the union proposal.

PATCO leadership recommended that the controllers reject the proposal, which they did. The 12,000 controllers went on strike on August 3, the first time that federal employees embarked on a national strike officially called and sanctioned by their union. President Reagan immediately warned the controllers that their action was illegal and that, if they did not return to work within 48 hours, they would be terminated. When a large majority of the controllers did not respond to the president's ultimatum, he ordered the FAA to begin proceedings to terminate the illegally striking employees. Eventually, the FAA removed 11,325 controllers from their positions.

Fallout from the strike was not confined to the controllers, the president, and the FAA. The nation's airlines struggled to adjust to the FAA-reduced schedules, down by 50 percent from normal operations; thousands of passengers were inconvenienced; and fears of bankruptcy for weaker carriers were prevalent. Within a week, however, more optimistic attitudes in the industry developed as it saw less disruption than initially feared. In a spirit of cooperation, the airline industry pledged to back the Reagan administration's stance on the controllers and to cooperate with the FAA's plan for reduced operations through the spring of 1982. Using nonstriking controllers and supervisory personnel, the FAA set in motion a plan called Flow Control 50, which called for the carriers voluntarily to cancel 50 percent of their peak-hour flights at the 22 major airports. The agency separated flights by up to 30 miles, compared to the normal five-mile separation, for added safety. Because the commercial aviation industry accounted for the largest portion of FAA services and had suffered losses approximating $50.6 million per day at the onset of the strike, the FAA tailored its policies to the needs of this segment of the industry.

The focus after the strike shifted from one of immediate economic concern to that of longer term accommodations. The two main problems were the fate of the controllers and status of the aviation industry. The

Reagan administration, exuding confidence that it had successfully stopped an illegal strike, realized nevertheless that steps needed to be taken to rebuild and modernize the traffic control system. The controllers and their union found themselves pariahs among their union brethren, who feared that the controllers' challenge to Reagan's authority might backfire and hurt the whole labor movement. The labor leaders themselves took a wait-and-see approach.

The second question related to safety and recovery of the nation's airlines. When critics charged that air travel in the United States was not safe as a result of the strike, administration officials, pilots, and nonstriking controllers countered that, with the FAA's reduced flights and contingency planning, safety on the nation's airways was within reasonable tolerances. Moreover, the FAA announced plans to replace 25 percent fewer controllers than were fired because of changes in operational procedures, upgraded training, and acquisition of more automated equipment. Additionally, the agency announced that it would embark on a massive refurbishing of control-system equipment by including advanced computers, communication hardware, and navigation aids.

## *Ethical Questions*

- Did the controllers have substantial grievances?
- Were the grievances of sufficient magnitude to warrant a strike?
- During the prestrike period, did the FAA behave ethically?
- Is there any procedure or mechanism that might be employed to adjudicate fairly the grievances of federal employees?

## The Years Ahead

Scoping future problems and prospects for strengthening union-management relations within a single chapter is obviously impossible. But some beginnings can be made. Handling selective strikes and more recent labor tactics means that managers play in a new ballgame. Other new rules are appearing. In April 1990 the Supreme Court, in a 5 to 4 decision, nullified the NLRB's old policy that assumed that replacement workers were antiunion and, therefore, employers who hired them need not deal further with the union. When the NLRB reversed its policy, the question was stated somewhat differently but stuck to the same issue: can a presumption be made that replacement workers are antiunion?[44] TWA, International Paper, Boise Cascade, Phelps Dodge, and, most recently, Greyhound, had operated on that premise. The Court's decision meant reliance on the old premise was no longer wise.

The Supreme Court case arose with Curtin Matheson, a small Texan company that bought and sold laboratory supplies. When its workers struck, the corporation hired 29 replacements and refused to bargain further with the union. When an appeal was made in 1987 to the NLRB, the board ruled for the union, citing its revised policy against presuming that new workers would be automatically and instinctively antiunion. The majority of the Supreme Court, speaking through Justice Thurgood Marshall, said that it was the Court's position to give deference to policies adopted by specialized administrative agencies and that when the NLRB declared after its long experience that its earlier presumption (antiunionism among workers hired to displace the strikers) was incorrect, the NLRB view should be honored. In a dissent, Justice Anthony Scalia put the matter this way: "Since the principal employment-related interest of strike replacements (to retain their jobs) is almost invariably opposed to the principal interest of the striking union (to replace them with the striking members) it seems to me impossible to conclude on this record that the employer did not have a reasonable good-faith doubt regarding the union's majority status."[45]

Unions were not without their worries when they found themselves in court during the spirited election between incumbent Lloyd McBride and challenger Ed Sadlowski in the steelworkers' election of 1982. A good part of Sadlowski's $200,000 campaign contributions had come from outsiders—a tactic that outraged the incumbents. The union had adopted a rule in 1978 that barred nonmembers from contributing to any of its election campaigns. The constitutional question turned on the First Amendment, which gives Americans who contributed funds to campaigns for public office the right of free expression. Did such a right extend to a union election? By a close 5 to 4 decision the Supreme Court upheld the union.[46] Some observers complained that the rule barring outside contributions allowed unions to impose unreasonable restrictions on union democracy and was not pertinent to the steelworkers' world. The union did not face the possibilities of communist infiltration, gangsterism, or management stooges. But the Court's ruling is precarious. Changes in personnel and consequent changes in ideology do not assure the sanctity of closely split decisions.

## *Ethical Question*

- Is it unethical to bar contributions from outsiders to union election campaigns?

In addition to procedural changes foisted—or likely to be foisted—on management and labor in their bargaining process are issues that are only now simmering. In the early days of blue-collar unionism, brought to the bargaining table was an entrée consisting primarily of meat and potatoes—with money being the meat and seniority the potatoes. With time, however, the menu became flavored by such savories as shorter workweeks, paid vacations, unemployment compensation, and health retirement benefits. Although business continued to insist on management prerogatives (the right to establish corporate policies, production goals and processes, market strategies, capital investments, and the like) worker participation in such decisions, once considered a savory, is becoming standard fare. Noteworthy in the increasing number of savories in the worker's meat-and-potatoes dinner is the implication it has for the ideal of justice. In both labor's and management's original idea (a fair day's wage for a fair day's work), the view of justice was held strictly to a concept of exchange: workers received what they earned—no more and no less.[47] Under the narrowly construed notion of exchange justice, a worker might, for example, not deserve a bonus. Yet receiving one may be a part of a better concept of equity.

Bonuses, incidentally, raise another ethical question. By and large, employees have never been miffed by the high salaries earned by corporate executives—so long as the workers felt that the salary was *earned*. But they become very incensed if corporate executives are rewarded when the company posts a mediocre performance. Such was the case when CEO Robert Mullane of Bally Manufacturing Company (which makes pinball machines) received $2.5 million despite the company's mediocre performance; in contrast, the head of Digital Equipment, Kenneth Olson, received less than a million for leading his company to an outstanding record.[48] Even without the bonus question, workers now feel that they properly should share in an enterprise's good fortune. They, after all, make the company work; they often give their working lives to a single company—quite unlike fickle stockholders, who move in and move out with a casualness that, to workers, is as brazen as it is unethical.

One certainty is that when management and labor meet over the bargaining table, money will continue to be a priority item. But things once thought luxuries become, once granted, necessities. A first example would be health-care benefits. Faced by rapidly rising financial outlays for the estimated $100-billion annual bill for medical insurance, companies have pressured unions to share some of the expenses. At this point the corporate desire ignites a union fire. When, for example, Boeing sought to impose a $200 insurance deductible on single employees for the first time and raise deductibles substantially for married employees, the union threatened to walk out. Management, seeing the signals, accepted a union contract in October 1983 that assured some 26,000 workers the same medical benefits that they had enjoyed under previous contracts.

In that same year, Chrysler's negotiations with the United Auto Workers collapsed, largely because the company wanted to reduce cost-of-living pay increases if the union would not help the corporation to lower its health-care expenses by $50 million a year. Chrysler experienced the same union reaction as did Boeing. When some 60,000 UAW workers threatened to strike, the corporation backed down. But backdowns are not the end of the story. Health-care costs have continued to escalate. For example, such costs at Ford tripled between 1975 and 1985 despite a 34 percent reduction in the work force; AT&T reportedly spent about $1.5 billion in 1985 on workers' health care, with costs increasing around 17 percent annually between 1978 and 1983.

Interestingly, unions have been more willing to make wage concessions for a troubled firm than they are to make concessions over health benefits. Symptomatic of that view was the contract negotiated by the American

Federation of Teachers for some 215 high-school teachers in Mill Valley, California. Under the agreement teachers would pay up to $60 a month more to maintain their medical-insurance benefits in return for a modest pay raise. Within a year the teachers voted to leave the AFT in favor of its rival, the National Education Association. Chrysler workers, who made $1 billion in wage and benefit concessions from 1979 through 1981, refused to give an inch on medical benefits. The future is far from clear. The aluminum, brick, and glass workers, for example, accepted increased deductibles from the Aluminum Company of America and from Reynolds Metals.[49]

Another high sensitivity issue relates to pension funds. By 1990 it was estimated that more than 60 percent of workers were getting less or no retirement benefits after a termination. When, for example, Occidental Petroleum terminated its pension plans ($95 million was absorbed by management) 5,800 workers claimed foul play; Reliance Electric took $129 million from its workers' pension plan, leaving 11,000 workers without future retirement benefits. Companies respond that, because all they are doing is skimming off the excess in pension funds, the money legitimately belongs to them. Unions, on the other hand, counter that what seems overfunded today may be needed desperately tomorrow. Higher interest rates during the 1980s have, in fact, made some plans so overfunded that employers have not put money into them for a number of years. Funds continue to grow, nevertheless, because of employee contributions and interest on past contributions. Unions, therefore, demand that managements address this question: why should employers have the right to take funds unto themselves that, to a large extent, represent earnings on employee contributions? If there is any excess, insist the unions, workers should share in them through modest redistributions, or, better still, retain them for future pension-fund increases.

## Summary

With declining memberships, union leaders have looked for new tactics to bring concessions from managements and looked to new fields—particularly in the white-collar sector—to recruit workers to offset declining memberships. The changing demographics of the work force has led unions to concentrate on such white-collar professions as teaching, nursing, and government employees. Strikes by workers in these areas raise new ethical questions. And our social engineers have not been overly successful in bringing forth new procedures to resolve conflicts peacefully. How to apply the moral principles of adequate disclosure standards that meet the test of truth, the proportionality standard found in old theories about a just war (is even victory worth the costs?), the ideal of protecting innocent third parties who nevertheless have a vital stake in the outcomes of management-labor disputes, and, finally, a modification of adversarialism as the guiding principle in all management-labor relations are all challenges to leadership both in unions and in corporations, and in governing bodies that employ or regulate union members.

For workers, overriding all other issues is job security. Unions have seen work contracted out to firms in foreign lands; they have viewed hostile takeovers as a kiss of death; they are aware that downsizing must come; they are sensitive to declining union memberships. Getting a job and keeping a job may turn out to be the most difficult issue in all future labor-management negotiations. Managements, in turn, know that a world economy means world competition—competition with companies in countries having drastically different values, living standards, and aspirations. When business adjusts out of necessity, so will unions.

## *Questions for Discussion*

1. Does the right to work come before the right to unionize?
2. Is the two-tier wage system ethical?
3. Should troublesome issues between management and labor in such fields as medicine and nursing, teaching, and transportation be handled through compulsory arbitration?
4. Are secondary boycotts ethical?
5. Why are managers paid salaries and employees paid wages? Does the difference raise an ethical problem?
6. Are strikes by civilian government employees ethical? By military personnel?
7. Does ethical behavior require full disclosure by management to union members of pre- and post-tax earnings, capital investments, insurance costs, and labor overtime figures?

## Ethical Quandaries

### *Mary Allen*

After graduating from State University in 1980 with a bachelor's degree in nursing, Mary Allen returned to her hometown, an economically depressed city, to work in Community Hospital. As might be expected in such a city, salaries were substantially below the wages earned by nurses in the two nearby large cities.

Mary's dedication and competence led quickly to a series of promotions. By 1990 she was earning a comfortable salary as a supervisor. However, the relatively low wages of her subordinates troubled her so much that, when asked, she indicated a willingness to support a unionization drive. When word of Mary's position reached senior management, she was told in no uncertain terms that she was considered part of management, distinct from those who carried out operations under her direction. But Mary, holding her ground, argued that the community, despite its economic plight, was able to pay teachers more than nurses, firefighters and police more than nurses, and even trash collectors more than nurses. Because everyone knew these facts Mary wondered aloud why nurses were being so shabbily treated.

The encounter with management stiffened Mary's resolve to support a union. And when union organizers won the NLRB-supervised election, Mary rejoiced. Her joy, however, was short-lived. In the past, nurses on her floor would walk the extra mile to help patients; they were always willing to resolve day-to-day problems through informal discussions. Now, however, they talked only about going by the book. Slowdowns increased, as did employee turnover. Mary's disenchantment peaked when the union called a strike in the middle of a flu epidemic; management asked the union to accept binding arbitration, a risky move in light of the institution's financial plight. The union refused. Connected to the refusal, however, was a stated willingness to move critically ill patients without cost to a hospital in a city 17 miles away. The union had done its homework well because the nearby hospital indicated a willingness to receive the transfers.

Mary watched the rising tensions with growing concern. Her own decision depended on how she answered two questions. Should she stay with the striking colleagues? Or stay with her stricken patients? Mary opted for the second course, recognizing that her future managerial effectiveness might be jeopardized by her defection from the union ranks. "Scab" was a nasty scar to carry. But to Mary, the patients came first. And moving them to another city could be perilous for some.

## Questions

- Was Mary Allen a bleeding heart or a Benedict Arnold?
- If you were in a similar situation what would you think is the ethical course?
- Do you think health care professionals should resolve their differences with management through binding arbitration?
- If you were a recruitment officer for a large unionized hospital would you hire Mary Allen?

## The Pittsburgh Protesters

Until fairly recent times, the white- and blue-collar cultures of Pittsburgh were separate but equal. Steel workers often earned more money than white-collar managers in downtown corporate headquarters. Mill workers had comfortable homes, small boats, and cars; they felt secure within their neighborhoods, where social stability was promoted by ethnic clubs, unions, and churches. Between 1979 and 1984, however, more than 100,000 workers in steel and related industries lost their jobs. Homestead, "the steel center of the world," saw more than one-third of its population, mostly young people, migrate in search of work. Nearby towns like Clairton, Monessen, and McKeesport were similarly hard hit. New service-economy businesses helped to offset the erosion of Pittsburgh's industrial base, but most jobs went to well-educated newcomers. They lived in affluent enclaves like Shadyside, only a few miles away from the suffering towns.

On January 12, 1983, over 600 people affected by job losses jammed into the First United Methodist Church in McKeesport to protest against plant closings. Other clergy-led protests followed. Ministers from Baptist, Episcopalian, and Lutheran churches became especially involved. Recognizing their inexperience, the group hired Charles Honeywell, who had been trained in the confrontational tactics of Saul Alinsky.

Mellon Bank, then the 12th largest bank in the country, became the primary target. Honeywell reasoned that (1) the steel industry itself could offer little support, (2) poor people did not like bankers, and (3) Mellon's foreign loans (nearly $3 billion) comprised nearly a quarter of its total loan portfolio, at a time when foreign-made steel was anathema to American steelworkers. Shouting crowds blocked entrances to branch banks, threatening customers with physical violence. Protesters also entered the banks, throwing bagfuls of pennies through tellers' windows and noisily demanding receipts for their "deposits." Mellon's chairman, J. David Barnes, was at first surprised and then angry.

A second prong of the strategy was an appeal to Pennsylvania Governor Dick Thornburg to declare a disaster area. This could result in state funds and, perhaps even more important, might prod the federal government to follow suit. During the protest, Lloyd McBride, the conservative president of the United Steel Workers, weighed the protesters' petition to USW for open support. Eventually, four men found themselves in the eye of the ethical storm: bank chairman Barnes, Governor Thornburg, UAW chief McBride, and Reverend Douglas Roth, pastor of the Lutheran Church in Clairton.

*Reverend Roth.* Lutheran Bishop Kenneth May watched the behavior of the protesting ministers with growing unease. For him it was not simply a matter of public opinion (the *Pittsburgh Post Gazette,* the area's most influential newspaper, had turned solidly against the contrived tactics of Honeywell). More serious were the disruptions at some Protestant churches, especially in Shadyside, in which Roth had participated. Most alarming, however, were authenticated reports that Roth's own parishioners were badly split over their pastor's behavior. In fact, tempers were so high some of the group were bringing baseball bats to Sunday services. In light of these facts Bishop May decided to reassign Roth to a church not serving the idle steelworkers.

When the bishop's letter arrived, Reverend Roth's thoughts might have been these: "My heart and soul are in this protest movement. We are called by Christ to help the oppressed. On the other hand, if I disobey my bishop, my future as a minister is jeopardized."

## Question

- What do you think Reverend Roth should have done? Why?

*J. David Barnes.* Barnes reminded critics that, in a world economy, Mellon did not have the luxury of confining its operations to one city or one state; furthermore, Mellon's investments abroad helped to provide Pennsylvanians with 84,000 jobs in the export trade. The bank was ready to make loans to steelmakers, but they were diversifying into everything except steel. Finally, the bank held over $100 million in Industrial Development Corporation's low-interest loans intended to create local jobs.

In response, the protesters asked two questions: Why was Mellon investing so heavily in foreign enterprises that competed directly with the domestic steel mills? Why did not Mellon take the lead in applying far more of its resources to create new jobs? Given the bank's financial power, its $100 million investment in the Industrial Development Corporation was paltry.

At this point Barnes' thoughts might have been these: "As an ethical person and as a successful banker, should I pour more money into the Industrial Development fund? Go to Harrisburg to plead with the governor to declare a disaster area? Or mind my own business? I am not a politician. I am not a savior of cities."

## Question

- What do you think Barnes should have done? Why?

*Governor Dick Thornburg.* The governor received the protesters' petition to declare a disaster area. As he considered all of the ramifications, his thoughts might have included these: "I see the desperate plight of these petitioners. I see our example as possibly influencing the federal government to help. At the same time I see a state with mounting deficits. And I see the possible effect if we help the steelworkers this year. Next year it will be the farmers, then the miners, and God knows what will be next. What is my ethical obligation?"

## Questions

- How would you have counseled the governor if you were the comptroller general of the state?
- Would your advice be different if you were state chairman of his political party?

*Lloyd McBride.* As McBride contemplated the protesters' request for support, he might have said to himself: "We ought to do something to help these ministers. But they are steadily losing ground. Joining losers when we already have a declining and disgruntled membership is hardly the best way to ready ourselves for next year's tough bargaining round. On the other hand, Mellon has just foreclosed on Mesta Machine Works. Barnes will collect his loan, but the workers will be lucky to collect their pensions. I know the bank has carried Mesta for over a year and a half—a decent thing to do. Does the foreclosure give me ample reason to throw the support of our 120,000 membership to our friends? Doing that would give me a good feeling."

## Question

- What do you think McBride should have done? Why?

## Notes

1. Commonwealth v. Pullias, Philadelphia Court of Common Pleas (1806).
2. Commonwealth v. Hunt, Mass. Sp. Ct. (1842).
3. Jean Tussey, ed., *Eugene V. Debs Speaks* (New York: Pathfinders Press, 1972), 52.
4. Derek Bok, "Reflections on the Distinctive Character of American Labor Laws," *Harvard Law Review* 84 (1971): 1394–1460. Bok reflected the traditional interpretation, which saw workers as largely uninterested in reforming society.
5. William F. Forbath, "The Shaping of the American Labor Movement." *Harvard Law Review* 102 (1989): 1111–1164.
6. *General Electric Relations Newsletter*, June 26, 1963, 1. See also, Herbert Northrup, *Boulwarism* (Ann Arbor: University of Michigan Press, 1964).
7. Neil Chamberlain, "The Corporation and the Trade Union," in *The Corporation and Modern Society*, ed. Edward S. Mason (Cambridge: Harvard University Press, 1959), 122.
8. F. L. Acuff and Michael Dillere, "Games Negotiators Play," *Business Horizons* 19 (February 1976): 70–76. How such games might be played according to ethical rules was explored by Frederick R. Post, "Collaborative Collective Bargaining: Toward an Ethically Defensible Approach to Labor Negotiations," *Journal of Business Ethics* 9 (June 1990): 495–508.
9. Thomas C. Shelling, *The Strategy of Conflicts* (Cambridge: Harvard University Press, 1966).
10. These elements have become essential parts of game theory as developed initially by John Von Naumann and Oskar Von Morgenstern, *Theory of Games and Economic Behavior* (Princeton: Princeton University Press, 1947).
11. Patricia A. McIntyre, "Labor Law and Unfair Labor Practices," *University of Akron Law Review* 17 (1983–1984): especially 261–275.
12. Quoted by James Kuhn in Clarence C. Walton, ed., *Enriching Business Ethics* (New York: Plenum, 1990), 63.
13. Jerry Capeci, "Did Union Officials Lie?" *The National Law Journal*, November 21, 1983, 13.
14. Norman E. Bowie, *Should Collective Bargaining and Labor Relations Be Less Adversarial?* (Newark, Del.: Center for the Study of Values at the University of Delaware, 1987).
15. John T. Dunlop, "Have the 1980s Changed U.S. Industrial Relations?" *The Monthly Labor Review* 3 (May 1988): 29–34.

16. Harry C. Katz, Thomas A. Kochan, and Jeffrey H. Keefe, *Industrial Relations and Productivity in the U.S. Automobile Industry* (Washington: Brookings Papers on Economic Activity, No. 3, 1987), 685–728.
17. Ibid., 687. See also, Werner Chilton, "Labor Costs and International Competitiveness in Manufacturing Industries" (New York: Citibank Corporation, November 10, 1981), 5.
18. Donald Alexander McLean, *The Morality of the Strike* (New York: P.J. Kenedy & Sons, 1921), 19–20.
19. State of Delaware v. General Teamsters Union Local 326, Del.Sp.Ct.321 A 2d 123 (1974).
20. Fred S. Hall, *Sympathy Strikes and Sympathy Lockouts* (New York: American Management Association Press, 1968).
21. Atkinson v. Sinclair Oil Refinery Co., 50 LRRM 2420 (1974).
22. Eazor Express v. International Brotherhood of Teamsters Local 326, 85 LRRM 14 15 (January 23, 1974).
23. See note, "International Unions' Leadership Responsibility for Wildcat Strikes: The Carbon Fuel Case," *Syracuse Law Review* 31 (Fall 1980): 1007–1039.
24. Richard A. Givens, "Liability of Individual Employees for Wildcat Strikes," *Employee Relations Law Journal* 4 (Spring 1979): 552–561.
25. Lucas Flour Co. v. Teamsters Local 174, 369 U.S.S. Ct. 95 (1962).
26. See the fascinating study by Ivar Berg, "Corporations, Human Resources and Grass Roots: Community Profiles," presented at the Columbia University Center for Law and Economic Studies, March 1983.
27. Gail Bronson and Jeffrey H. Birnbaum, "How the Textile Union Finally Wins Contracts at J. P. Stevens Plants," *The Wall Street Journal*, October 20, 1980, 1.
28. Denise Giardina, "Solidarity in Appalachia," *The Nation*, July 3, 1989, 12.
29. Robin Taylor, "Coal Miners Strike Nonviolently," The *National Reporter*, June 16, 1989, 3.
30. Rick Wartzman, "UMW Takes Contract Dispute to Pittston's Own Turf," *The Wall Street Journal*, January 27, 1989, B-2.
31. Ibid.
32. *The Wall Street Journal*, August 3, 1983, 23A.
33. Whipsawing is, of course, only one of the tools that managements, driven by global competition, have used to contain labor costs; other practices include expanding contracting-out arrangements and increased use of part time workers to "make employees flexible." Audrey Freedman, "How the 1980's Have Changed Industrial Relations," *Monthly Labor Review*, 111 (May 1988): 37.
34. Typical was the full-page advertisement carried in the *Philadelphia Inquirer*, November 2, 1983, 5-B.
35. Hogan v. Unemployment Compensation Board (1951).
36. *Weekly Digest* (Harrisburg, Pa.: The Pennsylvania School Board Association, July 28, 1989) 1.
37. David Colton and Edith Graber, *Teacher Strikes and the Courts* (Lexington, Mass.: Lexington Press, 1982), 127.
38. Lazlo Hetenyi, "Unionism in Education: The Ethics of It," *Education Theory* 28 (Spring 1978): 91.
39. Theodore C. Wagenar, "Activist Professionals: The Case of Teachers' Strikes," *Social Science Quarterly* 55 (September 1974): 371–379.
40. NLRB v. Yeshiva University Albert Einstein Medical College, 247 NLRB 639 (February 20, 1980).
41. For background, see Kenneth Mortimer and T. R. McConnell, *Sharing Authority Effectively* (San Francisco: Jossey-Bass, 1978).
42. Based on a case prepared by William Bradford, *The FAA Air Traffic Controllers' Strike* (Baltimore: University of Maryland, 1990, mimeographed).
43. Edmund Preston, *Troubled Passage: The Federal Aviation Administration During the Nixon-Ford Term, 1973–1977* (Washington, D.C.: Government Printing Office, 1987).

44. N.L.R.B. v. Curtin Matheson, 110 S. Ct. 1542 (April 17, 1990).
45. Lind Greenhouse, "Companies' Anti-Union Tack in Strikes Blocked by Court," *The New York Times*, April 18, 1990, A 22.
46. Sadlowski v. United Steel Workers 457, U.S. 102 (October 10, 1982).
47. "Moral dessert" is a term in philosophy about which differences of opinion occur. John Rawls, *A Theory of Justice* (Cambridge: Harvard University Press, 1971), 311, argued that the idea of moral dessert is not, strictly speaking, part of the idea of justice. But Joel Feinberg, "Justice and Personal Dessert" in *Nomos VI: Justice*, eds. Carl J. Friedrich and John W. Chapman (New York: Atherton Press, 1963), 69–97, disagreed. Philosophers will find the differences between the two men interesting to explore.
48. Graef S. Crystal, "The Wacky Wacky World of CEO Pay," *Fortune*, June 6, 1988, 68.
49. Whether workers' determination not to yield on health benefits will continue throughout the decade is problematic. Merck's unionized workers agreed in the summer of 1991 to pay 20 percent of all medical costs. "Trends," *Monthly Labor Review* 114 (August 1991), 41. See also Thomas Burke and Rita S. Jain, "Trends in Employer-provided Health Plans," *Monthly Labor Review* 114 (February 1991), 24–30.

CHAPTER 9

# Advertising

## The Nature of the Industry
The Stakes
Definitions
Truth: Who Cares?

## Deceptive Advertising
FTC Rulings
Government and Industry Definitions
The Knowing-It-When-You-See-It Concept

## Special Forms of Advertising
Comparative Advertising
Puffery
Harmful-Product Advertising
Advertising to Children

## Institutional Controls
Intervention
Self-Policing
Two NAD Investigations

## Ethical Appraisals
Scrutiny of the Industry
Advertisers' Accountability
Specific Issues
*General Foods*
*The Surgeon General's Report*
*Nestlé*

## Summary
Questions for Discussion
Ethical Quandary

*A*dvertising has been around ever since the Romans painted murals to announce gladiator spectaculars and the Phoenicians used the first billboards along heavily trafficked roads to promote their products. A wall unearthed in Pompeii revealed a political poster, perhaps the first, which extolled the virtues of a particular politician—and signaled the need for truth in advertising. The Bible also tells of advertisements over shop entrances. Town criers, thought to be employed only to shout the hour to clockless households, actually worked for merchants to advertise their goods or services. Skilled artisans signed their work because they knew that even a good product had to be promoted—possibly the origin of brand names.[1]

Gutenberg's printing press, which appeared in 1453, drastically transformed advertising from one-shot messages to repetitive ones. Handbills could be quickly produced and newspapers became the advertiser's dream. The first American newspaper ad appeared in the Boston News Letter in 1704; Ben Franklin's Pennsylvania Gazette was one of the first to offer illustrated advertising; other publishers added their creative touches by using larger than normal type size to attract attention. So sophisticated had advertising become that Dr. Samuel Johnson (whose fame was assured by the success of his Dictionary of the English Language in 1755) said that advertising was so near perfection by the mid-18th century that it was hard to propose any improvements. Indeed, until the early 20th century, when Sears started to advertise do-it-yourself houses, few innovations came about.

As Gutenberg made newspapers and magazines possible after 1453, compulsory education, which began in Massachusetts in 1813, made them profitable. The number of literate people increased sharply. Something else also happened. Advertising began to change its emphasis from information to persuasion. Americans once skipped advertisements unless they were looking for some specific item; now they read the ads to find out not what they necessarily needed but might be led to want. As a matter of fact, advertising's roots may even be traced to literary criticism, which seeks to mirror what readers (i.e., consumers) really desire.

To support this somewhat novel thesis, advertisers have been urged to think of themselves as writers of stories and visions, not unlike the allegories of the Middle Ages. Advertising and poetry are similar in that both use metaphorical arts. Poetry is commonly defined as the "language of metaphor," whose persuasive power had first been identified by Aristotle. Having a sense of metaphor was the mark of genius, and to make metaphors meant *having an eye for resemblances. As an art form, therefore, advertising continues the centuries-old tradition of writing by providing insight into concepts that are used by "bards of Madison Avenue."*[2] *Bards is one description of advertisers; "bad men" is another.*

*The advertising world is fascinating. With considerable tongue-in-cheek prescience,* Advertising Age *editors began their publication on January 11, 1930, by asking whether advertising managers were people, noting rumors "to the effect that advertising managers, as a class, were in the same condition as the Indians, the buffalo, woolen underwear and open automobiles—in other words, they belong to a vanishing race." The race has not vanished and the question is not whether advertisers are people but, rather, what kind of people. And the answers tell much about the meaning of consumer sovereignty.* ■

## *The purposes of this chapter are:*

1. To trace the roots of the advertising industry, noting specifically the pressures that led advertisers to place persuasion before information.
2. To examine the intricacies involved in the word deception, using examples to illustrate the theories.
3. To identify the special kinds of advertising and the specific ethical problems each generates.

## The Nature of the Industry

### *The Stakes*

By the 1990s the advertising industry was a giant fast approaching the $100 billion sales figure annually and handling more money than many large corporations and even many nations. Size attracts the lightning of criticism. And when the giant's purpose is to persuade the consumer pygmies to buy the wares they trumpet, the lightning becomes more dangerous, threatening both the persuader and the persuaded. Every day, over five billion advertising messages pour forth from our daily newspapers, millions of others from 8,151 weeklies, and 1.4 billion more each day from 4,147 magazines and periodicals. There are 3,895 AM and 1,136 FM radio stations that broadcast an average of 730,000 commercials a day, and 770 television stations that use 100,000 commercials a day. Millions of people are confronted daily with 330,000 outdoor billboards; with 2,500,000 car cards and posters in buses, subways, and commuter trains; with 51,300,000 direct mail pieces and leaflets; and with billions of display and promotion items.[3] As the flood of commercials continues to rise, millions of Noahs in the consumer ranks wonder why monitoring groups do not build more and better arks. Perhaps battleships is the better word for this $20-billion-per-year business. But why did the industry grow so fast?

Advertising grew out of necessity. With the industrial revolution, which meant mass production for mass markets, corporate America searched for ways to publicize its products. Branding became a tool used by producers to distinguish their products from those of other producers, and advertising enabled audiences with specific buying characteristics to be targeted. National advertisers can be credited with bringing growth to the advertising industry, being responsible for well over 50 percent of all advertising expenditures today. Whether widely circulated newspapers, periodicals, radio, and television networks would have developed so quickly without national advertising is unclear. Certainly they grew together. Procter & Gamble, Goodyear Tire, and Ford transformed national advertising from a mere source of information to a sharp tool of persuasion.

The stakes are enormous. Few care that the Unclaimed Freight Company no longer buys most of its goods from "unclaimed" stockpiles of merchandise. But consumers are very much concerned whether or not two Tylenol tablets are more effective in stopping pain than two Advil tablets, especially when the concern is largely the result of mass advertising between large corporate rivals. In terms of purchases, two little Tylenol or Advil tablets seem so insignificant. In terms of sales, two billion tables are so much!

## *Definitions*

Because discussions about advertising's merits to the public are so hotly debated, it is useful to make some preliminary distinctions between (1) transactions and negotiations and (2) local and national advertisers.

A *commercial transaction* is a single event between buyer and seller whereas *negotiations* include a series of events that leads to an exchange. Sellers hawk their wares to entice consumers into buying; customers can listen, ignore, or reject what sellers claim. When they listen seriously, customers enter, sometimes unconsciously, the negotiating stage. One ethical problem is this: *When are advertisers morally justified to continue negotiations?* Three theories give three answers. The first two are clear-cut. Under the economic concept of consumer sovereignty (people buy only what they want when they want it), the answer is: as long as it takes to get a customer to buy. Time is the key. Under a deontological ethic, negotiations may continue so long as facts are clearly presented and products are safe. Truth is the key. Under the utilitarian ethic, however, the answer becomes more detailed. Advertisers may continue efforts to persuade people to buy so long as the product or service (1) is at least as beneficial for the customer as any other product or service, (2) serves the public good, and (3) preserves the free market by not allowing one firm to set prices. The distinction between transaction and negotiation means that advertising is a process carried out more in the second than in the first category—an ongoing process between experienced negotiators, on one hand, and less experienced negotiators on the other.

The second distinction exists between *local advertisers* like "mom and pop" stores or independently owned dry cleaning shops and *national ad-*

*vertisers* like Procter & Gamble or Johnson & Johnson, whose enormous advertising budgets are designed to reach targeted audiences in large market sectors.

## *Truth: Who Cares?*

During the Great Depression, the challenge for most Americans was to make ends meet: they purchased essentials, not luxuries. When producers were hurt by a dormant economy, so also were advertisers. Indeed, the advertisers were hit even harder than producers. With the end of World War II, however, a new era began. As population increased dramatically, so did affluence. There were so many more new products that the life cycle of nearly 98 percent of them became extremely short. As a result, advertising that promoted only the virtues of the product fell by the wayside. Instead, advertisers used delusively alluring images or made extravagant claims to serve corporate clients who knew that their product's life cycle was short, or that quality control was poor. Persuasion was the driving force. Information became secondary. Truth was often a casualty.

Major advertising agencies eventually became aware that their messages were too often tinctured by half-truths. But was there any cause for alarm in a society that had come to treat truth quite cavalierly?[4] If, as has been suggested, advertising has its authentic roots in literature, then part of the problem may be caused by writers. Talented novelists like Tom Wolfe and Norman Mailer illustrate the point. Wolfe's 1979 novel, *The Right Stuff*, is a fairly accurate account of the Mercury space program during the early 1960s; yet throughout the book, factual and contrived statements appear side by side. Wolfe imagined the thinking of the astronauts and made their "thoughts" his own. Terms like *esprit* and *joie de combat* spice the speech of space adventurers. Nor does Wolfe let a fact get in the way of a punch line, as when he claims that "more fighter pilots died in automobiles than airplanes." Norman Mailer called his *Executioner's Song* (1979) a "true-life novel, as accurate as one can make it." Yet the account of Utah murderer Gary Gilmore rested largely on unconfirmed third- and fourth-hand information. By tinkering with dialogue and documents, Mailer turned a cowboy convict into an eloquent philosopher who wonders, "What will I meet when I die? . . . Will my spirit be flung about the universe faster than thought?" Neither writer shows where fact ends and fantasy begins. Yet their great financial and critical success spawned imitators and even infected prominent reporters. In *The Brethren* (1979), Bob Woodward and Scott Armstrong of the *Washington Post* recreated Supreme Court justices' moods and thoughts based on interviews with clerks. The public has come to accept as routine the obfuscation of politicians and the "real-life" simulations of the advertising industry. Such "habitual acceptance of little fibs," novelist John Hersey warned, "leads to the swallowing whole of world-shaking lies."[5]

Commercial artists have also been caught in the web of half-truths. Nearly 500 companies own computer equipment that can quickly alter a photo's colors or move its elements around; by the mid-1990s, that number is expected to triple as the systems become less expensive. Altering photographs is commonplace. Editors of *National Geographic* moved two of the pyramids at Giza close enough to fit the magazine's cover; *Newsweek* forbids retouching news photos but permits it for feature or fashion pictures; *Time* stirred howls of protest when its "Picture Week" showed Raisa Gorbachev and Nancy Reagan together even before they had ever met. "Who knows what is real anymore?" sighed Len Kaltman, director of marketing for Comstock, a firm that catalogs and sells thousands of photos in New York.[6] The public's mood was expressed by an Ohio man who wrote:

*We live in a time when lies are so outlandish and so incredible that we simply ignore them. We don't believe them, but then, we don't believe what we see on television when the news reports something outlandish. We see it, we hear it, but like the commercial message that follows, it makes just a subliminal impression. From the televangelists to the junk-bond dealers to the lies about our involvement in everything from Panama to the S&L scandals, we just don't give a hoot....*[7]

Imagining that exaggeration and half-truth are characteristics only of contemporary Americans is itself a half-truth. Europeans have generally believed that Americans bragged, exaggerated, and twisted facts to suit their moods. "Exaggeration is an essential characteristic of American humor," wrote the editors of *Advertising Agency Magazine*: "It is a product of the civilization of the west, and to expect that it can be routed completely from our advertising writing is to expect a great deal indeed." The magazine said that it would be a sorry day indeed if "the element of fantasy, of poetry, of showmanship" were eliminated from advertising. Gray Advertising Agency proclaimed a similar view that "if all advertisers stuck to the plain unvarnished truth for one month, the people would put up a howl of boredom. The public not only liked but expected ads to be spiced with exaggeration."[8] Flights of fancy were part and parcel of our national mores. Today's national slogan may be the old Latin maxim: "*Mundus dulta decipe*—the world likes to be fooled."[9] If this is humanity's wish and Americans' unique application of wish to reality, it is not surprising that advertisers would respond.

Industry leaders, aware of Americans' casual love affair with quasi-truth telling, knew that toying with consumers' affections (or inflictions) had begun as early as 1920 and reached such excesses that the advertising community itself urged its members to remember the "Seven Maxims" by avoiding:

1. False statements or misleading exaggerations
2. Indirect misrepresentation of a product or service through distortion of details, either editorially or pictorially
3. Suggestions offensive to public decency
4. Statements that attributed to a competitor's products, generally, faults and weaknesses true only of a few
5. Misleading price claims

6. Pseudoscientific advertising, including claims insufficiently supported by accepted authority, or that distort the true meaning or application of a statement made by professional or scientific authority
7. Testimonials that do not reflect the real opinion of a competent witness[10]

Despite 70 years' experience with codes, problems remain—and will remain so long as (1) public indifference to truth remains, (2) technological innovation and product obsolescence exist, and (3) competitive markets prevail. The first one may in time decrease but the second pair will likely intensify. The policy goal, therefore, is not the elimination of all untruth but support for institutions organized to minimize it. The evolving story about the many deceptions reveals the obstacles that make such controls difficult to achieve.

## Deceptive Advertising

Prior to the creation of the Federal Trade Commission, advertisers and product manufacturers had to obey few enforceable rules concerning the legality of product claims. Although the common law did prohibit certain blatant kinds of false advertising, the unwritten principle was that it was the buyer's responsibility to examine goods before purchasing them. In addition, courts generally treated advertising claims as statements of opinion rather than fact that, as a consequence, should be treated by consumers with a certain skepticism. When hearing cases concerning false advertising, courts followed the legal requirement of *scienter*, according to which any misrepresentation could not be declared illegal unless the source's fraudulent behavior—specifically, his conscious knowledge of falsity and intent to use this falsity to deceive—was proved. This stance put consumers at a tremendous disadvantage.

### *FTC Rulings*

Formation of the FTC in 1914 was government's recognition that the rules of the game were so stacked against the consumer that elimination of some inequities was needed. Congress's admission that inequities existed between seller and consumer was the starting point for reform. There was no longer any doubt about the government's intention to regulate and verify advertising claims. However, due to limited time and inadequate financial and manpower resources, direct protection of the buying public took a back seat to the goal of providing fair competition in the marketplace.[11] This posture started to change in the late 1970s, when the FTC began to examine more instances of deceptive advertising, thereby putting protection of consumers first. For example, in January 1981, the FTC ruled that surveys conducted specifically for corporate marketing executives may not be substantial enough to warrant their use in external advertising. It was the FTC's position that external advertising surveys must meet a higher set of standards than surveys conducted strictly for internal use. The premise was that such imperfect research, when handled by knowledgeable marketing executives, may serve its intended purpose quite well. But FTC Commissioner Paul Rand Dixon wrote: "Consumers are not well situated to judge a survey's shortcomings. For this reason . . . surveys that are used as the basis for advertising claims must be held to higher standards."[12]

Another important problem was recognized by the FTC, namely, the freewheeling practices of some so-called experts. More often than not, testimony in cases of deceptive advertising came from people whose special training and experience allowed them to interpret advertising in ways that normal consumers might not. It was not hard to imagine qualified experts being found to support opposite sides of a case; this being so, "the facts of the case often got lost in attempts by both sides to discredit expert witnesses and to win the case on legal technicalities."[13] This practice came under critical review when the FTC began putting behavioral scientists on the witness stand to testify about possible deficiencies in their own research. Possibly more important were efforts to present the results of consumer surveys.[14] Although these avenues do not solve all of the problems faced by the FTC in protecting consumers from deceptive advertising, they point in the right direction.

By introducing the use of behavioral data reflected in consumer surveys, however, the FTC encountered still another problem, namely, that of determining how many consumers needed to be affected by an advertising claim in order to call it deceptive and, more important, how intelligent must the consumers be to catch the full meaning of subtly designed ads. Currently, the FTC attempts to protect the general public by sometimes defining it as the unthinking and the unsophisticated. This definition has been termed the "least reasonable man" theory by advertisers.

To be certain that all consumers are protected at all times, advertisers are therefore forced to aim their messages considerably below the comprehension of the average individual. It should be emphasized that the concept of the least reasonable man is an exception to the general rule of law.[15] The judicial system uses not the least reasonable concept but the "reasonable man" principle to describe one who is responsible for his or her own actions, capable of exercising sound judgment in practical matters and making decisions with some degree of care. If the FTC was given unlimited resources to prosecute all deceptive advertising, contemporary advertising might not survive. This difference leads to important moral questions.

## *Ethical Questions*

- Should advertisers follow the least reasonable man approach?
- Should the FTC be permitted to demand "corrective advertising" by forcing companies to admit publicly that they lied?[16]

## Government and Industry Definitions

The foregoing indicates how difficult it is to establish clear legal guidelines for consumer protection against the advertising world's formidable array of talented persuaders. Outright lying can be detected and the advertiser or producer who uses it can be punished. But the gray areas—comparative advertising, puffery, children's advertising, and unsafe products that some consumers want—remain difficult to handle. In one study that compared the deceptiveness of six sources of information—advertising, union leaders, government leaders, business leaders, local newspapers, and network television news—advertising was found to have the highest percentage of intentionally false or misleading messages.[17] It seems strange that what everyone talks about still has no definition acceptable to both sellers and buyers, to public regulators and self-policing agencies. Under a strictly Kantian ethic no form of calculated deceit is permissible; however, neither the public nor the industry seems prepared to accept this ideal.

One reason for the lack of a precise definition is the past record of the FTC—a series of defeats in trying to curb major advertisers on the deception issue. The commission's current approach is to concentrate on whether the deception was deliberate, not on whether a consumer was deceived; therefore, obviously deceptive statements that do not really deceive consumers are judged nondeceptive because the intent of the advertiser was honorable—or, at least, not dishonorable. "Mr. Isuzu" illustrates the point.

The FTC recognized the problem it has helped to create. In a 1982 statement, the then FTC chairman, James C. Miller III, asked Congress to "amend the law so actionable fairness and deception are defined more precisely."[18] To Miller, "a deceptive act or practice is a material representation that (a) is likely to mislead consumers, acting reasonably in the circumstances, or (b) that the representor (advertiser) knew or should have known would be misleading."[19] Only noting Miller's use of words like "should have known" and "likely" suggests that the commissioner's contribution was more an expression of hope than of definitional clarity. It was nonetheless clear that a heavy burden was being placed on advertisers for something called deception, which was subject to different interpretations.

To help themselves to clear the air, three major advertising associations (Association of National Advertisers, American Association of Advertisers, and American Advertising Federation) defined deceptive advertising as (1) consisting of material representations known to be false, or (2) made in reckless disregard of their truth or falsity, or (3) may foreseeably result in substantial economic injury to unsuspecting consumers.

Their definition is similar in some respects to the FTC's definition, but the industry was obviously determined to lighten its legal burden by using such words as "reckless disregard for truth" and "substantial injury." Like smart debaters who know that defining the issue in their terms is the first step toward victory, the FTC and the industry jockeyed for position. In February 1980 industry representatives sharply criticized the FTC before a Senate subcommittee, charging that the agency's 1972 rule harmed the advertisers. The rule stated that every claim must be substantiated and that prosecution would follow if it was not—even if later testing showed that the claim was true. Unfairness should mean untruthfulness, said the industry. Unfairness should mean anything that takes advantage of consumers, countered the FTC.

Because the differences between government and industry definitions of deception were not removed, other definition makers sought an end to the impasse. Among the definitional candidates, two are most promising— even if each is quite technical. The first sees deception occurring when customers (1) listen to the claim, (2) are positively influenced by it, (3) remember the claim for a long time, (4) are given directly or by implication false information, and (5) decide on the basis of the claim to purchase the advertised product.[20] Most interesting in this definition is the inclusion of two factors not previously emphasized—the ad's potential for attracting attention and the customer's potential for remembering it.

A second definition of deceptive advertising is the following: If an advertisement leaves the consumer with an impression and/or belief different from what would normally be expected if the consumer had reasonable knowledge, and that impression and/or belief is factually untrue or potentially misleading, then deception exists.[21] This definition varies from the others only in a small but very important detail. It emphasizes the advertisement's relationship to the consumer's accumulated beliefs and experience. The irony in the government-versus-industry definitions of deception is that each side seemed to think that the other's definition was itself deceptive.

## *The Knowing-It-When-You-See-It Concept*

Useful to the experts, the knowing-it-when-you-see-it concept provides two methods for detecting deception. First is the normative-belief technique, which seeks to establish product-class norms on the basis of information gathered from consumers and experts. It then asks consumers to view advertisements for a particular product to see if they actually believe the specific product had all the qualities of the product brand. The second method is already used by advertisers, namely, pretesting. Consumers would view advertisements and then answer a number of questions concerning claims made. If the consumer perception agreed with the claims made, the advertisement would be considered nondeceptive.

## Special Forms of Advertising

The effort—indeed, the struggle—to reach acceptable and adequate definitions of deception can be traced through the various forms that advertising takes in dealing with certain competitors (comparative advertising and puffery), certain products (cigarettes and alcohol), and certain audiences (the very young and the very old).

## Comparative Advertising

Comparative advertising is exactly what the words mean: one product or service is compared with another named product offered in the same general area. During the 1980s, restrictions on comparative advertising diminished substantially, offering new opportunities for advertisers and causing new headaches for regulators and competitors. Even the automobile giants got into the act in 1990 with a vengeance, leading caustic critics to urge motorists to turn on their windshield wipers because carmakers were slinging so much mud. Subaru pitted itself against Volvo; Oldsmobile confidently asserted that its Cutlass Supreme was better than the Ford Taurus; Chrysler's Dodge Spirit and Plymouth's Acclaim were said to outperform the Honda. The rivals' head-on bashings produced as many headaches as heart warmings.[22] The advertising industry feels that the real problem is caused by the ineffective review systems used by the television networks. Ford charged Chevrolet with getting away with "mistruths" about Ford trucks. Then Coca-Cola was so outraged by the network's handling of a complaint it filed against Diet Pepsi that it demanded—and got—the networks' approval for having outside independent panels of research experts to verify ad claims before they are used.

What comparative advertising can do, and not do, for the seller may be best seen through the lens of the Avis–Hertz controversy, although the Listerine–Scope battle and the Schick–Remington clash had their shares of drama.[23] In 1926, John Hertz, the man who gave the company its name, was bought out by General Motors. With the shortage of gasoline, tires, and automobiles during World War II, Americans turned increasingly to car rentals. By the mid-1950s, despite a number of worn-out vehicles, people continued to rent Hertz cars in large numbers. After the war, the firm launched a major advertising campaign to wean motorists away from car purchases to car rentals. The multimillion dollar project was primarily to tell consumers of the cost and convenience of rental cars while emphasizing the car rental industry rather than the Hertz name.

The success of the program encouraged others to enter the rental field. One was Avis, founded in Detroit just after World War II by Warren Avis. However, it was not until after a syndicate, headed by Richard Robie, purchased the company in 1955 that Avis began advertising nationally. Spending less than $200,000, Avis emphasized the advantages of its service for business and pleasure trips. By 1959, ad spending had risen to $4 million, but the company operated at a loss throughout the late 1950s and early 1960s. In 1962 Lazard Freres acquired control of Avis and one of the first things that the new chief executive, Robert Townsend, did was search for a new advertising agency. In interviewing agencies, Townsend told them he had a $1 million ad budget and needed $5 million worth of impact. Most agencies were not interested, but one, Doyle Dane Bernbach, told Townsend to give the agency 90 days and a promise not to change a single thing in the ads it created, not even a comma.

What the agency came up with was the then controversial and now classic "We try harder" campaign. Consumers were told outright that though

Avis was second in rental cars, they should nevertheless choose Avis. Ad copy said Avis would never allow dirty ashtrays, half-empty gas tanks, unwashed cars, low tires, or heaters and defrosters that did not work. The campaign provoked widespread criticism, but by year's end Avis reported a $1,200,000 net profit, the first in 15 years. Profits the following year were up to $3 million. The "No. 2" campaign lasted through 1967, although the "We try harder" line was carried over to a subsequent campaign intended to show the variety of "bugs" that could plague rental car customers.

At Hertz, in the meantime, management decided to strike back by showing why Avis was number two—and would remain so. Despite increasing popularity, comparative advertising aroused deep suspicions. The spokesperson of the N. W. Ayer Company, the nation's oldest advertising firm, said that comparative advertising that knocks the competition does nothing to sell the product, but it does lots to push the ad business closer to the jungle. Richard Wirthlin used a different simile: comparative advertising is "like throwing a grenade in the other guy's foxhole and it comes right back to blow him up."[24]

## *Ethical Questions*

- Does knocking the competitor's product violate the principle of constructive effort mentioned in the chapter on competition?
- Is comparative advertising unethical if the criticism it contains is accurate?

## *Puffery*

Puffery is a word far gentler than its cousin, lying; it is congenial to the American penchant for bragging; it seeks not to put the other fellow down as much as it strives to put the "puffer" up; it is home to superlatives; it states no facts explicitly and thus appears as opinion. Advertisements containing puffery had previously gone unchallenged because of the FTC's belief

Table 9.1  Survey Respondents Who Reported Well-Known Puffery Advertisements to Be True

| Product Slogan | Respondents Who Listed as True |
| --- | --- |
| "When you care enough to send the very best" (Hallmark) | 62% |
| "Kodak makes your picture count" (Kodak) | 60 |
| "The quality goes in before the name goes on" (Zenith) | 49 |
| "Today, aluminum is something else" (Alcoa) | 47 |

Source: Survey by R. H. Brushin Associates, New York City.

that the exaggerated claims were immediately recognizable by consumers as either false or opinionated. However, the agency's decision had been made according to criteria established prior to the coming of human-behavior research. But a later study put these traditional criteria in doubt when it showed that nearly 40 percent believed them. See Table 9.1.

The results raised anew the the relevance of the "least reasonable man" theory. As already noted, courts now give consumers the benefit of the doubt in tort cases—to a point where the caveat emptor principle has been completely shredded of its old meaning. Furthermore, more buyers today are more literate: they can read the fine print. Nevertheless, in present markets, numerous advertisements, like puffery, may confuse some consumers. A few examples illustrate the point.

The results raised anew the relevance of the least reasonable man theory to truth as viewed by some courts and regulators. Numerous ads in today's market may, like puffery, be considered deceptive, among them:

1. Campbell's vegetable soup ads that were photographed by placing marbles in the bottom of the bowl in order to get the vegetables to rise to the top
2. The Stroh's Light commercials in which Alex, the dog, fetches, opens, and consumes a bottle of beer
3. The popular "lying" Isuzu commercials

These are usually considered to be ethically indifferent because there is no intent to mislead consumers. But there are hundreds of other instances in which the norm of truth may be violated. If advertisers are in doubt, consumer groups often are not, and their pressures have been felt by the titans and the tiny. Mighty McDonald's, for example, learned to its dismay how pressures by consumer groups got the FTC to act. Pressure by consumer groups has also spurred officials in three heavily populated states—New York, California, and Texas—to ask McDonald's to remove advertising that portrayed its food as wholesome and healthy. In one ad, McDonald's claimed that the sodium content of its food was "down across the board." The government contended that the salt level was not reduced in at least four of the menu items listed in the ads: regular-size french fries, regular cheeseburgers, six-piece chicken McNuggets, and the vanilla shakes. McDonald's countered in an ad that said: "for over thirty years, millions of people have included McDonald's food as part of a healthy and balanced diet."

## Ethical Question

- Did McDonald's make an ethical end run in its advertising response to consumer and government criticism?

## Harmful-Product Advertising

As states have become more involved in regulating advertising, federal enforcement, rather slight during the early Reagan years, is beginning to get tough again. During the summer of 1986, the Supreme Court ruled that states not only may restrict, in addition to untruthful advertising, even advertising for legal but socially undesirable products or activities. This ruling came primarily against the tobacco and gambling industries. What came to be known as the cigarette crisis started on January 11, 1969, when Surgeon General Luther Terry made public copies of his Advisory Committee's "Report on Smoking and Health." The report stated that among male smokers cancer of the lung was 1,000 percent higher than among nonsmokers. The report also cited chronic bronchitis and emphysema to be of far greater incidence among smokers. Additionally, the committee found that the incidence of coronary artery disease, the leading cause of death in the United States, was 70 percent higher among smokers. The bombshell cast a pall over the tobacco industry—a pall that deepened because, a quarter century later, the Surgeon General's Report of 1989 showed that half of all living Americans who had ever smoked had quit. The Marlboro Man, symbol of macho independence, became a Casper Milquetoast—or so it seemed.

In late 1986, the FTC sued the R. J. Reynolds Company over ads that maintained that the debate about smoking was only a debate over "facts" that were far from clear. The FTC alleged that, in view of the overwhelming body of scientific evidence linking smoking to cancer, the Reynolds' claim constituted deceptive advertising. The tobacco industry was undaunted. In 1990 Philip Morris launched a $30 million national campaign featuring the Bill of Rights as the stalwart bulwark of individual choice. Because the choice to smoke was being severely curtailed in many jurisdictions, the ads were interpreted as a subtle defense of smoking. One outraged commentator wrote:

*Philip Morris has been a power in the smokers' rights cause, a big loser in the 1980s. Three years ago it came up with "American Voices: Prize Winning Essays on Freedom of Speech, Censorship and Advertising Bans." The self-published, self-serving 444-page book, heavier than a carton of Marlboros and twice as fumy, was presented, according to the president of Philip Morris, as "a refutation of censorship." Proposed advertising bans against cigarettes are a threat to free speech, he believed. With tens of millions of Americans dead, dying or gasping from cigarette smoking—what C. Everett Koop called the most documented cause of disease in history—here is Philip Morris huckstering the bizarre notion that it is the victim.*[25]

In 1986, however, cigarette manufacturers, whose financial futures had been clouded by a spate of lawsuits from smokers with health problems, won a major victory. A federal court in Philadelphia ruled that the cigarette-package health warnings mandated by federal law protected tobacco companies from claims that they failed to provide adequate notice of smoking's hazards. The decision cut out much of the legal ground from nearly 100 then-pending lawsuits against the tobacco manufacturers.

Notwithstanding the decision, the tobacco industry is still not home free. George and Dania Deschamps-Braly (a husband-wife legal team from

Oklahoma) filed a $147 million suit against the United States Tobacco Company. The facts in the case were clear: A teenager named Sean Marsee (once voted the outstanding athlete on his high school's track team) died in 1983 at age 19 from mouth cancer. Marsee had begun using U. S. Tobacco's brand snuff at age 13 after he had received a free sample while attending a rodeo. The Bralys accused the company of deliberately targeting the young for its market and of concealing evidence that nitrosamine, a chemical proved to be carcinogenic to animals tested in laboratories, might be dangerous to humans. Although makers of smokeless tobacco had never indicated that anything other than taste differentiated their products, studies have found that some brands of snuff contain levels of nitrosamine as much as 40 times higher than others.

The Bralys alleged that the makers of smokeless tobacco knew from research that changes in processing could substantially reduce nitrosamine content and they chose to ignore the fact. Investigator Dietrich Hoffmann claimed that his study of smokeless tobacco showed that nitrosamine levels in snuff ranged from 5,900 parts per billion in one U.S. brand to 240,000 in a Canadian brand. Over the 12 years he had measured nitrosamine levels in smokeless tobacco, he found no significant changes among U.S. brands. Because manufacturers closely guard their processing technology, exactly why the levels vary so widely was not known. Hoffmann's published research did not name the brands tested, but in a deposition given under subpoena for the Marsee case, he said that Copenhagen, the nation's best-selling snuff, contained nitrosamine levels of 37,000 parts per billion. The government limit for the substance in beer and bacon is ten parts per billion.

## *Ethical Question*

- Do manufacturers act reprehensibly when they give customers whatever they want?

Consider also a Benson & Hedges' full-color, double-page ad in a popular women's magazine. Three attractive young people—a male sitting at one table and two women, one of whom is not smoking, seated at an adjacent table—are shown in a plush dining room. The advertisement prominently displays the surgeon-general's warning about the health hazards of smoking to pregnant women. The caption, "For people who like to smoke" is not reinforced by any sales pitch—but the Benson & Hedges label is prominently displayed. On the opposite page the two smokers are seen engaged in lively conversation while the nonsmoking woman looks on. The purpose of the advertisement is clear. The subtleties are well managed—so well, indeed, that those who prepared the ad deserve kudos for their imaginative presentation.

## Ethical Question

- Was the Benson & Hedges advertisement ethical?

A strong case can be made that it was: consumers were warned, no one was urged to smoke; the setting was decorous. But critics would contend that the purpose is obvious—and evil in light of a February 1990 government report that smoking was lethal. Yet the public, while believing that tobacco and alcohol are dangerous, did not want them prohibited. Although there is no great grassroots support for outlawing either product, more than half support a ban on advertising them. One poll showed the results in Table 9.2.

**Table 9.2 Percentages of Consumers Surveyed Who Favor or Oppose Restrictions on Marketing Tobacco and Alcoholic Beverages**

|  | Favor | Oppose | Don't Care/Don't Know |
|---|---|---|---|
| ***Alcohol*** | | | |
| Require warning labels about the dangers of alcohol | 68% | 16% | 16% |
| Require equal time for public health messages | 60 | 20 | 20 |
| Have alcoholic beverage companies contribute $1 to charity for every $10 of sales | 58 | 24 | 18 |
| Ban all ads for beer and wine from TV | 48 | 31 | 21 |
| Eliminate ads for liquor from magazines and newspapers | 42 | 34 | 24 |
| Prevent bars from selling a patron more than one drink per hour | 35 | 43 | 22 |
| Outlaw alcoholic beverages | 15 | 69 | 16 |
| ***Tobacco*** | | | |
| Have cigarette manufacturers contribute $1 per carton to charities | 59 | 24 | 17 |
| Eliminate all cigarette machines so minors can't buy them | 57 | 25 | 18 |
| Eliminate cigarette ads in magazines and newspapers | 54 | 23 | 23 |
| Ban smoking in all public places | 52 | 36 | 12 |
| Increase the tax on cigarettes to $1 per pack | 39 | 43 | 18 |
| Make tobacco products illegal | 24 | 58 | 17 |

Source: Alin M. Freedman, "More Temperance in Marketing," *The Wall Street Journal*, November 14, 1989, B1 and B6.

The issue of cigarette advertisements is as cloudy as the famous smoke-filled rooms of politicians. The American Medical Association has proposed a blanket ban on cigarette advertising and promotion, and legislation has cleared Congress to implement the proposed ban. The proposal extends the present advertising prohibition in the broadcast media to the print media and to other means of promoting tobacco products. Immediate and negative response to the proposed ban came from a broad spectrum of diverse political and economic interests. Opponents of the plan range from the Tobacco Institute to the American Civil Liberties Union.

Opposition to the ban centers on the underlying assumption made by ban proponents that the elimination of advertising will curtail cigarette consumption and thereby support the government's legitimate interest in public health. Opponents of the ban argue that advertising does not induce people to begin smoking or otherwise significantly affect industry demand, but rather serves primarily to allocate the relative market shares of competing firms within the cigarette market. Also, media and advertising interests argue that the ban is a form of censorship in violation of the First Amendment. Their free-speech argument is founded on the evolving commercial speech doctrine, a doctrine that has provided significant constitutional protection for commercial advertising.[26] On balance, constitutional lawyers have concluded that the AMA's proposal was "supported by national public policy, but not by a proper reading of the Supreme Court's free commercial speech cases."[27]

## *Ethical Question*

- Prescinding from the legal issue for the moment, which public policy do you favor on ethical grounds—prevent or permit cigarette advertising?

## *Advertising to Children*

Because advertising space on television and radio has limits, advertisers sought other methods of promotion. The two that have caused most controversy are the turning of Saturday cartoons into feature-length advertisements and the placing of products in films shown in theaters. Here the use of cleverly disguised advertisements for the toys and games in the shows takes on a new meaning because audiences are usually between 2 and 8 years of age. During the late 1970s, an FTC inquiry into the methods of advertising to children produced considerable evidence of harm, but there was little action to curb the abuses. By 1990 there were over 50 Saturday cartoon shows featuring action toys such as Rambo, G.I. Joe, and He-Man. Naturally, all of these shows feature toys that are available in the stores.[28] Although there may be no direct manipulation of truth in these children's programs, the wholesale bombardment of the young has raised problems that child psychologists say in some instances can be very harmful. The other form of subliminal advertising to children—placing products in movies—has become so lucrative that several brokerage firms have appeared whose only business is to introduce movie producers to product merchants who want to place product brands in the theater.

Parents have not escaped the advertiser's attention. To illustrate, television advertising aired during children's programming featured an expert spokesperson who stated: "I recommend new Cabbage Patch Kids Chewable Vitamins because they are naturally flavored with fruit juices and contain no table sugar, no salt, no artificial colors or flavors." The same expert was quoted in a signed statement on the package labeling: "I urge parents to provide their children with vitamins in a form as natural as possible. The advantage of Cabbage Patch Chewable Vitamins is that they are in the purest possible form and do not contain sucrose (table sugar), glucose, lactose, salt (sodium), artificial colors, artificial flavors or additives found in so many of the other children's chewable vitamin preparations. . . . They are the *only* brand of children's vitamins that contain Calcium Ascorbate, Beta Carotene, and natural-source Vitamin E."

Bewildered parents may have scratched their heads but an alert competitor questioned the accuracy of the description, stating that the placement of such advertising on children's programming contravened industry practice not to advertise drugs and nutritional supplements directly to children. The banned practice was mentioned in the Children's Advertising Guidelines, first published in 1955 by the National Advertising Division of the Better Business Bureau. Subsequently, the advertising community established the Children's Advertising Review Unit (CARU) to serve as an independent manager of the industry's self-regulatory programs. CARU revised the guidelines in 1977 and again in 1983. Five ethical principles were suggested:

1. Advertisers should always take into account the level of knowledge, sophistication, and maturity of the children.
2. Realizing that children are imaginative and that make-believe play constitutes an important part of the growing-up process, advertisers should not exploit that quality in children.
3. Recognizing that advertising may play an important part in educating children, information should be communicated in a truthful and accurate manner.
4. Advertisers should develop advertising that, wherever possible, addresses itself to social standards generally regarded as positive and beneficial—such as friendship, kindness, honesty, justice, generosity, and respect for others.
5. The prime responsibility to provide guidance for children remains on the parent.

## Institutional Controls

### Intervention

Concern for the child brought early action from the FTC. Over 20 years ago (August 24, 1971), the FTC issued a complaint against the ITT Baking Company, alleging that its Wonder Bread advertisements were false, misleading, deceptive, and unfair. ITT claimed that its bread (1) was an outstanding source of nutrients, distinct from other enriched breads, and (2) provided children aged one to 12 with all the nutrients, in recommended quantities, that are essential to healthy growth and development. A further pitch was made to parents who were told that the optimum contribution they could make during the formative years of growth was to assure that the child consumed Wonder Bread regularly.

When challenged, ITT admitted that Wonder Bread did not have the nutritional qualities claimed for it but denied that the advertisements represented that the bread did have those qualities. The case turned, therefore, on the meaning of the advertisements themselves. A psychiatrist, appearing on behalf of ITT, emphasized the importance of family and other influences on children's perception of television commercials. He testified that, while a normal young child viewing the fantasy growth sequence might "hope that maybe this would happen to him," discovering that he would not in fact grow instantaneously by eating Wonder Bread would be a normal learning experience without harmful impact.

The administrative judge, concluding that the government had failed to prove any of ITT's claims were false, misleading, and deceptive, dismissed the complaint in its entirety. However, the FTC rejected the judge's conclusion and found instead that "the challenged Wonder Bread television advertisements represented to viewers that Wonder Bread is an extraordinary food for producing dramatic growth in children." The commission relied principally on its interpretation of the advertisements themselves "when viewed in their entirety." It pointed to the verbal content of the commercials, which included numerous references to child growth and the value of Wonder Bread in aiding such growth, as well as to the visual fantasy growth sequence. The commission stated that "the inferences to be drawn from the sequence, and others, is clearly misleading, apart from whether or not most consumers would regard the literal import of the sequence with skepticism."[29]

As a result of court cases, state involvement, and tightened FTC regulations, the advertising industry has become more cautious. It is relatively easy for a competitor to halt an advertising campaign via a court injunction, and the prospect of large fines makes the risk of being caught too high for many companies.[30] The ad industry would prefer to clean its own house rather than have it cleaned by others. The industry is fearful of other developments. For example, in early 1990 the FDA warned food manufacturers that they risked regulatory intervention if they proceeded with plans to label and advertise health foods carrying the Heart Guide seal—a seal of approval developed jointly by the American Heart Association and the Food Processors. A further vulnerability is the way scientific evidence fluctuates. To illustrate, manufacturers of food products containing oat bran proclaimed its cholesterol-reducing potentialities, a claim that was challenged immediately by medical experts.[31]

Satisfactory criteria may come by answering four questions:

1. Does the ad create misleading impressions, even if the statements made are factually correct?
2. Are important facts about the product or service concealed or omitted?
3. Is consumer attention diverted from the actual terms or conditions made in the original offer?
4. Are false and/or misleading comparisons to competitors made?

After this has been done, a closer scrutiny is undertaken to determine if the ad qualifies as deceptive advertising practice according to four criteria:

1. *Bait and switch.* This technique is used to draw consumers into a store for an advertised special, but the salesman, following instructions, suggests that the consumer buy another in-store model of higher quality and price.
2. *Misquoted "sale prices."* Advertising is considered deceptive when the original price of the merchandise is overstated to give the impression of greater savings associated with the sale.
3. *Extra charges.* Ads that fail to include additional charges required for shipping, handling, installation, tax, delivery, and the like misrepresent the total cost of an item. To circumvent the law, advertisers use small print. For example, television commercials for automobiles may quote a price that does not include tax, tags, and dealer prep costs, and the omission is noted only in small print.
4. *False product comparison.* Ads are deceptive that compare products in a limited fashion rather than in the comprehensive way needed to provide an overview showing the consumer not only where the promoted product excels, but also where its shortcomings are in relation to comparable products on the market.

When evaluating advertisements, some practices are documented as clearly deceptive in terms of the criteria just given, but many are decided on a case-by-case basis, the reason being that the FTC is often obliged to examine not only a specific product but the competitive nature of a given industry.

## Self-Policing

There are two ways advertisers seek to encourage truth telling, one internal-cooperative and the other external. The internal-cooperative mechanisms work rather well; the following summarizes what generally happens in the various media:

- *Television and radio networks.* Each has a staff of people, mostly lawyers, who review and pass judgment on the accuracy, honesty, and taste of every commercial before it is shown on their network.
- *Magazines.* Each individually sets its own standards for the acceptance or rejection of specific advertising. Some publications use laboratory testing of the product to evaluate the accuracy of its advertising. Some

publications reject the advertising of entire product categories (cigarettes and hard liquor).

- *Newspapers.* Each has its own set of advertising requirements. Being a local medium, each paper can reflect the taste-standards of its own community.
- *TV and radio stations.* Like newspapers, they set standards of taste acceptable to their local communities. When they carry network commercials, they benefit from the stringent requirements imposed by network reviewers.
- *Media associations.* Associations offer standards of business conduct for the benefit of each member. These standards, if carried out, are designed to reflect favorably on the entire medium. All major media have such associations, including the outdoor-advertising and direct-mail industries.
- *Ad agencies.* Successful agencies are as careful with the products they release as are successful manufacturers. Some agencies depend on a legal staff to screen their advertising for accuracy, legality, and taste; others require that all advertising receive the approval of a central management committee. The American Association of Advertising Agencies (4A's) offers its members a comprehensive code as a guide to honesty and taste in the advertising they produce.

Major advertisers subject their advertising to extensive internal review by legal, technical/medical, and public affairs executives who carefully examine the product proposed. When things go awry they often use their own industry's oversight mechanisms because they are less expensive. In 1978, the National Advertising Review Board (NARB) appointed a consultive panel from among its members to determine how well advertising's self-regulatory process was working. In doing this, the panel was to ask two questions: (1) what should be self-regulated and what should not? and (2) why should some things be self-regulated and why should others be under government control? Because consumer complaints were one way to measure how well advertising's self-regulatory process was working, the panel commissioned the Gallup organization to make a national survey.

Half the respondents told Gallup that there had been at least one time in the past year when they had wanted to complain about an advertisement. While the major complaint was that advertising was not truthful or accurate, this complaint was expressed by only 10 percent in the national sample. Truth is the area in which the National Advertising Review Board is primarily charged to monitor. The NARB performed very well in dealing with questions of false or deceptive advertising. Many consumer complaints, however, are in the area of *taste* (the advertising of feminine hygiene products, advertising that "insults the consumer's intelligence," advertising that exploits sexuality, and advertising that is too loud, too repetitive, or quantitatively excessive). However, only 16 percent of those wanting to complain had ever expressed their discontents to anyone. Thus, the Gallup survey provided an attentive ear to complaints that might otherwise have remained unspoken.

After finishing its review, the panel told the NARB and the National Advertising Division (NAD) of the Better Business Bureau that they could reduce the level of consumer complaints by taking the following steps:

1. The NAD should institute a project to persuade major media—with the advice and assistance of their trade associations—to try to find ways to screen out any inaccurate or untruthful advertising that they now accept.
2. Industry groups should organize to identify advertising that insults the intelligence of the consumer or that offends because of sexual or other objectionable appeals. Such identification would normally be for the use of advertisers themselves.
3. Major advertising associations should organize a consumer-education program designed to reduce complaints against advertising by explaining why some advertising cannot, or should not, be changed.
4. The NARB should repeat the Gallup survey every other year and appoint a new panel to review its findings and recommend appropriate action.

The recommendations were well received.

Advertisers often bring their complaints to a nongovernmental agency for adjudication because the process before an industry-run group is less expensive and, above all, noncoercive. The policy of the NAD, judicious and flexible, is expressed in these words:

> The fact that advertising has been modified or discontinued ... is not to be taken as an admission of impropriety on any advertiser's part. In some cases, advertisers have voluntarily changed or discontinued advertising in cooperation with NAD's self-regulatory efforts. In others, advertisers have discontinued challenged advertising for their own reasons but have agreed not to run it again without consulting NAD or furnishing appropriate substantiation, if not previously supplied. NAD works with the National Advertising Review Board (NARB) to insure truth and accuracy in national advertising.[32]

*The NAD is first to review such cases; if, after its examination, NAD and the advertiser fail to agree, the former takes two steps: (1) it publishes a summary of the case that has the effect of putting everyone on alert and (2) it forwards the case to the NARB for a final determination. While the NARB decision is not binding, rarely will ad agencies continue the ads if the NARB voices a criticism. Typical of NAD practice and advertisers' responses are the following two cases.*

## Two NAD Investigations

AMF Incorporated, manufacturer of the Head Director Tennis Racquet, used a television commercial showing two experienced players in a singles match and claimed: "To serious players it was no contest. In independent play tests Head's new over-sized Director racquets were overwhelmingly preferred over Prince." An accompanying chart showed the Head preferred in 15 out of 16 categories. A second magazine advertisement made similar claims for the aluminum racquet under the headings, "With test results like these their [Prince's] racquet should have stayed in the locker room. Head's new Tournament Director overwhelmingly preferred over Prince Pro 110." Both print advertisements offered complete test results to respondents. Chesebrough-Pond's, manufacturer of the Prince Graphite and Pro 110 racquets, challenged the claims, saying the tests were flawed.[33]

The NAD reviewed the challenge. Complete records of the tests in question were supplied, supplemented by a later study employing players over age 40 using graphite racquets. After review and discussions with the advertiser, NAD defined a number of concerns in relation to the experimental design. These included: the test-selection process tended to exclude or reduce the participation of important classes of players, including experts, over 35-year-olds, and previous purchasers of the two major brands; follow-up efforts to expand the surveys were not totally successful; the questionnaire could encourage repetitious responses; the racquets were not strung in strict accord with manufacturers' instructions with the result the Prince Graphite racquets were strung at lower than the recommended tension for advanced players.

After attempts to resolve these concerns failed, and following established rules of procedures, the advertiser joined with NAD in requesting review by the National Advertising Review Board. In its statement, AMF Head disagreed with the implications of each concern raised by NAD in this matter and said it was the firm's view that the independent market research study was appropriately designed, validly executed in all respects (including stringing all racquets in accordance with manufacturers' instructions), and that the advertising accurately reflected and was fully substantiated by the research. "AMF Head therefore welcomes the opportunity for review of the matter by NARB."[34] A compromise was reached when AMF modified its advertisements, though not admitting to any form of deception.

A second case that shows the extent of a NAD investigation involved the Bristol-Myers Company. The inquiry involved Bufferin magazine advertising addressed to arthritics that was headlined: "Arthritics: If you use Tylenol you may be hurting more than you have to. Use Bufferin instead. Bufferin can reduce painful swelling and inflammation. Tylenol cannot. And with Bufferin, like Tylenol, there's far less chance of stomach upset than with Bayer or Anacin." The primary question for NAD was whether aspirin (Bufferin's analgesic ingredient) at over-the-counter dosage levels could reduce inflammation associated with rheumatoid arthritis. While aspirin is the drug most often prescribed by physicians for relief of this painful affliction, the dosage level prescribed is often higher than that recommended for over-the-counter aspirins. NAD considered numerous studies from the medical literature on aspirin therapy in rheumatoid arthritis, several of which supported the Bufferin claim. Therefore, NAD felt that Bufferin's claimed advantage over Tylenol in relieving inflammation associated with rheumatoid arthritis at over-the-counter dosages had been adequately documented.

During its review, NAD recognized that the term arthritis represented numerous disease states and programs of treatment. Even aspirin therapy prescribed by a physician can differ significantly from one patient to the next. NAD had also recognized that many medical experts, including the Arthritis Foundation, opposed any consumer analgesic advertising that encouraged self-medication. The Bufferin advertising addressed to arthritics attempts to respond to the arthritic's need for appropriate medical attention by voluntarily including the warning: "Because arthritis can be serious, if pain persists more than ten days or redness is present, consult your doctor immediately. If under medical care, do not take without consulting a physician." However, because there is such a great propensity for arthritics to self-medicate, NAD felt that this warning might better serve the public interest if featured more prominently in the advertising. In a spirit of cooperation, the advertiser significantly enlarged the type size used for the warning statement.

## Ethical Appraisals

The much maligned advertising business is impressive in its willingness to air dirty linen in public—something that professions like medicine, accounting, and law find distasteful because individual reputations are at stake.[35] Nevertheless, if its procedures are admirable, are advertising practices and products equally honorable? At this point ethical judgments come into play.

Of all industries, television advertising has seen some of the largest and most rapid changes during its brief history. As a result, the networks are challenged constantly to relax the standards of what can and cannot be said or shown on television. Advertisers maintain that their controversial ads only reflect society's evolving standards of acceptability; the network censors, on the other hand, feel that because their medium is national they should not use the lowest common denominator in determining the acceptability of a particular theme. Nevertheless, a Gresham's Law of Ethics seems to be at work. Thirty years ago commercials showing double beds and bathrooms were taboo; 20 years ago, the showing of women's undergarments and deodorant soaps began; 10 years ago advertising "personal care" products was still banned. Today all such products are allowed under the evolving guidelines of the network censors.[36]

### Scrutiny of the Industry

Competitive advertising, puffery, the nature of the audience, the quality and safety of the product, the product's potential for causing problems to a segment of an audience the vast majority of whom want and need the product, the uneven record of FTC enforcement against deceptive advertising—all are factors that, when aggregated, confuse the heads of regulators and regulated. Nevertheless, continued efforts are made to answer constantly arising problems. Because of its power, the industry invites special scrutiny. And the scrutinizing takes the form of five questions.

1. *Does advertising make goods cheaper or more expensive? Or neither?* The first positive answers are that it (1) decreases prices because it significantly increases demand, which, in turn, provides economies of scale that reduce unit costs; (2) spurs competition; (3) gives information to customers about the availability of products; and (4) alerts manufacturers to changing consumer tastes. Given such conditions, the market guides profit-seeking producers to allocate economic resources in ways that optimize the aggregate satisfaction of demand. The process is dynamic and progressive. On the other hand, some economists have argued that (1) advertising's creation of consumer loyalty makes it more difficult for new competitors to enter the market and (2) advertising is expensive and the added costs adversely affect the buyer's pocketbook.[37]

2. *Does advertising add value to goods and services?* In certain cases it does.[38] Placebos take away pain without the dangers of medication; brand name cosmetics make a person feel special; signature jeans may make an otherwise underdressed person feel well dressed. These are all definite positives. But the consumer again pays a price. The perfume Obsession costs a few dollars per ounce to make—much the same cost as for any other perfume—but retails in exclusively contracted outlets for 50 times its actual costs. Heublein produces three brands of vodka that are virtually the same in composition, taste, and production costs. The high-end product, however, sells for nearly three times the price of its low-end cousin. Clearly advertising adds a perceived value to goods. In the competitive world, where should the line be drawn between real and unreal differences?

3. *Does advertising cause people to buy unneeded things?* Of course it does. Vance Packard once argued that if businesses catered only to people's needs, they would be selling tents instead of ranch houses, horses instead of automobiles, and animal skins instead of high fashions. It is the wants and desires people have—not their needs—that allow both advertising and business to prosper.[39]

4. *Does advertising tell the truth? If not, are there enough monitoring agencies able to prevent major errors?*

The last two questions have been of greatest interest to lawyers and to moralists. On the positive side is the fact that the advertising community is held accountable to a variety of organizations—federal and state agencies, industry-established policing institutions, and, not unimportant, organized consumer groups. Ralph Nader's name has special appeal. Honor graduate from Princeton and product of the Harvard Law School, Nader passed up a profitable career in corporate law to become the voice of consumer conscience.[40]

## *Advertisers' Accountability*

Probably the greatest disciplinarian of deceptive advertising is the growing tendency of companies to challenge their competitors in court. In the spring of 1990 a case occurred that might reveal a significant new trend. Princeton Graphics (a unit of a holding company named Intelligent Systems) sought $25 million from a Japanese electronics giant, the NEC Corporation, after a court ruled that NEC ran false ads about its personal-computer monitors. Princeton contended that NEC's false advertising cost it not only sales, but hurt its potential acquisition price. The reason for the latest trend is found in a November 1989 congressional amendment to the Lanham Act regulating advertising. The amendment clarified the right to sue over false claims and also provided for treble damages in some cases. In past cases, the plaintiffs were to some degree satisfied simply to get an injunction. But with the law strengthened, more claims for cash will be undertaken.

Reliance on the law is not enough, and the alert reader will note that advertising itself has not been found morally suspect. But there are business ethicists who condemn the whole enterprise on a variety of ethical criteria. Among the charges leveled against the industry are the following:

1. Individuals are inundated with ads no matter where they go or what they do. The net effect is brainwashing.[41]
2. Advertising represents attempts to diminish the individual's autonomy.[42] The logic for the indictment runs along the following lines:

   *It is immoral to invite another to act irrationally (in his interactions with you) at the same time you are acting rationally, even calculatingly, and when part of your reason for asking the other to behave irrationally is that such behavior will more efficiently promote your ends than would dealing with a rational, aware individual. This violates the assumption of the market as a place where buyer and seller meet freely in an attempt to pursue their own ideas of personal profit. It is also immoral because it asks the other party to assume a burden he/she could avoid when there is no good moral reason for him or her to compete on less than equal terms. In effect, you are asking that person to set limits on pursuit of goals and so end up with less than might otherwise have been in order that part of the loss can become your gain. And you won't even ask this as a favor; rather, you are in effect trying to distract the other person while you sneak one over on him/her, hardly a morally savory position.[43]*

3. Advertising is not only manipulative, it contributes to a sneer-and-sneak conduct.
4. Advertising induces forms of unacceptable hedonistic behavior: the eat-drink-and-be-merry philosophy that precedes society's fall.

Softening the rigors of a harsh buyer-beware maxim represents a moral good because advertisers know more about their product's quality than do buyers—and may even know more about the buyer's psychology than buyers know about themselves.[44] Nevertheless, as there are moral defects in an exaggerated form of caveat emptor, so, too, are there defects in the exaggerated form of caveat vendor. If advertisers are asked to refrain from doing anything that leads a buyer to behave irrationally, in itself a laudable ideal, it means that advertisers decide *a priori* what is rational for each potential buyer—an order of such magnitude that, carried to its conclusion, invades the very individual autonomy that philosophers and economists praise. A subtle but pronounced form of paternalism results when Big Brother (government or nongovernment) tells buyers that they are rational only on terms decided by others. More modest but more meaningful maxims could be stated in negative terms: (1) avoid deception, direct or indirect, in promoting products that are safe to use; (2) avoid tasteless and vulgar advertising; and (3) avoid advertising to other societies goods that have been found harmful in our own.

## *Specific Issues*

The problems are far from being resolved, as the following three issues illustrate.

**General Foods.** Former president of General Foods, C. W. Cook, said:

> *There is currently much debate about what precisely is a consumer need, and how far society should go in satisfying a desire, be it for a pornographic peep show, or a $75,000 Rolls Royce. But this is really a matter more of social philosophy than of commercial practice or economic theory. Business has traditionally operated on the basis that if there is a commercial demand for a product or service that is not illegal or socially destructive, the businessman is entitled to meet that demand at a profit.*
>
> *Another problem that concerns advertisers is the effort to use advertising for purposes other than selling merchandise, and to compel this through the regulatory process. For example, there have been proposals that all advertising of food—including even a 30-second commercial—be required to include helpful information on good nutrition, in addition to the commercial message. There are two problems here. First, there is barely enough time in a 30-second commercial to deliver an effective commercial message, and even in a one-minute commercial, there is not a whole lot of elbow room. If the advertiser were forced to "piggy-back" material on nutrition also, it might well kill the commercial and he would not run it. So the educational message would not get on the air in any case.*
>
> *But there is a deeper problem. For more than a half century the major food companies have made serious and persistent efforts to educate consumers about nutrition. The success rate has been conspicuously low. They have found it terribly difficult to interest a mass audience in theory and practice in this field. The most*

*promising challenge so far has been to work through home economics teachers in the schools.*[45]

## Ethical Question

- Do you agree with Cook?

**Surgeon General's Report.** Shortly after he left office in 1989 as Surgeon General, Everett Koop told a distinguished audience in Washington:

> *In one of the most disgraceful examples of private enterprise gone amok, the cigarette industry is focusing its high-powered marketing attention on the unprotected citizens of third-world nations in Asia, Africa, and South America. As a result, those nations are now beginning to experience the same rise in smoking-related diseases that we experienced a generation ago—heart disease, stroke, and cancer of the lung, mouth, esophagus, and stomach. As Surgeon General I was—and as a private citizen, I am—appalled by this behavior of American companies and, further, I am shocked by our own government's support of such behavior. We will justly earn the title of "The Ugly American" as we continue to export disease, disability, and death to the third world which will never be able to pay the health bill down the road.*[46]

## Ethical Question

- Do you agree with Dr. Koop? If you do, what would you do about it?

**Nestlé.** In 1981, when the Nestlé infant formula was being hotly debated, 118 nations of the World Health Organization voted to ban advertising of infant-formula foods. Only the United States dissented, saying that commercial free speech was being threatened.[47]

## Ethical Question

- Do you agree with your country's position?

## Summary

A decade ago Harvard professor Theodore Levitt wrote a delightful article on the questionable morality of advertising.[48] His major point was that distinctions between embellishment and mendacity were hard to make. Many years have elapsed since the Levitt article appeared. Despite heroic efforts by the FTC and the NAD, the distinctions still remain elusive. As Charles Revson of Revlon observed, "In the factory we make cosmetics; in the store we sell hope." Advertisers are great at selling hope.

Revson's comment, however, points up significant differences in the products sold. A woman may be disappointed with her perfume or her diamond. A driver will be devastated by an automobile that is a lemon. And the observation of Revson omits the different capabilities of purchasers: the very old and the very young are audiences especially vulnerable to manipulative advertising. As already detailed, new evidence suggests that even others are easily deceived.

Yet substantial progress has been made since Levitt chastised advertisers for their shameful failure to mount vigorous programs to protect and inform consumers. Truth-in-advertising efforts have improved labels and packages; the drive for factual accuracy continues to progress. What has not meaningfully diminished is the oppressive vulgarity of so much of contemporary advertising. Those who see advertising as intrinsically evil are relatively few; those who see the industry as essentially manipulative are many.

But, as Levitt noted, consumers suffer from an old dilemma: they want truth and they want fantasy. The result? Levitt answered: "Business is caught in the middle. There is hardly a company that would not go down in ruin if it refused to provide fluff, because nobody will buy pure functionality. Yet, if it uses too much fluff and little else, business invites possibly ruinous legislation. The problem therefore is to find a middle way."[49]

## Questions for Discussion

1. Are advertisers unethical when they emphasize persuasion to the neglect of consumer education?
2. If you rejected the FTC's least reasonable man theory, could you develop a substitute theory to guide advertisers?
3. Should cigarette ads have been banned totally on television?
4. Should children's ads be first approved by a panel of randomly selected parents before being aired on television?
5. Should differences between the FTC and the industry over definitions of deception be resolved by professional arbitrators?

## Ethical Quandary

### The Client's Confidence

As head of a large and successful advertising agency you have learned over the years how to deal with various kinds of clients—from the shady to the saintly. In the latter category is Bill Sharp, CEO of a modest-sized drug manufacturing company, who has been a client for nearly 20 years. In your view Sharp's word is as good as gold.

One afternoon Sharp paid a surprise visit. He had just returned from one of many trips to Washington, where he had tried, unsuccessfully, to have the FDA speed its process for approving a drug that he is convinced will alleviate the sufferings of terminally ill cancer patients. He wanted you to develop advertisements that say:

> *Drug X relieves suffering of cancer patients. The FDA has not yet approved the drug but we have total confidence in its efficacy. So should you.*

You refused, pointing out that selling a nonapproved drug violates the law and that a warning is not sufficient to protect patients who, in their pain, might be prepared to buy anything. Sharp countered that cigarettes can cause cancer, yet the FDA permits the tobacco industry to advertise so long as its ads carry the appropriate warning. When you insisted that his argument was based on a non sequitur, Sharp left in a huff, saying that he might "look around for a more creative ad agency." You cringed, but held your ground.

Two weeks later Sharp returned with a new proposal. Why not advertise the drug in Latin American countries where government regulations over new drugs are lax? When you asked what would happen if the drug's unforeseen consequence was to accelerate the coming of death for users, Sharp replied: "If local doctors assert that there is a causal relationship between the drug and early death, I will use company profits to compensate the victims' families." But he hastened to say: "I expect no such payouts. The drug relieves pain. The patient will not die in agony. Finally, the users are doomed to die anyway. Meanwhile I help millions abroad and hasten the day when I can help millions at home."

## Question

- Would you accept Sharp's advertising business?

## Notes

1. Daniel Pope, *The Making of Modern Advertising* (New York: Basic Books, 1983). See also the helpful book by Michael Schudson, *Advertising* (New York: Basic Books, 1984).
2. Barbara B. Stern, "Medieval Allegory: Roots of Advertising Strategy for the Mass Market," *Journal of Marketing* 52 (July 1988): 84.
3. Lawrence P. Feldman, *Consumer Protection: Problems and Prospects* (St. Paul, Minn.: West, 1980), 115.
4. Ibid., ch. 6.
5. John Hersey, "The Legend on the License," *The Yale Review*, Autumn 1980, 1–25.
6. Clare Ansberry, "Alterations of Photos Raise Host of Legal, Ethical Issues," *The Wall Street Journal*, January 26, 1989, B1.
7. Bill Gordon, "Letters to the Editor," *The Wall Street Journal*, February 21, 1990, A14.
8. Quoted in Joseph Seldin, *The Golden Fleece* (New York: Macmillan, 1980), 197.
9. The quotation was used by Walter Kauffman in his introduction to Martin Buber's *I and Thou* (New York: Charles Scribners, 1970).
10. Hugh W. Sargent, ed., "Extracts from the Advertiser's Copy Code," *Frontiers of Advertising Theory* (Palo Alto, Calif.: Pacific Books, 1972).

11. David M. Gardner, "Deception in Advertising: A Conceptual Approach," *Journal of Marketing* 39 (January 1978): 40–46.
12. "Internal Surveys Not OK for Ad: The Litton Order," *Advertising Age*, January 19, 1981, 20.
13. Gardner, "Deception in Advertising," 41.
14. Herbert J. Rotfeld and Ivan L. Preston, "The Potential Impact of Research on Advertising Law," *Journal of Advertising Research* 21 (April 1981): 9.
15. Isabella C. Cunningham and William Cunningham, "Standards for Advertising Regulation," *Journal of Marketing* 41 (October 1977): 92.
16. Feldman, *Consumer Protection*, 128–129.
17. Franklin Carlile and Howard Leonard, "Caveat Venditor! The Skepticism of the Rational Majority," *Journal of Advertising Research* 22 (August–September 1982): 17–19.
18. Quoted by Stanley E. Cohen, "A New Law Legalizing Some Deception?" *Advertising Age*, April 19, 1982, 50. For moral perspectives on the issue, see Alan Donagan, *The Theory of Morality* (Chicago: University of Chicago Press, 1977), ch. 3; and the detailed analysis by Sisella Bok, *Lying: Moral Choice in Public and Private Life* (New York: Pantheon Books, 1978).
19. Richard L. Gordon, "FTC and Regulation Hearings Bog Down," *Advertising Age*, July 26, 1982, 58.
20. Terence A. Shimp and Ivan L. Preston, "Deceptive and Nondeceptive Consequences of Comparative Advertising," *Journal of Marketing* 45 (Winter 1981): 24. See also *Advertising Age*, February 4, 1980, 6.
21. Gardner, "Deception in Advertising," 42.
22. Jacqueline Mitchell, "More Car Ads Challenge Rivals Head-on," *The Wall Street Journal*, June 25 and October 23, 1990, B1.
23. Nancy Giges, "Comparative Ads: Battles That Wrote Dos and Don'ts," *Advertising Age*, September 29, 1980, 59–64. For excellent background on comparative advertising see two other articles by the same author, "Comparative Ads: Better Than . . .?" *Advertising Age*, September 22, 1990, 59–62, and "Comparative Ads: The Headache of Analgesics," *Advertising Age*, October 6, 1990, 63–66.
24. Round Table Discussion: "Products Battles Lead to Negative Ads," *Advertising Age*, September 24, 1987, 76.
25. Colman McCarthy, "Theodore Hesburgh: Marlboro Man," *Washington Post*, May 19, 1990, A25.
26. The constitutional validity of a total ban on cigarette advertising was clearly questionable under the standard of protection accorded commercial speech in the landmark case of *Central Hudson Gas & Electric Corp. v. Public Service Commission*. However, the Court's recent decision in *Posadas de Puerto Rico Associates v. Tourism Co. of Puerto Rico* casts serious doubt on a First Amendment impediment to the proposed ban.
27. Michael J. Garrison, "Should all Cigarette Advertisements Be Banned? A First Amendment and Public Policy Issue," *The American Business Law Journal* 25 (Summer 1987): 169–205. See also, the editorial commentary in *Barron's*, March 2, 1987, 11; the article by Gordon L. Dillon, "The Hundred Year War Against the Cigarette," *American Heritage*, February–March 1981, 44–107; and the article by Allan M. Brandt, "The Cigarette, Risk and American Culture," *Daedalus* 119 (Fall 1990): 155–176.
28. Jonathan Rowe, "Babes in Toyland," *The Christian Science Monitor*, January 29, 1897, 16.
29. FTC v. ITT, 539 F.R. 2d, 1976.
30. David Scott Clark, "Advertising Standards Get Tighter Rein," *Christian Science Monitor*, November 10, 1986, 23.
31. *The New England Journal of Medicine* (January 15, 1990).
32. *Report of the Conference on Self-Regulation* (Washington, D.C.: Ethics Resource Center, 1982).
33. *NAD Case Report*, vol. 13 (New York: Better Business Bureau, September 15, 1983), 28–30.

34. Ibid., 25.
35. Priscilla A. La Barbera, "Advertising Self-Regulation: An Appraisal," *MSU Topics*, (Summer 1980), 55–63. After noting the strengths of NAD/NARB, La Barbera suggests the addition of more "public membership" on the review panels (p. 61).
36. The trend toward relaxed standards in clothing has reached areas traditionally thought off limits, namely the use of sexually suggestive ads. See the editorial, "Sex Oriented TV Shows and Ads," *Advertising Age*, January 19, 1987, 16.
37. John Kenneth Galbraith, *The Affluent Society* (New York: Mentor Books, 1951), 127 ff.
38. Alan Goldman, "Ethical Issues in Advertising," in *Original Essays in Business Ethics*, ed. Tom Regan (Philadelphia: Temple University Press, 1987), 235–240.
39. Vance Packard, *The Hidden Persuaders* (New York: David McKay Co., 1957).
40. Alan LeMond, *Ralph Nader: A Man and a Movement* (New York: Warner, 1972), 18.
41. David Braybrooke, *Ethics and the World of Business* (Totowa, N.J.: Rowman and Allenheld, 1983), 327–328.
42. Robert L. Lippke, "Advertising and the Social Conditions of Autonomy," *Business and Professional Ethics Journal* 8 (Winter 1989): 35–58.
43. Kendral D'Andrade, *An Advertising Ethic* (Newark, Del.: University of Delaware Center for the Study of Values, 1987). Andrade added: "A good ad provides good reasons for buying the advertised product or service. That comes not only from my standard but from the traditional justification for advertising. One of the best ways to make an informed decision is by first sampling all the likely alternatives. In that spirit I offer the following modest proposal: let each advertiser devote 10 percent of his advertising budget to some form of free samples of his product or service. I suspect that few advertisers would favor such a proposal; what reasons could they give? In effect this proposal challenges the advertiser to promote consumer-oriented choosing, which he does by producing ads which are maximally helpful to the individual consumer in aiding him to make rational choices. I wonder how many view that as the major goal of their advertising, and how many worry that better-informed buyers would mean fewer sales. Obviously businessmen in the second group are acting improperly when they invite consumers to make choices against their own interests." (p. 15)
44. John Waide, "The Making of Self and World in Advertising," *Journal of Business Ethics* 6 (1987): 73–79.
45. "Responsibilities of Advertisers to Society," *Proceedings of the First Panel Discussion of the Councils of Better Business Bureau* (New York: Better Business Bureau, 1979, Mimeographed report).
46. C. Everett Koop, "Address to the Cosmos Club" (Washington, D.C., October 19, 1989), 20–21.
47. Stanley Cohen, "WHO Vote Is a Disaster for Advertising," *Advertising Age*, June 8, 1981, 24. Cohen's condemnation of WHO elicited a storm of protest.
48. Theodore Levitt, "The Morality (?) of Advertising," *Harvard Business Review Ethics for Executives* (1979), 97–106.
49. Ibid., 106.

CHAPTER 10

# Tort Law

## Evolution of the Law
Early Views
Critical Dates
The Current Scene

## Consumer Opposition to Protective Legislation: Three Examples
Motorcyclists
Saccharinites
AIDS Victims

## Judicial Trends and Ethics
Fault and Strict Liability
Admissible Evidence
The Law's Reach
Deep Pockets
Single and Collective Liability
*Single-Party Responsibility*
*Plural Responsibility*

## Guidelines
Fuller's Counsel
FDA Guidelines

## Summary
Questions for Discussion
Ethical Quandaries

*C*ustomers who have exercised personal due diligence and yet are harmed by sellers merit compensation for the injuries, even when no contract exists between the two. Tort law seeks to provide just compensation to the injured in such instances. A classic case that law students are frequently asked to analyze occurred in 1928. Helen Palsgroff, enroute to Rockaway Beach, was standing on the station platform of the Long Island Railroad when a train, bound for another station, stopped. Two men ran forward to board it. One of the men reached the platform of the car without mishap, though the train was already moving. The other man, carrying a package, jumped aboard the car, but when he seemed about to fall, the conductor reached forward to help the unsteady individual into the car while another guard on the platform pushed him from behind. During the pulling and the shoving, the small package, covered by a newspaper, fell onto the rails. The packet contained fireworks, but there was nothing in its appearance to give notice of its contents. The fireworks exploded when the package fell and toppled some scales at the other end of the platform. The scales struck Palsgroff, causing injuries for which she sued. Judge Caradozo ruled against her. This old ruling would possibly be in jeopardy today.

Because facts in tort cases are often hard to uncover and responsibility is therefore difficult to ascertain, tort law has generated wide confusion over whether its purposes (provide compensation to injured individuals and deter carelessness in others) are being adequately achieved. It is possibly more than mere coincidence that the Latin word **tortus**—from which the English noun is derived—means twisted. In its development tort law has been indeed twisted by the growing body of product liability law to the extent that the legal system seems more gladiatorial than judicial. Ethical analysis would join legal analysis in holding that reasonable liability for the harmful consequences of a product is sensible. More and more, however, this principle is being translated into an assumption that every product must always be safe no matter how used and no matter how infrequently the unanticipated harms occur—an assumption that almost certainly violates the way the universe is constructed. The relatively little interest in this reality prompted one analyst, Robert Frosch, to say:

> The basic facts about probability and the manner by which things are really designed and manufactured are quite unknown to those who have not been educated in any way in engineering and science. The legal profession, regulatory and judicial, appears not

only to be proceeding in considerable ignorance of science, but is, in fact, developing a set of rules of evidence that is quite independent of, and in contradiction to, what is known about natural events. Legislation is frequently even further removed from any scientific relevance. Unfortunately, the counterbattle of industry against this difficulty, as well as some of the problems of regulation, has not always been rational or entirely honest throughout. The legal defenses of corporations have frequently been based on countering irrationality with irrationality; the whole process becomes a jousting contest rather than a procedure seeking justice. A battle of foolishness has ensued.[1]

*What is foolish to some is wisdom to others. Distinguishing between the two through consideration of actual cases is an efficient way to introduce the problem:*

- *Everyone knows the hazards of flying in outer space and no one is forced to do so. The family of Michael J. Smith, the Navy commander who piloted the ill-fated Challenger, filed a claim in 1986 for $15 million on the grounds that NASA officials had been negligent. Should NASA pay?*
- *In August 1985 a jury awarded $180,000 to Karen Friedman, who had been hit by a foul ball during a baseball game at the Houston Astrodome. Should she be compensated? If so, by whom?*
- *The parents of a young man sued the boy's high school for failure to teach their son how to read, write, and reckon. He had received a high-school diploma but, when he was found not to have the basic skills to hold a job, his parents took the school district to court. Is the school morally negligent?*
- *University of Michigan student Bob Higgins asked $550,000 for the mental anguish he suffered because he received a B instead of an A grade. Would university counsel be unethical to insist that Bob see a university psychiatrist?*
- *A mechanical engineer named Stanley, who at the time of this incident worked for the ABC Corporation, had earlier been president of Sapphire Manufacturing, a press builder. In 1966 Sapphire went out of business. In 1977 Stanley was sued because of an accident at a punch press built by Sapphire. Sapphire had been out of business for 11 years; the possibility that the press was more than 40 years old was irrelevant because there is no statute of limitations on this sort of thing; the summons and complaint offered no clue on what happened; the cause of the accident may have rested with the tooling and/or its setup; it may have been with a careless or incompetent operator; or it may have been with the press, which nevertheless managed to function for at least 11 years without causing an accident. Nothing is known about the full facts except that somehow, in some way, the press builder and Stanley were held legally culpable. ABC (Stanley's present employer) was also named as a defendant. On the basis of the foregoing facts, do you think Stanley is legally culpable? Morally culpable?*

- *Two men who stuffed a hot-air balloon into a commercial laundry dryer, which then exploded, received awards from the manufacturer of the machine on the grounds that no warnings about drying balloons had been placed on the machine. Do you agree that the injured men were entitled to awards?*
- *The policy of McDonald's fast food chain restaurants is to encourage employees to do after-hours cleanup work at one of the company's playgrounds. No salary is paid but employees know that participating in such work can help their careers. Evans, a McDonald's worker, spent part of an evening with some coworkers performing such chores. Afterward the workers went to the home of another McDonald's employee, where they socialized until early morning. Driving home, Evans collided with a motorcycle driven by Martin O'Connor. O'Connor lost his leg. He sued Evans and McDonald's. The Court of Appeals overruled the town court, which had distinguished between Evans' work and Evans' fun. Which decision do you support?*

These are a very small sampling of the kinds of problems that regularly confront society, companies, and individuals. ■

### The purposes of this chapter are:

1. To trace the evolution of tort law.
2. To explore current approaches for determining liability.
3. To look at the use of evidence by the courts.
4. To give a sense of the law's reach.
5. To consider the implications of deep pockets.
6. To note recent decisions in tort law.
7. To examine the concepts of single and collective guilt.

## Evolution of the Law

Given the tumult that marks litigation over torts, it is somewhat surprising that a distinguished teacher of tort law and dean of the Yale Law School, Guido Calabresi, has written that the doctrine of torts could be taught in two days.[2] The good professor devotes a full semester course to tort law, which suggests that his statement must be viewed with care. But Calabresi was seeking to emphasize that many things besides law enter into decisions regarding wrongs done, albeit unintended, to others: the claims of victims and victims' families, the rights of the "victimizer," and the interests of society. Because these are matters of special interest to moralists, it is highly worthwhile to consider how one distinguished law professor reasons on such issues.

Calabresi employs a puzzle-swapping technique; that is, he looks at how old legal quandaries were resolved by the courts and adds to such quandaries a new puzzle. Instead of concentrating on statutory law or on court decisions, the way to begin is the way managers and ordinary people begin: use common sense. And that means asking new questions. As an example, if the first question deals with how accident victims receive compensation for their losses when manufacturers are negligent, Calabresi goes on to ask: Should behavior based on the victim's belief systems have any role in awarding compensations? An actual case involved a Jewish woman who jumped from a ski lift, which had stalled because of negligently made equipment, in order to avoid having to sleep with her rather aggressive male companion. She acted because of her religious conviction that simple acquiescence in sexual activity violated God's law. Had she not jumped, however, she would not have injured herself. Should the woman recover? The courts said yes. But, to add a new puzzle, suppose that in her jump the woman fell on a bystander and seriously injured her. Should the court accept the jumper's defense? Not likely. Nevertheless, in tort cases religious convictions have been generally more widely accepted than other beliefs.

The overall result is that tort law impels judges and jurors, plaintiffs and defendants to take value questions seriously into account. Therefore the court's role is not simply to *decide* among disputants but to *instruct* both sides so that each protagonist emerges from the proceedings with a clearer understanding of the values that are involved and how such values might be used to construct a more just and humane society. Calabresi is, in short, a ethician in much the same way that managers are moral philosophers when confronted by hard choices. Seeing how tort law has evolved is part of the learning process.

## Early Views

That the law of torts did not loom large in the common law before the 19th century is clear from the fact that not a single treatise on the subject was published in English before that time.[3] Before 1800 negligence was not a separate tort. In England's common law, liability was attached indiscriminately to acts causing injury, regardless of the actor's degree of culpability. In the famous 1466 *Case of Thorns,* Judge Bryan stated the view generally held when he wrote: "When any man does a thing, he is bound to do it in such a way that his act shall cause no hurt or harm to others. Thus if, when I am building a house and the timbers are being reared, a piece of timber falls on the house of my neighbor and breaks into it, he will have a good action against me; and yet the building of my house was lawful, and the timber fell against my will."

In the mid-19th century, however, this hallowed legal doctrine was rejected in the *Winterbottom* case when an English court denied a passenger (riding in a mailcoach that collapsed and injured him) the right to collect from the one who had contracted to maintain the coach in good condition. The court reasoned that, if recovery were allowed, merchants would be forced out of business under the pressure of litigation. This was a harsh ethics—made even harsher during the century's abominable working conditions, low wages, and massive poverty. The Winterbottom doctrine of negligence surfaced in the United States in 1850 when Chief Justice Lemuel Shaw of Massachusetts declared in *Brown v. Kendall* that plaintiffs must come prepared with evidence to show either that the intention was to harm or that inexcusable carelessness was present.

What breathed new life into the body of torts was the industrial revolution. Before that time, bodily injury from accidents was not much of a social problem. People were often hurt—and for efficiency in mangling people there was nothing like the modern machine. Ancient doctrine provided that one could sue for damages if another inflicted an injury without justification, but only in the late 19th century, when industrialism was at full flower, did tort law develop its intricate network of rules to protect the manufacturer. There is dispute on how this body of law was built: the rules and concepts that came first; how and why they changed; the precise relationship of tort law to the felt needs of the times, and so on.

## Critical Dates

In the history of American tort law 1873 is a critical date, for it was then that Justice Holmes spoke in uncharacteristically Kantian terms of a duty of all to all. The idea enabled Holmes and his successors to apply a limited-liability principle to help victims of accidents by holding accountable, on grounds of negligence, those who were at fault. This negligence principle, difficult to apply during the industrial revolution, became even more difficult to apply during the recent technological revolution, when, for example, more than 41,000 medical devices were introduced in the health market, ranging from bedpans and brainscans to new wonder drugs and electronic scanners at supermarkets. In the aftermath of this technological revolution, liability was extended into hitherto unheard-of areas: parent-child relations, psychic and emotional trauma, liability of municipalities and other local governments, liability of professionals—in short, liability of almost anyone for almost everything.[4] The principle enunciated in the old *Case of Thorns* was becoming the modern view: consumers did not have to prove negligence; sellers had to prove innocence. Shifting the burden of proof from the consumer's shoulders to the manufacturer's shoulders was a momentous development in tort law.

A critical step in the change process had been taken by New York's highest court in 1916 when it determined (*MacPherson v. Buick Motor Company*) that a person who bought an automobile from a dealer could, despite the absence of contract, recover from the manufacturer who failed to inspect the car or when the dealer failed to discover the defect. In a strong dissent, the chief judge recalled *Winterbottom* and the numerous decisions that had relied on it; but the majority pointed out that an automobile was intended to operate at high speeds so that a defective wheel was more than likely to cause serious injury.

The decision changed the whole meaning of liability, the importance of which can be appreciated by viewing the courts' definition of warranty. A warranty action for product liability could always be brought under contract so long as a direct relationship existed between manufacturer or seller and the ultimate consumer of the product. In fact, this condition was a prerequisite for all product liability suits until *MacPherson*. Over 40 years later the New Jersey Supreme Court, as was noted previously, ruled that under modern marketing conditions, when a manufacturer introduced a new product into the stream of trade and promoted its sale, an implied warranty that it was reasonably suitable for use accompanied the product into the hands of the ultimate purchaser.[5] The absence of agency between the manufacturer and the dealer who made the ultimate sale was immaterial.

## *The Current Scene*

The number of tort cases has been on the rise for a long time, but the pattern of growth is uneven. According to a 1987 RAND study of caseload trends, the rate of tort case filings grew overall about 3 percent per year during the early 1980s, with the growth being slightly faster in the federal courts than in state courts. Again, the picture is clouded. Although the routine tort categories (mainly automobile accidents) changed little, high-stake cases such as medical malpractice and product liability rose sharply. A 1986 study by the Department of Justice's Tort Policy Working Group showed very high growth rates in federal courts between 1974 and 1986—75 percent in product liability cases. This is possibly an exaggerated figure because asbestos-related cases between 1974 and 1986 accounted for roughly 50 percent of the increase, with Dalkon Shield and Benedictin representing an added 4 percent.

Cool analysis of torts is difficult because the issue has been politicized. Once the exclusive province of judges under the common law, such cases have recently become a platform from which state legislators rant against "careless corporations," "selfish salesmen," and "insensitive" insurance companies. Sometimes the adjectives fit the realities. Sometimes they do not. The fact is that 41 states have passed tort laws. When criticized, the legislators point to stories of injured people left with mangled hands and crushed bodies. Inspiration for the stories often comes from plaintiffs' lawyers, who use such evidence before juries that are frequently anti-corporation and anti-insurance company in the first place. Tort rules developed through courts and through legislatures may produce different outcomes for social policy. Different decision makers with different motives, different resources, and different processes generate a different kind of tort law. Judges, unlike politicians, need not posture, need not exaggerate, and need not defend their decisions before angry interest groups.

The presumption, however, that coolheaded jurists provide sounder social policies than hotheaded legislators has been challenged. The reason is seen in the changed views of judges toward corporations. During the

1960s, courts viewed compensatory awards as insurance whose costs were best handled by spreading them across various industries. At that time firms were seen in a quite favorable light because they provided quality goods for a mass market at reasonable prices. In the 1970s, however, corporations began to be defined as greedy, insensitive, and reckless monsters run by people not quite like, but not that very much unlike, Cornelius Vanderbilt with his vulgar public-be-damned philosophy.

Measuring the effect of increased tort cases, as well as the substantial size of some awards, is difficult but important. Although the impacts of large awards (discussed in greater detail in the following chapter) is hard to determine, a preliminary observation is timely. Large awards could eventually persuade the best manufacturers to leave a market; make insurance so costly that people needing a financial backstop are unable to get one at any cost; persuade doctors to leave a field they perceive to be very susceptible to malpractice suits; increase the public's tax burden (more judges to handle more cases); and even adversely influence corporate governance if boards are denied able outsiders who fear being held personally liable.

Complaints do not end here. There are fears that current tort practices encourage a form of insurance expressed in higher prices. The poor are hurt far more than the middle and upper classes. Moreover, when poor persons are injured, the compensation they are likely to receive is lower than the amounts given to the more affluent because courts, in determining the monetary amount for injuries, estimate on the individual's potential earning power. Because the poor presently earn less, they are likely to earn less over their lifetimes than better paid employees. In short, the poor pay more and get less.

A particularly disturbing problem is that courts have drawn some confusing distinctions between products and services. California, for instance, holds that blood sold to others is a service, not a product. But mounting mumbers of infected blood puts California's definition into question. In Oregon pet skunks are products. In Illinois they are not. Because makers of defective products are punished more severely that providers of defective services, the law places burdens on the former that are far heavier than the law's burden on the latter. For this reason, strict product liability laws have been denounced as not only impractical but immoral.[6] The confusion began in a 1955 decision (*Escola v. Coca Cola Bottling Company*) when the California Supreme Court put the burden of proof in negligence cases on the manufacturer.[7] The perplexity continued after the 1983 *Greenman v. Yuba Power Products*, another decision rendered by the California Supreme Court. Justice Roger Traynor's majority opinion laid down the general rule for strict liability: *make sure that the costs of injuries resulting from defective products are borne by manufacturers, not by injured persons, who are powerless to protect themselves.* A final point is that tort law is being transformed by the moral perceptions of ordinary women and men who are called to jury duty. Torts, therefore, provide classic examples of decisions that reflect—or change—the moral foundations of American society.

## Consumer Opposition to Protective Legislation: Three Examples

Complicating the problem of liability is the fact that consumers, facing conflicts between their perceived economic interests and their physical well-being, often opt for the former. Individual consumers and consumer organizations have supported restrictions on business in order to protect the public's health and safety; they have been less diligent about their own behavior. Labor unions, too, have moved to place their own economic interests over the general welfare.[8] In the mid-1970s, for example, the United Auto Workers union was as unenthusiastic as General Motors about the government's effort to require carmakers to install ignition interlocks on new automobiles. The reasons were that the $50 added cost might depress sales; depressed sales mean lower profits; and lower profits mean fewer jobs. Property owners who stand to gain when additional housing construction is legally limited have generously supported environmental groups that have backed the restrictive legislation—and environmentalists do not bite the hands that feed them. How consumers themselves have opposed government's efforts to protect them are seen in the controversies over motorcycle helmets, saccharin, and AIDS.

### *Motorcyclists*

By 1975, California excepted, all states had adopted mandatory helmet requirements. The cyclists, resisting angrily, staged demonstrations before state capitols and on the streets of Washington. Politicians heard the roar of the throttles and by 1980 only 21 states required helmets. Motorcyclist deaths had declined 40 percent after state mandatory-helmet laws went into effect in the late 1960s, but, after lawmakers took the requirements off the books, deaths recorded between 1976 and 1979 increased by 46 percent. Motorcycle accidents claimed 3312 lives in 1976; in 1979, the number was 4850. There was a threefold increase in the frequency of head injuries and nearly a fourfold increase in the severity of head injuries among motorcyclists in those states that had repealed their laws. Another study estimated that the repeal led to a $16 million to $18 million increase in unnecessary medical expenditures—a significant share of which was borne by taxpayers, because many motorcyclists had little or no health insurance.

### *Ethical Questions*

- In return for helmet-free rides, do motorcyclists take major responsibility for injuries caused by themselves?
- If the previous question is answered negatively, what should society do to (or for) the disabled cyclists—let them fend for themselves? cover their medical expenses? resurrect the old helmet requirements?

## Saccharinites

The saccharin story began in 1969 when the FDA forbade the use of cyclamates, an artificial sweetener, because it feared using this sugar substitute increased the risks of cancer. When, therefore, the FDA proposed in 1977 to ban saccharin, the only other sugar substitute, a consumer howl deafened the ears of congressmen. The FDA's decision was mandated by the Delaney Amendment to the Food, Drug and Cosmetic Act of 1938, which stated that no additive is deemed to be safe if it is found to induce cancer when ingested by man or animal. Although saccharin had been defined as a carcinogen, the American Cancer Society (ACS) declined to support the FDA because a ban might harm many while protecting only a few. ACS pointed out that diabetes and obesity posed more dangers to Americans than the possible cancer-causing effects of saccharin. Aligned with the ACS were the American Medical Association and the American Diabetes Association. Supporting the FDA's position, namely, that economic factors should never be weighed against health risks, were Ralph Nader and the Environmental Defense Fund. Congress acted to prohibit the FDA from maintaining the saccharin ban.

## Ethical Question

- What kind of ethical reasoning could Congress (and its supporters) and the FDA (and its supporters) have used to support their respective positions?

## AIDS Victims

Before 1962, pharmaceutical companies had to show the FDA that every new drug was safe. But Senator Estes Kefauver from Tennessee in 1962 persuaded his congressional colleagues that, before a drug could be marketed, manufacturers had to show that the new product was not only *safe* but *effective*. The results were drastic. The average cost of developing a new drug increased from $1.3 million in 1960 to $50 million in 1979; in 1979, it took the average drug approximately 10 years to get through the FDA's testing process, four times longer than it took before 1962. Further, although the United States remained the leading producer of new drugs, it ranked ninth among 12 nations in making new drugs available to the public.

In the mid-1980s came AIDS, a fatal disease then affecting primarily male homosexuals. The politically articulate gays used picketing and demonstrations to make the point that drugs were needed immediately. Responding to the pressure, the FDA modified its usual drug approval procedures in 1988, the first such action since 1962. In order to make at least one drug available for the treatment of AIDS, AZT was approved within 18 months—faster than any other drug in FDA history. The agency took another drastic step when it suspended the third testing stage for seriously ill people. This last step involved giving the drug to a large number of patients and giving an equal number of placebos in order to obtain a statistically meaningful measure of the drug's effectiveness. The first two stages involved dispensing the drug to both healthy individuals and to a limited number of patients in order to monitor it for toxicity and significant side effects. But the third stage added two to three years to the drug's approval time—even though only 10 percent of drugs that successfully completed Phase II ever failed to complete Phase III.

Now, for the first time, the FDA officially sanctioned the concept of risk-benefit analysis when it said that safety is not absolute (i.e., no drug is free of risk); rather, a new drug must be assessed in light of the condition the drug treats. This is particularly true in treating life-threatening diseases, when quite toxic drugs may nevertheless be considered safe under the circumstances. The stories reveal a common consumer trait: faced with unwelcome health or economic impacts, consumers expand their risk-taking proclivities and, by doing so, tend to reduce the ethical responsibility of the manufacturers. They become, in effect, co-defendants before the bar of justice.

## *Ethical Questions*

- Facing rapidly escalating costs for employee health benefits, which threaten the firm's profit margins, the CEO tells the manager of human resources not to hire people who appear excessively vulnerable to illnesses or accidents. Is the CEO acting ethically?
- A life insurance company refuses to write premiums on gays. Is the company ethical?

## Judicial Trends and Ethics

Business has watched with growing fear and moralists have watched with increasing confusion the recent meanderings of tort law in the courts. Fears and confusions have been intensified by developments related to five issues: (1) fault and strict liability, (2) admissible evidence, (3) the law's reach, (4) deep pockets, and (5) single and collective liability.

To individuals harmed by a product they have used, the novelty of recent court decisions in tort law represent social innovation at its best and ethics at its finest. To defendants the novelty is alarming because it stretches the meaning of responsibility beyond what is reasonable. Because recent judicial decisions stimulate moral reasoning in provocative ways, it is useful to examine some of the specific features of court principles and processes.

### *Fault and Strict Liability*

It may be recalled that traditionally there have been two main approaches to placing the responsibility for their behavior on individuals and groups: (1) fault in the 19th century and (2) strict liability in the 20th. Whereas fault means negligence or carelessness, strict liability means that the cost of compensating victims is considered insurance, regardless of the behavior of the parties concerned. It is not asked by society whether companies or persons behaved badly or were unreasonable; it is asked only that companies clearly understand that they are legally responsible because they are in the best position to make choices between safety and profits. By making good choices, manufacturers reap the profits; by making bad choices they bear the costs. The guiding principle is simple: choose carefully when deciding what to make and market.

The doctrine of strict liability, however, has expanded so much that the law itself has created a jungle of confusion. Originating in the 1960s, for example, the doctrine of enterprise liability held that firms are responsible for *any* injuries caused by products they introduce into commerce, even if the products when marketed were as safe as state-of-the-art technology allowed. This is entirely different from the old common law view that, with few exceptions, there is no liability when there is no fault. While countries like England and Australia adhere to the fault standard, American tort law has become an instrument to promote what courts think is social justice.

Calabresi put the justice issue well when he said that judges who make decisions on whom to burden are also deciding "whether we wish to become callous or whether, instead, we think that as a society we would be better off if we continue to view some things as shocking, offensive, and even abominable."[9] Morality counts. The culture—or lived ethic—provides society's definition of what is shocking, offensive, and abominable; philosophers provide the conceptual framework from which a given culture's ideas of good and evil are measured; judges and jurors use both the lived ethic and the philosophical ethic to determine which acts are repugnant.

Courts have uniformly recognized negligence on three bases: (1) product defects, (2) design defects, and (3) failure to warn. The use of a failure-to-warn rule to sustain a negligence claim came in 1984 when Carol Ann Feldman contended that her teeth turned gray from using Declomycin, an antibiotic that she received periodically from her physician-father to control respiratory problems and other infections. Lederle Laboratories, the manufacturer, said it did not know of the side effect at the time the Declomycin was first marketed, and two lower courts accepted this argument; in 1963 the company began, however, to issue warnings about possible tooth discoloration from using the drug. In its ruling, the New Jersey Supreme Court did not deny drug manufacturers the state-of-the-art defense *but it changed the burden of proof from customer to manufacturer*, saying that the drug company was in a better position to sense potential danger in its products than were its customers.[10] The company itself did the testing; the company itself knew the latest scientific data; and the company was obligated to monitor the product's effect over time. The line between product defect and failure to warn was blurred. Traynor's influence was evident.

What might be called the blur effect was extended by a federal judge in Texas named Robert Carter, who held that the duty to warn was violated even if the manufacturer did not know of the danger at the time the product was manufactured. But the questions multiply: Warnings over what and how? Could warnings become a cry-wolf story? Would warnings frighten off the very people who needed the drug most?

Pharmaceutical firms felt especially vulnerable because they knew that the same substance that had uniquely beneficial powers in a new drug might eventually cause the greatest harm. The result was a drug maker's nightmare. If a company invented and sold a drug that, used in the prescribed way, cured cancer, but caused polio in 10 percent of its users, and if that knowledge were imputed to the manufacturer, the drug's design would not be defective; nothing could be done to alter the key ingredient without impairing the usefulness of the product. If, on the other hand, the same post-manufacturer knowledge could be imputed to the manufacturer in a failure-to-warn claim, the manufacturer would be liable. A drug firm could avoid liability only when its product had to be used in a strictly prescribed way to bring about beneficial effects. Even then, manufacturers could escape liability only if the warning led to safer use, rather than (as in medical malpractice warning cases) allow consumers to make a more informed choice.

Without question, the expanded meaning of torts has buttressed the *caveat vendor* principle. Unwary consumers are no longer vulnerable to the line once handed out by traveling salesmen that their wares would cure everything from frostbites to liver disorders. In this sense the law's development has been salutary. The nagging moral question is the departure of American law from English law, which still respects the ethical principle of guilt through fault. But proving fault was not easy and, under the old rules of negligence, few plaintiffs could afford to assemble and pay the expert witnesses usually needed to buttress the plaintiff's claims. Out-of-court settlements normally meant that victims received half a loaf when they deserved all the bread.

The changes also reflect a growing awareness that adjudicating torts under contract law was often catastrophic for victims. As an example, the Massengil Company in 1937 began shipping a sulfa drug in a raspberry extract and alcohol base that had never been tested for safety. One hundred users died. Massengil was apologetic, but little more: if the users wanted a guarantee of safety, the company conveniently reasoned, they should have demanded one before buying the product. Shortly after World War II, American litigants began to denounce such one-sided contracts and the courts set out to redress the imbalance—which they did. No longer could companies get away, perhaps literally, with murder. Judges also expanded the scope of jurors' powers.

By far the greatest change in liability, however, occurred in product safety. At one time, strict liability meant that cause and effect must be proved but negligence need not be. Now manufactured products—from playpens to pantyhose—fall under the strict-liability rule. Originally the product needed to be defective in and of itself, but soon it was sufficient to show that another manufacturer had a better designed product or merely that a better design was feasible. It also became immaterial that a consumer had bought an inherently weaker design in order to save money. Thus a jury fined Honda $5 million for its "reckless" act of using materials lighter than those used by other manufacturers.

Courts also began to rewrite insurance policies if it turned out the policyholder failed to buy enough of the right coverage; they also discarded virtually every legal rule that had previously allowed insurers to define risk pools with workable precision. The result was that private insurance would inevitably decline. Intangible injuries, such as unintentional infliction of severe emotional distress, had been traditionally limited for the obvious reason that, if carried to extremes, practically anyone could be made liable to practically anyone else for practically anything. This wall, too, has been crumbling, with teachers now collecting damages for the mental trauma of being unconstitutionally exposed to prayers said in student assemblies. Already burdened by legal complications weary managers feel they need no more—but another exists.

Built into the product liability approach is a concept called risk assessment, which raises two new questions: What is the relative size of the tolerable risk that can result in injury? What is the magnitude of the harm when injury does take place? Trying to answer the questions, risk assessors deal with uncertain or incomplete scientific findings. Prudence becomes, therefore, not a matter of acting effectively to remedy a suspected source of injury, but of waiting for better scientific results. The results are a mixed bag. Remedial action by lawmakers tends to be postponed, leaving to judges sole responsibility for deciding cases when adequate scientific findings are unavailable. Ethical reasoning may enrich the law by first asking this question: Do present legal rules for admissible evidence promote justice?

## *Admissible Evidence*

With good reason lawyers have sought to define the nature of admissible evidence.[11] As a general rule, hearsay evidence is taboo, but there are at least 30 exceptions to the general principle in the federal rules of evidence. Consider, however, the case of a four-year-old boy who told his mother that he was beaten by his father while she was at work. When taken by the mother to the hospital, the child told the pediatrician the same story he had told his mother. X-rays confirmed the nature of the injury. However, when the case came to trial, the child and mother had left town, fearing that the accused man would seek revenge and harm them. When called by the prosecution to testify under oath, the pediatrician told the jury what the child told her—but the evidence was dismissed by the judge because it was hearsay. The point is that the legal rules of evidence can be moral nonrules that prohibit jurors from hearing relevant information. A Tucson judge described the dilemma when he wrote:

> *I have sat on the bench for eleven years now, and day in and day out, month in and month out, I apply rules that belie common sense. It wouldn't be right to suggest that we change some of those rules. But in the name of justice, we should at least change the*

*oath that suggests that the witness will be telling "the truth, the whole truth and nothing but the truth."*[12]

Barring hearsay evidence is, of course, not intrinsically wrong. Suppose, in the above story, for instance, the mother was the one who injured her son and cajoled him into accusing the father. Because the mother disliked her husband intensely, she had motive; however, automatically dismissing all hearsay evidence smacks of too much arbitrariness. Absent opportunity to cross-examine the two major witnesses for the prosecution in the case of the abused child, the court possibly had no other recourse but to forbid the pediatrician's testimony. But the probable result was a miscarriage of justice.

Evidence was also very much an issue in the famous Pinto case. The state of Indiana had accused Ford Motor Company of making and selling a compact car when it knew that its gasoline tank might explode in a rear-end collision. The case arose in August 1978 after three teenaged girls were burned to death when their 1973 Pinto was hit in a rear-end collision. Some asides are pertinent: the prosecutor reportedly had a budget of $20,000 and volunteer help from law professors and students interested in the case; the Ford company allegedly had a budget of $3,000,000 to support over 20 attorneys and public relations people. In addition, former Watergate prosecutor James Neal reportedly received $1,000,000 to oversee the Ford team.

Prior to the trial, the prosecution leaked evidence that appeared to put the Ford Motor Company in the wrong. Most of this evidence, however, was never brought before the jury because the judge ruled against its admissibility. The court allowed evidence involving only Pintos manufactured in 1973; it mandated that every document had to be authenticated; it permitted no personal testimony because such testimony might pull at the jurors' heartstrings; and it prevented major prosecution witnesses from testifying before the jury. One such witness was Frank Camps, a retired Ford engineer, who had worked on the company's crash-test program. With the jury out of the room, Camps testified that Ford employees were told to do whatever was necessary to enable vehicles to pass certification tests. The judge did not permit jurors to hear this testimony. As a result, only a dozen or so of the 200 documents (many gathered from Ford's records) were allowed. However, the *Chicago Tribune* gained access to these inadmissible documents suggesting that, after completing its cost analysis, Ford concluded that the extra $11 per vehicle needed to make 12.5 million cars safer would be almost three times greater than the costs stemming from persons killed or injured in vehicles made without the new design.

Another nonadmissible document from Ford's files indicated that the automaker considered putting the gas tank in a safer location but rejected the idea because it would reduce luggage space. One of the documents the prosecution was permitted to introduce was a 16-page report from the Transportation Department's National Highway Traffic Safety Administration that criticized the Pinto model as being unsafe; however, the report lacked crash-test results for the 1973 model. The prosecution nevertheless argued that Ford had ample time to change the fuel system but did not do so in order to save money.

Ethicists would ask: If witnesses were available and if documents were available, would not the search for truth have been better served than by denying them to the jury? If the burden of proof was already on the plaintiffs, had not the judge, by his procedural decision, added to their burden? In fairness to Ford, it should be noted that the company felt it was already unfairly burdened by application of criminal law, which would drastically expand common conceptions of criminal offenses. This, however, is a different issue. Equally distant from the problem of evidence was Ford's claim that Indiana had no business bringing such a case because the auto industry was federally regulated and the 1973 Pinto model met all federal standards; Ford also protested using an Indiana law passed in 1977 (a corporation could be charged with criminal acts) to judge its 1973 cars.

So far as evidence was concerned, Ford was allowed to show the jurors exhibits and nine miles of test-crash films that demonstrated that the Pinto was as safe as rival subcompacts; in addition, several witnesses were allowed to testify that the driver of the ill-fated Pinto told them that the car had been stationary when hit. After several months of litigation, Ford was acquitted of reckless homicide. The jury, which deliberated four days, held a press conference to justify its verdict, stating that they simply felt there was not enough evidence to convict Ford of a criminal act—a position applauded by the judge and by the editors of the *Chicago Tribune,* the paper which had earlier published the long article on Ford's "secret" reports.[13] A nagging question persists: had the jurors heard the evidence the judge disallowed, would a different verdict have been reached? Was the leaking of selective facts by the prosecution ethical? Was Ford unfairly treated if its Pinto was as safe as other subcompacts accepted by the federal government?

Nonlawyers may be excused from wondering about the evidence issue— especially when the Pinto case is contrasted to a decision rendered by the Arizona Court of Appeals in December 1978. Recall that in Pinto, the judge prohibited testimony on cars other than the 1973 model. Only the specific characteristics of a specific model could be considered. In an Arizona case, the state judges, on the other hand, accepted evidence from experiments that showed the general traits of a product.[14]

In light of the Indiana-Arizona approaches, a moralist could reason that, with a whole-truth-and-nothing-but-the-truth jurisprudence, jurors themselves should be allowed to decide what to believe and to disbelieve. Attorneys, trained to detect flaws in testimony, would shield jurors from too readily swallowing flimsy secondhand reports. To deny the admissibility of alleged facts, even if acquired indirectly, is to exclude information that presiding judges may know is relevant. From a moral standpoint, relevancy is at least as important as admissibility. If there is no constitutional abridgement of freedom for the press, should there be abridgement on the freedom of those in a position to provide information? Even though perjury is now frequently ignored, perjurers can be severely punished. Sloppy testimony is easily demolished and all jurors are not stupid.

An indictment of present rules of evidence having been made, it is necessary to present the counterargument: strict regulations on what is admissible evidence make for more accurate presentations. Jurors are not forced to choose between witnesses. They are forced to accept facts. In addition, jurors have neither the time nor the abilities to become investigative reporters who check multiple sources before coming to a single conclusion. Moreover, the Pinto case is not symptomatic of something intrinsically wrong with the current rules of evidence. And, interestingly enough, if the rules are relaxed, corporations might have more to lose than plaintiffs because constant repetition of hearsay testimony could make the Big Lie the juror's truth. Beyond this issue is still another ethical question regarding jurisdiction: in how many places can and should manufacturers and sellers be legally accountable?

## *The Law's Reach*

In 1878, the U.S. Supreme Court (*Pennover v. Neff*) voided a judgment rendered against a nonresident of one state who had not personally been served with a process in that state. Approximately a century later, the Fifth Circuit Court of Appeals allowed an action against a Japanese manufacturing company that had never had an office, place of business, servant, employee, or director anywhere in the United States. The case was one of several responding to so-called long-arm statutes passed by states in their attempt to hold manufacturers and sellers responsible for accidents occurring within their jurisdictions—even though the maker and/or seller did not conduct business within that state.

This issue came to the Supreme Court in 1980 in a case where the facts were uncontested. In 1976 Mr. and Mrs. Harry Robinson had purchased a new Audi from a dealer in New York. The following year, the Robinson family left their New York home for a new residence in Arizona. While driving through Oklahoma, their car was struck by another car, causing a fire that severely burned Mrs. Robinson and her two children. The Robinsons then brought a product liability action in an Oklahoma state court against the New York dealer, the regional distributor, the importer, and the manufacturer in Germany. The majority of the Court said:

> *We find in the record before us a total absence of those affiliating circumstances that are a necessary predicate to any exercise of state court jurisdiction. Petitioners carry on no activity whatsoever in Oklahoma. They close no sales and perform no services there. They avail themselves of none of the privileges and benefits of Oklahoma law. They solicit no business there either through sales persons or advertising reasonably calculated to reach the State. Nor does the record show that they regularly sell cars at wholesale or retail to Oklahoma customers or residents or that they indirectly, through others, serve or seek to serve the Oklahoma market. In short, respondents seek to base jurisdiction on one isolated occurrence.*[15]

Justice Brennan, in a dissent, took the position that Oklahoma had contacts with the dealer and the distributor because each of the latter intended the automobiles to be used in travel. It was therefore difficult to see why the Court should distinguish between a case involving goods that reached a distant state through a chain of distribution and a case involving goods that reached the same state because consumers—using them as dealers knew they would—took them there. In Brennan's view, once a product is made for mass markets, responsibility ends ultimately with maker and/or seller.

## *Ethical Question*

- Which of the two arguments (majority or minority) strikes you as being more responsive to ethical criteria?

Shortly after the decision against the Robinsons, and in a somewhat similar case, the Fifth Circuit Court handed down a decision in favor of one Mrs. Oswalt who was seriously burned when a Catch 98 lighter, distributed in the United States by Scripto and manufactured in Japan by Tokai-Seiki, allegedly malfunctioned, causing her pajamas to catch fire.[16] Tokai-Seiki, incorporated under the laws of Japan, had no officers, employees, or directors in the United States or in Texas, where the accident occurred. It seemed that the ruling against the Robinsons should govern. The appeals court, however, took a different tack by finding that Tokai-Seiki had made no attempt in its negotiations with Scripto to restrict sales from certain states. When, therefore, a corporation purposefully availed itself of the privilege of conducting activities within a state, it had clear notice that it was subject to suit there. It can alleviate the risk of burdensome litigation by procuring insurance, thereby passing the added costs to customers or, if the legal risks are too great in a given state, severing its connection with that state. In the court's view the home state did not exceed its powers under the due-process clause when it asserted jurisdiction over a corporation that delivers its products into the stream of commerce with the expectation that they will be purchased by customers in that state.

## *Ethical Question*

- Reviewing your response to the Robinson case, do you find the court in Scripto using a different ethical criterion to justify its decision?

The overall result of the Oswalt case reveals a significant extension of the states' jurisdictional powers. In drawing a conclusion based on ethical reasoning, it appears that the added protection for customers can be defended on both deontological and utilitarian grounds. But the Supreme Court itself issued a warning when it said that foreseeability alone has never been a sufficient benchmark for *personam* jurisdiction under the due process clause. If foreseeability were *the* criterion, a local California tire dealer could be forced to defend in Pennsylvania when a blowout occurred in Pittsburgh; a Wisconsin seller of a defective automobile jack could be hauled before a distant court for damage caused in New Jersey; and a Florida soft-drink concessionaire could be summoned to Alaska to account for injuries happening there. Viewing these cases, one lawyer wrote as follows:

> *Clearly, jurisdiction does not exist in, and must not be allowed to be extended to, situations where the only contact with the forum state is that the plaintiff is a resident or that his lawyer is licensed to practice there; otherwise, "forum shopping" will become the order of the day. Finally, care must be taken by our courts to avoid decisions which chill the constitutional liberty of a citizen to travel to another state and consider engaging in even the simplest business venture ... such as those which would dissuade a Louisiana service station from installing a tire on a vehicle with out-of-state license plates.*[17]

Problems with a state's jurisdiction over liability issues arise because court decisions are ambiguous or even contradictory. The moral confusion intensifies when judges jeopardize consistency. For instance, Illinois has a reputation for being a smart place to bring product liability class-action suits, and Kansas is known as a good state for suing oil companies over natural-gas royalties. Shopping sprees became even more widely practiced after a superior court ruling when Irl Shutts, a Kansas resident who owned natural-gas leases, sued Phillips Petroleum in a Kansas state court over interest on royalties owed him. Shutts' attorneys brought suit not just on his client's behalf or the 600 parties in Kansas but for 28,000 royalty owners from 11 states. Phillips said it was improper to sue in Kansas on behalf of all these class members because 97 percent of them lived outside of Kansas and 99 percent of the leases did not involve Kansas land. Furthermore, evidence in one case should not be used as evidence in all cases. The Kansas court upheld Shutts' right to include out-of-state members so long as they had received proper notice of the suit and were allowed to opt out. The Supreme Court validated the Kansas ruling.[18]

## *Ethical Question*

- Is justice better served if the royalty owners were asked to "opt in"?

## *Deep Pockets*

Deep pockets have become another hotly debated issue in tort cases. Deep pockets occur when state laws permit a person injured by one who has been identified as primarily responsible for the accident to extend the claims to others who might be only minimally related to the injury-causing incident. Lawyers have been quick to exploit such legal provisions when the primary defendant is relatively poor and the remote agent is relatively rich—the one with the deep pockets. On the whole, public authorities have adopted a policy of benign neglect toward protests by manufacturers and insurance companies over this trend. When, however, public authorities themselves felt the sting, new attitudes began to appear.

The story is best told through a California case.[19] In 1982 Am Sporer-Schiff, a high-school teacher from San Jose, visited San Francisco on a sightseeing excursion. She decided to visit Lombard Street, "the crookedest street in the world," and a justly famed tourist attraction. From the top of Russian Hill, at the intersection of Hyde and Lombard streets, is a fantastic view of the bay—from the Golden Gate to Treasure Island. Down Hyde Street from Lombard are the cable cars climbing "halfway to the stars." In the background is Alcatraz Island, the former site of a prison for the nation's most hardened criminals. The Lombard Street view, widely reproduced on posters and tourist booklets, offers one of the city's most spectacular attractions.

While sitting on a railing at the bottom of Lombard Street, Ms. Sporer-Schiff was struck by an automobile. The accident cost her a leg; she was saddled with heavy medical bills and hampered in performing even the most menial household tasks. At the pretrial hearings, the driver, perceived by both sides as having been primarily responsible for the injury, had only $25,000 in insurance coverage. However, there was available a deep pocket—the city and county of San Francisco. Ms. Sporer-Schiff's attorney, using generally accepted legal theory, proposed to submit evidence to show that the negligence that caused the debilitating injury should be shared between the automobile driver and the city. Admitting that the driver was 98 percent liable due to his carelessness and faulty brakes and that the city was only 2 percent negligent due to failure to erect crash barriers along the sinuous route of Lombard Street, the plaintiff's attorney nevertheless used the deep pocket doctrine, which holds that a defendant having only a small portion of negligence must nevertheless pay the bigger amount for the plaintiff's pain and suffering when the primary defendant is unable to do so.

The city's attorney, realizing the probable result of a jury verdict, settled out of court for $350,000. Both lawyers acknowledged that it was likely that the jury would attach, at a minimum, substantial liability for the accident to the city. The result was that taxpayers had indemnified Ms. Sporer-Schiff for the financial loss she would have suffered if only the car's driver was held financially accountable. The deep pockets doctrine had effectively put the city in the role of a liability-insurance underwriter for the motorist. When asked to comment about results on taxpayers, Ms. Sporer-Schiff's attorney replied that "it was only fair and just that the financial responsibility for pain and suffering fall to a solvent responsible party rather than on the shoulders of an unfortunate victim." In the lawyer's view, without deep pockets his client would have been left without adequate compensation. Ms. Sporer-Schiff's own comment was brief: "The City continues to lure tourists to Lombard Street with Chamber of Commerce propaganda. It cannot absolve itself of responsibility for personal injury that occurs on city streets."

## *Ethical Questions*

- Is the woman's view the ethical one?
- Or should compensation be paid by each party in proportion to its share of responsibility?

By the early 1980s, the public outcry against perceived perversions in the liability system had become boisterous. To the critics the legal system was treating liability cases with a simplistic Robin Hood maxim: take from the rich and give to the poor—regardless of who was at fault. One of the first to rebel against the deep pockets doctrine was California, one of the few states where the public may legislate directly through the initiative process, thus bypassing the legislative and executive branches of government. Proposition 51 (the Fair Responsibility Act) sought to amend the Civil Code to change the rules governing who must pay for so-called noneconomic damages (pain and suffering), while limiting the liability of each responsible party to that portion of noneconomic damages equal to the responsible party's share of fault. The courts still could require one party to pay the full cost of economic damage if other responsible parties were not able to pay their shares. By limiting noneconomic damages to the proportion of the defendant's share of the fault, the deep pocket would effectively be shortened because virtually all of the large deep pocket awards have been for such noneconomic damages as pain and suffering or injury to one's reputation. In the typical cases involving death or debilitating injury, the noneconomic damages are usually five to ten times greater than the economic damages.

Californians who opposed the amendment were backed by Ralph Nader, who insisted that the reason Proposition 51 appeared on the ballot was that incompetently run insurance companies still were able to dupe people into believing that a crisis existed in California's liability laws. In their view, insurers during the early 1980s were so busy investing funds at the then prevailing high-interest rates that they became oblivious of the actuarial realities of the business they were underwriting. On this point they had the backing of a report by the National Association of Independent Insurers, which revealed how many companies had willingly risked underwriting losses so they could make huge profits by investing the premium dollars that were rolling in. The bubble broke in 1984, when interest rates crashed and red ink started to flow; most casualty business the insurance companies had on the books was losing money, and the companies responded by wholesale cancellations of policies. What little coverage was available was being sold at exorbitant rates. Insurance companies were accused of blaming their problems on the "lawsuit crisis" to divert responsibility from themselves. Insurance critics pointed out that in 1985, the year of the so-called crisis, insurers paid out $8.3 million in claims to California cities while receiving $26.9 million in premium payments from them. Although it can be argued that the deep pocket system unnecessarily shifted the burden of restitution for negligent acts to the cities, it cannot be shown that the practice is bankrupting the insurance industry.

Proponents of Proposition 51 argued that charges of mismanagement by insurance companies missed the point. Aberrations in the insurance industry were due to temporal shifts in interest rates and such aberrations usually work themselves out over several years as rates stabilize. The real issue is the fairness of shifting the victim's burden to those who least caused the injury. If deep pockets seemingly offers justice to plaintiffs, it is because some defendants with large resources are treated unjustly. The moral appeal here is to the deontological ethic that harm cannot be inflicted on an innocent party in order to help an injured party. Therefore, any legal system in which the scales of justice are so heavily balanced on one side cannot be countenanced. In the deontological analysis a further point was made to the effect that deep pockets might be tolerated in certain cases if the victims actually received the bulk of the judgments. The reality, however, was that lawyers took from 30 to 50 percent of the plaintiff's award under the contingency payment system. In light of such fees, the call by plaintiff lawyers to keep deep pocket awards flowing to hapless victims seemed hollow. Perhaps the hollow tone rings for both groups: the trial lawyers who bankrolled the effort to defeat Proposition 51 and the insurance companies that did much the same thing to sustain it.

## *Ethical Question*

- Under present circumstances does Proposition 51 promote justice?

Is it possible that in all the din the voice of justice has been muffled? Or has the California focus on deep pockets served to call attention to several related aspects in handling liability cases, one of which is the jury system itself? Robert Slatter, an appellate judge in Connecticut, has argued that the use of juries to assess damage awards is tantamount to using a lottery system because jurors (1) are novices at the law, (2) receive only vague instructions from judges, and (3) serve so infrequently that they do not award damages in a consistent manner. A review of the judge's criticisms shows, however, that the second indictment is the fault of judges themselves and that his criticism conveniently ignores inconsistencies that have come from the bench.

## *Ethical Questions*

- If the jury system is indeed inefficient in tort cases, who supports its continuance? Why?
- Is procedural and substantive justice the same thing?

The liability crisis has become a battle of the blame throwers. In early 1986 New York Governor Mario Cuomo called for empowering the state insurance superintendent to set limits on how much an insurer could raise or lower rates for liability coverage. He also urged restrictions on cancellations of coverage and supported the right of municipalities (and other public entities) to form their own insurance pool under the state's administration. The governor asked for changes in the civil justice system but rejected Republican efforts to limit awards for pain and suffering to $250,000. Governor Cuomo also backed proposals that allowed large monetary settlements to be paid out over time, instead of in lump sums, and provided stiff penalties for lawyers who brought "frivolous" lawsuits. And he also supported efforts to make it more difficult, in cases in which several parties were found to be responsible for an injury, to shift payments for the full settlement to one party. In awards or settlements for pain and suffering, for example, each party would be responsible only for its share of the damages; such a provision would be especially helpful to municipalities—as shown in the San Francisco case when plaintiff's lawyers defined the city's pocket as the jugular vein.

The New York governor's fears were amply justified. In 1988 alone, four of the top ten jury awards involved governments and two of the four were in Cuomo's own state.[20] The facts of the two New York cases are worth recording because they show real-world issues in heart-wrenching terms.

In July, 1981 John Amistadi was driving on New York City's rain-slicked Interborough Parkway when his car collided with a westbound vehicle. Amistadi's car careened over the foot-high median into oncoming traffic, striking a Chevy van driven by 25-year-old Kenton Ames. Ames, who sustained massive internal injuries, multiple fractures of the pelvis, and facial disfigurement, testified that he had aspired to be a male model and already had assembled a portfolio. But he lost 14 teeth and three inches of jaw as a result of the collision. As early as 1970, city and state inspectors reported that the Interborough Parkway was among the most dangerous roadways in the state; engineers had testified that, in light of the parkway's accident record, a center barrier—as opposed to the "center demarcator"—should have been installed. The central issue was whether Amistadi was driving carelessly or whether the city had too long neglected a dangerous road condition. In November a jury awarded Ames over $14 million, including $6 million for pain and suffering and $7 million for loss of quality of life. The city paid!

Earlier in the same year a woman named Fatima Delosevic and her three children were crossing a five-way intersection in Greenwich Village. The four, who had just begun crossing when the "Walk" sign changed into the flashing "Don't Walk" phase, were halfway across the street when the traffic light changed from red to green. Truck driver Stephan Rapczak, distracted by nearby construction, began to drive slowly through the intersection, but his high driver's seat prevented him from seeing the four pedestrians immediately in front of him. The truck's wheels pulled two children into the undercarriage and crushed them to death. After unknowingly dragging the children 50 feet, Rapczak heard the mother's screams and stopped his truck. Fatima, who was injured, was rushed to a hospital. Thirty minutes later, when she asked about her third child, an eyewitness rushed out of the building and found the baby lying in the truck's undercarriage, injured but alive. The intersection had long been rated one of the five most dangerous in the city.

In May 1988, a jury found the driver 44 percent liable, New York City 28 percent liable, and the truck manufacturer (Higgins Trucking Company) 28 percent liable for not installing proper mirrors. A $25 million verdict included $10 million for wrongful death, $9.5 million for emotional distress, and $5 million to Fatima's husband for loss of consortium.

## Ethical Question

- In both the Ames and the Delosevic cases, should the public officials directly responsible for not installing safety devices be punished?

A Maryland story turned out quite differently. A drunk driver's truck struck a pedestrian named Ashburn and severely injured him. Minutes before the accident, a Maryland county police officer saw Millham, the trucker, slumped over the wheel of his vehicle, clearly intoxicated. The officer told the man not to drive but did not follow a regulation requiring him to detain the intoxicated man. Ashburn sued Millham as well as the county and its police department. Although a Maryland court of appeals ruled that the governmental entities were immune, the jury awarded Ashburn $17.5 million. But Millham's insurers, Globe American Casualty, paid only $20,000—generous in its view because of Millham's intoxicated condition while driving.

## Ethical Question

- From an ethical standpoint, did the exoneration of Maryland officials make sense?

## Single and Collective Liability

**Single-Party Responsibility.** Use of the words "single-party responsibility" suggests that the legal issue is one of determining who, of many parties to a case, is at fault. But there is far more to the problem than identifying a culprit from a rogue's gallery. Already noted is the fact that in most jurisdictions persons injured by design-defect products, or failure to warn, may argue on one of three bases: (1) negligence, (2) strict liability in tort, and (3) breach of contract. However, proof differs vastly for each base. Plaintiffs relying on negligence must show that manufacturers unreasonably exposed them to harm; in claims based on breach of warranty and strict liability, on the other hand, the focus is on the condition of the product, not on the conduct of the defendant. Rather than decide whether the defendant acted reasonably, jurors are instructed to decide whether the product was unmerchantable because it violated the warranty or because the product was otherwise defective—the strict liability doctrine.

Viewed simply, warranty (stated or implied) is a form of contract between buyer and seller, but every warranty can turn out to be tricky. Relevant is the Arizona Supreme Court's handling of the Salt River Project dispute. The antagonists were two giant corporations that went to court to determine who should pay for a $2 million fire loss. The blaze occurred when a control mechanism for operating gas turbines malfunctioned. The manufacturer disclaimed liability for such losses under a Uniform Commercial Code (UCC) contract. The court agreed that this disclaimer was proper. Most people would have thought that the ruling concluded the matter and the court acknowledged that this normally would have been the case. However, after analyzing the two parallel product–liability systems (warranty and strict liability), the court went on to say that the legislatively approved method for disclaiming warranty liability for defective products was not good enough because the parties did not use the judicially prescribed language. Although the buyer's agreement to disclaim can be made through agents recognized by the UCC, such agents *must be expressly approved by the buyer's responsible officers.* One marvels at the ingenuity of the judge's reasoning in determining the responsible agent.[21]

The individual's responsibility was emphasized in 1985 when two plaintiffs were rebuffed in effort to get a $4.29 million award, $3.9 million of which was for punitive damages. The suit began in 1977 after Larry Hale of Sheldon, Missouri, was injured when trying to inflate a tire mounted on his truck. Two parts of the tire rim, types that were phased out during the 1960s, were made by Firestone and the third was made by Budd. A three-judge panel ruled that the district court erred in failing to instruct the jury about contributory fault. The panel said there was ample circumstantial evidence that Hale knew of the dangers of inflating a tire still mounted on a truck, because he owned and operated a truck stop and a garage and bought tire-inflation safety equipment for his employees (*Hale* v. *Firestone Tire and Rubber Company*, 1985).

Another decision held that a machine manufacturer was not liable for an operator's injuries, despite its knowledge of the purchaser's intent to cut holes in the machine's safety shield. Responsibility for the willful choice of the purchaser to bypass a built-in safety feature did not fall on the manufacturer, whose duty is to design a finished product that is safe when it leaves its control. Third-party alterations, however foreseeable, that destroy the utility of a key safety device work a substantial change in the product and thereby relieve the manufacturer of liability (*Robinson* v. *Reed-Prentice Division of Package Machinery Company*, 1980). Although the single-party principle cuts two ways (against manufacturers and against buyers), it is more frequently applied to consumers.

In buyer-seller relationships, contemporary moralists have been, by and large, less inventive than judges in projecting new theories. One exception is Alan Gewirth of the University of Chicago, who defined responsibility on three principles: *informed control, intervening agency,* and *probability of harm*. The informed control principle requires persons not to perform actions that they have good reason to believe will result in serious injury to—or death of—others.[22] But Gewirth recognized that this principle fails on practical grounds; automobile makers know from mortality rates that a number of people will be killed annually in car accidents and pharmaceutical firms know that, despite rigid laboratory controls, lethal side effects may appear. Does the informed control principle prohibit the marketing of such products? To arrive at his negative answer, Gewirth posited the intervening agency principle, which transfers primary responsibility to the careless consumer. But what of drug users? Now the third principle is introduced—probability of harm. Because drugs are highly addictive, users know they are on a suicidal track. If willing to embark on that path, drug addicts have no one but themselves to blame. If the Gewirthian approach gives insufficient attention to society's vested interest in public health, it most certainly focuses attention on the responsibilities of each individual and of each manufacturer.[23]

**Plural Responsibility.** The DES (diethylstilbestrol) crisis of the past decade is a prime example of how courts have extended liability from the one to the many. DES (a drug used to prevent miscarriage at birth, premature delivery, late pregnancy toxemia, and uterine death) had been marketed since the 1940s but was later found to be related to vaginal cancer in the female children of mothers who used DES. This meant that cases were initiated 20 or more years after the sale of the drug. A California Supreme Court ruling in the *Judith Sindell v. Abbott Laboratories et al.* case used a novel theory of market-share liability. When plaintiffs could not identify which of the five manufacturers sold them the drug, the court said that the entire industry was responsible. The court reasoned that when an injury-inducing drug was made by different manufacturers from identical formulas, liability must be divided among them on the basis of market share.

Writing for the majority, Justice Mosk noted that advances in science and technology create goods sometimes harmful to consumers that cannot be traced to any specific producer. In such instances the courts can either adhere rigidly to the prior doctrine of single responsibility (thereby denying recovery to those injured by such products) or they can fashion new remedies to meet needs. Mosk reasoned that, if monetary damages were to be awarded to the plaintiffs, those damages should be assessed in proportion to the estimated amount of the drug marketed by the different companies even if, because of passage of time, the market share could not be accurately determined. The New York courts went further by holding a company liable even when it demonstrated that the plaintiff's mother did not use the pill.[24]

When the market-share principle in plural liability was later embraced by courts in Washington and Wisconsin, pubic policy seemed to be moving toward a Traynor-like judicial and moral theory that holds that a manufacturer is indeed guilty unless proven innocent. If, for example, Johnson & Johnson had 50 percent of the market for a certain drug X, Merck 30 percent, Wyeth 15 percent, and three other pharmaceutical firms the remaining 5 percent, the harmed user of the drug—who may have actually bought it from the lowest share-of-the-market manufacturer—might collect millions from Johnson & Johnson. Of further interest was the California court's ruling that only firms having a substantial percentage of the market need be included in a suit, the implication being that small manufacturers were not under the gun. Defendants were liable unless they could show conclusively that they did not make the dangerous product. On balance, the judge's remarks sounded sweetly reasonable but afterthoughts suggest that the reasoning was not far removed from that of the grade-school teacher who punished the whole class because of inability to identify the lad who loosed the snake on the classroom floor.

Faced with similar questions about plural responsibility, a New Jersey appellate court took an opposite position, holding that a DES victim could not sue manufacturers as a group when the specific maker was not identified. The plaintiff, Gail Mann, had brought suit in 1981 against 44 DES manufacturers, arguing that, because she could not identify the seller, all should be held liable for her injuries. The court rejected the argument, saying that adopting industry-wide liability would result in taking the property of all the named defendants in order to pay for harm that may have been caused by only one—or even by one who is not a party to the lawsuit. In addition, said the court, the plaintiff's argument (that the dilemma arising from complexities of identification should shift the burden of proof to each defendant) was unacceptable because there was nothing in the record to suggest that any defendant was in a better position to make the required identification than was the plaintiff. To make an entire industry liable, reasoned the judge, would result in total abandonment of the well-settled principle that manufacturers were responsible only for damages caused by their own defective products and that the defects arose while the products were still under their control. This principle was later reaffirmed by the New Jersey Supreme Court which said that following California's Sindell rule would turn manufacturers into insurance companies.[25]

## Ethical Question

- Which of the two courts (California or New Jersey) made the better moral argument?


The plural-responsibility doctrine, already frightening to manufacturers, took a new turn over the DES drug on April 3, 1989 when the New York Court of Appeals, the state's highest judicial body, refused to accept the joint responsibility theory (all are responsible unless they can prove they did not sell to the plaintiff) and ruled instead that all manufacturers of DES could, in fact, be held liable under the share-of-the-market theory—even if they could prove that they were not manufacturing DES at the time a woman began to use the drug or began to suffer. The Wisconsin Supreme Court added another dimension when it decided that victims of cancer-causing

DES could recover full damages from any DES manufacturer, even if the company did not produce the medication that injured them. The plaintiff needed only establish by a preponderance of evidence that a defendant produced or marketed the type (e.g., color, shape, markings, or other identifiable characteristics) of DES taken by the plaintiff. The court reasoned that even though an innocent manufacturer may be sued, "we must accept this as the price the defendants and, perhaps ultimately, society must pay to provide the plaintiff adequate remedy under the law."[26]

Ethical questions arise in all DES cases. If plaintiffs are forced to bear the burden of proof even when they cannot identify the particular producer of the ingested DES, the costs of the innocent's suffering may never be recompensed; further, the consequences of an entire industry's error will possibly be forgotten and a forgotten mistake is an invitation to future carelessness. On the other hand, forcing manufacturers to bear the entire cost, or even partial cost, of a specific wrong when it has not been shown that the company's product caused the injury raises other problems.

On these questions ethicists divide as regularly as do judges. It seems, however, that utilitarians would be inclined to defend the pharmaceutical industry against shared responsibilities on grounds that (1) a great social good is served by science, (2) there are understandable risks in using certain drugs, and (3) reasonable people (doctors who prescribe and patients who use such drugs) know these things and must, therefore, assume responsibility when appropriate warnings are given. Drug companies would argue, and perhaps justifiably so, that when they have done everything duty required under the state of technology at the time of manufacture, users, not providers, should at least be required to identify the company brand.

In addition, drug companies complain that the new judicial theories are both unworkable and unfair. What, for instance, accurately defines market share? Is it a nationwide or a regional percentage? Is it the company's share at the date of injury or its current share? The drug companies argue further that, if a market-share theory is asserted, not all defendants may be brought to court and thus they may be liable for much more than their fair share. They feel it is unjust to saddle the industry with the sins of companies that no longer exist, may have been negligent, or cannot be identified. If, in fact, a whole industry is guilty under the collective responsibility doctrine, why should one company alone ever bear the costs even when it has been identified as the culprit? One certainty exists: collective responsibility opens the door to plaintiffs whose lawyers target the big and rich companies on the deep pockets principle, itself a dubious practice in the minds of some moralists.

The concert-of-action approach will likely make companies reluctant in the future to share information and thus hinder further scientific development; it is also relevant that companies involved in the voluntary pooling of clinical data (through what is called the Small Committee) did so at the prompting of the FDA, the one public agency having most clout over them. What is done to satisfy one government agency is sometimes punished by another. Perhaps it is easier to blame governments or corporations instead of concentrating on other factors (lack of public funding for research, lack of capital, and diversion of talent into other fields of study) that are at the root of the problem.

Many arguments from industry have cogency, but uncertainty over accepting them at face value persists because of these questions: Do drug companies race too quickly to capture a dominant market share? Is there, as Nader alleged, too cozy a relationship between manufacturers and their government watchdogs? Or does Nader himself have too close a relationship with tort lawyers, as a *Forbes* writer has suggested.[27] Is the argument that the concert-of-action approach will hurt research more rhetoric than reality given that each firm has a vested interest in reaching the market first? Why was not DES first tested on animals prior to selling the drug to humans? Finally, has there been created for scientific products an illusion of total efficiency that prompts everyone to engage in a mindless pursuit of total safety?[28]

## Guidelines

### Fuller's Counsel

Given the confusion that reigns, temptations to despair over solutions are understandable—and wrong. Theorists from philosophy and jurisprudence could profit by starting with Professor Lon Fuller's 1983 classic, *The Morality of Law*, wherein he warned of seven ways to ensure disasters:[29]

1. Failure to reach any rule at all so that every issue is decided on an *ad hoc* basis
2. Failure to publicize the rule that everyone is expected to obey
3. Abuse of retroactive legislation that undercuts the integrity of existing rules and puts companies and individuals at risk
4. Failure to make rules understandable to reasonable people
5. Enactment of contradictory rules
6. Demand of conduct beyond the powers of the affected party to observe
7. Making of such frequent changes in the rules that the subject cannot plan his or her actions with any consistency

While obviously partisan to business, General Motors lawyer Charles Babcock, Jr., made a telling point when he argued that the product liability system meets none of Fuller's criteria.[30] Babcock's specifics were these:

- Legal decisions are made on an *ad hoc* basis and long after the product leaves the manufacturer—a violation of Fuller's first criterion.
- Manufacturers are not told the rules that judges will use to instruct jurors—a violation of the second norm.
- Court decisions are always hindsight judgments and, when legal precedent and/or present law is sidestepped, Fuller's third principle is violated.

- Jury decisions and judges' determinations encourage opinions that are often unclear, thus ignoring the fourth maxim.
- Manufacturers often find their designs criticized in different and often contradictory ways by different agencies and different juries—violation of Fuller's fifth norm.
- Manufacturers are often condemned for a defective design when the "defect" is incapable of elimination—as in the 1979 case of *Caterpillar Tractor v. Beck*—and thus norm six is bent.
- Using the "maximum possible protection theory" enunciated in 1979 by the Texas Supreme Court (*Turner v. General Motors*) violates the seventh Fuller criterion.

The last point invites speculation. Suppose a manufacturer designed a small car that provided the maximum possible passenger protection in a rear-end collision. The manufacturer, aware that tractor-trailers weighing 70,000 pounds are sometimes driven negligently, knew that his automobile might be back-ended by the large vehicle. Because the national speed limit for trucks is 55 mph, the manufacturer asked his engineers how a crash into his automobile at that speed would allow the car's occupant to walk away unscathed. A solution: add 16 feet of structure (usable crush space) to the rear of the automobile so that the manufacturer's original 10-foot-long car is now about 27 feet long.[31] Would Americans be willing to pay considerably more for the safe car, considerably more for fuel and car maintenance, and considerably more in taxes and insurance? Not likely.

There is another legal anomaly in light of court rulings on pornography, libel, and defamation of character, respectively. Washington lawyer Peter Huber wrote that "the new liability rules are very strict with manufacturers of goods and extraordinarily lenient with manufacturers of lies."[32] Two standards of justice defended on the freedom-of-speech principle do not increase confidence that legal and ethical standards are in harmonious relationships.

## *FDA Guidelines*

A semblance of order *may* come if companies respond effectively to three guidelines issued by the FDA for company recall policies. This is an important step for everyone, especially the food industry, where almost one thousand food recalls were made in fiscal 1985. Makers and sellers may make policy on the basis of three FDA classifications:

- *Class I.* These recalls are for products that could cause *serious* health problems or death. A 1980 example was a batch of frozen peeled shrimp imported by Red Lobster Inns that contained sulfites in excess of 100 parts per million.
- *Class II.* These recalls are for products that might cause a *temporary or reversible* health hazard. A 1986 example was iron-enriched white hominy manufactured by Beatrice Specialty Products, which had unsafe levels of niacin. Niacin causes the skin to redden and prickle but is not

usually harmful. Iron salts, on the other hand, and especially ferrous glucanate, the one used in food supplements, can be quite toxic.
- *Class III*. These recalls are for products that are *unlikely* to cause any adverse health reactions but are deficient. One example is a cinnamon with additives that Sphite Company of Roanoke sold as pure.

Recall policy is, of course, an admission that dangerous and/or defective products continue to enter the market, that unthinking consumers can make good products dangerous, that good manufacturers can market bad products, and that, in some instances, both manufacturer and consumer are at fault. Unhappily, Solomon is not around to teach ethicists or judges in such gray cases.

# Summary

It is widely believed that "the microsocial frames of contemporary life form a world of sales presentations in which someone is typically attempting to close a sale on some else."[33] One result is the commercialization of life: everyone and everything has a price. In the world of unionized labor, the employer's price is the worker's wage as determined by collective bargaining. In fields like law, the client's cost is the attorney's income, which is generally fixed not by negotiations but by the profession itself. In the world of torts, the victor's reward is the tortfeasor's price, which may be established through bargaining (out-of-court settlements) or by third parties like judges and juries, who act as society's agents. If there is some semblance of logic in what unionized workers and professional employees are paid, there seems to be considerably less logic in the way compensatory and/or punitive damages are determined in tort cases, an issue to be explored further in the following chapter.

How does society discharge justice to those who have been inadvertently harmed by others? How does society deter those who have the potential of causing great harm, even when they are trying to do good? The two answers to the two questions constitute the goals of tort law in the United States. But this country has taken some very interesting routes toward the goals—paths not followed by the British, from whom Americans received their first instruction in torts. In the 15th century our English mentors taught that liability fell on anyone whose acts hurt others, regardless of the harmdoer's innocence. Five centuries later, the doctrine was modified when negligence had to be proved before judgments against manufacturers or merchants would be made. Remember Dean Calabresi's statement that the doctrine of torts can be taught in two days. If true, what may be so quickly taught is so slowly learned. Inconsistencies abound.[34] Adding to the confusion is the fact that makers of hand guns are practically immune under the law.[35]

## *Questions for Discussion*

1. Are court decisions ethical that hold a pharmaceutical company liable when the plaintiff cannot identify the brand that caused the damage?

2. Should aggrieved individuals in tort cases carry the burden of proof in negligence issues?
3. Should the government set up special funds obtained through an industry-wide tax to compensate victims of unintended and unforeseeable harm?
4. Should funding for government health-related R&D be prioritized according to mortality rates—the more who die from a particular disease, the more research money that disease should receive?
5. Should each state have jurisdiction over all manufacturers of all products that cause injury while being used within the state?
6. People wanting something desperately (smokers, motorcyclists, olympians, etc.) are prepared to take high risk to reach their goals. Relevant is the story told on Sunday, October 2, 1988, by an NBC newscaster. The 1984 Olympic participants were asked in a poll: "Would you take a steroid if you knew that it would enable you to win a gold medal but that it would cost you your life within five years?" Over 50% of the respondents said that they would take the steroid.

Now write a different scenario. After embarking on a business career, you are told that following a certain course of action would bring you to the top of your organization within ten years, but that you would die within ten years after reaching the top. What ethically should you do? What legally may you do? What would you do?

## Ethical Quandaries

### The Professor

You are taking a course from a professor whose lectures are as difficult to follow as his A grades are difficult to get. As class was ending one day, a classmate became violently ill. You and the professor help the stricken student into your car. At the professor's imperious instructions to "get to the hospital fast," you drive 60 miles an hour in a 30-mile zone. You strike a pedestrian, but thinking him "only nicked"—the professor's words after he looked through the rear window—you continue to race toward the hospital. Unfortunately, the accident victim is seriously injured.

### Questions

- Who has primary ethical responsibility for causing the accident?
- If the professor has much higher insurance coverage than you, should he pay the higher proportion of any damage award?
- Hearing that this is your third traffic violation for speeding this year, and seeing how distraught you are, the professor offers to tell the sum-

moned police that he was driving when the accident occurred. Would you accept the offer?

## The Research Business

While working for your doctorate in chemistry you become a close friend of another degree candidate working in the same area. After graduation you go your separate ways—he to a research assignment at the National Institutes of Health (NIH) and you to resume work with Wyeth Pharmaceutical Company. In time you lose contact with your friend, but at a ten-year class reunion you meet again. You discover that your respective research experiments have given both of you enough information to believe that a drug to relieve AIDS patients can be produced at relatively low cost. You had thought of starting your own company with some of a $5 million legacy from your father. You delayed taking the plunge, fearing that your own knowledge might prove to be inadequate for the work and fearful, too, that the product, even if carefully and successfully manufactured, might have unintended side effects.

From the exchange with your classmate you know that (1) he is seeking capital to start his own firm and (2) he is confident that a safe drug can be made within a year's time. Moreover, he would welcome you as a cofounder of the business—even though he is totally unaware of your inheritance. The prospect of working together, the prospect of "hitting it big," and, above all, the prospect of helping millions of desperately ill people prompt you to call your friend to discuss this most exciting venture.

Just before the scheduled rendezvous, you mention your idea to the family lawyer—a highly trusted and extremely competent attorney. Having heard your story, the lawyer warns of the danger of liability suits if ever anything untoward should happen. You respond that your assessments of the drug's safety and efficacy mirrored your friend's assessment—a million-to-one shot that something unexpected might happen. Nevertheless, counsel urges you to protect yourself. With the lawyer's help you prepare a contract for arm's-length negotiations. Under the contract you will provide and prepare the needed venture capital. You will accept neither co-ownership nor a seat on the board. In return for your money you want two things: (1) a chance to work on the project as a company employee and (2) a secret clause guaranteeing you a fixed percentage of the profits. Surprised by the terms, your friend asks time to consider the offer. Within a month your proposal is accepted and the contract is duly signed and witnessed.

The following years prove to be the most exciting in your professional career. The research breakthrough occurs. The drug is approved by the FDA and patented. The sales are heavy and the profits are handsome. Because your friend is as ethical as he is brilliant, the terms of the contract are scrupulously met. For seven years the sun shines across blue skies. Then the dreaded unexpected event happens. Three patients who had used the drug die. Lawyers for their survivors sue you (as principal *de facto* owner) and the company. While company lawyers are preparing briefs, your friend confides to you that he feels obligated to take the drug off the market and to compensate the victims' survivors. But he cannot make compensation because of insufficient funds. He asks you to advance 10 percent of your profits to help repay the plaintiffs. Without such funds, he will have to declare bankruptcy.

## Questions

- With appropriate safeguards would you advance the money?
- If you had invested the returns in other profitable ventures, what would you do?
- Should the judge apply some form of collective-responsibility doctrine to make you provide the money that the company cannot?
- Is a state-of-the-art defense ethically sound?

## Notes

1. Robert Frosch, *Technological Innovation in the Eighties* (Englewood Cliffs, N.J.: Prentice-Hall, 1984), 78–79.
2. Guido Calabresi, *Ideals, Beliefs, Attitudes and the Law: Private Law Perspectives on a Public Law Problem* (Syracuse, N.Y.: Syracuse University Press, 1985), 23. See also his early study, *The Costs of Accidents* (New Haven: Yale University Press, 1970).
3. G. Edward White, *Tort Law in America* (New York: Oxford University Press, 1980), especially 37–62. See also, W.S. Landes and Richard A. Posner, *The Economic Structure of Tort Law*. Cambridge: Harvard University Press, 1987.
4. Harry W. Jones, "Lawyers and Justice: The Uneasy Ethics of Partisanship," *Villanova Law Review* 23 (September 1978): 957–958. See also, David Luban, "The Risk of Talking about Risk," *Philosophy and Public Policy* 6 (Spring 1986): 9–11. For a more detailed view of Luban's position, see *The Good Lawyer: Lawyers' Roles and Lawyers' Ethics* (Totowa, N.J.: Rowman & Allanfeld, 1983).
5. Henningsen v. Bloomfield Motors, Inc., 32 N.J. Sp. Ct. 358, 161 A. 2d(1960).
6. Peter Huber, *Liability: The Legal Revolution and Its Consequences* (New York: Basic Books, 1988).
7. Escola v. Coca Cola Bottling Works of Fresno, 24 Cal. 2d 453, 461, 150 P. 2d 436, 440 (1940). There is little doubt that the trailblazer in tort law change was Judge Roger John Traynor of the California Supreme Court. Shortly after his death in May 1983 Traynor was hailed as a judge's judge, the "ablest judge of his generation," a judicial giant. Editors of the *California Law Review* dedicated the July 1983 issue to Judge Traynor.
8. David Vogel, *When Consumers Oppose Public Protection* (St. Louis, Mo.: Washington University Center for the Study of American Business, November 1988).
9. Calabresi, *Ideals, Beliefs, Attitudes and the Law*, 83. N.J. Sp. Ct.
10. Carol Ann Feldmann v. Lederle Laboratories, 479 A. 2d 374 N.J. (1984) 7.
11. William Twining, *Theories of Evidence: Bentham and Wigmore* (Stanford, Calif.: Stanford University Press, 1985). 8.
12. Lillian S. Fisher, "The Rules of Evidence," *Newsweek*, September 29, 1986, 8.
13. Editorial: "Ford Motor's Acquittal," *Chicago Tribune*, March 17, 1980, Sec 4, 2. Publication of Ford's alleged secret documents came in an article by Lee Strobel, "Ford Ignored Pinto Fire Peril: Secret Memos Show," *Chicago Tribune*, October 13, 1979, 1 and 5.
14. Rayner v. Stauffer Chemical, Arizona Ct. of Appeals (Dec. 1978).

15. World-Wide Volkswagen, v. Charles Woodson, 62 L. Ed., 2d U.S. Sp Ct. 490 (January 21, 1980) U.S. Sp. Ct. (1980).
16. Oswalt v. Scripto, 616 2d 5th Cir. Ct. of Appeals (1980).
17. James R. Sutterfield, "In *Personam* Jurisdiction: How Long is the 'Long Arm' in Products Liability?" *Insurance Law Journal* (August 1980): 460. This article provided the basis for the writer's analysis of the jurisdictional issue.
18. Irl Schutts v. Phillips Petroleum, 472 U.S. Sp. Ct. 797 88 L. Ed. 2d 628, 105 U.S. Sp. Ct. 2965 (June 26, 1985).
19. A Sporer-Schiff v. City of San Francisco, Cal. District Ct., San Francisco (1983).
20. Marshall Sella, "The Ten Largest Jury Awards of 1980," *The American Bar Association Journal* (March 1989): 45–50.
21. Morris G. Shanker, "Judicial Gospel on the Strict Tort and UCC Warranty Relationship," *The National Law Journal* 11 (February 10, 1986): 18.
22. Alan Gewirth, "Human Rights and the Prevention of Cancer," *American Philosophical Quarterly* 17 (April 1980): 117–125. See also, Alan Schwartz, "Responsibility and Tort Responsibility," *Ethics* 97 (October 1986): 270–277.
23. Eric Von Magnus, *Rights and Risks* (Newark, Del.: University of Delaware Center for the Study of Values, 1980), unpublished paper.
24. Sindell v. Abbott Laboratories, 26 Cal. 3d 588, 607 P. 2d 924 Cal. Rptr 132 (1980) and *Hymowitz v. Eli Lilly* N.W. 2d 487, 539 N.E. 2d 1069, 541 N.Y. 5 2d (1989). *See also* Sheila L. Birnbaum and Barbara Wrubel, "Products Liability," *The National Law Journal* (December 19, 1983): 22–26. See also, Rhonda L. Rundle, "DES Firms Acted in Concert," *Business Insurance*, March 2, 1981, 28; and O. L. Reed and A. Davison, "The DES Cases and Liability with Causation," *American Business Law Journal* 19 (Winter 1982): 519–539.
25. Ferrigno v. Eli Lilly, 175 N.J. Super. Ct. 551, 420 A. 2d (1980).
26. Jerry Geisel, "Wisconsin Court Says Victims Can Sue Any DES Defendant," *Business Insurance*, March 13, 1984, 3.
27. "Ralph Nader, Inc.," *Forbes*, 146 (September 17, 1990) 117–132.
28. Walter Guzzardi, Jr., "The Mindless Pursuit of Safety," *Fortune*, April 9, 1979, 54–64.
29. Lon Fuller, *The Morality of Law* (New Haven: Yale University Press, 1967).
30. Charles Babcock, Jr., "Product Liability: Problems in Jurisprudence," *For the Defense* 23 (February 1983): 18–23.
31. Relevant here is Talbor Page, "Responsibility, Liability and Incentive Compatibility," *Ethics* 97 (October 1986): 240–262.
32. Peter Huber, "The Press Gets Off Easy in Tort Law," *The Wall Street Journal*, July 24, 1985.
33. Guy Oakes, *The Soul of the Salesman and the Moral Ethos of Personal Sales* (London: Humanities Press International, 1990), 13.
34. Cases which support the ruling that manufacturers are responsible for unforeseen damages because it forces companies to do everything possible to reduce hazards include Escola v. Coca Cola Bottling Works of Fresno, 24 Cal 2d 453, 461, 150 P 2d 436, 440 (1940), which reinforced the classic English case that held that those who do damage, even innocently, must pay; Rylands v. Fletcher 14 L.R. 523, 526 Exchr 265, 280 (1886), which concluded that even failure to use R and D to anticipate future hazards made companies culpable; and Beshada v. Johns-Manville Product Co., 90 N.J. 191, 447 A. 2d 539 (1982). A Massachusetts court ruled that class actions were acceptable because injured individuals might otherwise go uncompensated: Payton v. Abbott Labs., 83 F. R. 382 D Mass. (1979). However, when drug companies are involved, other jurisdictions stress the need to impose only strict liability, which is the traditional and narrower responsibility: Woodill v. Parke Davis and Co., 79 Ill. 2d, 26, 402, N.E. 2d 194 (1980). Also relevant is Feldman v. Lederle Laboratories, 931 N.J. Super Ct., App. Div. (May 12, 1983).
35. Martin v. Harrington and Richardson Inc., 743 F. 2d 1200 7th Cir. Ct. (1984).

CHAPTER 11

# Tort-Related Issues

### Punitive Damages
Origin of the Doctrine
Problems in Application
*Net Recovery to the Plaintiff*
*The Judge's Power*
The Constitutional Question

### Defense Tactics
Withdrawal from the Market
Bankruptcy
Shifting the Blame
*The Lawyer–Insurer Dogfight*
*The Insured's Costs*
Institutional Reform
Ethical Input

### Life's Monetary Worth
Economic Theories
Legal Theory
Moral Theory

### Summary
Questions for Discussion
Ethical Quandary

*B*uilding on materials discussed in Chapter 10, this chapter looks carefully at some of the questions that the tort controversy has already brought to law and business, especially in regard to punitive damages. Certainly corporate executives are asking whether American law has gone astray in its use—or misuse—of punitive damages. Business enterprises need legal predictability. Manufacturers also wonder whether it is sensible to stay in fields where the risks of tort awards threaten company solvency. Finally, managers ask whether the liability crisis is the fault of irresponsible insurers or greedy lawyers—or both.

Notable in the discussions on tort law is the singular gap between judicial and moral reasoning in the sense that moralists have not been particularly imaginative in applying their insights to the area of greatest importance in tort litigation, namely, the monetary value of human life. This moral value has, of course, roots in the biblical traditions of the Judeo-Christian story in Genesis, in which a distinction is made between the physical universe as a reflection of God's power and the human person who alone is the image and likeness of God's being. Mohammed kept tradition alive in Islamism and the Hindus in their devotional book, **Bhagavad Gita**, which teaches that because each person (otman) has qualities of the divinity (Psaratman), everyone is sacred.

If the theme of the sanctity of each person permeates all the major religions, the theme of stewardship emerges most clearly in Genesis: reaching God comes by touching others kindly and treating nature wisely. Both the "touching" and the "treating" are at the core of the principle of stewardship. To hurt people and to harm nature are plainly wrong. And when harm (even when unintentional) is done, wrong must be righted. Tort law seeks to provide the remedy. ■■

## The purposes of this chapter are:

1. To consider the nature and meaning of punitive damages, as well as the judge's power to second-guess jury decisions regarding appropriate amounts of compensation.
2. To look at the tactics adopted by corporations, insurers, and lawyers to defend themselves in liability suits.

3. To examine the theories (economic and legal) that are currently applied to determination of a life's worth.
4. To explore the prospects for original contributions by moral philosophers to the life's-worth question.

## Punitive Damages

### Origin of the Doctrine

One of the most complex issues in tort law and in ethics is the punitive-damage principle. Unlike Nebuchadnezzar's maxim of an "eye for an eye and a tooth for a tooth," which was a straightforward way of determining punishment, today's concept of justice takes a circuitous route by including punitive damages. A jury, under the hybrid legal doctrine of punitive damage, imposes a civil fine against a harmdoer to express its moral indignation over injury to the innocent and to deter other potential malefactors from doing something similar. However, a jurisprudence that places in private hands the use of a public punishment to deter others requires careful legislative and moral scrutiny. Jurors are not legislators. Neither are judges. When punitive damages are excessive, Nebuchadnezzar's law can look quite gentle.

The idea of punitive damages appeared in the English common law around the middle of the 18th century when a government official was held liable for wrongly imprisoning an innocent man (*Huckle v. Money*, 1863). In subsequent cases a broader interpretation was allowed when pecuniary damages were difficult to quantify, especially for intangible losses. But punitive damages had always been strictly limited in England and no statute specifically provided for them; thus, allegations of punitive damages were extremely rare in Great Britain and had no application to situations in which they were routine under American law.

There are few doctrinal differences in the tort law of the United States, Europe, and Japan: all countries use a negligence standard for medical practice and "strict liability" for product design defects. The United States is different in that a variety of ancillary factors provide strong incentives to injured parties to use tort law more intensively than victims in other industrialized countries. Several factors, mostly outside the narrow field of tort law, are responsible: the use of juries to decide cases, the American system of contingent attorneys' fees (present in Japan but not in England, where losing parties pay winners' lawyers' fees); the more liberal rules allowing plaintiffs to recover damages for pain and suffering (the one tort-specific doctrine that may be important); and more liberal discovery rules in the United States for all types of litigation. The importance of these nontort factors should warn those who believe that, just by modifying certain tort doctrines, the net benefits of the overall system can be significantly improved.

## Problems in Application

In the United States the frequency of punitive-damage occurrences, the wide variations in awards for similar hurts, the numbers of judicial interventions into jury awards, and, finally, some unprecedented actions by judges in handling punitive judgments have turned the issue into a battleground for all and a nightmare for many. Examples give indications of the problem.

- A California jury awarded $1.5 million in punitive damages to a Nevada woman whose silicone breast implants ruptured and leaked gel into her body. The jury also directed Dow Corning Corporation of Midland, Michigan, the maker of the implants, to pay the woman $211,000 to compensate her for her injuries. The punitive-damage award was over seven times larger than the compensatory award.
- A Texas trial judge approved $20 million in punitive damages against Ford Motor Company in the case of a 19-year-old driver who burned to death in a Mustang II. That was a victory of sorts for Ford because the jury had awarded $200 million. An $180,000,000 differential between a jury's and the judge's estimates of the appropriate amount raises eyebrows.
- The Colorado Supreme Court affirmed $6.2 million in punitive damages against A. H. Robins Company to a woman who used its Dalkon Shield contraceptive device and had to have a hysterectomy. With interest added, the penalty came to nearly $9 million.
- A Kansas jury ordered Lederle Laboratories of Wayne, New Jersey, to pay $8 million in punitive damages for injuries resulting from the use of Lederle's oral polio vaccine.

**Net Recovery to the Plaintiff.** The dimensions of the punitive-damage problem affect what lawyers and plaintiffs receive, as shown in Table 11.1. The table underscores not only the fact that punitive-damage awards vary widely but that net recovery to the plaintiff is sometimes less than the adjudged actual loss; moreover, attorney fees, despite the complexities of the four cases, were consistent—a third of the total award. What prevails is a lawsuit lottery in which only the lawyers can win.[1]

**The Judge's Power.** In looking at the judge's power to change punitive damages awarded by juries, two Kansas cases are relevant. In the spring of 1985 a federal jury awarded $10 million to the estate of Betty O'Gilvee, a 21-year-old woman who died of toxic shock syndrome after using a tampon manufactured by International Playtex, a subsidiary of Beatrice Companies. On March 24, 1985, U.S. District Judge Patrick F. Kelly reduced the jury-awarded punitive damages from $10 million to $1.35 million after Playtex took tampons off the market. Kelly had made plain his willingness to consider reducing the jury's verdict if the tampons were taken off the market (which International Playtex did) and to admit that its product was dangerous (which the company did not do). While denying that its tampons

### Table 11.1  Net Recovery of the Plaintiff in Four Cases

**Libel Case**

| | |
|---|---|
| $6,700,000 | Adjudged actual damages (loss of business) |
| 2,500,000 | Punitive damages |
| $9,200,000 | Total |
| −3,066,666 | Attorney's fee |
| −   50,000 | Costs |
| $6,083,334 | Net recovery; $616,666 less than the plaintiff's actual loss |

**Medical Malpractice Case**

| | |
|---|---|
| $1,000,000 | Adjudged actual damages |
| 1,000,000 | Punitive damages |
| $2,000,000 | Total |
| −  666,666 | Attorney's fee |
| −   10,000 | Costs |
| $1,323,334 | Net recovery; $323,334 more than the plaintiff's actual loss |

**Product Liability Case A**

| | |
|---|---|
| $247,000 | Lost salary, medical expenses, money loss |
|   50,000 | Pain and suffering judgment |
| $297,000 | Total |
| −  99,000 | Attorney's fee |
| −   1,000 | Costs |
| $197,000 | Net recovery; $100,000 less than the plaintiff's actual loss |

**Product Liability Case B**

| | |
|---|---|
| $  45,000 | Actual financial loss |
|   50,000 | Pain and suffering judgment |
|  250,000 | Punitive damages |
| $345,000 | Total |
| −115,000 | Attorney's fee |
| −   3,000 | Costs |
| $227,000 | Net recovery; $132,000 more than the plaintiff's actual loss |

---

caused toxic shock syndrome, Playtex said that the judge's offer was one of several factors that led to its decision for a "voluntary" recall. The previous year, in a Wichita case involving General Host and its American Salt division, Judge Frank G. Theis awarded $3.1 million in actual damages and $10 million in punitive damages to a group of farmers whose ground water had been polluted. But Theis said he would consider reducing the punitive-damage award if the company took steps to clean up the affected area.

These two actions have triggered sharp debate between (1) those who felt that judges had a clear responsibility to control verdicts and (2) those who thought that by so doing the plaintiff was unfairly disadvantaged. In the latter view, trials are litigated on the basis that the most at stake was a particular amount of damages, not whether a particular product line should be discontinued.[2] Kelly admitted that he had no authority to make the adjustments, and that there were no legal precedents for so doing, but that he acted nonetheless because he thought it was right.[3] In the judge's analysis, there was no inherent reason to justify placing jury decisions above bench decisions.

These different opinions illustrate how utilitarians and deontologists would approach the problem. The former would support the judge's intervention in jury awards on grounds that such interventions promote the greater good for society; deontologists, on the other hand, feel that, when 12 disinterested jurors had determined what was fair restitution, the judge's intervention is actually judicial interference. People who received less than their due were harmed.

## *Ethical Question*

- Was justice served better by Judge Kelly's award than by the jury's decision?

## *The Constitutional Question*

Obscured in the debate is another, and possibly more important, point, namely, the primary purpose of punitive damages. If they exist to correct a public problem, why should private citizens and their lawyers walk away with the money? The plaintiff is compensated for loss and the lawyer compensated for work. Because neither was primarily concerned with a public problem, the punitive-damage awards are simply add-ons that properly belong to the public.[4] This is a problem of social justice. It is also a constitutional problem. One irate partisan wrote:

> *Just as cancer in the body is a wild, undisciplined growth—an aberration of the normal body processes—so punitive damages are a cancer of the judicial system, an aberration of the normal judicial processes. Although punitive damages have been known in the law for more than two hundred years, it is only recently that they have become a serious problem for insurance carriers, corporations and even some individual defendants. For insurance carriers, punitive damages represent a cost to policyholders that cannot be justified. Under this system, money is being transferred, for basically insubstantial reasons, from people who earned it to people who did not.*
>
> *We are convinced that if the question is put to the United States Supreme Court, punitive damages will be found unconstitutional as presently administered. Purely and simply, punitive damages are punishment. They are in fact punishment without the protection of the U.S. Constitution.*[5]

The Supreme Court, however, seemed reluctant to tackle the problem. Only after considerable hesitation did it agree on December 6, 1988, to hear an appeal by Browning-Ferris Industries challenging a $6 million punitive-damage award. At issue was a jury decision favoring the Kelco Disposal Company, which had sued Browning-Ferris for attempting to monopolize the industrial-waste disposal business in Burlington, Vermont. The jury found that Browning-Ferris had indeed engaged in illegal predatory pricing because, by reducing its prices below costs in 1982, it tried to put Kelco out of business, thus violating both federal and state antitrust laws. On the state-law claims, the jury awarded $51,146 in compensatory damages and $6 million in punitive damages—a hundred times more than the compensatory amount. When a federal appeals court in New York upheld the verdict in April 1986, Browning-Ferris sought certiorari on grounds that the punitive-damages award was excessive and hence a violation of the Eighth Amendment.

In June 1989, the Supreme Court answered the constitutional question only in part when it said in a 7 to 2 decision that the Eighth Amendment was designed to protect people from property harm by the government and not harm by private parties. The opinion, written by Justice Harry Blackmun, traced the history of the clause back to the time of the Magna Carta. Citing numerous legal scholars and ancient English cases, Blackmun concluded that the excessive-fines clause only constrained public authorities, a conclusion not totally pleasing to Justice Sandra Day O'Connor.[6]

The Court did not rule on whether unrestricted punitive damages might run afoul of the due process clause of the Fourteenth Amendment and dodged this issue by saying that, because Browning-Ferris failed to raise its due process argument before either the district court or the court of appeals, and because it made no specific mention of it in its petition for certiorari to the Supreme Court, it would not consider its effects. A straw in the judicial wind may nonetheless be seen in the June 1980 ruling by the Supreme Court of Maine, which said that proof for awarding punitive damages had to go from a preponderance of evidence to a clear and convincing evidence. The shift is significant for a state that has lived in relative peace with a doctrine it had introduced in 1863.

## Defense Tactics

Worried about criminal indictments, staggering fines, tarnished images, and legal uncertainties, executives today consult their lawyers as monarchs once consulted their confessors. But there is a big difference between the two. Kings had a good sense of what penance they faced and needed only to heed the priest's injunction to "sin no more." CEOs have little idea what the penance will be and even are unsure when certain acts are sins. In their dilemmas managers have basically four options: (1) follow the Browning-Ferris example by staying in business and fighting back; (2) leave the troubled product field altogether; (3) declare bankruptcy to minimize the costs, or (4) help to identify the real culprit. The last three merit special comment.

### Withdrawal from the Market

Companies withdraw from the market if the risk of suit threatens financial stability. G. D. Searle, for example, stopped selling IUDs not because they were unsafe but because the firm kept getting sued as an aftermath of the

Dalkon Shield problem. Searle had successfully defended IUDs in eight lawsuits, three brought against the company by the same lawyer, but the suits kept coming and Searle exited. In the 1980s six companies quit making football helmets, and the two that continue in the business (Bike Athletic and MacGregor Sporting Goods) worry that insurance coverage may exceed the cost of manufacturing and force them out.

Merrell Dow's experiences are particularly illustrative. The company took Bendectin (the only drug available to help pregnant women with severe nausea) off the market, not because the company ever lost a lawsuit or that the drug was found to be dangerous but because of the trial publicity and higher insurance premiums. In 1984 the company had agreed to pay $120 million to settle claims that the drug caused birth defects, despite the publicly stated belief by the FDA that Bendectin was safe and despite victories in two court cases. The company quit because the trials themselves caused an avalanche of new cases with the probability of skyrocketing legal fees. The result, therefore, was that no drug is available for morning sickness.

Because of exits from the market, Merck is now the only manufacturer of the combined measles, mumps, and rubella vaccine; Lederle and Connaught Laboratories are the only companies that sell diphtheria, tetanus, and pertussin vaccine; Lederle is the only company making the oral polio vaccine; and only two manufacturers, both foreign owned, make anesthesia gas machines for hospitals. Companies now bring lawyers into product design, documenting and justifying every decision and putting warning labels on everything about possible misuse. Editorializing on the issue, *The New York Times* correctly noted that the central issue in these cases, causation, remains unresolved.

> *Satisfying the FDA's safety requirements should not absolve a company of liability for unexpected damage caused by its drug. But federal safety review, if properly conducted, ought to count for something. Courts are a necessary forum for second guessing the FDA and resolving scientific uncertainties. But in the case of Bendectin, they did neither. With Bendectin (and Agent Orange), the law has made a devastation and called it a settlement.*[7]

Fairness, however, requires an addendum. In highly sensitive cases, Congress (and state legislatures) seek to pass laws that offend as few influential people as possible. Tough choices are avoided and the consequence is that courts and regulatory agencies have to "bite the bullet" and "take the heat" of public criticism. And while this goes on, some companies try to avoid the heat by taking the bankruptcy route.

## *Bankruptcy*

In ancient times, bankruptcy laws were harsh on debtors. Prior to the adoption of early Roman laws, a debtor who could not pay was either killed, enslaved, imprisoned, or exiled; bankruptcy law in Italian society existed not to relieve the debtor but to help creditors to collect. A similar philosophy prevailed when Henry VIII ordained bankruptcy laws for England in 1543.

Although the English later permitted modifications to help honest debtors avoid imprisonment, most debtors were still severely punished by having their benches or trading places destroyed—*banca rotta*.

In the history of bankruptcy the most famous—or infamous—case of the 20th century involved the Johns Manville Company, the major manufacturer of asbestos products. A fibrous mineral, asbestos is an excellent insulator widely used in cement products, brake linings, sewer pipes, protective gloves, and a number of roofing and flooring products. Unlike drug compounds, which are designed and made by humans, asbestos is found directly in nature itself. Romans used woven asbestos to make napkins that were dry cleaned by being thrown in the fire; asbestos outerwear, used to prevent damage from fires, was worn during the early 1800s; building codes required the use of asbestos in spaces where there was serious danger of fires.

Because the facts about asbestos are disputed, ethical judgments do not come easily. That constant exposure to high levels of asbestos causes serious health problems is beyond debate, but the key variables are "constant" and "high levels." A World Health Organization study of 1986 reported that, for the general population, the risks of mesothelioma attributed to asbestos cannot be quantified.[8] Some researchers became convinced that the populace's fears had reached a hysterical level because the public did not understand that asbestos, instead of being a single product, is a family of six different chemicals, each of which poses different health hazards.[9] Lung tumors in people exposed to asbestos, for example, are rare in nonsmokers. Yet asbestos and lung cancer have become almost synonymous in the public mind.[10]

No one denies that inhaling asbestos fibers could lead to asbestosis—a clogging and scarring of the lungs that can result in impaired breathing—or to mesothelioma, which is a fatal cancer of the lining of the chest and abdomen. And while most uses of asbestos are banned today, it is everywhere. Some 30 million tons of the fibrous mineral were mixed into plaster to insulate walls during the past hundred years. When the material ages and begins to crumble, the tiny particles that cause lung cancer and other respiratory diseases are released into the air. Asbestos-related diseases often take 15 to 40 years between exposure and manifestation. Most deaths occur in patients over age 60.

Not until 1964 was the public alerted to the product's dangers by Irving Selikoff of New York's Mount Sinai Medical Center; however, as early as 1920 the first signs of respiratory disease related to asbestos appeared. In 1938 a study of asbestos-related respiratory diseases, published by the U.S. Public Health Service, indicated what were unacceptable levels of exposure; later studies led to the formation of the National Institute of Occupational Safety and Health (NIOSH), which permitted only one-fifth as much exposure as was allowed by previous studies. Approximately a million workers have been exposed to asbestos fibers in the past 45 years, with many being initially endangered during World War II in government-run shipyards. Like many crises of the type, conclusive evidence is hard to come by.

School children have been given special attention. In 1980 Congress enacted the Asbestos School Hazard Detection and Control Act, which required public and private schools to inspect buildings and to report findings of flaking asbestos and other hazards to federal authorities. Parents and school boards were expected to take protective action. However, Congress provided no funds for inspections or cleanup and the majority of the nation's schools have yet to complete the necessary tests.[11] While Congress claimed that no funds had been requested to implement the legislation, the EPA in 1986 fined a New Hampshire school $24,000 for not reporting asbestos in its buildings.

At the Mount Sinai School of Medicine, Dr. William J. Nicholson concluded that 75 to 90 deaths a year will result from exposure to asbestos in schools. So there is "suit" trouble for the school systems of America because many school districts, strapped for money, have elected to ignore the removal problem. One need not tarry long over the agonizing moral problem school boards face when the hour of reckoning arrives.

Anxieties continued to grow over the potential threat to 36 million students. Cleanup costs are extremely expensive—$100,000 for a single medium-sized building and over $3 billion (possibly $6 billion) nationwide. A similar program for all public and commercial buildings could, estimated the EPA, cost $51 billion. Local school districts have carried the cost burden (Maine and Oklahoma were the only states to assume major costs); asbestos dangles from cafeteria ceilings and may be inches deep in attics. Horror stories of children throwing pencils and pens at the ceiling to watch it snow led critics to blame Congress itself for creating alarm over "friable" asbestos.[12] The reasons for the original installation in schools between 1940 and 1965 were to insulate pipes and ceilings and to deaden sound; but, say critics, more than sound will be deadened.

Asbestos removal (possibly more dangerous than any other form of exposure) has been complicated by human error and human greed. Removal is difficult and the federal government has issued reams of complicated cleanup rules: insulation must be sprayed with water and stashed in airtight containers; special air-circulating machines are recommended; workers must don masks and gear that look like space suits. But removals have not always followed the federal guidelines. In Philadelphia, just across the street from the EPA office, workers had collected asbestos debris with brooms, much as a garage would be cleaned; in another case, eight teenagers were discovered removing asbestos with their bare hands in an abandoned school that was being converted into a condominium in Salem, Massachusetts. When the Justice Department filed suit against the developer, Granite Development, company officials said they did not realize that asbestos was in the school. Neither did the youths employed to remove it. To error must be added evil. The EPA, for example, discovered a Texas contractor who hired dozens of homeless street people who were not told of the danger to remove asbestos from a San Antonio hotel;[13] in Manhattan, a non-English-speaking porter was told to remove the material from pipes, which he did with his bare hands.

At the center of the storm was Johns Manville, which elected to file for bankruptcy in 1982. Manville's attorneys were charging the company some $2 million a month, which included more than half the average $40,000 it cost the company to dispose of each case. Shortly thereafter, bankruptcy lawyers in six firms demanded more than $2 million in fees and expenses to cover costs incurred between the August 26 filing date and December 31; five other firms handling general litigation during that period were seeking more than $1 million. A further factor in the company's decision was the behavior of its insurers, who asked hard legal and ethical questions. Did coverage begin when a victim was first exposed to asbestos? Or at the manifestation of the disease? Were insurers obligated to pay for the legal defense of a suit even after the policy's liability limits had been exceeded? The stakes were high because Manville had demanded $600 million from the insurers and the proposed settlement from its three major insurers was about half that amount.

Others became involved. Labor leaders have been disturbed by alleged tardiness on the part of government enforcement agencies. Because acquiring the appropriate technical data had been a major problem, it was not until November 1985 that OSHA acted by issuing new emergency standards on workplace exposure—its first such action since 1978. Unions were moderately pleased; industry was dismayed. The predictable result was another round of suits against both government and businesses.

Partisan politicking was another by-product of the asbestos controversy. A 1985 report prepared by the Democratic-controlled House Subcommittee on Oversight and Investigations said that Republicans had deliberately obstructed proposed rules that would ban some asbestos products completely and gradually eliminate most others over a ten-year period. Republican legislators countered that the attack was unjustified and that the OMB itself, though part of a Republican administration, was engaging in a pervasive pattern of intrusion into the rule-making authority granted to federal agencies by Congress. Further irony was added when it was discovered that Democratic Senator Gary Hart of Colorado had introduced a bill to transfer the cost burden of Johns Manville, the Colorado-based company, to the taxpayers.

If the scientific evidence divided the engineering and medical experts, and if the government mechanisms for meeting the asbestos danger were caught in a political quagmire, there was no doubt about Manville's situation. It was far from broke ($2 billion in assets and a favorable cash flow) yet it feared that claims could break the company. Facing such facts and fears, management decided to file for bankruptcy. W. T. Stephens, Manville's CEO, said that when he dived into one of the biggest messes in corporate America he learned that "the use of Chapter 11 to deal with the Manville situation was right and ethical," but "that we in industry must completely change the way we approach product safety and product liability. No one has the right to sell a product that can harm someone else and not warn them about that risk. Stated very simply, the days of 'let the buyer beware' are over. Today, it is 'let the seller beware,' and it's as it should be."[14] But an attorney for one of the plaintiffs, Charles O'Reilly, angrily declared: "Trying to dismiss claims for people who don't even know they are sick is a reprehensible way to act."[15]

It was not the filing for bankruptcy that alone unsettled moral sensibilities. Some 60 years ago (in 1933, to be precise) the company had settled with 11 workers who claimed that they had contracted asbestosis for less than $3000 apiece, with a guarantee from their lawyer that they would never sue again. The directors knew the danger; in 1948 they were more precisely informed by their own medical director, who reported a high incidence of asbestosis and recommended that those afflicted not be told so they could live and work in peace. The company would also have the benefit of their many years of experience.

Before attempting to answer questions regarding the ethics of bankruptcy, it is necessary to examine what the law means.[16] Creditors generally share in assets of the estate ratably in accordance with the value of their nonbankruptcy entitlements. Bankruptcy is the way to constrain them and others from promoting their individual interests to the disadvantage of other claimants. Bankruptcy rules should, therefore, be viewed as a way to develop a system that rational creditors would agree to privately—the so-called credits'-bargain theory. The purpose is to keep the size of the asset pool as large as possible. Slicing the asset pool is a function of bankruptcy, but prioritizing the claims is not inherently a bankruptcy function.

The current system of creditor priorities is laid out in the Uniform Commercial Code, which divides creditors into those with secured claims and those with unsecured claims. Secured claims are protected by a lien on the property of the estate whereas unsecured claims are not. The priority system places creditors first in line who have loaned money for the purchase of a specific asset, which then secured repayment of the loan. Unsecured interests are general creditors who have no such security interest but are entitled to payment—such as suppliers or advertising agencies. Finally, there is the first-in-time, first-in-right principle, which rules that early interests have priority over later interests in the same category. Because by definition a bankrupt firm does not have sufficient assets to cover its debts, the secured interests usually receive full payment while unsecured interests (including tort claimants) usually receive partial payment or none at all. The asbestos victims are, of course, tort claimants.

The theory behind the bankruptcy system thus assumes that credit agreements are based on a consensus among those who have knowledge of the system. This assumption, however, is not true for tort claimants, who are at the lowest level of priority. Some basic goals of tort law are to compensate injured parties, to allocate costs of injury to the one best able to bear them (those with deep pockets), and to prevent future harm by promoting socially beneficial conduct. That these goals are realized is essential to justice. In the Manville case none was.

A widely held belief is that insurance will compensate the tort claimants for their injuries but, as demonstrated in the Manville case, this is simply not true. A federal bailout program would not be effective either, because it would remove incentives for companies to be careful and it would treat individuals differently because of political assessments of the importance of industries. A superfund (requiring industry-wide participation in paying victims' costs) would also not link payment to a specific firm's behavior because it, too, would reduce the firm's incentive to take precautionary measures.

One way to resolve the dilemma is to give tort claimants a status equal to secured creditors—or even above the secured creditors. If tort victims were given equal status with secured creditors, the priority between the two would be based on the first-in-time, first-in-right principle. This is, however, morally undesirable because victims have no control over the timing of their claims; they know only when the injury appeared, not when the injury occurred. This is especially important given the long latency period for asbestos-related diseases.

Changing the status to one of super-priority is therefore the preferred alternative, because it induces creditors to monitor closely the activities of the firm in terms of necessary precautionary measures, price increases to cover these costs, and insurance to cover the claims. Although the full range of facts in this complicated case cannot be exposed, enough information has been given to warrant raising several questions.

## Ethical Questions

- Because Manville hoped to derive substantial benefits by following the bankruptcy course, did its sidestepping of claims violate the rights of others?
- Was Manville the only culprit in the asbestos story?
- Because large corporations affect the lives and fortunes of millions, is corporate survival the organization's first ethical responsibility?[17]

One way to judge Manville's behavior from a moral perspective is to ask whether the firm acted in bad faith when it sought relief through bankruptcy. Traditionally, four types of cases can be dismissed because of bad faith; they involve attempts (1) to deceive the court, (2) to settle internal organizational disputes, (3) to pretend there is a reasonable chance for rehabilitation, or (4) to hinder or delay payments to harmed claimants. Manville does not appear to have violated the first three criteria. Though asbestos claimants charged that Manville tried to deceive the court, their claims remain unproven; the filings are clearly necessary because of external, not internal, problems; successful reorganization is definitely feasible and not a pretense.

The relevance of the fourth criterion (to avoid payments in tort cases) is more debatable. Asbestos victims claim that the intent of the filings was to hinder or delay payments. But courts have always been reluctant to use this norm unless delay appears to be the *sole* reason for the filing; moreover, the purpose of bankruptcy laws is to protect debtors who are unable to meet their liabilities. The real problem, therefore, is the priority in which the assets of the firm are distributed to claimants.

Moralists, approaching the questions from deontological or utilitarian perspectives, reason along these lines. Deontologists, emphasizing the duty to do no harm, could say that Manville harmed not once but twice by knowing of the danger for a long time and by refusing to compensate the first victims adequately. Manville's special moral obligations to its employees were independent of the general good. Deontologists would therefore look unfavorably on Manville's action. Utilitarians, stressing the consequences of Manville's behavior, *might* defend the company on grounds that corporate survival is good for stockholders, for employees, and for society. Letting an important company go broke is therefore counterproductive. But utilitarians might hedge their bets in light of the claim by company managers that they never saw anything wrong in using asbestos—which is highly implausible.

A definitive ethical judgment on Manville itself is hard to make because (1) the victims' illness appeared years after the first exposure to asbestos, during which time other practices, such as smoking, may have been the primary factor; (2) the law of bankruptcy is stacked against tort claimants; (3) the company has every right to use the law in its own defense; (4) the law of torts allows punitive damages that, in the aggregate, could bankrupt the company; and (5) society itself is unlikely to provide any high-level bailout as it did in the Chrysler case, Hurricane Hugo, and the California earthquake of 1989. On balance, however, Manville will not be present for the choir's rendition of the old song, "When the Saints Come Marching In."

## *Shifting the Blame*

Aware of the seemingly never-ending procession of tort cases, corporate executives assumed a sour mood—and for good reason. As courts became clogged with complex cases, long queues of importunate claimants formed. Everybody blamed somebody else: judges and juries were blamed; government agencies like OSHA and EPA were blamed; lawyers and insurance companies were blamed; corporations were blamed. A dog-eat-dog mentality spread within business itself. To illustrate, in 1986, when W. R. Grace was convicted of polluting the drinking wells in Woburn, Massachusetts, it hired high-priced lawyers to defend it. After losing the case, Grace demanded that its three major insurers (Maryland Casualty, Continental Casualty, and Hartford Insurance Company) pay the $2.5 million assessed against it. Insurance companies had good reason to fear the making of a precedent because at least 45 lawsuits had been filed between 1982 and 1985 by industrial companies in efforts to force insurers to pay legal expenses.

A basic problem for insurers is that many of the liability policies on which today's cases are based were written as much as 40 years ago when few could foresee that scientific advances would bring harmful effects from commonly used substances, that illnesses would surface after years of incubation, that the public would develop a penchant for litigating, and that court rulings would greatly change the meaning of liability. Insurance companies limit their liability to "sudden and accidental" pollution and to damage done to a neighbor's property, contending that their policies do not cover cleanup and legal costs.

**The Lawyer-Insurer Dogfight.** The lawyer-insurer game played earlier in California, when each side blamed the other for the liability crisis, was later played on the national canvas. It was a bitter battle worth telling even though some of the details are similar to the California experience. The American Bar Association's 1986 report said that the liability insurance crisis was based on "anecdotes and horror stories" rather than the facts. Although punitive awards in excess of $1 million had generated tremendous publicity, the median award in such decisions was less than $50,000. Stephen Daniels, a sociology professor at Northwestern University who conducted the study on which the lawyers based this claim, cautioned that his research should be regarded as preliminary; nevertheless, the lawyers seized upon its findings to bolster their defense—evidently on the theory that there was relatively little need to worry about minor aches and pains caused by legal costs. Another study by the National Center for State Courts found that civil cases stemming from torts, contracts, property, and small-claims disputes had actually declined by more than 10 percent since 1981. And while it was true that there were more million-dollar awards than ever, more than two-thirds of the "winners" had suffered permanent paralysis, brain damage, amputations, or death. Insurers failed to mention these facts.

The lawyers received support from *The New York Times* in a 1986 editorial:

> *Liability insurance has a 'long tail'—the years of legal proceedings between a loss and ultimate payment of damages leaves insurers with huge cash reserves for investments in financial markets. When interest rates or stock prices were high, insurers had an incentive to pile up cash by selling coverage at what looked like bargain rates, confident that investment profits would more than cover any losses on claims. When financial markets cooled off, the insurers found that reduced investment profits required them to raise premiums and drop riskier types of coverage altogether. As interest rates soared in the late 1970s, the insurers cast a wide net for cash. In the 1982 slump, when interest rates plunged, they should have raised rates to cover future obligations but they were still fat with cash. Now they are rushing belatedly to drop high-risk customers.*[18]

Driven to the ramparts by the lawyers' attack, insurers admitted that, although investment income traditionally had more than made up for losses on policies, unforeseen changes had suddenly occurred. In 1982, for example, the industry suffered an underwriting loss of $10.4 billion—about 64 percent greater than the $6.35 billion loss suffered in 1981. Insurance leaders

CHAPTER ELEVEN  Tort-Related Issues    345

saw ominous problems in the figures. The underwriting loss ratio was 110, meaning that for every $100 collected in premiums, $110 was paid out for claims and expenses. Worse was the fact that, with declining interest rates, insurance companies garnered considerably less investment income that could offset their underwriting losses.

The changing interest rates hit the industry just at the time when it was contending with major liability claims. Asbestos claims alone could run from $4 to $10 billion. Love Canal and related disposal sites claims have been estimated at $10 billion. Because insurers cannot legally charge customers higher premiums to make up for past claims, the prospect that they might have to pay huge sums in such cases caused them to reassess their financial responsibilities and adjust their premiums accordingly. To insurers the prime culprits are overzealous lawyers whose earnings depend heavily on contingency fees.

**The Insured's Costs.**   Business itself has tended to say to both lawyers and insurers, "A plague on both your houses." But public opinion may be shifting more against the legal profession if Edward Court is representative. Court, who started his own business in 1969, wrote:

*In less than three years, my product liability insurance has risen from $6,000 to $40,000 per year. And the $40,000 this year buys only one-tenth of the coverage I had three years ago. For the past nineteen years, I have built my security gate manufacturing and installation business to a point where it now employs forty-five people. All I have worked for—and the jobs of my employees—could be lost in one single judgment in which I believe is a "lawsuit lottery" for the money-grabbing plaintiffs and attorneys. Like playing Russian roulette, every gate I install raises the odds against my company. And the most frustrating part of this gamble is that a judgment against me may have little or nothing to do with the quality or performance of my product. At first, I felt a lot of resentment towards the insurance industry. My feeling was that they had created another sort of "gas embargo" for the purpose of raising my premium rates while reducing my coverage. As time went on and my understanding of the problem grew, I realized that for the most part, insurance companies were reflecting their cost of doing business today. I found that most insurance companies were not willing to quote me product liability and that many of them were getting out of the product liability field altogether. That is not the kind of response you see if there is money to be made....*

*The amount of money paid out, just in California, by insurance companies in 1984 on behalf of their insured was $1,552,744,000. Over one billion dollars of that amount was paid not to fix a broken arm or leg, but for noneconomic damages; mostly pain and suffering. Legislation like Proposition 51 in Cal-*

*ifornia will help but, unfortunately, it does not put any limit on the amount of noneconomic damages that can be awarded....*

*There are some very powerful interests on the receiving end of the dollars spent for insurance: plaintiffs' attorneys (who get between 30 percent and 50 percent of every award given), medical providers, defendants' attorneys, and professional witnesses to name a few. If the cost of our insurance is to be reduced, we will be taking those dollars away from these special interest groups. And that's not going to be easy. We need reforms limiting liability.... We need reforms to control the many greedy attorneys and the many greedy so-called victims who see dollar signs every time someone has an accident.*[19]

As the battle between lawyers and insurers raged, liability insurance costs rose astronomically and some could not get any insurance at all. The Piper Company paid $75,000 insurance for each plane it manufactured, more than the total manufacturing costs for its smaller planes; the Maryland town of Skyesville received a liability insurance increase of 700 percent in one year; more than 500 Ohio schools had their liability insurance canceled. Frustrated by insurers, people vent anger on them and on lawyers when litigants are forced to dole out large sums of money to counsel. Ultimate costs are incalculable. Taxpayers pay more when dockets are crowded; the economy suffers when scarce resources are diverted into essentially nonproductive uses; and public confidence in the judicial system erodes when different courts reach different conclusions in similar situations.

As insurance costs have skyrocketed, so, too, have legal costs. The Rand Institute for Civil Justice found that plaintiffs in asbestos-related suits alone netted only 37 cents on every dollar spent by all parties in cases closed over the past decade. The remainder was spent on litigation costs by both plaintiffs and defendants. The Rand study also reported that the average total compensation claim paid by all defendants and their insurers was about $60,000 each and total defense litigation expenses were an additional $35,000 per claim. Of the one billion dollars expended up to 1982, two-thirds was paid by insurers and one-third by defendants; plaintiffs used 41 percent of the compensation they received to pay for their own litigation expenses.

Taxpayers were also hard hit by the flurry of legal activity. Some 661,000 tort cases had been filed in state courts of general jurisdiction in 1980 alone at an estimated expenditure of $264 million. This excluded cases filed in small claims courts and in most municipal courts. With 32,315 U.S. district court tort filings in 1980, the annual federal expenditure was an estimated $56 million—yielding a total of $320 million. However, government expenditures were only a small fraction of the total costs of tort cases because other private costs, which account for the majority of the total costs, included plaintiff and defense attorneys' fees, witness fees, investigative work, and other costs.

In short, the liability crisis raised so many complex ethical issues—for governments and businesses, for lawyers and doctors, for insurers and public-interest groups—that it was difficult to identify heroes and villains. But there was growing consensus that changes had to be made.

## Institutional Reform

Reform is easier said than done—a truism that came brutally home to Montana legislators in 1986. Efforts in that state to resolve the tort-liability "crisis" ended in a bitter partisan deadlock over how to amend the Montana constitution. Business and professional interests lobbied for caps on private liability, contending that they and municipalities faced the same problem, namely, unaffordable (or even unavailable) insurance and that the problem itself was created by the state court's liberal development of tort law, which greatly expanded the covenant of good faith and fair dealing. On the other side was the Montana Trial Lawyers Association, which argued that limits would strip away fundamental civil rights.

Shortly before the Montana deadlock the federal government had also begun to move. In 1985 the Reagan administration and the American Bar Association appointed committees to review tort reform—a move so worrisome to the Association of Trial Lawyers that it appointed its own "reform" commission. However, the ABA itself was not above suspicion because its first commission (chaired by former U.S. Attorney General Griffin Bell) had issued a thousand-page report that defended the contingency-fee system and rejected the notion of a federal products-liability cap. It did endorse a "discovery rule" statute of limitations for toxic-tort cases. The committee also suggested that judges be more assertive in throwing out frivolous tort cases and provide closer reasoning about why they impose punitive damages.[20] It was hoped by many that the new ABA panel would take a more comprehensive view of the public's need. It did not.

Congress was also aroused and first signs of its interest appeared in 1983 when separate bills were proposed by Representative Norman Shumway of California and by Senator Robert Kasten of Wisconsin. Both bills would have a jury determine whether punitive damages should be awarded but would have the judge determine the actual amount. The bills were designed to prevent runaway jury verdicts; in addition, both bills strictly defined "reckless disregard" for consumer safety by the manufacturer and required plaintiffs to prove that the manufacturer acted in an irresponsible manner. States like Minnesota and Wisconsin had already required plaintiffs to show conclusively that the defendant was guilty of reckless conduct before punitive damages could be awarded. Moving through this haze-maze is difficult but it is obvious that tort law has become in too many cases a mad tea party to which justice has not been invited.[21] For example, Howard Specter, president of the Association of Trial Lawyers in America, spoke eloquently of the public interest while holding steadfast to his association's own private interests.[22]

## Ethical Input

Judicial and ethical reasoning work from two common premises: (1) conflicts between individuals and groups are as natural to humans as night and day are to nature and (2) peaceful conflict resolution continues only so long as society believes that the chance of getting justice is open to everyone. Because the gap between premise and policy is so wide, ethicists try to expound on the meaning of right and wrong in the tort world by venturing to suggest guidelines that, in a few cases, depart from current legal definitions and practices. These guidelines include the following:

- Individuals and organizations are not morally responsible for harm they cause others provided they intended no harm and provided, further, that they took all reasonable measures to protect consumers from unintended harm.
- Innocent individuals who have been hurt by others deserve sufficient compensation to make them economically whole again. This demands a societal response.
- Punitive damage is society's way to deter wrong doing and money derived therefrom should go back to society, not to individuals.[23]
- Size of awards should be suggested by experts, but determined by jurors or judges. To transfer the decision to experts simply relieves society's agents from making the hard choices.
- Conflicts should be resolved expeditiously. Delaying tactics used to force concessions are unethical.
- Lawyers should be paid for services rendered, not according to percentages of the total award.[24] Clients who feel the fees are excessive should be able to have the presiding judge resolve the issue.
- Or, conversely, lawyers should bid on cases much as contractors bid on building projects. Cost overruns would have to be justified.
- Insurers should reduce rates in rough proportion to reduced litigation and settlement costs.
- Going to court should be the last, not the first, recourse.[25]

A variation on the foregoing was made by *Forbes'* editors, who offered the following ten commandments:

1. Thou shalt not find parties liable who did not cause the harm done.
2. Thou shalt not permit joint and several liability judgments that force a marginally responsible defendant to pay the entire claim.
3. Thou shalt strongly encourage litigants to seek alternative dispute forums to the courts.
4. Thou shalt penalize parties who pointlessly force cases into lengthy court wrangles. [Note: Because this could lead to more wrangling over whether the first wrangle was really pointless, tight procedural rules are required.]

5. Thou shalt make federal statutes which clearly define the limits of product liability.
6. Thou shalt keep thy regulators watchful of insurance companies.
7. Thou shalt forbid punitive damages except in cases of gross negligence.
8. Thou shalt encourage structured settlements that disburse payments over time.
9. Thou shalt not covet expert witnesses who are not truly expert.
10. Thou shalt honor judges who control abusive discovery proceedings. [Note: This is not easily achievable because judges rarely, if ever, do so.][26]

In all the foregoing, trade-offs are required. But the burden of proof should be on naysayers to the reform effort. And in all discussions over institutional change looms the one question on which ultimate answers must be based: What is the value of a human life?

## Life's Monetary Worth

The most difficult of all tort issues relates to the financial value of a human life. Various cultures have defined that value differently. The Chinese, for example, disposed of female babies more easily than male infants; primogeniture in Western Europe gave priority to men over women; early qualifications in the United States denied women their property rights. So far as business was concerned, the history of life insurance is most apposite. Until the late 19th century, most Americans deemed it immoral to put a price on a human life and stories circulated about widows refusing to take benefits because they were "blood money." That attitude prevails even today in Spain and some countries within the Spanish tradition. The essential question—what is human life worth?—has led to intensive searches. Economists and lawyers have taken the lead but ethicists show growing interest.

### *Economic Theories*

Economists have disagreed over the exact monetary value of a human life, but they have reached rather substantive agreement on reasons for such calculations. No better rationale has been provided than that given in 1924 by the father of life insurance education, Solomon Huebner, of the Wharton School. In a keynote speech to the National Association of Life Underwriters that is worth extensive quote, Huebner declared:

> *In our economic life only two types of values exist, namely, human life and property values. The life values consist of the character, industry, technical and managerial ability, power of initiative, and judgment of individuals. They have heretofore been regarded as intangible, economically indefinite, and difficult if not impossible of scientific treatment. The property values comprise land, buildings, machinery and equipment, raw materials, finished goods,*

*and business goodwill. Being tangible in character, and thus more easily comprehended than the life values, these material things have for years been regarded as capable of scientific organization and management. They are therefore subjected to appraisal.... But with lessons so admirably evolved in the field of property values and with this information to guide us, may we not ask why life values should not be treated equally scientifically and be made equally tangible and definite? Is it not ridiculous for a human being to make himself more and more valuable all the time and then all of a sudden, just when that value is greatest to his business and his family, have it disappear entirely because of death or disability? Does it seem reasonable that life values should be treated thus carelessly, especially since we owe a duty to others— to family and business associates—when the lessons of foresight, so fully prepared in connection with property values, are before us for imitation?*

*The most important new development in economic thought will be the recognition of the economic value of human life. I confidently believe that the time is not far distant when, in wholesale fashion, we shall apply to the economic organization, management, and conservation of life values the same scientific treatment that we now use in connection with property.... Scientific treatment of life values is justified because of their monetary importance in our economic affairs. Human life values—the factors of personal skill, industry, judgment, and driving force, that mean so much to business success—greatly exceed in importance all property values. These personal factors are, after all, the real source of all other economic values. Were it not for them, there would be no property values. Were I called upon to make an estimate of life values in the United States, based on the current earning capacity of our adult population, capitalized at an ordinary rate of interest, I would place the total valuation at not less than six to eight times the aggregate of the nation's material wealth.*[27]

Huebner's approach was tinctured with the so-called *human-capital* approach used by economists. The theory assumed that life's monetary value was worth whatever that person's expected lifetime earnings would be. Calculations done in 1975 yielded life values of roughly $500,000 in today's prices for an American male worker in his late twenties; for a woman, the estimate was $350,000. Earnings potential was the key variable. The formula, however, came under sharp attack from those who said it was flawed (a) by being unidimensional and (b) by its implication that nonworkers and workers like housewives had no economic value.

An alternative to the human-capital theory was the *willingness-to-pay* approach proposed in 1968 by Thomas Schelling of Harvard.[28] In this model, life's monetary worth is what a person would demand for accepting a small risk of death or, alternatively, the payments he or she would willingly make to reduce the risk. To explain his model, Schelling said we should imagine that individuals are invited to join a group of 10,000 persons, one of whom would be randomly selected for execution. If an individual was willing to pay $200 for insurance, then that person estimated his or her life to be worth $2 million (10,000 times $200). This does not, of course, mean that the person would accept certain execution. In another Schelling scenario individuals were forced to play Russian roulette but they had the right to buy back various numbers of bullets for a price, with the price and odds again dictating a life value. The offered price became the base number on which the life was valued.

Insurance experts are predictably skeptical of results based on survey data, arguing that when people fill out questionnaires, they do not think deeply or answer truthfully questions on how they would behave in real situations; therefore, efforts have been made to derive life values from people's actual behavior. Paul Portney of the Resources for the Future, a Washington-based think tank, published a study in 1981 that derived values from a person's willingness to pay extra for homes in areas with little pollution. Portney reached a life value of around $600,000 to $900,000. Today the price would be much higher.

Federal regulators came from still another direction. To them the data that determine human value should be derived from labor-market studies on the interaction between job safety and pay. The data on workers have some built-in advantages, reflecting as they do the judgments and preferences of an enormous number of Americans who are knowledgeable about pay-safety trade-offs. W. Kip Viscusi of Northwestern University made this point in a 1983 study commissioned by OSHA. Armed with such data one might assume that government agencies involved in assessing life's value would have rather similar conclusions. The facts are different. OSHA's assessment of a life value had a whopping spread: from $2 to $5 million. The EPA's range was between $1 to $72 million. The FAA's number was $650,000.

That controversy should attend every formula-making effort is understandable because the practical implications in court cases are so significant. For example, during the asbestos crisis, a congressional committee attacked OMB for making recommendations that estimates of the costs and benefits of regulating asbestos should apply a discount on the value of a human life for the years it takes for cancer to develop. OMB officials insisted that the practice of discounting reflected the amount of time it takes to get a return from money spent now to protect lives; therefore, discounting allowed available resources to be used more rationally to save more lives. But Congress attacked the agency's discounting theory as morally repugnant. To the legislators the plan, if widely adopted, would thwart regulation of many toxic substances through the application of cost-benefit criteria. The result was that the nation would fail to protect future generations from many serious chemical hazards.

Perhaps managers themselves will determine the price of a worker's life because, ultimately, the monetary value of a human life will depend on a broad range of management decisions, including the problems of wrestling with vexatious questions about, for example, how much should be spent to make products and the workplace safer, how much employees should be paid, and what benefits are due when injuries occur. In a world in which some level of risk is inevitable, but some higher level of risk is unacceptable, management decisions will gradually approach the level that Americans view as reasonable.

## *Legal Theory*

Not to be outdone by economists, lawyers have added their estimates of an individual's life value by adding to the economic estimate a hedonic calculus, that is, a person's capacity for pleasure and joy. Its kinship to the principle that punitive damages are appropriate when the victim can demonstrate this or has mental anguish or damage to reputation is evident. The hedonic principle was first enunciated in 1984 when a federal jury in Chicago awarded $850,000 in hedonic damages to the family of a 19-year-old man killed by a policeman in 1979. The damages, which made up more than half of the jury's $1.6 million judgment, marked the first time a jury made an award in a wrongful death case based on data related to the enjoyment of life, rather than on the more traditional principles of future lost earnings or some other form of pecuniary loss. "Very simply, hedonic damages measure the taking away of the pleasure of being alive," said presiding U.S. District Judge George N. Leighton.[29]

It has been calculated that hedonic value ranges from 3 to 30 times more than a person's economic value. But placing dollar signs on one human's capacity for happiness is well-nigh impossible. To illustrate, some proposed life-saving programs have shown that the median cost of saving a life was $50,000 to the Consumer Product Safety Commission, $64,000 to the National Highway Traffic Safety Commission, $2.6 million to the EPA, and $12.1 million to OSHA. The differences suggest that some wild figures are in the cards as courts and companies, legislators and judges, are asked more frequently to apply the hedonic calculus to specific cases.

Notwithstanding the difficulties in fixing a figure, the willingness of the courts to accept a hedonic calculus in determining awards in tort cases strikes many lawyers and judges as a reasonable endeavor. The idea, after all, resonated in Jefferson's pursuit-of-happiness rhetoric in the Declaration of Independence. And long before the political declaration, theologians acknowledged the role and purpose of suffering and happiness in human life.

## *Moral Theory*

If the unimaginable could be imagined (agreement is reached on the monetary value of a single life), theologians and philosophers still feel that more is needed. And the added element is the sacredness of human life. Contemporaries have their own ways of expressing the sacred value of life: helping crash victims in automobile accidents; saving airline pilots and passengers lost at sea; retrieving under gunfire a wounded or dead warrior in battle;

halting work designed to make mines safer in order to mount a rescue mission for a single trapped miner; and supporting individual medical treatment rather than providing more public health research. All of these defy economic sense and, as a consequence, suggest that life has a value that cannot be cashed out exclusively in economic or hedonic terms.[30]

From moral perspectives, evaluating human value begins with the meaning of the word person. Its etymology is instructive. The world may be of Etruscan origin because persons referred to the mask worn by the devotees of the goddess *Phersu*; later, it made its way into the Roman theater, when the mask was fashioned according to the character being portrayed. With a play on words, the Romans called the mask the "persona" (*per sonare*, or to speak through) because it was the mask through which the actor spoke. In the beginning, the "persona" was a visual, acoustic, and dramatic device, but by the time of Cicero in the first century B.C. the word had assumed the meaning of a juridical being with legal rights and duties.[31] These same Romans also began to use the word *corpoia* (from which our early notion of the corporation was derived) in several different ways.[32]

Less evident in the Greco-Roman discussions was appreciation of the intrinsic value of the human person—a question often discussed by early theologians who noted how Old Testament prophets tied faith to justice, and justice to persons. Society was judged especially by the presence—or absence—of fairness in dealing with widows, orphans, and strangers, the marginalized people of the times. The Jew's standing before God depended heavily on the Jew's standing with others, especially with the weak and the oppressed. Christians added the Incarnation to the theological meaning of the word person. In the Old Testament, God made people like unto himself; now God made himself like unto us. This need for association with others is an implicit acceptance of Aristotle's view that persons are social animals.

Building on this theological premise philosophers like Boethius (475–525) began to say (1) that each individual is not only separate from all others but also is independent of the physical home to which it gives life and (2) that, although separate, each is driven to seek association with other individuals in order to fulfill itself.[33] A person is therefore subject to will and to reason. Persons had dignity because they were created like God.

Giving specificity to such terms as human dignity, rights, duties, and community has been a formidable assignment. Knowing, therefore, how the definition of person has been framed for moderns is important if for no other reason than that we are prisoners of our past. In classical economics, for example, a person is the maximizer of self-interest. This view, often attributed to Adam Smith, ignores the Scottish philosopher's insistence that self-interest never justified greed, that market competition worked only when mutual cooperation and coordination existed, and that justice governed all human interactions.

If justice is sovereign, people have moral claims on others—what Americans call "certain unalienable rights." Scholars like John Rawls, Michael Walzer, and Ronald Dworkin have written much on the meaning of justice. Less known are names like Leo XIII (whose famous 1891 encyclical on labor and private property was important in shaping the attitudes of immigrant workers toward unions); and Walter Rauschenbusch (1891-1918), who promulgated the Social Gospel as a reminder to fellow Protestants that American workers were not being treated as individuals with rights, but only as hired hands with muscles. It is an easy step to conclude that, if each person's intrinsic worth is recognized at the workbench, each person's intrinsic worth should be recognized in tort law.

But how does this intrinsic-worth idea add to the debate? Recall that economists calculated a person's monetary value on the basis of potential earnings. Those who were not in the marketplace (children, housewives, ministers) were excluded. Lawyers later introduced the hedonic principle to estimate a person's financial worth on the basis of that individual's capacity for happiness. Emphasis by the economists and the lawyers is on what a person *does* and what a person *enjoys*. Although very important, such concepts can be expanded to include what a person *is*. Moral theory would, therefore, shift American business away from its ideological commitment to individualism toward a more communitarian posture. If human beings fulfill themselves through interactions with others, such interactions are also intended to help other human beings fulfill themselves.

The theory is illustrated by a simple example: Child psychologists have long noticed how the coming of the first child to a couple intensifies the sense of solidarity for the entire family. With time the infant moves from "I" identification ("I want," "give me," and other expressions of a crude ethical egoism) to a concern for others. Without such concern, the individual grows in physical size, but diminishes in moral stature. Adults recognize that viable communities depend on Martin Buber's "I-You" ethic: the self cannot be selfish.[34]

Although he cast them primarily in terms of the individual's relationship to God, Buber made the telling points that all living is a "meeting" with others that is "not exclusively defined by the intellectual life."[35] Meetings are for mutual enrichment. One gets and one gives. From this point it is easy to ask the questions not raised by economists and lawyers: In a tort case, what did the harmed person do for others? What did he or she give? What could the person continue to give if not injured or killed? Specifics can be added to make answers more practical. Did the person serve as a nonpaid member of the local school board? Serve on United Way committees? Help scout troops? Manage Little League teams? Work as a volunteer firefighter? Serve as an unpaid nurse's aide? The list, easily expandable, illustrates only the barest possibilities. For each activity, rough estimates could be made on the community's loss because of injury or death of a person who enriched the lives of others.

For those who remain skeptical, it need only be recalled that economic (earnings) and legal (joy) criteria have already been accepted by courts, despite the controversy that characterizes the definitions and the results. It is not implausible to believe that society will come to accept the moralist's contribution because the ethical question goes beyond a view of a person as wage earner and beyond a view of a person as Benthamic agent of pleasure. It goes to the ideal of service to others. It can be roughly measured just as other criteria are roughly estimated. And it has one advantage that economic and legal theories of life's worth in tort cases lack, namely, a sense of the community's profound stake in the potential contribution of each person to others. In a "me-too" world, the value of such a perspective is ignored only at the price of a diminished value of everyone and every community.

## Summary

Entrepreneurs regularly contract with others (suppliers, competitors, and customers). When the contract is broken the aggrieved party can go to court. But anyone can sue if harmed through the negligence of others. Tort law imposes an implied contract.

No area of business activity is more vexed by legal and moral problems than the one concerned with consumer protection in the use of goods that are often not what the manufacturer had in mind when the product was first introduced. A century-old experience with the Sherman Antitrust Act and its successors has given business a fair—if incomplete—sense of what the ground rules are in pricing policies, advertising, competition, monopoly, and so on. No comparable experience exists for torts. Each year, in and around the American home, 30,000 people are killed, 110,000 permanently disabled, and 585,000 are hospitalized. It has been estimated that because of accidents related to commercial products, more than 20 million people are injured seriously enough to require medical treatment or to miss work a day or more. The estimated annual cost to the economy of these occurrences is over $6 billion.[36]

For years manufacturers of consumer products felt that "safety doesn't sell." The new message is that "nonsafety costs a bundle." Today's most pressing ethical problems turn more to what people need and not what they want—drugs to maintain or restore health and food to sustain life. Meeting human needs is ethically more important than meeting human wants. However, there are risks in using drugs and even eating certain kinds of food. Because risk taking is an individual choice, it is easy to leave the matter there. But the heart of ethical decision making is choice, and desperate people have no choice: the starving will take any kind of food and the grievously ill any kind of medicine. Producers in these areas, therefore, carry a heavier moral burden than producers of such consumer goods as skis or skates, sables, or satins.

When, then, are manufacturers morally culpable? Perhaps the debate is best closed by recalling Justice Cardozo's reasoning on the meaning of negligence. Given the expansion of the word in recent years, was this great jurist right or wrong when he wrote the following in the *Palsgraf* case of 1968?

> *Negligence is not a tort unless is results in the commission of a wrong, and the commission of a wrong imports the violation of a*

> right. . . . *If the harm was not willful [the plaintiff] must show that the act as to him had possibilities of danger so many and apparent as to entitle him to be protected against the doing of it though the harm was unintended. Affront to personality is still the keynote of the wrong.*[37]

When affronts, intended or unintended, occur, society has puzzled over how much to compensate the affronted individual. Confronting the puzzle, economists have produced the life-earning and risk-avoidance themes to determine the worth of a human life. Lawyers have added the pleasure principle (the joys of living) to the economic concepts. These ideas are likely to be retained. Suggested in this chapter is a moral theory of human worth that correlates what individuals can take from others to what individuals can provide to others. The moral theorem is still nebulous. If, however, society is to move away from the view of a person driven only by egoistic ethic (satisfy oneself) to a larger ethic (serve others) that takes into account Adam Smith's vision of the human personality, ethicists need to articulate a theory that social engineers can someday implement.[38] One step toward a further refinement in tort law can occur if the monetary worth of the individual's voluntary nonpaid contributions to society can be roughly estimated. But more must be done: "By focusing on the presence of fault in a just theory of liability, moral philosophers largely have ignored the question of who should bear a loss when no candidate for it is at fault. Consequently, philosophers have stopped contributing to the dialogue at that very point where their contribution is needed most."[39] This chapter suggests moral philosophers have even more to offer.

## Questions for Discussion

1. In general terms, are tort victims "victimized" by their lawyers because of contingency-fee practices?
2. Are companies fearing liability suits unethical if they leave a product field essential to human well-being—especially when they are the sole providers of such products?
3. Should inexpert "experts" be punished for testifying in fields beyond their competence?
4. Does the hedonic calculus represent sound ethics?
5. When contradictory regulations are promulgated by different government agencies, is it ethical to abide by the least demanding rule?
6. Can you think of any way to introduce the philosopher's theory of the human person into the law of torts?
7. Do you agree with the late Roger Traynor of the California Supreme Court that, when harm is done to a consumer, the working assumption is that the manufacturer must prove its innocence?

## Ethical Quandary

### The Commuter

An investment banker, you commute daily to your office in the city. Driven by financial exigencies to cut costs, management of the commuter railroad has removed most of the lights from the station platform at your stop. The steep wooden stairs are shrouded in darkness each evening.

One evening, an elderly man would have fallen down the darkened steps if you had not stretched forth a supporting arm. The next morning you telephone the head of railroad maintenance to report the incident and to ask that new lights be installed. You are told that provisions for new lamps have already been made and that they would be installed the very next day. When the lighting is not improved, you again telephone the chief of maintenance to report the problem and again you receive assurances that the lamps would be promptly installed. They are not. Again you telephone to protest. Again you receive the same assurances.

The cat-and-mouse game continues. Toward the end of the second week, when a dinner party requires you to stay late in town, you decide to drive and park in a nearby public parking garage. Returning home around midnight after consuming a couple of martinis, you get out of the car to open the garage door. Suddenly your feet slip on the rain-slick driveway, and you feel a thud as your head hits the pavement. The emergency room doctor at the neighborhood hospital diagnoses a concussion and a broken wrist.

Asked what caused the accident, you answer, "I fell down some steps." This answer leads to a calculated plan to vent your frustrations against the railroad. You write the following letter to the president of the commuter line:

> I have repeatedly phoned your head of maintenance to protest the lack of appropriate lighting at Aurusville station. Each time I was told that problem would be corrected the next day. Last night when I took the 11:48 train to my home in Aurusville, I arrived at 12:11. Descending the dark stairs whose conditions I had so often called to your attention, I fell. Though dazed, I was able to phone my wife, who took me immediately to the hospital, where I was told I had suffered a broken wrist and a brain concussion.
>
> My lawyer is presently out of town but when he returns I plan to discuss the possibility of suing the railroad for $25,000 in compensatory damages and $250,000 in punitive damages.

You have no plan to file a suit. Your only strategy is to prod the railroad to action. That evening your return to Aurusville was "brightened" in the full physical sense of the word.

### Questions

- Did the railroad act ethically?
- Did you act ethically?

## Notes

1. Jeffrey O'Connell, *The Lawsuit Lottery: Only Lawyers Can Win* (Chicago: University of Chicago Press, 1990). O'Connell indicts tort lawyers for having created a "manipulative, deceptive, subterranean world of tort litigation," 27.
2. Michael Siconolfi, "Novel Punitive Damage Approach," *The Wall Street Journal*, September 17, 1985.
3. Ellen Schechet, "Judges Bargain with Damages," *The National Law Journal*, August 12, 1985, 13.
4. Clarence C. Walton, "Punitive Damages: New Twists on Torts," *Business Ethics Quarterly* 1 (July 1991): 269–291.
5. Kenneth C. Tyler, "Punitive Damages: A Judicial Cancer," *Best's Review*, April 1985, 16, 22. See also, Stephen Sugarman "Doing Away with Tort Law," *California Law Review* 73 (January 1987): 558–664.
6. Browning-Ferris Industries v. Kelco Disposal Co., et al. U.S. S Ct No 88-556 Slip opinion (June 26, 1989).
7. Editorial: "Morning Sickness: Legal Miscarriage," *The New York Times*, July 30, 1987, A20. See also the article by Michael Brody, "When Products Turn into Liabilities," *Fortune*, March 3, 1986, 20–24; and the four part series by Paul Brodeur, "The Asbestos Industry in Crisis." *The New Yorker* 61 (June 10, 17, 24 and July 11, 1985).
8. *Asbestos and Other Mineral Fibers* (Geneva: World Health Organization, 1986). The Royal Commission Study of Ontario concluded that "the risks which asbestos posed to building occupants was insignificant." *Report of the Royal Commission on Matters of Health and Safety Arising from the Use of Asbestos* (Toronto, Ontario, Canada: 1984).
9. Brooke T. Moosman and J. Bernard L. Gee, "Asbestos Related Diseases," *Journal of Medicine* 320 (June 29, 1989): 1721–1729.
10. P. Saracci, "Asbestos and Lung Cancer: An Analysis of the Epidemiological Evidence on the Asbestos-Smoking Interaction," *International Journal of Cancer* 20 (1977): 323–331.
11. Kathy Koch, "Congress Ready to Examine Asbestos Compensation Issue," *Congressional Quarterly Weekly Report*, March 26, 1982, 205.
12. Editorial: "Scary Asbestos." *Wall Street Journal*, Oct. 12, 1987, 20.
13. *The Wall Street Journal*, March 5, 1986, 1.
14. *Report of Bentley College's Seventh Annual Conference on Business Ethics* (Waltham, Mass.: Bentley College, 1987), 17.
15. James S. Grenelli, "The Future Claims Fight," The *National Law Journal*, April 4, 1983, 28.
16. "The Manville Bankruptcy: Treating Mass Tort Claims in Chapter 11 Proceedings," Note in *Harvard Law Review* 96 (1983); and Christopher M. E. Painter, "Tort Creditor Priority in the Secured Credit System: Asbestos Times, the Worst of Times," *Stanford Law Review* 36 (April 1984): 1045–1085.
17. The questions were suggested by Brad Johnson, B. R. Baliga, and John D. Blair in their article, "Chapter 11: Strategic Advantage and Social Anathema," *The Journal of Business Ethics* 5 (1986): 51–61. Helpful is Andrew Sigler, "Uses and Abuses of Bankruptcy Laws," *Ethikos* 5 (October 1991): 1–5.
18. Editorial: "Liability Insurance in Crisis," *The New York Times*, March 4, 1986, B 26.
19. Edward R. Court, "Attorneys at Fault—Liability Crisis," *The Journal of Business Ethics* 7 (September 1988): 711–714. See also, Richard Posner, "Can Lawyers Solve the Problems of the Tort System?" *California Law Review* 73 (May 1985): 747–754.
20. *Commission to Improve the Tort Liability System* (Chicago: American Bar Association, 1987).
21. Gilbert Simonetti, Jr., and Andrea R. Andrews, "The Liability Crisis: Make Room for Fairness at the Mad Tea Party," *Price Waterhouse Review* 30 (1986): 57–59.
22. Editorial: *U.S. News and World Report*, December 20, 1982, 58. For ATLA's official position see *The American Trial Lawyers Reporter* (Washington: ATLA, 1985).

23. Judge James J. Richards. *Civil Justice Roundtable* 1 (February 1984): 1. See also Timothy B. Atkison and George Neidich, "A Status Report on Proposals for a Federal Product Liability Act," *The Business Lawyer* 38 (February 1983): 623–639.
24. Martin Zuger and Sean Mooney, *Public Attitudes toward Civil Justice* (New York: Insurance Information Institute, 1983), 5.
25. Honorable Warren E. Burger, "Litigation: Is It out of Control?" *The Journal of Insurance* 43 (May–June 1982): 6–7. See also, *Statement by the Research and Policy Committee of the Committee on Economic Development* (New York: Committee on Economic Development, 1989), chs. 4 and 5.
26. "*Ten Commandments for Tort Reform,*" *Forbes*, 138 (August 11, 1986) 78.
27. Mildred F. Stone, *The Teacher Who Changed an Industry* (Bryn Mawr, Pa.: The American College, 1977), 46–47.
28. Thomas Schelling, *Choice and Consequences* (Cambridge: Harvard University Press, 1984).
29. Lucien Sherrod v. Willie Berry, Fred Breen, and the City of Joliet, US DC nd, Ill. 589 F. Supp. 433–438 (June 15, 1984). The case's relationship to Gertz v. Robert Welch, Inc., (1974) is worthy of note.
30. Douglas Maclean, "Risk Analysis and the Value of Life," *Report from the Center for Philosophy and Public Policy* 6 (Winter 1986): 13. For an expanded treatment of Maclean's views, see his book, *Values at Risk* (Totowa, N.J.: Rowman and Littlefield, 1980).
31. Kenneth Schmitz, "The Geography of a Human Person," *Communs* 13 (Spring 1986): 29.
32. How the Romans prepared the modern mind for the idea of corporation is traced by Jeffrey L. Patterson, "The Development of the Concept of Corporation from Earliest Roman Times to A.D. 476," *The Accountancy Historians Journal* 10 (Spring 1983): 87–98.
33. Hugh Fraser Stuart, *Boethius: The Theological Tractatus* (London: W. H. Meineman, 1918). See also, Clarence C. Walton, ed., *Enriching Business Ethics* (New York: Plenum Press, 1990), chs. 2 and 3; and John Courtney Murray, *We Hold These Truths* (New York: Sheed and Ward, 1960), 295–336.
34. Martin Buber, *I and Thou* (New York: Scribner, 1985). See also, David Gauthier, *Morals by Agreement* (New York: Oxford University Press, 1986), 87–90.
35. Martin Buber, *The Way of Response* (New York: Schocken Books, 1966), 48 and 54.
36. Guido Calabresi, *The Cost of Accidents* (New Haven: Yale University, 1970).
37. Palsgraf v. L. I. RR, 248 N.Y. 339, 162 N.E. 99 (1928).
38. Norman Bowie, "Challenging the Egoistic Paradigm," *Business Ethics Quarterly* 1 (January 1991): 1–21.
39. Jules L. Coleman, *Markets, Morals and the Law* (New York: Cambridge University Press, 1989), 183. An exception is Henry J. Steiner, *Moral Argument and Social Vision in Courts: A Study of Tort Accident Law* (Madison: University of Wisconsin Press, 1987), esp. Ch. 5.

PART FOUR

# The World Stage

CHAPTER TWELVE
**Multinational Corporations**

CHAPTER THIRTEEN
**The Environment**

CHAPTER 12

# Multinational Corporations

## Multinationals: What They Are
Multinationals Defined
Evolution of an MNC

## Relations with Host Countries
The Scope of the Problem
Liberation Theology versus Liberating Theology
*Gutierrez's Thesis*
*Novak's Thesis*
*Underlying Demographics*
Ethical Considerations
Practical Steps for Improvement

## Multinationals and Advanced Countries
The Rise and Fall of Nations
The MNC-versus-Government Struggle
Public-Private Multinationals

## American Multinationals and the European Community
Early Mistakes of American Multinationals
European Economic Interest Grouping

## Strengths and Weaknesses of Multinationals

## Summary
Questions for Discussion
Ethical Quandaries

*Compound words and phrases that include "national" have something of an eerie quality. International diplomacy, for example, suggests lying and spying but rarely dying for mother country or fatherland; its redeeming quality is that all is done on behalf of what is perceived to be a noble institution. International banking creates the image of a small coterie of stuffed shirts stuffing their own pockets at the expense of hapless borrowers. Their only loyalty is to the Jolly Roger flag, which they never display but steadfastly honor. For some people, the term multinational has an equally negative connotation, suggesting a dracula that sucks the lifeblood of relatively weak countries peopled by the poverty stricken. Yet institutions come into being to serve, and when the service is either no longer needed or has become morally loathsome, they die. Examples of institutional death in the Western world include feudalism, the Holy Roman Empire, the city-state, and slavery.*

*For the foreseeable future, the multinational—or global—corporation shows no symptoms of terminal illness, which suggests that it must be doing something right. Illnesses may come, and one of the assignments of corporate and political leaders is to treat the patient promptly and effectively.* ■

## *The purposes of this chapter are:*

1. To note the different meanings attached to multinational organizations.
2. To contrast the arguments of those who criticize the multinational and those who defend it, with special emphasis on the differences between liberation theology and liberating theology.
3. To treat the reciprocal relations between the host country and the corporate visitor from both historical and ethical perspectives.
4. To examine the argument that multinational corporations threaten the sovereignty of the host nations.
5. To consider recommendations for turning multinational corporations into public-private bodies.
6. To consider the significance of the European Community on the multinational corporation.

# Multinationals: What They Are

Among large organizations, 20th-century multinational/global corporations (MNC) constitute the fastest growing segment.[1] And in this undulating world of power shifts among major organizations, the multinational corporation—only an adolescent a half century ago—appears to many as the powerful young adult ready to challenge governments. The likely answer to the question of which will be the victor in this match has some people worried and others pleased. Attitudes are shaped by facts and biases. Many people are in the tent pitched in 1971 by Harvard professor Raymond Vernon, who worried because "the multinational enterprise is not accountable to any public authority that matches it in geographical reach and that represents the aggregate interest of all the countries the enterprise affects. Suddenly, it seems, sovereign states are feeling naked."[2]

## *Multinationals Defined*

Can the multinational be curbed by uniform rules applied by an authoritative public international body? Is it the duty of the nation that allowed its incorporation to assume control? Definitions proffered from four sources are used as starting points for answers to these questions.

- *A scholar*: Multinationals are merely American organizational supergiants doing business in a number of countries and acting on the basis of a strategy directed by a corporate center that is unconcerned about national boundaries.[3]
- *A British competitor*: "A multinational corporation is an American registered company manufacturing its products where labor is cheapest and channeling its profits to another country whose taxation is lowest and possibly nonexistent."[4]
- *The U.S. Senate*: A multinational corporation is any company whose foreign sales have reached a ratio of 25 percent of its total sales.[5]
- *A business executive*: Adequately defined, a multinational should meet the following five criteria: (1) it must do business in many countries that are in different stages of economic development; (2) it must have foreign subsidiaries with the same R&D, manufacturing, sales, services, and so on, that a true industrial entity has; (3) there should be nationals running these local companies because they have a better understanding of the local scene, and this helps promote good citizenship; (4) there must be a multinational headquarters, staffed with people from different countries, so one nationality does not dominate management decisions; and (5) the stock must be owned by people in different countries.[6]

Observers of, and participants in, the multinational game punch holes in one another's definition. The scholar's description has been attacked on grounds that it is unclear about the types of primary activities involved—manufacturing, marketing, investments, advertising, and so forth. To illustrate, Tinto Zinc is devoted to extractive industries and local processing whereas Unilever is interested in locally produced consumer goods. And both differ from General Electric or IBM. Companies also can have different organizational patterns (tight centralized controls versus considerable local autonomy), different impacts on the host countries, and different investment policies.

The English executive's definition conveniently overlooked the existence of European multinationals like British Petroleum, Shell, and Phillips, and the fact that half of them are chartered outside the United States and have achieved higher growth rates than American multinationals. Members of the Senate Finance Committee neglected to note the uneven sales and profit records that global competition intensifies. And the executive, after compiling his list of criteria, ruefully admitted that if they are strictly applied there are no multinationals in the world.

The simplest definition—and possibly the one nearest reality—was given by the Commission of the European Economic Community: *The multinational is an undertaking with production facilities in at least two countries.* As such, the multinational organization is practically synonymous with investments abroad.[7] Seeking to encompass all the characteristics of these transnationals, Arvind Phatak of Temple University wrote:

> *A multinational company is an enterprise that has a network of wholly or partially (jointly with one or more foreign partners) owner-producing and marketing affiliates located in a number of countries. The foreign affiliates are linked with the parent company and with each other by ties of common ownership and by a common global strategy to which each affiliate is responsive and committed. The parent company controls the foreign affiliates via resources which it allocates to each affiliate—such as capital, technology, trademarks, patents, and manpower—and through the right to approve each affiliate's long- and short-range plans and budgets.*[8]

There is one point of agreement: MNCs operate in a global environment that is the sum total of the environments of separate nations, each of which is identifiable through its own legal, cultural, economic, and political elements. Culture collisions are common experiences for multinationals. Contrasts between the United States and the United Kingdom illustrate the point. To a large extent, practices in England parallel practices in the United States; but even the culturally "kissing cousins" have their differences. In the United States, the public fears monopoly and corporate managers fear government intrusiveness. Americans live under an ideology that prescribes an arm's length relationship between private enterprise and government. Indeed, the distance between government and business is such that each learns about the other's foreign operations more through newspapers than through official channels. Britain, on the other hand, exercises a form of benignity toward cartels that is due in part to another British characteristic—"the tendency to assume that any class of enterprise that has for a long time exercised some given prerogative in the economy, whether by law or custom, whether formal or informal, has an equitable claim to the continuation of that advantage."[9]

There are, of course, other differences. The British manager is more relaxed. The American is more tense. British executives work comfortably with government officials when their companies do business abroad. Americans prefer to be left alone. But the differences have proved rather easily manageable—something that cannot be said of France. Corporate rights in the United States and in the United Kingdom may be acquired simply by durability—doing a job for so long a time that no one questions the organization's right to exist. In France, on the other hand, legitimacy is acquired through specific statutes that spell out rights and duties in detail. Organizational and political stability are important to the French whereas organizational innovation and rapid changes are preferred by Americans. Ignorance of cultural values has led many Americans doing business in France into trouble. Between non-Western underdeveloped countries the cultural differences are even more pronounced.

The personality of the multinational has, however, remained rather consistent: its primary goal is profits; its policies are often weakened by managerial ignorance of other cultures; its measures to judge performance are imperfect; fixed assets appear to be less difficult to reproduce than in domestic companies; and management, concerned with maintaining employee loyalty and initiative over the long run, is prepared to modify the classic return-on-investment calculations to keep the principal members of the team in play. Another quality of the multinational personality includes the capability to repay obligations at an accelerated pace—an important factor during a currency crisis—as well as the ability to avoid some of the more onerous regulations that domestic companies encounter. Finally, there is managerial belief that the MNC is always a boon to the host country.[10]

## *Evolution of an MNC*

As a domestic company evolves into a full-fledged multinational enterprise, it goes through several distinct but overlapping stages. It may start as an import or export business; or it may flow from countertrade that involves barter, clearing arrangements (two countries specify the goods that may be exchanged at stipulated prices), buybacks, and the like. Very often the MNC does assembly abroad because of cheaper shipping costs for unassembled products, lower tariffs, and reduced labor costs. Production abroad and integration of foreign affiliates to the parent organization are, however, the most visible signs of the mature global organization. Probably 4000 multinationals do about 40 percent of total global business. As global competition deepens, the numbers will likely shrink through mergers, hostile takeovers, or government expropriation. However small their numbers become, their powers will remain formidable. Of the hundred largest economic units in the world, 50 are nation-states and the others are the world's largest 300 multinationals. As in the United States, the MNCs dominate key industries like oil, automobiles, computers, and pharmaceuticals. Of the American corporations with the largest sales in 1990, all were multinationals.[11]

In times past, international trade was primarily in cotton and cotton textiles, coal and steel rails, wool and foodstuffs. These products were shipped and sold through intermediaries who never saw the customer and sometimes were even unaware until the very last moment of the destination where they could get the highest price. Before 1914, for example, American grain ships waited for a signal from Land's End to learn where in Europe was their best market. For this kind of trade there was no need for a multinational. However, modern industrial enterprises, mainly in manufacturing, sell at prices preestablished to assure a profitable return. Therefore, they need power—power over planning and production, power over market strategy, power over prices, and power to influence the host state not to destroy one or other of these operations.[12] Yet multinationals have been accused of (1) turning host countries, especially in the Third World, into vassals; (2) threatening to replace the nation-state as the primary institution in the world; (3) destabilizing the international monetary system; and (4) subverting the trade union movement. So formidable an array of charges requires comment.

## Relations with Host Countries

### The Scope of the Problem

When considering the multinationals' impact on host countries, it is difficult to escape the ideological struggle between socialists and free-market advocates. The dimensions of the struggle were evident when the United Nations asked a group of eminent persons to assess the implications of MNCs. Responding to this request, the UN Economic and Social Council at its 57th session in late 1974 established an Inter-Governmental Commission on Transnational Corporations. Composed of representatives from 48 member states, the commission acted as a forum within the UN for consideration of all major (and sometimes minor) issues relating to transnationals. Free-market advocates feared the UN group because it embraced a state planning ideology rather than a capitalistic bias. Emeric Blum, one of the UN Eminent Persons Group, said it was necessary to realize that multinationals are part of an international economic system that, as is generally accepted today, rests on inherited privileges and relationships of exploitation and neocolonialism. Global corporation managers who have never been called eminent winced at this widely shared view.

Churches have also taken a keen interest in moral questions related to the multinationals. The World Conference of Churches, headquartered in New York and representing most of the Protestant leadership in the United States, has been particularly critical of their behavior. To the Conference, multinationals epitomize the worst features of a capitalistic system already corrupted by its impersonal and exploitative treatment of workers.[13] The Catholic church has been no less concerned. Popes Paul VI and John Paul II have urged the developed nations—and by implication the corporations domiciled therein—to take a hard look at the results of their involvement in foreign countries.[14] Lying below the surface in the church responses is a bitter debate between exponents of liberation theology (a polemic that has been evident with special force in the case of Latin America) and what has been called liberating theology.[15]

## Liberation Theology versus Liberating Theology

**Gutíerrez's Thesis.** The celebrated spokesman for liberation theology is Gustavo Gutíerrez, whose book, *A Theology of Freedom*, impressed many North Americans as the authentic voice of the oppressed.[16] Relying heavily on the studies of two Latin American economists, Fernando Henrique Cardoso and Enzo Faletto, Gutíerrez defines the Latin American reality as dependence rather than underdevelopment. Because underdevelopment in the Third World is the inevitable consequence of development in the First World, Latin American development will never proceed properly until economic dependence is broken—and this can occur only in the context of a worldwide class struggle.[17]

The thesis rests on the premise that the multinationals are central to the oppression of the many by the few. They have gone beyond the past forms of imperialistic presence that created enclave economies (mines and plantations) to a new form of investment capitalism in which the more dynamic elements of native industry bind the host countries into even greater dependency on international capitalism. Gutíerrez views this as beneficial only to the vested interests—that is, the local elites who collaborate with the transnationals as well as with foreign stockholders. Although his theory is revolutionary, Gutíerrez's advice to leaders and workers in the oppressed countries is vague: does liberation theology mean expropriation of the assets of the transnationals? recourse to violence (Gutíerrez's background suggests that violence would be the poor's very last desperate move)? worker control of plant operations or employee benefits? Liberation theologians have come under sharp attack from Pope John Paul II, who fears that the emphasis on worldwide class struggle is only a religious expression of an already discredited Marxism.

**Novak's Thesis.** Opposed to liberation theology is liberating theology—terms that are close in sound and wide apart in meaning. Liberating theology sees the large corporation as both the great engine for production—the results of which help everyone in the long run—and as the instrument for free people to express themselves. One of the most forceful advocates of the view is Michael Novak, himself the son of a poor Catholic immigrant couple who settled in a small western Pennsylvania town. Novak's thesis is that capitalism itself is a moral system.[18] In a forum sponsored by *Harpers Magazine* in the fall of 1986 (and despite strong opposition from a number of fellow panelists) Novak insisted that capitalism encourages the moral virtues of self-reliance and responsibility, work and creativity.[19] If noncapitalist countries were undeveloped they had themselves largely to blame. Rather than carp at the multinationals for creating dependencies, observers should praise them as change agents that awaken slumbering peoples from their lethargies. Supporting this view is the widely known economist, John Kenneth Galbraith. He asked why

> in an adult industrial world, there should be apology for this kind of international development. International trade always had to be defended against those who saw only its costs, never its advantages; who saw only the intrusion of foreign competitors, never the resulting efficiency in supply or products or the reciprocal gains from greater experts. The multinational corporation comes into existence when international trade consists of modern technical, specialized, or uniquely-styled manufactured products. Accordingly, it should be defended, as international trade was defended, for its contribution to efficiency in production and marketing, to living standards, and to reciprocal opportunities in other lands for the enterprises of the host country.[20]

Joseph Ramos, a South American economist whose research supported Novak, challenged the Gutíerrez dependency theory by pointing out the following:

1. Only 5 percent of U.S. investment goes abroad.
2. U.S. investment in Latin America represents less than 1 percent of the United States GNP.
3. The after-tax return on U.S. capital in Latin America is approximately 10 percent.
4. If U.S. investors in the Third World take out more than they invest, that is only what occurs in all sound investments.
5. U.S. corporate profits do not depend heavily on investments in the Third World. Figures on U.S. overseas profits vary from year to year, from company to company.
6. The United States has a chronic balance of payments problem.[21]

For Ramos and Novak these six facts demolish any theory that explains Latin American underdevelopment (and, by implication, underdevelopment elsewhere) in terms of United States' development. The real problem is that Latin American poverty is a consequence of the internal structures common to that area. On the other hand, democratic capitalism, despite its imperfections, is the most promising model of development and the multinationals that make it work are the best instruments for promoting the common good. Leaders of developing countries know this. Zimbabwe's Robert Mugabe, the socialist prime minister, begged Union Carbide to stay in his country; the clamor for withdrawal from South Africa would never have arisen if the multinationals operating there were not doing some good. Why else bother if their positive impacts were negligible? Examples could be multiplied to show that, in the absence of global corporations, the likelihood that the world would be more prosperous, freer, more peaceful, and more healthful is slim.

**Underlying Demographics.** The facts on which to base moral judgments are nevertheless clouded. In developing countries important advances in economic growth and human well-being were recorded during the 1960s; life expectancy rose and infant mortality rates fell in most developing countries; people in developing countries in 1985 could expect to live an average of about 60 years compared to about 51 years in 1965; literacy has spread dramatically and primary-school education is now a reality for most children in the developing world; secondary school enrollment rates have also increased. However, despite measurable progress, the poor are still very poor and, because of population growth, there are now more of them. Roughly one in five of the world's five billion people lives in absolute poverty, struggling with malnutrition, illiteracy, disease, infant mortality, and short life expectancy; in addition, a disproportionate number of people living in poverty are women. In a September 1988 address to the World Bank Board of Governors, Barbara Constable, president of the World Bank, said: "Poverty on today's scale prevents a billion people from having even a minimally acceptable standard of living. To allow every fifth human being on our planet to suffer such an existence is a moral outrage. It is more: It is bad economics, a terrible waste of precious development resources. Poverty destroys lives, human dignity and economic potential."[22]

There is still another factor at work. Poverty varies markedly from region to region. In East and Southeast Asia, slower population growth rates and steady advances in per-capita income have contributed to a significant reduction in poverty. In South Asia, where roughly half of the world's poor live, modest rates of growth have barely kept pace with the expanding population. And in sub-Saharan Africa, where two-thirds of the people live in poverty, rapid population growth rates exacerbated economic deterioration. Falling or stagnant farm production—as well as natural disasters—have contributed to widespread malnutrition and decreased social welfare. Finally, economic stagnation in most developing countries in the 1980s has reversed many hard-won gains of earlier decades. For 16 African and Latin American countries, per capita income was lower in 1985 than in 1965, and additional troubled countries in the two areas showed per-capita income growing by less than 1 percent during the past decade.

## *Ethical Considerations*

Under a strict exchange ethic there is little reason for multinational executives to be concerned with the unfortunate people in developing countries at this time. Providing fewer skills and fewer dollars than people in industrialized countries, they are more drag than benefit to the industrialized countries and their global corporations. As investment opportunities, they scarcely exist. Yet only the morally callous reject Barbara Constable's charge that poverty on such measured scales is a moral outrage. Because of her position as head of the World Bank, Constable's message may carry more persuasive power than if the same charges were made by various popes or by various church groups. But is relief of poverty the obligation of multinational corporations? or of the entire community of nations? Business entities exist not to give aid but to provide help while making money. Because the moralist's job is to offer criteria that help such decision makers, the following guidelines have been offered:

- *The principle of the moral minimum*: Do no intentional harm to the host country. Harm may come through careless use of pesticides, industrial waste, or slave wages.
- *The principle of respect*: All people in the host country must be recognized as bearers of basic human rights. Apartheid, unsafe and unsanitary working conditions, child labor are anathema. On the positive side, recognition of human rights requires multinationals to support minimum wage laws, the right to strike, the right of all adults to vote, and other forms of corrective legislation.
- *The principle of restraint*: The values of the local culture should not be undermined by the multinational unless—and this requires great sensitivity—they hurt members of the host country themselves. One example is women's rights, which in local mores are often subordinated or ignored.
- *The principle of obedience*: Many multinationals successfully work to avoid or evade restrictions placed by governments on domestic businesses. The moral assignment is to promote abroad what is urged upon large corporations at home, namely, the previously defined level playing field principle.[23]

Unfortunately, violations of these principles do occur. Of the sad stories told about the multinationals' behavior, two are illustrative. On May 5, 1983, a Monday morning, 289 women workers of a Honduran garment factory found the factory doors closed. Posted on the portal was a brief note of "regret" that the factory had been closed permanently. Executives of the parent company, the American multinational NCC Industries, were the decision makers. NCC had a long history of antiunionism and its action on Honduras was only an extension to its Latin American affiliate of its practices in North America. Word of the decision quickly spread and Hondurans still remember "grim Monday" as one in a long series of Yankee acts of imperialism.[24]

A second example occurred thousands of miles away in South Africa. In 1987, some 340,000 pit miners of the National Union of Mineworkers went on strike against the Anglo-American Mining Company. The company was founded in 1917 by Sir Ernest Oppenheimer; son Harry took over leadership in 1962. The Oppenheimer family continues to control a company that has 46 percent of South Africa's gold production, 80 percent of the world's trade in rough diamonds, and large holdings in food processing, steel, electronics, banking, insurance, and other industries. Its assets total an estimated $15 to $18 billion. In view of its power, the company not surprisingly brought the union to its knees.

What is intriguing is the Jekyll-Hyde character of Anglo-American Mining. Harry Oppenheimer has been acclaimed for his opposition to apartheid and for his substantial gifts of money to urban development programs for blacks. The company permitted unionization when other firms opposed it. Yet the company's wages were among the world's lowest and its black employees earned a quarter of what whites were paid. And while white miners were given heavily subsidized modern homes, utilities, and schools, blacks were crowded into compounds that resembled prison camps. Yet the company does have one black on its 28-member board—a rare occurrence in South Africa, even if he plays no significant role, because the small all-male and all-white executive committee makes the critical decisions.[25]

On the other hand, it has already been reported how host countries aggressively woo multinationals. Pepsi Cola operates in over 115 countries and has over 500 bottling plants outside the United States. The important thing about the Pepsi story is that, as far back as the 1960s, both production and marketing facilities were owned by the nationals of those countries.[26] The fact is that, while subjects like capital flow have been rigorously examined, few individual companies have been examined over a long enough period to warrant complete support for sweeping moral judgments.

When facts collide, broad generalizations are risky. So far as Gutíerrez's dependency thesis is concerned (multinationals systematically operate to make developing countries dependent), the supporting evidence may be incomplete but some is there. Multinationals have been slow to develop an international outlook and the result is a myopia that leads managers to weigh their effectiveness only in terms of the good of the company.[27] Multinationals have sometimes behaved callously toward the host's culture. And although some companies have come to recognize the need for a geocentric orientation, more needs to be done. The dependency factor, therefore, cannot be summarily pushed aside—as Brazil's experiences have shown.[28]

On the other hand, no one can summarily dismiss Novak's thesis (multinationals have benign effects) either. There is evidence that South Americans' problems have been related to the ineptitude or corruption of the local Latin elites. Former slaves in northeastern Brazil simply vanished into a larger, free, and poorer rural population.[29] It is an old, familiar, and sad story of native elites joyously joining foreigners in the plunder of their own people; in Argentina, the Spanish crown "depended on the economic practices of the dominant local groups in Buenos Aires, including smugglers, to advance its interest. These local elites, in turn, were intertwined with the administrative and military structure they helped to create."[30] The popularly acclaimed Golden Law of freedom in Latin American was for many slaves the iron law of destitution.

If the history of one British gold-mining company provides a paradigm, neither Gutíerrez nor Novak explains the whole story. The performance of the St. John d'el Rey Mining Company is relevant. Founded in 1830 the firm had a century of remarkable success. Despite the usual tensions that accompany absentee landlords/local residents relationships, the company produced gains for England and for Brazil. Its collapse in 1960 was due to management ineptitude in London and the indifference, possibly venality, of the local managers in Brazil—as well as rising Brazilian nationalism that expressed itself in great hostility toward the British.[31] Providing clear instruction on the ethical performance of a single multinational over the long-term is, to repeat for the sake of emphasis, hard to come by.

## *Practical Steps for Improvement*

Among the practical steps that can be taken by multinationals to improve relations with host countries are the following:

1. Be not only a good guest, but a helpful guest: "The successful global firm in Latin America can't simply adjust to its environment; there isn't that much to adjust to. Instead it must turn environment-builder, engineering this work into everyday operations."[32]
2. Concentrate on the efficient use of all resources (human, physical, economic) for the purpose of rewarding stockholders *and* the local community.
3. Explore market opportunities in neighboring countries where profitable links can be established, especially in auxiliary systems like hospitals, schools, and other support areas.
4. Discern and cooperate with the economic goals of the host company, unless the goals are clearly unrealistic. If this is the case, the multinationals can make this point clear to government officials and offer expertise in the particular areas in which the goal statement is weak.
5. Provide full disclosure on a regular basis.
6. Use a self-imposed "tax" to support building up the host country's infrastructure.
7. Take practical steps (including scholarships to U.S. universities) to train local managers for greater responsibilities.[33]
8. Support human rights programs even though risks are involved.
9. At a minimum avoid cooperation with dictatorial regimes.[34]

On the other hand, host countries have an obligation to reciprocate. And reciprocity includes elimination of gross corruption and a demonstrated willingness to help themselves. Too often multinationals have been victimized by their hosts. One of the best-known cases that came to public attention is United Brands and the suicide of Eli Black, a devout Jewish rabbi and a financial wizard. Even today there is dispute over naming the real villain. Shortly after Black leaped from his office window overlooking Fifth Avenue, it was discovered that he had approved the payment of a $2.5 million bribe to a Honduran official to cut back the enormous tax increase Honduras had placed on banana exports.

In one view, Black was, despite the tragic circumstances surrounding his death, a villain who simply got cold feet when he knew that his bribe could no longer be concealed. According to this version, the "Honduran arrangement" was only the tip of the iceberg, part of a pattern at United Brands that predated Black's ascendancy and persisted long after his demise. The corporation was involved in the U.S.-sponsored coup that overthrew the populist government of President Jacob Arbenz in Guatemala in 1954. Its violent repression of a militant labor movement in 1959 was inexcusable, as was its refusal in the mid-1960s to implement the recommendations of a study done at the company's request by the International Basic Economic Corporation (IBEC) to construct decent workers' housing in the Honduran plantations. Finally, its efforts to repress union activities and grower cooperatives from 1975 on are hardly reconcilable with the picture of United Brands as a benevolent—even minimally decent—company.[35]

Looking at the same facts, two Notre Dame professors, John Houck and Oliver Williams, saw a quite different scenario. They stressed Black's faithfulness to the Jewish tradition of "tzedakah" (the love that does justice), which was reflected in the policies of United Brands.[36] As evidence, they cited Black's decisions to raise the wages of the company's farm workers to nearly six times that of competitors and to upgrade housing for plantation workers as well as his efforts to know Caesar Chavez better in order to bring a more fruitful relationship with Chavez's United Farmworkers Union.[37] They recalled Chavez's eulogy: "Mr. Black's life was proof that farm labor and management could work for the betterment of all." To the Notre Dame observers, Honduras, not Black, was the real villain.

The point of the Black story in the Houck-Williams account is its vivid portrayal of the multinational's weakness before a determinedly aggressive host country that acts under the cloak of legitimacy. Taxes can be raised suddenly; expropriation can be threatened; workers can be mobilized by government agents to participate in wildcat strikes; getting licenses to operate can become very expensive and getting them may become inordinately time-consuming; and important and critically needed goods can be halted without notice. In short, the mighty multinational can be humbled by its tiny host.

## Multinationals and Advanced Countries

Another troublesome question is whether the multinational, indifferent as it is to natural boundaries, poses a threat even to industrialized nations. Countries and empires rise and fall but commerce goes on forever.[38] In less than a half century the British, French, and Dutch have seen their empires vanish.[39] And no one was prepared for the shocking events of 1989 and 1990, when a mighty Russian empire began to wither on the vine.

### *The Rise and Fall of Nations*

Very recently the theme of rise and fall of nations was expressed in persuasive terms by Paul Kennedy, whose thesis merits extensive summary because of its relevance to the role of multinationals.[40] According to Kennedy, the relative strengths of the leading nations in world affairs has never remained constant, due largely to the uneven growth among different people, and technological and organizational breakthroughs that help one community to surpass others. The coming of the long-range gun and the sailing ship, and the rise of the Atlantic trades after 1500 were not uniformly beneficial to all European nations; the later development of steam power—and of the coal and metal resources upon which it relied—added immeasurably to the relative power of certain nations. Once productive capacity was enhanced, a country could sustain the costs of armaments essential to its security in both peacetime and wartime. Economic power is usually needed to sustain military power, and military power is needed to protect wealth. After 1890, for example, when the United States began to export more than it imported, a great American navy came into being. If, however, too large a proportion of the state's resources is diverted from wealth creation, national power is weakened over the long term.

Since the 16th century, the history of the rise and decline of the leading countries in the Great Power system (Spain, the Netherlands, France, Britain, and now the United States) showed a significant long-term correlation between productive and revenue-raising capacities, on one side, and military strength on the other. There was, of course, always the possibility that one state might acquire sufficient resources to surpass the others, and then to dominate the European continent. For about 150 years after 1500, a dynastic-religious bloc under the Spanish and Austrian Hapsburgs threatened to do just that, but after 1660 former Great Powers like Spain and The Netherlands dropped into the second rank, and by 1815 the five major states were France, Britain, Russia, Austria, and Prussia. It was a period in which France, first under Louis XIV and later under Napoleon, came close to controlling Europe—just as Germany under Hitler came close to doing it in the 20th century.

Toward the latter part of the 19th century the pace of technological change quickened, leading to uneven growth rates that made the international system more unstable than it had been 50 years earlier. After 1880 the Great Powers competed for additional colonial territories in Africa, Asia, and the Pacific, partly for gain and partly out of a fear of being eclipsed. Arms races and military alliances marked the period: France and England buried a century-old feud in 1904 with the *entente cordiale*; Germany, Russia, and Austria-Hungary responded with the Triple Alliance; and the two blocs went to war in 1914.

After World War II, the United States and Russia moved to the forefront, and because both interpreted international problems in bipolar, and often Manichean, terms, their rivalry drove them into an ever-escalating arms race that no other power could equal. Then suddenly the 1989–1990 explosions in Eastern Europe signaled the disintegration of Russia's empire. The question for the United States as a nation and as an economic power is how its leaders will interpret the future. Europe is over its wartime paralysis and the European Community has become the world's largest trading unit. Other momentous alterations have occurred: China is leaping forward economically; Japan's postwar economic growth has been so phenomenal that by some standards its GNP is larger than Russia's; by contrast, both the American and Russian growth rates have become relatively sluggish and their shares of global production have shrunk since the 1960s. The world is again multipolar. Today's five large power centers are China, Japan, the European Community, the Soviet Union, and the United States.

## The MNC-versus-Government Struggle

In today's multipolar world the multinationals play a leading role. Russia has created its own multinational. In February 1990, Gorbachev called for a return of private property and creative adaptations of the market system; and at the same time, thousands of Muscovites lined up before the golden arch of McDonald's, the first hamburger shop in Russia. Symptoms of greater changes to come were everywhere and the turmoil led political leaders of advanced countries to share fears already raised for developing countries. First was fear over the MNCs' control of a few key industries; second was fear that decisions important to their futures were being made by foreigners; finally was a Gutierrez-type fear that infusions of foreign capital increased the dependency of the host country.

But industrialized nations can strike back with more power than can impoverished countries.[41] Australia, for example, which for many years had encouraged foreign investment, took steps that included (1) abolition of tax incentives to mining companies, (2) state takeover of oil and gas from the North West Shelf, and (3) close monitoring of proposed capital investment by foreign countries. The Australian national telecommunications administration standardized production requirements for the MNC subsidiaries from which it buys equipment. As a result, the L. M. Ericsson subsidiary often ends up manufacturing ITT-designed equipment, and vice versa. In the past, the well-known practice of switching technology was not a major problem; but in the 1970s, allocating to one company the production of another's equipment has made it difficult for multinationals to protect new proprietary switching information. Canada, another country highly receptive to direct foreign investment, limited the degree of foreign ownership in such key sectors as broadcasting and banking; introduced policies to extend Canadian ownership or directorship participation; and tightened proposed takeovers of Canadian business by nonresidents. The Canadian moves must be seen in the context of its business world, where some three-quarters of its largest corporations are foreign owned.

Another example of counterattack strategy is India. Until 1970 the primary type of diversification among MNC subsidiaries in India had been based on linkages with existing competencies of the parent company in distribution and marketing, production technology, or the exploitation of R&D. This related diversification changed after 1975, however, when unrelated diversification took priority. This shift resulted mainly from the government's attempt to restrict the strategic power of the multinationals in India's economy.[42] Now MNC executives take a hard look at India because its rewards can be so high and its constraints ever higher.[43] In that country exists what is euphemistically called license-cum-permit Raj, which is the bureaucracy composed of innumerable departments, secretariats, and ministers whose approvals are necessary even before production can begin. IBM fought off the Indian governments's attempts to weaken its autonomy for over a decade before calling it quits. Burroughs, on the other hand, stayed to profit modestly and suffer much.

Fears that multinationals would destroy the sovereignty of nations have been exaggerated; on the other hand, the global corporation's power to make, withhold, or withdraw heavy investments makes the MNC a constant threat. When the global corporation's teeth become too large and too menacing, however, governments seem to have the resources either to file them down or extract them. What is likely to appear is a rough replication of the struggle of corporations versus government in the United States. Domestic corporations once crossed state boundaries just as multinationals now cross national boundaries. When the crossings became intrusive, states reacted; and when state responses proved inadequate, the federal government stepped in. Today no organization in the international community possesses power like that of Congress over the domestic economy, but some form of international legislation is coming, and the European Community may be the first to create it.

Developing countries in South America, West Africa, and the Far East often demand joint ownership of local MNC subsidiaries. The workers' codetermination schemes, now gaining momentum in the developed countries of Europe, may ultimately have the same effect of forcing MNC subsidiaries to share their strategic decision making with representatives of local constituencies. Spain established explicit sales and export volume conditions before allowing Ford to establish production facilities there. High on the reform list is the idea of public-private ventures.

## *Quasi Public vs Private Multinationals*

If examples of rectitude are sought from the history of state-private multinationals, they are not found in the early behavior of such organizations. Neither the Dutch East India Company (founded in 1602 to monopolize trade between the Cape of Good Hope and the Straits of Magellan) nor the less successful Dutch West India Company (established in 1621 to monopolize trade in South America and Africa) is remembered for kindly behavior toward the host countries. Treatment of the American Indians by English multinationals was not much better. Exploitation, sometimes softened by paternalism, left such bitter memories that the violent outbreaks of nationalism throughout all the nondeveloped countries should have surprised no one. That it did is probably the greatest surprise of all. But advocates of state-private global corporations insist that the past is not prologue, a conviction that can be tested against the experiences of Exxon, which had no government ties, and of British Petroleum, which had close connections to Parliament.

The operations of Exxon, headquartered in New York City, span the globe from North America to the Far East, from Alaska to the South Pacific. Its 1990 revenues of $117,000 million exceeded the GNP of many countries in which it operates.[44] Because the organization's interest is the interest of the thousands of stockholders who own bits and pieces of the company, the board keeps a wary eye on the effect of its action on stock prices and dividends. This single-mindedness of purpose was defined by the company's founder, John D. Rockefeller. In 1911 when Standard Oil was dissolved into 34 companies, the largest piece by far was Standard Oil of New Jersey with $285.5 billion in net assets. It was renamed Exxon in 1972.[45] Exxon's legacy from Jersey Standard included an organizational structure with a powerful board of directors, a grand market strategy, and a preference for a low public profile.

Led by its active board, the company has historically relied on decentralized committees to oversee the various subdivisions. These committees reviewed one another and reported back at the frequent board meetings. This corporate check-and-balance system provided many employees with opportunities to share in decision making, yet maintained a unity and corporate-wide awareness of all divisions. Exxon's productivity strength has always been in the refining and storage areas; its weakness was in the exploration and retail marketing areas. The other major areas of Exxon's strength rested in its financial commitment to maintain enormous cash holdings that could be used for interest income and for a stock strategy. Stockpiling and financial strength proved invaluable when the oil industry was hit by the political and economic thrusts of OPEC.

Special note must be given to Exxon's secrecy. In the past, public and private hatred of Rockefeller and of Standard Oil forced both to a policy of oleaginous silence. Rockefeller stirred antagonisms by the underhanded, even malicious, behavior he exhibited in acquiring his empire. But it was the secrecy of Rockefeller's methods, "as much as his ruthlessness, that made him such a special figure of hatred. As his trade and refineries expanded, his rivals never knew quite what was hitting them."[46] As his company grew to mammoth proportions, Rockefeller began to circumvent even the few laws that governed business behavior. The Sherman Antitrust Act proved insufficient and it was not until 1911 that the government finally mustered the necessary force to break up the empire. Since that time, distrust has never disappeared completely from either party. Suspicion, however, never deflected Exxon from its legacy of aggressive competition, long-term profit maximization, silence, and global strategizing.

In contrast to Exxon, the private and close-mouthed American corporation, is British Petroleum, the fifth largest corporation in the oil industry. It has extensive reserves in the North Sea and in Prudhoe Bay, Alaska. It is a typical quasi-public corporation. The government plays a major role in its operations, resource-allocation decisions, and selection of strategic objectives. Managers recognize a primary duty to government and country as opposed to the self-interest goal of Exxon. Its evolution provides interesting insights into an MNC's transformation from an exclusively private to a quasi-government enterprise.

The Anglo-Persian Oil Company was founded in 1909 by William Knox D'Arcy as a wholly British-owned and operated company to find oil and to develop land concessions in over four-fifths of Iran. At the beginning, D'Arcy gave Iran 20,000 shares in his company and made a commitment to pay the host government 16 percent of all oil revenues. Although a purely private organization at this point, the Anglo-Persian Oil Company relied heavily on the home government's persuasive power to convince the Shah to cooperate with the English investor. Government assistance included bribery, subterfuge, and intrigue.

The efforts led to a long marriage between the company (which changed its name to British Petroleum) and the British government. By 1914, when BP's modest success in drilling for oil had been negated by rising costs of transportation, bankruptcy loomed. However, First Lord of the Admiralty Winston Churchill convinced the government to bail out the failing company because the navy, rapidly converting from coal to oil, needed a reliable supplier—which meant a government-controlled oil enterprise—for strategic purposes. When the time came for government and company to join forces, the purchasing agreement had several interesting provisions:

1. The company would always remain an independent British company but each director would be a British subject who, it was assumed, would always maintain a "sense of duty" to support the government and its policies.

2. The British government would appoint two of the company's directors and have power to veto company decisions that threatened the strategic interests of the nation.

3. The company would always be bound to "help and enrich" British subjects at home and abroad. This meant that the company (1) had social responsibilities to build houses, schools, roads, hospitals, and the like; (2) would concentrate its production technology on specific products the government desired (such as navy distillate), and (3) would be devoid of a marketing structure because it was government's intention to insulate it from competition.[47]

The framework established by the Churchill-inspired government buyout would stay with British Petroleum for decades. From 1914 on, the company's actions were characterized by aversion to competition and cooperation with, and reliance on, the government. This arrangement contrasted sharply with the antitrust and adversarial postures that characterized relationships between the U.S. government and American oil companies, including Exxon.

By 1947, several oil-well discoveries close to Great Britain increased British Petroleum's ability to help the homeland. Shortly after the discovery of Scottish shale oil, the government, seeing an opportunity to keep alive a home industry that employed many thousands, built refineries in South Wales at Llandarey and in Scotland at Pumplerson. Still lightly committed to refining products like gasoline, the company was largely oriented toward upstream products (such as distillate oil for ships) that undergo few, if any, value-adding processes before sale. Around this time, too, British Petroleum moved to obtain complete control of crude oil products in Iran. To BP, the

"16 percent of profits clause" reached under the original agreement was just and equitable to the people of Iran. It believed that it had met its social responsibilities to the host country.

Buttressing its beliefs were substantial contributions. By 1951, British Petroleum employed 70,000 Iranians and had built 30 schools, a technical college, three hospitals, 35 dispensaries, 40 bridges, and 1250 miles of road. Yet, what the British believed to be ethical, was judged unacceptable by the Iranians, whose sense of outrage was orchestrated in 1951 by Dr. Mossadegh in a coup that resulted in the expulsion of the Shah and all Westerners. The National Iranian Oil Company was started and took ownership of three-fourths of the reserves formerly belonging to British Petroleum. After 1953, when a CIA-managed coup restored the Shah, BP regained nearly 40 percent of its reserves.

The upheaval had lasting effects. The first was that British Petroleum realized that it walked a tightrope. As a publicly owned company it needed to remain subservient to the government yet had to reduce reliance on it in order to make money. The company had been appalled when Parliament stood "idly by" during the Iranian nationalization. Despite its frustration, British Petroleum still recognized a duty not to question Parliament's reasons. The second major effect was that BP recognized that it was itself a target because of its status as an extension of the Empire. To reduce its vulnerability it embarked on a wave of oil explorations unmatched by any other company. By 1953, BP had developed major wells in Libya and Nigeria; in 1958, it acquired Alaskan leases to Prudhoe Bay; and in 1962, it made major oil finds in the North Sea. Today, only one-fifth of the British Petroleum reserves remain in the Middle Eastern countries.

The first expensive efforts were only prelude to other large ventures. British Petroleum bought a majority stake in Standard Oil of Ohio, a refiner and marketer of oil in the midwestern United States. Because the purchase was made by exchanging the first 600,000 barrels per day of North Slope crude oil produced from Prudhoe Bay, British Petroleum obtained a U.S. presence and a strong downstream organization without spending a penny. The move had the added benefit of allowing BP to use the debt-free balance sheet of Standard Oil of Ohio to finance future operations in Prudhoe Bay. In 1981 it purchased Kennecott Corporation, a copper mining company, and Purina Mills for $500 million. With both acquisitions, British Petroleum acquired healthy companies with strong managements. Its management philosophy is "hands off" the Americans in order not to impose on the subsidiaries either the corporate culture of an oil world or the organizational culture of a company that never lost its sense of obligation to the British government and to the British people.

The story of BP management and the British government took a new turn when, in an agreement with Saudi Arabia, Parliament agreed to sell 132 British warplanes worth over $7 billion, Britain's biggest military export deal. The terms of the agreement called for BP to buy Saudi crude oil for refining and marketing on the world market. The Saudis would then pass proceeds of the sale into a British defense ministry account, from which the contractors for the military equipment would be paid. The venture was not profitable; it was unfair to shareholders; it diverted company attention from its main job. Nevertheless, BP felt it had an obligation to thousands of British workers on the aircraft production lines. The final irony was that, despite BP's demonstrated fealty to England, the Thatcher government sold its 31.7 percent stake in the company as part of the Conservative government's move toward a free-market economy.

The stories of Exxon and British Petroleum are interesting because they raise important legal and moral questions about the virtues and vices of either public or private global corporations, two of which stimulate larger discussions about the role of the multinational in a complex world:

## *Questions*

- Would it be fair to stockholders who invest in private companies to turn U.S. multinationals into quasi-government corporations?
- Is it fair to host countries to promote multinationals that are, in effect, instruments of American foreign policy?

## American Multinationals and the European Community

No analysis of the multinational can close without mention of the European Community and its impact on global corporations, especially American multinationals. Postwar Europe, composed of insular, protected national markets, has been economically stagnant compared to the United States and the Far East. European companies have lacked a home market of sufficient size to support the investments necessary to compete with aggressive Japanese and American competitors in industries of the future—electronics, information technology, biotechnology, and telecommunications. Indeed, the fragmentation of the European marketplace, with its multiplicity of regulations, economic conditions, cultural preferences, tensions, and jealousies, has made doing business in Europe an unpleasant experience.

This fragmented, chauvinistic Europe is now disappearing and a dynamic, integrated market grows in its place. The year 1992 will be remembered as the historic date for the European Community's formal baptism but only decades after that event will the true implications be known. Never before have 12 nations voluntarily yielded so much of their individual sovereignties; never before have American managers had to listen to the voice of one, not 12, governments in economic matters; never before have American multinationals (which traditionally developed local strategies for each European country) needed to develop a pan-European strategy; never before have Americans had to worry about a united Germany as the dominant party in the European household. The list of "never befores" could be extended.

## Early Mistakes of American Multinationals

One "before" act that cannot be repeated is the reaction of Americans in 1957 to the European Common Market, when they naively assumed that Europe would become a relatively integrated marketplace like the United States. Americans tried to choose manufacturing locations and set up distribution networks much as they might have done in the United States—to serve a common market. They were disappointed to discover that Europe was not one market but many, with subtle and not-so-subtle barriers to multinational trade: regulations, transport barriers, national tastes, and cultural prejudices, to mention just a few. Americans did get over the pan-Europe misconcept some time ago, but they are only now beginning to develop a European strategy, or even to move toward the formation of organizations capable of creating a European strategy. In late 1988 Coca-Cola announced a reorganization of its European, African, and Middle Eastern management to form a new focused team with responsibility for the European Community. Colgate-Palmolive, with manufacturing operations in nine EC countries, appointed a pan-European management board. Heinz, probably one of the more European of U.S. companies, proclaimed in its annual report for 1988 that "the potential for an integrated European market engages the Heinz imagination." Even IBM, considered by many Europeans the prototypical pan-European corporation, may have to develop a different marketing program to complement its nationally oriented sales organizations.

## European Economic Interest Grouping

For the multinationals, the new European market is an opportunity. To illustrate, the European Economic Interest Grouping is a new legal form that facilitates the operation of a network of national subsidiaries as a single coherent business. An EEIG is not a "European company" or a form of joint venture. It is a contractual association operating under the laws of one designated home country that provides for the allocation of revenues and profits among association members in accordance with the terms they themselves stipulate in the contract. The concept, first employed in the Airbus consortium, the Euromissile project, and the Carte Bleu banking system, can greatly simplify operating a coordinated business in a multiple tax and legal jurisdiction.

Suppose, however, that an American multinational joins an EEIG group. Should U.S. antitrust laws govern the group's activities? If environmental harm is done by an American-sponsored EEIG to Spain, does the EPA have a voice? Should American audit standards prevail if five members of the EEIG are non-American companies?[48] The challenge is not simply legalistic; it is ethical as well. Definitions of fairness, obedience to other countries' laws, and respect for other nations' cultures will occur in the coming decade not only between developed and developing economies (which has gotten most attention so far) but between companies and cultures far older than America's. If anything, the EC forces managers in the United States to consider those basic ethical norms that measure all cultural values, not only those of specific countries.

The moral challenge will become especially acute when Americans consider Europe's social costs for health care, disability training and the like which are much higher than in the United States. Will American workers in an EEIG, for example, settle for less benefits than those available to their coworkers on the continent? The questions are as endless as the opportunities are dazzling.

## Strengths and Weaknesses of MNCs
### Strengths

- They tend to diminish counterproductive nationalism.
- If multinationals enrich themselves, they also improve the economy of the host country, especially through the transfer of technology and management skills. Unilever's research and development program, to take just one example, is conducted in 33 countries.
- They speed the transfer of technology. It took 20 years for the U.S. rotary printing press to be introduced into Britain. In the 1950s and 1960s the average time lag between original production of a major semiconductor device to first production outside the innovating country was about two years. Within one year of Wilkinson's introducing stainless steel razor blades in 1962 to the United States there were competing products on the world market.
- MNCs are a major force in international monetary stability. For them, currency fluctuations are a threat, not an opportunity.
- The MNCs are generally seen as good employers, offering conditions at least equal to the most progressive domestic companies. They perceive that it is in their interest to behave well because of their visibility and vulnerability as "foreigners." One old study in the British Kingdom, for example, of the behavior of the U.S. subsidiaries of MNCs (about 1600 of them in 1969) indicated that they had good reputations because of above-average wages and superior working conditions.
- Talk of destroying American jobs ignores the report of a Harvard research team showing that foreign investments in manufacturing created more jobs for U.S. workers than they destroyed. Had the U.S.-based corporations not made the foreign investments, the cost to American employees would have been high—an estimated 250,000 production jobs lost, another 250,000 jobs in the main offices of the MNCs, and 100,000 supporting jobs. However, the investments did tend to alter U.S. trade patterns, which, in turn, upset employment in some U.S. sectors, a serious problem but less serious than any total dislocation.[49]

## *Weaknesses*

- Multinationals have usually opposed unionization of workers. What expressly arouses resentment is that part of the incentive offered by some governments is antiunion. Strikes against foreign companies in South Korea are illegal. The Malaysian government offers new industries a three-year period during which no trade union can operate.
- Multinationals are runaway firms roaming the world in search of profits by using cheap labor abroad. A classic example of highly labor-intensive industries leaving the home country is the shifting of electronics production to Far East countries. Hong Kong, Taiwan, Singapore, the Philippines, and South Korea are all countries that have attracted companies such as Phillips, RCA, Zenith, and IBM.
- Multinationals play games with taxing authorities. They can minimize the tax bill by establishing an artificial transfer price that will inflate the profits of subsidiaries located in countries where the tax burden is low and limit the profits earned in countries where taxes are high. The tax authorities in the various countries, not having access to all the relevant data of the parent firm and its affiliates, cannot determine the consolidated profits or evaluate the reasonableness of the transfer prices. They must therefore base their tax assessment on the book profits of the enterprise within their jurisdiction.
- Multinationals, having too much control over key industries, often induce destabalizing results. Oil in the Middle East is an obvious example. An organization of bauxite-producing countries brings together such unlikely partners as Australia, Guyana, Jamaica, Yugoslavia, Guinea, and Surinam. Spain and Morocco have been active in setting up a mercury producers organization. Phosphates, tungsten, and chrome ore are other cases. The MNCs will be affected directly by this changed balance of power. The implications, both for the country and for world trade, are great.

## Summary

Multinationals are here to stay. Their presence may spur countermeasures by nations that feel harmed by the foreigner; may result in moves to establish an internal commercial court to enforce an international code of company conduct; and may induce labor leaders to form an umbrella organization—an international labor movement—that could flex its muscle throughout the world. Farseeing executives know these things. They know that attention now focused on Japan and the Soviet Union, Europe and America will turn in the next century to China, a country where they will see a baffling combination of traditional Confucius values, enormous ethnocentrism, a complicated bureaucracy, and enormous resources.

Multinational managers also know that world reforms can be directed by the passionate or by the principled. In the making is a drama more exciting than any one previously experienced by the multinational. Codes of conduct for individual corporations, joint ventures, increased roles for local managers, investments in schools and hospitals, support of human rights, and innovative programs for social ordering are among the tools that can be used to build a more humane world community.[50] French Jesuits working in North America and Spanish Franciscans working in Latin America were seen as a *force civilatrice* during the 18th century. With enlightened leadership the multinational can become the civilizing force of the 21st.

That fulfillment of the vision will be difficult is seen in the frustrating decade-long effort by the United Nations Commission on Transmutual Corporations to produce a code of behavior. Perhaps incrementalism will be the final solution when companies like IBM, General Motors, General Electric, and Dow Corning share their own experiences in code building for a multinational world.

## Questions for Discussion

1. If you were the CEO of a multinational company that could make a financial killing by accepting the invitation of corrupted officials to invest in their country, would you go?
2. Would you accept a three-year assignment to a project designed to establish an international code of conduct for multinationals? Even if it meant financial sacrifice?
3. Should American multinationals siphon a fixed percentage of their annual profits to help the world's poor?
4. Are unions necessary in countries where jobs are scarce and skills are low?
5. Should multinationals accept as a moral duty the task of job training for unskilled workers of the host countries?
6. Should American multinationals insist that one condition for their involvement in South Africa be government-endorsed affirmative action programs?

## Ethical Quandary

In its notice and proxy statement for its annual 1991 stockholders meeting, IBM included a stockholder proposal regarding company policy in South Africa and the board's response. Both illustrate what has been a classic debate on multinational policy.

*Stockholder Proposal:* This resolution is supported by IBM employees and religious organizations. In 1988, 6 IBMers cosponsored a similar stockholder resolution. In 1989, 91 IBMers cosponsored or endorsed. In 1990, 368 IBMers from Europe, Japan, and the United States cosponsored or endorsed the resolution.

Upon emerging from prison after 27 years, Nelson Mandela called on the international community "to continue the campaign to isolate the apartheid regime."

IBM has sold more computers to South Africa than any other company, and IBM has acknowledged that nearly all its customers in South Africa are white.

IBM's reply to the 1989 stockholder resolution further acknowledged that technology shipments strengthen the South African economy to the point where South Africa can be "competitive with other industrialized nations." In other words, technology shipments help overcome existing sanctions and the inefficiencies of apartheid.

IBM's customers include major military contractors in South Africa: Grinaker Electronics, Plessy, Dorbyl, and Phillips. Technology helped South Africa overcome a worldwide arms embargo and build a sophisticated armaments industry. The weapons have been used to repress dissent and attack neighboring states. Arms are now South Africa's largest manufactured export item.

IBM also supplied computers to run production at two South African oil refineries that supply fuel for military vehicles and that help South Africa overcome the impact of the worldwide oil embargo.

IBM further assists Pretoria by leading the campaign against local government laws restricting purchases from companies dealing with South Africa. IBM's campaign is less than forthright:

1. IBM tells local government officials that it cannot sell to the South Africa military or police—but IBM omits mentioning that it legally sells to South African companies that design and build weapons for the South African military.
2. IBM advertises its donations for education but the truth is that the donations are tiny compared to IBM sales to the apartheid rulers.

By selling to South Africa, IBM is hurting its image and risking legitimate business in the United States, a market for IBM products at least 100 times larger than South Africa.

We believe the bottom line is this: IBM's sales to South Africa strengthen apartheid, put human lives at risk, make IBM tacitly complicit with apartheid rule, and jeopardize IBM's reputation and profits.

RESOLVED, shareholders request that IBM proceed immediately, within the law, to stop all direct or indirect sales and services to South Africa until apartheid ends.

*The Company Response:* This resolution continues a dialogue of several years duration concerning the most appropriate method for achieving the objective which IBM and the proponents both share: ending the morally repugnant system of apartheid in South Africa.

Since South Africa now seems set on the road to meaningful economic and political participation by blacks and other non-whites, it is imperative that the country's economy remain strong enough to support a peaceful and orderly transition. It is our view that responsible business activity and social programs carried out by American and other companies in South Africa have contributed to ending apartheid and creating a post-apartheid economy and society.

For example, when the deteriorating economic and political situation made it necessary for IBM to sell its South African subsidiary to an employee trust in 1987, we announced that the new company, Information Services Management Ltd. (ISM), would continue to market IBM products and services in order to meet our responsibilities to our former employees and to our customers. Today, ISM continues to honor IBM's commitment to fair employment and equal opportunity; it continues to comply with U.S. export control laws which prohibit sales to South Africa's police and military. . . .

Further, within the American constitutional system, foreign policy is entrusted to the President and the Congress. Now that the South Africa government has satisfied most of the conditions set by the U.S. Congress for reducing or removing sanctions—and with European governments having already begun the process of reducing their sanctions—unilateral termination of IBM's sales to South Africa is particularly counterproductive.

What the proponents advocate would effectively put ISM out of business, along with any possible contribution IBM products might make to a post-apartheid South Africa. We firmly believe that this would be a profound disservice to blacks and other non-whites in the transition to a new South Africa.

## Question

- Which position do you think is the better ethical statement?

## Notes

1. Mira Wilkins, *The Emergence of the Multinational Empire* (Cambridge: Harvard University Press, 1970). See also, Orville L. Freeman, *The Multinational Corporation: Instrument for World Growth* (New York: Praeger, 1981), especially chs. 1 and 2.
2. Raymond Vernon, *Sovereignty at Bay* (New York: Basic Books, 1971), 3.
3. Ibid., ch. 1.
4. Sir Arnold Hall, chairman of British-based Hawker Siddeley Ltd. John Humble. Quoted in John Humble, *The Responsible Multinational Enterprise* (London: Foundation for Business Responsibility, 1973) 2.
5. United States Finance Committee Hearings, 1973.
6. Jacques G. Maisonrouge, president of IBM World Trade Corporation, in comments to the International Academy of Management, New York, September 19, 1989.
7. Neil Jacoby, *Social Responsibility* (New York: MacMillan, 1973).
8. Arvind V. Phatak, *International Dimensions of Management*, 2d ed. (Boston: PWS Kent Publishers, 1989), 4.
9. Vernon, *Sovereignty at Bay*, 216.
10. Ibid., ch. 5.

11. *World Almanac 1989*, 1401.
12. John Kenneth Galbraith, "The Defense of the Multinational," *Harvard Business Review* (March–April 1978): 83–93. Corporate disclaimers about power and corporate claims of political neutrality are throwbacks to a model of operation taught in neoclassical economics. The disclaimer and the claim put the multinational in the position of a hypocrite and liar—and yet their leaders may believe their own rhetoric.
13. Dennis McCann offered a perceptive analysis of the ideological/theological nexus in his article, "Political Ideologies and Practical Theology: Is There a Difference?" *Union Seminary Quarterly* 36 (Summer 1981): 243–257.
14. Paul VI, *On the Progress of People* (Washington, D.C.: 1967); and John Paul II, *Laborem Exercens* (Washington, D.C.: National Catholic Conference of Bishops, 1981).
15. Dennis P. McCann, *God's Controversy with the Multinational Corporation* (Chicago: DePaul University, 1987). Unpublished monograph.
16. Gustavo Gutíerrez, *A Theology of Freedom* (New York: Orbis Books, 1973). Reverend Robert McAfee Brown is a good example of a prominent Protestant theologian who is also committed to liberation theology.
17. Ibid., 87.
18. Michael Novak, *Toward a Theology of the Corporation* (Washington: American Enterprise Institute, 1981).
19. "Symposium": *Harper Magazine*, December 1986, 37–40.
20. John Kenneth Galbraith, "The Defense of the Multinational Company," *Harvard Business Review* (March–April 1978): 88.
21. Joseph Ramos, *Neoconservative Economics in the Southern Cone of Latin America, 1973–1983* (Baltimore: The Johns Hopkins University Press, 1986).
22. Quoted by John W. Sewell, "The Metamorphosis of the Third World: U.S. Interests in the 1990s," in *The Global Economy*, eds. William Brock and Robert Hormonts (New York: N. W. Norton, 1990), 129. Sewell's article, one of many fine essays in the collection, forms the basis for the author's analysis.
23. Richard T. De George, "Five Moral Rules for Multinationals Operating Overseas," *Ethikos* 1 (January–February 1988): 7–10. Thomas Donaldson, *The Ethics of International Business* (New York: Oxford University Press, 1989), sees a need to distinguish between minimal and maximum obligations; even the former are woefully inadequate in Third World countries (ch. 2).
24. Anne M. Street, "Multinationals Square Off against Central American Worker," *Business and Society Review* 52 (Winter 1985): 45–50.
25. Robert Thurow, "The Golden Goose Finds it Unleashed New Threats," *The Wall Street Journal*, July 30, 1990, A4.
26. Donald Kendall, "Corporate Ownership: The International Dimension," *Columbia Journal of World Business* 3 (March–April 1968): 13–21.
27. Howard Perlmutter, "Multinational Corporations," *The Columbia Journal of World Business* 4 (January–February 1969): 9–19.
28. Gary Gereffi, *The Pharmaceutical Industry and Diplomacy in the Third World* (Princeton: Princeton University, 1983); and Peter Evans, *Dependent Development: The Balance of Multinational, State, and Local Capital in Brazil* (Princeton: Princeton University Press, 1979).
29. Rebecca Scott, "Exploring the Meaning of Freedom: Post-Emancipation Societies in Comparative Perspective," *The Hispanic American Review* 61 (August 1988): 421.
30. Zacharias Moutourkais, "Power, Corruption, and Commerce: The Making of Local Administrative Structures in Seventeenth Century Buenos Aires," *The Hispanic American Historical Review* 68 (November 1988): 171–172.
31. Marshall Eakins, "British Imperialism and British Enterprise in Brazil: The St. John d'el Rey Mining Company, 1830–1960," *The Hispanic American Historical Review* 66 (November 1986): 696–741.
32. Enno Hobbing, "The Good Corporate Guest Helps Build the House," *Columbia Journal of World Business* 2 (September–October 1967): 39–40.

33. T. A. Litvak and C. J. Marcelle, "Guidelines for Multinational Corporations," *Columbia Journal of World Business* 3 (July–August 1968): 35–43.
34. Risks are involved. One thinks of ITT and the violation of human rights in Chile by Pinochet Augusto Urgarte, Genaro Arriagarda, *Pinochet: The Politics of Power* (Winchester, Mass.: Lexington, 1989). Trans. Nancy Morris. See also, Ariel Dorfman, "Adios General,' *Harper's*, December 1989, 72–76.
35. Penny Lernoux, *Cry of the People* (New York: Doubleday, 1980), 108–110.
36. John Houck and Oliver Williams, *Full Value: Cases in Business Ethics* (New York: Harper & Row, 1978).
37. Ibid., 144–151.
38. Frank Tannenbaum, "The Survival of the Fittest," *Columbia Journal of World Business* 3 (March–April 1968): 13–21. See the extended treatment in the paper by Richard G. Baumgart, "Multinational Corporations: New Dimensions in Community Power Research," delivered to the Society for the Study of Social Problems, August 23, 1975.
39. Richard and Margaret Baumgart, "Multinational Corporate Expansion and the Nation-State Developments," paper prescnted to the 73rd annual meeting of the American Sociological Association, September 6, 1978.
40. Paul Kennedy, *The Rise and Fall of the Great Powers* (New York: Vintage Books, 1898), xv–xxv.
41. John Humble, *Social Responsibility Audit: A Management Tool for Survival* (New York: American Management Association, 1973), 21–30.
42. Yves L. Doz and C. K. Prahalad, "How MNCs Cope with Host Government Intervention," *Harvard Business Review* (March–April 1980): 149–157.
43. Dennis J. Encarnation and Sushil Vachan, "Foreign Ownership: When Hosts Change the Rules," *Harvard Business Review* (September–October 1985): 153–160.
44. Exxon Corporation, *Annual Statement, 1990.*
45. William N. George, *Strategies of the Major Oil Companies* (Ann Arbor, Mich.: JMF Research Press, 1985), 7.
46. Anthony Sampson, *The Seven Sisters* (New York: Bantam Books, 1975), 28. See also, Robert Engler, *The Brotherhood of Oil* (Chicago: The University of Chicago Press, 1977).
47. George, *Strategies of the Major Oil Companies*, 241.
48. Thomas Dunfee and Aryeh Friedman, "The Extra-Territorial Application of United States Antitrust Laws: A Pyramid for an Interim Solution," *Ohio State Law Journal* 45 (1984): 883–992.
49. This old study (1971) has not been refuted. See David W. Ewing, "MNCs on Trial," *Harvard Business Review* (May–June 1972): 130–142.
50. Humble, *Social Responsibility Audit*, 33.

CHAPTER 13

# The Environment

### Threats to a Safe Environment: Scientific Perspectives
Domestic Dangers
Global Phenomena
Technology's Side Effects

### Key Questions Concerning the Common Good
How Safe Is Safe?
Do We Know What to Do?
Will Americans Pay for Their Own Safety?
Is Industry Doing Enough?
Will Americans Sacrifice for Others' Safety?

### Toward a New Environmental Ethic
Two Ethics?
Rolston's Maxims
A Short Checklist
Short-Term Problems: Two Examples
*Ecotage (Ecological Sabotage)*
*Midtown Pulp*

### Summary
Questions for Discussion
Ethical Quandary

### Appendix 13A
### Protection of the Ozone Layer: Chronology of Key Events

*T*he Bible speaks of "man's dominion over the earth." Man (meaning men and women everywhere) has gone about the business of establishing the fiefdom with enthusiasm—some would say with a vengeance. Forests have yielded to farms, farms to factory towns, factory towns to sprawling cities. Change is the constant among multiple variables as the aging face of Mother Earth loses more and more of her clear and resilient skin. But nagging questions arise: Has king man of the Western world debased servant earth of all humankind? Has he forgotten these words of the Chinese warning in the Tao Te Chung?

> Those who would take over the earth and shape it to their will never, I note, succeed.[1]

Before the Europeans came to America, Native Americans saw mystery in the sun and the moon, the rain and the rock. The physical world was treated with reverence. Now the imprint of giant footsteps record a series of revolutions—scientific, industrial, technological, and electronic—that move man toward greater and greater dominion over the earth. Americans today eat better and live longer than their forebears; they travel farther and more frequently than their grandparents; they enjoy air-conditioned houses and swim in their own pools; they sleep in better beds and ride on better roads. Few would exchange their complex, comfortable world for the simple life of the past.

And, ironically, what damage humans forget to do, nature herself remembers: floods and fires, volcanos and earthquakes, hurricanes and typhoons. The Johnstown flood in 1889 took over 2,200 lives; the Galveston hurricane of 1900 claimed 6,000 lives; a Martinique volcano in 1920 caused over 30,000 immediate deaths. In 1989 fires at Yellowstone, earthquakes in California, and floods in Louisiana taught Americans anew that their dominance over nature had to be understood in relationship to nature's dominance over them. One lesson is clear: Nature strikes back against intrusions by humans and is often devastating of its own accord. The Creator is the unseen player in a global chess game.[2]

As we learn more, we discover more natural hazards. Radon is a good example. After the manmade nuclear problem at Pennsylvania's Three Mile Island in 1979, concern for protection from mistakes made at nuclear facilities led to the discovery of radon, a chemical formed by the radioactive decay of uranium. When sucked into houses and inhaled, radon can cause cancer. One Pennsylvania worker's home was found to have a radon dose equivalent to smoking 220 packs of cigarettes a day. Radon is especially prevalent in the Reading Prong, which stretches from northwest New Jersey into Pennsylvania and New York.

Twelve percent of America's 75,000,000 homes are believed to have radon in amounts sufficient to constitute a major health problem. Polluted air, polluted water, toxic waste dumps, and pesticides on farms and in food are signs of the times. Southern California's once Eden-like city of the angels and Colorado's once pristine pure city on the mountain have become centers of smog; northeast forests have been hurt by acid rain spewed out by midwestern factories; New Jersey beaches have been awash in New York City's garbage. For too long a time Americans wanted to keep their cake and eat it, too. Today is the moment for trade-offs, when the costs of doing things have to be weighed against the costs of not doing things. In a sense the moral question from a homocentric point of view is simple: Will people sacrifice enough today so that tomorrow will come with enough for others? Perhaps the economics of environment, more than the economics of scarcity, will recall the relevance of the old Puritan ethic: work today and save today in order to enjoy tomorrow.

Traditional economic theory is under attack for its alleged overriding concern with individuals as consumers interested only in themselves and for its gross neglect of individuals as citizens shaped by their collective history and concerned with their collective identity. Economists concentrate on trade deficits and budgeting deficits when they should be concerned with earth deficits. Now others, describing themselves as ecological economists (nearly 400 of them met in May 1990 in a conference at the World Bank) or as environmental ethicists, emphasize a theme forcefully articulated by Thomas Berry, a Dominican priest:

> Seldom does anyone speak of the deficit involved in the closing down of the basic life system of the planet through abuse of the air, the soil, the water, and the vegetation. As we have indicated, the earth deficit is the real deficit, the ultimate deficit, the deficit in some of its major consequences so absolute as to be beyond adjustment from any source in heaven or on earth. Since the earth system is the ultimate guarantee of all deficits, a failure here is a failure of last resort. Neither economic viability nor improvement in life conditions for the poor can be realized in such circumstances. These can only worsen, especially when we consider the rising population levels throughout the developing world.
>
> This deficit in its extreme expression is not only a resource deficit, but the death of a living process, not simply the death of a living process, but of *the* living process, a living process which exists, so far as we know, only on the planet earth. That is what makes our problem definitely different from those of any other generation of whatever ethnic, cultural, political, or religious tradition, or of any other historical period. For the first time we are determining the destinies of the earth in a comprehensive and

irreversible manner. The immediate danger is not possible nuclear war, but actual industrial plundering. Economics on this scale is not simply economics of the human community, it is economics of the earth community in its most comprehensive dimensions.[3]

*Interest in the environment dates back to 1962 and publication of Rachel Carson's* Silent Spring. *Carson's conclusions (that man will end by destroying the earth and that the free-market system is the prime culprit in the deadly process) became the public's conclusions despite accusations of lack of evidence and lack of logic.*[4] *Since that time, environmentalism is to moderns what chastity was to the Victorians. Even motherhood and apple pie do not compete for public esteem with environment. As a consequence, environmentalists are angels and their adversaries are the devils.*

*But the environmentalists are realists and the campaigns they wage are carefully chosen, partially because Congress, during the past two decades, has come to rely heavily on private enforcement of public laws. In the early 1980s there was a surge of suits related to violations of the Clean Water Act (passed in 1970 and first amended in 1977), which was left to private groups for enforcement. The surge was not due exclusively to a further decline in water quality, or to an enfeebled congressional interest, but rather to careful calculations by environmentalists about the deep pockets of big industries.*

*Two features of the Clean Water Act were especially helpful to the environmentalists. The first was a provision that allowed private citizens to sue not only for injunctive relief but also to enforce the civil-fines provision of the act. District courts can impose civil penalties of up to $25,000 per day per violation. Legally, these fines are payable to the government but, faced by long and costly trials as well as threats to their image, corporations settle out of court for a sum that can be pocketed by the plaintiff, not by the government. The other feature attractive to the environmentalists was the requirement that the EPA record the permits granted to firms for using waters to dispose of waste and the further requirement that companies that violated the law report the incident promptly. The environmentalists did not need to spend money searching for corporate culprits. The villains, having identified themselves, were willing to settle out of court.*

*Another writer who had a powerful impact on public opinion was entomologist Paul Ehrlich, who spoke of a population bomb caused by too many people, too many factories, too many machines, too little public outcry, too little government action, and too little federal-state coordination.*[5] *His solution was creation of a government agency designed to discourage reproduction through personal incentives and practices and the injection of temporary sterilants into the water supply. Following Carson and Erlich, others have poured forth their anguish in books with titles expressive of their feelings—*The End of Nature *and* The Deluge and the Ark.[6]

*Whether applauded or dismissed, Carson's and Ehrlich's findings have become so well known that the word environmentalism has joined words like sexism and racism as symbols of deeper problems. Acid rain, smoggy skies, escaping gas from industrial plants, and toxic waste are the threats—with the disposal of dangerous waste emerging as the most pressing concern. Toxic dumps with steel drums that have been left to rust and leak, letting poisons seep into the earth for decades, are scattered in virtually every county of every state. They present a potentially irreversible threat to water supplies, public health, and the economy. It was no pejorative when the EPA declared in 1980: "America has a ticking time bomb ready to go off." Chemicals with once strange names—dioxin, vinyl chloride, PBB, and PC—as well as familiar toxins such as lead, mercury, and arsenic are now household words for deadly poisons.* ■

## *The purposes of this chapter are:*

1. To convey the scientists' sense of the magnitude of the environmental problem.
2. To indicate what government and business are doing about it.
3. To examine the Lockean ethic of private property as it relates to pollution.
4. To report (and challenge when appropriate) Rolston's maxims for an environmental ethic.

## Threats to a Safe Environment: Scientific Perspectives

### *Domestic Dangers*

Renaissance man Frances Bacon (1561-1626) called on humans to storm and occupy the outermost boundaries of the globe. In Bacon's time, there was little chance that occupation of the castles would do significant harm. Today that danger is real and polls show that Americans know it. Acting on such knowledge is a different story. If we seek environmental safety, the Dakotas look most inviting, but Americans have settled heavily in New Jersey, the most densely populated of all 50 states and the one with the largest number of jobs (95,000) in the chemical industry. It ranks only after Texas in chemical production but its environmental threat is far worse because a great number of companies are located next to residential neighborhoods. In one case a plant that stored tons of phosgene, a gas produced during World War I, was located ominously close to a day-care center. By the 1950s the Garden State became known as Cancer Alley.[7] Yet by 1985, when the New Jersey rate was close to the average, the early assumption that industrial pollutants were the cause was challenged.

Prior to the Love Canal crisis, which made headlines throughout the 1970s, toxic waste management was treated with the respect accorded to national defense and the space program: too complex to be understood by the public and too important to be monitored by the regulators. By the

1980s, with some 50,000 chemical waste sites in the United States—2,000 of them posing health hazards—and with nearly 30 percent of the nation's large water systems contaminated, the matter was no longer the preserve of experts.[8] The public has reason for worry. Examples tell part of the grim story:

- From 1853 to 1959 a series of chemical, leather, and glue manufacturing companies operated in Woburn, Massachusetts. In this country's first toxic-waste disposal site are 800 acres of land and wetlands containing open arsenic pits, chromium lagoons, and buried animal hides.
- Located in a rural area near Louisville, Kentucky is the so-called Valley of the Drums, five acres of which were used for the disposal of drums containing dangerous chemical wastes. Thousands of canisters were deposited in the valley between 1967 and 1978, and many have corroded and leaked.
- In Jackson Township, New Jersey, a municipal landfill has been used by the community since 1972 for the disposal of solid and septic wastes. Wastes from the landfill, percolating through the earth into an underground aquifer, has contaminated much of the drinking water.
- Denver has 39 sites that contain buried radioactive tailings produced from the refinement of uranium into radium during the early part of the 20th century.
- In southern California, the Stringfellow site was used for toxic waste disposal between 1956 and 1972. The area has a series of artificial ponds containing over 32 million gallons of waste material from DDT, acids, and other carcinogens.
- Alkali Lake in south central Oregon, during a short period in 1969 and 1970, was used as a storage for drums containing toxic wastes. It has become highly dangerous.

These six are part of a large family of danger points in the United States. Examples could be offered almost endlessly. In 1979, a small Pennsylvania company was found to have illegally dumped toxic waste into the Susquehanna River near Pittston after leaking chemicals burned eight playing children. In 1980 the Pine River in Michigan was discovered to be polluted with chemicals dumped into an area adjacent to the river by the Michigan Chemical Company. Each day seemed to bring a new threat and each year the threats raced ahead of the solutions. Americans everywhere express fear over environmental issues. Fairly representative of public opinion was the report by the Field Institute's survey of Californians showing that respondents rated toxic waste, sewage, air pollution, and acid rain at their primary worries.

These problems form the main agenda for American environmentalists everywhere. Which of them constitutes the major hazard is hard to determine because below-surface problems tend, for understandable reasons, to be downplayed. Water is a good example. For every gallon of fresh water in America's rivers and lakes, another 24 are hidden underground. This vast natural resource is being consumed at an enormous rate—from 34 billion gallons a day in 1970 to 85 billion by 1980. The penchant to rob Peter to pay Paul was evident in responses to federal efforts to protect surface water. When more waste was sent by chemical companies to levels as deep as a mile below the earth's surface, the injections caused waste to seep upward to poison surface water.

While chemical companies have been the primary targets of outrage, a new culprit, the farmer, is coming into range. Intensive cultivation of wheat, corn, soybeans, and cotton has led to extensive topsoil erosion—almost three billion tons per year—and has reduced the true value of agricultural output by some $40 million annually. What seems especially shameful to environmentalists is that effective techniques to combat erosion are available. Conservation tillage, contour planting, strip cropping, and terracing are measures known to reduce erosion rates by 60 to 90 percent.

Not all, however, agree with the environmentalists on this issue. Some agricultural experts contend that erosion control itself may involve other environmental insults—such as those resulting from the increased use of herbicides that accompany scientific farming. The farm dilemma is easy to state: Do Americans want greater production (the total amount of commodities produced by each farmer) or greater productivity (the ratio between economic input and output)? Ironically, greater productivity has not consistently resulted in greater production because, when farm prices fall below costs, there is no reason to increase production.[9]

Because new fertilizers have already increased productivity to the point that farming is one of our most efficient industries, it may make sense from ethical and economic perspectives to curb use. Pesticide, herbicide, and fertilizer residues have contaminated an estimated 20 percent of U.S. wells with nitrates that are potent carcinogens. According to various U.S. geological studies, Iowa and Florida are hardest hit but others suffer.[10] Residues of pesticides were identified in more than two-thirds of the wells in northeastern Iowa; in Florida's citrus growing regions, pesticides such as ethylene dibromide (EDB) have turned up in the drinking water; California, Nebraska, Colorado, Oklahoma, and Texas are states where poorly managed irrigation threatens ground water's purity.

But California commands greatest national attention because the San Joaquin Valley has become a disaster area. In early 1985 the reservoir at the Kesterson National Wildlife Refuge was so polluted that the refuge was declared a toxic dump. In 1980, high levels of salinity in the Colorado River cost regional taxpayers more than $100 million from tainted soil, killed crops, and escalated water treatment costs.[11] Toxic chemicals spewing into the air continue to draw major attention. Between 1980 and 1985, approximately 6,928 accidents involving toxic chemicals occurred in the United States, killing more than 135 people and injuring nearly 1,500.[12] Estimates suggest that only modest improvement was made in the second half of the decade. Moreover, the statistics underestimate the total danger because data were secured only from certain regions.

## Global Phenomena

To ignore the worldwide dimensions of the environmental topic is to play false with ethics and folly with policy. In this arena, experts first concentrate on population growth in the developing countries as well as the circumstances in which it occurs and the actions it triggers. Because people in the developed nations do not have many children, the inference was made that, if other regions industrialized, they too would avoid environmental problems assumed to be related to dense population. New obstacles, however, are now appearing to what looked only a few years ago to be the prospect of an orderly process of universal development. Although population has been increasing slowly and steadily for a long time, only in recent years have people heard about the greenhouse effect, acid rain, pollution of the oceans, and the decline of fish populations. The sudden appearance of these environmental phenomena, contrasted with the only gradual increase of population, suggests they have little connection, and indeed this conclusion has been drawn. That population has little part in causing the environmental damage is argued from the fact that the population growth started to decelerate during the 1970s and 1980s. The world rate of growth was 2 percent 20 years ago. If it was 2 percent then, how can the present rate of 1.8 percent be harming the planet?

In the past the strongest case against population growth had been based on the loss of nonrenewable resources, because nature appeared to fix the total supply of oil, metals, land, and other commercial minerals. This argument has been rendered obsolete by the facility with which new supplies have been discovered; moreover, technical advances have created substitutes with such speed that the apparent overcoming of the classical "increasing marginal cost" has caused many to think that nature offers no further resistance to the expansion of population and economy. Malthus as prophet had failed.

However, other factors are at work. Soils, forests, wild animals, and especially fisheries have been harvested from time immemorial and have been referred to as renewable resources. Wholly different rules were applied to these from those governing minerals. But now there seem to be adequate amounts of the nonrenewable resources, and it is the renewable ones whose shortage will traumatize humanity. In an odd turn of language, resources called nonrenewable are the ones that will not run short, while renewable resources like forests and water will be the areas of shortage. According to this line of reasoning twice as many fish eaters will normally eat twice as much fish; therefore, a doubling of population will double the stress on the aquatic system. The inference is correct, however, only at those low harvesting levels that have existed throughout history. Empirical study of the past relations between population and fish supplies, however, can be totally misleading when the scale of exploitation changes. One or two fishermen in a lake are an easily assimilated element in the biosystem of the lake, the slightly greater mortality of mature fish being offset by better survivorship of the young. However, if the fishermen become dozens, then thousands, and if the lake is not large, they do affect the biosystem.

Consumption may be a linear function of population when technology and style of life are given, but the resulting strain on the environment is distinctly nonlinear. Once the woodcutting or fish consumption outpaces the normal mortality of the trees or the reproductive capacity of the fish, then any increment of population (again with given technology and style of life) changes the ecology permanently. Through eutrophication a lake loses its ability to support commercially valuable fish, and they are replaced by worthless species, as in Lake Erie. A dry area kept fertile by artesian wells becomes desert when its fossil water is exhausted.

Sudden changes can take place without clear warning. Once population has moved beyond the level that can be supported by the natural resource at equilibrium, a new feature of the interaction between the human population and resources comes into play: less and less exploitation is sustainable. The less productive resource has to be harvested more intensively: smaller trees are cut for firewood, smaller fish are eaten, the search for hidden resources intensifies. The response to a diminishing resource and a burgeoning market is higher prices, which provide economic incentives to use even more ingenuity and more effective technology to hunt down and capture whatever of the resource remains. It may take more effort to catch smaller fish, but the effort still pays because of higher prices.

One of the most dramatic examples was the Korean trawlers in the Mediterranean that picked up unnumbered marine creatures while pulling nets 15 miles long and extending 40 feet down. Contrast the volume of water swept through per crew member per day with that for the Eskimo fisherman spearing fish through a hole in the ice. A quick calculation shows that it can easily be a million times as great. What applies on a local scale to a lake or to a sea applies on a world scale once markets have become larger than the sustainable catch. Even the fisheries of the vast Pacific could be turned into desert by superefficient trawlers. And this nonlinear relation between population (and the stress it causes) applies to all resources on all levels.

## *Technology's Side Effects*

Lively controversy continues between the neomalthusians and those who believe that science can save future generations as it has saved the present generation. One development in particular that has attracted scientists' attention is ozone and the greenhouse problem. Ozone has been called the single most important chemically active trace gas in the earth's atmosphere. Two singular characteristics of this remote, unstable, and toxic gas make it critical: (1) certain wavelengths of ultraviolet radiation that can damage and cause mutations in animal and plant cells are absorbed by the extraordinarily thin layer of ozone molecules dispersed throughout the atmosphere, particularly in the stratosphere; and (2) differing quantities of ozone at different altitudes can have major effects on global climate, which of course is related to life itself.

In 1973 two University of Michigan scientists, Richard Stolarski and Ralph Cicerone, while exploring the possible effects of chemical emissions from NASA rockets, theorized that chlorine in the stratosphere could unleash a complicated chain reaction that would continually destroy ozone for decades. A year later Mario Molina and Sherwood Rowland at the University of California at Irvine identified certain peculiar properties of manmade chlorofluorocarbons (CFCs). Unlike most other gases, CFCs were not chemically destroyed or rained out quickly in the lower atmosphere, but migrated slowly up to the stratosphere where they remained intact for decades or more. The CFCs, not naturally present in the stratosphere, are eventually broken down by radiation and thereby release large quantities of chlorine. The implication of these two hypotheses was that CFCs might cause significant depletion of the ozone layer. The enhanced levels of ultraviolet radiation—which would then reach the earth's surface—might have disastrous impacts on human health and the environment, causing skin cancer, eye cataracts and blindness, suppression of the human immune system, losses in food production, damage to plastics and other materials, and intensification of the greenhouse heat-trap effect.

Much attention had already been fixed on the undesirable effects of burning coal because it emits sulfur and nitrogen oxides that have destructive effects on ecology and health. The carbon dioxide content of the atmosphere would be increased by such combustion and that of other carbonaceous materials. This could lead to a global warming. When, during the 1980s, summer temperatures in the United States were noticeably warmer than in the past, concern about a possible causal linkage between energy use and climate change increased. Most of the serious analytical work, plus a spate of popular articles, suggested that if man's consumption of fossil fuels had not already committed us to significant climatic change, continued use of such fuels, as well as changes in the amounts of some other trace gases in the atmosphere, will.

This is not a new theory. Scientists have long realized that, were the earth not endowed with an atmosphere containing a substantial amount of carbon dioxide, it would be covered with ice and would be about 34 degrees centigrade colder. That it is relatively warm is due to the so-called greenhouse effect. This arises because carbon dioxide and water vapor (along with some other trace gases in the atmosphere) are nearly transparent to light in the visible part of the electromagnetic spectrum where solar radiation peaks, but are strongly absorbing in some parts of the infrared spectrum. Because an atmosphere containing these greenhouse gases cradle the earth, absorbing some of the infrared radiation from it, the earth's surface is heated to a significantly higher temperature than would be the case for a planet without such an atmosphere. If the amount of carbon dioxide in the atmosphere changes, equilibrium temperature of the earth will change with it. Although it has not been proven that relatively low carbon dioxide concentrations led to the ice ages, a strong correlation exists between atmospheric levels of carbon dioxide and global average temperatures in ice ages and interglacial periods.

But change in average temperatures is only the beginning of the story. Second-order effects (patterns of cloud cover, precipitation, winds, ocean currents, and glaciation) depend sensitively on average surface temperatures and partially on seasonal and geographic differences in temperatures. Until the industrial revolution, the composition of the earth's atmosphere changed slowly; the carbon dioxide concentration increased from about 195 parts per million (ppm) during the last ice age (18,000 years ago) to 280 ppm in the late 1700s. It is 352 ppm today and increasing. Additionally, other greenhouse gases arising from man's industrial and agricultural activities—notably methane, nitrous oxide, tropospheric ozone, and chlorofluorocarbons (CFCs)—are being added to the earth's atmosphere at accelerating rates. They are now estimated to be about as significant in their collective impact on climate as the changes in carbon dioxide composition that had occurred in the last century.

Most of the change in atmospheric GHG concentrations is directly attributable to energy use. Almost 80 percent of the carbon dioxide increase is due to the burning of fossil fuels (the remainder mostly to the burning of tropical forests and production of cement). Some of the methane increase is due to mining of coal and leakage from gas pipelines, wells, and refineries. The tropospheric ozone is due mainly to the use of internal combustion engines, which are major factors in the creation of photochemical smog. Some of the CFC loading is due to leakage from refrigerating and air conditioning equipment. Thus, the greenhouse problem is seen largely as one of energy use. If focus is on the possible effects of energy use on global climate, the greenhouse issue is *the* problem. Nevertheless, it is one of many. Therefore, attentive to the needs of the living and still-to-be born makes an Earth Day even more important than remembrances of the dead on Memorial Day.

Even so, considerable doubt exists about how large and serious the challenges are. Although substantial efforts have been made to model climate, the problems are formidable, and the results so far are anything but definitive. Many nonlinear processes, competing effects, and feedback loops are involved, so that great uncertainty attaches to attempts to estimate the magnitude of the effects, despite a growing consensus in the geophysical community that continuing increases in GHG content of the atmosphere will likely lead to climate change that will be noticeable sometime in the next century. Uncertainty also exists over the magnitude of change as a function of the level and the rate of increases of GHGs, as well as about future patterns of energy use and GHG levels. Finally, because the amount of carbon dioxide is 25 percent higher than it was a century ago and because, further, a 1989 report by staff at the National Oceanic and Atmospheric Administration showed no detectable warming trend, optimists point out that policymakers should move cautiously in adopting measures urged upon them by the fearful. The optimists further believe that members of the Worldwatch Institution give insufficient recognition to the fact that when carbon dioxide pumps more water vapor into the air, resulting in a warming effect, it also forms clouds that have a cooling effect; moreover, a buildup of carbon dioxide in the earth's atmosphere offsets a decline that has been going on for millions of years and which, if unchecked, would bring a new ice age.

In view of the scientific uncertainties, speculation seems to be all that we have. With the world facing a more rapid rate of temperature increase than has ever occurred in the past (based on GHG emissions that have occurred during this century and those that can be reasonably projected for the next decade or two), a question arises: Will humans, their institutions, and other biological species be able to adapt? Many people, especially those in industrial societies, are not likely to face unusual problems of adjustment. In the United States particularly, people and industries have moved readily in response to economic pressures and opportunities; moreover, movement has become easier than in times past when most Americans were farmers. For such industries as information processing and light electronics, location is essentially irrelevant except insofar as the environment—including availability of housing, cultural opportunities, and so on—must be attractive to workers.

For those in the developing world, however, adjustment to climatic change may be more difficult—indeed, impossible. Poverty implies less mobility and less flexibility. For the Dutch, building higher dikes as a hedge against rising sea levels and greater frequency of storms is a realistic possibility. Not so for the Bangladeshis. Their choices are likely to be attempts to migrate to an already overpopulated India or death by drowning or starvation. The Soviet Union, on the other hand, might benefit from global warming. Winters would be less severe; productive agricultural land would increase (particularly because the northern parts of the country were not stripped of top soil by glaciation in the last ice age, as was the case in much of Canada); access to ice-free waters would be improved; and any increases in sea level would be proportionately less troublesome than for most other industrial nations. The moral question is this: *Will the less harmed help the grievously harmed?* That this has not happened to any great extent in the past is the worrisome part of the answer—so much so that the hypothetical question raised in the first chapter of this book now becomes a practical one: How much national sovereignty must be sacrificed for the common good of all?

## Key Questions Concerning the Common Good

Central to the debate over national sovereignty versus the common good are five questions:

1. How safe is safe? (*a technical question*)
2. Do we know what to do and how to do it cost effectively? (*an economic question*)
3. Will Americans pay for their own safety? (*a political question*)
4. Is industry doing enough to promote safety? (*a business question*)
5. Will Americans sacrifice for others' safety? (*an ethical question*)

## How Safe Is Safe?

This question appeared in the chapter on torts and the same answer will be given: no one knows with certainty.[13] Foreseeing changes is much easier than predicting what such changes mean.[14] The issue is whether it is presently possible to establish scientifically a hierarchy for what is known, can be known, and is unknowable. What is occurring is that the process of assuring minimal risk is proceeding increasingly by a random establishment of things to be controlled, and without any particular examination of the hierarchy of dangers to which anyone or anything is exposed. Perhaps it is impossible to do better while preserving everyone's rights in a democratic society.

The one certainty is that the lack of precise knowledge and the presence of growing fear mean that the regulation of risk will become intensely political: "although it does not carry a warning label, our political system may be hazardous to our health."[15] In a risk-averse society both politicians and regulators are forced to be cautious; and when carried to extremes the corporate community deals not with a lovely wonderland, but with a costly blunderland.

Approaches to environmental safety require reconsideration of two related concepts—biotic communities and ecosystems. A biotic community is an assemblage of species of plants and animals inhabiting a common area and having, therefore, effects upon one another. It is the combination of a biotic community and its physical environment that makes up the ecosystem. Chemicals from air, water, and soil supply the building blocks of these systems; the sun's energy activates the chemicals of the ecosystem and the life processes of the biosystem's organisms. Air, water, soil, and sunlight make human survival possible. What people are doing to the environment that supports them and what they can do without endangering it and themselves are the questions. The pessimists believe that an environmental crisis is coming and may lead to a breakdown of society and to famine and disease—both within the lifetime of children alive today.[16] Others argue that this pessimistic reading of the signs is grossly inaccurate. There is time to remedy errors of our technological development, which are not nearly so crucial as the environmentalists suggest because large reserves of materials and energy exist and because of resiliency in our life support systems.

## Do We Know What to Do?

Again disagreements exist in the scientific community, a good example of which has been given by the discussion on ozone. Spring and summer are the ozone seasons and, like acid rain, ozone is transported sometimes hundreds of miles from its origin. A total of 88.6 million Americans live in counties that exceed the 0.12 parts per million standard set by the EPA in 1987. Water pollution has seemed more susceptible to correction than, for example, the ozone problem and states have responded with a variety of maneuvers, one of which was the three-state effort by New York, New Jersey, and Pennsylvania to cleanse the Delaware River of its pollutants.[17]

Congress responded by passing laws governing environmental management, air and water pollution, and control of solid waste and toxic substances. In 1980 it passed the Comprehensive Environmental Response, and the Compensation/Liability Act (ERCLA) which, among other things, placed the financial burden of cleaning up contaminated sites on the parties responsible for causing the contamination. It held liable four classes of persons: (1) the current owner and operator of a vessel or facility, (2) any person who formerly owned or operated a facility at the time the hazardous substance was disposed, (3) persons who arranged for disposal or treatment of a hazardous substance at any facility owned or operated by another person, and (4) transporters of such substances to a facility. Especially interesting to moralists is the fact that, according to the circumstances, a parent corporation and even its officers and individual stockholders may be held liable. Accountability was both institutional and individual.[18]

Muddying the ethical waters was an action taken on April 26, 1991, by the U.S. Sentencing Commission, which voted to make effective on November 1, 1991, more drastic penalties on corporations convicted of federal offense. Under the commission's guidelines corporations could be fined a staggering $290 million for serious offenses. Not only the magnitude of the fine worries corporate managers; under federal criminal laws a corporation could be convicted for any employee's wrongdoing if the proscribed action occurred on the employer's premises, within the employee's prescribed duties, and ostensibly to advance the corporation's interests. Only if the corporation already had an effective compliance training program would the fines be lessened. Moreover, what is effective in the organization's mind might be ineffective in the government's mind.

Dissatisfied with inadequacies in the Clean Air Act, Congress, with the strong support of President Bush, ended years of controversy in October 1990 by tightening regulations. The deadlines set are shown in Table 13.1. This wide-ranging law forced factories, power plants, cars, gasolines, and other commercial products to be less polluting. The estimated costs to industry and business for the year 2000 was over $20 billion a year. Within 15 years, the law aimed to clean up the smog in all cities except Los Angeles, partly by forcing oil companies to develop cleaner burning gasoline. For the first time, it attacked the acid rain problem, widely accused of harming lakes and streams in New England, by forcing coal-fired utilities to reduce emissions sharply. Factories nationwide had to install new antipollution equipment to protect people living and working nearby from dangerous fumes. The how-safe-is-safe question was answered by the Senate: no more than 1 in a 10,000 risk of cancer for people living near the offending facilities. The House, on the other hand, refused to specify. Corporations faced different problems. As the fifth largest polluter, DuPont was hit hard—its consolidated coal division expected to lose jobs in order to comply with the statute's acid rain provisions. Oil companies like Sunoco, Gulf, and Amoco faced heavy outlays for new emission-control equipment. Such private losses are seen as public gains.

## Table 13.1  Clean Air Deadlines

**Cities and Towns**

1993: "Marginal" areas must reach ozone standard (39 cities).

1996: Deadline for "moderate" nonattainment areas (32 cities).

1999: Deadline for "serious" areas (16 cities).

2005–7: Deadline for "severe" areas (8 cities).

2010: Deadline for "extreme" areas (Los Angeles).

**Cars, Trucks, and Buses**

Model Year 1994: 60 percent less nitrogen oxide. 35 percent less hydrocarbons.

MY 1998: Cars must be equipped with emission control systems with a "useful life" of 10 years or 100,000 miles.

MY 2003: Stage Two tailpipe standards would go into effect subject to EPA veto.

**Motor Fuels**

1992: Cities with $CO_2$ nonattainment must use gasoline containing 2.7 percent oxygen, unless EPA delays the standard.

1995: Nine smoggiest cities must sell only reformulated gasoline. Volatile organic compounds (VOCs) and toxic emissions must be cut 15 percent.

1996: 150,000 "clean fueled" vehicles must be sold in California.

1998: Fleet program requires 80 percent emissions cut for cars and 50 percent cut for trucks.

**Utilities**

1995: 111 dirtiest coal-fired plants must cut $SO_2$ emissions.

2000: Annual $SO_2$ emissions limited to 10 million tons.

**Other Industries**

1995: EPA must regulate 90 percent of the 30 most serious toxic pollutants emitted by dry cleaners, gas stations, and other "area" sources. Cancer risks must be reduced 75 percent.

2003: Major sources (chemical plants, oil refineries, etc.) must apply best available technology to reduce emissions of 189 toxic chemicals by the average of the 12 cleanest similar plants. "Residual" cancer risk to most exposed persons must be reduced to 1 in 10,000.

2020: Extended "residual risk" deadline for coke ovens, which must meet tougher interim standards.

Source: Alyson Pytte, "A Decade of Acrimony in the Glow of Clean Air," *Congressional Quarterly* (October 27, 1990), 358.

One side effect of the drive to protect the environment has been an increase in the number of administrative bodies, probably the most significant legal trend of the century, one that continues and remains controversial. The first Clean Air and Clean Water acts left managers and lawyers with difficult issues bred of the statutes' length and complexity, inept drafting, the difficulty and cost of compliance, as well as continuance of the substantial civil and criminal penalties imposed in 1980 by ERCLA—penalties that, as noted, can be imposed on "any person, or responsible corporate officers," and, even in certain cases, on lawyers themselves.[19] To remove such confusions was a major goal of the 1990 law. The law also reflected the legislators' unhappy reactions to the Environmental Protection Agency (EPA), which was having rollercoaster experiences with the hazardous-waste management problem. Dr. Jack Moore, an EPA official, offered a comment that illustrated the difficulty of the agency's problem: "It took us ten or twelve years before it [the EPA] figured out what it wanted to do about pesticides [but] the problem is that we are ten years behind where we should be."[20] Whether the 1990 law compresses the time lag remains the big question.

## Will Every American Pay $450 Each Year for Their Own Safety?

Over the decade EPA programs will cost $1.6 trillion. As noted, the group first hit by the cost factor is business, especially the chemical industry, which does so much with—and to—the world's physical resources. A *New Yorker* cartoon reflected a rather common view when it showed two smiling executives looking at their smoke-belching factories and saying, "Where there's smoke, there's money." But for whom? The head of EPA, Lee Thomas, noted that the costs of cleaning a polluted earth eventually reaches consumers. When Thomas established regulations in 1990 to limit nitrogen-oxide and particulate-matter emissions from heavy-duty trucks and buses, the resulting increase in production costs was quickly translated into price.[21]

The term acid rain was first used in 1972 by English chemist Robert Angus Smith to describe precipitation falling on England's industrial city of Manchester. Because acid rain results from burning coal and oil, no one doubted its connection to industrial pollution. Acid rain is worldwide, falling in Brazil, China, South Africa, the Arctic, and North America as acidic snow, sleet, fog, and dust. In the United States the nine largest coal-burning states are in the Ohio-Basin-Midwest area. They contribute roughly two-thirds of all sulphur dioxide depositions within the eastern states—the area first hit hard by the silent invader. However, by June 1984, acid rain had moved into 13 southern states and ranged from West Virginia to Florida. Unlike the Midwest-Northeast connection (where one area pollutes and the other suffers), the South itself is primarily responsible for its own problems.

It was a cruel irony for Americans to learn that acid rain was actually increased by the very laws Congress had passed to encourage industries to build towering smokestacks intended to reduce pollution in areas where they were located. What happened, however, was that the smokestacks released fumes high into the atmosphere. In 1969 the United States had fewer than 12 smokestacks taller than 500 feet; ten years later, there were 180. A lesson became painfully clear—the higher the stack, the worse the consequences.

## Is Industry Doing Enough?

Corporate executives seem to accept the fact that the old Kantian injunction (do no harm) makes sense. To prevent harm, industries are using a new specialist called the environmental auditor. Celanese, DuPont, Reilly Tar and Chemical, and the Olin Corporation are among the pacesetters. Although such audits cost as much as $500,000, executives feel they are worth the cost.[22] Such voluntarism is generally to be preferred to coercion by regulatory bodies, whose costs in reduced productivity growth, lost jobs, and consequently, increased government social spending, have been well documented.

As has been the case with other health-related problems, however, the courts, not regulators or legislators, may provide the final remedies.[23] In 1985 the Justice Department's Environmental Crimes Unit began an intensive effort to bring to court violators of various environment-protection laws. Many laws relating to environmental matters reflected a Kantian ethic by providing criminal sanctions only in cases of "willful" or "knowing" wrongdoing. Not to will harm (or not to know harm was being done) suggested that enforcement of the law would be indeed difficult.[24] But judges saw it differently—as the 1985 case involving Johnson & Towers illustrated. The company owned a plant in Mount Laurel, New Jersey, where large motor vehicles were repaired and overhauled. Degreasers and other industrial chemicals used at the plant contained some chemicals that were classified as hazardous wastes under the Clean Water Act. Waste chemicals from the operations were drained into a holding tank and, when the tank was full, pumped into a trench that flowed into a tributary of the Delaware River. Generators of such waste must obtain from the EPA a permit for disposal. Johnson & Towers had not. The indictment named as defendants the company and two of its employees (Jack Hopkins, a foreman, and Peter Angel, a service manager in the trucking department). When the court found the company guilty and the two individuals innocent because neither was an owner or operator, an appeal was made. This time the court ruled that the first verdict was too narrowly constructed and that workers in responsible supervisory positions could be just as guilty as owners.[25] Knowing and willing need only be inferred, not directly proved, in cases of violations.[26] Presumption of innocence until proved guilty was a casualty.

## Will Americans Sacrifice For Others' Safety?

This question is difficult to answer, not simply because it involves a my-brother's-keeper ethic but because it is hard to know what the brother is himself doing. At what time the international community became aroused over environmental deterioration is hard to specify. But the issue's emergence into the realm of high politics became clear by the spring of 1987 with the publication of a United Nations report called *Our Common Future*. After nine reprintings in little more than one year, the "Brundtland Report," as it is also known, had changed the terms of international debate by convincingly demonstrating to a broad audience that environmental degradation is a survival issue, especially for the developing nations. Interest accelerated after Brundtland gave resounding support to the environmentalists.

In March 1989, Prime Minister Margaret Thatcher of England called an international meeting to discuss stratosphere ozone depletion. Representatives of 123 nations attended. One week later, the prime ministers of The Netherlands, France, and Norway sponsored a conference to consider global atmospheric change generally, and especially greenhouse warming. The resulting Declaration of the Hague, signed by 24 heads of state, called for "the development of new principles of international law, including new and more effective decision-making and enforcement mechanisms" and proposed that a "new institutional authority" be established within the UN framework, empowered with "such decision-making procedures as may be effective even if, on occasion, unanimous agreement has not been reached." This extraordinary document accurately reflected a prevailing sense that changes in the environment demand action that is, in the Declaration's words, "vital, urgent and global."

The developing nations joined the swelling chorus in May 1989 at the Non-Aligned Summit Meeting in Belgrade. In a keynote speech, Indian Prime Minister Rajiv Gandhi noted that the costs of development must integrally include the costs of conservation, which, if not paid for now, will surely be extracted later. He proposed a Planet Protection Fund to which all the developed and developing countries (except the 30-odd least developed) would contribute a fixed and equal percentage of gross domestic product (GDP). Contributions of as little as 0.1 percent from so many countries, he noted, would produce $18 billion annually. The question of international controls had been broached earlier in 1977 by the United Nations Environment Program (UNEP) under the vigorous leadership of Mostafa Tolba of Nigeria.

How the United States fits into the international effort remains to be seen. Crises in the Mideast, Soviet interventions in Lithuania, a grinding national debt, unfavorable trade balances, Congressional difficulties in getting its own house in order and, particularly, uncertainty over the intentions of West European industrialists to cooperate in the cleanup clouded the picture. The United States and the 12-nation European Community that dominated the market for chlorofluorocarbons accounted for over 80 percent of the world's output in 1974. Notwithstanding a common political, economic, and environmental orientation, critical differences marked their approach to potential threats to the ozone layer. Whereas the ozone depletion theory had captured the imagination of the American public (possibly because of U.S. journeys into space), it had relatively little impact in Europe.

Differences between American and European industrialists reflected the strength of public concern in the United States. Worried American consumers had cut their domestic market for spray cans by two-thirds even before Congress's landmark legislation of 1977 authorizing the EPA to regulate "any substance . . . which *may reasonably be anticipated* to affect the stratosphere, especially ozone in the stratosphere." Following this legislation, the United States banned CFCs as propellants for nonessential aerosol sprays in early 1978, affecting nearly $3 billion worth of sales in a wide range of products. This action was followed by action in Canada and by Sweden, Norway, Denmark, and Finland. However, under heavy pressure from the European chemical industry, the EC waited until 1980 before following suit. It then enacted a 30 percent CFC aerosol cutback from 1976 levels, together with a cap on production capacity.

Such actions by the Europeans seemed almost hypocritical to Americans because European sales of CFCs for aerosols had already declined by over 28 percent after 1976, while capacity was deliberately defined as a 24-hour operation, which would enable output to increase by over 60 percent. The EC measures were clearly dictated more by commercial than by environmental concerns. They were painless actions, fully supported by European industry, which gave an appearance of control while permitting unhampered expansion for two more decades. It seemed to Americans that while Europeans snuggled in the inn, they shivered in the cold.

Yet maneuvering abroad did not excuse the United States. Its power and prestige thrust upon it the same leadership role that was thrust on it after World War II. Americans may not want prime responsibility but they have it, and in their own self-interest, if not their moral interests, firm action must be made. The complications that make positive and early responses difficult are seen in the way Americans have handled the vipers in their own garden—DDT, paraquat, dioxin. DDT is the best weapon for fighting malaria among the Third World's impoverished peasants; paraquat, one of the most versatile tools in farming, controls weeds and speeds harvest on 10 million acres in the United States; and dioxin is important to forest management. Yet each can have serious side effects.

## Toward a New Environmental Ethic

### *Two Ethics?*

Distinctions have been made, often unfairly, between a religious or humanistic ethic, which sees physical resources as useful to humans, and a naturalistic ethic, which holds that physical objects have intrinsic values. The distinction was made by UCLA professor Lynn White, Jr., who felt that the religious ethic was responsible for abuses of the environment because it not only established a dualism between man and nature but asserted that God willed that humans should dominate the earth and exploit the universe for their own ends.[27] White noted that before Judaic Christian ethics took hold, pagan animism viewed every tree, plant, animal, rock, and the like as something with its own sacred spirit. Thus man thought twice before destroying a natural object and releasing the spirits.

Western religions, on the other hand, provided a comfortable ideology for modern technology and the two, having joined forces, must be held accountable. The need therefore exists to develop a new religious ethic or reformulate the old one along lines inspired by St. Francis of Assisi, whom

White has called the greatest radical since Christ.[28] Francis rebelled against the technology of his time; his preaching of humility challenged the view of man as master over the world. Though Francis tried, he failed. But his failure cannot be the moderns' failure.

White's argument is compelling—until tested against certain facts. Prehistoric man exploited the environment long before the coming of the Jews and Christians; examples are the fire-drive technique of hunting and the flooding of the Nile. The ancient Greeks and Chinese created environmental problems long before a Christian culture was formed. On the other hand, few managed resources more productively and preserved the environment more effectively than the followers of Saint Benedict. White's assertions have value nonetheless because they are reminders that the power to rule the universe, like other forms of power, must be exercised wisely and well. As banker Louis Lundborg noted, "environment and other social problems should get at least as much corporate attention as production, salary, and finance. The quality of life in its total meaning is, in the final reckoning, the only justification for any corporate activity.[29] This quality of life consideration has been extended in the naturalistic ethic from people to animals and inanimate objects: animals want to feed, trees want to grow, flowers want to blossom. Their interests must be included in moral terms if an authentic ethic is to be found.[30] The Ten Commandments are not enough.

## Rolston's Maxims

At this point the views of Professor Holmes Rolston III become relevant. To him the traditional religious ethic was still vital but its theology, even when supported by the philosophers' logic, needed to go beyond the interests of the human community to think of nature as a community first and a commodity second.[31] The wisdom of the Native American should be joined to the wisdom of the early missionaries so that a wiser and more humane ethic could be forged. Humans cannot live without a healthy environment and a healthy environment cannot live without humans. There is life in both. Recognition of this relationship is the beginning of wisdom. Rolston posited, therefore, not 10 but 30 commandments to guide corporate executives:

1. *The stakeholder maxim:* Assess costs suffered by persons not party to your business.
2. *The countryside maxim:* Do not assume that what is good for the company is good for the country.
3. *The sunshine maxim:* Do not keep company secrets that may vitally affect those from whom the secrets are kept.
4. *The legacy maxim:* Do not disclaim responsibility for inherited problems.
5. *The no-discount maxim:* Do not discount the future environmentally, because we do not altogether use up natural resources but partly convert them to capital that others inherit.

6. *The unconsumption maxim:* Minimize the throwaway economy, which does not urge efficiency on anyone.
7. *The reconsumption maxim:* Maximize recycling.
8. *The priority maxim:* Understand that the more vital and irreplaceable the resource, the more worthwhile should be the use to which it is put.
9. *The toxin-is-trumps maxim:* Know that an ounce of permanent toxicity is worse than a ton of passing good—one man's profit never permits another man's poisoning.
10. *The steady-state maxim:* Accept no-growth sectors for the economy.
11. *The reversibility maxim:* Avoid irreversible change in the environment.
12. *The diversity maxim:* Maximize the use of natural kinds of goods.
13. *The natural selection maxim:* Respect an ecosystem as a proven efficient economy.
14. *The scarcity maxim:* Understand that the rarer an environment, the kinder it ought to be treated (grasslands are common, gorges infrequent). Rare environments are not usually essential to regional ecosystems and hence humans can do without them. But the earth cannot.
15. *The aesthetic maxim:* Understand that the more beautiful an environment, the more tenderly it should be treated.
16. *The china-shop maxim:* Understand that the more fragile an environment, the more lightly it should be treated. Fragility alone, like rarity, is hardly a value but it has a way of figuring in a constellation of natural qualities.
17. *The life maxim:* Respect life—the more sentient, the more so. As the English jurist-philosopher Jeremy Bentham said, "The question is not can they reason or talk but can they suffer?"[32]
18. *The life-specific maxim:* Respect at times the species more than the individual. Extinction is irreversible; to lose the diversity, beauty, and genetic resource of a natural wonder is to lose a souvenir of the past. Underlying this is a religious reason: life is sacred.
19. *The parental maxim:* Love your neighborhood as you do yourself.
20. *The buck-stopping maxim:* Do not use complexity to dodge responsibility. (Examples of companies that have paid considerable attention to the environmental impact of projects they have financed are John Hancock Life Insurance Company, Equitable Life Assurance Society, and Aetna Life and Casualty.)
21. *The no-cosmetics maxim:* Do not use public relations to confuse yourself or others; deeds come before words.
22. *The second-mile maxim:* Remember that morality often exceeds legality. The environmental novelties that are still unfolding ignore state jurisdictions.
23. *The burden-of-proof maxim:* Recognize a shifting asymmetry in environmental decisions by simply remembering that between 1941 and

1977 the volume of manufactured synthetic chemicals increased 350 times, with many of these quite toxic to natural systems and to human biology.
24. *The full-circle maxim:* Extend moral judgments through the whole event in which your business plays a part. Although the buck should not pass outside a given company, the scope of judgment should not stop at the boundaries of that business, because each enterprise is linked to others.
25. *The grand maxim:* Think for decades ahead. The Weyerhaeuser timber cycle is half a century and no other big company can afford less than such telescopic vision.
26. *The do-it-yourself-first maxim:* Impose on others lower risks than you impose on yourself. An illustration for censure are fishermen who work both the contaminated James River and its uncontaminated tributaries and mix both catches for public sale—but take home only uncontaminated ones for their own consumption.
27. *The togetherness maxim:* Work for benefits that can be had only in concert. What one firm cannot afford, all working together can.
28. *The question-authority maxim:* Understand that judgment is a high-class business skill that persons other than business managers have. Rachel Carson was right about DDT; Ralph Nader was right about automobile exhausts and air pollution; the Alaskan pipeline was built better because of its critics.
29. *The greening maxim:* Remember that the bottom line should not be black unless it can also be green.
30. *The Hemingway maxim:* Esteem highly everything and everyone. When a bell tolls, it is for you.

## *A Short Checklist*

If Rolston's maxims threaten to overwhelm harried policymakers into silence, a shorter list of natural laws and cultural observations—plumb lines, so to speak—might be more helpful. The following are relevant.[33]
1. *Nature is ethically normative.* Nature itself needs controls. To act as though humans, with their technologies, are the only source of the problem is to blot out reality. Humans regularly ingest toxicants without adverse effects.
2. *Environmental risk is defined by society's culture.* People define and prefer a certain way of life so that the culture dictates risk selection: "The risks we select to control or mitigate, individually and collectively, are a product of the choices we make concerning the best way to organize social relations, to protect shared values, and to devise institutional mechanisms for providing informed consent in the formulation of social policy."[34] Risk selection is the result of prior allegiance to a preferred form of social organization and shared values.

3. *The collectivity's risk-aversion is higher than the individual's risk-aversion.* Each of us would do less for ourselves than we would insist that the government do for us. Watch the politicians and those who manipulate them.[35]

4. *Living involves trade-offs.* Always establishing a contradiction between risks and benefits conveys the impression that there is a clear way to have one without the other. Biostatistical predictions must therefore be compared to naturally occurring biohazards.

5. *The greater good is not always served by government and environmentalists.* Because individuals and groups have different goals, politics plays the dominant role. For example, fairly wide agreement exists among scientists that the best way to reduce acid rain is to switch from the dirty coal mined in the northern Appalachians to the clean coal found in states like Wyoming. But here a glitch appears. Mining the Appalachian coal are members of the powerful United Mine Workers (UMW); mining the western coal are unorganized workers—or members of weak unions. When the quest for sulfur-emission control ran into the special interest groups on Capitol Hill, lawmakers like Senators Metzenbaum of Ohio and Byrd of West Virginia successfully blocked the clean-coal option. In 1977, they prevailed on Congress to amend the Clean Air Act to require new power plants to use expensive scrubbers on the coal they burn no matter how clean it was to start with.[36] The amendment was defended as a way to save existing coal jobs, and it has done so; but a lot of low-sulfur coal has stayed in the ground. The scrubber option is roughly three to four times costlier than the clean-coal option. Yet environmental organizations joined the unions and pro-miner political groups.[37] The story is the same for farmers, who are one of the largest single sources of pollution and are outside the EPA's effective jurisdiction.[38]

6. *Ownership's benefits include responsibilities.* Boundaries are mapped by society and crossing the lines in ways that hurt others is forbidden. When midwestern factories belch smoke that eventually falls on other people's property, the factory owners are invaders. Those who cause public harm should pay to the public purse. (Note: One obstacle to complete acceptance of this theory of justice is that it implies wrongdoers can continue to do wrong so long as they are willing to pay the price.)

7. *Scientific uncertainty is no excuse for political indifference.* Political leadership has an obligation to teach before it taxes; it must therefore learn by sponsoring research that benefits its mentors as well as the public.

8. *Corporations are more responsive than government to crises in a free market.* To exploit the market's strength, business should be given incentives to innovate.

9. *National security rests on global security.* National security was a zero-sum concept in its original military sense: the greater one nation's se-

curity, the less would be another's. Contemporaries have learned, however, that the economic strength of one is the economic strength of all. They are now learning that (1) the environmental health of one nation affects the environmental health of others and (2) that energy efficiency must become a top priority in the global agenda.[39]

10. *Negotiation is the key to peaceful solutions.* As the nation-state was the revolutionary idea of the 16th century, the regional state is the revolutionary idea of the 21st. As it evolves, the nation's leaders should engage in labor-management types of collective bargaining with the leaders of other countries because global environmental problems are immune to solution by one or a few countries. Peaceful solutions require compromise and compromise requires negotiation.

## Short-Term Problems: Two Examples

While long-term strategies unfold slowly, short-term problems press relentlessly. How we respond in the short term now may provide clues on how responses will be made for the long term. The following examples may encourage readers to compare the two.

**Ecotage (Ecological Sabotage).** A tactic called ecotage has been used by some environmentalists to call immediate attention to the problem of deforestation. Ecotage has resulted in environmentalists' toppling power lines, destroying machinery, and slashing tires. In the Pacific Northwest an ecotage group came up with a new idea to preserve that region's glorious forests: drive spikes into trees to break chains on power saws. The group said that its previous efforts at persuasion had been rejected by officials of lumber companies and that the mad destruction could be halted by no other means. Loggers knew that danger might lurk in every treetop and, if they voluntarily took the risks, that was their own responsibility. The activists pointed to the risks they were taking (fines, jail sentences, beatings) and said other risk takers should also be prepared to pay the price. They further argued that lawmakers had a vested interest in the lumber industry because it meant tax revenue; unions had a vested interest because it meant jobs; courts had a vested interest in the lumber industry because it meant protecting property rights. In such an environment, ecotage becomes a last resort.

Others denounced such arguments, pointing out that fewer trees meant higher prices for houses, which the rich could afford and the poor could not. To its foes, ecotage is environmentalism gone mad. So it seems when extremes of environmentalist fervor are cited:[40]

- A rare butterfly that lives only seven days a year was used to block a mountainside development of badly needed moderate-income housing in a San Francisco suburb for years.
- A Maryland environmental group refused to join a battle to keep a hazardous waste dump out of Hawkins Point, one of the nation's oldest and poorest African-American communities.

- A National Wildlife Federation lobbyist was at odds with hard-pressed shrimpers and merchants on the Texas coast over a federal plan to burn hazardous wastes at sea.

In answer to such charges, the ecotage practitioners say that the examples cited are irrelevant because their goal is to promote the long-term prosperity of all Americans, not the short-term prosperity of a few. Extreme action is sometimes justified when significant change in thinking about values is needed.

## *Ethical Question*

- Do you agree?

**Midtown Pulp.** Years ago, a small town in western Pennsylvania known as Tyrone was famous for its pulp and paper mill and infamous for the stench the mill created. The mill was abandoned shortly after World War II. Now suppose that in another area of the county was a community that here will be given the fictitious name of Midtown. Here also was the paper company of Midtown Pulp, which traced its history back to 1895. Unlike the Tyrone mill, it had managed to survive and even turn a modest profit. For years Midtown was the city's largest employer and, although people complained of the odor, they liked the sweet smell of the dollar. In 1980 a new electronic plant came to the area, Lightomatics Inc., which made specialty parts for the defense industry. Unlike Midtown Pulp, its facilities were clean and its employees were recruited from local technical schools. As Lightomatics expanded, its work force doubled. Its employees bought new homes, and they demanded better schools—and cleaner air. In 1990, a group of Lightomatic employees approached the mayor to demand that "something be done about Midtown's stench." The mayor expressed a desire to act but noted that "Midtown has been here as long as the town itself" and that he was unaware of any technology to remove the smell. "We've sorta got used to it," was his parting comment.

Angered, the group traveled to the state capital to meet with the Pennsylvania Environment Agency (PEA). As a result, PEA inspectors visited the Midtown Pulp plant, which they found to be in full compliance with state laws. The next move of the disgruntled Lightomatics group was to write to the EPA to describe the problem and ask for relief. However, when two inspectors from the federal agency arrived at Midtown, they were met by the firm's angry workers as well as angry managers. When the federal inspectors sought to have Midtown Pulp undertake voluntary cleanup efforts, they were told that the company had already considered such a project and rejected it because the costs were astronomical. Even with some public funding, a satisfactory cleanup job was out of the question. To back its refusal, Midtown Pulp offered the following arguments:

1. The company had been in the community almost 90 years longer than Lightomatics.

2. Lightomatics managers knew of the odor problem but decided on the Midtown location because the community had good rail and road service, possessed a quality work force, had a favorable tax base, and was beautifully situated along the bank of a small river.
3. No one had ever proved that the Midtown's evil-smelling air was a source of any disease.
4. The rules of the game should not be changed by newcomers or by "arbitrary" outsiders from the federal government.
5. If harassment continued, the owners would close the marginally profitable mill completely and older workers would be thrown out of their long-tenured jobs.
6. Lightomatics employees were unfair to their less advantaged fellow townspeople.

## *Ethical Questions*

- From an economic standpoint do you agree with Midtown Pulp? Or Lightomatics?
- From ethical perspectives, do you support Midtown? Or Lightomatics?

Of course, other questions are being raised, the answers to which are bitterly dividing political and business leaders. Rather than awaiting replies from others, it is useful for ourselves to make responses. By so doing, our personal moral philosophies may be exposed.

## Summary

It is not unrealistic to expect that the natural scientists may do more to improve the environment than moralists. Over sixty years ago, when physicists invented quantum mechanics, they declared that now all problems of chemistry were solved. Yet between 1960 and 1970, chemistry experienced its most revolutionary period—and more is on the way. Chemists now talk of 2020 as a time when HF will be replaced by less toxic acids, and CFCs by molecules that are less threatening to the stratospheric ozone. Moreover, research in artificial synthesis may lead to the making of molecules that will permit the direct conversion of sunlight and abundant raw materials into high-energy chemicals, as well as into fuels to heat homes, make electricity, cook, run cars, and so forth. A main goal is to produce hydrogen gas as the fuel. Since hydrogen is very energy-rich and clean burning, giving only water as the product, pollution problems could be reduced tremendously. The very extensive network of natural gas lines could be used with some modification to pipe hydrogen around the country. In principle there could be an enormous energy network based on hydrogen produced from solar energy.

The chemists' confidence boggles the mind. The ethician's diffidence disturbs it. A partnership may bring the required balance that decision makers need during the interim, long or short, when environmental dangers increase.[41]

## Questions for Discussion

1. Do Americans have any ethical obligation to help countries in Eastern Europe—such as Czechoslovakia (whose drinking water is over 50 percent polluted), Southern Poland, and East Germany—that have wantonly destroyed their environment?
2. Should Americans make conservation their first choice for action because of the acid rain poured down by American factories?
3. Is it ethical to impose heavy taxes on American corporations for environmental cleanup in situations where the scientific community is divided over the need?
4. If one company, unaware of the problem, purchases the plant of another company that has polluted the environment, should the former owner be made to pay all the cleanup costs?
5. Do you think that an authentic environmental ethic should hold all forms of life to be equally sacred?
6. Would it be unethical for the United States to refuse to join any international organization established to attack the world's environmental problem if joining meant possible diminution of its national sovereignty?
7. Were Senators Byrd of West Virginia and Metzenbaum of Ohio unethical when they opposed legislation designed to clean the environment because the law might result in unemployment for workers in their respective states?
8. Plum Creek Timber Company used advertising to assure residents of the Pacific Northwest of its concern for the environment. Depicting a forester tenderly planting a seedling, one advertisement proclaimed: "Our Roots Are Here." But so are its tree stumps. The board's effort to maximize shareholder values by ignoring the problem threatened to leave an enduring mark on the land and contribute to an economically crippling regional timber shortage in future decades. Is ecotage ethical under these circumstances?

## Ethical Quandary

### The Zealous Lobbyist

University of Georgia Professor Dwight Lee asks us to consider the statements of some of those who hold themselves up as environmental experts. For example, Richard Benedick of the U.S. State Department, while on assignment with the Conservation Foundation, said, "A global climate treaty must be implemented even if there is no scientific evidence to back the greenhouse effect." Stephen Schneider, a highly publicized environmental activist, went further in stating, "We have to offer up scary scenarios, make simplified, dramatic statements, and make little mention of any doubts we may have. Each of us has to decide what the right balance is between being effective and being honest." Senator Timothy Wirth of Colorado advised, "We've got to ride the global warning issue. Even if the theory of the global warning is wrong, we will be doing the right thing anyway in terms of economic policy and environmental policy.[42]

## *Questions*

- Which, if any, of the statements are ethically defensible?
- If you were an environmentalist lobbying before Congress, would you follow the advice given by Benedick, Schneider, and Wirth?

## *Notes*

1. Huston Smith, *The Religions of Man* (New York: Harpers, 1958), 262.
2. J. C. Furnas, "The Ant and the Twig: On the Dark Side of God," *The American Scholar* (Winter 1983–1984): 63–81.
3. Thomas Berry, *The Dream of the Earth* (San Francisco: Sierra Book Club, 1988), 72. See also, Mark Sagoff, *The Enemy of the Earth: Philosophy, Law, and the Environment* (Cambridge: Cambridge University Press, 1988), especially chs. 1 to 5. See also, *Final Report of the Seventy-Seventh American Assembly* (New York: Columbia University, 1990), 5. Technical information for this chapter has been drawn from the collection of essays edited by Jessica Tuchman Mathews, *Preserving the Global Environment* (New York: W. W. Norton, 1990).
4. Thomas DiLorenzo and James Bennett, *The Politics of Environmentalism* (St. Louis: Washington University Center for the Study of American Business, 1986). For an earlier treatment of their views, see *Destroying Democracy: How Government Funds Partisan Politics* (Washington: Cato Institute, 1985).
5. Paul Ehrlich, *The Population Bomb: Population Control or Race to Oblivion?* (New York: Ballantine, 1968), 66 ff.
6. William McKibben, *The End of Nature* (New York: Random House, 1989); and Dale Peterson, *The Deluge and the Ark* (New York: Houghton Mifflin, 1989).
7. The National Cancer Institute, *The Atlas of Cancer Mortality for U.S. Counties, 1950–1969.*
8. Robert M. O'Brien, Michael Clarke, and Sheldon Kamieniecki, "Open and Closed Systems of Decision Making: The Case of Toxic Waste Management," *Public Administration Review* 44 (July–August 1984): 334–340.
9. Mark Sagoff, "Ethics, Agriculture and the Environment," *Report from the Center for Philosophy and Public Philosophy* 7 (Winter 1987): 9–12.
10. The Department of Interior has published a large number of *U.S. Geological Survey Reports* during the past 20 years. A constant theme in these reports is the ever-growing danger to the environment.
11. Stuart Diamond, "US Toxic Mishaps in Chemicals Put at 6,928 in 5 Years." *The New York Times*, October 3, 1985, 1, D–22. See also, Christopher H. Schroeder, "Rights Against Risks," *Columbia Law Review* 86 (April 1986): 495–562; and Judson W. Starr, "Count-

ering Environmental Crimes," *Boston College Environmental Affairs Law Review* 13 (Spring 1986): 379–395.

12. See the series of articles by Stuart Diamond, Matthew Wald, and Philip Shabencoff in *The New York Times* (November 25, 26, and 27, 1985).

13. A sense of the difficulties inherent in efforts to answer the question may be found in B. Fishoff et al., "How Safe Is Safe Enough? A Psychometric Study of Attitudes toward Technological Risks and Benefits," *Policy Sciences* 9 (1976): 127–152.

14. James M. Utterbeck, "Environmental Analysis and Forecasting," in *Strategic Management: A New View of Business Policy and Planning*, eds. Daniel E. Schendel and Charles W. Hofer (Boston: Little Brown, 1979). Reprinted in John F. Veiga and John N. Yanouzas, eds., *The Dynamics of Organization Theory* (St. Paul: West, 1984).

15. Harvey M. Sapolsky, "The Politics of Risk," *Daedalus* 119 (Fall 1990): 83. See also, Dixie Ray Lee, *Trashing the Planet* (Chicago: Regnery Gateway, 1990); and Robert Frosch's commentary in the American Assembly study, *Innovation in the 80s* (Englewood Cliffs, N.J.: Prentice-Hall, 1984).

16. Brian Harvey and John D. Hallett, *Environment and Society: An Introductory Analysis* (Cambridge: MIT Press, 1977), 62.

17. Bruce A. Ackerman et al., *The Uncertain Search for Environmental Quality* (New York: Macmillan–Free Press, 1974), 142–145.

18. FTC v. Rubberoid Co., 343 U.S. 470, 487 (1952) (Justice Jackson dissenting).

19. "Air and Water Enforcement Problems: A Case Study," *The Business Lawyer* 34 (January 1979): 665–666.

20. Philip Shabecoff, "Pesticides Finally Top List at EPA," *The New York Times*, March 6, 1986, B12.

21. Lee Thomas, "Public is Willing to Pay Price for Pure Air and Water," *U.S. News and World Report*, July 8, 1985, 41–42.

22. Lee Harrison, "Big Business's Pollution Problems," *The New York Times*, May 17, 1981.

23. It has been rightly said that "few corporate activities have been influenced by law as much as the environmental area." Frank B. Freidman, "Corporate Environmental Programs and Litigation: The Role of Lawyer-Managers in Environmental Management," *Public Administration Review* 45 (November 1985): 766.

24. Ralph Kagan and Eugene Bardach, *Going by the Book: The Problem of Regulatory Unreasonableness* (Philadelphia: Temple University Press,1982).

25. Ben A. Franklin, "Justice Speeds Up Pace of Hazardous Waste Cases," *The New York Times*, May 15, 1983, Sec 1, 17.

26. John R. Wheeler, "Potential for Criminal Liability of Personnel under the Federal Acts," *The National Law Journal* 7 (March 24, 1985): 22–25.

27. Lynn White, Jr., "The Historical Roots of Our Ecological Crises," in *Western Man and Environmental Ethics*, ed. Jane Barbour (Boston: Addison-Wesley, 1973).

28. Ibid., 28.

29. Louis B. Lundborg, *Future without Shock* (New York: W. W. Norton, 1974), 128.

30. Robin Attfield, *The Ethics of Environmental Concern* (New York: Columbia University Press, 1983). See also, Lewis Hinchman and Sandra Hinchman. "Deep Ecology and the Record of Natural Rights," *The Western Political Quarterly* 42 (September 1989): 221–240.

31. Holmes Rolston III, "Environmental Issues," in *Just Business*, ed. Tom Regan (Philadelphia: Temple University Press, 1983).

32. Jeremy Bentham, *Principles of Morals and Legislation* (London, 1789). Quoted in *The New Dictionary of Questions on Historical Principles from Ancient and Modern Sources*, ed. H. L. Mencken (New York: Knopf, 1942), 45.

33. This approach was suggested by Professor Margaret Maxey of the University of Texas at Austin, *Managing Environmental Risks. What Difference Does Ethics Make?* (St. Louis, Mo.: Washington University Center for the Study of American Business, 1990), 13–21.

34. Ibid., 17. See also, Aaron Wildasky, "Rich Is Safer," *The Public Interest* 60 (1980): 23–29.

35. Aaron Wildasky and Mary Douglas, *Risk and Culture* (Berkeley: University of California Press, 1982).
36. As the former chairman of the Council of Economic Advisers said, "Like the rest of us, Congress wants a cleaner environment, but fears special interest groups." Murray Weidenbaum, *Protecting the Environment* (St. Louis, Mo.: Washington University Center for the Study of American Business, 1989), 5. See also other studies issued by the Washington University Center, especially those prepared by Melinda Warren and Kenneth Chilton, *Clearing the Air: Regulating Ozone in the Public Interest* (1988), and Kenneth Chilton and Anne Sholtz, *Battling Smog: A Plan for Action* (1989).
37. Walter Olson, "Dirty Coal, No Clean Air," *Barron's* November 30, 1987, 11.
38. Mary Gison, ed., *To Breathe Freely: Risk, Consent and Air* (Totowa, N.J.: Rowman & Allanheld, 1985). See also, William Byron, *Toward Stewardship: An Interim Ethic of Poverty, Pollution and Power* (New York: Paulist Press, 1975), ch. 3.
39. Flora Lewis, "The Red Game Line," *The New York Times*, April 10, 1990, A 21. Also see, Robert Malpas, "Moving Toward Greater Energy Efficiency," *Scientific American* 203 (September 1990), 184; readers interested in the energy question will find this special issue most helpful.
40. Michael Parfit, "Earth Firsters Wield a Mean Monkeywrench," *Smithsonian Magazine*, April 1990, 184–187. Another lively treatment is Trip Gabriel, "If a Tree Falls in the Forest They Hear It," *New York Times Magazine*, November 4, 1991, 34–38.
41. How the philosopher sorts through technical and moral issues was beautifully illustrated by Michael Hoffman of Bentley College in his presidential address to the Society for Business Ethics, August 10, 1990. See also, Harry B. Gray, "A 20–20 Vision of Chemistry," *The Chemist* 67 (July–August 1990): 4.
42. Dwight Lee, *The Perpetual Assault on Progress* (St. Louis, Mo.: Washington University Center for The Study of American Business, 1991), 13.

# Appendix *13A*

*Protection of the Ozone Layer: Chronology of Key Events*

**Late 1974** Theories of CFC/chlorine-induced ozone layer depletion published.

**March 1977** Washington: U.S. hosts UNEP meeting, which recommends "World Plan of Action on the Ozone Layer" and establishes an annual science review.

**1977** Ozone protection amendment to U.S. Clean Air Act.

**March 1978** U.S. bans use of CFCs in nonessential aerosols, with Canada, Denmark, Finland, Norway, and Sweden taking similar action.

**1980** European Community reduces aerosol use by 30 percent and enacts capacity cap.

**March 1985** Vienna: *Convention for the Protection of the Ozone Layer* adopted. Covers research, monitoring, and data exchange, but negotiators fail to complete protocol on CFC controls.

**May 1985** British scientists publish data showing seasonal Antarctic ozone hole.

**July 1986** WMO/UNEP assessment, *Atmospheric Ozone 1985*, published.

**Dec. 1986** Geneva: first round of negotiations on ozone control protocol; subsequent sessions in February, April, June, and September 1987.

**June 1987** Venice Economic Summit declaration lists stratospheric ozone depletion first among environmental concerns.

**Sept. 1987** Montreal: final round of negotiations—*Protocol on Substances that Deplete the Ozone Layer* adopted.

**Jan. 1988** Washington: trade fair on CFC substitutes.

**March 1988** Washington: Ozone Trends Panel releases new evidence that CFCs are causing both global ozone depletion and the Antarctic ozone hole.

**March 1988** DuPont announces phaseout of CFCs.

**April 1988** U.S. ratifies Montreal Protocol (Sept. 16, 1987), which established rules and procedures to reduce the production of CFCs.

**Sept. 1988** Vienna Convention enters into force.

**Dec. 1988** Commission of the European Communities, together with eight of twelve member countries, ratifies Montreal Protocol. (Other four members ratify separately.)

**Jan. 1, 1989** Montreal Protocol enters into force.

**May 1989** Helsinki: first meeting of Parties to Vienna Convention and Montreal Protocol. Declaration calls for complete phaseout of CFCs and halons.

**Aug. 1989** Nairobi: meetings of working groups to consider revisions to protocol.

**June 1990** London: second meeting of Parties to Vienna Convention and Montreal Protocol.

Source: Richard Elliot Benedick, "Protecting the Ozone Layer: Directions in Diplomacy," *Preserving the Global Environment* (New York: W.W. Norton, 1991, 150–151) Ed. Jessica Tuchman Matthews. To the foregoing may be appended the chronology of major federal laws on the environment carried in Appendix I of Norman J. Zig and Michael C. Kraft, eds., *Environmental Policies of the 1990's*. (Washington: Congressional Quarterly Press, 1990), 301.

# Conclusion
# An Abelardian Valedictory

## Why Abelard?

Ending a book on law and ethics in the business environment with reference to medievalist Peter Abelard (1079–1142), best remembered by young romantics for his love letters to Heloise, is something of an oddity. But Abelard's relevance becomes clear if it is recalled that, as a student, he was considered an obnoxious gadfly by the professors he regularly taunted and was later adored by students who found in him the kind of intellectual maverick that appeals to restless young minds. His tract, *Sic et Non* (*Yes and No*), which Abelard used to quell critics who accused him of grievous omissions when he discussed the early church fathers, provides a convenient point for summation.

Having finished a book replete with references to statutes and court decisions, management-union engagements, corporate encounters with other corporations, philosophers' commentaries, and historians' narratives, the reader may understandably experience a measure of ennui. Memory, even for that fortunate few having great retentive powers, is a sieve that loses as much as it retains. But certain issues, certain conclusions, and certain debates will be remembered. On such remembrances, readers enlarge their perspectives and deepen their insights. Such enlargements may come from agreement with the author on certain points or—and frequently this is the most important contribution a writer can make—from disagreements. Every class and every organization needs some Abelards to make their *yes or no* clear to themselves. For this reason, the following are to be seen not as conclusions but as prods to further reflection. The book's ending is the reader's beginning; the author's validictory is the student's commencement, a commencement made less frustrating when each statement is accepted for what it is: a broad generalization, the answers to which can be used to sort out personal values that may someday shape—or be shaped by—corporate policies.

## Yes and/or No (Sic et Non)?

Although impossible to distill all major points, it is—given the author's purpose—not only possible but necessary to offer several ideas for recall and reassessment. The following—*not all of which represent the writer's views*—invite attention.

1. The first step in judging ourselves and others is to make explicit in our personal *sic et nons* our own understanding of human nature. On this point, the two canonical statements in American history are the Declaration of Independence and the Constitution. Taken together, they reveal our forefathers' view—at once trusting (popular sovereignty) and at once cautious (checks and balances). Because each person is the ultimate judge of her or his self-interest, each must be free. But because freedom is easily abused, each person's liberty must, at times, be restrained. On this proposition of the nation's founders rests reasons for the legitimacy of democratic governments and of market systems.

   As the country moves toward a new millennium there is worry that freedom is turning into license. Some citizens treat freedom to vote by refusing to exercise it; some Wall Street brokers define liberty as a right to lie; some savings and loan owners conceive liberty as a right to loot; some media pundits use freedom of the press to write half-truths; some politicians legislate to entrench and enrich themselves; some lawyers see liberty as a procedural bulwark to foil justice. *In most current exercises of liberty, freedom marches without accountability.*
   Yes or no?

2. In his famous Essay II in *The Federalist*, James Madison assured Americans that they would have little to fear from factions because, in a large country like the United States, the principle of countervailing power would come into play whenever one special-interest group began to acquire too much strength. Madison's opinion was reassuring to his fellow Virginians and to other southerners who were becoming restive over the growing financial and commercial power of the North. Except for the Civil War, Madison's insight seemed unassailable. Large corporations did garner to themselves enormous powers that they frequently abused, but eventually Big Government and Big Labor were able to challenge Big Business; midwestern farmers fought northern financiers; and the political system was, of course, never in total equilibrium. This has been the country's past.

   Now arises a different kind of self-interest group. The real danger to political and social stability comes not so much from domination by a single bloc but from a single group's power to block publicly desired legislation. To illustrate, the American Rifle Association's belief that widespread possession of guns is good—even when police departments throughout the country say it is bad—has not been repudiated by Congress; the trial lawyers' association has been able—at least so far—to

thwart efforts to reform tort law; the American Medical Association uses its large resources to hamper passage of legislation to control runaway health-care costs. The essence of the problem is this: *Special interest groups may not always be able to get what they want (Madison predicted they never would) but they are able to block what the majority wants.*
Yes or no?

3. Bribes are both illegal and unethical. In this, law and morality join hands. Payoffs, on the other hand, are legally and morally justifiable when the survival of the firm and the survival of jobs are threatened by corrupt public officers if their demands are not met. *However, if payoffs help an evil regime to retain its power, they are justified only when the United States maintains normal diplomatic relationship with the extortionist country.*
Yes or no?

4. "Tort law" have become fighting words in the United States. Critics insist that excessive awards, especially in the form of punitive damages, result in such expensive insurance premiums that consumers who pay them in higher prices are unfairly treated. That there are bizarre awards in the tort saga is undeniable. Defenders of punitive damages, on the other hand, argue that awards are not nearly so excessive as critics claim and that, generally speaking, when high awards have been made they are deserved by the innocent victims and serve the further purpose of warning all manufacturers to be careful in what they make and what they market. Current tort law, according to its defenders, helps individuals and society.

As usual, when Congress delays, the courts act. On March 4, 1991, the Supreme Court ruled that the punitive damage of $1,077,978 levied by a jury against Pacific Mutual Life Insurance should stand. In a 7 to 1 opinion, the justices concluded that caps on awards were not required by the Constitution under the Fourteenth Amendment. Writing for the majority Justice Blackmun opined that, although unlimited jury discretion in the fixing of punitive damages may invite results that jar one's constitutional sensibilities, the constitution calls for only "general concerns of reasonableness and adequate guidance from the court when the case is tried by a jury." The only dissenter, Justice Sandra Day, said that without standards of reasonableness, which the courts have failed to provide, juries can run amok. Extreme PDs may be the exception. But so were scud missiles during the Gulf War. When courts fail to provide reasonable norms, the present PD system is wrong. *Justice Day is right.*
Yes or no?

5. Advertisers believe that they are—and should be—more than purveyors of information. Accepting their role as persuaders, advertisers try to make their presentations as lively and imaginative as possible. Sometimes the effort leads advertisers to stray from the path of truth. They are not hidden persuaders—Vance Packard's famous descriptive—but overt manipulators. It remains somewhat of a puzzle, however, that the meaning of deception has been so widely contested. The Federal Trade Commission had one view and the National Association of Advertisers had quite another. But it is widely believed that the advertisers' main street, Madison Avenue, is a thoroughfare for slicksters and hucksters whose patron saint is P. T. Barnum—"A sucker is born every second."

A contrary view has been expressed in this book. TV ads may offend the viewers' tastes but opinion polls suggest that public tastes are already low. And on this point of truth telling the advertising community itself (with nudges from the FTC) is doing a reasonably good policing job. The NAD and NARB investigate thoroughly; experts testify; testimony is weighed; if necessary, additional evidence is sought; the judgments are made public; and the record of compliance with legally uninforceable opinions is remarkable. There is, of course, a weakness. Action is taken only when one company charges another with making fraudulent claims. If intramural rivalry is slight or nonexistent, two companies may stretch the truth. Hertz, for example, ignored Avis for years. In this climate the consumer may be misled by companies from the same industry. *However, in its attempt to prevent deception the advertising industry in the United States deserves high moral marks.*
*Yes or no?*

6. Seeking to restore muscle to its tired body, unions have turned more and more to organizing efforts among white-collar workers—nurses and teachers, secretaries and lab technicians, writers and musicians, federal and state employees, and the like. It is a truism that unions come when managements have behaved shabbily. It is also true that in a society like America—in which material goods are very important—any group of workers whose income is substantially less than others will seek to organize. People working in the same general area are less prone to tolerate wide variances in wage scale. To illustrate, nurses ask why doctors earn so much and they so much less; firefighters want as much as police; and carpenters want as much as bricklayers. But certain occupations are so essential to the public that the thesis that *all workers have a right to organize but not all workers have a right to strike is the ethical right.*
*Yes or no?*

7. Americans instinctively fear large corporations—a fear expressed in the maxim that big is bad. Some folks were initially concerned that the

merger mania of the past decade would leave American customers under the dominion of corporate giants and that an economy of corporate Goliaths and consumer Davids was unfair. As time went on, however, the Goliath syndrome seemed less threatening because the takeover artists were less interested in running companies than in running off with money. Billion-dollar acquisitions were made but billions of dollars in assets were sold. To spectators it often appeared that big was not bad—it was just dumb.

Whether takeovers, hostile or friendly, are good for America has been hotly debated. The Reagan administration, supported by economists like Michael Jensen, pointed to the economic advantages of the merger/takeover movement. To the experts takeovers were the only way to oust indulgent managers who had become fat and lazy. Others, like Louis Lowenstein and Peter Drucker, saw leveraged buyouts and hostile takeovers as dangerous developments: managers were deflected from their real work; employee morale plummeted; downsizing was effectuated incompetently and ruthlessly; and productivity was not enhanced. *Hostile takeovers, in short, were bad for business and bad for America.*
*Yes or no?*

8. Insider trading has been declared legally anathema by a Congress that has never defined it. The Supreme Court has also had a hard time making up its mind what insider trading is and when it takes place. Defenders of the practice say that part of the legislators' and judges' difficulty is due to the fact that what could be legally wrong in precise statutes is morally right. So long as the trader's own clients are not hurt, and so long as lying and theft are not involved, the insider plays a constructive role in the financial world. By their diligence they learn what is going on in the marketplace; by their alertness they start capital flowing to where it is needed; and by their willingness to bet on the future they exhibit the desirable trait of entrepreneurs everywhere.

   Opponents of insider trading are not impressed by such assertions. They feel that the insider takes advantage of information that properly belongs in the public domain. By so doing, insiders violate the basic rule of a competitive economy, namely, the ethical principle of the level playing field. They also insist that innocent investors are hurt by the greedy few in a silent club that turns capitalism away from an investment world into a casino society. *In short, inside traders get rich unfairly.*
   *Yes or no?*

9. In collective bargaining both labor and management are expected to come to the negotiating table with certain information concealed from the opponent's view. Bargaining theory that takes into account this

fact is, however, not always reconcilable to moral theory because truth telling can too easily become a casualty in such a bargaining game. When General Electric announced its Boulware policy (make public all relevant facts), union leaders were aghast. Boulwarism became synonymous with paternalism, with Big Daddy telling his workers what is relevant and what management accommodations will be made.

Defenders of Boulwarism say that it is the only way to end a bargaining process that Columbia Professor Neil Chamberlain once called a time-consuming charade. Boulwarism serves to end the posturing that both sides in the collective-bargaining process adopt. Moreover, workers know what the facts are and this knowledge helps them to determine whether their representatives are really committed to their interests. Corporations are not given to abuses because any corporation that failed even once to put its cards on the table would forfeit the game forever. *Boulwarism makes sense because, in the long run, complete openness and total honesty are best for sound and ethical collective bargaining.*
Yes or no?

10. The debate between advocates of *liberation theology* (multinationals make developing countries too dependent on them) and *liberating theology* (multinationals enrich the lives of other people) shows no sign of diminution and for one very good reason: facts can be selectively marshaled to support either position. Indeed, in every form of capitalistic exchange—whether between worker and employer, rich nation or poor nation, lender or borrower—changes in equality between the two participants result in disappropriate profits for the stronger.

    Liberating theology, on the contrary, claims that host countries are invariably benefited when a global corporation does business in their midsts. People wallowing in inertia are awakened from their slumber; local firms prosper; technology transfers increase the host country's potentials for productivity gains; schools and hospitals are built—either by communities receiving more tax revenues or by global corporations themselves.

    Although conditions vary widely from country to country and from region to region, a conclusion can be made to the effect that *multinationals are a force for good in Third World countries.*
    Yes or no?

11. Economic theory, as two economists noted, "has trouble in explaining strikes."[1] Yet Americans have little trouble today in accepting strikes as the expression of a fundamental human right. That recognition has been sharpened by awareness that, in the recent past, that right was generally not accepted by courts and only grudgingly conceded by a skeptical public.

As demographics change the work force, and as global competition forces companies to downsize, union leaders have looked to organizing white-collar workers to offset the deplenishing supply of blue-collar workers. This group, generally better educated than their blue-collar associates, has looked to unions to protect them when their interests are threatened. Teachers have struck. Doctors have struck. Nurses have struck. Government employees have struck. In all such cases the public seems both bewildered and frustrated. Now is the time to lay down a general rule: *workers in organizations or professions that provide essential services on a timely basis do not have the right to strike.*
*Yes or no?*

12. When are manufacturers and consumers at fault? This was the question submitted in March 1991 to the Supreme Court. The case, stemming from the death of Mr. Cipollone's wife from lung cancer in 1984, had attracted wide attention because the first jury verdict required a cigarette manufacturer to pay $400,000 in damages to relatives of a smoker who died of cancer. A federal appeals court in Philadelphia overturned the verdict and ordered a new trial. But the appeals court barred Mr. Cipollone from pursuing any claims against tobacco companies that occurred after 1966—the year Congress required warning labels on cigarette packs and in cigarette advertisements.

    The appeals court ruling in the Cipollone case was thought to say that warning labels immunize cigarette makers against claims dating since 1966. Before that date the tobacco industry advertised widely and pushed sales aggressively. Once consumers begin to smoke, the practice becomes almost addictive.

    No matter how the question is phrased before the courts, an ethical argument can be made to the effect that *if consumers are adequately informed in time for them to avoid using a particular nonessential product, the individual, not the manufacturer, is responsible.*
    *Yes or no?*

13. To offset declining sales in the domestic market, the tobacco companies are exporting to Third World countries and marketing aggressively. When criticized, the firms defend themselves by saying that their manufacturing and export sales provide (1) jobs for unskilled workers who most need jobs, (2) dividends to stockholders, (3) taxes to both the local community and the federal government, and (4) considerable satisfaction to people who live in squalid conditions. The defense rests on a rather unique interpretation of the utilitarian ethic. In reality, the company is hypocritical. *Exporting toxic products even with prominent warning labels is unethical.*
    *Yes or no?*

14. On January 2, 1990, the governor of Rhode Island closed all banks and credit unions in the state to protect the financial system from total collapse. Although state officials blamed the embezzlement of $13 million by a small bank called Heritage Loan and Investment for the crisis, the reality is that a state report in 1985 predicted a banking collapse if reforms were not introduced promptly. Nothing happened because the industry had influential friends in the legislature, the state house, and the regulatory bodies themselves.

Four years before the state report was made public, a Peat-Marwick accountant named Karl Ericson voiced his concern about the industry-owned insurance company called Rhode Island Share and Deposit Indemnity Corporation (RISDIC). In the Rhode Island legislature, however, were committee chairmen and many others who had close ties to the heading-for-disaster RISDIC. The power of the banking industry's lobbyists was awesome.

The Rhode Island story is not unique among the states. Unlike the President and the Congress, state officials are less under the glare of the media's searchlights and consequently can more easily escape the heat. If state and local officials were carefully examined a conclusion would be reached: *grassroots democracy is as venal as the federal government—and perhaps more so.*
Yes or no?

15. Aware of the laxity that exists in state governments, and convinced that certain states (Delaware and New Jersey, particularly) are too accommodating to large corporations, Ralph Nader has advocated placing them under tighter control by the federal government. Nader's mechanism for taming the "corporate beasts" is federal chartering. If getting a federal charter required corporations (1) to make full disclosure of their finances, (2) identify codes of conduct, (3) abide by affirmative action laws, (4) protect the environment, and (5) guarantee to workers a bill of rights, *Nader is on the right track.*
Yes or no?

16. It was widely believed that the civil religion that required minimum religious commitment from individuals (belief in God the Creator of persons in the image of their Maker with certain inalienable rights) was enough to hold American society together. From the civil religion flowed, it was said, certain values of honesty and decency. Today offense has been taken by many to the vulgarity of Robert Maplethorpe's photographs of homosexual behavior and Bret Easton Ellis's novel *American Psycho*, the story of a Wall Street psychopath who murders bums, prostitutes, street children, and even acquaintances. Those appalled by such photographs and such novels use them as examples of the nation's loss of innocence. *The conclusion is this. The personal*

*values of Americans are at a very low moral level.*
*Yes or no?*

17. The market system depends on trust. However, the antics of Wall Street operatives like Levine, Boesky, and Milken raise warning signals about the stock market. Overcharging the government by big corporations raises ethical questions about large defense contractors. Union racketeering among teamsters and dock and construction workers raises questions about unions. Even if one concedes that the net of evil has snared relatively few, enough wrongdoing is going on to warrant the conclusion that *the United States is a money-driven society where cash is more important than character.*
*Yes or no?*

18. It has been hypothesized that, because environmental abuses are an international problem, the world needs some form of international regulatory agency. Establishing and forming such an agency would, of course, require the United States to surrender some of its sovereignty. Unhappy experiences with certain United Nations' agencies make this country's leaders suspicious of international bodies whose jurisdiction might cover American corporations and unions. What might overshadow our Environmental Protection Agency is a Multinational Protection Agency (MEPA). Although many fears are justified, *the time has come for the nation to declare support for an MEPA and similar organizations to deal with global problems.*
*Yes or no?*

19. Because the United States has, albeit slowly, moved to adopt affirmative action laws, it should move aggressively to promote such laws in places like South Africa, India, and the Middle East, where racism and ethnic and gender discrimination exist on a wide scale. *Large American corporations should support the government's effort to improve the recruiting and employment practices of countries practicing any discrimination.*
*Yes or no?*

20. A CEO of a company in the powerful and prestigious Business Roundtable examines the agenda set for that organization's next meeting. Among the topics for discussion are two that pose serious problems. One involves support for increased taxes to meet the needs of the homeless and the unemployed. The other deals with efforts by groups like the Council for Competitiveness, the National Association of Manufacturers, and the Electronic Industries Association to persuade Con-

gress and the President to provide federal funds to improve the country's technological expertise. Without government economic help the United States will lose its share of the world markets in computers, electronics, car manufacturing, and pharmaceuticals. The CEO's own fears about the country's relative decline in applied technology are reinforced when he reads that, if the Patriot missiles (used so successfully to destroy deadly Iraqi scuds) were built today, defense contractors would have to rely on computer parts made in Japan.

Also in the day's mail is a letter from Kent Hughes, president of a Washington-based think tank called the Council on Competitiveness, who wrote that "the single most important thing Congress needs to do when it is making law is to put on a pair of competitiveness glasses and think about how it will affect the long-term economic health of the country."[2]

The CEO's humanitarian instincts collide with his economic interests. He wants to support both welfare and research programs even if they mean increasing corporate taxes. But there is the annual budget deficit and an astronomical national debt. He knows the debt has to be reduced. Government officials know it has to be reduced. As a consequence, trade-offs are inevitable, one of which is a reduction in federal aid to welfare programs. He decides to support an increase in R&D for applied technology only. *The CEO has made the right ethical decision.*
Yes or no?

21. The *Economist* made the following dreary assessment:

*Accountancy is in a sorry state. In America the country's seventh-biggest firm, Laventhol & Horwath, has filed for chapter 11 bankruptcy. Ernst & Young, the mega-merger of Arthur Young and Ernst & Whinney, has run advertisements reassuring clients that it is in a very strong financial condition. Auditors face a series of humiliating lawsuits from the savings and loan mess. Standard Chartered has sued Price Waterhouse for $800 [million] following its (Standard Chartered's) purchase of an unsuccessful bank in Arizona; punitive damages could push the claim over $2 billion.*

*Accountants deserve most of the stick they are getting. Like advertising agencies and investment bankers they fell for the 1980s fad of the service conglomerate. The big eight firms became the big six as they merged and remerged, struggling to push under one roof a whole range of business services, like tax advice, management consultancy, corporate finance and, yes, insolvency. This left them woefully dependent on non-recurring fee-businesses like consulting; it also encouraged them to cut auditing charges to win other business.*

*Lackluster scoring and divided loyalty go hand in hand. All the accountants' problems have a common origin: they are no longer seen to be impartial. Too often it looks as if they are bending over backwards to help the people who write their cheques, the managers, rather than the people who pay for them, the shareholders.*[3]

*The Economist is right on target.*
*Yes or no?*

22. The war against Iraq led many clergy to denounce it as immoral. Although no prelates were involved, the feisty editor of *The American Spectator* wrote as follows in March 1991.

*America's mainline clergy are doing more than merely neglecting to respond to evil. They are hamming it up, reiterating all the vacuous platitudes of yesteryear, as though the Gulf were Vietnam and Vietnam had made war unconscionable and forever futile.*

*Thus the greasepaint moralizers again afflict us. In Paramus, New Jersey, Msgr. Frank LoBianco of Our Lady of Visitation Roman Catholic Church urges that parishioners ignore "the country's call to duty because it takes a lot of love to forgive those who are evil and unjust to others."*

*In Croton-on-Hudson, New York, the Rev. Linda Kimmelman of the Asbury United Methodist Church asks rhetorically "Why war?" and responds cleverly, "Because human greed, lust for power and national self-interest are alive and well. Ask yourself, if the primary export of Kuwait were broccoli and not oil, would we be in this war?" Rev. Kimmelman, that is a good one. But if broccoli provided the energy to run hospitals, to heat schools, to run a country, surely we would have some moral obligation to ensure the flow of broccoli at stable prices. But to those who see the world as it is, some wars are eminently moral.*

*The barbarities committed by our enemies vindicate our resort to arms. In violation of international law and of the conventions of decency, Saddam's troops invaded Kuwait. They have tortured, raped, and pillaged. They have repeatedly fired on a non-combatant nation, Israel; and they aim not at military installations but at civilian neighborhoods. In past wars they have used weaponry banned by international law. They now commit brutal war crimes against prisoners of war. Still, from comfortable pulpits the clergy sing of virtue. Have they ever heard of sins of omission?*[4]

Although this may have been expressed in overly florid terms, the fact is that *most church leaders are both antimilitary and antibusiness.*
*Yes or no?*

23. The savings and loan crisis of the late 1980s and early 1990s will cost taxpayers billions of dollars. The story involved five senators known

as the Keating Five: Cranston, Riegel, DeConcini, Glenn, and McCain. Keating was a fundraiser for the senators, asking in return that his bank, Lincoln Savings and Loan, be freed from intrusive regulators. The only one charged with wrongdoing by the Senate Ethics Committee was Alan Cranston of California, who had already announced his intention to leave the Senate because of heart problems.

Less publicized were the roles of federal regulators themselves. One was Michael Patriarca, the federal bank's head of enforcement, who resisted heavy political pressures to drop the inquiry. However, Patriarca's bosses, Danny Wall and Rosemary Stewart, later ordered Lincoln Savings removed from his jurisdiction, allowing it to stay open more than two more years until it was closed in April 1989. The bank's failure was expected to cost taxpayers $2.3 billion. Ms. Stewart defends her office's record on grounds that there were never enough lawyers to handle the high case load.

*Ms. Stewart and others like her in the regulator's office are guilty of gross negligence.*
*Yes or no?*

## A Final Comment

The 23 illustrations may elicit 46 different responses. How do readers answer? How do policymakers answer? Both can follow public polls, being content to be *told* what to do. Or they can assume the risk-laden role of social engineers and *teach* others what to do. In either case, responses are shaped by legal rules and ethical values. Involvement in the process of questioning, answering, and implementing is heady business. The young dream of position and power. Those who achieve both often do not know quite what to do about them. However, confusion is not chaos; doubt is not defeat. Whether one is contemplating a career in business or already launched on a career, it is always salutary to dwell on the words of philosopher Alfred North Whitehead:

*The general functions of a university can be at once translated in terms of the particular functions of a business school. We need not flinch from the assertion that the main function of such a school is to produce men (and women) with a greater zest for business. It is a libel upon human nature to conceive that zest for life is the product of pedestrian purposes directed toward the narrow routine of material comforts. Mankind, by its pioneering instinct, and in a hundred other ways, proclaims the falsehood of that lie.*

*In the modern complex social organism, the adventure of life cannot be disjoined from intellectual adventure. Amid simpler circumstances, the pioneer can follow the urge of his instinct, directed toward the scene of his vision from the mountain top. But in the complex organisations of modern business the intellectual adven-*

*ture of analysis, and of imaginative reconstruction, must precede any successful reorganisation. In a simpler world, business relations were simpler, being based on the immediate contact of man with man and on immediate confrontation with all relevant material circumstances. Today's business organisation requires an imaginative grasp of the psychologies of populations engaged in differing modes of occupation; of populations scattered through cities, through mountains, through plains; of populations on the ocean, and of populations in mines, and of populations in forests. It requires an imaginative grasp of conditions in the tropics, and of conditions in temperate zones. It requires an imaginative grasp of the interlocking interests of organisations, and of the reactions of the whole complex to any change in one of its elements. It requires an imaginative understanding of laws of political economy, not merely in the abstract, but also with the power to construe them in terms of the particular circumstances of a concrete business. It requires some knowledge of the habits of government, and of the variations of those habits under diverse conditions. It requires an imaginative vision of the binding forces of any human organization, a sympathetic vision of the limits of human nature and of the conditions which evoke loyalty of service. It requires some knowledge of the laws of health, and of the laws of fatigue, and of the conditions for sustained reliability. It requires an imaginative understanding of the social effects of the conditions of factories. It requires a sufficient conception of the role of applied science in modern society. It requires that discipline of character which can say 'yes' and 'no' to other men, not by reason of blind obstinacy, but with firmness delivered from a conscious evaluation of relevant alternatives.*

*The universities have trained the intellectual pioneers of our civilisation—the priests, the lawyers, the statesmen, the doctors, the men of science, and the men of letters. They have been the home of those ideals which lead men to confront the confusion of their present times. The Pilgrim Fathers left England to found a state of society according to the ideals of their religious faith; and one of their earlier acts was the foundation of Harvard University in Cambridge, named after that ancient mother of ideals in England, to which so many of them owed their training. The conduct of business now requires intellectual imagination of the same type as that which in former times has mainly passed into those other occupations; and the universities are the organisations which have supplied this type of mentality for the service of the progress.*[5]

If readers leave with a more imaginative reconstruction of the business environment and of the laws and ethics that govern it, the author's goal will have been achieved-and Abelard pleased.

## Notes

1. Raquel Fernandez and Jacob Glazer, "Striking for a Bargain Between Two Completely Informed Agents," *The American Economics Review* 81 (March 1991): 240. The authors show that even strikes between two fully informed parties can be inefficient but nonetheless rational.
2. Alissa J. Rubin, "Proponents of Technology R and D Emphasize Competitiveness," *Congressional Quarterly Weekly Reports*, 49 (March 2, 1991): 534.
3. Comment, "Blowing the Whistle on Accountancy," *The Economist*, Dec. 22, 1990, 15.
4. R. Emmet Tyrell, Jr. "Fathead Bishops," *The American Spectator*, 24 (March 1991): 8.
5. Alfred North Whitehead, *The Aims of Education and Other Essays* (New York: Macmillan, 1966), 140–142.

# Index

Abelard, Peter, 421
Abraham, Henry, 41n
Abstention doctrine, 29
Accounting profession, 69–70, 430–431
  and ethics, 69–70, 73, 74
Acid rain, 405
Ackerman, Bruce A., 418n
Acquisitions, 139. See also Mergers/takeovers
Acuff, F. L., 258n
Adams, Brooks, 12n
Adams, John, 19, 20, 21, 28
Adler, Nancy J., 108n
Administered pricing, 131–133
Admissible evidence, 307–310
Adversarialism, and collective bargaining, 234–236
Advertising, 262–293, 424
  advertisers' accountability in, 287–288
  agency self-policing and, 282
  associations in, 270
  to children, 278–279
  comparative, 272–273
  consumer complaints about, 282–283
  criteria for, 280–281
  deceptive, 268–271
  definitions in, 265–266
  ethical appraisals of, 285–289
  government and industry definitions for, 270–271
  harmful-prooduct, 274–278
  industry scrutiny of, 285–286
  industry size, 264–265
  institutional controls on, 279–285
  intervention as control over, 279–281
  local vs. national, 265–266
  nature of industry, 264–268
  puffery and, 273–274
  self-policing as control over, 281–283
  Seven Maxims in, 267–268
  special forms of, 271–279
  and tobacco industry, 275–278
  truth in, 266–268
AFL. See American Federation of Labor
AFT. See American Federation of Teachers
Agency theory, 49
Agres, Ted, 191n
AIDS victims, and consumer legislation, 303–304
Airport and Airway Development Acts, 249
Akins, Oran, 209
Alcoholic beverages, marketing restrictions on, 277
Alderson, Wroe, 135n
Alexander, Charles, 192n
Allen, Herbert A., Jr., 202
Allsop, Dee, 40n
Althusius, Johannes, 17
America. See United States
American Association of Advertising Agencies (4A's), 282
American Cancer Society, 303
American culture, 83–91
American Express Company, ethics of, 117
American Farm Bureau Association, 61

American Federation of Labor (AFL), 62–65
American Federation of Teachers (AFT), 247
  and health benefits, 252–253
American Medical Association, and cigarette advertising, 277–278
American Overseas Airlines (AOA), 231
American Railroad Union (ARU), 228
  and Pullman strike, 237
American Rifle Association, 422
American Surgery Company, and insider trading, 202–203
American Telephone and Telegraph, breakup of, 157
American Tobacco Company, 140
AMF Incorporated, advertising by, 283–284
Anderson, Gary M., 78n
Andrews, Andrea R., 358n
Anglo-Persian Oil Company. See British Petroleum
Ansberry, Clare, 291n
Antitrust acts, 120–122
Antitrust issues, 140, 141. See also Mergers/takeovers
Aquinas, Thomas, 17
Arbenz, Jacob, 374
Arbitration, and strikes, 238
Argyris, Chris, 108n
Aristotle, 17, 353
Arkes, Hadley, 108n
Arkwright, Richard, 48
Armstrong, Scott, 266
Arriagarda, Urgarte Genaro, 389n
Arrow, Kenneth, 1
Asbestos removal, 338–341
  ethics of, 342–343
Asbestos School Hazard Detection and Control Act, 339
Ashland Oil, 209
Asia, 6
  poverty in, 370
Associations, in advertising, 270
Atkins, James, 14
Atkison, Timothy B., 359n
Atlantic Refining Company, 130
Attfield, Robin, 418n
Atwood, James, 135n
Auerbach, Joseph, 185
Australia, 376
*Autobiography* (Benjamin Franklin), 90
Aviation industry, and traffic controllers' strike, 247–250
Avis, Warren, 272
Avis-Hertz controversy, 272–273
Axelrod, Robert, 105n

Babcock, Charles, Jr., 322
Bacon, Francis, 394
Baida, Peter, 77n
Baier, Annette, 166n
Bait and switch tactics, 281
Baliga, B. R., 358n
Bally Manufacturing Company, 252
Bankers, investment, 200

435

# 436  INDEX

Bankruptcy, 337–342
   and credit agreements, 341
Barber, Bob, 77n
Barbour, Jane, 418n
Bardach, Eugene, 418n
Bargaining, 229–230
Bargaining theory, 233–234
Barry, Marion, 172
Barton, Nancy E., 165n
Barzun, Jacques, 11n
*Basic Inc. v. Levinson*, 151
Bathtub theory, 126
Baumgart, Margaret, 389n
Baumgart, Richard G., 389n
Baumhart, Raymond, 98, 119
Baxter, William, 142
Bayles, Michael, 80n
BCI Holdings, 146
Beatrice Company, leveraged buyout of, 145–149
Bebéar, Claude, 93
Bechtle, John, 232
Bell, Daniel, 12n, 107n
Bell, Griffin, 347
Bellah, Robert N., 106n
Bendix, 155
Benign neglect policy, 313
Bennett, James, 417n
Benson & Hedges, 276
Bentham, Jeremy, 100, 410
Berg, Ivar, 78n, 259n
Berk, Richard A., 106n
Berle, Adolf, 49, 55
Berry, Thomas, 392
Bethlehem Steel, 140
Beveridge, Norwood P., 78n
Bids, two-tiered, 142–143
Bird, Frederick B., 108n
Birnbaum, Jeffrey H., 259n
Birnbaum, Sheila L., 328n
Bituminous Coal Operators' Association (BCOA), 214–243
Black, Eli, 374–375
Blackburn, Virginia, 165n
Blackmun, Harry, 336, 423
Blair, John D., 358n
Blase, Vincent, 21n
Blitzstein, David, 243
Block, Dennis L., 165n
Bloom, Allan, 39n
Blough, Roger, 132
Blum, Emeric, 367
Blumenthal, W. Michael, 2
Blumstein, Michael, 22n
Blyton, Paul, 77n
Bobo, Jack, 129
Bodin, John, 111
Boesky, Ivan, 142, 143, 147, 195, 201
Boethius, 353
Bok, Derek, 258n
Bok, Sisella, 292n
Bolingbroke, Viscount Henry St. John, 16, 39n
Bond, Langhorne, 248
Bondholders, 157
Bonuses, and labor-management conflicts, 252
Borders, William, 12n
Bork, Robert, 31, 33
Bossism, 65
Boulding, Kenneth, 106n
Boulton, David, 223n
Boulware, Lemuel, 230

Boulwarism, 230, 426
Bourrough, Daniel, 135
Bowie, Norman, 79n, 111, 235, 359n
Boycotts, 240
Bradford, William, 259n
Bradley, Joseph C., 137n
Bradley, Michael, 166n
Bradley, Phillips, 40n
Brandeis, Louis, 32–33, 136n
Brandt, Allan M., 292n
Brandt, Richard, 108n
Brannigan, Martha, 79n
Brant, Peter, 203
Bratton, William W., Jr., 79n
Braybrooke, David, 293n
Brenner, Steven N., 107n, 135
*Brethren, The*, 266
Brewster, Kingman, 135n
Bribes and payoffs, 206–207, 423
   definitional examples of, 207–212
   gifts as, 212–213
   moral assessments of, 217–220
   and U.S. government, 214
Brigham, Eugene F., 164n
Brill, Steven, 164n
Briloff, Abe, 197
Bristol-Myers Company, advertising by, 284–285
British Petroleum, 379–381
Britton, Herchell, 174
Brock, William, 388n
Brodeur, Paul, 358n
Brody, Michael, 358n
Brokers. *See* Insider trading
Bronson, Gail, 259n
Brooks, John, 164n
Brown, Donaldson, 131
Brown, Peter Megargee, 72
354, Brown, Robert McAfee, 388n
Browning-Ferris Industries, 335–336
*Brown v. Kendall*, 299
Bruck, Connie, 164n
Brudrey, Victor, 165n
"Brundtland Report," 406
Buber, Martin, 291n, 359n
Bucy, J. Fred, 181
Bullinger, Heinrich, 17
Bumpers, Dale, 26–27
Bureaucracy. *See* Regulators; United States government
Bureaucratic organization, 51
Burger, Warren, 32, 33, 69–70, 359n
Burgess, Anthony, 41n
Burke, Thomas, 260n
Burton, John, 73
Bush, George, 403
Businesses, noncorporate, 60–61. *See also* Corporations
Butcher, Charles, 11n
Byron, William, 419n

Cadbury, Adrian, 83
Calabresi, Guido, 297–298, 305, 324, 359n
Calame, Byron E., 223n
Calicchia, Marcia, 40n
California
   liability laws in, 313–315
   San Joaquin Valley in, 396
Calvin, John, 84
Camenisch, Paul, 80n
Camps, Frank, 308

# INDEX 437

Canada, 376
Capeci, Jerry, 258n
Capitalism, 45–46
   corporations and, 46–61
   institutional, 49–50
   managerial, 49
Cardoso, Fernando Henrique, 368
Caradozo, Benjamin, 54, 295, 355
Carey, Ronald, 231
Carley, William M., 108n
Carlile, Franklin, 292n
Carlton, Dennis W., 222n
Carnegie, Andrew, 88
Carpenter, David, 202
Carper, William B., 165n
Carr, Albert Z., 107n, 135n
Carrington, Tim, 164n
Carson, Rachel, 393
Carter, James E., 216
Carter, Robert, 305
Carter, Stephen L., 41n
*Case of Thorns*, 298, 299
Categorical imperative, 101–102
*Caterpillar Tractor v. Beck*, 323
Caveat vendor principle, 306
Chamberlain, Neil, 55, 232, 233, 426
Chandler, Alfred D., 77n
Change
   cultural, 5–6
   economic/business, 6
   political, 8
Chapman, John W., 260n
Chavez, Caesar, 240, 374
Chazen, Charles, 224
Cheit, Earl, 106n, 136n
Chiarella, Vincent, 203–204, 205
Children, advertising to, 278–279
Chilton, Kenneth, 418n
Chilton, Werner, 259n
China, 7
Chlorofluorocarbons (CFCs), 399, 400
Chonko, Lawrence B., 199n, 15n
Chrysler Corporation, and UAW, 252
Church, Frank, 215
Churchill, Winston, 379
Cicerone, Ralph, 398
Cigarette advertising, 275–278
CIO, 62
Cities Service, 155
Clark, David Scott, 292n
Clark, John Maurice, 78n
Clarke, Michael, 417n
Clayton Act, 121
Clean Air Act, 403
   deadlines of, 404
Clean Water Act, 393, 403
Clothing and Textile Workers, 240–241
Cluett Peabody (CP), 153
Coal and environment, 399
Coca-Cola, 155–156, 382
Cochran, Thomas C., 77n
Cocom. *See* Coordinated Committee for Multilateral Export Controls
Cohen, Laurie P., 165n
Cohen, P., 79n
Cohen, Stanley E., 292n
Cohen, William, 191n
Coleman, James, 59
Coleman, Jules L., 359n
Colgate-Palmolive, 382

Collective bargaining, 232–236, 425–426
   and adversarialism, 234–236
   and bargaining theory, 233–234
   cooperative techniques in, 235
Collegial organizations, 51, 52–53
Colton, David, 259n
Commercial intelligence, 173
Commercial professions, 66–74
Commercial revolution, 47
Commercial transactions, 265
Communism, 45
Comparative advertising, 272–273
Compensation/Liability Act (ERCLA), 402–403
Competition
   ethical and legal rules for, 110–137
   and ethical criteria, 115–120
   evolution of economic, 112–115
   issues relating to, ranking of, 119
   and litigiousness, 113–114
   negative aspects of, 115
Comprehensive Environmental Response, 402
Computer crime, 176–177
Computer technology, theft of, 178–180
Conan, Joseph, 224
Concert-of-action approach, 321
Congressional Budget Office (CBO), 97, 98
Congress of the United States, 36
   election to, 22–24
Constable, Barbara, 370
Contitutionalists, 50
Constitutional organization, 51–52
   attributes of, 52
Constitution of the United States, 16–22
   challenges to, 20–22
   framers of, 18–20
   ratification of, by state, 21
Constructive effort principle, 116–117
Constructive insider, 205
Consumer Product Safety Commission (CPSC), 34
Consumers, 427
   and advertising, 270
   and protective legislation, 302–304
Contract, 318
Contract law, 227
Conwell, Russel, 106n
Cook, C. W., 288
Cooperative movement, 60–61
Cooper Industries, 159
Coordinated Committee for Multilateral Export Controls (Cocom), 181
Copperweld Corporation, 126–127
Cornfort, Chris, 77n
Corporate raiders. *See* Mergers/takeovers; Raiders
Corporate social responsibility (CSR) doctrine, 54–60
   CSR-1, CST-2, 59
Corporations, 424–425. *See also* Economics; Ethics; Noncorporate businesses
   capitalism and, 46–61
   employees and, 50–53
   growth of, 46–49
   internal reform of, 161–162
   management vs. ownership in, 49
   multinational, 362–389
   and organization structure, 51–52
   politicizing, 53
   power of, 53–60
   regulation of mergers and takeovers, 162
   and tort law, 300–301

## INDEX

Corwin, Edwin S., 32
Cosmopolitanism, 91–92
Court, Edward R., 345
Cox, Archibald, 27–28
Craswell, Richard, 137n
Crevecoeur, Hector de, 84, 86
Crimes, electronic, 176–177. *See also* Information gathering
Cromwell, Oliver, 170
Crystal, Graef S., 260n
CSR. *See* Corporate social responsibility
CSR-1, CSR-2, 59
Cultural change, 5–6
Cultural determinism, 3–4
Culture, definition of, 83–84
Cunningham, Isabella C., 292n
Cunningham, William, 292n
Cuomo, Mario, 315, 316
Cutler, Neal E., 11n
Cybernex Corporation, 183
Czepiec, Helena, 191n

Dahl, Robert A., 77n
Dalkon Shield, 333
  Searle and, 336–337
Dalton, Leonard, 78n
Dandrade, Kendral, 293n
Daniels, Stephen, 344
Danley, John, 223
D'Arcy, William Knox, 378
Darwin, Charles, 88
Davison, A., 328n
Davison, Sol, 79n
DDT, 408
Debs, Eugene, 228
Deceptive advertising, 268–271
  detecting, 271
Declaration of the Hague, 407
Declonycin, 305
DeConcini, Dennis, 432
De George, Richard, 108n, 388n
Delotte, Mark, 202
*Democracy in America*, 86–87
Demographics, and MNCs, 370
Demography, 4–5
Denhardt, Robert, 41n
Denzau, Arthur T., 40n
Deontological ethics, 159
Deontology, 101–102
Derivative liability, 204
Derra, Skip, 191n
Deschamps-Braly, Dania, 275, 276
Deschamps-Braly, George, 275, 276
DES crisis, 319–322
Design defects, 323
Developing countries
  ethics and, 370–373
  and MNCs, 368–370
Dialog Information Services, 173
Diamond, Stuart, 417n
Dillere, Michael, 258n
Dillon, Gordon L., 292n
Dillon Read, 141
Di Lorenzo, Thomas, 417n
Dioxin, 408
Dirks, Raymond, 204–205
Divorce, 93
Dixon, Paul Rand, 269
Doctors, strikes by, 244–245. *See also* Medical profession

Dodd, P., 165n
*Dodge Brothers v. Ford Motor*, 57–58
Doig, J. W., 42n
Dole, Robert, 182
Donagan, Alan, 292n
Donaldson, Thomas, 388n
Dorfman, Ariel, 389n
Dorsey, Robert, 213, 214
Double Pac-man defense, 155
Douce, William, 143
Douglas, Mary, 418n
Douglas, Paul W., 241, 243
Doz, Yves L., 389n
Drexel Burnham Lambert, 144
Drucker, Peter, 11n, 49, 425
Drug companies, liability of, 319–322
Dulles, Foster Rhea, 106n
Dunfee, Thomas W., 223n, 389n
Dunkel, E. B., 78n
Dunlop, John T., 258n
DuPont, 119
Durkheim, Emile, 51
Dutch East India Company, 47, 377
Dworkin, Ronald, 135n

Eastern Europe, 7
Ecology. *See* Environment
Economic/business change, 6–8
Economic competition, evolution of, 112–115
Economic Information Systems, 173
Economic productivity, 92–93
Economic relations, and change, 6
Economics, and ethics, 155–161
Economic systems. *See also* Capitalism
  capitalism, 45–46
  market, 45
  planned, 45
  traditional, 45
  types of, 45–46
Economic theories, and monetary value of human life, 349–352
Economizers, 50
Ecotage, 413–414
Education, 114–115
  and American culture, 89–90
EEIG. *See* European Economic Interest Grouping
Eells, Richard, 78n, 191n
Ego ethic, 100
Ehrlich, Paul, 393
Elections, of U.S. officials, 22–23
Electronic data bases, and information gathering, 173
Electronic data theft, 176–177
Ely, John, 41n
Employees, corporation and, 50–53
Employers, union encounters with, 226–260
Encarnation, Dennis J., 389n
Energy use, 400
Engler, Robert, 389n
Enlightenment, 85–86
*Enquiry Concerning the Principles of Morals*, 101
Enterprise liability, 305
Environment, 390–420. *See also* Ozone
  domestic dangers to, 394–396
  ecotage and, 413–414
  ethics for, 408–415
  global dangers to, 396–398
  industry and, 405–406
  international concern for, 406–408
  and Multinational Protection Agency, 429

## INDEX 439

ozone layer and, 419–420
risk and, 401–402
technology and, 398–401
threats to, 394–408
Environmental Crimes Unit, 406
Environmental hazards, 391–392
Environmental Protection Agency (EPA), 393, 404
EPA. *See* Environmental Protection Agency
Epstein, Edwin M., 135n
Erdman, William, 178
Ericson, Karl, 428
Erikson, Robert S., 40n
Erlichman, John, 34
*Escola v. Coca-Cola Bottling Company*, 301
Espionage, 172. *See also* Security
industrial, 174–175, 178–180
Esso, administered oil price of, 132
Ethical criteria, and legal criteria, 120–122
Ethical egoism, 159
Ethical issues, and horizontal price fixing, 122–125
Ethical principles, 116–120
Ethics, 1. *See also* Advertising; Corporations; Economics; Moral philosophies
in advertising, 285–289
of Americans, 428–429
competition and, 110–137
economics and, 155–161
ego, 100
environmental, 408–415
expediency, 100
and Foreign Corrupt Practices Act, 218–220
in global terms, 362–389
and insider trading, 205–206
and Johns Manville, 342–343
and labor-management conflicts, 229–232
and professions, 72–74
of size, 138–166
survival, 99–100
and tort law, 304–322, 348
Etzioni, Amitai, 135n
Europe, tort law in, 332
European Community, 6
American MNCs and, 381–383
European Economic Interest Grouping (EEIG), 382–383
Evans, Don Alan, 12n
Evans, Peter, 388n
Ewing, David, 227, 389n
Exclusive dealings, 127–129
*Executioner's Song*, 266
Expediency ethic, 100
Export Administration Act, 181
Export controls, 181–182
Extortion, and payoffs, 213–215
Exxon, 377–378

Face, 103
Failure to warn, 305
Fair Responsibility Act, 314
Fair-trade laws, 125–126
Faletto, Enzo, 368
Falk, Carol, 223n
Family structure, 93–94
Farr, Robert, 191n
Fault, and strict liability, 304–307
FDA, 303
and AIDS drugs, 303–304
recall guidelines of, 323–324
Federal Aviation Agency (FAA), and PATCO strike, 247

Federal Charters, 53–60
Federal Corrupt Practices Act, 210
*Federalist, The*, 21, 22
Number 10, 24–26
and self-interest groups, 422–423
Federal regulators, 34–37
Federal Trade Commission (FTC), 36, 121
and deceptive advertising, 268–269
and government/industry definitions, 270–271
Feinberg, Joel, 260n
Feldman, Lawrence P., 291n, 292n
Feldmann, Carol Ann, 305
Feldstein, Stuart, 173
Fernandez, Raquel, 434n
Fiduciary obligation, 160
Fiorina, Morris P., 42n
Fischel, Daniel R., 166n, 222
Fisher, Lillian S., 327n
Fishoff, B., 417n
Flax, Steven, 191n
Flexner, Abraham, 68
Flexner Report, 68, 70
Flint, Jerry, 11n
Flow Control 50, 249
Fogg, Joseph, 166n
Foner, Philip, 79n
Food manufacturers, advertising regulation of, 280
Food recalls, 323–324
Forbath, William F., 258n
Ford, Gerald, 215
Ford, Henry, 57
Ford Motor Company, Pinto and, 308–309
Foreign Corrupt Practices Act, 206, 216–217
and ethics, 218–220
moral assessments and, 217–220
Foreign trade, and industrial espionage, 178–180
Francis, Jack, 200
Francis of Assisi, 408
Frankfurt, Harry, 108n
Franklin, Benjamin, 20, 90, 263, 418n
Frantz, Douglas, 222n
Frederick, William, 58
Frederickson, H. George, 40n
Fred Myers Company, 151–152
Freedman, Alin M., 277n
Freedman, Audrey, 259n
Freedom of Information Act (FOIA), 173, 182–183
Freeman, Harry, 117
Freeman, John, 79n
Freeman, Orville L., 387n
Freeman, Richard, 79n
Free market system, 7
Freidman, Frank B., 418n
French, Peter, 78n
Freund, James C., 148, 164n
Fried, Charles, 102
Friedman, Aryeh S., 223n, 389
Friedman, Milton, 78n, 111
Friedrich, Carl J., 260n
Friedson, Eliot, 73, 74
Fritschler, A. Lee, 40n
Fromson, Brett Duval, 165n
Front-end, two-tiered bids, 142
Frosch, Robert, 295–296, 418n
Fuggers, House of, 170
Fuld, John, 191n
Fuller, Lon L., 77n, 322–323
Furnas, J. C., 417n

## 440  INDEX

Futrell, Charles M., 135n
Futter, Victor, 78n

Gabriel, Trip, 419n
Galbraith, John Kenneth, 293n, 369, 388n
Galenson, Walter, 79n
Gardner, David M., 292n
Gardner-Denver Company, 159
Garrison, Michael J., 292n
Garvin, David, 107n, 165n
Gauthier, David, 359n
Gee, J. Bernard L., 358n
Geisel, Jerry, 328n
Gellhorn, Ernest, 135n
General Electric Company, and labor-management conflict, 230
General Foods, and advertising ethics, 288–289
General Motors
 and labor-management relations, 235–236
 and management labor tactics, 243–244
George, William N., 389n
Gereffi, Gary, 388n
Germany, 7
Gewirth, Alan, 80n, 108n, 318, 319, 328n
Ghent, W. J., 108n
Giardina, Denise, 259n
Gifts, 206, 212–213
Giges, Nancy, 292n
Gildern, George, 164n
Ginsberg, Benjamin, 41n
Gison, Mary, 419n
Givens, Richard A., 259n
Glazer, Jacob, 434n
Gleason, Thomas, 230
Global corporations. *See* Multinational corporations
Global managers/workers, 6
Global warming, 399–401
Goldman, Alan, 293n
Gold standard, 48
Gomory, Ralph, 10
Gompers, Samuel, 63–64
Goodpaster, Kenneth E., 78n
Gorbachev, Michail, 45, 376
Gordon, Bill, 291n, 292n
Gospel of wealth, 88
Gothman, Alan H., 80n
Government employees, strikes by, 247–250
Graber, Edith, 259n
Grace, W. R., 343–344
Graglia, Lino, 41n
Graham, Edward M., 12n
Grange movement, 61
Gray, Harry B., 419n
Gray, William F., 137n
Great Depression, 49, 65
Greed, 160
Green, Mark, 78n
Greenfield, Jay, 136n
Greenhouse, Lind, 260n
Greenhouse gases, 400
Greenmail, 142–143
*Greenman v. Yuba Products*, 301
Greenwald, John, 164n, 223n
Gregg, Davis W., 11n
Gregory doctrine, 146
Grenelli, James S., 358n
Gresham's Law of Ethics, in advertising, 285
Greyhound, lockout and, 244
Grounded organizational constitutionalism, 52

Grovirz, L. Gordon, 165
Guardian Industries, 183
Gulf Oil Corporation, 155
 and extortion/payoffs, 213–214
Gulf War, morality of, 431
Gutíerrez, Gustavo, 368, 372
Guzzardi, Walter, Jr., 192n, 328n

Habermas, Jurgen, 77n
Hagedorn, Ann, 80n
Hagen, Willis W., III, 222n
Hagstrom, Jerry, 12n
Haldeman, H. W., 34
*Hale v. Firestone Tire and Rubber Company*, 318
Hall, Arnold, 387n
Hall, F. T., 79n
Hall, Fred S., 259n
Hallett, John D., 418n
Halperin, Morton, 192n
Halpern, Stephen, 41n
Hamilton, Alexander, 19, 20, 23, 40n
Hamilton, Walton, 77n
Hammond, Thomas H., 40n
Hannan, Michael T., 79n
Hanson Trust case, 153–154
Hardin, Clifford, 40n
Hardin, Russell, 108n
Hargrove, William, 232
Harmful-product advertising, 274–278
Harris, Robert G., 136n
Harrison, Lee, 418n
Hart, David K., 40n, 41n
Hart, Gary, 22n, 340
Hart, H. L. A., 77n
Hart-Scott-Rodino law, 151
Hartz, Louis, 39n
Harvey, Brian, 418n
Hay, George A., 137n
Hayes, Robert H., 165n
Health care, 114
Health-care costs, and labor-management conflicts, 252–253
Hearsay evidence, 307–308
Hedonic calculus, and human life value, 352
Heidenheimer, Arnold J., 223n
Heilbroner, Robert, 77n
Heinz, H. J., 382
 boycott of, 240
Held, Virginia, 78n
Heller, Harry, 222n
Heloise, 421
*Henningsen v. Bloomfield Motors*, 116
Henry, Patrick, 20
Herrnson, Paul S., 40n
Hersey, John, 266
Hertz, John, 272
Hetenyi, Lazlo, 259n
Hill, Samuel, Jr., 105n
Hiltzik, Michael A., 191n
Hinchman, Lewis, 418n
Hinchman, Sandra, 418n
Hitachi, 179–180
Hobbing, Enno, 388n
Hochman, Stephen A., 165n
Hofer, Charles W., 418n
Hoffman, Michael, 78n, 419n
Hofstadter, Richard, 106n, 136n, 223n
Holmes, Oliver Wendell, 107n
Hormonts, Robert, 388n
Horowitz, Donald, 41n

# INDEX

Hostile takeovers, 142–155
Houck, John, 374
Household International, 153
Huber, Peter, 323, 327n
*Huckle v. Money*, 332
Hudson, Richard, 223
Huebner, Solomon, 349
Human-capital approach, 350
Human life, monetary worth of, 349–355
Humble, John, 389n
Hume, David, 17, 100, 101
Hunt, S. D., 119n, 135n
Huntington, C. P., 214

IAM. *See* International Association of Machinists
IBM, 382
   and industrial espionage, 178–180
   and intellectual property rights, 183
Ichan, Carl, 142, 143, 144
Independent agencies, 35
Independent initiative principle, 116
India, MNCs in, 376–377
Indirect price discrimination, 124
Individualism, 87–88
Industrial espionage, 174–175
   globalization of, 178–180
   and security, 178–183
Industrialized nations, MNCs and, 374–381
Industrial revolution, 47–49
Industry, and environment, 405–406
Information, freedom of, 182–183
Information gathering, 168–192
   and electronic crooks, 176–177
   and intellectual property rights, 183–185
   and national security, 177–178
Information sources and kinds
   commercial intelligence, 173
   industrial espionage, 174–175
   legal and illegal, 170–172
   national espionage, 172
   political intelligence, 172
Ingrassia, Paul, 223n
*Ingredient Technology v. Nay*, 130
Innocent bystander principle, 231
Insider trading, 195–206, 425
   and Chiarella, Vincent, 203–204
   criteria for judging, 204–205
   definition of illegal, 202–205
   and Dirks, Raymond, 204–205
   ethical assessment of, 205–206
   and Winans, R. Foster, 202–203
Institutional capitalism, 49–50
Insull, Samuel, 145
Insurance
   lawyers, liability, and, 344–347
   liability and, 313–315, 331, 343–344
   and monetary value of human life, 349–352
   and tort claimants, 341–342
Insurance policies, and liability, 307
Integrity, 99
   moral, 102
Intelligence gathering, 170, 172
   commerical intelligence, 173
   political intelligence, 172
Interest groups, 24–26
International Association of Machinists (IAM), 64–65
International Longshoremen's Association, 230
International relations, and economic/business change, 6

Interorganizational/intraorganizational ethics, 1
Interstate Commerce Act, 34
Interstate/instrastate commerce, 120–122
Intervention, as advertising control, 279–281
Intuition, and moral rules, 98
Investext, 173
Investment bankers, 200
Investment pressure, 160
Investors, economics, ethics, and, 155–159
Irreducible organizational constitutionalism, 52
IRS, and takeovers, 146
ITT Banking Company, 279–280

Jackson, John E., 40n
Jackson, Robert, 148
Jacoby, Neil, 387n
Jacoby, Robert, 160
Jain, Rita S., 260n
Janeway, Eliot, 223n
Japan
   competitive capability of, 113–115
   and computer technology theft, 179–180
   economic productivity of, 92–93
   tort law in, 332
Jay, Anthony, 108n
Jefferson, Thomas, 23
Jennings, Edward T., 41n
Jensen, Michael, 12n, 156, 165n, 425
Jewell, Malcolm E., 41n, 42n
John Paul II, 367
Johns Manville Company, bankruptcy and, 338–341, 342–343
Johnson, Brad, 358n
Johnson, Elmer W., 77n
Johnson, Karen, 222n
Johnson, Keith, 165n
Johnson, Samuel, 263
Jones, Harry W., 327n
Jones, John Philip, 136n
Jorde, Thomas M., 136n
Joseph, Frederick, 147
Judicial and moral reasoning, 331
Judicial review, 29–32
Judicial trends and ethics, 304–322
   admissible evidence, 307–310
   deep pockets, 312–317
   fault and strict liability, 304–307
   law's reach, 310–312
   single and collective liability, 317–322
Judiciary, of United States, 36–37. *See also* Supreme Court of the United States
Judiciary Act, 29
*Judith Sindell v. Abbott Laboratories et al.*, 319, 320
Junk bonds
   leveraged buyouts and, 145–149
   and Milken, Michael, 201
Jurisdiction, 310–312
Justice Department, Tort Policy Working Group, 300

Kagan, Ralph, 418n
Kamieniecki, Sheldon, 417n
Kamm, Mark, 173
Kant, Immanuel, 101
Karl, Barry, 42n
Karst, Kenneth L., 40n
Kasten, Robert, 347
Katz, Harry C., 259n
Kauffman, Walter, 291n

# INDEX

Kaufman, Stuart, 79n
Keating Five, 432
Keefe, Jeffrey H., 259n
Keenan, Michael, 164n
Kefauver, Estes, 303
Kelly, Patrick F., 333, 334
Kendall, Donald, 388n
Kennedy, Anthony, 30–31
Kennedy, John F., 36, 90–91, 132
Kennedy, Paul, 374
Kern, George C., Jr., 164
Kessler, Sanford, 108n
Kilchel, Walter, III, 192n
Kim, Peter, 103
King, David C., 40n
King, William, 50
Kissinger, Henry, 4
Kitner, Earl, 136n
Kluge, John W., 197, 199
Krugman, Paul, 2, 11n, 12n
Knights of Labor, 63, 236
Knowledge worker, 7
Koch, Kathy, 358n
Kochan, Thomas A., 259n
Kohlberg, Lawrence, 97
Kohlberg Kravis Roberts, 146
Kolbert, Kathryn, 107n
*Komsolets*, 101
Koop, Everett C., 289
Korda, Michael, 108n
Korman, Abraham, 40n
Kraar, Louis, 77n
Kraus, Michael, 40n, 83
Kraynak, Robert P., 108n
Kreuger, Ivar, 145
Kripke, Herman, 78n
Kuhn, James, 258n
Kurland, Mark A., 191n
Kusserow, Richard P., 177
Kutak, Robert, 74, 80n
Kutak Committee, 74

La Barbera, Priscilla A., 293n
Labor force, women in, 93
Labor-management conflicts, 225–260
    and innocent bystander principle, 231
    and lockout, 244
    and management tactics, 243–244
    and moral suasion principle, 231–232
    procedural changes in, 251–253
    and proportionality principle, 230–231
    and reasonable disclosure principle, 229–230
    and union tactics, 239–243
Labor-management relations, and NLRB change, 250–251. *See also* National Labor Relations Board
Labor strikes, 236–238
    arbitration and, 238
    boycotts, 240
    definitions of, 237–238
    of Pan American pilots, 231
    and Pittston Coal Company, 241–243
    and positional power, 238–239
    by professions and government employees, 244–250
    selective, 239–240
    and Stevens, J. P., 241–242
    sympathy, 237
    and union positional power, 238–239
    and union tactics, 239–243
    wildcat, 237–238

Labor unions, 61–66, 424
    characteristics of, 62
    and employer encounters, 226–260
    evolution of, 63
    leadership styles in, 62
    legitimacy problems of, 65
    positional power, strikes and, 238–239
    recent tactics of, 239–243
    and steelworkers' election of 1982, 251
    strikes, boycotts, and lockouts, 236–244
Laderman, Jeffery M., 222n
Laitin, David, 105n
Lamb, Charles, 41n
Lamberti, Jean-Claude, 40n
Landauer, Jerry, 223n
Landrum-Griffin Act, 228
Lang, James, 165n
Lange, Mark, 164n
Langevin, Theodore, 176
Lanham Act, amendment to, 287
Larson, Magali Sarfatti, 80n
Larson, William L., 223n
Lasswell, Harold, 40n
Latham, Earl, 77n
Latin America, and MNCs, 368–370
Law. *See also* Tort law
    and advertising, 287
    and ethics, 111
    tort, 294–328
Law, Warren A., 166n
Lawrence, George, 106n
Lawsuits, 296–297
Lawyers, 67–68
    ethics of, 72–73, 74
    and insurers, 344–347
    litigiousness and, 113–114
Lays, Colin, 223n
LBOs. *See* Leveraged buyouts
Learned men/learned professions, 68
Lederle Laboratories, 305
Lee, Dixie Ray, 418n
Lee, Dwight, 419n
Legal criteria, 120–122
    antitrust acts, 120–122
Legal profession. *See* Lawyers
Legislation, consumer opposition to protective, 302–304
Lehn, Kenneth, 165n
Leigh, James H., 135n
Leighton, George N., 352
Le Mond, Alan, 293n
Leonard, Howard, 292n
Lernoux, Penny, 389n
*Letter Concerning Toleration*, 16
Level playing field principle, 118
Leveraged buyouts (LBOs), 145–149
Levine, Dennis, 195, 200, 201, 202
Levinson, Sanford, 106n
Levitt, Theodore, 289–290
Levy, Leonard, 40n, 41n
Lewis, Flora, 419n
*Lewis Service Centers v. Mack Trucks*, 126
Liability, 300, 301
    derivative, 204
    enterprise, 305
    and Fuller's counsel, 322–324
    guidelines for, 322–324
    institutional reform and, 347
    single and collective, 317–322
    strict, 304–307

# INDEX 443

Liability insurance, 313–315, 344–347
Liability laws
 in California, 313–315
 in Maryland, 317
 in New York, 315–317
Liberation/liberating theology, 368–370, 426
Liddle, Jeffery L., 137n
Liddle, William D., 39n
Lieberstein, Stanley, 192n
Life, monetary worth of, 349–355
*Limits to Growth*, 95
Lincoln, Abraham, 28
Lindsay, Ronald A., 166n
Lippke, Robert L., 293n
Lipton, Michael, 143, 144
Listerine-Scope issue, 272
Litigiousness, and competition, 113–114
Litvak, T. A., 389n
Livesay, Harold C., 79n
Locke, Gary, 1
Locke, John, 16, 17, 50, 52
Lockheed Aircraft, and payoffs, 214–215
Lockout, 244
Lodge, George Cabot, 78n
Logue, Dennis E., 165n
Lomasky, Lorene, 108n
Lombarde, Louis, 80n
Long-arm statutes, 310
Loomis, Burdett, 40n
Love Canal, 345, 394
Lowe, Herman J., 79n
Lowell, Francis Cabot, 170
Lowenstein, Louis, 165n, 425
Loyalty, corporate, 158
Luban, David, 327n
Lundborg, Louis B., 409
Lying. *See* Puffery

MacAndres & Forbes Holdings, Inc., 154–155
Machiavelli, Niccolo, 100
Maclean, Douglas, 359n
Maclean, John, 223
*MacPherson v. Buick Motor Company*, 299–300
Macroethics/microethics, 1
Madison, James, 19, 20, 21, 22, 24–25, 28, 422
Magazines, advertising in, 281–282
Magnet, Myron, 222n
Magnusson-Moss Act, 36–37
Mailer, Norman, 266
Maisonrouge, Jacques G., 387n
Malpas, Robert, 419n
Management
 labor conflicts with, 225–260
 social responsibilities of, 56–57
Management buyouts (MBOs), 151
Managerial capitalism, 49
Manifest Destiny, 84–86, 88
Mann, Horace, 89
Manner, Henry, 148
Manufacturers, and tobacco use, 427
Manville Corporation, 183–184
Marbury, William, 28
*Marbury v. Madison*, 28–29
Marcelle, C. J., 389n
Marglin, Stephen A., 78n
Marietta, 155
Market, withdrawal from, 336–337
Market economy, 45
Marketing, ethical issues and, 119–120
Market-share principle, in plural liability, 319–320

Marshall, Burke, 41n
Marshall, John, 28, 47, 60
Marson, Charles, 192n
Maryland, liability in, 317
Mascone, Cynthia, 11n
Mason, Edward S., 77n, 258n
Massengil Company, 306
Matheson, Curtin, 250–251
Mathews, Jessica Tuchman, 417n
Matthews, John B., Jr., 78n
Maxey, Margaret, 11n, 418n
Mayer, J. P., 106n
Mayflower Compact, 85
Mays, Bernard, 108n
MBOs. *See* Management buyouts
McBride, Lloyd, 251
McCann, Dennis, 388n
McCarthy, Colman, 292n
McCloy, John, 206
McConnell, T. R., 259n
McCormick, Joseph, 68
McCoy, Charles, 39n
McCraw, Thomas K., 136n
McCullough, John, 231–232
McDaniel, Morey W., 166n
McDavid, Janet L., 136n
McDonald, Forrest, 39n
McDonald's, advertising by, 274
McGowan, William, 146
*McGuffey Readers*, 90
McIntyre, Patricia, 258n
McKibben, William, 417n
McLean, Donald Alexander, 259n
McManus, Kevin, 192n
Means, Gardiner, 49
Media, advertising self-policing in, 281–282
Media associations, 282
Medical insurance, and labor-management conflicts, 252
Medical profession, 68
 ethics and, 72
Mencken, H. L., 418n
Merck, 260n
Mergers/takeovers, 139–166
 defensive tactics against, 152–155
 economic and ethical assessments of, 155–161
 and hostile takeovers, 142–155
 regulation of, 162
Merrell Dow, 337
Merton, Robert K., 77n
Mesa Petroleum, 154, 155
Metromedia, and insider trading, 197–198
Metzenbaum, Howard, 152, 412
Meyers, Gordon, 215
Middleton, Martha, 165n
Midnight judges, 28
Miles, Jason, 210
Milken, Michael, 144, 152, 201
 and Drexel Burnham Lambert, 145–149
Mill, John Stuart, 100
Millar, Victor E., 191n
Miller, Gary T., 40n
Miller, James C., III, 270
Miller, J. Irwin, 107n
Miller, Lee E., 166n
Millstein, Ira K., 166n
Misappropriation, 204–205
*Missouri v. Jenkins*, 30
Mitchell, Jacqueline, 292n
Mitsubishi, 179

## 444  INDEX

MNCs. See Multinational corporations
Molina, Mario, 398
Mollander, Earl A., 107n, 135n
Monetary value of human life
   economic theories of, 349–352
   legal theory of, 352
   moral theory of, 352–355
Monsanto, 126
Montesquieu, Charles-Louis, 16, 118
Mooney, Sean, 359n
Moore, Jack, 404–405
Moore, Jennifer, 223n
Moore, Thomas, 192n
Morality, 2
   American, 82–108
   and U.S. Constitution, 18–20
   modern, 2–4
*Morality of Law, The*, 322
Moral philosophies, 97–103
   deontology, 101–102
   and face, 102–103
   self-oriented, 99–100
   utilitarianism, 100–101
Moral reasoning, 331
Moral responsibility, in changing world, 91–95
Moral suasion principle, 231–232
Morgan, E. S., 39n
Morgan, J. P., 87
Morgan, Stanley, 222n
Morris, Betsy, 135n
Morris, Gouverneur, 20
Morris, Richard B., 79n
Morris, Walter S., 164n
Mortimer, Kenneth, 259n
Motorcycle helmet regulations, 302
Moutourkais, Zacharias, 388n
Mugabe, Robert, 369
Mullane, Robert, 252
Multinational corporations (MNCs), 262–389, 426
   and advanced countries, 374–381
   definition of, 364–366
   ethical responsibility of, 370–373
   and European community, 381–383
   evolution of, 366–367
   public-private, 377–381
   relations with host countries, 367–374
   strengths and weaknesses of, 383–384
   struggles with governments, 376–377
Munger, Michael C., 40n
Murray, John Courtney, 359n

NAD. See National Advertising Division
Nader, Ralph, 53, 286, 314, 322, 428
Nagel, Ernest, 11n
Naisbitt, John, 11n
National Advertising Division (NAD) of Better Business Bureau, 283
   investigations by, 283–285
National Advertising Review Board, 282
National Education Association (NEA), 247
National espionage, 172
National Grange, 61
National Institute of Occupational Safety and Health (NIOSH), 338
National Iranian Oil Company, 380
Nationalism, 15
National Labor Relations Act, 228
National Labor Relations Board (NLRB), 228, 229, 237
   policy changes in, 250–251

National Labor Union, 63
National security, 177–178
Nations, rise and fall of, 374–376
Nation-state, 15
NCC Industries, 371
NEA. See National Education Association
Neale, A. D., 136n
NEC Corporation, 287
Negligence, 298–299, 304–305
   bases of, 305
Negotiations, 262
   and mergers/takeovers, 149–152
Nehemkis, Peter, 191n
Neidich, George, 359n
Nelson, William E., 106n
Neoclassicists, and agency theory, 1
Nestlé, 289
Newcomen, Thomas, 48
New Deal, 65
Newman, Gerald, 106n
Newspapers, advertising in, 282
Newton, Lisa, 166
Newton's Law, 160–161
New Traditionalism, 96–97
New York State, liability laws in, 315–317
Nichol, Armand, Jr., 93, 94, 96
Nicholson, William J., 339
Niebuhr, H. Richard, 17, 18–19
Niekirk, Bill, 223n
Nietzsche, Friedrich, 91
Nisbet, Robert, 9
NLRB. See National Labor Relations Board
Non-Aligned Summit Meeting, 407
Noncorporate businesses, 60–61
Noonan, John, Jr., 223n
Noonan, Peggy, 5
Norlund, D. Craig, 217
Norris, Floyd, 164n, 165n
Norris-LaGuardia prohibition, and labor strikes, 238
North, Oliver, 22n
*North American Review, The*, 88
Northrop Corporation, 214
Northrup, Herbert, 258n
Novak, Michael, 368, 369, 372
Nozick, Robert, 108n
Nye, Joseph, 12n, 78n

Oakes, Guy, 328n
O'Brien, Robert M., 417n
O'Connell, Jeffrey, 358n
O'Connor, Sandra Day, 336, 423
OECD. See Organization for Economic Cooperation and Development
*Oeconomia*, 55
Office of Manpower Budget (OMB), and Congressional Budget Office (OBO), 97, 98
Olson, David, 41n
Olson, Walter, 419n
O'Neill, Shelly, 223n
O'Neill, William, 108n
Ontario Medical Association (OMA), strike by, 244–245
Operation Exodus, 181–182
Oppenheimer, Harry, 371–372
Ordway, Fred, 11n
Organization for Economic Cooperation and Development (OECD), 217
*Origin of Species, On The*, 88
Ornstein, Norman, 40n

## INDEX

*Oswalt v. Scripto*, 310
*Our Common Future*, 406
Owen, Robert, 61
Ozone, 402
    protection of earth's layer, 419–420

Pacific Mutual Life Insurance, 423
Packard, Vance, 293n
Pac-men, 155
Padding, 235
Page, Talbor, 328n
Paine, Lynn Sharpe, 116, 191n
Painter, Christopher M. E., 358
*Palsgraf* case, 355–356
Palsgroff, Helen, 295
*Panama Refining Company v. Ryan*, 35
Parfit, Michael, 419n
Parkhurst, Priscilla, 106n
Parsons, Gregory, 191n
Parsons, Talcott, 94
PATCO, 248–250
Patterson, James, 103
Patterson, Jeffrey L., 359n
Paul VI, 367
Payments, and bribes/payoffs, 206
Payoffs, 423
    bribes and, 206–207
    extortion and, 213–215
Peirce, Neal, 12n
*Pennover v. Neff*, 310
Pension funds, and labor-management relations, 253
Pension fund socialism, 49–50
Pensions, 152
Pepsi, 156
Pepsi Cola, as MNC, 372
Perlman, Selig, 79n
Perlmutter, Howard, 388n
Per se rule, 122, 123
Pertschuck, Michael, 126
Pesticides, 396
Peterson, Dale, 417n
Pfeffer, Raymond, 78n
Pharmaceutical firms, liability of, 306
Phatak, Arvind V., 365
Philadelphia Roofers Union Local, 231–232
Philips, Michael, 223, 224n
Phillips, Almarin, 136n
Phillips Petroleum, takeover of, 143–145
Philosophers, and value of human life, 353
Philosophy, moral, 97–103
Piaget, Jean, 97
Pickens, T. Boone, 142, 143, 144, 145
Pinochet Ugarte, Augusto, 389n
Pinto car, 308–309
Pirenne, Henri, 77n
Pittsburgh, Pa., Gulf closings and, 158–159
Pittston, Pa., 395
Pittston Coal Company, 241–243
Planned economy, 45
Plato, 17
Platt, George, 222n
Platt, Gerard, 94
Plural responsibility, 319–322
Poison pill, 144, 152–155
Political Action Committees (PACs), 26
Political change, 8
Political factions, 24–25
Political intelligence, 172
Political parties, 23–24

*Politics*, 17
Pooley, James, 191n
Pope, Daniel, 291n
Population growth, 396–398
Porter, Michael E., 191n
Portney, Paul, 351
Poser, Norman S., 164n
Posner, Richard, 136n, 358n
Post, Frederick R., 258n
Poverty, and MNCs, 370–371
Powderly, Terence, 63
Prahalad, C. K., 389n
Predatory pricing, restrictive covenants and, 130–131
Presidency of the United States
    and Congress, 36
    and judiciary, 36–37
    pluralized, 36
Preston, Edmund, 259n
Preston, Ivan L., 292n
Price, Charles, 136n
Price discrimination, indirect, 124. *See also* Price fixing
Price-earnings (PE) ratios, 140
Price fixing
    horizontal, 122–126
    vertical, 125–126
Pricing, predatory, 131
Princeton Graphics, 287
Procter & Gamble, boycott of, 240
Products
    defects, 305
    false advertising of, 281
    liability. *See also* Liability
    safety, 306–307
Products and services, and tort law, 301
Professions, 66–74
    accounting, 69–70
    characteristics of, 70–74
    legal, 67–68
    medical, 68
    strikes by, 244–247
Profits, ethical uses of, 155–156
Prokesch, Stephen, 166n, 191n
Property, and corporations, 50–51
Property rights, intellectual, 183–185
Proportionality principle, 230–231
Proposition 51, 314
Proxies, 144
Proxmire, William, 215, 216
Public-private multinational corporations, 377–381
Puffery, 273–274
Pugh, Emerson, 7
Pullman strike, 228, 237
Punitive damages, 331
    constitutional question and, 335–336
    doctrine of, 332–336
    and judge's power, 333–335
    and net recovery to plaintiff, 333, 334
Puritans, 84
Pytte, Alyson, 404n

Quinn, Kenneth P., 136n

Radio, advertising in, 281, 282
Radon, 391–392
Raiders, 142
    and MBOs, 151
Railroads
    mergers and, 140
    and strikes, 236

# INDEX

Ramos, Joseph, 369
Rand, Ayn, 100, 101
Randolph, Edmund, 20
Ransom, Harry Howe, 191n
Rawls, John, 260n, 353
Reagan, Ronald, 5, 31, 36, 141–142. *See also* Aviation industry
Reasonable disclosure principle, 229–230
Recall policy, 323–324
Reed, O. L., 328n
Reedy, George, 23
Referees, respect for, 118–120
Regan, Donald, 36
Regan, Tom, 293n, 418n
Regulators, federal, 34–37
  respect for, 118–120
Reid, Thomas, 58
Reisman, W. Michael, 223
Relativism, 6
Religion, and moral rules, 98
*Republic*, 17
Resale price maintenance (RPM), 125–126
Responsibility
  moral, 91–95
  personal and organizational, 58
  single-party, 317–319
Restrictive covenants, and predatory pricing, 130–131
*Revlon, Inc. vs. MacAndres & Forbes Holdings Inc.*, 154–155
Revolutionary War, 86
Reynolds, R. J., 275
*Reynolds v. Sims*, 29
Ribin, Alissa J., 434n
Richards, James J., 359n
Richardson, Elliot, 215, 216
Richelieu, Cardinal, 170
Richman, James D., 166n
RICO, 148
Rights, to intellectual property, 183–185
*Right Stuff, The*, 266
Riis, Jacob, 106n
Risk asessment, 307
Robie, Richard, 272
Robin Hood maxim, 314
Robinson, Harry, 310–311
Robinson, James D., III, 117
Robinson-Patman Act, 121, 123
  and predatory pricing, 131
*Robinson v. Reed-Prentice Div. of Package Machinery Company*, 318
Rochdale, England, cooperative movement in, 61
Rockefeller, John D., 100, 378
Rockwell Corporation, 158
Rogers, Ray, 240
Rohr, John A., 40n
Rollins Corporation, 212–213
Rolston, Holmes, III, 409
  maxims of, 409–411
Roosevelt, Theodore, 120
Röpke, Wilhelm, 77n
Ross, Bernard, 40n
Rossi, Peter H., 106n
Rotfeld, Herbert J., 292n
Rothman, Barbara Katz, 11n
Rourke, Francis E., 42n
Rouse, Philip, 39n
Rousseau, Jean Jacques, 90
Rowe, Jonathan, 292n
Rowe, Richard, 213

Rowland, Sherwood, 398
Rubinger, James, 136n
Rule-of-reason principle, 122
Rules, respect for, 117–118
Rundle, Rhonda L., 79n, 228n
Russia, multinational corporations in, 376

Saccharinites, legislation for, 303
Sachs, Goldman, 145
Sadlowski, Ed, 251
Sadowski, Ellen, 40n
Safra, Edmond, 117
Sagoff, Mark, 417n
St. John d'el Rey Mining Company, 372
Salerno, Anthony, 232
Sales prices, misquoted, 281
Saliby, Steven R., 223n
Salmon, William K., 191n
Salt River Project, 318
Sampson, Anthony, 389n
Santaquiliani, A. G., 11n
Santor, Susan, 117
Sapolsky, Harvey M., 418n
Saposs, David J., 79n
Saracci, P., 358n
Sargent, Hugh W., 291n
Saudi Arabia, and British Petroleum, 380
Savings and loan crisis, 431–432
Scanlon, Peter, 73
Scarfo, Nicodemo, 232
Schechet, Ellen, 358n
*Schechter Poultry Corporation v. United States*, 35
Schelling, Thomas, 350
Schendel, Daniel E., 417n
Scher, Irving, 136n
Schick-Remington, 272
Schlesinger, Arthur, Jr., 34
Schmitz, Kenneth, 359n
Schoen, Donald A., 108n
Schor, Juliet B., 78n
Schroeder, Christopher H., 417n
Schudson, Michael, 291n
Schumacher, B. F., 120
Schumpeter, Joseph, 60, 135n, 145
Schwartz, Alan, 328n
Schwartz, Barry, 11n
Science, 2
Scienter, 268
Scientific management, 3
Sciulli, David, 77n
SCM Corporation, 153–154
Scopo, Ralph, 232
Scott, Rebecca, 388n
Searle, G. D., 336–337
SEC. *See* Securities and Exchange Commission
*Second Treatise on Government*, 52
Securities and Exchange Commission (SEC), 151. *See also* Bribes and payoffs; Insider trading
  and insider trading, 198
Securities laws, 198
Security
  business costs of, 180–183
  consultants and equipment, 182
  firms, 174
  and industrial espionage, 178–180
  national, 177–178
SEI Center for Advanced Studies, 6
Seidman, Burke, 152

# INDEX 447

Seldin, Joseph, 291n
Selective strikes, 239–240
Self-interest, 51, 100, 159
Self-interest group, 422–423
Self-oriented philosophies, 99–100
Self-policing, as advertising control, 281–283
Seligman, Joel, 78n
Selikoff, Irving, 338
Sella, Marshall, 328n
Separatists, 85
Serpa, Roy, 166n
Sewell, John W., 388n
Shabencoff, Philip, 417n, 418n
Shanker, Morris G., 328n
Shapiro, Irving, 153
Sharp, Daniel, 19
Sharp Inc., 118
Shaw, Lemuel;, 227–228, 299
Shellhardt, Timothy, 223n
Shelling, Thomas C., 233
Sherman Antitrust Act, 7, 120–121, 123, 140
Sherwin, Douglas, 223
Shimp, Terence A., 292n
Shinn, Richard, 241
Sholtz, Anne, 418n
Shumway, Norman, 347
*Sic et Non*, 421
Siconolfi, Michael, 358n
Siegan, Bernard H., 41n
Sigler, Andrew, 358n
*Silent Spring*, 393
Silicon Valley, espionage and, 178
Silverstein, Marc, 41n
Simon, Julian L., 11n
Simonetti, Gilbert, Jr., 358n
Single and collective liability, 317–322
Single-party responsibility, 317–319
Singletary, Amos, 20
Sinkeldam, Michael S., 223
Skinner, B. F., 97
Slater, Samuel, 170
Smith, Adam, 17, 100, 112, 113, 120, 121, 136n, 353
Smith, Huston, 106n, 417n
Smith, Page, 39n
Smith, Robert Angus, 405
Smith, Roger, 5–6
Smithers, Peter, 40n
*Smith vs. Van Gorkom*, 154
Snooping, 169–170
Social Darwinism, 88–89, 99–100
Social fragmentation, in U.S., 94–95
Social Gospel, 354
Social responsibilities, of management, 56–57
Solomon, David, 147
Sonnett, Neal, 809n
Sorensen, Theodore, 34
Soviet Union, 7
Spauling, Stephanie G., 137n
Specter, Howard, 34S
Spencer, Herbert, 88, 99–100
*Spirit of the Laws*, 16
Spitalnic, Robert, 191n
Spray Rite Service Corporation, 126
Srivasta, Suresh, 108n
Standard Oil, 140, 378
Standard Oil of California, and quantitative substantiality test, 128
Standard Oil of Ohio, 380
Starr, Judson W., 417n

State (nation), intellectual development of, 16–18
States (of United States)
    judicial review and, 29
    legal jurisdiction of, 310–312
    role of, 37
    tort laws of, 300
Steel industry, 230–231
Steelman, John, 132
Steel Workers' Organizing Committee, 65
Steelworkers union, 251
Stegemoeller, Mark A., 165n
Stein, Benjamin, 199, 222n
Stein, J. C., 57
Steiner, Henry J., 359n
Stephens, W. T., 340
Stern, Barbara B., 291n
Stevens, Edward, 108n
Stevens, John Paul, 127
Stevens, J. P., labor strike against, 234, 240–241
Stevens, Uriah, 63
Stewart, James A., 191n, 192n
Stewart, Robert W., 191n
Stewart, Rosemary, 432
Stimson, James A., 40n
Stockbrokers, ethics of, 73
Stockholders. *See* Investors
Stock market, ethics and, 429
Stolarski, Richard, 398
Stone, Christopher, 78n, 111
Stone, Edward Durrell, 10
Stone, Mildred F., 359n
Street, Anne M., 388n
Strict liability, fault and, 304–307
Strikes. *See* Labor strikes
Strobel, Lee, 327n
Stuart, Hugh Fraser, 359n
*Study of Administration, The*, 35
*Study on Productivity*, 92
Sugarman, Stephen, 358n
Sumner, Charles, 89
Sumner, William Graham, 106n
Supreme Court of the United States, 28–34
    innovators and originalists and, 32–33
    power of, 33–34
Surgeon General of the United States
    advertising ethics and, 289
    and cigarette advertising, 275
Survival ethics, 99–100
Sutterfield, James R., 328n
Switzer, Barry, 22n
Sympathy strike, 237
Synott, Anthony, 108n
Szell, Gyorgy, 77n

Taft-Hartley Act, 72, 228
Takeovers
    hostile, 142–155
    mergers and, 139–166
Tannenbaum, Frank, 79n, 389n
Taste, of ads, 282–283
Taxation
    and liability crisis, 346–347
    and U.S. Supreme Court, 30–31
Tax system, 114
Taylor, Frederick Winslow, 3, 88
Taylor, Robin, 259n
Teachers, strikes by, 245–247
Teamsters, 231, 238
Technology, environmental effects of, 398–401
Television, advertising in, 281, 282

# 448   INDEX

Terkel, Studs, 149
Terry, Luther, 275
Theis, Frank G., 334
*Theology of Freedom, A*, 368
*Theory of Moral Sentiments*, 100
Third World. *See* Developing countries
Thomas, Cal, 107n
Thomas, Lee, 405, 418n
Thompson, Michael, 11n
Thornburgh, Richard, 12n
Thornton, Mary, 176
Thurber, John, 170
Thurow, Robert, 388n
Tobacco industry, 427
   advertising by, 275–278
   marketing restrictions on, 277–278
Tocqueville, Alexis de, 22, 23, 41n, 84, 86–87
Tollison, R. D., 78n
Tomlin, Christopher L., 79n
Tort law, 294–328, 423
   and admissible evidence, 307–310
   bankruptcy and, 337–342
   and corporations, 300–301
   deep pockets and, 312–317
   defense tactics and, 336–349
   evolution of, 297–301
   judicial trends, ethics, and, 304–322
   and monetary value of human life, 349–355
   punitive damages as constitutional problem, 335–336
   punitive damages doctrine, 332–336
   reform of, 347
   related issues, 330–359
   in U.S., Europe, and Japan, 332
Tower, Rachelle, 77n
Townsend, Robert, 272
Trading. *See* Insider trading
Traditional economy, 45
Traffic controllers, strike by, 247–250
Traitz, Stephen, Jr., 232
Traynor, Roger John, 301
Treadway Commission, 74
Trumka, Richard, 243
Tucker, Dean, 113
Tucker, Gordon, 219–220, 224n
*Turner v. General Motors*, 323
Tussey, Jean, 258n
Twining, William, 327n
Two-tiered bids, 142–143
*Two Treatises on Government*, 16
Tying agreements, 129–130
Tyler, Kenneth C., 358n
Tyson, Kirk W. M., 191n

UBCJ. *See* United Brotherhood of Carpenters and Joiners
UCC. *See* Uniform Commercial Code
Ullman, Lloyd, 79n
UMW. *See* United Mine Workers
*Unical Corporation v. Mesa Petroleum Company*, 154
Uniform Commercial Code (UCC), 318
   creditor priorities and, 341
Unions. *See* Labor-management conflicts; Labor unions
United Auto Workers, 252
United Brands, 373–374
United Brotherhood of Carpenters and Joiners (UBCJ), 64–65
United Mine Workers (UMW), 65, 237
   and Pittston Coal Company, 242–243

United Nations
   Economic and Social Council, 367
   Environment Program (UNEP), 407
United States. *See also* American culture; Competition; Morality; Multinational corporations; Tort law
   appointed officials in, 28–37
   competitive capability of, 113–115
   Constitution of, 16–22
   economic productivity of, 92–93
   elected officials in, 22–28
   government of. *See* United States government
   intellectual heritage of, 16–18
   interest groups in, 24–26
   money interests in, 26–28
   moral future of, 95–97
   political change in, 8
   political parties in, 23–24
   status of, 8–11
United States government. *See also* United States
   agencies of, 35
   and federal employee strikes, 247–250
   and Foreign Corrupt Practices Act, 216–217
   payoffs and, 214, 215–216
   and tort-liability crisis, 347
United States Sentencing Commission, 403
United States Steel, 132
*United States v. Trenton Potteries*, 123
Unruh, Jesse, 26
Utilitarian ethics, 159
Utilitarianism, 100–101
Utterbeck, James M., 417n

Vachan, Sushil, 389n
Values
   culture and, 84
   institutional impact on, 1–4
   need for, 96–97
Vance Security Asset Protection Company, 43
Vanderbilt, Cornelius, 140
Veiga, John F., 418n
Velasquez, Manual V., 78n
Vernon, Raymond, 364
Vertical price fixing, 125–126
Victims, and tort law, 297–298
Viscusi, W. Kip, 351
Vogel, David, 327n
Vogt, Stephen, 165n
Voluntarism, industrial, 405–406
Voluntaristic organization, constitutionalism and, 52
Von Magnus, Eric, 328n
Von Morgenstern, Oskar, 258n
Von Naumann, John, 258n

Waechter, Kiderlen von, 172
Wage demands, 230
Wagenar, Theodore C., 259n
Wagner Act, 65, 160, 228
   and collective bargaining, 233
Waide, John, 293n
Wald, Matthew, 417n
Waldron, Jeremy, 77n
Walsingham, Frances, 170
Walton, Clarence C., 77n, 78n, 106n, 108n, 135n, 137n, 191n, 192n, 224n, 258n, 358n, 359n
Ward, Gregory, 178
Ward, John William, 106n

## INDEX  447

Seldin, Joseph, 291n
Selective strikes, 239–240
Self-interest, 51, 100, 159
Self-interest group, 422–423
Self-oriented philosophies, 99–100
Self-policing, as advertising control, 281–283
Seligman, Joel, 78n
Selikoff, Irving, 338
Sella, Marshall, 328n
Separatists, 85
Serpa, Roy, 166n
Sewell, John W., 388n
Shabencoff, Philip, 417n, 418n
Shanker, Morris G., 328n
Shapiro, Irving, 153
Sharp, Daniel, 19
Sharp Inc., 118
Shaw, Lemuel;, 227–228, 299
Shellhardt, Timothy, 223n
Shelling, Thomas C., 233
Sherman Antitrust Act, 7, 120–121, 123, 140
Sherwin, Douglas, 223
Shimp, Terence A., 292n
Shinn, Richard, 241
Sholtz, Anne, 418n
Shumway, Norman, 347
*Sic et Non*, 421
Siconolfi, Michael, 358n
Siegan, Bernard H., 41n
Sigler, Andrew, 358n
*Silent Spring*, 393
Silicon Valley, espionage and, 178
Silverstein, Marc, 41n
Simon, Julian L., 11n
Simonetti, Gilbert, Jr., 358n
Single and collective liability, 317–322
Single-party responsibility, 317–319
Singletary, Amos, 20
Sinkeldam, Michael S., 223
Skinner, B. F., 97
Slater, Samuel, 170
Smith, Adam, 17, 100, 112, 113, 120, 121, 136n, 353
Smith, Huston, 106n, 417n
Smith, Page, 39n
Smith, Robert Angus, 405
Smith, Roger, 5–6
Smithers, Peter, 40n
*Smith vs. Van Gorkom*, 154
Snooping, 169–170
Social Darwinism, 88–89, 99–100
Social fragmentation, in U.S., 94–95
Social Gospel, 354
Social responsibilities, of management, 56–57
Solomon, David, 147
Sonnett, Neal, 809n
Sorensen, Theodore, 34
Soviet Union, 7
Spauling, Stephanie G., 137n
Specter, Howard, 34S
Spencer, Herbert, 88, 99–100
*Spirit of the Laws*, 16
Spitalnic, Robert, 191n
Spray Rite Service Corporation, 126
Srivasta, Suresh, 108n
Standard Oil, 140, 378
Standard Oil of California, and quantitative substantiality test, 128
Standard Oil of Ohio, 380
Starr, Judson W., 417n

State (nation), intellectual development of, 16–18
States (of United States)
　judicial review and, 29
　legal jurisdiction of, 310–312
　role of, 37
　tort laws of, 300
Steel industry, 230–231
Steelman, John, 132
Steel Workers' Organizing Committee, 65
Steelworkers union, 251
Stegemoeller, Mark A., 165n
Stein, Benjamin, 199, 222n
Stein, J. C., 57
Steiner, Henry J., 359n
Stephens, W. T., 340
Stern, Barbara B., 291n
Stevens, Edward, 108n
Stevens, John Paul, 127
Stevens, J. P., labor strike against, 234, 240–241
Stevens, Uriah, 63
Stewart, James A., 191n, 192n
Stewart, Robert W., 191n
Stewart, Rosemary, 432
Stimson, James A., 40n
Stockbrokers, ethics of, 73
Stockholders. See Investors
Stock market, ethics and, 429
Stolarski, Richard, 398
Stone, Christopher, 78n, 111
Stone, Edward Durrell, 10
Stone, Mildred F., 359n
Street, Anne M., 388n
Strict liability, fault and, 304–307
Strikes. See Labor strikes
Strobel, Lee, 327n
Stuart, Hugh Fraser, 359n
*Study of Administration, The*, 35
*Study on Productivity*, 92
Sugarman, Stephen, 358n
Sumner, Charles, 89
Sumner, William Graham, 106n
Supreme Court of the United States, 28–34
　innovators and originalists and, 32–33
　power of, 33–34
Surgeon General of the United States
　advertising ethics and, 289
　and cigarette advertising, 275
Survival ethics, 99–100
Sutterfield, James R., 328n
Switzer, Barry, 22n
Sympathy strike, 237
Synott, Anthony, 108n
Szell, Gyorgy, 77n

Taft-Hartley Act, 72, 228
Takeovers
　hostile, 142–155
　mergers and, 139–166
Tannenbaum, Frank, 79n, 389n
Taste, of ads, 282–283
Taxation
　and liability crisis, 346–347
　and U.S. Supreme Court, 30–31
Tax system, 114
Taylor, Frederick Winslow, 3, 88
Taylor, Robin, 259n
Teachers, strikes by, 245–247
Teamsters, 231, 238
Technology, environmental effects of, 398–401
Television, advertising in, 281, 282

Terkel, Studs, 149
Terry, Luther, 275
Theis, Frank G., 334
*Theology of Freedom, A*, 368
*Theory of Moral Sentiments*, 100
Third World. *See* Developing countries
Thomas, Cal, 107n
Thomas, Lee, 405, 418n
Thompson, Michael, 11n
Thornburgh, Richard, 12n
Thornton, Mary, 176
Thurber, John, 170
Thurow, Robert, 388n
Tobacco industry, 427
  advertising by, 275–278
  marketing restrictions on, 277–278
Tocqueville, Alexis de, 22, 23, 41n, 84, 86–87
Tollison, R. D., 78n
Tomlin, Christopher L., 79n
Tort law, 294–328, 423
  and admissible evidence, 307–310
  bankruptcy and, 337–342
  and corporations, 300–301
  deep pockets and, 312–317
  defense tactics and, 336–349
  evolution of, 297–301
  judicial trends, ethics, and, 304–322
  and monetary value of human life, 349–355
  punitive damages as constitutional problem, 335–336
  punitive damages doctrine, 332–336
  reform of, 347
  related issues, 330–359
  in U.S., Europe, and Japan, 332
Tower, Rachelle, 77n
Townsend, Robert, 272
Trading. *See* Insider trading
Traditional economy, 45
Traffic controllers, strike by, 247–250
Traitz, Stephen, Jr., 232
Traynor, Roger John, 301
Treadway Commission, 74
Trumka, Richard, 243
Tucker, Dean, 113
Tucker, Gordon, 219–220, 224n
*Turner v. General Motors*, 323
Tussey, Jean, 258n
Twining, William, 327n
Two-tiered bids, 142–143
*Two Treatises on Government*, 16
Tying agreements, 129–130
Tyler, Kenneth C., 358n
Tyson, Kirk W. M., 191n

UBCJ. *See* United Brotherhood of Carpenters and Joiners
UCC. *See* Uniform Commercial Code
Ullman, Lloyd, 79n
UMW. *See* United Mine Workers
*Unical Corporation v. Mesa Petroleum Company*, 154
Uniform Commercial Code (UCC), 318
  creditor priorities and, 341
Unions. *See* Labor-management conflicts; Labor unions
United Auto Workers, 252
United Brands, 373–374
United Brotherhood of Carpenters and Joiners (UBCJ), 64–65
United Mine Workers (UMW), 65, 237
  and Pittston Coal Company, 242-243

United Nations
  Economic and Social Council, 367
  Environment Program (UNEP), 407
United States. *See also* American culture; Competition; Morality; Multinational corporations; Tort law
  appointed officials in, 28–37
  competitive capability of, 113–115
  Constitution of, 16–22
  economic productivity of, 92–93
  elected officials in, 22–28
  government of. *See* United States government
  intellectual heritage of, 16–18
  interest groups in, 24–26
  money interests in, 26–28
  moral future of, 95–97
  political change in, 8
  political parties in, 23–24
  status of, 8–11
United States government. *See also* United States
  agencies of, 35
  and federal employee strikes, 247–250
  and Foreign Corrupt Practices Act, 216–217
  payoffs and, 214, 215–216
  and tort-liability crisis, 347
United States Sentencing Commission, 403
United States Steel, 132
*United States v. Trenton Potteries*, 123
Unruh, Jesse, 26
Utilitarian ethics, 159
Utilitarianism, 100–101
Utterbeck, James M., 417n

Vachan, Sushil, 389n
Values
  culture and, 84
  institutional impact on, 1–4
  need for, 96–97
Vance Security Asset Protection Company, 43
Vanderbilt, Cornelius, 140
Veiga, John F., 418n
Velasquez, Manual V., 78n
Vernon, Raymond, 364
Vertical price fixing, 125–126
Victims, and tort law, 297–298
Viscusi, W. Kip, 351
Vogel, David, 327n
Vogt, Stephen, 165n
Voluntarism, industrial, 405–406
Voluntaristic organization, constitutionalism and, 52
Von Magnus, Eric, 328n
Von Morgenstern, Oskar, 258n
Von Naumann, John, 258n

Waechter, Kiderlen von, 172
Wage demands, 230
Wagenar, Theodore C., 259n
Wagner Act, 65, 160, 228
  and collective bargaining, 233
Waide, John, 293n
Wald, Matthew, 417n
Waldron, Jeremy, 77n
Walsingham, Frances, 170
Walton, Clarence C., 77n, 78n, 106n, 108n, 135n, 137n, 191n, 192n, 224n, 258n, 358n, 359n
Ward, Gregory, 178
Ward, John William, 106n

Warranty, 300, 318
Warren, Earl, 29, 30, 32, 33
Warren, Melinda, 418n
Warrington, Eric, 39n
Wartzman, Rick, 259n
Washington, George, 20, 23
Washington University, 247
Water, pollution of, 395–396
Watergate, 172
Watkins, W. P., 79n
Watts, James, 48
Wealth, Gospel of, 88
*Wealth of Nations, The*, 100
Weber, Max, 51, 77n
Wechsler, Herbert, 33
Weidenbaum, Murray, 12n, 418n
Weingarten, Palomba, 148
Weisberg, Herbert, 40n
West, William F., 42n
Westinghouse Electric Corporation, fairness of, 217–218
Weston, J. Fred, 164n
Wharton, Joseph, 214
Wheeler, John R., 418n
Whicher, Stephen E., 106n
Whinston, Michael D., 137n
White, G. Edward, 327n
White, Lawrence J., 164n
White, Lynn, Jr., 408
Whitehead, Alfred North, 432–433
White knight, 144
Whittaker, Robert, 248
Wiedenbaum, Murray, 78n, 165n
Wiedrich, Bob, 223n
Wilbur, James B., 78n
Wildavsky, Aaron, 105n, 418n
Wildcat strikes, 237
Wilkins, Mira, 387n

Williams, Harold, 54
Williams, Oliver, 374
Williamson, Oliver E., 136n
Willingness-to-pay approach, 350–351
Wills, Gary, 1, 39n
Wilson, James, 20
Wilson, Woodrow, 35
Winans, R. Foster, 202–203
*Winterbottom* case, 298–299
Winthrop, John, 85
Wiretapping, 176
Wirthlin, Richard, 273
Wittgenstein, Ludwig, 212
Wohlgemuth, Donald W., 184
Wolf, Arnold Jacob, 149
Wolfe, Christopher, 41n
Wolfe, Tom, 266
Woll, Jerry, 174
Women, and family structure, 93
Wonder Bread, advertising of, 279–280
Wood, Gordon S., 39n
Woodward, Bob, 266
Woodward, Richard B., 107n
Workers, and labor unions, 61–66
Workers' bill of rights, 428
Workers' codetermination schemes, 377
World Conference of Churches, 367
Wright, Gavin, 79n
Wrubel, Barbara, 328n

Yago, Glenn, 164n
Yanouzas, John N., 418
Yeshiva University, 247
Yoder, Edwin M., Jr., 31

Zimmerman, Thomas, 232
Zuger, Martin, 359n
Zwieback, Burton, 108n